Fields of War:

Fifty Key Battlefields
in
France and Belgium

Robert J Mueller

A Visitor's Guide to Historic Sites

 French Battlefields
Arlington Heights

ii

 French Battlefields
PO Box 4808
Buffalo Grove, Illinois 60089-4808
Email: contact@frenchbattlefields.com
Web address: frenchbattlefields.com

Cover photographs: Color: Notre-Dame de Lorette Cemetery, Lantern Tower, and Basilique;
Time line: Jeanne d'Arc at the siege of Orléans. Painting by Jules Eugène Lenepveu
Napoleon after abdicating at Fontainebleau. Painting by Paul Delaroche
Bredow's Death Ride at Mars-la-Tour (detail). Canadian Illustrated News, 1870
Canadian infantry sheltering in a front line trench during the First World War. LAC
Australian soldier checks a fallen comrade during the Battle of Passchendaele, November, 1917. LAC
US troops land at Omaha Beach on 6 June 1944. NARA
German attack troops during Ardennes Offensive, December 1944. NARA
Spine: 'The Brooding Soldier' - Canadian Memorial at Vancouver Corner, St-Juliaan near Ypres.

Abbreviations used:
IWM: Imperial War Museum
LAC: Library and Archives Canada
NARA: National Archives and Records Administration

Excerpts from 'The Break-Through on the Meuse' and 'Invasion 1914' in *The Rommel Papers*, copyright 1953 by B.H. Liddell-Hart and renewed 1981 by Lady Kathleen Liddell-Hart, Fritz Bayerlein-Dittmar and Manfred Rommel, reprinted by permission of Houghton Mifflin Harcourt Publishing Company.

Excerpt from *Their Finest Hour* by Winston Churchill. Copyright 1949 by Houghton Mifflin Company, renewed 1976 by Lady Spencer-Churchill, the Honourable Lady Sarah Audley, the Honourable Lady Soames. Reprinted by permission of Houghton Mifflin Harcourt Publishing Company. All rights reserved.

From *A Time for Trumpets* by Charles B. Macdonald
Copyright 1985 by Charles B. Macdonald
Reprinted by permission of Brandt & Hochman Literary Agents, Inc.

A Storm in Flanders by Winston Groom. Copyright 2002 by Winston Groom.
Used by permission of Grove/Atlantic, Inc

From *Requiem for a Nun* by William Faulkner, published by Chatto & Windus. Reprinted by permission of The Random House Group, Ltd.

This book is dedicated to my one love,

Nancy

The past is never dead. It's not even past.

- William Faulkner, *Requiem for a Nun*

Contents

Introduction

Since a childhood visit to Little Round Top on the American Civil War battlefield near Gettysburg, Pennsylvania, I have felt an emotional draw to locations where fateful events took place. Over the years, a growing interest developed in the great conflicts which directed the course of Western history. Long referred to as the 'Cockpit of Europe' the geographic region which now constitutes northern France and Belgium hosted many of the famous engagements in history. From Crécy to the Ardennes, the armies of Jean d'Arc, Marlborough, Wellington, Napoleon, Moltke, Foch, Rommel, and Patton demonstrated their mastery of military arts in this relatively small area. The impact upon future events was notable. On terrain within one-half day's drive of Paris, the English crown's claims to the throne of France, French royalist claims upon the west bank of the Rhine River, and German attempts at European hegemony were all decided over the course of six hundred years of bloody conflict that culminated in the twentieth century's two great wars. The result, acquired at a high price of the fields of gravestones which dot the countryside from Normandy to the Rhine, may hopefully be a lasting peace in the European Union.

Battlefield touring provides views of militarily important terrain features, surviving or reconstructed structures, and post engagement memorials – but also much more. All too frequently, tourists to France do not venture outside Paris or pass quickly through the countryside to Provence. They never see the real France of orchards, expansive woodlands, flat plains, forested hillsides, winding rivers, and straight canals. They never taste the regional cuisines, stimulating beverages, or fresh produce of local market days. They miss the religious and architectural France of Amiens or Reims Cathedral, Pierrefonds Château, and the medieval Cloth Hall of Belgium's Ieper. Touring battlefields forces one to escape the traffic and congestion of large cities for narrow country lanes and small rural villages. It encourages interaction with farmers, shopkeepers, and fellow battlefield visitors.

Regardless of the best constructed tour route, it is the unexpected that frequently makes a visit most memorable. The author recalls the French farmer who offered an invitation to his barn to view a personal collection of First World War artifacts; or the formal military burial of a recently discovered British soldier who died on the Somme in 1916; or the casual meeting with a soldier's relatives who traveled from Australia to remember their fallen uncle and brother. Fortunately the dead animals, the devastated landscape, and the smells of battle are long gone. The dead men and women remain, nevertheless, their trials and tribulations never far below our consciousness. This book is in tribute to the soldiers of all nations who, willingly or not, suffered the cold, hunger, fear, and hurt of battle.

How to Use this Book

The objective of this guide is to bring visitors to the specific site of important battlefield events, but it can also be seen as an account of the varied tapestry of historical events of this fascinating area. The book has been organized chronologically to facilitate study of a particular historical period. Selection of sites

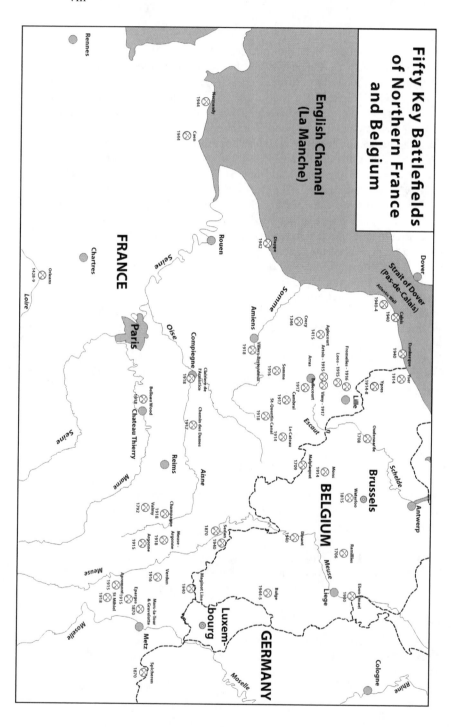

Fifty Key Battlefields of Northern France and Belgium

of interest from the map of the included battlefields allows geographically expedient tour routes which are attuned to the visitor's individual interests to be constructed.

The battlefields' proximities to Paris, Calais, and Brussels allow for short visits to a particular site of interest. Longer excursions to review the key engagements of an entire conflict are also possible with appropriate planning. For the purposes of this book, the stage has been stretched a bit to include sites within 400 kilometers of Paris. This allowed the inclusion of two of the Second World War's most decisive battles – the invasion of Normandy and the Ardennes Offensive (best known to Americans as the Battle of the Bulge).

Anyone who attempts to establish such a compendium is faced with issues of inclusion and exclusion. The shear number of potential battlefields, especially from the First World War, is overwhelming. The predetermined size of the book required a careful process of selection. Battlefields were chosen because of their proximity to Paris, the presence of identifiable landmarks, the quality of their associated memorials, and the significance of the engagement. In keeping with the theme of the book, that is, to provide guidance to the sites of events of great impact, a few included sites retain little to note their importance. While not all locations have seen their proper remembrance, most are marked by grand structures of monuments, museums, and memorials, and, unfortunately, cemeteries. This guide includes those sites that are most visited, most evocative, provide an overview of the battlefield, or are simply among the author's favorites. No guide can be all-inclusive.

I have chosen to include some locations which do not receive the attention of English speaking visitors that they rightly deserve. The great French battles against the Germans in Champagne and Lorraine are frequently ignored by the crush of visitors to Ieper, Somme, or Normandy. Almost forgotten and with few grand memorials to the missing, these battlefields of enormous struggle and loss remain undisturbed. In the Forêt d'Apremont one can see what trench warfare was really like; the battle lines still very visible, with the trenches neither re-constructed nor artificially preserved. Vauquois, Éparges, or Chemin des Dames offer opportunities to witness the effects of the 'war of the mines'; gruesome underground battlefields where men fought in semi-darkness, cold, and constant fear of entombment.

Each chapter begins with a brief summary of the political and military events which precipitated the conflict. A 'fact box' summarizes key information and a detailed battlefield map assists in following the action and locating selected sites. The 'Battle' section describes each commander's objectives and troop movements. Frequently an 'Aftermath' section notes results of the fighting and significant events which occurred after the engagement. A 'Consequences of the War' section summarizes the political events following from the conflict. The major section of each battle is devoted to the 'Battlefield Tour'. Each tour starts at a nearby city or major, well-signed location. Clear driving instructions, highlighted in boxes for easy reading, are designed to bring a visitor to various positions of major importance on the battlefield. A brief explanation of the significance of the site is included. 'Recommended Readings' are offered for those interested in expanding upon the historical aspects of the war. Because of their duration and complexity, the two world wars have been presented in several chapters representing separate time periods in the conflict.

Besides the recommended tours in this guide, local tourist organizations may have established routes to a larger number of sites. For example, the NTL (Normandie Terre-Liberté) Totems in Normandy identify sites along eight routes, each of which focuses upon a different period of the Battle of Normandy. Bastogne, Belgium has fifteen well-done site markers with period photographs and explanations of the local action in four languages. The battlefield visitor is encouraged to explore these additional sites. Up-to-date road maps are necessary for off-route touring. The 1:50,000 scale maps prepared by the *Institut Géographique National* (IGN) are available at many bookstores, autoroute service areas, or over the internet from www.ign.fr (unfortunately the website is in French only). Detailed Belgian maps are more difficult to obtain; bookstores or tourist offices are one's best bet.

Distances between sites are for the recommended route or swiftest route if specific directions are not given. The maps presented in this book generally show a mix of original and modern roadways; orientation is always with north upwards. They should never be considered a substitute for current highway road maps as new or modified roadways are constantly being constructed. Farm or forest roads are generally not drivable without four-wheel drive vehicles. Driving times are not provided as they depend too greatly upon traffic conditions and one's inclinations to stop; however, most of the tours can be completed in one day.

Spelling preferences have been chosen to facilitate finding each site on a map or local road sign. Most locations are thus spelled in their native language not the anglicized version, such as the French Dunkerque for Dunkirk or the Dutch Ieper for Ypres. A few exceptions have been retained due to well-known spelling. Belgium is a trilingual country using Flemish in the north, French in the south, and German in a small eastern sector. In this country road signs frequently appear in more than one language. The identification of informational signs or museum labels as being trilingual implies French, German, and English, although Dutch or Spanish is sometimes found and will be so indicated.

Twenty-four hour military time is in use in Europe; therefore operational hours in this book are so presented. Museum hours and content are thought to be accurate at the time of writing, but they are notoriously subject to change. If access to a certain site is of paramount importance, it is best to contact it in advance. American visitors must accommodate the use of the metric system as it is the measure used on local road signs and maps.

Military ranks are at the time of the events described. French military ranks and German names have not been anglicized; for example using Wilhelm, not William. The indicated positions of military units on the battlefield maps are approximate and do not necessarily indicate army headquarters locations.

Battlefield casualty statistics are a subject of great controversy; sources present non-comparable numbers. Chroniclers of ancient battles only concerned themselves with the nobility. Even in modern battles, statistics are subject to wide variation. In wartime, it was common to exaggerate the enemy's losses, and understate your own to maintain home front morale. In reference to casualty figures, British wartime Prime Minister Herbert Asquith suggested that his War Office 'kept three sets of figures, one to mislead the public, another to mislead the Cabinet, and the third to mislead itself.' The totals presented here are the author's best determination taking various sources into account.

Sources of cemetery statistics have narrower variations due to the continued exhumation and reburial of individual soldiers. German counts for mass graves are estimates at best as battlefield clean-up was performed by POWs who had little interest in keeping exact numbers. French, British, German, and most other nationality's cemeteries are not fenced and thus are always open to visitors. American Military Cemeteries maintain fixed hours, open daily from 9:00 to 17:00 except on January 1 and December 25. Only American cemeteries provide on-site assistance in locating specific graves.

General Tourist Information

The book has been written with the intent of touring battlefields by automobile. For those unable or unwilling to provide their own transportation, several of the larger and most-toured battlefields are serviced by tour companies which offer a reasonable alternative providing transportation, experienced guides, and sometimes arranging for meals and accommodations. Public transportation to battlefields is seldom a viable option.

Every region, department, and many communities in France have tourist offices which can provide helpful information regarding accommodations, cultural and historic sites, walking or cycling routes, and hours of operation for museums. Belgian battlefield cities such as Ieper and Bastogne have excellent facilities for assisting tourists. Regional Michelin Green Guides are highly recommended for their presentation of general tourist information. They make an excellent accompaniment to this book and offer general touring advice in addition to listing historic and cultural locations, market days and festivals, public holidays.

Outside of the major French metropolitan areas, tourist offices, many museums, most retail shops, and all banks honor the French custom of closing during midday. Weekday and Saturday morning hours are frequently restricted to 9:00 to 12:00 and 14:00 to 17:00. On Sundays and public holidays almost all establishments are closed with even many restaurants closing after the noon meal. Belgian hours are more liberal. Those sites open on weekends are frequently closed on Mondays or Tuesdays. Some variations exist, especially later closing hours during the summer tourist season. Many sites operated by volunteer organizations such as Maginot Line fortifications are open summer weekends only. Few museums are handicap accessible; those that advertise to be are indicated Most British and American military cemeteries are accessible.

The information contained herein is believed to be accurate at the time of printing, however roadways are improved or re-routed, intersections reconstructed, museums opened or closed, and new monuments are commemorated. France is now undergoing a renumbering of their National Roads, changing them from their historic 'N' designation to 'D' or departmental road identifier.

Local citizens are remarkably tolerant of battlefield visitors; however private property should be respected and never accessed without owner's permission. Crops are the farmer's livelihood and trampling planted fields should be avoided, although a field boundary often provides a useful walkpath. Forests may be the scene of the autumn shooting season and care should be exercised.

Finally, an additional word of caution: abandoned bunkers or off-trail battlefield terrain frequently retain dangerous spikes, barbed wire, or even unexploded ordinance. Each year, farmers in France and Belgium uncover hundreds of thousands of pieces of First World War ordinance known as the 'iron harvest'. They move them to the roadside where they are collected by bomb disposal experts. Although ninety years old, many of these relics contain potentially lethal gas or still-active explosives. The potential danger presented by old ordinance should not be under-estimated. Never touch, prod, or in any manner move shells, bullets, grenades, or containers of any type. To do so may risk serious injury or death.

Military Symbols

Unit Size:

⊠	Company	⊠	Division
⊠	Battalion	⊠	Corps
⊠	Regiment	⊠	Army
⊠	Brigade	⊠	Army Group

Unit Type:

⊠	Airborne	◢	Cavalry
	Airborne, Artillery	E	Engineering
⌒	Airforce	⊠	Infantry
⊖	Armored (Panzer)	⊠	Infantry, Motorized
⊠	Armored, Reconn.	⊠	Special Forces
·	Artillery	TD	Tank Destroyer
⊙	Artillery, Armored	⊠	Opposition (Infantry example)

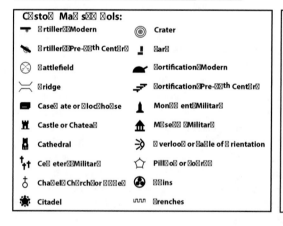

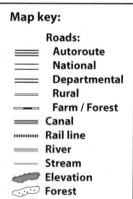

Map key:

Roads:
- Autoroute
- National
- Departmental
- Rural
- Farm / Forest
- Canal
- Rail line
- River
- Stream
- Elevation
- Forest

Chapter One

Hundred Years War
1337 - 1453

Medieval warfare was a contest of power for territorial dominance. Forces were drawn to one side or the other by payments, promises of plunder, or grants of estates. The French king was the most powerful ruler in western Europe, and his military power was founded upon French knights. The code of loyalty to the king provided a fighting capability that dominated Europe. Lords called upon their vassals to provide knights and auxiliary troops. Nobles often impressed the lower ranks, and collected the rewards of their service. Mounted knights were the most powerful military weapon of their day. Chain mail covered their bodies; helmets and plate armor shielded critical areas.

Mercenary armies were common and often switched sides for a better offer. Of paramount importance, a ruler needed to levy and collect taxes to attract, outfit, and retain soldiers. Plunder as compensation drove an invading army to rampage, loot, and otherwise destroy the enemy's territory. Weakly defended towns, unprotected villages, and the open countryside were put to the torch in expeditions of destruction known as *chevauchée*. Rape and slaughter of civilians was commonplace, however individuals of higher birth or well-known clerics were often spared since they offered the potential for ransom. The devastation was often so complete that the populace did not recover for decades. Such destruction was a strategy to deny tax income to the opposition.

Whereas the French monarchs had been successful in centralizing much of the political authority during this time, by the mid 14th century, feudal lords felt less obligated to provide military service to the king in exchange for their landed estates.

Dynastic rivalry between the royal houses of France and England dated from William the Conqueror's invasion of England in 1066. The English king ruled in his island possessions; however, he owed hereditary allegiance to the king of France for his fiefs of Guyenne and Ponthieu. With the death in 1328 of Charles IV, the last king of the Capetian dynasty, the legitimate ownership of the French crown was left in question. The count of Valois lost no time in getting himself proclaimed King Philip VI by a Paris assembly.

Edward III assumed the English throne in 1327 after his own struggle against his mother, Isabella. She was Charles IV's sister, and some thought that her Edward had a better claim to the French throne than did Philip. Edward was militarily weaker than Philip, leaving him little choice but to offer his allegiance or risk losing his French possessions. Edward's income and England's economic prosperity were tied to retaining its wool markets in Flanders, where Flemish nobility had long resisted control from Paris. They switched sides frequently, and influenced other nobles in the region to do the same. Eventually Philip arrested all English merchants in Flanders, and withdrew Flemish trading and guild privileges. Further increasing the antipathy between the two monarchs was the exiled king of Scotland, who received refuge in France where he raised troops and funds to press his claim for an independent Scotland.

For years Edward and Philip had been squabbling over the borders of Guyenne, and cross border attacks were common. In May 1337, King Philip declared that Edward had forfeited Guyenne when Edward had repudiated his homage to Philip. Edward responded by laying claim to the French throne based upon his mother's Capetian kinship. This claim and counterclaim thus started a 116-year period of conflict known as the Hundred Years War; years that were filled with intrigue, *chevauchée*, and treaties, but few fixed battles.

Initially the French waged a bloody, three-year invasion of Guyenne, threatening the English stronghold at Bordeaux. Philip's superior naval forces raided

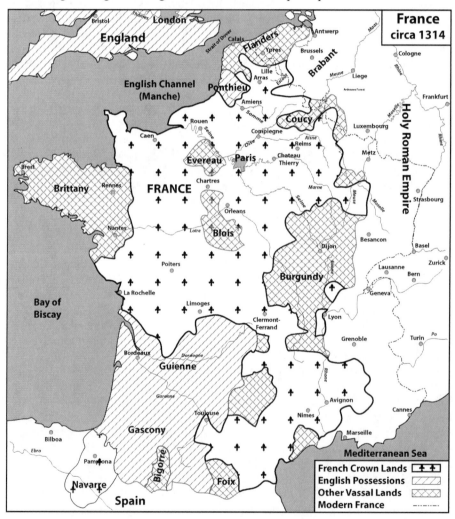

English ports, burning Portsmouth and Southampton, and thereby denying Edward taxes from wool and wine trades as well as his ability to support his troops in Guyenne. In 1340, Edward attacked the French fleet while it was in harbor at Sluys, Flanders. English archers swept the French and their Castilian and Genoese allies from their decks in a nine-hour battle that first revealed the firepower of the English longbow. In autumn 1342, Edward invaded Brittany, but Philip refused to be brought out into full-scale battle. Edward plundered the countryside but, without siege equipment necessary to capture fortified cities, he returned to England.

#1

Battle of Crécy
26 August 1346

OBJECTIVE	To defeat the French Army and establish Edward III as king of France
FORCES	
FRENCH:	30,000 men (King Philip VI)
ENGLISH:	11,000 men (King Edward III)
RESULT	Although greatly outnumbered, the English produced a stunning victory.
CASUALTIES	
FRENCH:	10,000 killed and wounded including 1,500 named knights
ENGLISH:	Historically believed to be less than 100
LOCATION	Abbeville is 176 km north of Paris; Crécy-en-Ponthieu is 20 km north of Abbeville

In the early summer of 1346, Edward sailed from England in hundreds of vessels transporting a professional army of 15,000 paid, well-trained English and Welsh troops. In total secrecy, the army landed on 12 July at St-Vaast-la-Hougue on the Cotentin peninsula in Normandy. Edward's campaign strategy was to capture Paris while Philip's forces were occupied by other English troops in Gascony and Brittany. The English marched through Norman towns, pillaging and burning every structure, torturing peasants to disclose hidden goods, and indiscriminately raping and murdering their women. Neither monasteries nor their religious inhabitants were spared. French knights who were taken prisoner were held for ransom. Total war had arrived in France.

After a brief battle on 26 July, English forces entered Caen, and occupied the great *Abbaye-aux-Hommes* of William the Conqueror. While the English troops continued to move along the coast, Edward ordered the captives and plunder loaded onto his ships, and sent back to England. The fleet left Ouistreham, carrying the spoils back to England but also closing off Edward's path of retreat. Edward continued towards Paris moving along the west bank of the Seine River.

Philip VI had gathered his forces at Rouen on the west bank of the Seine, but refused to offer battle. Edward traveled up the left bank toward Paris, while the

French army mirrored his movements along the right bank, destroying bridges ahead of Edward's arrival. The English army approached within sight of the walls of Paris, and Philip issued the chivalric challenge to do battle; but now it was Edward who wished to avoid fighting the greatly enlarged French force. His men repaired the bridge at Poissy, finally enabling a crossing of the Seine, and turned north to avoid a major fixed battle or encirclement.

Edward intended to join forces with his Flemish allies to the north, but Philip's vanguard, commanded by Jean de Luxembourg, King of Bohemia, had overtaken Edward, and reached the Somme River to deny Edward use of its bridges. Edward was hence trapped on the Somme estuary with his back to the sea. Legend states that a local Frenchman succumbed to English bribery, and pointed Edward to an outcropping of white chalk known as Blanché taque which crossed the sandy riverbed. The English army waited for low tide, and then forded the Somme below Abbeville, fighting against a stubborn defense by 4,000 French knights and Genoese infantry. They completed the passage minutes before the arrival of Luxembourg's leading light cavalry, whose pursuit was stopped by a rising tide.

After escaping the trap, Edward and the bulk of his army spent the day in defensive positions south of the Forêt de Crécy. He had planned to continue north into Flanders, but with the coastal route impassable due to flooding, he circled to the south of the Forêt de Crécy. His movements were forcing him closer to the pursuing French. The hard marches of the six-week-old campaign had taken their toll on his men; their clothes were now in tatters, and their shoes worn through. Edward realized that he could no longer outrun the French, and decided to find an advantageous place for battle. He encamped near the small village of Crécy-en-Ponthieu. The topography was to Edward's liking for fighting a defensive battle in which he could use his longbow men to maximum advantage

Due to casualties and defections, the English army had shrunk to approximately eleven thousand men. They fought dismounted with their horses and the baggage train secured in the Bois de Crécy Grange. Edward arranged his forces in an 1800-meter line across the forward slopes of the *Vallée aux Clercs* between the towns of Crécy and Wadicourt. Two groups of dismounted men-at-arms were placed on the downward terraced fields. On the right were four thousand men, including two thousand archers commanded by his son, Edward, Prince of Wales, who later became known as the Black Prince. On the left was a reserve of five hundred men-at-arms and another twelve hundred archers commanded by Thomas Hatfield, Bishop of Durham. The archers formed lines in the shape of an outward pointing 'V' between the massed infantry. Their position was to provide open fields of fire down the slope and flanking fire into the attacking enemy. They dug small holes in front of their positions to topple the charging horses of the French mounted knights. Iron-tipped, wooded spikes may also have been driven into the ground to protect the archers, and funnel the attacking French horsemen toward the infantry, further exposing their flanks to the archer's arrows. The king commanded seven hundred men-at-arms and two thousand archers. He established himself in a windmill on high ground to the rear of the vanguard.

King Philip, after spending the night at Abbeville, and attending early morning Mass to pray for victory, arrived after a 20 km march that was tiring for the heavily laden French knights and their mounts. In addition, some detachments, misled by bad information about Edward's position, had made a futile detour. To complete the march and engage a prepared enemy would put his army at a disadvantage; therefore Philip planned to make camp on a plateau near the village of Estrée-les-Crécy. Emboldened by the previous night's pre-battle celebration, enraged by the slaughter inflicted upon French cities by the marauding English, and not wanting the see the English decamp, and again avoid battle, the French Army could not be restrained even by their king. They were ready for battle, and wanted English blood.

Battle

A detailed description of the battle does not exist, and medieval chroniclers' accounts are in disagreement. French forces were nominally divided into four groups, with Philip commanding the reserve; Jean de Luxembourg and the Count d'Alençon, Philip's brother, commanding two groups of mounted men-at-arms; and six thousand Genoese mercenary crossbow men commanded by Antonio Doria and

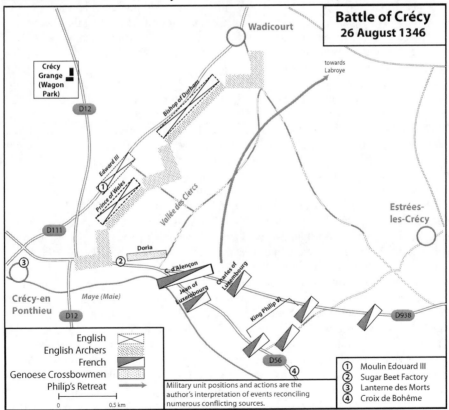

Carlo Grimaldi. In transit, however, the army fragmented, and units intermixed. Some obeyed the king's initial instructions to camp for the night while others forced their way through stationary troops to confront the enemy. Late in the afternoon, with major portions of his thirty thousand-man army still arriving onto the field, Philip realized that battle that day was inevitable. The Genoese crossbow men had marched the distance from Abbeville in full battle array carrying their weapons but without their protective shields which were in the trailing baggage train. Upon reaching the battlefield, they were greeted by a sudden, drenching thunderstorm, which ended quickly but soaked their bowstrings and muddied the field. Philip ordered the Genoese into the valley and up the hill, straight toward the English men-at-arms. The mercenaries moved forward, and uttered a great cry intended to intimidate the English. Despite a second great cry, and another leap forward, the well-disciplined English stood fast. With a third small advance, the Genoese released a volley, but their wetted strings limited the crossbow's range and accuracy, and most bolts fell short.

The English archers responded by taking one step forward, and filling the air with a rain of arrows. The longbow had a range of approximately 250 meters – slightly less than that of the crossbow – and it was less accurate; but its advantage was speed of fire of up to ten arrows a minute. In a few minutes, thousands of the Genoese were killed, and the survivors broke rank and ran discarding their weapons. Disgusted at the apparent Genoese cowardice, the Count of Alençon charged his mounted men-at-arms through and over the retreating crossbow-men, his knights using their swords to open a path to the enemy.

The English longbow men continued to find their marks on the charging knights, the arrows piercing the mail of riders and horses alike. The frenzy resulted with wounded horses and riders mixed on the muddy ground. Philip's ally, the blind King Jean of Bohemia, ordered his personal guard to lash themselves together and take him forward so he could strike at least one blow for France. They fought valiantly through the archers, and reached the men-at-arms commanded by the Prince of Wales. The prince's flank was thus hard pressed by the attack of King Jean as well as the French, German, and Savoyard cavalry charges led by the Count d'Alençon. A messenger was sent to King Edward asking his assistance, but the king responded that it was the day for the Prince of Wales to earn his spurs and sent no help, although timely assistance arrived from Durham's reserves. The next morning, King Jean and his knights were found dead with their horses still lashed together.

Hand-to-hand fighting followed the cavalry charges. During the intervals when the French drew back, Welshmen rushed forward and slit the throats of fallen French knights. While evening turned into night, fresh troops struggled forward in the oncoming darkness to continue the slaughter. Edward may have had three early cannons, the explosions of which would have terrified the horses and added to the mayhem. In the gloom of late evening, a slightly wounded King Philip led the fifteenth and last feeble assault. Failing to make progress, he was led off the field by John of Hainault, and their party retired to the Château de Labroye 15 km away. Edward remained in the mill for the duration of the battle, never putting on his helmet and never committing his reserves. The English did not even know the extent of the slaughter until the noise of battle diminished and they explored the battlefield under the light provided by the burning windmill, which they torched for that purpose.

Aftermath

The slaughter wrought upon French knighthood was devastating. Bodies of men and horses were in layers due to the successive waves of the attack. The bravest and noblest of France were dead. Estimates of the losses vary with the source. Seward reports that French losses were 'certainly well over 10,000' with 'more than 1500 lords and knights' individually identified.[1] Mourned by English and French alike, the body of Jean de Luxembourg was returned to Luxembourg, and in homage to his courage, the Prince of Wales added Jean's motto '*Ich Dien*' (I Serve) to his coat of arms.

English losses were less than one hundred. Edward had won one of the greatest victories in the history of warfare; in so doing he proved the fighting potential of a small professional army over feudal conscripts, and hence changed military strategy with the firepower of the longbow over armored horsemen.

Instead of pursuing Philip toward Paris, Edward marched north toward Calais, the last French town on the coast before entering Flanders and the port closest to England. Capturing Calais proved difficult because of the strong city defense works, stubborn resistance, and the lack of siege equipment strung out the English timetable. Although cut off from re-supply by sea due to an English naval blockade, and abandoned after a half-hearted relief attempt, Calais held for nearly one year before surrendering. The Truce of Calais was signed on 28 September 1347, and Calais remained an English bridgehead on French soil for the next 210 years. Edward apparently gave up the idea of a French crown and returned to England on 12 October, and military operations ceased completely in 1348 with the appearance of the Black Death in Western Europe.

Battlefield Tour

> Proceed from Crécy-en-Ponthieu toward Wadicourt / Dampierre-sur-Authie (D111); the battlefield is 1 km north of the village.

The village of Crécy-en-Ponthieu is situated on the north bank of the Maye (or Maie) River. The English army stood directly east of the current D111 between Crécy and Wadicourt on the downward slopes of the long ridge. Hardly any evidence of the great events that took place here remains –even the roadside sign simply states 'Crécy – 1346'; however the battlefield has changed little in 650 years. The burned windmill has been replaced by a now slightly dilapidated and graffiti-marred **Moulin Edward III** observation tower that nevertheless provides superb views over the battlefield. A line of shrubs camouflages the village's underground water reservoir.

---

[1] Desmond Steward, *The Hundred Years War: The English in France 1337 - 1453* (London: Constable and Company, 1978), 67.

The tower overlooks the battlefield from all perspectives in the valley. Immediately before the tower is an unplowed pasture, whose long grass pulls the eye down the slope and into a north/south running depression called *Vallée aux Clercs*. The valley is flanked on both sides by rolling hills that rise 50 – 70 meters in height marked by *rideaux*, steep drops of two to five meters. It drains into the Maye, to the right; uphill is the neighboring village of Wadicourt. On the south side of the pasture before the start of the village which has spread toward the battlefield, there is a shear drop of almost 4 meters. This spot was probably the position of the Prince of Wales' men-at-arms and archers. The steep drop may have provided protection on his flank. To the left of the pasture, a farmer's lane provides access between planted fields down the hill and into the valley. The natural contours of the land would have a tendency to funnel undisciplined troops toward the middle of the English line. The distance from the tower to the valley bottom is approximately 1.3 km. Edward's defensive formation and the potholes dug by his troops must have occupied at least one half of the distance to the valley; probably down the hill to the flat spot about 600 meters from the valley bottom.

A sugar beet factory is on the far right at the entrance to the valley, and it marks the starting point of the Genoese attack. Modern academics theorize that the French forces were funneled piecemeal into the valley from this point. Never able to bring their full force against the English lines, the small groups were destroyed. Others believe that the French charged from over the opposing hillside into the valley and up the near side against the English position. Several rideaux on the opposing slope, however, would have precluded this movement by heavily armored horsemen. Because of contradictions in the chronicled descriptions of the battle by eyewitnesses, a lively debate about actual events during the battle continues.

In this field, many of the richest, most honored, proudest scions of the best families of France fell and bled. In the days that followed the French dead were stripped of weapons and valuables, and dumped into hastily dug pits on the right and left of the battlefield – essentially where they fell the thickest. The exact locations are no longer identifiable even with modern search equipment. The English wagon park was probably in the vicinity of the current D12. The English wounded were given to the protection of the monks at nearby Crécy Grange. Those that died were buried in a still unplowed field there.

Return to the center of Crécy-en-Ponthieu.

If Edward had not selected the ridge northeast of Crécy for his defensive stand, nothing would be known of this small market village. It's history before and after the battle is mostly speculation. In the center of the place de Luxembourg stands a black stone memorial 'To Jean de Luxembourg, King of Bohemia and all his comrades in arms, dead for France at Crécy 26 August 1346.' At the foot of the place is a brick monument known as **Lanterne des Morts**. The structure's origin is somewhat uncertain, but it is believed to date from the end of 13th century, and it was erected by Edward I, king of England, in posthumous homage to its wife Eléonore de Castile, countess of Ponthieu.

Leave Crécy-en-Ponthieu toward Brailly (D56) and continue for 2.5 km.

A further commemoration to Jean de Luxembourg stands upon a modern stone plinth, which is adorned daily with the French tricolor. The battered and weatherworn **Croix de Bohême** marks the legendary spot of Jean de Luxembourg's death. The centuries' old memorial is shrouded in some mystery. The location may be more figurative than literal as it is well behind the assumed location of the French lines, and not near the fierce action against the Prince of Wales as described by historians.

Other Sites of Interest: Some French wounded did escape and many of them sought refuge at the **Abbaye de Valloires** near the village of Argoules 17 km to the northwest. Originally a Cistercian abbey founded in 12th century, the abbey was totally destroyed during the Hundred Years War and again in the Thirty Years War (1618 – 1648). The current structure was rebuilt in the 18th century. The abbey is now more famous for its extensive gardens, which are open to the public for a slight fee, but worth the visit.

#2

Battle of Agincourt
25 October 1415

OBJECTIVE	To prevent the English army from reaching safety at Calais
FORCES	
FRENCH:	10,000–20,000 men-at-arms and 2,000 crossbowmen (Charles d'Albret, Constable of France)
ENGLISH:	Approximately 1,000 men-at-arms and 4,000–7,000 archers (Henry V, King of England)
RESULT	An overwhelming victory for the English defeating a much superior force
CASUALTIES	
FRENCH:	8,000–10,000 killed; 2,000 taken prisoner
ENGLISH:	100–400 killed
LOCATION	Calais is 290 km north of Paris; Azincourt is 75 km south of Calais

King Philip died in 1350, and the war was taken up by his son, King John II. English military leadership transferred to Edward's son, Edward, Prince of Wales, the Black Prince. He led the English forces in September 1356 at the battle of Poitiers, where King John was captured and sent to England, where he died in captivity eight years later. The prince was never to hold the crown, dying in 1376 one year before his father.

Turmoil continued in France as *chevauchée* and invasions followed in rapid succession. French King Charles V regained much of the land lost to Edward III. His son, Charles VI, fell into madness, and the territorial ambitions of the Burgundian and Armagnac / Orléanist factions produced a civil war that provided the English with another opportunity as both sides traded French lands for English support. In 1399, Henry IV deposed the tyrannical Richard II to take the English throne, which passed to his son Henry V in 1413.

Battle

Henry V was a professional soldier raised in the military service of his father. He had developed his martial skills putting down rebellions in Scotland (1400) and Wales (1402 – 1405). Almost immediately upon assuming the English throne, Henry planned to re-establish England's claim to the French throne by launching an invasion to reclaim the duchy of Normandy. Gathering his forces at Southampton, he crossed the Channel, striking first at the Norman seaport of Harfleur with the intent of creating another English bastion on French soil as Edward III had at Calais 69 years earlier. The five-week siege of Harfleur delayed Henry's advance toward Paris, however, giving the French nobility time to gather their forces at Rouen. The delay also weakened Henry's men; food was short, and they suffered from dysentery.

Charles d'Albret, a career soldier, was constable of France, the titular leader of its army. He was not, however, the overall commander of all the lords, dukes, and counts eager for glory from destroying the detested English invaders.

Henry, now without transport back to England, decided to leave his heavy equipment at Harfleur and take his weakened army to the protection of Calais. He intended to cross the Somme at Blanché taque, the same ford used by Edward III before the battle of Crécy, only to find it and most other crossings effectively blocked by French advance detachments. Henry was forced deeper into French territory to find an undefended crossing point, until he eventually succeeded near Péronne.

The French main body left Rouen to intercept the English, opting for direct confrontation with the decidedly smaller force. After days of maneuvering, the French host closed in on Henry, and blocked the road to Calais near the village of Agincourt. By now Henry's provisions were almost depleted, his men were exhausted from marching 420 km in seventeen days, and the autumn weather had turned foul. His army was also outnumbered five to one.

In the early morning of 25 October, Henry positioned his nine hundred men-at-arms across a recently planted wheat field bounded on two sides by woods, between the villages of Agincourt and Tramecourt. On each wing were his archers, protected by sharpened staves plunged into the ground to form a prickly defense like a hedgehog. Despite the odds, Henry's army was prepared for battle with high spirits and confidence in their king, according to Shakespeare's description in *Henry V,* in which the king gives a spirited exhortation:

From this day to the ending of the world,
But we in it shall be remembered-
We few, we happy few, we band of brothers

Constable d'Albret's larger army was arranged 900 meters distant in three battles (divisions). The first two ranks were dismounted men-at-arms with a detachment of crossbowmen in between and cavalry detachments on either wing. In the rear were the majority of the French mounted knights. The seasonal rains that had plagued the English army's progress had turned the soil into a gooey muck. The previous night's rains had further sodden the field. At mid-morning therefore, with

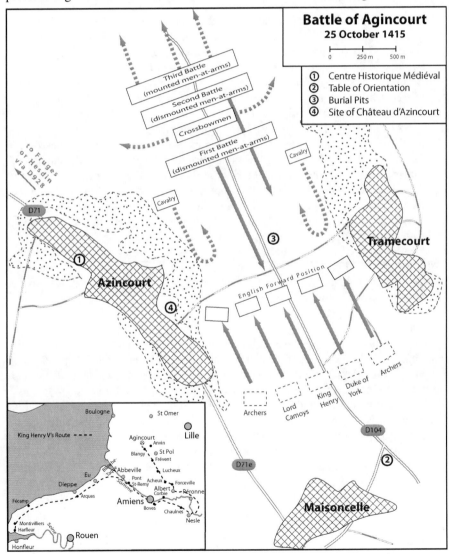

the toss of a baton as a signal, the English made the first move, slowly advancing to within arrow range (180 meters) of the French front. Henry's archers re-planted their stakes, and began to loose their arrows into the French host. This action was not a movement of attack as much as an attempt to provoke the French knights. The French cavalry responded, both wings charging against the English archers. Their charge was repulsed, however, by the stakes and accurate fire of the English longbow. The survivors of the cavalry charge turned their steeds toward the rear and, in their flight, disrupted the ranks of the advancing men-at-arms.

The now disorganized French first battle, personally led by d'Albret, moved forward struggling across the now churned mud. In addition, the men became squeezed by the woods bounding the field and the heavy flights of arrows fired into their flanks. By the time they met the English line, the press became so great as to prevent many from swinging their swords. Those who fell wounded by arrows were unable to rise, exhausted by the effort to cross the field or pinned to the ground by other wounded. As an English recorder of the events stated, 'the French stood immobilized whilst our men wrenched axes from their hands and felled them in the same way as if they were cattle'[2].

Leading his knights, Henry charged the French second line, adding to the pressure. A general mêlée ensued with King Henry and his retinue in the thick of the fighting. The clang of slashing swords, cries of anguish, and shouts of encouragement and warning mixed in a brief, but closely fought battle. Their arrow supply depleted, the archers dropped their bows, drew swords, and merged into the mêlée, stabbing at vulnerable points in the knight's armor. Within hours both French lines were reduced to a seething, dying mass. The mounted third battle, witnessing the slaughter but lacking maneuvering room to intervene, rode away.

At this point, with the battle won, Henry perceived a French threat against his lightly defended baggage train stationed to the rear. Fearing the release of captured French knights who were in the train, Henry ordered the captives to be slain, and many died before the perceived threat abated.

Aftermath

The losses at the battle affected nearly every noble family in France decimating the ruling class of the country. The Constable was slain along with over six hundred dukes and knights and hundreds of men-at-arms and bowmen. Two thousand prisoners were taken for ransom to Calais. The fighting season was over, and Henry returned to England to accolades and triumphant processions. The battle at Agincourt was decidedly an English victory, but it meant little in the outcome of the war until Henry returned to France in 1417 to lead a five-year campaign which saw the successful siege of Rouen and return of Normandy to English rule. Eventually married to Charles VI's daughter and designated as Charles' official heir, Henry was worn out by the deprivations of life as a soldier; he died in 1422 at age 34 before assuming the French crown.

---

[2] Anne Curry, *Agincourt: A New History* (Stroud, England: Tempus Publishing, 2005), 212.

Battlefield Tour

The Agincourt battlefield remains essentially unchanged, although the forests that bound the field are much reduced from their 15th century size. The tour starts in the center of the farming village of Azincourt (as it is now called) and follows a route around the battlefield to an observation point behind Henry's battle line. It continues along a highway which bisects the battlefield toward French positions before returning to the village across the line of attack.

The **Centre Historique Médiéval** presents 15th century France and the opposing forces at Agincourt through large poster displays and audio enhanced, holographic images of key participants. Whereas authentic artifacts from the period are sparse, an audio-visual presentation uses a large scale projected battlefield to describe the action. The centre, with displays of interest to children and adults, makes an excellent start to the battlefield tour. The centre is open daily April through June from 10:00 to 18:00; July and August from 09:30 to 18:30; September and October from 10:00 to 18:00; from November through March from 10:00 to 17:00, closed on Tuesdays. All materials are bi-lingual or use bi-lingual audio headsets. Fee.

Leave the Centre Historique south through Azincourt (D71e). Bear left and pass through Maisoncelle and continue to the next major intersection (D104).

The tour approaches the battlefield by-passing the early eighteenth century church and modern houses of the farm community of Maisoncelle, where Henry spent the night before the battle. The thin tree line bounding the rural road (D71e) may also have shielded the French cavalry sortie against the English rear that led to the slaughter of the prisoners. The roadway now traverses the rear of Henry's position and approximately the area of his baggage train just to the north. Much of this location is not visible due to the sunken nature of the road, but at the next major intersection, a collection of monuments commemorates various anniversaries of the battle and includes a ceramic **table of orientation** showing the placement of forces. The location of the monuments is unfortunate because it is quite a distance from the actual site of most of the fighting, and views across the slightly higher battlefield terrain are difficult. The road (D104) to the right leads to Blangy-sur-Ternoise; the direction from which Henry's army approached the battlefield. They probably had their first view of the assembled French nobility upon cresting the ridge.

Turn north from the commemorations.

The road passes through the middle of the unchanged and nondescript battlefield, approaching the French line through the center of the English positions. The terrain between Azincourt and Tramecourt offers a particularly flat piece of ground, unusual among the generally more rolling hills of Artois. Considering the heavy armaments of the period, it presented excellent ground upon which to conduct medieval warfare; however, in 1415, movement across the field was nearly impossible due to the recent rainfall.

The woods, visible to the left and right but less extensive than in 1415, still mark the sides of the contest. In the distance on either side the ground falls away, the slopes having offered some protection to Henry's flanks. A rural road to the right leads to Tramecourt. St-Leonard's parish church, which sits adjacent to the private, walled eighteenth century **Château de Tramecourt**, presents a charming example of village religious architecture. Henry's initial front line was roughly parallel to the line of the church in Tramecourt as indicated by its steeple.

The crossroads ahead marks the approximate final position of the English front line, with the French just slightly to the north. The small copse ahead on the right may indicate the center of the engagement; from it the fighting lines extended to the left and the right. The **copse** also marks burial pits that were dug to dispose of the almost six thousand slain of lesser rank; most of the bodies of the nobles were recovered and transported home. The calvary on the site dates from the late nineteenth century.

Turn right, ignoring the garish wooden soldiers that line the roadway.

The road returns to Agincourt, passing the area of the left half of the English battle line. Upon re-entering Azincourt, the farm on the right occupies the location of the long-since ruined Château d'Azincourt, ancestral seat of two minor nobles killed in 1415. At last visit, the battlefield was once again sown with winter wheat, as it was 600 years ago.

#3

Siege of Orléans
12 October 1428 to 8 May 1429

OBJECTIVE	To capture the last royal stronghold north of the Loire River
FORCES	
FRENCH:	French forces varied greatly over the course of the siege but by May 1429, 3,800 men plus an unknown number of militia and 72 cannon remained in the city (Bastard of Orléans later known as comte Jean de Dunois)
ENGLISH:	3,500 men and approximately 50 cannon (Thomas Montagu, Earl of Salisbury, then William de la Pole, Earl of Suffolk)
RESULT	The siege was lifted and the English were forced to withdraw from the Loire valley. A long decline in English fortunes ensued, resulting in their expulsion from France by 1453.
CASUALTIES	
FRENCH:	Uncertain
ENGLISH:	Uncertain
LOCATION	Orléans is 131 km south of Paris

The Hundred Years War had raged off and on for 84 years. Five years after the French defeat at Azincourt, the terms of the Treaty of Troyes (1420) stipulated that the English king, Henry V, would marry Catherine, the daughter of the then French King Charles VI. Upon Charles' death, Henry would rule both France and England as a united kingdom. Meanwhile, Charles' son, the Dauphin, was effectively declared a bastard and disinherited. The treaty provided an ideal finale to the Hundred Years War: one king for both countries by agreement, not by conquest. Unfortunately for the people of France, Henry and Charles both died at young ages in 1422. The proposed King of England, Henry VI, was less than one year old, and the rivalries for succession to the throne of France started anew.

The enmity between the House of Burgundy and the Houses of Orléans and Armagnac dominated French internal politics. In revenge for the murder of Louis of Orléans, John of Burgundy was assassinated by the Orléanists in 1419. In their efforts to suppress the influence of the Orléanist/Armagnac faction, the Burgundians allied themselves with the English. The English successfully occupied Paris and most of the territory north of the Loire River, and laid siege to the critical Loire city of Orléans.

Battle

Orléans controlled a major crossing of the Loire, and was the home of the anti-Burgundian Armagnac forces. The capture of Orléans by the English offered the possibility of control of the entire Loire valley and the eventual subjugation of Dauphin Charles' southern provinces. The invading army, commanded by the Earl of Salisbury, rapidly seized Loire crossings at Beaugency, Meung-sur-Loire, Jargeau, and Châteauneuf – effectively isolating Orléans by holding the river both up and down stream.

Orléans' medieval bridge was built in the 12th century and required twenty spans to cross the wide, shallow Loire River. Numerous houses, businesses, and water-powered mills were situated on top of and below the bridge. For defensive purposes, drawbridges marked both ends of the structure with the southern drawbridge dominated by the two stone towers of Les Tourelles. At the northern end of the bridge was the great Châtelet citadel. The city walls incorporated thirty-two towers and six main gates. Each gate was further protected by stone- and timber-strengthened earthen embankments called *boulevards*.

The English siege of Orléans started on 12 October 1428, when Salisbury's main force joined the English vanguard commanded by the Earl of Suffolk, which was then encamped at the southern end of the bridge. The French destroyed suburban neighborhoods and numerous churches including the Convent des Augustins to deny the English cover for their cannon or shelter in the approaching winter.

During the night of 23/24 October, after an intense cannonade by English guns, the French abandoned Les Tourelles, which now became the main English defensive position, further isolating Orléans from the king's supporters to the south. During the retreat they destroyed spans of the bridge, prohibiting the English from using their position for a direct assault on the city. By a lucky French cannon-shot across the Loire, Salisbury was killed, and the less aggressive Suffolk assumed command.

The English recognized the folly of further attacks against the heavily defended city and decided to besiege it into starvation. The construction of siege-works or *bastille* around Orléans was started but, because of the size of the city, never completely eliminated delivery of provisions and reinforcements due to the less well-defended eastern suburbs. Orléans' commander, known as the Bastard of Orléans, later comte de Dunois, led numerous sorties to delay construction of siege towers, but the work continued. English attacks against the western defenses

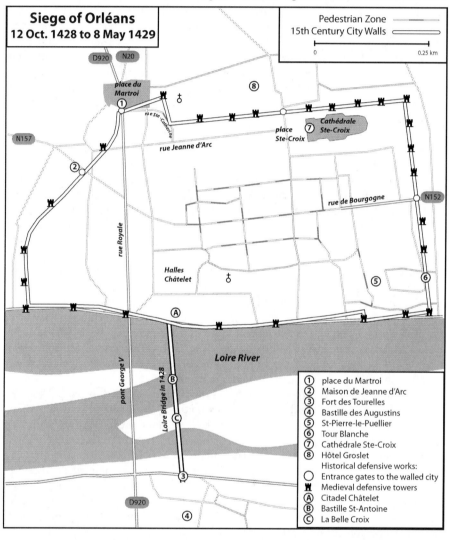

Siege of Orléans
12 Oct. 1428 to 8 May 1429

Pedestrian Zone
15th Century City Walls

0   0.25 km

① place du Martroi
② Maison de Jeanne d'Arc
③ Fort des Tourelles
④ Bastille des Augustins
⑤ St-Pierre-le-Puellier
⑥ Tour Blanche
⑦ Cathédrale Ste-Croix
⑧ Hôtel Groslet
Historical defensive works:
◯ Entrance gates to the walled city
♜ Medieval defensive towers
Ⓐ Citadel Châtelet
Ⓑ Bastille St-Antoine
Ⓒ La Belle Croix

increased while the towers were completed and offered shelter for the supporting cannon. After a hard winter on reduced rations, the French garrison was dwindling through injury and desertion. By March the English were attempting to close the communications route from the east by constructing the Bastille de St-Loup on the northern shore.

No historical figure has had as dramatic an impact in as short a time as a 17-year-old peasant girl from the small Lorraine village of Domrémy, who appeared at Charles' court at Chinon begging for an opportunity to defend France from the invaders. No one has come from more obscure beginnings or has remained more controversial. As France's youngest and most revered hero and as patron saint of the country, homages to her are found throughout the land. For a person of whom no formal portrait exists, her image is the most reproduced in France. Few figures from this period have had their every move and utterance as well documented, translated, or analyzed as Jeanne d'Arc, Maid of Orléans.

Jeanne was allowed to join the army commanded by the Bastard of Orléans that was assembling at Blois to relieve the siege of Orléans. The three to four thousand man relief army approached Orléans on 29 April 1429. Although badly needed provisions were delivered through the Porte de Bourgogne, the army remained south of the river and later returned to Blois. Jeanne, in her white armor and mounted upon a white warhorse, led 200 men-at-arms into the city to a tumultuous reception from the besieged city's inhabitants.

The French, re-victualized and re-energized by Jeanne, began sorties in strength against English defenses. On 4 May, the Bastard of Orléans attacked the English Bastille de St-Loup, which was threatening to cut off the remaining access to the city. When Jeanne heard the noise of the fighting, she donned her armor and rushed to the scene, only to be met by bloodied and retreating Frenchmen. With Jeanne leading the way, and with her war banner plainly visible, she rallied the almost-defeated French and stormed St-Loup. With a few exceptions, mainly due to Jeanne's intercession, the defenders were all killed. The next day the small Bastille de St-Jean-le-Blanc also fell. The English, ostensibly holding siege on the French, were becoming the besieged.

On 6 May, against the wisdom of the town's more experienced military commanders, Jeanne led a sortie against the Bastille des Augustins on the site of the ruined convent. By courageous force of arms, it was taken, and the English again retreated into Les Tourelles. That night a critical war council was held and, aware of an approaching English relief column, a frontal assault against the intimidating Les Tourelles was decided upon for the next day.

In a bloody age that saw few bloodier confrontations, this was an all-out attack upon a walled fortification held by five hundred select troops led by Sir William Gladsdale and supported by numerous cannon. After thirteen hours of repeated attempts to scale the landward ramparts, during which Jeanne received the first of her many battle wounds from an arrow in the shoulder, the English position held. While night approached, the wounded Jeanne returned to the fighting. Using her banner as a signal to advance, a final assault carried the *boulevard* before the Tourelles while a second force attacked from the city over planks laid across the destroyed drawbridge. The English attempted to retreat into the towers of Les Tourelles; however, the French had floated a flaming barge under the drawbridge connecting the *boulevard* with the main towers. When the heavily armored English men-at-arms tread upon the drawbridge, it collapsed, throwing them into the river. With their leaders dead, the English garrison lost heart, and the two hundred survivors surrendered.

The next morning the Earl of Suffolk, realizing that the siege was broken, tried to force an open field battle, but the French did not accept. The English army then abandoned their fortifications and retreated toward Jargeau. The celebration within the city was long remembered as the city's greatest, and all the glory of victory was attributed to Jeanne's intercession.

Aftermath

Jeanne's inspiration led to an enlargement of French forces which quickly recaptured English-held towns along the Loire, and destroyed a large English relief column at the battle of Patay (18 June 1429). Jeanne witnessed the Dauphin's coronation as King Charles VII at Reims as she had promised. She was captured by Burgundians during a sortie outside the gates of Compiègne in 1430, sold to the English, and burned at the stake for sorcery in Rouen on 30 May 1431. The English dominance in France had been broken, however, and after defeat at the battles of Formigny (1450) and Castillon (1453), the Hundred Years War unceremoniously ended.

Battlefield Tour

Modern Orléans bears little resemblance to the city of Jeanne. Heavily bombed in the Second World War, the rebuilding process cost it much of its medieval appearance, and the city now looks like many other modern, commercial cities, including the attendant traffic, one way streets, and congestion. The Vieil Quarter, however, standing between the cathedral and the river retains numerous historic structures. The scale of central Orléans encourages exploration because it is small enough to walk but large enough for a variety of old buildings, especially near the Châtelet and the rue de Boulogne, where medieval-looking buildings remain. A 3.3 km (2 mile) walking tour covers important sites in the lifting of the siege in 1429 and includes much of the city of Jeanne's time. The French fortifications of 1429 ran 0.9 km along the Loire River from the rue Notre-Dame de Recouvrance west of Pont George V to rue de la Tour Neuve to the east. They extended north approximately 0.5 km to include the Cathédrale Ste-Croix.

Immediately after Orléans' liberation, the city became a favorite place of rest for Jeanne, and the city adopted a special devotion to her. That relationship has remained strong over the past 580 years, and Orléans holds a Jeanne d'Arc fete every May with a local girl selected to portray Jeanne in a dramatization of her ride into the besieged city.

Parking convenient for the walking tour is available in garages near the place du Martroi or at Halles Châtelet.

The **place du Martroi** is in the heart of Orléans on the rue Royale and is the logical starting place for tours of the Jeanne sites. The place has been mostly pedestrianized and presents an open expanse at the intersection of three major streets. The square retains its 18th century classical buildings and the equestrian statue (from 1855) of Jeanne whose plinth is decorated with bronze plaques commemorating events from her life. Leaving the place du Martroi to the southeast is the pedestrian-only rue Ste-Catherine. Its old storefronts and narrow passage present an image of what medieval Orléans may have been like.

Turn right onto the rue Jeanne d'Arc; the great Cathédrale Ste-Croix is visible at the eastern end of a street lined with buildings of classical design. The street runs from the place du général de Gaulle to the place Ste-Croix. We will return to the cathedral later in the tour but for now proceed west.

Jeanne d'Arc frequently stayed in the house of Jacques Boucher, the treasurer of the duc d'Orléans, while residing in the city during and after the siege. The house was originally built against the western ramparts of the city, and marks the limit of the medieval fortifications. Located at 3, place du général de Gaulle, it now houses the **Maison de Jeanne d'Arc**. The original building was destroyed during the Second World War; the current structure is a slightly smaller reconstruction of the original half-timbered house, and contains a small museum which presents scenes and models of events in Jeanne's life. The first floor has a diorama showing Jeanne's triumphant entry into the city and a larger diorama of the battle for Les Tourelles with considerable detail, including miniature figures. External lighting illuminates relevant parts of the diorama, corresponding to the audio explanation which is available in French, English, Spanish, German, and Italian. The museum is open from 2 May through October from 10:00 to 12:00 and 14:00 to 18:00 (closed Mondays); and afternoons only from November through April. Fee.

Leave the museum to the southeast on rue du Tabour and turn right onto rue Royale, an attractive shopping street of upscale stores and restaurants. Arcades on both sides allow pedestrians to walk protected from the weather. The rue Royale leads directly to the Pont George V (1760).

After crossing the river turn left onto quai du Fort Tourelles, which shortly changes name to quai des Augustins. Unlike its wooden predecessors, the 12th century Pont des Tourelles was constructed of stone and crossed the river between what is now rue des Hôtelleries and rue Ste Marceau, approximately 100 meters east of Pont George V. Sixty meters to the east is a small overlook which provides a viewpoint of the city back across the river. A wooden cross tops a stone column below which a very faded plaque identifies the location as the entrance to **Fort de Tourelles**. The shrub-covered islands in the river are all that remain of the foundations of the original bridge.

Forty meters farther along the Quay du Fort Tourelles is a triangular square with another bronze statue of Jeanne. This one was erected in the 19th century. The original, erected during the lifetime of Jeanne's mother, was destroyed during the 16th century religious wars. Bounding the square is the rue Croix-de-la-Pucelle, at the far end of which a small cross-topped column marks the location of the Bastille des Augustins. Its plaque states, 'In memory of Jeanne d'Arc, called la Pucelle, the pious heroine who on 8 May 1429 in this same location by her valor saved the city, France, and her king.'

Return across the Pont George V and proceed right on rue Jean Hupeau, then right on rue des Halles. The **Châtelet** stretched from the present rue des Hôtelleries to rue au Lin. The citadel was formed by four sets of buildings surrounding a courtyard. The courtyard became the present rue d'Albret when the fortress was dismantled in the 17th century. The only remnant is the medieval corner tower at 9 rue au Lin. In the 20th century, the 'Halles Châtelet' covered market was built north of where the fortress used to stand. Today the indoor food market presents fresh fish, meat, cheese, and fruits among other delicacies. The individual stalls specialize in particular foods, and all are very fresh.

Turn left on rue du Petit Puits, pass Église St-Donatien, and then turn right onto rue de la Charpenterie. After 250 meters bear right on rue des Sept Dormants, passing the Cloître St-Pierre-le-Puellier across the square on the right. The Romanesque church of **St-Pierre-le-Puellier** is crowded by neighboring structures in narrow alleys. Built in the 12th century, it is the oldest remaining church in Orléans. Isabelle Romain, Jeanne d'Arc's mother, was one of its parishioners. The church became a salt storage facility during the French Revolution, and today is a cultural center.

Proceed on rue des Africans to rue St-Flou. Visible on the right is the **Tour Blanche,** the only remaining element of the medieval fortifications. From this tower, the French cannon bombarded the Fort des Tourelles. The foundation, visible on the rue St-Flou, is from the 4th century. The upper section is from the 14th and the beginning of the 15th century. The tower lost its defensive importance when the city walls were extended to the east. A good view of the tower can be obtained by proceeding to rue de la Tour Neuve.

Return past St-Pierre-le-Puellier and turn right on rue St-Gilles, which becomes rue de l'Université. Turn left and continue along the rue de Bourgogne which contains numerous restaurants and cafés offering a wide variety of local and ethnic cuisines. Jeanne's triumphant entry into the city on 29 April 1429 probably led down this street, then a major thoroughfare. At rue Parisie turn right and continue into the place Ste-Croix in front of the **Cathédrale Ste-Croix**.

A church has been on this spot since the 7th century. After being destroyed by fire in 989, Hugh Capet, founder of the Capetian dynasty, ordered construction of a new cathedral. At least one king of France (Louis VI) was crowned here. After a partial collapse in 1278, a Gothic structure in which Jeanne celebrated her victory took its place. The 13th century church was burned by the Huguenots in 1568, and the reconstruction took over 200 years due to the later religious wars. Gutted by bombing in World War II, the building has been restored to its prewar grandeur.

The five great portals of the façade are surmounted by three rose windows. The structure is crowned with two square towers which complete the impressive, symmetric front. Peaking out from behind the towers is the central spire, which is sited directly over the transept crossing. Inside, the main aisle is flanked on each side by two side aisles. The tall interior roof is capped by a gothic vaulted ceiling. Extremely colorful stained glass windows depict events in Jeanne's short career whereas the plain glass windows are a reminder of the Second World War's destruction. The north transept to the left of the main altar has a statue of Jeanne supported by two lions. The altar is carved with battle scenes, including the conquest of Les Tourelles. Upon nearby pillars are two plaques commemorating the more than one million dead from the British Empire who fell in the First World War, and the more than one half million Americans who gave their lives fighting in two world war in France. Stone decorations on the side altars and ambulatory show time's wear. Bullet holes at the rear of the nave are still visible. Many of the church's treasures as well as tours of the tower for views over the city are by guided tour only (in French) as arranged by the tourist office. The foundations of the original 4th century structure can still be seen in the crypt. The cathedral is open daily 10:00 to 12:00 and 14:00 to 17:00 (18:00 during the summer season). No admission charge.

The old **Hôtel Groslot**, a 16th century Renaissance building, is north of the cathedral in the place d'Etape. The red brick building was once a residence for French kings. Another Jeanne statue, wearing a dress, is in front of the stairs. The building contains Jeanne artifacts and noted Renaissance paintings. If possible, walk through the building to a small park where the façade of the 15th century chapel of St-Jacques has been reconstructed after being moved from the Châtelet district.

Return to the place Ste-Croix, go west on the rue Jeanne d'Arc back to the rue Royale. The place du Martroi is to the north.

Recommended Reading

Ayton, Andrew and Philip Preston: *The Battle of Crécy, 1346*. Woodbridge, England: Boydell Press, 2005. Modern experts offer a revised analysis of the battle.

Burne, Lieutenant-Colonel Alfred H: *The Crécy War: A Military History of the Hundred Years War from 1337 to the Peace of Brétigny, 1360*. Ware, England: Wordsworth Editions Limited, 1999. A detailed account of actions preceding and following the battle. Originally published in 1955.

Curry, Anne: *Agincourt: A New History*. Stroud, England: Tempus Publishing, 2005. An academic look at ancient chronicles about the battle and the men who fought it.

Keegan, John: *The Face of Battle*. New York: The Viking Press, 1976. An analysis of how medieval battles were fought.

Livingstone, Marilyn and Morgen Witzel: *The Road to Crécy: The English Invasion of France, 1346*. Harlow, Great Britain: Pearson Education Limited, 2005. A day-by-day account of the English army's movements and of the battle.

Sackville-West, Vita: *Saint Joan of Arc*. New York: Doubleday, 1991. A biography of Jeanne d'Arc.

Steward, Desmond: *The Hundred Years War: The English in France 1337 – 1453*. London: Constable and Company, 1978. The classic account of the Hundred Years War and its many engagements. Originally published in 1979.

Tuchman, Barbara W. *A Distant Mirror: The Calamitous 14th Century*. New York: Alfred A. Knopf, 1978. A vivid description of Europe and its society in the Middle Ages.

Chapter Two

War of Spanish Succession
1701 – 1714

During the late 17th century, King Louis XIV of France engaged in a series of wars in Holland, Sicily, Germany, Italy and Spanish Netherlands (much of current day Belgium), and France become Europe's most populous and affluent country. By 1700, however, he felt surrounded by powerful enemies; England across the Channel, Spain across the Pyrenees, Hapsburg Austria to the east, Spanish Netherlands to the northeast, and the German states across the Rhine. Louis encouraged the heirless King Charles II of Spain to name Louis' grandson, Philippe d'Anjou as successor. Austrian Emperor Leopold I's son, Charles, had an equally strong claim on the Spanish throne, the battle for which became the War of Spanish Succession.

Louis XIV was well served by the greatest of military engineers, maréchal Sebastian le Prestre de Vauban who designed a system of fortifications each of which could be overcome only by lengthy siege. Military campaigns thus became slow, indecisive affairs mainly focused upon maneuver and siege with few pitched engagements. Those battles that did occur involved ranks of musket-carrying infantry firing at close quarters, cannon tearing large holes in the linear ranks of infantrymen, and sword-wielding cavalrymen slashing their way through anything in their path.

Although hostilities were conducted in Italy, Iberia, and the Mediterranean, the decisive battles were in Flanders and Germany. The greatest of all English military commanders, John Churchill, the Duke of Marlborough, led allied forces in Spanish Netherlands. In 1704, Vienna was under threat by an advancing Franco-Bavarian Army when Marlborough marched his English-Dutch army 400 km across Germany to a stunning victory at Blenheim.

#4

Battle of Ramillies
23 May 1706

OBJECTIVE	To defeat Villeroi's army before additional French forces arrived
FORCES	
FRENCH:	62,000 men and 72 guns (maréchal François de Neufville, duc de Charost et de Villeroi)
ALLIES:	60,000 men and 120 guns (John Churchill, Duke of Marlborough)
RESULT	A decisive victory for Marlborough, opening much of Flanders to English allied occupation.
CASUALTIES	
FRENCH:	6,700 killed, 5,300 wounded, 5,800 taken prisoner and 4,000 scattered
ALLIES:	4,200 killed and wounded
LOCATION	Namur, Belgium is 310 km northeast of Paris; Ramillies-Offus is 22 km north of Namur

Battle

In 1706 French Marshals Villeroi, Vendôme, and Villars led armies in Spanish Netherlands, Italy, and Germany. Marlborough's campaign plan was limited by his Dutch allies to pressuring French defensive lines in Spanish Netherlands. By 22 May, the Duke advanced from Merdorp toward Namur moving along the Mehaigne River. Maréchal duc de Villeroi wanted to attack because he was confident of victory and eager to engage Marlborough. He left Louvain, proceeding south toward Tienen, under orders to capture Leuze.

On 23 May, reconnoitering the ground beyond the Mehaigne River near

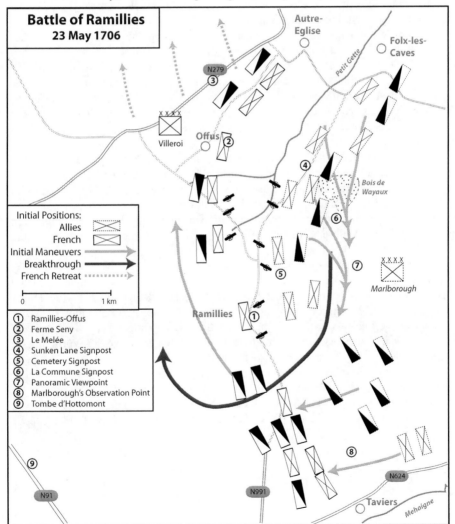

Folx-les-Caves and planning to camp on the Mont St-André plateau west of Ramillies, Marlborough's Quartermaster General William Cadogan stumbled into a patrol of French hussars at 08:00 just as the thick morning fog began to lift. A few shots were exchanged, and the French force retired. With visibility increasing as the sun burnt off the mist, Cadogan sighted Villeroi's advanced guard on the high ground beyond Ramillies. Both armies proceeded to establish lines of battle.

Villeroi immediately assumed a defensive posture, centering upon the village of Ramillies. A brigade of infantry occupied the hamlets of Franquenée and Taviers, anchoring the French right on the Mehaigne. Between Taviers and Ramillies were one hundred squadrons of cavalry interspersed with infantry commanded by Maximilian Emanuel II von Wittelsbach, Elector of Bavaria. The elite *Maison du Roi* cavalry were initially stationed upon the slopes of the Tumulus d'Hottomont. The French center at Ramillies was sufficiently elevated to provide uninterrupted views to the north and east; there Villeroi stationed twenty battalions[1] of infantry supported by cannon. Meanwhile, his left was guarded by strongpoints in Offus and Autre-Église. It was a strong disposition of troops.

The English spent three hours establishing their initial position on the plateau de Jandrenouille, with Marlborough's slightly convex front running from the Mehaigne near Franquenée to Folx-les-Caves. In keeping with his proven tactics, Marlborough planned feint attacks on both flanks to draw the enemy's strength from its center, where he meant to establish superiority for the decisive thrust. He did not give the order to attack until 14:00.

The fighting started with George Hamilton, Earl of Orkney and commander of the right flank, ordering his troops across the Petit Gette against Offus and Autre-Église. Despite the marshy lowlands swollen by the previous day's heavy rainfall and withering French musket fire, English infantry, stopping only to volley, forced their way up the hill to the outer buildings of Offus and Autre-Église. Fearing a turn of his left flank, Villeroi sent reinforcements from his center into the increasing struggle for Offus.

Simultaneous with Orkney's movement, Dutch Guards commanded by Count Hendrik van Nassau, Lord of Ouwerkerk (Overkirk), attacked Franquenée and Taviers while their cannon reduced French defenses. Responding to the Dutch advance, fourteen squadrons of dismounted dragoons and two battalions of Swiss mercenaries rushed forward – only to be repelled by the Dutch. They were then cut down by Danish cavalry commanded by Karl Alexander, Duke of Württemberg, while struggling to withdraw across the marshy lowlands.

As he was about to capture both villages, Lord Orkney retired, having received the command delivered by several aides and finally by Cadogan personally to force the reluctant Orkney's obedience. Nevertheless, Villeroi's attention was fixed upon Orkney and the scarlet jackets of the English formations on the Petit

---

[1] By the 18th century, military formations nominally held one hundred fifty horsemen per squadron and four hundred to six hundred infantrymen per battalion although actual size was frequently reduced by casualties, disease, or desertion.

Gette as he had been warned to do by Louis XIV. The battle's focus shifted to the center when Marlborough executed the main effort against Ramillies.

German infantry battalions fought their way into the outlying buildings of Ramillies, locking French defenders into a struggle for the village. Ouwerkerk's cavalry, with Dutch, German, and Swiss infantry, clashed with French and Bavarian cavalry between Ramillies and Taviers. Thirteen squadrons of the elite *Maison du Roi* smashed into the advancing troops, threatening a breakthrough and flanking the infantry engaged in Ramillies. The advance was stopped only by Marlborough's personal intervention. Marlborough gradually gained the advantage by adding squadrons of cavalry into the struggle – first eighteen and then twenty-one more whose movements from the Gette were concealed from Villeroi's view by the fold of the Quivelette stream. By late afternoon Marlborough established numerical superiority and drove into Villeroi's middle.

The Danish cavalry advanced beyond Taviers, taking the French right flank. They wheeled from the south and drove through the lines of the *Maison du Roi*, falling upon their rear. By 17:00 the center was penetrated and the right flank pushed back like a gate on the hinge of Ramillies. The French line collapsed in disorder.

Villeroi attempted to repair the situation by ordering his cavalry to form a new line facing south to cover his army's retreat. The stench of defeat was in the air, however, and the cavalry fled. Villeroi and Maximilian, caught up in the congested roadways, were nearly captured while English cavalry slaughtered stragglers. Maréchal Villars, waging his own campaign in Germany, described the defeat as 'the most shameful, humiliating, and disastrous of routs.'[2]

Marlborough's victory so early in the campaigning season permitted him to sweep into Flanders capturing Antwerp, Dunkerque, Menen, Brussels, Ghent, and Bruges before the campaign season ended.

Battlefield Tour

Rolling hills of arable land around Ramillies are broken only by an occasional copse or village and hence presented ideal terrain to deploy troops with room for maneuver and with sufficient natural features to disguise troop movements. The Mehaigne and Petit Gette are lazy, narrow creeks which wander over the countryside. Individually they present no great obstacle, but each nurtured boggy wetlands which in 1706 were substantially engorged by recent rainfall.

The tour passes French strongpoints in Ramillies, Offus, and Autre-Église before crossing the battle area to the Allies' initial position and proceeding to the location of the final struggle.

Approach Ramillies-Offus from Namur on highway N991 (not to be confused with the nearby N91).

---

[2] Correlli Barnett, *Marlborough* (Ware, United Kingdom: Wordsworth Editions, 1999), 170.

The roadway loses its numbered designation and changes names several times while it approaches and passes through the village. The east-west N624 approximates the course of the Mehaigne River along the southern limit of the battlefield, passing through Franquenée and Taviers.

A Roman road runs approximately parallel to the N624 one half kilometer to the north. It once linked Cologne and Bavay and still runs along the ridge crest separating the watershed of the Escaut River (which includes the Gette) from that of the Meuse (which includes the Mehaigne). The ridge once constituted the fortified northern border of the Roman Empire. After the empire's fall, the Cologne to Bavay road remained the route of choice for successive invaders from the east up to and including the German penetration of the Gembloux Gap in 1940. On the eve of the battle of Ramillies the allied army covered the distance from the outskirts of Waremme to the battlefield along that very road.

The Ramillies battlefield is still a rural location. Many of the roads are very narrow and some retain their 19th century cobblestones; therefore one can drive slowly and study the terrain without encountering heavy traffic. The tour is a short 22 km but does not follow the action chronologically because the fighting shifted from the flanks to the center.

Enter **Ramillies-Offus**, where red brick is still the dominant building material as it was in Louis XIV's time. The town square is along the highway and in front of the church. Its heavily rusted First World War German *minenwerfer* (trench mortar) is enclosed within a low iron fence that also contains the war memorial. The first of several descriptive and attractive multi-language **signboards** which identify key battlefield locations is also here. The village was the focus of the battle and strongly defended along its eastern outskirts. Late in the battle, while the French front collapsed to the south, allied battalions broke through Bavarian infantry into this now sleepy central square, eventually capturing the Bavarian commander, Alessandro, marquis de Maffei.

Continue north on the highway. Turn left toward Offus (Chaussée Oliver Dehasse), then right on rue de Fagneton, and finally right toward the church (rue L. Delhache).

At the intersection of rue L. Delhache and rue du Fôdia is the old ***Ferme Seny***. The red brick walls enclose a courtyard that was typical of the time. The slit openings may have been for muskets because the site provided a strong defensive position. The buildings are topped with black slate roofs, the sway of which indicates their age. The rue du Fôdia, which proceeds east from the courtyard gate, provides a view of the Petit Gette and the slightly farther away Bois de Wayaux. The road ultimately leads to an intersection of rural paths at Fôdia, from which Lord Orkney brought his English and Scottish infantry to the outskirts of the two villages. The poplars now lining the course of the Petit Gette were not present in 1706; their place was occupied instead by low reed banks and scrub brush.

Proceed west on the rue L. Delhache back to the rue de Fagneton and turn toward Autre-Église.

To the left, before entering Autre-Église, is an area known as **Le Melée** where the final actions of the battle took place. The French cavalry attempted to move south to form a new defensive line but instead ran into the French baggage train and retreating infantry. Panic set in, and the cavalry joined the rout, completing the French defeat.

In the village turn right at the 'T' intersection, then a quick left toward the church. If interested, continue straight to the small square which contains a large caliber German artillery piece from the First World War; otherwise turn right toward Folx-les-Caves (rue de Folx-les-Caves).

The terrain drops, hiding Autre-Église from view while crossing the barely noticeable Petit Gette stream.

Turn right before entering the village onto the rue de la Tannerie. The road changes name several times while it approaches the Bois des Wayaux on the left.

Along this area Orkney launched his initial, nearly successful assault toward Offus and Autre-Église. The land becomes sunken, and shortly afterwards another **signboard** is on the right.

Sunken lanes radiate in all directions and are typical of this part of Belgium. They played an important part in the battle of Ramillies because they hid troop movements. During the French retreat they proved fatal for fleeing troops who were attacked and trampled by the pursuing English cavalry. Paths to the west were followed by the allied army in its decisive assault upon the French center.

Continue on what is now rue J. Guilleaume where it re-enters Ramillies. Exit the town square to the northeast on rue de Wayaux and follow it to the town cemetery where there is another **signboard**.

Ramillies was strongly defended and this location marks the critical point on the battlefield. To the east is the long, gradual slope which gave defenders a perfect field of fire. Four brigades of infantry approached from this direction, their orderly ranks pouring musket volleys on the Bavarian and the Swiss defenders. The infantry fought their way up this slope and, despite heavy casualties, forced its way into the village.

Proceed down the hill toward the Fermes du Wayaux (indicated on maps as *La Commune*) in the opposite direction of the allied advance.

Before arriving at the farm buildings, a dirt track to the left rises up the hill. A couple hundred meters along the track is another **signboard**, which identifies the route taken by the Danish cavalry when it shifted from northern flank to south in support of Ouwerkerk. The Quivelette tributary of the Petit Gette flows through the Bois du Wayaux, past the farm, and behind the hill.

Continue past the Fermes du Wayaux and turn right onto an unnamed, narrow road and proceed to any convenient parking spot (perhaps at the next intersection at which turn left).

The location provides a great view of the entire battlefield. Visible through a 360° panorama are the farm of Wayaux and the Bois du Wayaux woods beyond, the Offus church tower, the closer church tower at Ramillies, and the traffic on the N624 highway to the south. From any of the next several locations, the spire of the church in Ramillies is visible and it helps retain orientation.

Turn left and proceed south; turn right at the next lane which is the Chaussée Romaine.

The Roman road is drivable; however, it is one of the narrow, one-car wide roadways so prevalent in this rural area. Stop at the next intersection and walk to the ridge crest ahead where the road crosses the ridgeline between Ramillies and Taviers. Slightly to the north is the **highest elevation on the battlefield**, and Marlborough established himself here with a view of the entire battlefield. In this area the final struggle for the center of the French line took place with a cavalry mêlée of 25,000 horsemen, during which Marlborough personally rallied his troops, though he was unhorsed in the process and nearly captured. In this famous incident, two Swiss infantry battalions rushed to Marlborough's protection, repelling the furious onslaught of French horsemen. Later Colonel Bringfield, Marlborough's horseman, was holding a spare mount for the Duke when he was decapitated by a cannonball. Ouwerkerk's forces moved from here against the French first line to face the *Gardes du Corps* and *Mousquetaires* of the *Maison du Roi*. Lord Orkney described the intensity of the fight, 'indeed I think I never had more shot about my ears – both musketry and cannon.'[3] With the support of the Danish cavalry and after two hours of conflict of the most deadly kind, he drove the French flank back west of Ramillies.

Do not continue straight ahead because the road deteriorates. Turn left to intersect with the N624 between Franquenée and Taviers.

---

[3] Robert Parker, *Military Memoirs of Marlborough's Campaigns 1702 – 1712*, ed, David Chandler (London, Greenhill Books, 1998), 61.

The white turreted farm visible to the east dates from 1659. The low swampy areas where the dragoons and Swiss met defeat at the hands of allied cavalry are visible to the south.

> Continue west toward Noville-sur-Mehaigne (N624); then turn right toward Leuven (N91). After 1.75 km a small rural road to the right is on the political border between the two provinces. The approach from the north has a sign 'Tombe d'Hottomont'; however, it is not signed coming from the south.

Another **signboard** near the tree- and brush-covered hillock describes the history of the Roman road and the uncertain origins of the tomb. **Hottomont Tumulus**, erected on the edge of the Roman road, is 11.5 meters high and 50 meters in diameter. These mounds were usually constructed to hold the remains of renowned generals. In the fields to the left and right the Elector of Bavaria's units were driven back upon the infantry around Ramillies.

> Do not continue forward but return to the N91.

#5

Battle of Oudenaarde
11 July 1708

OBJECTIVE	To regain Ghent and Bruges for the Allies while France threatened the last fortification along the Scheldt, the lifeline to the Channel coast.
FORCES	
FRENCH:	85,000 men (Louis, duc de Bourgogne, and Louis-Joseph, duc de Vendôme)
ALLIES:	80,000 men (John Churchill, Duke of Marlborough, and Prince Eugène Francis of Savoy-Carignano)
RESULT	Marlborough and Eugène destroyed half of the French Army.
CASUALTIES	
FRENCH:	4,200 killed and wounded; 9,800 taken prisoner; 15,000 scattered
ALLIES:	3,040 killed and wounded
LOCATION	Lille is 220 km north of Paris; Oudenaarde is 62 km northeast of Lille

In the year following the stunning victories of 1706, maréchal duc de Vendôme, now commanding the French Army, and Marlborough engaged in a series of maneuvers without significant result. In 1708 Vendôme was joined by the king's grandson, duc de Bourgogne (Burgundy), who, being a royal, was titular commander. France regained supremacy in Flanders when local Catholic burgers in Ghent and Bruges threw open the city gates in an insurrection against the hated

Protestant Dutch. After executing some diversionary maneuvers along the Rhine, Prince Eugène of Savoy left his army and joined Marlborough. Marlborough had positioned himself between the French Army and France; conversely the French were now between Marlborough's predominantly Dutch army and Holland. Marlborough and Vendôme then maneuvered for control of the Scheldt River and the fortified city of Oudenaarde.

Battle

The battle of Oudenaarde was a battle of encounter taking place on terrain

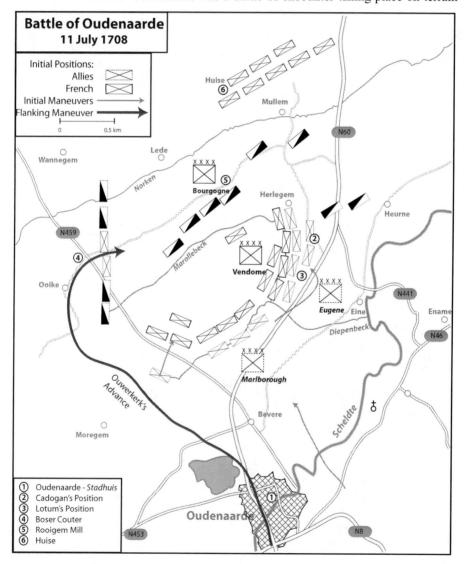

Battle of Oudenaarde
11 July 1708

Initial Positions:
Allies
French
Initial Maneuvers
Flanking Maneuver
0   0.5 km

① Oudenaarde - *Stadhuis*
② Cadogan's Position
③ Lotum's Position
④ Boser Couter
⑤ Rooigem Mill
⑥ Huise

of neither side's choosing. Marlborough's forces were strung out across the countryside in a forced march, as a consequence of which, they reached the battlefield in a piecemeal manner.

In the early hours of 11 July, Major-General William Cadogan left the allied camp and headed toward the Scheldt River crossing at Oudenaarde with sixteen battalions of infantry and eight cavalry squadrons. He arrived at 09:00 and saw the French Army lazily crossing the river 10 km to the north at Gavere. He immediately set his engineers to work erecting five pontoon bridges across the river between Oudenaarde and Eine. Shortly before noon, Cadogan's force crossed the river and established positions behind the Diepenbeck creek where they routed a French foraging party. When word of the Allies' presence reached Vendome, he was stunned by the rapidity of the enemy's advance.

Marlborough arrived and extended the line to the west protected by the marshy Diepenbeck. Burgundy, the inexperienced commander, and Vendôme, the veteran, were at odds as to how to respond, while allied troops continued to cross the river. Under Burgundy's orders to prepare for battle, Vendôme organized his forces along the high ground which extended in both directions from Huise.

The allied commanders joined Cadogan at his advanced position, and they could see the French Army deploying along the partially wooded ridge behind the Norken River. Not until 15:00 did Marlborough and Prince Eugène feel that they had sufficient strength to engage the enemy. Cadogan swept through Eine and Heurne, capturing three Swiss battalions and decimating a fourth. His Hanoverian cavalry tauntingly charged the French left wing, capturing prisoners and disengaging before the full weight of the French was brought to bear.

As the allied forces continued to stream across the bridges – minus most of their cannon which were too cumbersome to maneuver in the crush to cross the river – Burgundy decided to advance. The French struck Cadogan's exposed position and would have overwhelmed it if not for their slow progress on the impossibly entangled terrain, which was no place for the effective deployment of France's superior cavalry. Cadogan's defense to French assaults was skillfully managed and well supported by twenty Prussian squadrons gathered around Groenewoud. Newly arriving reinforcements for each side extended the line westwards. The arrival of the Duke of Argyll's twenty battalions temporarily secured Cadogan's left, where the two allied corps faced fifty battalions of French infantry. Intense musketry merged with hand-to-hand fighting while the lines swung to and fro. Vendôme was personally leading French infantry to recapture Groenewald instead of standing by Burgundy's side offering the advice (some say orders) expected from him. The French fought fiercely to cross the Diepenbeck and approach the pontoon bridges. Twenty German battalions, commanded by General der Infanterie Philipp von Wylich und Lottum, arrived to prevent the engulfment of Argyll's left and drove the French back. Prussian cavalry charged past Herlegem through the French cavalry and against French infantry toward Rooigem. In the approach they were charged upon by the *Maison du Roi* and in the ensuing confrontation lost three-quarters of their number but entered cavalry history.

Vendôme, recognizing the weakness of the allied right, sent messages for a French assault by units near the Ghent road. Burgundy, believing in the existence of an intervening marsh, refused the attack but sent an aide to inform Vendôme. The aide was killed en route, and Vendôme was unaware that the assault would not occur.

By 18:00, Ouwerkerk's twenty-five thousand Dutch troops had crossed the Scheldt via separate bridges in Oudenaarde. Marlborough left Eugène in charge on the right and moved west, where he ordered Ouwerkerk to move across more open ground to the northwest in order to sweep around the French flank and into its rear. All the while, the battalions and squadrons of the French left stood firm behind the Norken. Four brigades of Dutch infantry and twelve squadrons of Danish cavalry moved from Ooike Hill toward Rooigem, delivering a deadly blow against the French right. The force rolled over French infantry and through the *Maison du Roi*, which had wheeled right to face them.

As the sun was setting, Dutch infantry and cavalry from Ooike surged into the French rear, while Cadogan's strengthened flank broke through and turned the left side of the French center near Herlegem. The Allies had encircled nearly fifty thousand French troops. The confused engagement continued into the gloom until darkness forced Marlborough to call a halt.

Burgundy and Vendôme, after a loud and public argument, withdrew with the largely intact left wing to Ghent. Marlborough desired to bring the war to northern France, but Lille's Vauban-built citadel would have to be taken first. Maréchal Louis duc de Boufflers conducted a brilliant defense, holding off the Allies for four months while the French rebuilt defensive lines. The citadel did not fall until 8 December, a very late ending to the campaign season.

Battlefield Tour

Urban expansion has encroached upon the Oudenaarde battlefield. The land between the city center and Eine, where Marlborough's pontoon bridges were erected, has been developed. North of the city, where Ouwerkerk battalions and squadrons reformed after the constriction of crossing the stone bridges into the city, the sprawling Bruwaan Industrial Park has been built. Lowlands that figured in the battle, especially around the Diepenbeck creek, have been drained by ditches. The Scheldt has been canalized and no longer shows the meandering banks from the 18th century. The Ghent road is now the high-speed N60 highway, but it occupies essentially the same ground. With the exception of the initial rout of the French advanced guard, most of the action on the allied right flank took place to the north and west of this highway. No monuments or museums to the battle exist. The tour of this compact battlefield covers only 18 km.

Place names in Flanders are in Dutch, which can create some confusion with French texts and the Anglicized spellings found in English language histories – most notably in the substitution of vowels. Many of the villages mentioned in historical accounts are now a mere half dozen structures, and their names do not appear on most roadmaps. Do not be disconcerted because they are not as important as the terrain which encompassed them. People who have difficulty driving the area's narrow roads are encouraged to remain on the N60 and N459 highways. The other roads on this route are mostly one car wide – with two-way traffic. The occasional wide spot allows for opposing cars to pass.

Begin the tour in the city center.

Oudenaarde dates from the construction of an 11th century fortress for Baldwin IV to exert control over river traffic. The late **Gothic *Stadhuis*** was completed in 1530 and stands today much as it did on the day after the battle, when Marlborough and Eugène were cheered by their soldiers in the Grote Markt. The city presents many other examples of fine architecture.

Proceed northeast to the Tussenbruggen but do not cross the Scheldt; instead turn left and follow the road (Marlboroughlaan) along its left bank. Although the road changes names several times, follow its course along the bank of the river for good views. Approximately 1 km from the Tussenbruggen is the area of the allied pontoon bridges; however, nothing distinguishes the site now. Continue along the river to the interchange with the highway toward Ghent (N441) and proceed in that direction. Continue until the large roundabout intersection with the Ghent road (N60) and again turn toward that city. Carefully turn left at the second opportunity, after the roundabout onto Leistraat, one of the famous Belgian narrow, one-lane roads. Continue down the lane, which becomes Beekstraat, until you reach a small widening of the road where one car can pass the other.

The surrounding farm fields are very flat, criss-crossed by hedges, and spotted by copses and thickets, representative of Groenewoud. Beekstraat eventually crosses the **Marollebeek,** which appears to be little more than a drainage ditch and now belies its impact in 1708. A cluster of houses to the northwest is all that remains of Herlegem. Here along the Marollebeek, Cadogan faced infantry led personally by Vendôme. From the south Argyll's twenty battalions of British infantry marched to enter the fray along Cadogan's flank.

Return to the Ghent Road (N60) and turn toward Oudenaarde. After 2 km turn right (Doorn); just before this turn the road crossed the Diepenbeck, hardly identifiable in this built-up area except for the poplars delimiting its course to the west. Continue through a corner of the Industrial Park. Turn left (Trompestraat) and carefully follow it through the semi-rural countryside.

The route passes between and parallel to the Diepenbeck and Marollebeek streams, crossing the battleground where Lottum's twenty battalions drove the French back across the **Diepenbeck** to the rear. Marlborough later moved Lottum's units to the right flank in a daring and well-executed exchange with newly arrived Hessian and Hanoverian infantry which took up positions here.

Trompestraat becomes Ooikestraat in an area of very old farm buildings, open fields, pear orchards, sugar beet fields, and cow pastures, which again presents the difficult nature of the terrain.

Follow Ooikestraat to the intersection with the N459 highway.

This highway marks the route of Ouwerkerk's swing around the French right flank, occasionally referred to as the '*Boser Couter*.' The terrain slopes gently but consistently down toward the Scheldt River. At approximately this intersection General Week, commanding Ouwerkerk's vanguard, led sixteen battalions to the northeast in an attack upon the French right flank which was fighting with the Hanoverian forces.

To the north is a ridge which runs essentially in the same direction as the approach to the highway. The ridge shielded Ouwerkerk's movement from French view. Turn right and proceed toward Wannegem.

Continue 1.4 km and turn right (onto Loweg, but named Ooikeplein on the other side of the main highway).

The road moves along the crest of a higher, second ridge where Ouwerkerk's detachment led by the young Prince of Orange, future King George II, fell upon the enemy rear. After 0.6 km, a high spot with a clump of trees sits on the right and presents a view of the entire terrain including Oudenaarde to the east.

Continue along Loweg to the clump of trees and brush standing along the road in front of the red-roofed barn on the left.

Rooigem Mill was once located here and provided the best physical location to view the battlefield because it is on very high ground with clear visibility onto the wide, sweeping depression where the bulk of the battle was fought. In this mill Burgundy and his staff, advisors, and couturiers watched the battle develop.

Turn left at the mill; do not proceed straight because the roadway turns into a very rutted, potholed farm track. Turn right at the next intersection, then left toward Huise (Driesstraat). Before entering Huise, the road crosses the Rooigembeek (Churchill called this the Norken River, others called it the Molenbeek). Continue into Huise.

The village church is a fine example of the small town, gray stone edifices found throughout Flanders. Vendôme and Burgundy met in the village after the battle and exchanged heated words. Vendôme then abandoned his men and left for Ghent.

Wannegemstraat starts immediately opposite the front doors of the church. Upon exiting the western edge of the town, Wannegemstraat traces along the south slope of the ridge crest which was the position of the French right flank before it moved forward over the slopes to join the battle. The roadway provides a perfect view over the battlefield. A short distance west of Huise is a windmill which provides a fine example of the type used by Burgundy to observe the battle from Rooigem.

Follow Wannegemstraat back to the N459 highway.

#6

Battle of Malplaquet
11 September 1709

OBJECTIVE	To attack French positions blocking the approach into France.
FORCES	
FRENCH:	80,000 men and 60 guns (maréchal Claude Louis duc de Villars, then maréchal Louis duc de Boufflers)
ALLIES:	107,000 men and 105 guns (John Churchill, Duke of Marlborough, and Prince Eugène Francis of Savoy-Carignano)
RESULT	A Pyrrhic victory for Marlborough whose allied army was so debilitated as to be unable to pursue the retreating French.
CASUALTIES	
FRENCH:	4,500 killed and 8,000 wounded
ALLIES:	6,500 killed and 14,000 wounded
LOCATION	Valenciennes is 210 km north of Paris; Malplaquet is 30 km east of Valenciennes

Both sides were weary of the war, and Louis was willing to concede Spain to the Habsburgs; however, the Allies overplayed their hand, insisting upon terms too onerous for Louis to accept. Since the Allies feared French hegemony of Europe and Louis XIV strived to retain his conquests, the war continued. Marlborough pressured France's barrier fortresses, rejoined by his co-commander at the battle of Blenheim, Prince Eugene of Savoy, who was leading the Imperial army. In 1709, the allied commanders, after a successful but too lengthy siege of Tournai, moved their armies to invest Mons, the fall of which would allow invasion into France. They then moved south to face France's best general, maréchal duc de Villars, who had established entrenched positions northeast of Bavay in front of the small village of Malplaquet.

Battle

Villars, now well familiar with Marlborough's tactics, expected the main attack to come in the center; therefore he strongly fortified it with redans and cannon. Gaps were left between the redans to permit cavalry to pass. Additional French guns and all of the French cavalry were stationed behind the redans. His infantry, including Swiss, Irish, and Bavarian units, were in a long front positioned behind the defense works and anchored in the Bois de Taisnières and Bois de Sars (now collectively the Bois de Blaregnies) to the north and the Bois de la Lanière to the south.

Marlborough spread two hundred fifty squadrons of cavalry and one hundred twenty battalions of infantry across a 6 km front. The right flank, commanded by the Prince of Savoy, was to penetrate the Bois de Taisnières using forty battalions of German and Danish infantry, under Major-General Alexander von der Schulenburg, before an assault in the center could begin. To his left a strong force of Prussian and Hanoverian infantry and guns commanded by General Lottum was to feint an attack on the French center but at the last moment veer to the right to engage the southern edge of the Bois de Taisnières. Meanwhile a smaller force of

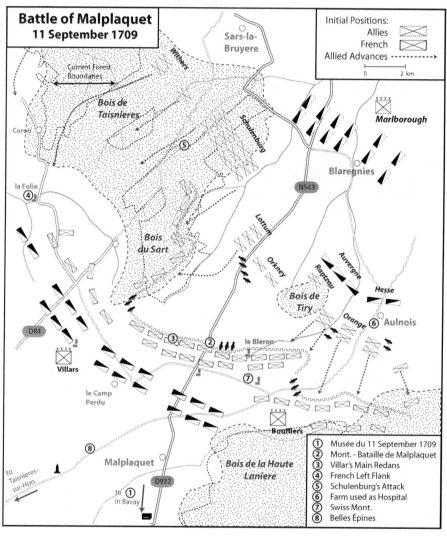

Battle of Malplaquet
11 September 1709

Sars-la-Bruyere

Initial Positions:
Allies
French
Allied Advances ----------►
0   2 km

Withers

Current Forest Boundaries

Bois de Taisnieres

Schulenburg

Marlborough

Coroy

⑤

Blaregnies

la Folie
④

N543

Lottum

Bois du Sart

Orkney

Auvergne

Rapteau

Hesse

Bois de Tiry

Orange ⑥ Aulnois

D84

Villars

③ ② le Bieron

⑦

le Camp Perdu

Boufflers

⑧

Malplaquet

Bois de la Haute Laniere

to Taisnieres-sur-Hon

to ①
in Bavay

D932

① Musée du 11 September 1709
② Mont. - Bataille de Malplaquet
③ Villar's Main Redans
④ French Left Flank
⑤ Schulenburg's Attack
⑥ Farm used as Hospital
⑦ Swiss Mont.
⑧ Belles Épines

nineteen battalions, commanded by Lieutenant-General Henry Withers, attempted to circle through the forest and fall upon the French left flank. His ten squadrons made a still wider circuit. A nineteen hundred-man force commanded by Brigadier Gauvain moved into the gap between Withers and Schulenburg. The main assault was to be led by Orkney with a moderate force of fifteen battalions facing the French redans; however, Marlborough's hammer of over one hundred seventy squadrons of cavalry was hidden behind the Bois de Tiry to exploit any success. Finally, the much-smaller force of the Prince of Orange was on the left, facing the Bois de la Lanière.

At 07:30, while the morning mist started to lift, the batteries commenced exchanging salvos. At 09:00, a mass artillery discharge signaled the beginning of the battle. Schulenburg's infantry marched in three ranks toward Bois de Taisnières, where General Albergotti's five brigades of French infantry waited behind lines of earthen ramparts and abattis[4]. The forest's edge exploded in fire when determined French musket volleys depleted the approaching first rank before it even reached the wood. General Lottum's twenty-two battalions struggled to cross the marshy rau de la Roulerie while rapidly repositioned French batteries poured enfilade fire into its ranks. General Withers' nineteen battalions entered the wood farther north but quickly became entangled in the dense brush.

The Prince of Orange's thirty battalions fell upon twice that number on the French right commanded by maréchal Boufflers in the Bois de la Lanière approximately thirty minutes later. His advance was enfiladed by French guns hidden in a small depression. The effect was cataclysmic when twenty cannon erupted with a roar of ball and grapeshot that scythed down entire ranks of Dutch, Swiss, and Scottish infantry. Survivors were raked by mass musket volleys from their front. The Prince was de-horsed, and the enthused French, sensing victory, left the protections of their palisades to pursue the survivors – only to be met and driven back by Prince Hesse-Cassel's cavalry. The Allies regrouped and attacked again with a similar result. Thirty minutes of such action produced five thousand casualties, such a terrible loss that the Dutch were all but eliminated as a fighting force for the remainder of the war.

Back on the French left, Lottum and Schulenburg's four to one numerical advantage began to show when they breached the French breastworks and entered the murky shadows of the forest. Schulenburg's infantry attacked against chained logs angled as in a Vauban fortress to allow flanking fire. The lines of fire and disciplined ranks dissolved, resulting in a desperate hand-to-hand mêlée. Bayonets flashed in the sun and musket balls sliced through foliage amid screams of anger and agony. This engagement was unusually savage for the time but foreshadowed European combat to come. Wrote a German observer, 'They hewed them to pieces all they found before them – even the dead when their fury found no more living.'[5]

---

[4] Abattis: felled trees whose sharpened branches pointed outwards and were so arranged as to form a deadly entanglement

[5] Winston Churchill, *Marlborough: His Life and Times* (Chicago: University of Chicago Press, 2002), 611.

Villars moved more troops to his endangered left wing, but they could not halt the allied advance. Schulenburg's infantry, supported by seven cannon, emerged from the forest to find the French defenders manning a second defensive line 250 meters away. Lottum's and Withers' infantry joined Schulenburg's as equal forces of twenty-five thousand men faced each other in lines 1.5 km long. Intense fire erupted, and musket fire shattered Villars's knee and killed several of his local commanders. Villars attempted to lead his army from a chair but soon passed into unconsciousness. The shaken French left flank began to retire from the field.

By 13:00 the French center had been so depleted as to hold only a few battalions of French Guards. Totally outgunned, the infantry abandoned the redans with little resistance, and they were occupied by Orkney's comparatively weak infantry battalions. Boufflers, now commanding, held back his cavalry in anticipation of Marlborough's actions. At 13:30 Marlborough launched thirty thousand Dutch, British, Prussian, Hanoverian, and Imperial cavalry toward the front, supported by forty guns. Boufflers personally led the two thousand *Maison du Roi*, who forced back the allied horsemen six times only to have their advance stopped each time by Orkney's infantry entrenched in the French redans. Additional allied cavalry pushed the French back to the plain in front of Malplaquet, which became a sea of swirling sabers, snorting mounts, and anguished cries along with a rising dust cloud that obscured identification. The action raged for almost an hour.

Orange renewed the attack on the right, again supported by Prince Hesse-Cassel's cavalry. With both wings falling back, Boufflers, to retain the last remaining army in France, ordered retreat. The exhausted Allies could not gather the strength to follow. Although in command of the field of battle, Marlborough's army had incurred casualties amounting to one fifth of their number. In a letter to his king after the battle, Villars wrote, 'If our enemies win one more such victory, they are ruined.'

Aftermath

Malplaquet was the greatest battle of European history before the time of Napoleon and was the last of Marlborough's four famous victories. The magnitude of the bloodshed shocked both opponents. Lord Orkney wrote afterward, 'I hope in God it may be the last battle that I may ever see. A very few of such could make both parties end the war very soon.'[6] The battle's outcome, especially the dramatic efforts of its two marshals, however, stirred French morale, and Villars was credited with saving France. Cracks appeared in the alliance, and Louis became intransigent.

Although larger armies took the field in 1711, their commanders henceforth avoided direct confrontation. Deceptive maneuver and siege dominated for the remainder of the war. By 1714, the French, British, and Dutch were exhausted and signed the Peace of Utrecht, drawing a new map of Europe and the New World.

Battlefield Tour

The terrain at Malplaquet did not provide ability to maneuver as Ramillies or Blenheim. The village sits upon a hilly ridge where passage and visibility is

---

[6] Correlli Barnett, *Marlborough*, (London: Wordsworth Edition, 1999), 239.

limited to the 2 km gap between dense woods. The land is crossed by water-filled ditches and serviced by only mud-choked lanes, except to the south where the Chaussée Brunehault runs through the Bois de la Lanière. The forests, which were the major scenes of the battle, were dense with underbrush and low-hanging branches. Since the battle, the forests have been significantly reduced in size with the Bois Tiry all but disappearing. Names have changed, and the expanded road network can be confusing; however, the rural nature of the battlefield has remained and repeatedly crossing the federal borders is no longer an issue. The area sports few monuments, no remnants of the French fortifications, and little in the way of tourist comforts. A fine small private museum is located in Bavay, however, and there the tour begins.

Bavay was an ancient Gallo-Roman market town as archeological excavations east of the town center prove, and remains so today. A roadmap shows seven rays emanating from the city; the remnants of the great northern European Roman road network, of which Bavay was a critical junction. Parking is plentiful near the town's banks, pharmacies, and restaurants. The **Musée du 11 September 1709** is located at 6, rue des Juifs just off the town's main square and around the corner to the right of the Hôtel-de-Ville. The building looks old and small from the outside. Few battlefield relics from that long ago remain except corroded metal objects and assorted cannon balls, but it presents numerous diagrams and pages from early books with depictions of the main characters in their long white wigs and flowing gowns. The hand-drawn maps are very professional and describe the movements of units during the engagement. A chart locates current battlefield sites with numerous photographs. The museum is open every day from 09:00 to 18:00 from April to November. Fee.

Exit Bavay toward Maubeuge (D932) and follow it 6.7 km to the village of Malplaquet.

Visible in the fields on the left are Second World War blockhouses that formed part of the French defenses along the Belgian border. The final installation is at the intersection immediately before entering Malplaquet. It carries a plaque remembering two Resistance fighters executed here by the Nazi SS in September 1944. A smaller monument ahead celebrates the village's liberation by US 3rd Armored Division on 2 September 1944.

Continue through the village to a slight rise amid the open fields to the stone obelisk.

The **Monument to the Battle of Malplaquet** marks the French center. It was erected on the 200th anniversary of the engagement and presents profiles of the two French generals, Villars and Boufflers. On this spot a twenty gun French battery supported the redans which stretched across the field to the left rear.

Ahead is a mud rut toward the right that leads to Ferme le Bléron, which stood in front of the major French positions and where Marlborough spent the night after the battle. The farm track is almost exactly on the old French-Belgian border, as the abandoned customs offices attest. British and Prussian infantry advanced across these fields to occupy the French redans, after which allied batteries here and those similarly positioned near Bois de Taisnières engaged Boufflers's cavalry charges in a deadly crossfire.

Carefully reverse direction toward Malplaquet. Shortly after passing the Malplaquet monument, turn right toward le Camp Perdu (chemin de la Bondoise).

The crest of the ridge to the north held Villars's main redans and shielded French cavalry movements from Marlborough's view. Turn right before entering le Camp Perdu onto chemin de Jean Sart and follow it until the intersection with the highway (D84). The dairy farms and hay fields just passed on the left held the French rear position of cavalry squadrons.

Turn right toward Sars-la-Bruyère (D84). Almost immediately a rural road to the left (rue des Alliés) goes 1.2 km to la Folie farm, the limit of the French left flank. Nothing special remains; therefore, continue toward Sars.

Upon approaching the old border, one passes through the area of the final line of French infantry. The road's name changes from Chaussée du Bois to Chaussée Brunehault, identifying it as an old Roman road. The surface turns to a charming cobblestone roadway where it passes through what remains of the **Bois de Taisnières**. This direction is the opposite of Schulenburg's attack, which took place in the forest to the right. The forest is managed now, and much of the dense undergrowth has been removed. A number of logging trails penetrate the forest toward where Schulenburg's and Lottum's troops encountered the French breastworks, but no evidence of the battle remains, and a walk is only recommended as a commune with nature.

After exiting the forest, follow the Chaussée Brunehault with a right turn followed by another right toward Blaregnies (N544). In the center of town, turn toward Aulnois (rue d'Aulnois) and follow the roadway to that town. Keep in mind that the road changes name several times.

Proceed to the village water tower, opposite of which stands a red brick farm that was used by the Dutch and Austrian troops as a **hospital**. Its arched entryway and slotted barn windows remain much as they were 300 years ago.

Proceed toward Taisnières-sur-Hon (rue de Malplaquet). Through this area the impetuous Prince of Orange engaged Boufflers. Bear right and pass near le Petit Bléron farm with its two white towers. Bear right again (chemin du Château Vert) to pass a **monument to the Swiss forces** located in front of the farm building.

Swiss mercenaries fought on both sides during the battle, most notably with the Dutch forces of the Prince of Orange. Similarly, Irish Catholic exiles in the French Army and the Royal Irish Regiment in the Allied army fought against each other in the Bois de Taisnières. The twenty-gun battery that inflicted so much death upon the Dutch was hidden by a depression in the field to the left.

Turn left toward Malplaquet (D932), then right at the next intersection toward Taisnières-sur Hon (Grand Chemin de Mons).

These open plains provided terrain for the massive cavalry mêlée in which squadrons of horsemen fought in the largest cavalry engagement in modern European history.

After approximately 1 km a black stone monument framed in red brick known as '**Belles Épines**' is dedicated to Villars and commemorates his wounding during the battle. Ahead is another stele remembering the murder of five patriots by the Nazi SS on 2 September 1944.

The tour ends in Taisnières-sur-Hon.

Recommended reading

Barnett, Correlli: *Marlborough*. London: Wordsworth Editions, 1999. Marlborough's life and his great military victories.

Churchill, Winston: *Marlborough: His Life and Times*. Chicago: University of Chicago Press, 2002. A massive biography in four volumes; book II (volumes III and IV) provides a detailed description of events during the War of Spanish Succession.

Weigley, Russell, F.: *The Age of Battles: The Quest for Decisive Warfare from Breitenfeld to Waterloo*. Bloomington, Indiana: Indiana University Press, 1991. History of warfare and how it developed in the modern era.

Chapter Three

Wars of the French Revolution and Napoleon
1792 – 1815

By 1792, the French Revolution had been raging for three years, with competing political factions propelling the country into an ever-deepening abyss. Each regime was followed by another that was more radical and more bloodthirsty. King Louis XVI and his queen, Marie Antoinette, were captured in Varennes-en-Argonne (35 km from Valmy) attempting to seek safety in Brussels and support from Europe's royal houses. The royal couple was returned to Paris and imprisoned in the Tuileries.

Austria and Prussia sought to unite European opposition against France into the First Coalition. Émigrés, who included many of France's military leaders and trained officers, agitated against the Revolutionary government. In November 1791, the Girondins, the current ruling party, forced a declaration of war on Austria, marking the start of the Revolutionary Wars. The following spring the French attempted to capture Flanders; however, the adventure was quickly brought to a halt by the indifference of the local population, the ill discipline of the French Army, and the general lack of a cohesive plan. In Paris French Revolutionaries saw treason in every defeat.

#7

Cannonade at Valmy
20 September 1792

OBJECTIVE	To eliminate the last Revolutionary force between the Prussian-Austrian Army and Paris.
FORCES	
FRENCH:	36,000 men and 40 guns (général François Christophe Kellermann, later the duc de Valmy)
PRUSSIAN:	34,000 men and 58 guns (Generalfeldmarschall Karl Wilhelm, Duke of Brunswick)
RESULT	A demonstration of the military potential of the French Republican Armies.
CASUALTIES	
FRENCH:	300 killed and wounded
PRUSSIAN:	184 killed and wounded
LOCATION	Châlons-en-Champaign is 160 km east of Paris; Valmy is 30 km east of Châlons

The esteemed Duke of Brunswick, accompanied by King Friedrich Wilhelm II of Prussia, led an immaculately dressed and rigidly trained sixty thousand man Prussian Army against French border fortifications. His force was enlarged by fifteen thousand French émigrés seeking to recover their lost wealth. Longwy fell on 23 August; Verdun fell on 2 September. Brunswick advanced, albeit at a glacial pace, to insert his army between French armies at Sedan and Metz. Once across the Marne at Châlons, he planned to march along the river valley to Paris. An additional forty-five thousand Austrian troops protected their flanks.

Général Charles François Dumouriez was given command of the French force – which largely consisted of half-trained recruits, although French artillery was considered the best in Europe. He planned to use the broken ground and dense forests of the Argonne plateau as a natural fortification. Only five routes were available to traverse the thickly wooded ground and each route was to be stoutly protected. The Austrians discovered a weakly defended opening, however, and forced passage. Dumouriez abandoned the defense of the Argonne and fell back to the area around Ste-Menehould, which straddled roads to Châlons and Reims. Général Francois Kellermann, commanding a twenty thousand-man force at Metz, was ordered to join Dumouriez at Ste-Menehould.

Battle

Although French forces were commanded by Dumouriez, Kellermann blocked the Prussian approach to Ste-Menehould. He established a strong position upon a windmill-topped plateau near Valmy, sent a detachment to Gizaucourt, and stationed cavalry along the Châlons Road. Dumouriez positioned his army to protect Kellermann's flanks.

Maneuver brought the Prussian Army between Dumouriez and Paris, but Brunswick could not tolerate the French Army sitting on his line of supply and retreat. The allied camp was already stricken with hunger, which was worsened by Dumouriez's instructions to denude the countryside. The duke's army was dependant upon Verdun for bread, and Dumouriez threatened to interdict those supplies should Brunswick make a move toward Châlons. The Prussians needed the high road between Châlons and Ste. Menehould to move their artillery. Kellermann's position effectively denied this avenue to them.

At dawn, the Prussians broke camp and proceeded from the west along the Poste Road to a road junction known as Cabaret de la Lune. The duke's plan was to push through the French center, separating their flanks which he could then crush in turn. Heavy mist shrouded the valleys and obscured views of enemy positions. Upon arriving at la Lune, the occasional French cannonball fell among Prussian ranks. The duke assessed Kellermann's positions as being too far forward and too unprotected.

As the sun burned through the mist and a bright blue sky appeared, the exchange of grape and canister became more forceful. It continued for approximately two hours, with the less experienced French getting the worse of the exchange. Brunswick expected the raw troops to dissolve into chaos as they had at other engagements. To further test French resolve, a division of Prussian infantry was sent up the slope toward the windmill. The division was met by withering salvos delivered by French cannoniers; the infantry wavered and fell back.

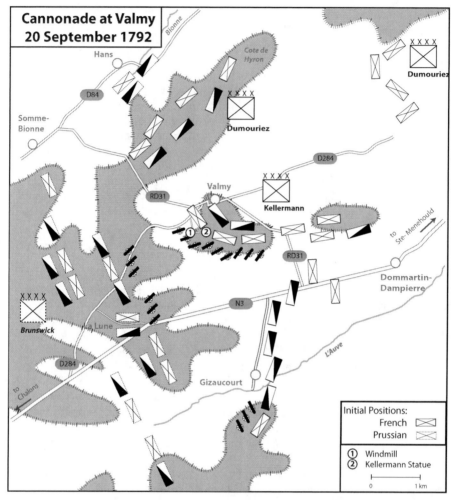

The artillery exchange intensified while Prussian cannonballs denuded the hillside approach to the French line. At one point Kellermann had a horse shot from beneath him while he strove to rally his men. The French rear was rocked by a violent explosion when a Prussian shell struck a munitions wagon. Kellermann rushed a reserve battery to fill the gap caused by the explosion. French infantry, restless with the inaction, became fearful but were rallied by Kellermann's cry of *'Vive la nation'* – a shout that was picked up by nearby battalions and quickly spread across the French ranks.

Brunswick saw the French agitation as an opportunity and again sent his infantry into a second assault. For 800 meters they advanced over the now exposed ground, all the while under heavy cannon fire. Before reaching the French line and after a moment's hesitation, they too fell back. Brunswick ordered no further efforts, and the firing just petered out by 17:00 with only light casualties on either side. Dumouriez's 16,000 men never entered the battle. The engagement is referred to as a 'cannonade' because of the lack of infantry involvement.

Aftermath

Brunswick was uncomfortable with the French held fortresses in his rear and generally disgusted with the entire affair. He lingered in the area for ten days before retiring to Longwy and entering winter quarters.

The allied army's failure to decisively defeat the French recruits was a momentous emotional victory, creating what eventually became the spirited army of Napoleon. On the same day as the battle, the National Assembly in Paris declared the establishment of the First French Republic. Later that year French Republican armies achieved further success in clashes along the Rhine and in the defeat of an Austrian army at the battle of Jemappes. The now doomed Louis XVI was guillotined in the place de la Revolution on 21 January 1793.

Battlefield Tour

The nearest Autoroute exit is #29 at Ste-Menehould, and Valmy is west of the provincial market town. The battlefield is well signed from the Châlons Road (N3). Valmy plateau is just south of the village and is accessed along the D284. A parking area is below the hill.

Unfortunately the A4 Autoroute slices through the battlefield south of Valmy, but it has little impact upon the tour. The lightly wooded area around Valmy marries the gradual rolling plains of Champaign to the ravine-ripped woodlands of the Argonne Forest. The battlefield memorial sits upon Valmy Plateau, and the few tour sites are within a short walking distance.

On the plateau was a prominent **wooden windmill** where grain was ground to flour. Kellermann ordered the original windmill destroyed because it provided a reference point for Prussian gunners. Subsequently it was reconstructed several times. The 1947 version was destroyed in the great storm of December 1999. The current reincarnation was constructed in 2005. Tours of the interior can be arranged through the tourist office in Ste-Menehould.

The plateau has four trilingual tables of orientation presenting the historical context and consequences of the battle. From here the full scope of the battlefield can be seen. Two km to the southwest, to the left of the modern radio tower, is la Lune, where Prussian artillery was placed and from which infantry brigades advanced across the open ground toward the mill. The fork in the road at la Lune is now little more than an intersection of the N3 with a farm track that leads to the hameau of les Maigneux. It is not visible from the hill.

Behind the mill and near the small chapel, Kellermann stationed his artillery, supported by the infantry that never was engaged. The rural road visible to the right of the chapel crosses the Châlons Road (not visible in the folds of the landscape) to Gizaucourt. Kellermann stationed infantry and cavalry along the main highway to block Brunswick's advance. Behind Valmy, the plowed ridge known as the Côte de l'Hyron is where Dumouriez's units provided flank support to Kellermann's position.

A pathway leads to a brick chapel containing the ashes of Kellermann's great granddaughter, Princess Ginetti. Farther along the path and at the end of a tree lined approach is a **statue of Kellermann** holding his saber erect and waving his feathered hat to encourage his troops. In recognition of Kellermann's feat, Napoleon – after he came to power – elevated him to maréchal of France and later to duc de Valmy. The statue was not erected until the centenary of the battle. On the far side of the plinth are inscribed the words of the German writer and witness to the battle, Johann von Goethe: 'From this place and from this day forth commences a new era in the world's history.' The cannon surrounding the monument are not from the battle, but are instead English models captured in a later engagement against the Dutch. A short, stone obelisk stands in front of the statue and contains the heart of the famous general, who willed that upon his death he should be buried near his comrades.

In an unusual juxtaposition of military commemorations, the village of Valmy contains a **statue of General Francisco de Miranda**, a Venezuelan officer who sought French help for Latin American liberation and served in the battle of Valmy. Facing Miranda is a bust of the great liberator of Venezuela, Simon Bolivar. In the same plaza are the town's First World War memorial and an American Sherman tank commemorating the town's liberation by American forces during the Second World War.

No commemoration of General Dumouriez or his contribution to the victory exists. After defeat at the battle of Neerwinden in 1793, Dumouriez came under suspicion by Jacobin revolutionaries and sought protection with the Austrians, eventually emigrating to England.

Rise and Fall of Napoleon Bonaparte

Conditions in France continued to deteriorate while the Reign of Terror beset Paris and portable guillotines spread the Terror to the countryside. The French Army carried the revolution beyond the country's borders and instigated the formation of coalitions to stop the revolutionary fervor. In the broth of corruption, civil unrest, and external threat arose the greatest general in French history, Napoleon Bonaparte. The diminutive Corsican took command of the French Army of Italy at age 26 in 1796 and brought about a succession of victories that resulted in French domination of most of Western Europe.

Guerilla warfare in Spain and the catastrophic losses incurred during the invasion of Russia bled France white. Enemies on all sides united, and, after the dramatic victory over Napoleon at the battle of Leipzig, marched on Paris. Napoleon abdicated but quickly regained his enthusiasm for warfare and left exile on the Mediterranean island of Elba to land in Provence on 11 March 1815. From there he marched north, gathering forces along the way.

#8

Battle of Waterloo
18 June 1815

OBJECTIVE	To defeat Wellington's Anglo-Dutch-Belgian Army.
FORCES	
FRENCH:	71,497 men and 246 guns (Emperor Napoleon Bonaparte)
ALLIES:	67,655 men and 156 guns (Field Marshal Arthur Wellesley, Duke of Wellington) and 45,000 men and 44 guns (Generalfeldmarschall Gebhardt Leberecht von Blücher)
RESULT	The Allies routed and destroyed France's last Grande Armée.
CASUALTIES	
FRENCH:	Estimated at 25,000 killed and wounded, 8,000 taken prisoner, and 15,000 missing
ALLIES:	Anglo-Dutch: 15,000 killed and wounded; Prussian: 7,000 killed and wounded
LOCATION	Brussels is 300 km northeast of Paris; the battlefield is 22 km south of Brussels

The leaders opposing Napoleon quickly chose Field Marshal Arthur Wellesley, the Duke of Wellington, to lead military operations against the returning emperor. The closest available forces were British and Hanoverian regiments, highly professional Germans in the English army known as the King's German Legion, and a twenty-eight thousand man Dutch-Belgian division commanded by the Prince of Orange. A strong Prussian corps was formed into the Army of the Lower Rhine, commanded by the ageing but still daring Prussian Generalfeldmarschall Gebhardt Leberecht von Blücher. Austria, Russia, and individual German states were assembling additional armies. Uncertain of Napoleon's intent, Wellington and Blücher aligned their forces across the Catholic Low Countries (now Belgium) from Ghent to Liège, with Wellington headquartered in the west in Brussels and Blücher to the east.

Napoleon knew that he could not face the combined might of the coalition armies. He determined to maneuver his forces so as to be able to attack and defeat each separately. After Napoleon's arrival at Charleroi on 15 June, Wellington and Blücher immediately started to concentrate their forces – Blücher at Ligny and Wellington around Brussels. The next day Napoleon's left wing, commanded by maréchal Michel Ney clashed against Wellington's vanguard at Quatre Bras. Ney nearly succeeded in turning the infantry's flank, but the timely arrival of English Guards restored the line, and little advantage was gained by either side. Ney's action, however, prohibited Wellington from aiding Blücher 12 km distant in Ligny.

Napoleon, upon hearing Ney's cannon engage Wellington at Quatre Bras, led his center and right wing against Blücher. During a savage six-hour battle, the Prussian center broke and was forced into a disorderly withdrawal. Since Napoleon believed Blücher was retreating toward Liège and away from Brussels, he felt secure to attack Wellington's forces. Although several of Napoleon's lieutenants had fought Wellington in Spain and had due consideration of his skills, Napoleon – who had never faced the great duke – was dubious of his inexperienced and rapidly assembled army.

17 June was spent in maneuver under violent thunderstorms with Wellington's army moving back toward Brussels to occupy previously identified positions at Mont St-Jean immediately south of Waterloo. Blücher reformed his troops 19 km to the east at Wavre. Napoleon moved his forces to join Ney at Quatre Bras. The heavy rainfall reduced the roads to rivulets of mud, and both man and horse struggled to make any progress.

Battle

The heavy rainfall of the previous day and night continued into the early morning of 18 June. By 09:00, however, the rain stopped, shafts of sunlight broke through the dark clouds, and a brisk wind arose to dry the fields of corn and rye. Wellington arranged his infantry units along a ridgeline that ran from Ohain to Braine-l'Alleud. He stationed the cavalry behind and the artillery in front. The second line and reserves stood on the downward slope north of the ridge and were thus not visible to the French as well as not exposed to cannon fire. The Nivelles Road ran in a ravine which secured Wellington's right flank; the villages of La Haie and Papelotte secured his left. Wellington established two outposts before his main line. To the right was the Château d'Hougoumont; in the center stood the smaller farmstead of La Haie Sainte.

The French were drawn up similarly in two lines on a parallel ridge three quarters of a kilometer to the south, with the Imperial Guards and cavalry held as a reserve in the center rear. Napoleon sought to smash the center of the English line and then send massed cavalry through the breach. This was to be a battle without artifice; a direct confrontation of firepower versus determination.

Napoleon waited a few hours until the soggy ground hardened sufficiently for his cavalry and artillery to maneuver. At 11:30, he launched a diversionary attack against Château d'Hougoumont – a large establishment with house, chapel, barns, and outbuildings enclosed within stout walls. The surrounding orchards were enclosed in turn by a barrier of hedges and copses. The château grounds were strongly defended by one thousand Hanoverian *Jäger*, a Nassau battalion, and two British Guards companies – all commanded by Lieutenant-Colonel James Macdonnell. Général Prince Jérôme Bonaparte, the emperor's brother, attacked Hougoumont with his 6th Division in a confrontation that escaladed throughout the day with the addition of more troops. Cannon fire, which started in this corner of the battlefield, soon spread across the entire line.

At 13:30, Napoleon ordered maréchal Ney to bring the four divisions of I Corps, commanded by général Jean-Baptiste Drouet, comte d'Erlon, in an attack upon the allied center and left, particularly against La Haie Sainte. They marched in parade ground perfection into the valley while English and French cannon exchanged fire over their heads. From within the walls of La Haie Sainte, the King's German Legion brought murderous fire upon the echeloned ranks of d'Erlon's 2nd Division,

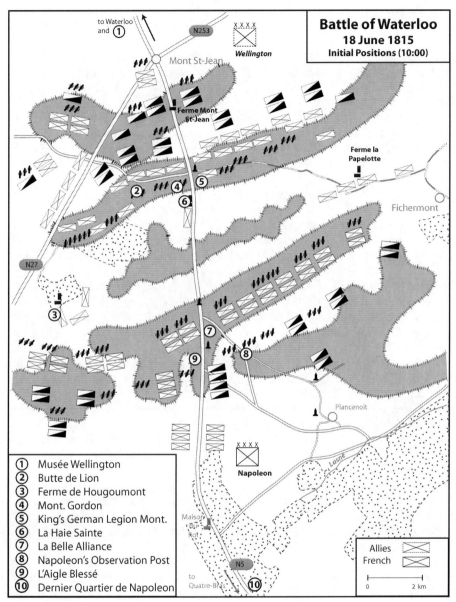

Battle of Waterloo
18 June 1815
Initial Positions (10:00)

to Waterloo and ①
N253
Wellington
Mont St-Jean
Ferme Mont St-Jean
Ferme la Papelotte
②
④ ⑤
⑥
Fichermont
N27
③
⑦
⑨ ⑧
Plancenoit
Lasne
Napoleon
Maison du Roi
to Quatre-Bras
N5
⑩

① Musée Wellington
② Butte de Lion
③ Ferme de Hougoumont
④ Mont. Gordon
⑤ King's German Legion Mont.
⑥ La Haie Sainte
⑦ La Belle Alliance
⑧ Napoleon's Observation Post
⑨ L'Aigle Blessé
⑩ Dernier Quartier de Napoleon

Allies
French
0   2 km

starting a daylong contest over this strategic position. East of the farm, the inexperienced militia troops of the Dutch-Belgian brigade broke under the force of the attack, but the second line, composed of four regiments of Scottish infantry,[1]

---

[1] The successors of the four Scottish regiments distinguished themselves in the First World War (the Black Watch, Cameron Highlanders, First Royal Scots, and Gordons).

under the command of Lieutenant-General Sir Thomas Picton, came forward. When the advancing French approached within 30 meters, Picton's line erupted in a wall of musket fire. A deadly exchange followed with the French gaining the sunken road (chemin d'Ohain). Picton drew his sword and ordered a bayonet charge; then he fell dead, shot through the head. The French staggered in surprised confusion, allowing Sir Henry Paget, Earl of Uxbridge's heavy cavalry to fall upon the French columns. The Union Brigade, led by General Sir William Ponsonby, of English, Scottish, and Irish dragoons pressed forward to a position which protruded in front of the French line. Ney had positioned a *Grande Batterie* of seventy-four guns there, and they were now rendered temporarily useless by the charge of the Scots Grays Regiment. French cavalry responded and drove the now exhausted intruders back, inflicting severe losses.

As previously agreed upon with Wellington, Blücher left a Prussian corps in Wavre to face maréchal Emmanuel maquis de Grouchy's 33,000-man army while the remainder of the Prussian Army marched all day toward Waterloo, pulling their cannon through flooded streams and along muddy roads. By 16:00, Lieutenant-General Graf Bülow von Dennewitz's lead elements exited Bois de Paris only 3 km east of La Belle Alliance. Napoleon dispatched the 3rd and 5th Light Cavalry Divisions – reinforced by a repositioning of VI Corps, commanded by général Georges Mouton comte de Lobau – to protect his right, but he discounted the potential size of the Prussian force, believing that général Grouchy had intercepted the main Prussian Army at Wavre. Two hours later Bülow's troops fell upon Plancenoit. The French Young Guards, who had been dispatched to Plancenoit, repelled repeated assaults by Bülow's infantry. His third assault carried Plancenoit and drove Lobau back. Prussian shells were falling upon La Belle Alliance. Napoleon sent eleven battalions of Imperial Guards in a line against the Prussian-held village, driving the defenders out once again. Each effort, however, required French reserves, lessening Napoleon's odds of victory.

As the day progressed, Jérôme ordered 9th Division to join the battle at Hougoumont, contrary to Napoleon's orders and depriving the main attack of extra striking power. The stronghold was almost surrounded and was set on fire, but still the greatly outnumbered defenders held out.

Napoleon repositioned his artillery on a central ridge that ran between the two armies, bringing his cannon into closer support of the French infantry. A drumming cannonade ensued while missiles were launched from the batteries into the ranks of infantry and artillery. Ney ordered a cavalry assault by five thousand cuirassiers on the allied right center. They rode immediately to the west of the Brussels Road and through the allied batteries, scattering artillerymen. The Third Cavalry Corps led by général François Etienne de Kellermann, son of the victor at Valmy, attacked German infantry near La Haie Sainte and proceeded onto the allied held ridge. They could not disrupt, however, the volley fire from the infantry squares. In a day of fearsome action, the repeated charges, conducted at a trot rather than a gallop because of the wet ground, were terrible encounters to behold. In front of every square was a carpet of agonizing horses and men struck down by musket fire. British infantry squares took on the appearance of abattoirs; the dead and dying so densely packed as to be underfoot of the fighting men. The din of cartridge and cannon was deafening; the dense smoke suffocating. Each respite from a French cavalry assault saw the artillery re-engage with ball and case shot. This pattern continued for almost two hours. Five successive attempts to break through the rows of bayonets were defeated by musket fire from the square's interior until the heavy cavalry was destroyed.

Sometime after 18:00, 2nd Division finally succeeded in capturing La Haie Sainte. They then used the strategic position to assault the allied center. French cannon were brought forward and fired grapeshot from a distance of 100 meters into the infantry squares. The center of Wellington's line was thinning, and no reserves were available. The attacking French, however, were exhausted by the struggle, and Ney's requests for fresh troops went unanswered. Efforts to stop Blücher's approach were failing, and Prussians were increasingly entering the field to the French right flank and rear.

Knowing that in the weeks ahead, additional allied armies would increase their numerical advantage for a march on Paris, Napoleon decided to risk all in a gamble for victory. Shortly after 19:00, while the weary troops continued the slugfest, he ordered the remaining six thousand men of the Middle and Old Guard to

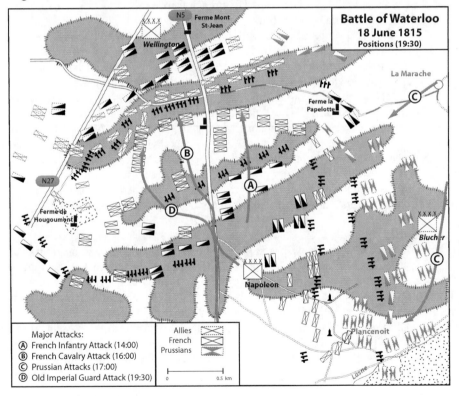

Battle of Waterloo
18 June 1815
Positions (19:30)

Major Attacks:
Ⓐ French Infantry Attack (14:00)
Ⓑ French Cavalry Attack (16:00)
Ⓒ Prussian Attacks (17:00)
Ⓓ Old Imperial Guard Attack (19:30)

Allies
French
Prussians

0   0.5 km

attack the allied right, moving between La Haie Sainte and Hougoumont. Passing before Napoleon while he stood upon a slight rise near La Belle Alliance, they shouted '*Vive l'Empéreur!*' These units had decided many of Napoleon's victories, and they were expected to do so again. To avoid the French cannon fire, British troops – strengthened by reinforcements released by the arrival of General Graf Ziethen's I Corps along the Wavre Road – were lying on the ground just below and behind the crest of the ridge. To the approaching French, the position looked barren except for the few mounted officers. When they marched forward, thirty allied guns on their left flank fired grapeshot, tearing holes in their ranks. Leading the assault, maréchal Ney fell to the ground when his horse was killed, the fifth of the day. He struggled to his feet and led the advance on foot.

At 50 meters distance, Wellington, who had spent the day moving across the battlefield from one crisis point to another, cried out the legendary phrase 'Stand up, Guards'[2] at which two thousand men jumped up and delivered a volley into the French column, dropping at least 300. Additional volleys followed while the French Guards scrambled to deploy. The final unit, the 4th Chasseurs Battalion of Imperial Guards, approached the same sector of the allied line. The British 1st Battalion, 52nd Light Infantry Regiment, stationed to the left of the advancing French, extended a line at right angle to the main defense. The French were caught in a deadly explosion of fire from front and flank. They broke rank and fled.

Taking advantage of the disruption to French ranks, Wellington ordered a general advance all along his line, and a rout ensued. Flooding rearward, some units attempted to form defensive squares, but for the most part, a crush of humanity and horses struggled down the road toward Charleroi. British cavalry slashed a path through the chaos with their sabers, only the gloom of nightfall affording a protective cloak to the defeated army. The Prussians pursued the French through the night while the vanquished enemy abandoned everything in a mad rush to safety. A bottleneck at the stone bridge crossing the Dyle River at Genappe 7 km south slowed the flow that did not stop until most of the officers and men recrossed the Sambre River the next day. Napoleon, protected within a square of Imperial Guard grenadiers, made his way back to his personal escort stationed at Le Caillou. From there he started a personal withdrawal that did not cease until he entered Paris.

Aftermath

The French defeat was complete. The Allies captured cannon, muskets, wagons, baggage, regimental colors, and all of the other paraphernalia of an army right down to Napoleon's sword and hat. Nothing remained of the Grande Armée. In Paris the Chamber of Representatives demanded Napoleon's abdication, which it received on 22 June. Napoleon escaped to Rochefort in an attempt to flee to America. The effort was futile, and on 15 July he surrendered to the captain of the English warship *HMS Bellerophon*.

Wellington, drained by his efforts, returned to the Waterloo inn where he slept fitfully for a few hours. The next morning he wept while the roll of killed and

---

[2] Albert A Nofi: *The Waterloo Campaign* (Pennsylvania: Combined Books, 1993), 246.

wounded was read. Afterwards he summarized the battle as 'the nearest run thing you ever saw in your life.'[3]

The Allies marched on to Paris, and on 3 July the city's capitulation ended 23 years of warfare. The Treaty of Paris was signed in November 1815. The Allies were not as severe with France as they could have been. The country's borders were reduced to those of 1789, certain frontier fortifications and Paris were subject to occupation for a period of three to five years, and a war indemnity of 700 million francs was imposed. Nineteen generals were put on trial by the now ruling King Louis XVIII. All were found guilty (fourteen in absentia) and sentenced to death. The royalists reserved the biggest trial for maréchal Ney, who was also found guilty and executed by firing squad. Napoleon died a British prisoner on the isolated island of Ste-Hélène in 1821 at age 52.

Battlefield Tour

Waterloo is the best-preserved 19th century battlefield in Europe and has been a major destination for British tourists for almost two hundred years. Although the surrounding communities, especially Waterloo to the north and Braine l'Alleud to the west, have expanded, the ground upon which the armies of Napoleon and Wellington clashed has remained undeveloped. To this day it remains plowed fields of corn or rye as in 1815.

One hundred and seventy thousand men dueled in a compact valley 4 km long and less than .8 km wide. The valley, strewn with hillocks and depressions, is formed by winding parallel ridges standing 30 meters above its bottom. The battlefield is bisected by the Brussels-Charleroi Road (N5) which gradually descends into the valley from La Belle Alliance and ascends the opposite ridge, topping it north of La Haie Sainte. Mont St-Jean is behind the center of the northern chain of hills. The sunken Nivelles Road, which forms the western boundary of the battlefield, has been dislodged by the R0 Autoroute. Walking paths cross the battlefield and allow intimate contact with the terrain. Singular events are well marked by monuments, and the site of Wellington's center is occupied by museums and monuments. The tour starts in the greatly expanded village of Waterloo and continues down the Brussels-Charleroi Road, now a bustling thoroughfare, to major locations.

Start the tour on the chaussée de Bruxelles (N5) in the center of Waterloo.

Wellington spent the nights before and after the battle in an inn in Waterloo, and the structure has been well preserved as **Quartier-Général du Duc de Wellington - Musée Wellington**. The building appears much as it did when Wellington strode through the arched entryway to survey his troops on the battlefield. The museum contains artifacts in rooms dedicated to each nation that participated in the battle. Multilanguage audio cassettes describe each display.

---

[3] Alessandro Barbero: *The Battle: A New History of Waterloo*. (New York: Walker Publishing Company, 2003), 309.

Across the courtyard in the old coach-house are illuminated maps of the battlefield, showing the positions of forces at several stages of the battle. The maps are a great assist in following the various movements ordered by Napoleon in his attempts to break the Anglo-Dutch army's line and to follow the arrival of the Prussians. The museum is easy to tour and a great overview for those not completely familiar with the actions during that day in June 1815. Open April through September from 09:30 to 18:30; October though March from 10:30 to 17:00. Closed Christmas and New Years Day. Fee. The domed **Église St-Joseph de Waterloo** opposite the museum was used as a hospital after the battle and now contains numerous memorials and commemorations. The adjacent presbytery now houses a helpful tourist office.

Proceed south toward Charleroi (N5), passing the **Ferme Mont St-Jean** on the left immediately after crossing the Autoroute (R0). At the next traffic light, turn right (rue de la Croix) to pass along the ridge of Wellington's line.

The battlefield's most dominating feature is the **Butte du Lion**, a 41-meter high perfectly conical mound erected in the 1820's to commemorate the Dutch soldiers who died here. The mound is located on the spot where the Prince of Orange was wounded while leading a charge against the Imperial Guards, and it marks the right center of Wellington's line. The summit of the butte is reached by 226 steps and offers views across the entire battlefield. It is topped with a cast-iron lion symbolizing both England and the Netherlands. Visible to the right front is a copse which hides the location of Château d'Hougoumont. The facing ridge to the south held the original line of the French. Much of the convulsive final battle took place on the ground directly below. At the time of the battle the south side of this road was higher forming a sunken lane, where Wellington's infantry received some protection from French cannonades. After the battle the soil was removed to construct the butte.

Butte du Lion Centre du Visiteur offers a full explanation of the battle's progress with a ten square meter lighted board that shows the movements of the formations and provides access to the butte. The Centre also presents a film depicting children reenacting a battle in the age of cavalry and muskets, a huge panorama painted by French artist Louis Dumoulion which extends 110 meters, and a wax museum with life-size figures of French and allied generals. All displays are labeled in four languages, but they are better understood with some prior knowledge of the events. Open generally the same hours as the Wellington Museum. A single discounted ticket may be purchased for admission to all of the attractions. The Visitor Center and Wax Museum are handicap accessible.

Leave the Butte complex toward Braine l'Alleud to cross over the Autoroute. Turn left toward Nivelles (N27) at the first intersection and left again onto a small lane (chemin des Vertes Bornes) which recrosses the Autoroute. At the next junction turn right (chemin du Goumont) and proceed to an unpaved wide spot in the valley.

Park and walk toward the **Hougoumont** buildings. Whereas the signs indicate private property, the owners permit visitors to walk around the farm as long as they remain outside the farm walls. The wooden gate at the main entrance was destroyed and never replaced. A simple iron gate now bars admission through the entryway that was used to receive supplies and reinforcements until attacked by encircling French. The low walls were never rebuilt to their original height, but some of the loopholes created by the defenders are still visible. Most of the buildings of Hougoumont were heavily damaged during the battle, and only one section of the château remains. The grass area inside the compound to the left marks the chapel's location.

Walk around the large barn to the south. The barn's thatch roof was set alight, and the burning embers ignited the hay and straw upon which the wounded lay. The older stonewalls are surmounted by red brick repairs. On the wall near the south gate a plaque commemorates the **Coldstream Guards** defense against repeated French attempts to force entry. After the battle numerous burial pits were dug in the surrounding fields.

Return to the Butte du Lion, continue toward the chaussée de Charleroi (N5), and cross the intersection to the parking area on the right.

Immediately to the left and almost hidden by large shrubs is a stone block **memorial to the Belgian soldiers** who participated in the battle. The terrain to the east was the center of général d'Erlon's first attack upon the British line early in the afternoon; the French coming from the right and up the gradual but nonetheless strenuous slope were repulsed by Picton's Scottish infantry. Across that ground over seven thousand infantry fought in a swirling mob, later joined by two thousand French and English cavalry. Upright stones along the side of the cobblestone roadway hold brass plaques commemorating the **27th Inniskilling Regiment of Foot** and the spot where Lieutenant-General Sir Thomas Picton died. Car travel farther down the road is not recommended, but the surface approximates the condition of the Brussels-Charleroi Road in 1815.

Return to the chaussée de Charleroi (N5) and turn south. Park beside the Hanoverian Monument on the left.

On the right is the fluted column of the **Monument Gordon**, erected in honor of Wellington's aide-de-camp, Lieutenant-Colonel Alexander Gordon, who was killed in the battle. The approach steps are badly overgrown, which makes accessing the monument difficult, and the inscriptions have all but disappeared. Since it was erected before the Butte du Lion, the base indicates the original level of the terrain south of the sunken road.

On the left and almost across from the monument, a solid stone block commemorates the Hanoverian troops of the **King's German Legion** who participated in the valiant defense of La Haie Sainte, the white buildings on the opposite side of the road and slightly to the south. The monument stands upon the sandpit, a site of much contention during the struggle for control of La Haie Sainte, which now contains the bodies of thousands of fallen soldiers.

Walk down the east side of the highway to a point opposite the **La Haie Sainte** gate. (Do not attempt to walk along the west side of the highway because no path exists. Please respect the owner's privacy and do not enter the yard.) Only 376 Hanoverian exiles protected this key position, which had not been prepared commensurate with its importance. Commanded by Major Georg Baron von Baring, the defenders fired through loopholes in the walls and held as long as possible before French engineers battered down the gates and their infantry flooded through them. Forty-two survivors escaped through the rear door of the house toward the main line.

La Haie Sainte is composed of a stone house, barn, and a small garden, enclosed within walls which incorporated the house walls to a large extent. The gate, house, and barn remain almost unchanged from the day of the battle. The shrub-hidden garden to the right was occupied by the French and demonstrates how close they were to Wellington's line. From this location French cannon devastated Wellington's center. The wall holds several **plaques** commemorating French and German participants in the struggle for control of the farmstead. The gentle swale to the left was used as a shelter to muster the Imperial Guard for its final assault while the nine battalions moved forward in echelon to the left. Continuing along the N5 to La Belle Alliance provides a better impression of the battleground.

Continue south to the old inn on the left at the next rural road (chemin de La Belle Alliance).

The **La Belle Alliance** complex, also little changed from the time of the battle, presents a slightly modified facade to the highway and side road. Although the inn was not a site of fighting, the view through the gates into the courtyard presents a look in an early 18th century inn's appearance. A short distance down the rural road, a marker indicates the hillock upon which Napoleon established his observation post at approximately 16:00. From this perspective, the terrain can be seen as Napoleon saw it. To the east, the Prussians approached through Plancenoit; directly north, d'Erlon's Corps failed to break the allied line; to the northwest, the cataclysmic final engagement. Wellington rode to La Belle Alliance after the victory to greet Marshal Blücher.

Return to the main highway and continue south.

Shortly on the right the monument known as 'L'Aigle Blessé' stands at the site of the French Imperial Guard's last infantry squares. The stone shows a wounded bronze eagle with bullet holes in its wing; one claw stubbornly holds the battle honors captured by Imperial Guards in earlier Napoleon victories.

Continue south on the highway.

The emperor selected Le Caillou Farm as his headquarters on the night before the battle, and the building has been preserved as the **Dernier Quartier général de Napoleon**. The five small rooms display a few of Napoleon's personal effects as well as weaponry of the period, all labeled in four languages. The men of his Imperial Guard straggled into the adjacent orchard during the night of 17 June to establish their sodden bivouacs. The farm grounds hold a small ossuary containing bones found on the battlefield. Open April through September from 10:00 to 18:30; October though March from 13:00 to 17:00. Closed Christmas and New Years Day. Fee.

Other Sites of Interest: The **Musée de l'Armée in Brussels**, which contains Belgium's major collection of weapons, documents, and artifacts, may also be of interest. Open daily except Mondays from 09:00 to 12:00 and 13:00 to 16:45; closed certain holidays. No Admission charge and handicap accessible.

Recommended reading:
The battle of Waterloo is probably the single most written about battle in history. The following recommendations do not denigrate the myriad of other fine accounts.

Barbero, Alessandro: *The Battle: A New History of Waterloo*. New York: Walker Publishing Company, 2003. A new and detailed account richly woven with descriptions of fighting in the Napoleonic area.

Creasy, Edward S.: *Fifteen Decisive Battles of the World: From Marathon to Waterloo*. New York: Da Capo Press, 1994. First published in 1851, chapter fourteen describes the battle of Valmy.

Hibbert, Christopher: *Waterloo*. Ware, England: Wordsworth Editions, 1998. Reprint of a somewhat dated but classic account of the battle, heavily quoting participants and their contemporaries.

Howarth, David: *Waterloo: Day of Battle*. New York: Atheneum Publishing, 1968. The battle told largely in the words of eyewitnesses.

Schom, Alan: *One Hundred Days: Napoleon's Road to Waterloo*. New York: Atheneum Publishing, 1992. Describes the events leading up to and including the battle of Waterloo.

Chapter Four

Franco – Prussian War
1870 – 1871

After the defeat of Napoleon, France underwent a series of governments that reflected the conflict between the forces of liberalization, which desired constitutional law, and the monarchists, who desired a return to one-man rule. The Bourbon dynasty returned under the leadership of Louis XVIII; Charles X followed upon Louis's death. Charles was overthrown in the Revolution of 1830 and replaced by Louis Philippe of the Orléans branch of the Bourbons. Another Revolution in 1848 abolished the monarchy and established the Second Republic. Legally elected as President of the Republic, Louis Napoleon Bonaparte seized full power in 1851 declaring himself president for life, then established the Second Empire in 1852 and declared himself Emperor Napoleon III.

By 1870, France had seen almost a century of revolutions and was engaged in yet another internal struggle of Republican versus Monarchist while watching the growing Prussian strength with alarm. The French saw themselves as a declining power, their prestige diminished by rising German nationalism. Napoleon III felt domestic pressure to be compensated for the establishment of the North German Confederation. He suggested that France receive either the Duchy of Luxembourg or Belgium, control of either country fulfilling Louis XIV's ambition of a position on the left bank of the Rhine. Although the southern German states of Baden, Bavaria and Württemberg remained independent, they felt threatened by Napoleon III's attempts secure Luxembourg, so they signed mutual defense treaties with Prussia.

Meanwhile the number of individual German States and principalities had been reduced from over three hundred to thirty-nine by 1815 through the conquests of Napoleon and the actions of the subsequent Congress of Vienna. Wilhelm I, King of Prussia, was victorious in uniting the northern German peoples into the North German Confederation under his leadership after a brief war with Austria in 1866.

War was thus inevitable between Prussia and France. The Prussian military had been planning on it for four years. The French leaders wanted an excuse for war, whether to regain the past glories of Napoleonic conquest, to distract the populace from internal discord, or to derail the seemingly inevitable Prussian economic supremacy on the continent. The events that triggered the war, however, emanated from Spain.

A Spanish revolution in 1868 against the ruling Queen Isabella II left the Spanish crown vacant. Prince Leopold of Hohenzollern-Sigmaringen, a member of the Roman Catholic branch of the Hohenzollern dynasty, was an acceptable candidate to the Spanish Cortes. The thought of a German ruling Spain while Prussia occupied the left bank of the Rhine, however, horrified the French and their emperor. Leopold at first refused the throne, but at the suggestion of Prussian Prime Minister Otto von Bismarck and without consultation with France, Leopold reconsidered and accepted. The French felt humiliated, and Wilhelm and Bismarck were furious at the audacity of the forwarded French demands. Through Bismarck's circulation of an altered report from his own ambassador, that France had insisted the Prussian king guarantee that he would never approve such a move became publicly known.

By now Paris was beyond making requests and demanded war. Some activists wanted nothing less than the destruction of the North German Confederation and occupation of the territory on the Rhine that France still considered to be her natural frontier. Attitudes of national pride and chivalry reappeared, and France was drawn into a potentially disastrous confrontation over its honor and its desire for territorial expansion. Napoleon III reluctantly, but with confidence brought on by recent successes in a campaign against Italy, made plans to attack, deluded by military planners who had simultaneously underestimated the speed of the Prussian mobilization and overestimated the speed of the French.

At 16:40 on 14 July, Napoleon III ordered his army to mobilize. France gained no allies because Austria and Italy wavered in their support, and early French defeats assured that they remained on the sidelines. The British declined Napoleon's request to become involved. Napoleon joined his still mobilizing army at the end of July and established the Imperial Headquarters at Metz with his chief military advisor, Minister of War maréchal Edmond Leboeuf. The mobilization was anything but rapid. Confusion reigned while men and their material were sent separately in criss-cross fashion around France from their homes and depots to mobilization centers while troops waited for their regiments to form. As a result, units arrived late for battles, under strength, without equipment or weapons, and with confused leadership. Everyone was giving orders; no one was in charge. Discipline was an early casualty when soldiers mocked their leaders and Napoleon.

Prussia[1] ordered mobilization on 15 July, and the Bavarian allies followed suit on 17 July. By early August, Prussia had 1.2 million men under arms with 320,000 men facing 140,000 French divided between Metz and Strasbourg. While the French struggled to assembly points inside France amid shortages of every conceivable commodity from bread to rifle cartridges, Chief of the Prussian General Staff Generalfeldmarschall Graf Helmuth von Moltke assembled fully operational army corps on the French border. He was thus able to grasp the initiative from the French and upset their plans of invasion into German territory.

#9

Battle of Spicheren
6 August 1870

OBJECTIVE	To assault French defensive positions.
FORCES	

---

[1] Sometimes the forces opposing the French are described as 'Prussian' and sometimes as 'German.' Strictly speaking there was no Germany at this time but the mixed nationality army of King Wilhelm I of Prussia was under Prussian command. As many of the fighting units were not Prussian, but rather from other German speaking states such as Bavaria, Württemberg, Baden, etc., the term 'German' is sometimes used to describe these mixed formations.

FRENCH:	II Corps with 28,667 men and 72 guns (général de division Charles Frossard)
GERMAN:	III Corps (Generalleutnant Konstantin von Alvensleben II) and VII Corps (General Henri von Zastrow) totaling 67,000 men
RESULT	The French were driven off a promontory overlooking the border but not before inflicting substantial casualties upon a much larger German force.
CASUALTIES	
FRENCH:	320 killed, 1,662 wounded, and 2,096 taken prisoner
GERMAN:	843 killed, 3,656 wounded, and 372 missing
LOCATION	Metz is 338 km east of Paris; Spicheren is 67 km east of Metz

Battle

The fighting started on 2 August when General Frossard's II Corps advanced against the city of Saarbrücken to gain control of that transit center on the French border. An attack upon the lightly defended outpost was strategically insignificant, but it resulted in a French victory that was highly acclaimed in Paris. The move left Frossard's flank exposed, however, to Prince Friedrich Karl's 134,000-man Second Army. Frossard voluntarily abandoned the city three days later.

The struggle for Spicheren focused upon the Rotherberg, the narrow spur of high ground which extends like an arrow from the Spicheren Heights toward Saarbrücken and which commanded the roadway through the Stiring valley toward Metz. The area was considered by général de division Sylvain de Laveaucoupet as a '*position magnifique*' for its defensive possibilities. Laveaucoupet had positioned two companies in trenches on the summit, with the remainder of his division on the heights to the south. French artillery occupied the high ground around the villages of Spicheren, Forbach, and farther south on the Pfaffenberg.

The Prussian First Army (General Karl von Steinmetz) was assigned responsibility for guarding the flank of the advancing Second Army. Steinmetz, not satisfied with this subsidiary role and in direct disobedience of orders, cut across Prince Friedrich's line of march and attacked Frossard's newly assumed but quite formidable defensive positions.

By midday, 14th (Westphalia) Division's artillery started a bombardment of the spur. With his visibility obscured by the dense forests surrounding the hills, General Kameke did not realize that he was facing an entire corps when he sent 27th Brigade (Generalmajor Bruno von François) to clear French artillery from the Rotherberg. Six battalions of his 74th Regiment advanced along a line from the Stiring Valley to Gifertswald[2]. Heavy French artillery and devastating volleys from superior French Chassepot rifles and *mitrailleuses* (machine guns) stopped the Germans and inflicted serious casualties. French attempts to formulate counter-assaults were blasted by the increasing number of German batteries arriving on the scene; French artillery being outmatched by the longer-range Prussian guns. Kameke

---

[2] Alternately known as Giffertwald

brought his 28th Brigade forward with orders to attack général de division Charles Vergé's division on the French left flank.

By 14:30, François rallied both the 74th Regiment's fusilier battalion and elements of the 39th Regiment and led his men up the reddish soil of the Rotherberg. François was hit by no fewer than five bullets and fell dead while the German assault reached the summit. Meanwhile, Vergé's troops hit Kameke's 28th Brigade in Stiring, dealing them a substantial defeat. Unfortunately, caution among the French generals kept them from pressing the advantage, and they remained on the defensive, awaiting the next German blow.

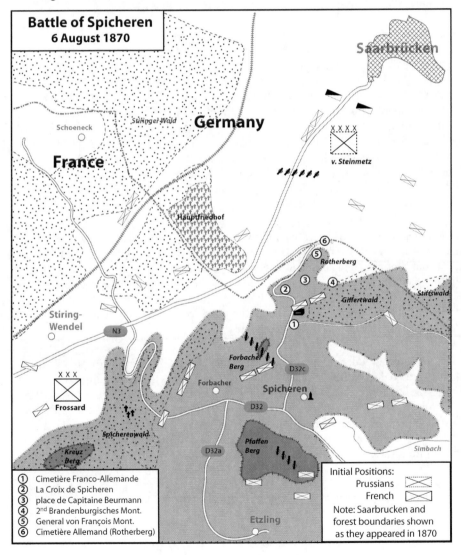

Battle of Spicheren
6 August 1870

Saarbrücken

Schoeneck

Süfinger Wald   **Germany**

X X X X
v. Steinmetz

France

Hauptfriedhof

⑥
⑤
Rotherberg
③ ④
②
Giffertwald   Stiftswald
①

Stiring-Wendel

N3

Forbacher Berg
D32c

Forbacher

Spicheren

X X X
Frossard

D32

Spicherenwald

Kreuz Berg

D32a

Pfaffen Berg

Simbach

Etzling

① Cimetière Franco-Allemande
② La Croix de Spicheren
③ place de Capitaine Beurmann
④ 2nd Brandenburgisches Mont.
⑤ General von François Mont.
⑥ Cimetière Allemand (Rotherberg)

Initial Positions:
Prussians
French

Note: Saarbrucken and forest boundaries shown as they appeared in 1870

General Alvensleben's III Corps responded to the sounds of battle, and his forces advanced toward the fighting. Alvensleben surveyed the situation and relieved Kameke of his command. Committing additional units when they arrived, Prussian 5th Division retook Gifertswald, and a force of mixed units from III and VIII Corps pushed Verge's division from Stiring back to Forbach. With the arrival of more reserves, Alvensleben pushed up the Forbacherberg, onto the ridge, and into Laveaucoupet's left flank while Zastrow's 13th Division was arriving against Forbach. The threat to Fossard's rear made holding the Spicheren heights any longer impossible. The sun was setting, and under the cover of darkness French forces abandoned the hills, retreating south toward Sarreguemines.

Battlefield Tour

While the threat to the French flank forced their nighttime withdrawal, the fighting upon the Spicheren spur was the most dramatic and hence is the focus the tour. The battlefield is compact and largely unchanged. It lies to the north of the village, essentially facing the now abandoned French-German border. The Germans celebrated their victory with the construction of numerous monuments on both sides of the border, most of which remain. Common burial grounds were used after the battle and also still exist. The Germans placed great significance upon their triumph, and the ground became a place of pilgrimage after the war. They fought to retain the heights toward the end of the Second World War, resisting the advance of the US 70th Division. A German cemetery and command bunker from that later war stand upon the approach from the Gifertswald.

The battlefield can be reached by following the A4 Autoroute east from Metz, then the A320 toward Saarbrücken. Use exit #45 at Stiring-Wendel toward Saarbrücken (N3), and continue to the east end of Stiring-Wendel to turn toward Spicheren (D32). Follow the road where it winds into the town; turn left toward the Mairie (rue des Hauteurs des Spicheren, D32c) and follow it to the far end of the town until a calvary backed by shrubs appears on the right at the intersection with the rue des Montagnes. Parking is available a short distance beyond.

Almost hidden behind the calvary is the small **Cimetière Militaire Franco-Allemande Gifertswald** dating from 1870. It contains 1,092 French and German soldiers killed on 6 August 1870, and they are buried in common graves marked by symbolic French white stone and German black iron crosses. Several individual German gravestones line the right side. At the far side of the parking area is the side entrance to the Spicheren Höhen Deutsche Soldaten Friedhof. Under its dark stone crosses lie 120 German soldiers from the Second World War.

Proceed toward the large white cross seen ahead on the left, and into its parking area.

To the right a German bunker that was part of the Westwall fortifications and a post-Second World War American M24 Chafee tank are visible. The forest path passes a sports field before continuing across the length of the Gifertswald.

The **La Croix de Spicheren** stands in the place du Souvenir Français and towers 15 meters above a sweeping left curve in the road. Erected on the 63rd anniversary of the battle, after the return of Lorraine to France after the First World War, the white cross commemorates the French fallen at the battle of Spicheren. Recently attached plaques on its sides list the French order of battle. Nearby is the rose granite memorial to the 70th Infantry who fought there during the winter of 1944/45.

Return to the rue des Hauteurs (chemin du général de Laveaucoupet, and later named the chemin de général Bruno von François), pass the Restaurant Woll – a structure erected in 1897, but a good place to stop for a battlefield lunch – and continue until the roadway ends in a small, tree-shaded parking area named the place de capitaine Charles-Auguste de Beurmann after an officer killed in the battle. Do not attempt to drive farther because the track deteriorates rather badly.

A German regimental monument is on each side of the parking area. On a rise to the right and surrounded by an iron fence is a stone obelisk dedicated to the **Fusilier Regiment *Fürst* Karl Anton von Hohenzollern Nr 40,** whose late afternoon attack near here drove the French Chasseurs from the heights. The elevation presents a good view of the Spicheren spur and the open summit that passes between the tree-covered slopes that were such a difficulty for the Germans to surmount. In the distance is the city of Saarbrücken. Opposite, a stone column mounted upon a stele commemorates the ***Niederrheinischen*** **(Lower Rhine) Fusilier Regiment *Nr 39,*** which joined forces with the 74th Regiment to establish a foothold upon the Rotherberg. Both monuments were erected shortly after the war and carry plaques listing casualties and regimental engagements from the war of 1870/71. They remain in remarkably good condition as do most of the monuments on the battlefield.

A short distance down the track, a forest road to the right enters the Gifertswald. The level road actually hugs the slope of the ridge that ascends the wood and provides a view of the steep climb faced by the German troops. Along this path a forest-shrouded stone column facing down the hillside toward Saarbrücken commemorates the **Grenadier Regiment *Prinz Carl von Preußen (2nd Brandenburg)* Nr 12.** Stones nearby outline a soldier's grave.

Return to the spur and continue along the path (Sentier des Héros) atop its spine. The ground drops precipitously on both sides. The French 10th Chasseurs were well entrenched along this ridge, supported from the rear by French artillery and a battery of *mitrailleuses.*

Down a slight drop, two monuments become visible on the left. The first is a single tombstone surrounded by a low iron fence, marking the location where **General Bruno von François** fell while leading elements of his 27th Brigade against the enemy. The Germans reached the spur crest at the cost of their general. In the clearing ahead is an obelisk dedicated to the fallen comrades and officer corps of the **1ˢᵗ Hannover Infantry Regiment** *Nr 74*. The monument lists the names of those killed in the fighting of 1870 to 1871 by battalion as well as by company, and is mounted upon a huge rock situated on the edge of the cliff which drops down to the D32c highway.

Return to the spur and continue to the north. On the right at the very edge of the spur is the ornately carved memorial to the **Infantry Regiment *von Stülpnagel** *(5ᵗʰ Brandenburg)* *Nr 48*; its front displays a stone Prussian Eagle. The regiment was part of the Prussian 5ᵗʰ Division.

Descending on the path through the thick, tangled vegetation to the interesting Rotherberg German Cemetery below is possible; however, the recommendation is to return to the parking area and follow the D32c past La Croix Souvenir Français to the hairpin left turn below the 1ˢᵗ Hannoverischen Infantry Regiment. Most maps do not indicate the recent roadway modifications completed in this former border area. Possible parking is available in a small side road. Walk along the brick and mud track (rue de la Frontière) to the final site on the battlefield tour.

The **Cimetière Militaire Allemand de 1870-1871 (Rotherberg German Cemetery)** is up the hill on the right, marked by its scattering of black iron Latin and Pattée Crosses indicating ancient graves. It is dedicated to the dead of the 74ᵗʰ Regiment. A walk path and benches offer an opportunity for a brief rest while gazing up the slope that cost the Prussians so dearly.

Other Sites of Interest: Numerous monuments and graves are located in **Forbach Cemetery**, around **Spicheren Church**, and in the **German-French Garden** in Saarbrücken. The **Saarbrücken** *Hauptfriedhof* is an enormous, park-like cemetery with burials from 1870 and a memorial to the *2ⁿᵈ Hannoversches Infanterie-Regiment Nr 77*.

#10
Battle of Mars-la-Tour (Battle of Vionville)
16 August 1870

OBJECTIVE	To intercept the French Army of the Rhine while it withdrew from Metz toward the fortress of Verdun.
FORCES	
FRENCH:	150,000 men and 340 guns of the Army of the Rhine (maréchal François Achille Bazaine)
GERMAN:	76,000 men and 210 guns of the Prussian Second Army (Generaloberst Prince Friedrich Karl)
RESULT	French indecision permitted the Prussians to block the French escape.

CASUALTIES	
FRENCH:	1,367 killed, 10,120 wounded, and 5,472 missing
GERMAN:	4,421 killed, 10,402 wounded, and 965 missing
LOCATION	Metz is 338 km east of Paris; Mars-la-Tour is 25 km west of Metz

After the defeat at Spicheren, the emperor attempted to gather his Army of the Rhine, commanded by the newly appointed maréchal François Achille Bazaine, into the great fortress of Verdun. The French evacuation from Metz, however, was rife with confusion and delay while units scrambled to cross the few bridges over the flooded Moselle River. Beyond the river, a single road ascended the escarpment west of the city before reaching open country at Gravelotte. The congestion on the road, worsened by the confusion of Bazaine's staff and the subsequent disheartening of his troops, slowed the movement of the French Army. On 14 August east of Metz, advance units of Steinmetz's 13th Division swept down upon the French rearguard of général de division Claude-Théodore Decaen's III Corps. Quickly escalating into the furious three-hour battle of Colombey (also named the battle of Borny) which cost Decaen his life, the action further disrupted the French withdrawal. Loses were substantial for both sides; the French suffering thirty-nine hundred casualties and the Germans forty-six hundred. The delay gave the Prussian Second Army of Prince Friedrich Karl time to cross the river south of the city, with three brigades of the 5th Cavalry Division of General Freiherr Albert von Rheinbaben taking up positions near Puxieux, south of Mars-la-Tour. The coming engagement was not to be a set-piece battle because both commanders wrongly guessed their enemy's intent, positions, and strength.

Battle

On the morning of 16 August, général Bazaine countermanded his orders given the previous night and granted permission for the troops on the Gravelotte plateau to pitch their tents in anticipation of the arrival of the remaining two French corps from the Moselle valley. Although enemy cavalry had been spotted near Mars-la-Tour the previous day and despite the lack of knowledge regarding the Prussian Army's location, no further reconnaissance was ordered.

Assuming that the French withdrawal had proceeded more rapidly than it had and that the espied French troops were a rearguard, Prussian X Corps commander General Konstans von Voigts-Rhetz ordered Rheinbaben's cavalry to attack the French encampment at Vionville despite his lack of infantry support. At 09:15, Rheinbaben's horse artillery fired upon the of encampment général de division marquis Henri de Forton's 3rd Reserve Cavalry Division, resulting in an immediately rout of the French force. One brigade of Frossard's II Corps moved forward to occupy the village, and an extended artillery duel ensued. Meanwhile General Alvensleben, in a daring move up the escarpment through Gorze, moved his III Corps against Flavigny and Rezonville from the south. The Prussian infantry was severely outmatched by the French Chassepot rifles; however, the superior all-steel, Krupp breech-loading Prussian batteries were pushed forward to maintain a toehold on the plateau. By late morning a massive artillery position of 105 guns ran from

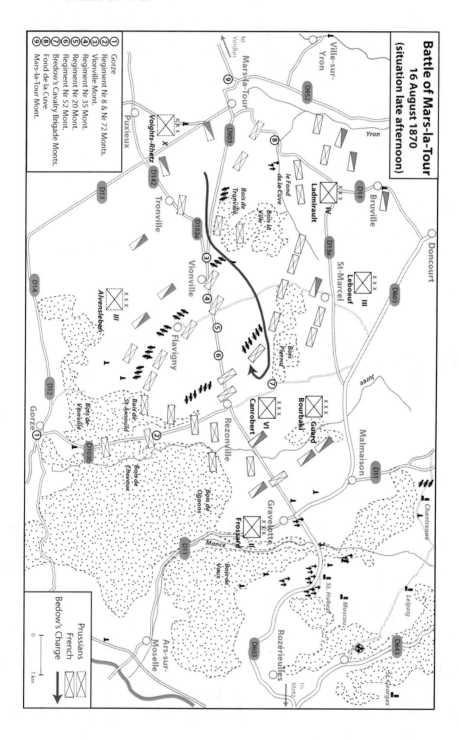

Battle of Mars-la-Tour
16 August 1870
(situation late afternoon)

① Gorze
② Regiment Nr 8 & Nr 72 Monts.
③ Vionville Mont.
④ Regiment Nr 35 Mont.
⑤ Regiment Nr 20 Mont.
⑥ Regiment Nr 52 Mont.
⑦ Bredow's Cavalry Brigade Monts.
⑧ Fond de la Cuve
⑨ Mars-la-Tour Mont.

Prussians
French
Bedow's Charge

0   1km

Bois de Tronville to Bois de Vionville, where Alvensleben faced the entire French Army with only two divisions. He later recalled, 'I had to match the physical inferiority of my numbers by the moral superiority of my offensive action.'[3] Displaying Prussian aggressiveness combined with incredible luck, he launched two infantry brigades against the now weakly defended Vionville from the vicinity of Tronville. After a short but bloody struggle, his guns overwhelmed the defending French 12th Chasseurs, and his advancing infantry occupied Vionville and Flavigny.

After a morning of indecisiveness, maréchal François de Canrobert aligned his VI Corps infantry along the road from Rezonville toward St-Marcel, placing artillery batteries in the gaps. The artillery bombarded the Prussian center around Vionville. Stationed behind Vionville was the last remaining uncommitted Prussian resource, the 12th Cavalry Brigade commanded by Generalmajor Friedrich (Adalbert) von Bredow. At 14:00, in what was to be the last successful cavalry charge in European history, Bredow led 804 Cuirassiers and Uhlans along a sunken track and shallow valley against Canrobert's artillery line. Achieving almost complete surprise, they rode through the batteries, the supporting infantry, and a second line of guns. Their fate was determined by Forton's cavalry, which had been routed earlier in the day but had since regrouped. Completely enveloped, only 400 of Bredow's men escaped; but 'Bredow's Death Ride,' as it became known, confused and demoralized the French as well as bought precious time for the Prussians.

General Leboeuf, pushed aside from his position as Minister of War and now commanding III Corps, finally brought his divisions to bear on the enemy positions. With overwhelming numerical superiority, he routed the Germans from Bois de Vionville and turned their left flank. At the moment of victory he hesitated, awaiting the arrival of comte Louis-René-Paul de Ladmirault's IV Corps. The delay bought time for elements of Voigts-Rhetz's X Corps to arrive and strengthen German defenses around Vionville. Displaying once again the temerity that had gripped the French commanders all day, Ladmirault drew back, abandoning the Bois de Tronville to the Germans.

Fearing for his exposed flank, Voigts-Rhetz ordered Generalmajor Richard von Wedell's 38th Infantry Brigade to advance against Bruville, which – unknown to Voigts-Rhetz – was the center of the French IV Corps. Five battalions of Wedell's infantry crested a slight rise to find unexpectedly a ravine known as le Fond de la Cuve. On the opposite side of the ravine were Ladmirault's two divisions, who fired intensely into the advancing Westphalian infantry. Over fifty percent of the 4,500-man force fell in a few minutes, and the brigade was destroyed. His left flank now in disarray, Voigts-Rhetz did what Alvensleben had done earlier in the day, ordering six hundred Prussian Guard Dragoons from Mars-la-Tour to attack the French infantry pursuing the 38th Infantry Brigade survivors. The sudden assault drove the French into a panicked retreat. Ladmirault, fearful that the attack was from a much larger force, withdrew behind the ravine. Once again the French had lost the opportunity to claim victory.

---

[3] Extract from *A Day of Battle: Mars-la-Tour 16 August 1870* by David Ascoli is reproduced by permission of Birlinn Ltd. www.birlinn.co.uk, 167.

By 18:30, German forces all along the line were hungry, exhausted, and short of ammunition. Although Stülpnagel's beleaguered 5th Division was receiving modest reinforcements south of Rezonville, the German left flank at Mars-la-Tour was dangerously exposed, protected by only a modest number of assorted cavalry regiments. Ladmirault ordered his cavalry to attack the German left flank, while nearly simultaneously Voigts-Rhetz ordered his cavalry to roll up the French right flank. On a flat plain near Ville-sur-Yron, 5,000 horsemen threw themselves at each other in a swirling storm of slashing sabers. In less than 15 minutes, the dust started to settle with neither side victorious.

For most of the day, Prussian forces had been outnumbered by at least four to one; however, through audacious attacks and the willingness to suffer outrageous casualties, two German corps stopped the French Army. Late that night Bazaine, short of supplies and ammunition, ordered his army to take up positions on the line from Rozérieulles to St-Privat with the intent of continuing its move toward Verdun by a more northerly route after re-supply from Metz. He voluntarily abandoned the ground so tenaciously held by his men during the day. Although still faced by a worn out and inferior force, he chose defense – and eventual defeat – over any opportunity for victory.

Battlefield Tour

The battlefield between Rezonville and Mars-la-Tour has remained unchanged since 1870. The largely agricultural fields and modest forests are undisturbed by modern development. By agreement in the Treaty of Frankfurt of 1871, French and German cemeteries and memorials are preserved in perpetuity. Thus, memorials erected by the conquering Germans still stand along the roadways, although some display bullet or shell damage from later wars. The tour route follows the action chronologically, and though not the shortest route to all of the sites, the compact nature of the field of action permits hardly any wasted time.

Whereas much of the action occurred along the Verdun-Metz road (D903), leave the Moselle Valley south of Metz at Novéant-sur-Moselle toward Gorze (D12).

The road follows the difficult route faced by the men and artillery of Stülpnagel's 5th Division in moving through the narrow valley before emerging onto the plain. **Gorze**, an ancient religious center, still has the twisted streets and timbered buildings of late 19th century France. During the battle, its houses filled with German wounded, with nearly every structure becoming a hospital or dressing station. A small local museum is in the same building as the Office of Tourisme near the Mairie.

Two routes were available to Stülpnagel to leave Gorze toward Rezonville. The first route toward Flavigny is no longer passable without a four-wheel drive vehicle. The second continues north (D103b) passing between the Bois des Chevaux and Bois de Vionville.

After exiting the woods, Stülpnagel's division came under the fire of French units around Rezonville. They immediately retired to the edge of the wood, and a day-long engagement ensued with little further progress possible against the strong French fire from Chassepot rifles and *mitrailleuses*. Where the road exits the forest and enters the grain fields, a granite stone on the right commemorates the fallen of **Leib-Grenadier Regiment Nr 8 (18ᵗʰ Division)**. Seventy-five meters down the road, surrounded by a cluster of tall trees and an iron fence, a tall, polished stone obelisk commemorates **Infantry Regiment Nr 72 (32ⁿᵈ Brigade, 16ᵗʰ Division)**. Both units came to the 5ᵗʰ Division's support during the late afternoon and suffered enormous casualties in their unsuccessful attempts to force passage into Rezonville, which by that time was defended by the French Imperial Guard.

Reverse direction and return to Gorze. In the town, return right toward Chambley-Bussières (rue de la Meuse, D12 which becomes D14) and follow for 5 km to the intersection with the D13. Turn right toward Mars-la-Tour and after 3.7 km, turn right again toward Tronville (D142).

The route just followed was that of Rheinbaben's 5ᵗʰ Cavalry Division in what began as a scouting mission and ended with the beginning of the battle of Mars-la-Tour. He established his horse artillery positions in the fields southwest of Tronville and moved them forward when their extended range and accuracy drove Forton's Cavalry Division out of the village.

Continue toward Vionville (D142, which becomes D103b) going through the heart of the Vionville battle area.

At the intersection with the Verdun-Metz Road (D903), two inscribed stones commemorate Prussian field artillery regiments; a cross-topped stele also commemorates the French dead of **Vionville** and marks their graves within the enclosing pipe fence. Across the main highway to the left is **Bois de Tronville**, a hotly contested site that changed hands numerous times during the fighting. Arriving from the south, Generalmajor Bredow's horsemen crossed the main highway near here and continued north through the swale still visible to the east of the Bois de Tronville. They then utilized a similar depression to ride east, parallel to the edge of forest that marks an old Roman roadway. We will continue his story below.

Turn east on the Verdun-Metz road; although the modern highway is heavily traveled, small turn-offs provide safe spaces for a car or two.

East of Vionville are more indications of the fierce fighting over Vionville and Flavigny to the southeast. A yellow sandstone stele set upon a stair-cased platform commemorates the battle and lists the casualties of **Brandenburg Fusilier Regiment Nr 35**. By noon on 16 August, 6ᵗʰ Division, commanded by General

Freiherr Gustav von Buddenbrock, had moved in between Vionville and Flavigny, opposed by the 12th Battalion of Chasseurs of général de division Henri-Jules Bataille's division. The fusiliers suffered mightily against the superior firepower and longer range of the Chassepots, but the Prussian artillery, moving forward under deadly enemy fire, drove the French back to Rezonville, and cut the main escape route from Metz to Verdun. The 35th Regiment was heavily involved, as can be attested by the long list of names on their memorial. The sandstone tower ahead is a memorial to the **Brandenburg Infantry Regiment Nr 20**, also of Buddenbrock's 6th Division, which later in the day defended the Bois de Tronville. Farther ahead a stone block monument is to the **Brandenburg Infantry Regiment Nr 52,** which lost a devastating 52 officers and 1,202 men in the day's fighting. The regiment calmly confronted a charging Imperial Guard Cuirassier regiment sent by Bazaine to retake Flavigny. The French cavalry absorbed a wall of metal and over 250 casualties without breaking the infantry's line. By then, however, the Germans were at the end of their resources, and they never did capture Rezonville that day. This last monument marks the front line at nightfall on 16 August.

In Rezonville, turn left between two closely spaced buildings onto a minor track toward Villers aux Bois (rue des Bois).

After 1.1 km, a sandstone stele on the right is dedicated to the **Schleswig-Holstein Hussar Regiment Nr 16**. In the field farther to the right is the ornately carved sandstone stele to the **Magdeburg Cuirassier Regiment Nr 7** and **Altmärk Uhlan Regiment Nr 16**, two units of Bredow's Cavalry Brigade. After crossing the main highway west of Vionville, they advanced using a swale parallel to the Roman road for cover. When the cover was broken, they whipped their mounts and crashed through Canrobert's gun line, which ran from the Roman road toward Rezonville to the west of the road just driven. Forton's cavalry stopped their advance in the field around the monument dedicated to them.

The handsomely carved white stone obelisk on the edge of the forest just off the curve in the road is dedicated to the **Brandenburg (Ziethen) Hussar Regiment Nr 3**. Well after nightfall, brigades of the 6th Cavalry Division, including the 3rd and 16th Hussar Regiments, were sent against the French line. The night attack was sheer folly and brought the Germans nothing but 700 additional casualties. The 3rd Hussar monument marks the approximate limit of their advance and happens to sit upon the Roman road.

Continue north through Villers aux Bois, then turn left toward St-Marcel (D13a). Three km after St-Marcel, the road merges with the D13 and continues southwest.

After approximately 1.7 km, a sweeping curve to the right indicates the approach into a ravine known as **le Fond de la Cuve**. To the left of the highway the two infantry regiments of Wedell's Brigade attempted to storm across the ravine from south to north. Unseen by them until the last second were the soldiers of général de division Ernest-Louis-Octave Courtot de Cissey's division. The ravine is now practically impassible due to dense brush covering its steep sides. The ground over which the vanquished Westphalian infantry retreated is now occupied by an abandoned train storage yard. Between the yard and the ravine are monuments enclosed within a low iron fence, remembering the 668 dead of the **Westphalian Infantry Regiment Nr 16**, one of its officers, and its sergeant-major.

> Continue into Mars-la-Tour and turn right onto rue de Metz. Pass to the western edge of the town to the rue du Château where the Verdun-Metz Road (D903) crosses over the rail line.

In a park setting also enclosed within an iron fence is France's major monument to the **Mars-la-Tour battle**. In a forlorn location below the highway bridge, the statue atop the stele represents France holding a dying soldier who is about to drop his rifle into the waiting hands of a child. The bronze sculpture by Frédéric-Louis Bogino was molded from four guns and erected in 1875. Two bronze reliefs were added later; the one on the southern face depicts the dramatic cavalry combat near Mars-la-Tour. The statue stands upon an ossuary containing 1500 bodies.

Other unit memorials are located at various sites; however, they are not as easily visited. The site of the grand cavalry engagement near Yron is in an unmarked open field just east of the village near the communal cemetery.

> By following the Verdun-Metz Road to the east one reaches Gravelotte, which is the starting point for the tour of the Gravelotte–St-Privat battlefield.

#11

Battle of Gravelotte – St-Privat
18 August 1870

OBJECTIVE	To attack French defensive positions
FORCES	
FRENCH:	112,800 men and 520 guns of the Army of the Rhine (maréchal François Achille Bazaine)
GERMAN:	188,332 men and 720 guns of Prussian First and Second Armies (Generalfeldmarschall Helmuth von Moltke)
RESULT	The Germans forced the French to withdraw into Metz, where they later surrendered.
CASUALTIES	
FRENCH:	1,146 killed, 6,709 wounded, and 4,420 taken prisoner
GERMAN:	5,237 killed, 14,430 wounded, and 493 missing
LOCATION	Metz is 338 km east of Paris; Gravelotte is 15 km west of Metz

After the events of 16 August, Bazaine felt ever more tied to Metz. The next day the French and Prussians re-organized and repositioned their armies. Bazaine's Army of the Rhine spent 17 August retiring to its new line from Rozérieulles to St-Privat; a few units did not arrive at their positions until after nightfall. Much of the day was spent constructing defenses and digging gun pits. Prince Friedrich took the remainder of his Second Army across the Moselle and up to the Rezonville plateau. King Wilhelm and his Chief of the Prussian General Staff, Helmuth von Moltke, established the Royal Headquarters near Flavigny. Moltke ordered Steinmetz's First Army into support positions south of Gorze. Guard and XII Corps were sent northward to intercept the French Army if it was evacuating along the northern roads to Verdun or to flank it if it was remaining near Metz.

Battle

In the early morning of 18 August, eight German army corps moved in an extended line sweeping to the northeast, seeking to engage the French. The pivot unit for this movement was General Steinmetz's VII Corps in the woods below Gravelotte and Rozérieulles. General Gustav von Manstein's IX Corps moved into the vicinity of Vernéville to engage the enemy; expecting to strike against the exposed right flank of the French Army, he encountered instead the center of the French line in Ladmirault's IV Corps occupying positions on either side of Amanvillers. Manstein, as per Prince Friedrich's orders, moved his artillery ahead of the supporting infantry. When they fired the first salvo at noon, his unprotected guns faced the artillery of Ladmirault's IV Corps, the enfilade guns and troops of Canrobert's VI Corps to the northeast, and Leboeuf's III Corps to the southeast – a deadly trap of his own making. After an hour of suffering heavy casualties, Manstein's surviving gunners withdrew to strongpoints in the Bois de la Cusse, and at Champenois and Chantrenne Fermes. Ladmirault did not move to the attack, granting Manstein time to bring his infantry forward and secure the German center. The engagement became a stalemate, and the action moved to the flanks.

Steinmetz, whose arrogant actions interrupted Prince Friedrich's march route on 6 August and who so recklessly initiated the battle of Spicheren, now engaged the French, contrary to specific orders. His First Army faced the French positions across the underbrush-covered Mance ravine east of Gravelotte. While moving forward, they came under intense fire from Leboeuf's III Corps at Moscou and at St-Hubert Fermes as well as from Frossard's II Corps on an elevated position known as Point de Jour. Steinmetz sent three brigades of infantry against the stone wall-enclosed farm complex of St-Hubert, which looked down upon the causeway crossing the Mance ravine. On either side of the causeway, devastating French fire shredded the German attack. Nevertheless, Steinmetz's batteries moved behind the infantry to the western edge of the ravine and put down overwhelming fire onto St-Hubert, driving the defenders into retreat. The farm was captured, but the German troops who now occupied it were under fire from French trenches on Point de Jour and the loopholed walls of Moscou Ferme.

Assuming that the French were in retreat across his front, at approximately 16:00, Steinmetz ordered his 1st Cavalry Division across the causeway in pursuit. Only one regiment made it across, and it fell under intense fire from Point de Jour. The scattered retreat through the bloody ravine added to the carnage already present. In the fading light of early evening, Steinmetz received the king's approval to launch the last of his army's reserves across the ravine. The infantry encountered a surprise burst of French rifle-fire, and at last the stoic German men broke and ran – most did not stop until reaching the relative safety of Rezonville, where King Wilhelm had

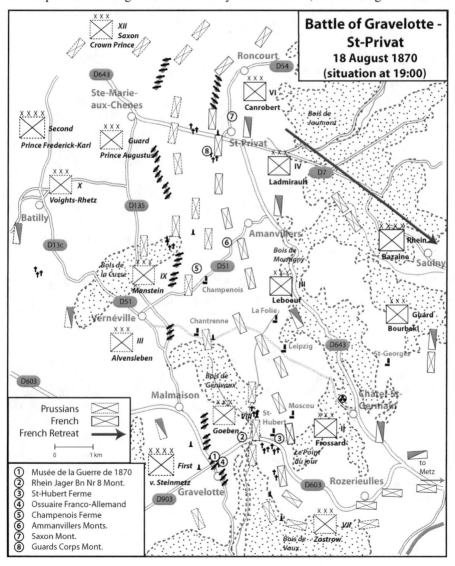

Battle of Gravelotte - St-Privat
18 August 1870
(situation at 19:00)

① Musée de la Guerre de 1870
② Rhein Jager Bn Nr 8 Mont.
③ St-Hubert Ferme
④ Ossuaire Franco-Allemand
⑤ Champenois Ferme
⑥ Ammanvillers Monts.
⑦ Saxon Mont.
⑧ Guards Corps Mont.

Prussians
French
French Retreat
0   1 km

relocated his headquarters. This rout before the very eyes of the king surely spelled the defeat of the Germans, but it was avoided by French failure to act. When the Prussian II Corps arrived at Gravelotte, it was temporarily assigned to Steinmetz's First Army. He ordered a fourth and equally futile assault, sending two more divisions of infantry into the ravine. The darkness and confusion now brought scattered German forces to fire upon each other. Exhaustion and darkness finally brought the engagement at Gravelotte to an end at nearly 22:00. The scene was described by a journalist who visited it the following day.

> The slope immediately beneath the French position, on the Verdun [road], was a frightful spectacle. Hundreds of Prussian corpses were strewed in quite a small space on the fatal slope. Where the Prussian battery had been placed ... there were thirty horses lying almost touching one another, many with the drivers beside them, still grasping their whips. Most of the corpses were on their backs, with their hands clenched. This position was explained by the fact that most of the men had been shot grasping their muskets, and their hands clenched as they dropped their weapons and fell. Many corpses of Prussian officers lay by those of their men, with their white glove on their left hands, the right ones being bare, in order better to grasp the sword. In the hollow road itself the bodies of men and horses lay thick; the corpses all along the sides of the road, for nearly 1,000 yards [920 meters], made one continually unbroken row. A little lower down I found the *tirailleur* corpses. Many of these men still had their muskets in their hands, many forefingers being stiff on the trigger.[4]

To the north, over the course of the day, Prince Friedrich's Second Army was having its own problems. Manstein's IX Corps was stretched from the northern limits of the Bois de Genivaux to the Bois de la Cusse, where it experienced continuous direct fire from Amanvillers and enfilade fire from St-Privat. At 16:45, the 3rd Brigade of Prince Augustus of Wurttemberg's Prussian Guard Corps emerged from the Bois de la Cusse into a storm of bullets and shells, which killed most of its officers and accomplished very little. Farther north 15 minutes later, 4th Guard Brigade moved from near St-Ail toward St-Privat. They proceeded at double time across the open ground until within range of the French Chassepots. Quoting the commander of the Guard Corps artillery: 'It was as if a whistling wind was blowing, as the hail of fire cut great swaths in the advancing battalions.'[5] The slaughter continued; 1st and 2nd Guard Brigades left the shelter of Ste-Marie-aux-Chênes to meet the same fate within 700 meters of St-Privat's stone houses. The French riflemen, within one hour, destroyed elite units of the Prussian Army, inflicting over 8,000 casualties.

---

[4] L.P. Brockett, *The Year of Battles: or the Franco-German War of 1870-1* (New York, 1871).

[5] Extract from *A Day of Battle: Mars-la-Tour 16 August 1870* by David Ascoli is reproduced by permission of Birlinn Ltd. www.birlinn.co.uk, , 278.

Only the XII Saxon Corps remained to rescue the day for the Germans. Their day-long march had finally brought them to the lightly defended northern flank of Canrobert's VI Corps, and they took up positions at Montois-la-Montagne and at Roncourt. Now bombarded from a great arc of over 200 German guns, the stout walls of St-Privat's houses were penetrated, and the village was set aflame. After stopping the Prussian Guard and suffering this bombardment, the French infantry was caught between Saxons to the north and the remainder of the Guard from the west. The fighting became house-to-house, under the ghastly lighting of burning buildings.

> The noise of explosions, combined with the horrible cracking of collapsing roofs and crumbling walls, the cries of the wounded mixed with the shrill whistle of bullets and the dull and impetuous shock of the shells and bombs turned the streets of the village into a splendid and horrible hell.[6]

Finally, with little left to give, the French started an orderly withdrawal that grew into a stampede to the safety of Metz. First the right flank turned, then Canrobert's Corps, then Leboeuf's, and finally Frossard's abandoned the field for Metz.

Aftermath

Despite the slaughter of some of its best troops and the stunning defeat of Steinmetz's First Army, the Prussian Army won the day largely through the ineptitude of Marshal Bazaine. Given numerous opportunities over two days to inflict a decisive blow against isolated German units, he remained steadfastly on the defensive. His corps commanders squandered advantages in firepower offered by the Chassepot rifle and by an early form of the machine gun – a lesson the Germans learned well in preparation for the next war. The 180,000-men Army of the Rhine was held under siege in Metz until its capitulation on 29 October. After the war, Bazaine alone was tried for treason for negotiating with the enemy; he was sentenced to death but escaped imprisonment to die in poverty as an exile.

Battlefield Tour

The French defensive line of 18 August ran along a ridge defined on the east by a valley running from Rozérieulles through Châtel-St-Germain to Amanvillers and on the west by the valley of the Mance, which flows into the Moselle at Ars. Upstream the Moselle crosses the national road east of Gravelotte, before petering out in the Bois de Genivaux. North of both valleys, the ground flattens into open plains at Amanvillers and runs north past St-Privat. Heights near Metz still show fortifications built for later French / German wars, especially the Groupe Fortifié Jeanne d'Arc situated upon an outcropping of rock east of St-Hubert. If continuing from the Mars-la-Tour battlefield tour, one enters Gravelotte from the west. From Gravelotte the tour continues north along the German side of the ridge until crossing

---

[6] Michael Howard, *The Franco-Prussian War* (New York: The Macmillan Company, 1962), 174.

the center of the battlefield before Amanvillers. It proceeds north into St-Privat and ends by proceeding to Metz along the route of French retreat.

In the center of Gravelotte the Verdun-Metz Road (D903) joins the National Road (N3) also coming from Verdun.

On the northeast corner of this intersection is the inn where Napoleon III spent the night of 15/16 August before taking leave of his army and going to the French military stronghold at Châlons. Adjacent to the inn is the temporarily closed **Musée de la Guerre de 1870**. The museum, dedicated to the battles near Metz, is undergoing a multi-year renovation which will incorporate artifacts from the long closed museum of Mars-la-Tour. The new facility is expected to open in December 2008.

Continue toward Metz (N3); near kilometer marker 3, a turn-off on the north side of the road enters the wood and leads to the largest of the commemorations in this area.

A monument to the **Rhein Jäger Battalion Nr 8** sits upon a yellow stone terrace extending from the side of the hill. Originally topped by a statue of a German Jäger, it now holds a stone Cross Pattée. On the edge of the valley below, a solitary gravestone marks the resting place of several of the battalion's officers, including its commander. This is the valley of death where the carnage of Steinmetz's attempts to capture Point de Jour fell in heaped masses. Here the Germans almost lost the battle of Gravelotte and brought their invasion of France to an ignominious end. Gravelotte was one of the first European battles to depend so extensively upon the entrenching tool, and the French infantry used it well in constructing tiered positions on the opposite slope and across the fields beyond, providing them with shelter and excellent fields of fire. The main highway now crosses the valley on an earthen embankment that in 1870 was a narrow and wreckage-strewn causeway.

Continue toward Metz (N3) and at the *Voie de la Liberté* kilometer marker 5 turn left onto the short bypass road. This is a difficult turn to make because of heavy, high-speed traffic, and it appears suddenly on a sweeping curve to the right. If missed, proceed several kilometers down the escarpment until a side road allows a safe place to reverse direction and return westbound on the N3; the bypass road is then easily navigated.

The farm buildings west of the bypass road are the current day incarnation of **St-Hubert Ferme**, minus the surrounding stonewalls of 1870. Within the barns and outbuildings the farthest German advance occurred on 18 August and led to the farm's capture by companies of the 28th and 67th Infantry Regiments. The bypass road and the N3 form a triangle within which stand French-German mass graves under a bullet-scarred obelisk to the **3rd and 7th Pomeranian Infantry Regiments Nr 14 and Nr 54** (3rd Division, II Corps). They were among the final units sacrificed in the fourth of Steinmetz's ill-fated attacks. Visible across the fields to the northeast are the still formidable buildings of **Moscou Ferme**, a French strongpoint defended by Leboeuf's III Corps. The road to the farm is not suitable for passenger vehicles; however, a short distance down the farm track, a logging road to the right accesses another bullet-scarred obelisk, this one commemorating the **3rd Rheinisches Infantry Regiment Nr 29**, part of II Corps' 16th Division. Across the highway are numerous crosses marking French-German mass graves below the impregnable French strongpoint of Point de Jour. Frossard's II Corps had dug a series of terraced trenches and gun positions which sheltered troops from view but afforded unobstructed fire into the ravine and upon the ground beyond. Although not easily accessible on the opposite side of main highway, the field of crosses gives an indication of the severity of the German losses.

Reverse direction and return to Gravelotte.

On the left, before arriving at the main roundabout, an easily missed entranceway provides access to the **Ossuaire Franco-Allemand à Gravelotte**. A stone path leads through the cemetery to a colonnaded courtyard where plaques commemorating individual unit casualties are affixed to the otherwise bare walls.

In Gravelotte, turn right toward Malmaison (N3) and upon entering that village bear right toward Vernéville (D11).

The route passes the heights from which King Wilhelm witnessed the events east of Gravelotte and from which he retired to Rezonville, thinking that the battle had been irretrievably lost. Not until after midnight did he and his entourage, including Moltke and Bismarck, receive word of the breaking of the French northern flank. To the east are the remains of the Bois de Genivaux and the fields that comprised the center of the French line.

Near Vernéville, turn right toward Amanvillers (D51) to cross the center of the German positions.

After 1.5 km, **Champenois Ferme**, a strongpoint occupied by the Germans early in the battle, is on the right. Visible to the left along a farm track opposite Champenois is a small copse with an eagle-topped boulder monument dedicated to one of the many Hessian artillery regiments of Manstein's IX Corps that held this ground against Chassepot-fire from Amanvillers. Over the rise but not visible is Bois de la Cusse, its scattered copses offering a little shelter on this otherwise open and exposed battlefield.

Continue 1.5 km to the S-curve in the highway where three additional German monuments are visible.

These monuments commemorate units of the **3rd Guards Brigade**, which rushed forward in the early afternoon to strengthen IX Corps and engaged both Ladmirault's IV Corps in Amanvillers and Leboeuf's III Corps in La Folie and Leipzig (also spelled Leipsic) Fermes.

Proceed into Amanvillers and turn left toward St-Privat (N43). Near the outskirts of the village, follow the road where it turns left and joins the D7. At the traffic light, turn right toward Roncourt (D54).

St-Privat has little resemblance to its 1870 appearance. The stone houses and their individual walled gardens that formed secure defensive positions now have a modern day, suburban appearance. On the northern fringe of St-Privat is the most outrageous monument on the Gravelotte–St-Privat battlefield. Dedicated to the dead of the **XII Saxon Corps**, the huge stone block is crowned with an iron medieval knight's helmet. Shields and swords adorn the sides. Although new housing now occupies the area, the ground to the north toward Roncourt presents the avenue of approach where the Saxons turned Canrobert's VI Corps' flank.

Reverse direction and return to the National Road (N43). Continue across the highway onto the residential rue de la Tour.

A large yellow sandstone structure resembling a chess piece is on the right. It is dedicated to the 307 officers and 7,923 men of the **Guards Corps** lost in the attack upon St-Privat. It and the accompanying cross-topped stele ahead, which is dedicated to 931 dead and wounded of the **Königin-Augusta-Garde Grenadier Regiment Nr 4**, mark the farthest advance of the Prussian Guards during their initial attack against St-Privat. The Autoroute ahead cuts its swathe across the fields, but visible before it are the white stone crosses of the mass graves of the German guards. The way was a deadly one, with many of the regiments suffering over one thousand casualties each before they and the Saxons routed the valiant French defenders from each house and garden. Numerous other monuments to German losses are between St-Privat and Ste-Marie-Aux Chênes if one desires to search for them.

Return to the National Road and turn right. Instead of continuing back toward Amanvillers, proceed straight at the next intersection toward Saulny / Metz (D7).

The road passes through the valley behind the French lines. Along this sunken road the now defeated French left the field and sought safety in Metz. The route leads directly to Metz, crossing the Canal de la Moselle and the Moselle River before entering the city near the pedestrian zone.

Other Sites of Interest: Metz was founded as a fortified Roman town built upon the intersection of several roads. It can trace its Germanic influences back to the

Kingdom of Lotharingia, created in 843 with Metz as its capital. Through the Middle Ages the city fought for independence from the dukes of Luxembourg, Lorraine, and Burgundy as well as against control by the bishop of Trier. The city became a French possession in 1552 after 600 years as part of the Holy Roman Empire (the first German Reich). Metz was occupied by the Prussian Army after Bazaine's surrender and transferred to Germany as part of the treaty in 1871, not to be regained by France until 19 November 1918 after the First World War's armistice.

After centuries as a border area and religious center, the city is well supplied with fortifications and churches – the gem being the massive but beautifully proportioned, yellow stone **St-Étienne Gothic Cathédrale**. Traces of the early walls are still evident, especially the 13th century **Porte des Allemands,** and the ramparts and towers to its north. The city offers a fine assortment of museums, accommodations, and restaurants and prides itself on its gloriously flowered parks and esplanade. South of the city, along the Moselle between Ars-sur-Moselle and Jouy-aux-Arches, are remnants of the **ancient Roman aqueduct**, sixteen stone spans that carried water across the river.

#12

Battle of Sedan
1 September 1870

OBJECTIVE	To intercept MacMahon's army while it was attempting to rescue Bazaine's army at Metz
FORCES	
FRENCH:	120,000 men and 564 guns (maréchal Patrice MacMahon duc de Magenta, then général Auguste Ducrot, then général Emmanuel de Wimpffen)
GERMAN:	220,000 men and 700 guns (Generalfeldmarschall Helmuth von Moltke)
RESULT	An overwhelming Prussian victory resulting in the surrender of the Army of Châlons and the capture of Emperor Napoleon III
CASUALTIES	
FRENCH:	3,220 killed, 14,811 wounded, and 104,000 captured or surrendered
GERMAN:	2,320 killed, 5,980 wounded, and 700 missing
LOCATION	Sedan is 250 km northeast of Paris and 133 km northwest of Metz

The only remaining force available to Napoleon III for halting the Prussian invasion of his country was the Army of Châlons, commanded by maréchal Patrice MacMahon. Under political pressure from Paris, MacMahon moved to join with Bazaine, who he thought was escaping from Metz toward Sedan. MacMahon started his army on a great flanking move through Reims to join with Bazaine.

While eight corps of the Prussian First and Second Armies saw to the entrapment of Bazaine, the remaining three corps formed the Army of the Meuse

(Prussian Fourth Army) commanded by Crown Prince Friedrich Augustus of Saxony. It and the Prussian Third Army moved on different axes in pursuit of MacMahon. Moltke expertly pushed his enemy into a trap.

Battle

I Bavarian Corps moved north in the early morning of 1 September, crossing the swampy lowlands south of Bazeilles at 4:30. To their north XII Saxon Corps was pressing toward La Moncelle, and still farther north the Guard Corps survivors of the St-Privat attack moved toward Givonne. While parts of three French corps fought ferociously to hold Bazeilles, maréchal MacMahon rushed to the scene of the action and was seriously wounded by a shell fragment. Général Auguste Ducrot was given command, and he ordered a vast retreat into the Bois de la Garenne north of Sedan. Shortly thereafter général Emmanuel de Wimpffen, appeared with a letter from French Minister of War Count Palikao, appointing him commander should MacMahon fall. Wimpffen countermanded Ducrot's retreat order; the two

conflicting directives within such a short period of time threw the French Army into confusion.

During the previous night, the German XI Corps had moved north on the left bank of the Meuse, and advance elements captured the remaining bridges at Dom-le-Mesnil and Donchéry. By dawn on 1 September, they had advanced as far as Vrigne-aux-Bois to command the road between Sedan and Mézières, cutting French escape routes to the west. Following XI Corps was V Corps; however, the road along the hairpin turn in the river was inadequate to handle two entire corps, and although unimpeded by the enemy, progress was slow. Lead elements of XI Corps were not seen north of Floing until after 6:00, while V Corps continued marching farther to the north to complete the encirclement. As was happening in the east, artillery positions were being established along the crest of the Floing-Illy ravine.

The French Army of Châlons was encircled, the heights around the city ringed with over 400 German guns. After the sharp infantry engagement at Bazeilles, the artillery put the issue to rest. The batteries of the Prussian Imperial Guard set fire to the Bois de la Garenne. Bombs and grapeshot fell on Givonne from a horizon exploding in flame. A circle of thunder surrounded the French, their camps becoming craters. The slaughter was occurring everywhere and all at once. The French had no weapons with the range to answer.

At the same time, elements of général Abel Douay's VII Corps had been driven from Floing by the heavy pounding of Prussian cannon on both flanks and the repeated infantry attacks by German XI Corps. German V Corps had found its way around the French flank, and repeated counterattacks could not stop its progress. In desperation général Ducrot called upon général Jean Margueritte's Chasseurs d'Afrique not only to bring a stop to the German advance but also to punch a hole in the German line through which his infantry could escape to the west. The effort was futile and led only to the cavalrymen's demise.

A final effort to escape the trap was led by de Wimpffen against the Bavarians at Balan. After a rapid but short advance, artillery fire proved too dense for further French progress. The troops sought shelter in Sedan's centuries old citadel. At 14:15, a white flag appeared briefly above the fortress' walls. Less than two hours later it reappeared at the order of the emperor, who was anxious to stop the bloodletting. Emissaries brought a personal note from Napoleon to King Wilhelm, offering his surrender and regretting his inability to die at the head of his army.

Early the next morning, an exhausted, ill, and war-weary Napoleon took leave of his soldiers and left Sedan by way of Donchéry. He was met by Bismarck near Frénois, and there, in a famous scene, the politically naive emperor and the conniving chancellor sat upon a log bench outside a weaver's cottage to discuss the events of the past months. Bismarck was purposely delaying Napoleon from a meeting with King Wilhelm until the surrender was completed. At the Château de Bellevue, Wimpffen signed the surrender that had been dictated by Moltke. Napoleon had his meeting with Wilhelm and then left for exile at Schloss Wilhelmshöhe in Prussia the next morning in a driving rain, never to see his army or his country again.

Aftermath

Although the emperor was in exile and his Army of the Rhine was entrapped at Metz, the war was by no means finished. Only three days after Sedan, the people of Paris proclaimed the end of the Second Empire.

The advancing Germans were able to complete the encirclement of Paris by 20 September. Paris was fortified by a wall eleven meters in height and by a moat three meters wide. Ninety-four bastions were in the wall, and fifteen smaller forts surrounded the city to keep modern artillery out of range. Storming such strong fortifications and then fighting a civilian army in the tangled streets of Paris had no appeal to Moltke. After months of siege, the bombardment of Paris finally began on 5 January 1871. The actual damage was superficial, but public opinion across Europe turned against Prussia.

On 18 January in the Hall of Mirrors in the Palace of Versailles, the King of Prussia was reluctantly acclaimed as the Kaiser of Germany, establishing the Second Empire of the Germans.

By late January, with food stocks down to a few days, even the Parisians had had enough. On 28 January an armistice was signed, and the Third Republic negotiated three basic terms with Bismarck: Alsace and northern Lorraine (including Metz) to become German provinces; a war indemnity of five billion French francs (then considered to be an astronomical amount); and a German army victory parade down the Champs Élysées.

Consequences of the War

The Franco-Prussian War had far-reaching consequences, establishing both the German Empire and the French Third Republic. With Napoleon III no longer in power to protect them, the Papal States were annexed by Italy, completing that nation's unification. Germany replaced Britain as the focus of French fears and apprehensions.

The German's crushing victory over the French consolidated their faith in Prussian militarism, which would remain a dominant force in German society until 1945. The Prussian system of conscript armies controlled by a highly trained general staff was soon adopted by the other great powers, effectively making large-scale conflicts more possible.

Most importantly, Germany's annexation of Alsace-Lorraine aroused a deep longing for revenge in the French people. The years from 1871 to 1914 were marked by an extremely unstable peace because France's determination to recover Alsace-Lorraine and Germany's mounting imperialist ambitions kept the two nations constantly poised for conflict. The mutual animosity engendered by the Franco-Prussian War proved to be the driving force behind the prolonged slaughter of the First World War.

Battlefield Tour

The valley of the Meuse is broad and marshy. The river flows in a northeasterly direction past Sedan before making a hairpin turn and continuing east. The large Bois de la Garenne runs across a series of hills behind Sedan to the north, only 11 km from the Belgian border. French troops became surrounded in a large triangle formed by the Floing River to the west, the Givonne River to the east and the Meuse River to the south.

The tour starts on the high ground south of the city and proceeds across the river to follow the eastern edge of the French positions. It continues around to the opposite (western) side to the site of the French cavalry charge and the citadel where the surrender was signed.

The Sedan battlefield is a logical next stop after touring the battlefields around Metz and covers some of the same ground as the Second World War Sedan tour. The most direct approach to Sedan from Metz is via the National Road (N43 / E44) via Longuyon, Montmédy, and Carignan. Leave the valley of the Chiers River at Carignan, turning toward Mouzon (D19) and the Meuse valley. Follow the left bank of the Meuse toward Remilly-Aillicourt (D27, becomes D4, becomes D6). In Pont-Maugis, turn left toward Noyers (D229a).

Traveling through Noyers, signs provide direction to the military cemeteries that are on the **Marfée Heights**, which at 340 meters dominate the Meuse valley. Down the right fork is the **Cimetière Militaire Français,** holding the dead from World War One, including 1,200 bodies in a mass grave. Near the cemetery, an informal overlook presents French and German information boards describing the major military actions that occurred near Sedan in 1870, 1914, and 1940. These heights, whose slopes were occupied in 1870 by IV Corps artillery, reward the steep, twelve percent grade drive with an overview of the Sedan battlefield including Sedan, its citadel, and the wooded hills north of the city. From the overlook, one obtains a view of a modern battlefield that is seldom possible. The entire terrain lies is spread before one's eyes all the way to the wooded slopes of the Belgian Ardennes.

The access road's left fork approaches the **Deutsche Soldatenfriedhof Noyers-Pont-Maugis**. The massive cemetery holds 14,055 dead from the First World War, many from the August 1914 invasion and later engagements in Champaign, and 12,785 dead from the Second World War, most killed during the defensive actions in 1944. The various sectors are identified by the different crosses.

Return to Pont-Maugis, where along the D6 to the north are remnants from both world wars. The simple, but classic **US 1st Division Memorial** stands above the highway between Wadelincourt and Pont-Maugis. The division liberated Noyers-Pont-Maugis on 7 November 1918. Numerous French concrete bunkers still guard the Meuse River crossings as they did in 1940. The most noticeable examples are at the northern entrance into Pont-Maugis and in Wadelincourt where the D6 crosses the rail line. The tour continues by turning southeast toward Remilly (D6); after 2.5 km turn left onto a narrow road which crosses first the canal then the Meuse on one-lane bridges.

General Ludwig von der Tann sent his 2nd Division of Bavarian infantry across the river on pontoon bridges at 04:00 in a thick mist to attack Bazeilles. Seventy years later, General Heinz Guderian's 1st Panzer Division performed the same feat in the opposite direction slightly farther north.

Enter Bazeilles on the rue de la Gare, which after a series of curves, joins the D764 in the center of the village.

The town, only 5 km southeast of Sedan, was defended by XII Corps and a detachment of French marines who had taken up positions inside the town's stone houses. A ferocious fight erupted, with the Bavarians being fired upon from every angle by French infantry, marines, and civilians. Both sides torched houses to flush out the enemy, and exploding Bavarian artillery shells added to the confusion.

In the center of Bazeilles a yellow stone obelisk in place de l'**Infanterie de Marine** commemorates the naval unit's sacrifice. Embedded in the stone pavement is the anchor emblem of the marines. The **French/German Ossuary** is down a tree-lined, 300-meter path west of the village center. It is easy to miss but identified by its iron gate, French flag, and obelisk on top. Two thousand French and Bavarian dead from the fighting in Bazeilles and Balan are interred below the brick and stone structure.

Continue to the avenue de la Derrière Cartouche (D764) less than 100 meters from the N43.

As the Germans pressed forward, approximately 30 officers and French marines led by commandant Arsène Lambert defended an inn on the outskirts of Bazeilles, whose position blocked passage from Bazeilles toward Sedan. Completely encircled by elements of the 15th Bavarian Regiment, the men fought for four hours until their ammunition was exhausted, and the survivors were forced to surrender. The Bavarians, enraged at the delay and the civilian support given to the defenders, took vengeance on the town by burning most of its houses and executing 40 civilians who they claimed participated in the defense.

The inn has remained as **Musée de la maison de la dernière cartouche** (The Museum of the House of the Last Cartridge) for over one hundred years. The door, hallway, ceilings, and window frames retain bullet holes from the fight. An unexploded canister is still visible in the facade to the left of the upper floor windows. The first floor is dedicated to commandant Lambert, and displays describe the contribution of the French Navy in the war. Pictures of French generals, swords, emblems, and shells are in glass cases for preservation. The flags in glass frames on the walls were from the battlefield. Unfortunately, nothing is labeled in English, and many items are not that well labeled in French either, but the three rooms are little changed since 1870. The museum has recently undergone a renovation and is now open 1 April to 30 September from 08:00 to 12:00 and 13:30 to 19:00; 1 October to

31 March from 09:00 to 12:00 and 14:00 to 17:00 (Closed Mondays). Fee. If the door is locked, ring the bell for the proprietor to come from the adjacent residence.

Continue toward Balan, passing under the Autoroute; upon entering Balan, turn right toward la Moncelle (D17).

On the north side of the Balan-la Moncelle Road (D17) in front of a low, stone wall sits **La Croix de MacMahon,** marking the location of général Mac-Mahon's wounding on the morning of 1 September.

Turn left toward Daigny / Givonne (D129), passing through Givonne to Olly.

The valley narrows where it passes through Daigny, the steady stream above Bazeilles becoming a mere trickle. On the east side, where sheep now graze in the pastures cut from the forest, the German guns were axle to axle; to the south stood those of IV Corps; farther north were those of XII Saxon Corps; around Givonne were those of Prussian Guard Corps. In all they covered the hilltops with Krupp, breech-loading cannon aimed at the batteries of outmatched French guns and massed infantry across the narrow stream. At approximately noon, Prussian Guard Cavalry met units of V Corps at Olly to close the circle around the Army of Châlons.

In Olly the highway makes a sharp turn and reverses direction toward Illy (D129). Stay on the main highway in Illy; at the village fountain, turn left (rue d'En Bas) and follow to the hillside above the town.

This height represents the northern peak of the triangle within which the French Army was trapped. The fenced area beside the rural road holds two crosses – one bears a Latin inscription – in addition to several large cut stones that may have been part of an ancient chapel. This area is the **Calvaire d'Illy,** from which général Margueritte's cavalry initiated their heroic charges.

The horsemen formed up for their charge in between Illy and the Bois de la Garenne. Margueritte himself became an early casualty, taking a bullet in the face but ordering the attack on the enemy while he collapsed. Two lines of horsemen moved over the top of the hill, through the lines of their infantry, and down the hill into the enemy. They could not break the German line which allowed the cavalry to approach within sixty paces before firing a volley. The horsemen, much depleted before even getting close to the German infantry, broke to the sides – one north, one south – and took more punishment while they sought to escape. Général Gaston de Gallifet, standing in for the wounded Margueritte, rallied the remaining cavalry and launched them again against the wall of fire. They charged three times only to be turned back with each attempt. On the last attempt the survivors were reportedly saluted by the German officers while they turned to return to the French positions.

By 14:00, Douay's men had abandoned the Calvaire and fled into the Bois de la Garenne. German infantry occupied the spot which provided clear fire into the woods now crowded with terrorized French troops. One can continue from the Calvaire south through Bois de la Garenne directly into Sedan. Whereas the forest drive is peaceful, no reminders of the battle exist, and the passage through Sedan's neighborhoods can be tedious.

Continue into Floing (D205), which approximately follows along the line of V Corps positions, to the junction with the D5. From the rue Charles de Gaulle (D5) in the center of Floing, turn toward the Mairie (D205), in whose square stands the statue of général Margueritte. Turn toward the church (Grandrue), then turn left in front of the church. Go around the church by making a right turn up a short but very steep street. At the 'T' intersection, make another right (rue des Braves Gens) and follow.

Below the road and in precarious condition is the **Franco-Prussian War Cemetery** where regimental mass graves are each marked by simple tombstones and metal crosses. The listing of units reads like a death notice of mounted troops, including regiments of Cuirassiers au Cheval, Lanciers, and Hussars. Farther ahead is the larger Floing Necropolis Nationale from World War Two.

The **Chasseurs d'Afrique Monuments** in Floing are difficult to find and somewhat dilapidated; however, considering the courageous attempt made by these noted warriors to break the Prussian encirclement, they deserve a visit. The monuments are located at the top of the hill. The heroic but futile charges came toward this position from the slopes to the east. Unfortunately, modern development has filled the hillside with houses, and the growth of shrubbery blocks the views. The site contains a line of identical, special memorial obelisks, each commemorating a regiment of the Chasseurs d'Afrique and all leading to the stone block monument whose bas reliefs have almost disappeared. Plaques added to the memorials denote actions in later wars. Gallifet was ordered by général Ducrot to continue the charges. His response is recorded on the monument 'As often as you wish my General, as long as there remains one of us.' The stone covered ossuary to the left holds the dead. The quoted phrase 'les braves gens (ah, good people)' is reported to have been uttered by King Wilhelm upon witnessing the Chasseurs charges.

Return to the main highway (D5) and follow it toward St-Menges / Vrigne-aux-Bois. Before Vrigne, bear left and continue through Donchéry (D24), across the Meuse bridge, and turn left toward Sedan (D764).

This section of road offers bucolic views of the Meuse valley; to the north is the loop around which two corps of German troops marched and within which the French soldiers were imprisoned after the battle under squalid conditions and with shortages of food and shelter. Bismarck and Napoleon met at the '**Maison du Tisserands** (weaver's cottage)' in Donchéry located on the rue de l'Entrevue (D764) and identified by a tourist sign.

Turn toward Glaire (D29).

Behind a tall hedge and among trees on a curve to the left stands the **Château de Bellevue**. With its boarded windows, the structure retains none of its original bourgeois style. Forlorn and abandoned, the building looks down upon the Autoroute (A203). As if in a final insult, a very large Second World War bunker occupies a corner of the château grounds. No access permitted.

> Return to the D764 and turn left toward Sedan. Continue into the city and past the Hôtel-de-Ville to the rue de Château. Turn right and proceed to the Citadelle de Sedan parking area on the left.

Built in approximately 1424, the **Sedan Citadel** is the largest feudal castle in Europe. Due to its strategic position on the eastern border of France, it was constantly extended, reinforced, and modernized by the powerful dukes of Bouillon. Sedan did not come permanently under the rule of France until 1642. By 1870, the structure had lost its military value other than as a storage depot. While the bombardment to the north grew in intensity, French units broke and ran for shelter within the château's thick walls. The château was used in the First World War by the Germans as a prison and place of execution for suspected spies.

A self-guided tour with audio headsets presents the citadel's history in three languages. An eleven-meter Panorama de Sedan by Louis Braun depicts the battle. The building has a number of stairs – some of stone, others not – but many are not suitable for those who have difficulty with uneven stairsteps. From the citadel's walls, one can look over the old quarter of Sedan with its many period houses. The hours vary by season and day so it is best to consult the Office of Tourisme.

Other Sites of Interest: The **castle of duke of Bouillon** in Bouillon is perched atop a rock escarpment above the Semois River. From Bouillon, Guderian's panzer divisions attacked Sedan in May 1940 by traversing the narrow Fond de Givonne.

Recommended reading

Ascoli, David: *A Day of Battle: Mars-la-Tour 16 August 1870*. Edinburgh: Birlinn Limited, 2001. An engaging history that also takes the reader onto the battlefields of Mars-la-Tour and Gravelotte. The book analyses the reasons for the French defeat and is highly critical of Bazaine.

Howard, Michael: *The Franco-Prussian War: The German Invasion of France 1870 – 1871*. New York: The Macmillan Company, 1962. The classic reference book on the Franco-Prussian War with detailed index and extensive but dated bibliography.

Wawro, Geoffrey: *The Franco-Prussian War: The German Conquest of France in 1870 – 1871*. Cambridge: Cambridge University Press, 2005 edition. A history of the entire war.

Chapter Five

The First World War
1914 – 1918

During the first years of the twentieth century, the great military powers of Europe established a system of mutual defense alliances that attempted to retain a balance of power in Europe. In the face of rising German economic and military power resulting from its unification and its victory in the Franco-Prussian War, France, Britain, and Russia formed the Triple Entente against the Triple Alliance of Germany, Austria-Hungary, and Italy. The assassination of Austria's Archduke Franz Ferdinand by a Serbian nationalist secret society precipitated the issuance of ultimatums and the implementation of army general mobilizations. In the summer of 1914, the belligerent countries lacked a great statesman who could have steered history onto a different course.

The French entered the war believing in the superiority of taking the offensive (*offensive à outrance*) and its commanders subscribed to Plan XVII, which held that the next war would be fought along the common French-German border. According to the Plan, the two southern-most French armies would advance into German territory to reclaim Lorraine and occupy the Saarland, while three others would guard against German moves into Belgium east of the Meuse River. The British Expeditionary Force (BEF) would occupy the left flank near the border fortress of Maubeuge, leaving the 160 km gap to the Channel ports defended by four weak French territorial divisions.

German military planners feared fighting a two front war – France in the west and Russia in the east. Their mobilization plans relied heavily on execution of the 1905 Schlieffen Plan, which called for the rapid defeat of French and Belgian armies before slow-to-mobilize Russia could transport its huge army against East Prussia. Schlieffen's plan called for victory in the west within 39 days before turning to face Russia in the east. German armies would be transported to the borders by a militarized railroad system and arranged with a preponderance of strength on the right (northern) flank. These northern 'hammer' forces would execute a sweeping hook through Belgium, encircling Paris from the west and trapping the five French armies and the BEF against the 'anvil' of German forces to the south. The plan was overly optimistic, lacking – as its creator pointed out – the superior numbers necessary to execute it and ignoring the responses of the enemy. Despite its shortcomings, it almost worked.

1. The Battle of Crécy as depicted in a 15th century manuscript of Jean Froissart's Chronicles. The English (right) are led by Edward III's banner, a quartering of the English Lion with the French Fleur de Lys.

The ancient Croix de Bohême sits upon its modern plinth.

Crécy battlefield viewed in the direction of the French attack. The row of hedges and three meter drop on the left may have protected the Prince of Wale's right. The observation tower on the crest of the ridge marks the windmill used by Edward III.

2. Agincourt battlefield viewed from the English starting positions near Maisoncelle. The field's heavy soil is visible in the foreground; the engagement took place in the distance across the field from left to right at approximately the distance of the barely visible vehicle.

Statue of Jeanne d'Arc in the place du Martroi, Orléans; the city has paid homage to Jeanne with a festival every May for 580 years.

3. Sunken roads, of the type that hid troop movements during the battle, are still to be seen in the vicinity of Ramillies. This one is west of the village whose church steeple is visible in the distance.

Ferme Seny is one on many ancient farmsteads in the area. Its stout walls could have offered protection to French troops.

4. Cannonade at Valmy from a 19th century military history of France by A. Hugo.
Painting by d'Arnaud Gaillard

French Cuirassiers charge into British infantry squares during the Battle of Waterloo.
Painting by Felix Philippoteaux

5. Waterloo: The King's German Legion defended the Ferme de la Haie Sainte behind its stout walls. The farm appears today much as it did in 1815; the gateway is visible on the extreme left.

Lord Arthur Wellesley, Duke of Wellington.
Painting by Sir Thomas Lawrence

View of Waterloo battlefield from Napoleon's observation point. The battlefield's most prominent feature, Butte de Lion, is on the left; Haie Sainte is to the left of the copse on the right.

6. The storming of Rotherberg by General Bruno von François' brigade during the Battle of Spicheren. Drawing by C. Röchling

Monument to Grenadier-Regiment Prinz Carl von Preußen in Gifertswald; the slope demonstrates the steep climb faced by the attackers.

7. The Metz – Verdun road crosses the Mance Ravine (valley of death), which was defended by extensive French entrenchments on the opposite slopes during the Battle of Gravelotte.
Napoleon III and Otto von Bismarck outside of the weaver's cottage after the French defeat at Sedan.
Painting by Wilhelm Camphausen

Musée de la Maison de la dernière cartouche in Bazeilles retains its bullet scarred façade.

8. Preserved trenches of the Dodengang curve along the west bank of the Yser River.
Inset: Demarcation Stone at the far end of the Trench of Death marks the farthest German advance
in this sector.

By November 1917 much of the city of
Ypres was in ruins; the Cloth Hall (right)
and St-Maartens-kathedraal (left). LAC

The reconstructed Gothic style Cloth
Hall houses In Flanders Fields Museum;
the attached Renaissance Nieuwerck
serves as the town hall.

9. Menin Gate Memorial stands along a section of moat which protected medieval Ypres.

Troops exit Ypres through the city's ramparts at the Menin Gate in September 1918. The Cloth Hall ruins are visible in the distance. LAC

Preserved trenches form part of the exhibits of the Sanctuary Wood Museum.

10. Canadian Memorial at St-Juliaan

Statue of General Paul Maistre stands near Notre-Dame de Lorette Memorial (background); his XXI Corps saw action at Vimy, Verdun and Somme battles.

The arcaded buildings of the Petit Place in Arras show the destruction wrought by German bombardments; Hôtel de Ville (left). (May 1917). LAC

11.   Abris du Kronprinz: Concrete shelter of German Crown Prince Wilhelm is one of several such constructions at this site in the Forêt d'Argonne.

Period photograph of the cratered summit and opposing trenches on Butte de Vauquois. NARA

The summit displays the shattered stones that are that remains of the Vauquois church which was located at the small stone marker. The Lantern of the Dead stands above the edge of the crater and indicates the farthest French advance in March 1915.

12. Tranchée de la Soif in the Bois d'Ailly winds through the re-grown forest for several hundred meters. Numerous such trenches are to be seen in the larger Forêt d'Apremont.

A Bavarian Command Post constructed in the Tranchées des Bavarois bears the slogan of the Bavarian regiments. A firing step is to the right.

13. Dud Corner Cemetery and Loos Memorial to the Missing; the British attack in the Battle of Loos went from left to right across the fields to the rear of the cemetery.

View to the west overlooking Ninth Avenue Cemetery showing the lack of cover for advancing infantry on the Loos battlefield.

14.   Road marker designation the Voie Sacrée supply highway into Verdun. On top is the French First World War 'Adrian' helmet.

Revitalized esplanade along Verdun's riverfront; the twin towers of the Cathédrale Notre-Dame are seen on the right rear.

Lieutenant-Colonel Emile Driant's command post in the Bois des Caures.

15. Aerial photograph of a barely discernable Fort de Douaumont in a 'forest' of shell craters during October 1916 French bombardment. NARA

Fort de Douaumont's 75-mm gun turret (right) and 1917 observation cupola (left). A 'zone rouge' is behind the signs on the right.

The Ossuaire de Douaumont holds the unidentified remains of 130,000 French and German soldiers.

16. A remaining segment of Londres (London) Trench as it winds towards Fort de Douaumont.

The entrance to Fort de Souville displays the vegetation which slowly overcomes the ruins. An astounding number of such structures can be found in the forest now occupying the Verdun battlefield.

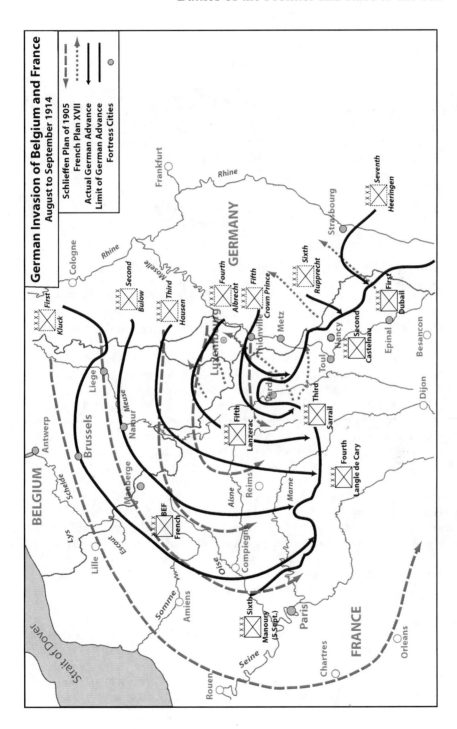

German Invasion of Belgium and France
August to September 1914

Schlieffen Plan of 1905
French Plan XVII
Actual German Advance
Limit of German Advance
Fortress Cities

#13

Battle of Mons
23 to 24 August 1914

OBJECTIVE	To march into Belgium and meet the German invasion.
FORCES	
BRITISH:	II Corps (General Horace Smith-Dorrien)
GERMAN:	First Army (Generaloberst Alexander von Kluck)
RESULT	The BEF successfully delayed the German advance across the French-Belgian border.
CASUALTIES	
BRITISH:	4,242, including a small number from I Corps
GERMAN:	Estimated by the British at greater than 6,000
LOCATION	Mons is 240 km north of Paris

German super heavy artillery made quick work of the fortresses at Liège and Namur that protected the open country of central Belgium. The grossly overmatched Belgian Army made a brief attempt to delay the German advance before retiring to fortress-ringed Antwerp. General Kluck's German First Army marched through Brussels toward the French frontier, uncertain as to the exact location of the BEF.

Commanded by Field Marshal Sir John French, the BEF landed in France between 12 and 17 August at Le Havre, Rouen, and Boulogne and then marched to take its place between French Fifth Army of général de division Charles Lanrezac and the Territorial divisions of Group d'Amade. Unknown to the British, général Lanrezac, under pressure from the German Second Army, commanded by Generaloberst Karl von Bülow, and grossly outnumbered, decided upon a strategic withdrawal which exposed the BEF's right flank. Lanrezac's actions would later make for recriminations between the Allies. Learning of Lanrezac's moves and the size of the oncoming German forces, French halted the BEF's advance. The British had already reached Mons, and General Horace Smith-Dorrien's II Corps, established a defense line along 25 km of the Condé-Mons Canal. I Corps, commanded by Lieutenant-General Sir Douglas Haig, was to the east and facing east. The canal was not an insurmountable obstacle, being only two meters deep and twenty meters wide. Kluck expected to meet the BEF coming from Lille, and his forces approaching Mons were strung out along kilometers of roads. They would, therefore, engage the British in an uncoordinated fashion.

Battle

In the early morning of 22 August, a patrol of the 4th Dragoon Guards encountered an advance unit of German Cuirassiers northeast of Mons, reconnoitering the approaches to the city. A few shots were fired, and a short chase took place, during which the dragoons caught the retiring Germans after 3 km and inflicting twenty-three casualties. Other skirmishes took place while the main

German force marched toward the French frontier, spreading across the countryside. During the night the British took up positions which ran along the canal line east from Condé, curved around to the north of Mons, then turned south from Obourg, forming a salient northeast of the city.

In the early mists of a drizzly rain the next morning, a short artillery bombardment from guns established on the high ground north of the canal fell upon the 4th Middlesex Regiment positioned south of Obourg. At approximately 09:00, they and the adjoining 4th Royal Fusiliers to their left at Nimy were surprised to see waves of German 18th Division infantry advancing across the meadows to the north. The Germans marched forward in tightly spaced columns as if fighting a Napoleonic battle. British professional infantry troops were especially well-trained in rapid-fire marksmanship, and the Germans fell in droves. A short time later the Germans, strengthened by regiments from the 17th Division, advanced again, extending the fight to the south. The German losses were again heavy, and their massed formations broke into smaller units which started infiltrating the British flanks.

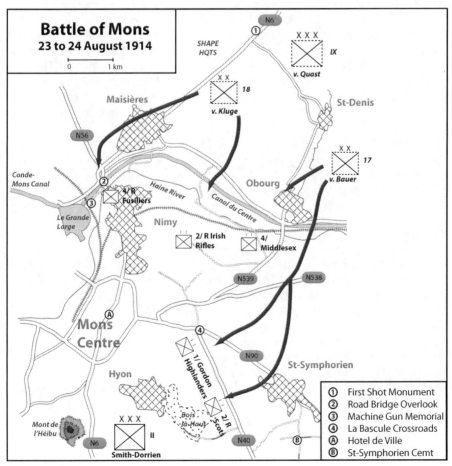

After a morning of steady pressure, the Germans crossed the Haine River, and at 14:00, British units in the salient started to withdraw under fire of German IX Corps artillery. 4th Middlesex Regiment fought a retreat across the eastern reaches of Mons, joined by the Royal Fusiliers who evacuated Nimy and withdrew through the city. Finally, the German Infantry Regiment Nr 75 struck against the 1st Gordon Highlanders and 2nd Royal Scots, who were defending the eastern slopes of the Bois Là-Haut along the Harmignies Road. British riflemen again performed admirably, and after suffering heavy losses, the Germans called an end to the assault. By 17:00, the enemy had entered the city center, and British artillery units were extracted from the Bois Là-Haut to a pre-established defense line farther south.

West of Mons British positions were along both sides of the essentially straight canal, clustered near the numerous bridges. Four divisions of German III and IV Corps fell upon British 5th Division like a rolling wave, starting at 11:00. The actions earlier in the morning were repeated while accurate and rapid British rifle fire decimated the closed ranks of German infantry. Walter Bloem, a German officer of Grenadier Regiment Nr 12 attacking the canal from Tertre, described the result: 'Behind us the meadow was dotted with little grey heaps. The hundred and sixty men that left the wood with me had shrunk to less than a hundred.'[1] Later Bloem wrote of the effect of the 1st Regiment's rapid fire, 'The enemy were firing like madmen again. The bullets hummed around me like a swarm of angry hornets.'[2] German indirect artillery fire was ineffective in finding targets. By midnight the German III Corps, having suffered enough casualties, ceased operations without any Germans having crossed the canal between Mons and Condé. 5th Division casualties were light.

With the forced withdrawal of 3rd Division from the canal salient, the positions of 5th Division were unsupportable. The BEF spent 24 August executing a fighting disengagement, suffering an additional 2,600 casualties. Through the discipline of concentrated rifle fire and the sacrifices of individual soldiers, II Corps was able to disengage and continue their fighting retreat farther south to Le Cateau.

Battlefield Tour

Mons, the capital of the Belgian province of Hainault, was a manufacturing, mining, and smelting center, whose slag heaps are still visible in the surrounding towns, especially to the west. The city is no longer the transportation hub that it was in 1914, and much of the manufacturing has also left the area leaving the soot- and grime-coated detritus common in old manufacturing centers. The headquarters of SHAPE (NATO's Supreme Headquarters Allied Powers Europe) is 6 km northeast at Maisières. The city has expanded to the east, engulfing much of the battlefield; however, important locations defended by the Middlesex and Royal Fusiliers have remained unchanged. The city retains its old world Grand Place, and the Hôtel de Ville has several memorial plaques to the 1914 fighting and the city's eventual

---

[1] Walter Bloem, *The Advance from Mons* (Solihill, England: Helion & Company, 2004), 42.
[2] Ibid ., 46.

liberation. The tour concentrates on the open area northeast of Mons, where the fighting first started and where the dramatic defense of the canal bridges took place.

The tour begins on the Mons-Brussels Road (N6) 8 km northeast of the city, a short distance past the entrance gates to SHAPE headquarters.

A dirty, gray **stone block stele** marks the point from which British troops first spotted the Germans. At 07:00 on 22 August, Corporal Drummer E Thomas of C Squadron, 4th Dragoon Guards saw the enemy coming over the rise on the roadway to the northeast and fired the first British shot of the First World War. Whether he killed his target is not known, but the Germans retired back along the road. Two troops of dragoons rode to the attack, led by Captain CB Hornby. A five-minute skirmish ensued 4 km northeast near an intersection known as A la Reine de Hongrie, with eight German cuirassiers taken prisoner and approximately twice that number killed.

In a great irony of the First World War, a **plaque** on the wall of a restaurant almost directly across the street from the stele identifies the position of the advance outpost for Canadian troops at 11:00 on 11 November 1918. For Britain the war started and ended at the same location.

Return toward Mons and park under the highway bridge that crosses the canal.

A stairway on the west side provides access to the bridge. In 1914, this was a swing bridge, which the British had opened cutting the Mons-Brussels road. A German infantryman swam the canal under British fire and operated the machinery to close the bridge, allowing the Germans to cross against the 4th Royal Fusiliers. From the bridge good perspectives of the battlefield are possible. To the east the canal curves around the area occupied by 4th Middlesex Regiment. The level, open meadow provided ideal fields of fire, and the Germans paid a heavy price fighting across the canal. To the west is the rail bridge that was heroically defended by 4th Royal Fusiliers.

Follow, by car or on foot, the narrow lane along the south bank of the canal to the rail bridge. Under the bridge a **memorial plaque** and small flower garden commemorate a sandbagged machine-gun position commanded by Lieutenant Maurice Dease VC, Royal Fusiliers, who denied the Germans use of the rail bridge across the canal. Holding off two battalions of the German Infantry Regiment Nr 84, Dease maintained fire despite several wounds. Upon Dease's evacuation to a field hospital (where he died), his place was immediately taken by Private Sidney Godley VC, who, although also badly wounded, remained to cover his unit's withdrawal. When the job was done, he dismantled his machine gun and threw the pieces into the canal. He was taken to a hospital by Belgian civilians, where he was later captured. The large body of water farther west is le Grand Large, a postwar barge turn-around that also connects the Canal de Centre to the old Condé-Mons Canal.

Return toward Mons and take the ring road east and south. Exit toward Charleroi / Binche (Chaussée de Binche – N90) and go 1.4 km to the Bascule crossroads (Chaussée de Beaumont – N40), which sits upon a commanding rise. Convenient parking is possible on chemin de Mourdreux, north of this confusing and very busy intersection.

In an attempt to block the British retreat, the Germans moved along chemin des Mourdreux to attack a makeshift unit of cooks and drivers defending the crossroads. Using a hastily repaired machine gun, forty men held off elements of 85th and 86th German Regiments for four hours before the assault shifted farther south. On one corner stands a **Celtic Cross** which commemorates the **Royal Irish Regiment**'s defense of the position. It also carries a plaque stating, 'Near this spot the 2nd Battalion commenced operations on 23 August 1914 and finished on 11 November 1918 after being decimated on four occasions.' Across the highway two stone columns, which once stood in the centre of Mons, commemorate the start and end of the war at Mons. The positions of the Gordon Highlanders and Royal Scots were along the present N40 highway to the southeast. Bois Là-Haut is 1.6 km directly south.

The battleground for the actions to the west of Mons is difficult to access and lacks distinguishing markers. The old Condé-Mons Canal (opened in 1818 and connecting the rivers Sambre and Schelde) has been replaced by a parallel extension of the Canal du Centre 3 km to the north. The Haine River / Condé Canal system still exists, but the E19 Autoroute runs along it, limiting access and obscuring the perspectives offered to the British riflemen as they fired at the advancing Germans. The Canal du Centre east of Nimy was started in 1882 but not finished until 1917 – by the Germans.

Other Sites of Interest: East of Mons in the village of Ville-sur-Haine, a canal-side plaque records the death of **Private George Lawrence Price, 2nd Canadian Division**, the last British soldier killed in the war at 10:58 on 11 November 1918. **St Symphorien Military Cemetery** is one of the most beautiful military cemeteries in Europe. Created by the Germans after the battle, British and German troops are buried in unit plots scattered around a rural, tree-shaded site. Lieutenant Dease and Private Price are buried near each other. The cemetery is south of St-Symphorien on a farm lane; it is hard to find (look for Commonwealth War Graves Commission (CWGC) signs in the village), but worth the effort.

#14

Battle of le Cateau
26 August 1914

OBJECTIVE	To delay the advancing Germans.
FORCES	
BRITISH:	II Corps (General Sir Horace Smith-Dorrien) and Cavalry Division

	(Major-General Edmund Allenby)
GERMAN:	III Corps (General der Infanterie Ewald von Lochow), IV Corps (General der Infanterie Friedrich Sixt von Armin), and II Cavalry Corps (General der Kavallerie Georg von der Marwitz)
RESULT	The delays at Mons and le Cateau impacted the timetable for the German advance on Paris.
CASUALTIES	
BRITISH:	7,812 casualties
GERMAN:	Estimated by the British at greater than 15,000
LOCATION	Cambrai is 175 km north of Paris; Le Cateau-Cambrésis is 24 km southeast of Cambrai

Battle

Under pressure from Kluck's German First Army, British II Corps retired from the engagement at Mons along the western side of Bois de Mormal. Progress was slow due to the fleeing refugees and the heat of a French August. On 26 August, Smith-Dorrien thought that his men were near exhaustion, but during a 02:00 conference with General Allenby at his headquarters in Bertry, the decision was that the enemy was too close and that II Corps would have to stand and fight, contrary to orders from General Headquarters (GHQ). British forces formed a 16 km-long, broken line along the le Cateau-Cambrai highway from le Cateau to Beauvois. 5th Division, augmented by 19th Brigade, was crowded on a hill southwest of le Cateau between the Selle River and Chaussée Brunehault. The open country around le Cateau was more conducive to the use of artillery than the built-up towns and slag heaps around Mons, and the Germans had a distinct advantage in artillery.

At 06:00, German guns began to roar out of the heavy mist along the entire British line, while German 14th Brigade infantry, entering the gap between Smith-Dorrien's II Corps and Haig's I Corps, passed through le Cateau and moved south down the valley of the Selle River. II Corps' right flank was to have been covered by General Haig's I Corps, but Haig was delayed due to fighting his own minor action at Landrecies on the previous day.

5th Division artillery had been pushed forward to only 200-400 meters behind the infantry and engaged German artillery east of Le Cateau. Outnumbered and outgunned, the British batteries slowly started to fade. The 11th Battery, Royal Field Artillery was a particularly hard hit target of German gunners. By 10:00, all of its officers were casualties and only one of its six guns remained operational.

By late morning, German infantry, sensing the opportunity, rushed to the attack. Hardest hit was 5th Division's 2nd Suffolk Regiment, which was at the point of the spur with 2nd King's Own Yorkshire Light Infantry (KOYLI) on their left above the Cambrai Road. In line to the west was 2nd King's Own Scottish Borders (KOSB). Although later reinforced by 2nd Manchester and 2nd Argyll and Sutherland battalions, the men on the hill were outnumbered five to one by three German infantry regiments, who also had massed machine guns across the road. Enfiladed from east and west and subject to fire from multiple Germans batteries, the infantry nevertheless put down withering rifle fire, and the forty guns from the seven batteries brought down the enemy's charges at close range over open sights. In a famous incident, 122nd Battery unlimbered its guns to face a German infantry platoon emerging from a depression. The battery's guns fired one simultaneous round to destroy the entire platoon.

By afternoon, German forces had been strengthened by the arrival of their 5th Division, whose Grenadier Regiment Nr 8 moved toward II Corps' rear via St-Benin and St-Souplet. One by one the British guns were put out of action by hits on their crews. The defenders held for an amazing six hours before the overwhelming pressure forced a withdrawal.

Smith-Dorrien's retreat order came – to those units who received it – at approximately 14:00. The cannon-short BEF was concerned about saving its batteries, and amidst the German infantry fire the limbers were brought up and the horses attached to pull the guns back. When the order to retire was received, 37th Battery's drivers rode forward despite German infantry fire and rescued four of their six howitzers. Asking for volunteers, their commander returned to rescue one more gun; he and two drivers earned Victoria Crosses for the action. Other batteries performed similar actions, with German machine-gun fire and shrapnel flying everywhere.

By 14:30, German Infantry Regiment Nr 26 was firing into 2nd Suffolk and Argyll's rear while they retired. To their left, the 2nd KOYLI never received the withdrawal order and by 15:30 was surrounded and annihilated. When the nineteen survivors exhausted their ammunition, the last remaining company commander, Major Charles Yates VC, led them in a final charge. Their sacrifice played a great role in the division's ability to disengage from the enemy. The same fate befell the 2nd KOSB to their left. The order also never reached a mixed group consisting mainly of 1st Gordons, the rearguard of 3rd Division near Caudry. Though surrounded, they held off two German regiments for six hours, ensuring their division's withdrawal. At 12:30, they finally attempted to retire but were intercepted by German infantry, and in a bitter fight in the dark, they were all but eliminated.

To the west, the newly arrived British 4th Division held the left flank. German units reeled under the effective British rifle fire, suffering enormous casualties. 4th Division had some difficulty disengaging when the order came, but the French Cavalry Corps held off further advance by German IV Reserve Corps and helped preserve the British flank.

The Germans fought heroically at le Cateau and suffered enormous casualties; therefore, they did not immediately pursue retiring units. The British losses were twice that of Mons, but Smith-Dorrien probably saved the entire BEF from envelopment. Over the next few days, isolated, small unit actions took place while the BEF continued to move south, eventually disappearing from German sight. It reappeared on 6 September, driving a wedge between Kluck's First Army and Bülow's Second Army during the turning point of the 1914 fighting at the First Battle of the Marne.

Battlefield Tour

Le Cateau, in the valley of the north-south running Selle River, is a pleasant market town which houses the Matisse art museum. The villages along the road to Cambrai – especially from Caudry to Beauvois – have expanded, obliterating any signs of the center and left wing portions of the battlefield. The site of the Suffolk Memorial, however, is of particular historical interest and provides a perspective of much of the eastern sector of the battlefield. Unfortunately, the location is somewhat difficult to find.

From the N43 in le Cateau, turn south onto boulevard Paturle. In the roundabout 'Carrefour de l'Europe' turn left onto rue du Pont Fourneau and almost immediately right on avenue des Essarts. Proceed until the chemin de Reumont and turn right. (The route is signed to 'Collège J. Rostand.') Once at the college, proceed uphill along the unpaved sunken track and then turn right at the fork. Park below and walk up the track.

The **Suffolk Memorial** is in a cluster of good-sized trees. A white stone block honors the officers and other ranks of the 2nd Battalion Suffolk Regiment, 2nd Battalion Manchester Regiment, 2nd Battalion Argyll and Sutherland Highlanders, and XV Brigade Royal Regiment of Artillery as well as lists the dead by unit and rank, including Lieutenant-Colonel CAH Brett, DSO, Suffolk's commanding officer. The Suffolks established their final position here, ignored German demands that they surrender, and withdrew only when German units appeared in their rear. The position afforded a good line of fire toward the German attack but offered little protection in its shallow defensive trenches dug in the hard, rocky soil. The site was also exposed to German positions to the north and east.

The hill is little changed except for the Collège J. Rostand, and from it the entire battlefield can be viewed. To the east, the ground dips precipitously; this valley covered the German troop movements while German III Corps marched to outflank the British right. To the north and slightly west of le Cateau are the hills toward Montay from where massed German batteries and machine guns poured shells and bullets upon the hill.

Other Sites of Interest: The adjacent **Le Cateau German and British cemeteries** are located at the top of the hill on the Chaussée Brunehault toward Montay (D 932) west of le Cateau. They contain the graves of 698 Commonwealth soldiers, most buried by the Germans after the 1914 battle; 5,576 German soldiers, mainly from the 1918 engagements that took place near here; and 42 Russian POWs. The site provides extensive views to the south and marks the position of the German machine guns which raked the Suffolks.

#15

Battle of the Yser
18 to 31 October 1914

OBJECTIVE	To destroy the Belgian Army and continue westward to capture Calais.
FORCES	
BELGIAN:	Six infantry divisions and one cavalry division of the Belgian Army (King Albert I) supported by French Marins Fusiliers (amiral Pierre Ronarc'h)
GERMAN:	III Reserve Corps (General der Infanterie Hans von Beseler)
RESULT	The Belgians, with French support, successfully stopped the German drive by flooding the polder.
CASUALTIES	
BELGIAN:	3,150 killed and 16,900 wounded
GERMAN:	At least 9,500
LOCATION	Ypres is 250 km north of Paris; Diksmuide is 24 km north of Ypres

During the First Battle of the Marne (not covered in this book), the hastily assembled French Sixth Army threatened Kluck's German First Army's exposed right flank. The BEF reversed direction, and moved northwards threatening to split Kluck from Bülow's German Second Army. On 9 September German Supreme Headquarters called for a withdrawal to the line of the Aisne River.

There ensued a steady series of troop movements known as 'The Race to the Sea' in which both sides attempted to turn the enemy's flank. French Marins Fusiliers, led by amiral Pierre Ronarc'h, and 6,000 men of the British Royal Naval Division attempted to reinforce the Belgium army still trapped in Antwerp by the German III Reserve Corps of General Beseler. On 10 October, the Allies, including the remnants of the Belgian Army, made their escape toward the French frontier surrendering the city. Generalleutnant Erich von Falkenhayn, who had replaced Generaloberst Helmuth von Moltke as Chief of the German General Staff for his failure to execute the Schlieffen Plan and quickly win the war, sent the German Fourth Army (Duke Albrecht of Wurttemberg) including Beseler's Corps against Flanders with the aim of capturing Calais. By 14 October, the Belgians were positioned behind the Yser and its canal, and the British 7th Division and 3rd Cavalry Division, forming the new IV Corps, were around Ypres. The front lines now extended to the North Sea near Nieuwpoort, Belgium.

Battle

The land around the Yser River (IJzer in Dutch) is polder – ground reclaimed from the sea the drainage of which is maintained by a complex network of canals, dikes, and pumps. The water table is never much below the surface, and holes quickly fill. At Nieuwpoort a complex of sluice gates set the water level in the numerous canals which meet there and in their outflow into the North Sea. Since the ground is almost perfectly flat, any high point provided an opportunity for observation and dominance over the enemy. The Belgian Army, while it fell back from Antwerp, established itself along the two prominent rises. One was the canalized embankment of the Yser River, and the other was several kilometers farther west, along the 19 km rail line running from Nieuwpoort south to Diksmuide.

Three Belgian divisions held the Yser River line with three more in reserve. Forward posts were at towns along the line of the current N369 highway. The Ieperlee Canal line from Diksmuide to Ypres was manned by the French 89th and Territorial 87th Divisions. Belgian and French cavalry screened the northern approaches to Ypres. Admiral Ronarc'h's French Marins Fusiliers took up positions outside of Diksmuide.

On 18 October, the Germans opened their attack with a heavy artillery bombardment along the entire Belgian line, and followed it with infantry incursions into the forward outposts at Sint Pieters Kapelle, Keiem, and Beerst. An attempt by the German III Reserve Corps to take Westende was beaten back by shellfire from three British monitors lying off the coast. Belgian reserves were largely committed over the next two days while the assaults continued – some forward positions changing hands several times. On 20 October, attention shifted to Mannekensvere, where General Beseler's corps sent three divisions against three Belgian regiments. Despite bombardment from German 210-mm howitzers, the Belgians held the city, even recapturing Lombardsijde on 22 October.

Also on 20 October, the German 43rd and 44th Reserve Divisions started their assault upon Diksmuide against général Meiser's brigade. On

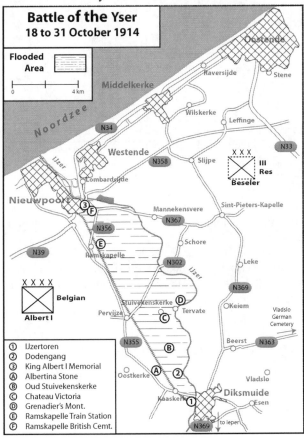

the roads leading into the city, Colonel Jacques and his 12th Regiment of the Line earned fame – and a statue in the Diksmuide town square – with his spirited defense of the approaches from the northeast, east and south. Ronarc'h's men held the west bank of the river, north of the city. The German preliminary artillery barrage set Diksmuide on fire, while heavy winds spread the flames from house to house across the narrow streets. The cycle of infantry attack followed by artillery fire continued throughout the day. On 24 October, the Germans launched their most determined effort to take the city, launching fifteen waves of infantry after an exceptionally heavy bombardment. The German effort ultimately failed, but the casualties and diminishing supplies of ammunition were weakening the Belgian resistance.

Meanwhile at Tervate, the German Reserve Infantry Regiment Nr 26 breached the Belgian lines during the night of 21 October by crossing the river on a temporary footbridge. Belgian counterattacks were not able to destroy the rapidly expanding bridgehead.

As the Belgian Army's situation became dire, a desperate plan was developed to flood the low land between the Yser and the rail line by opening the sluice gates to the North Sea. Engineers constructed small dams at each of the twenty-two culverts that crossed below the rail line and regulated the canal levels for eight days while the army slowly withdrew.

In a final effort the Germans again attacked Ramskapelle on 31 October, but with the water slowly rising around them and the strong Belgian resistance, they ended the offensive. Diksmuide finally fell to the Germans on 11 November in a separate assault.

Battlefield Tour

The tour of the Yser battlefield starts in Diksmuide and ends in Nieuwpoort, traveling only a short distance along the IJzer River to the Dodengang. Although following the riverside road north from Dodengang is possible, and would include the Tervate Bridge location, the drive can be tortuous. The significantly faster highway to the west of the railway embankment is recommended because the terrain is not very dissimilar from the battlefield. All of the ground has been reclaimed for farming, and except for the modern highway and buildings, the fields remain much the same in general appearance as in 1914.

In Diksmuide's medieval central square stands a memorial statue to Colonel Jacques (later **général-Baron Jacques de Diksmuide**). In the town park near the train station, a white wall commemorates the sacrifice of **Admiral Ronarc'h** and his French Marin Fusiliers in their defense of Diksmuide.

Leave Diksmuide to the west toward Veurne (N35). On the western edge of Diksmuide, only 1.5 km from the central square, turn south along the western bank of the IJzerdijk to the IJzertoren Memorial.

Ijzertoren, or Peace Tower, is a memorial to Flemish Emancipation as well as a museum to the history of Flanders. The entrance to the tower is through a rebuilt memorial (the original was destroyed in 1946) to Flemish leaders who died for protesting the French dominated army and central government. The issue remains a controversial subject in Flanders. Dramatic views over the Yser battlefield can be obtained from the observation room on the 22nd floor. A stunning panoramic photograph shows what the landscape looked like in 1914 and helps locate battle sites. Each floor has exhibits on Flemish history with special attention to the First World War. Open daily from 10:00 to 18:00 from April to September, shorter hours during the winter and closed Christmas holidays as well as the following three weeks. Fee.

From the IJzertoren proceed north along the canal for 2 km.

The **Dodengang** (also know as the Trench of Death or le Boyau de la Mort) is a well-preserved Belgian trench system dramatically revealing some of the most deadly local fighting that occurred for almost four years, even until the final allied Advance of 1918. After the end of the battle of the Yser, the Germans established a machine gun position near ruined petrol tanks on the west side of the canal. The Belgians started digging a trench northwards to recapture the site, not knowing that the Germans had started digging a trench southwards. These efforts resulted in the enemies being only meters from each other. Periodic strengthening of the positions took place with the construction – usually under enemy fire – of concrete pillboxes. The area hence experienced its own little war, with the Germans on three sides of the Belgian trench line. Snipers and bombers made the trench so dangerous that Belgian troops were assigned there for only a three-day rotation. All supply and reinforcement efforts had to be conducted at night over two footbridges across strips of the flooded zone.

A new visitor's center presents film clips and high quality photographs labeled in four languages of the Belgian fighting. An observation deck provides views of the entire trench line and a 1916 aerial photograph for comparison. From there one can descend into the trenches, which are lined with concrete 'sandbags', and explore the 400-meter long double trench lines as well as several pillboxes, including the most dangerous one called the 'Mousetrap' by the soldiers because its function was to catch any German soldiers attempting to infiltrate Belgian lines. At the far end of the trench is a Demarcation Stone erected by the Touring Club of Belgian to mark the farthest German advance in this sector. Fifty meters farther are the ruins of a German observation post. The visitor's center and Dodengang is open every day from April to 11 November from 09:00 to 17:00, except during the winter when it is open only on weekends. No admission charge.

Proceed north to the 'Y' junction and bear left onto Dodengangstraat; after 2.3 km, turn right toward Nieuwpoort (N35). In Pervijze continue toward Nieuwpoort (N355) for 4 km, bear right toward Ramskapelle (N356), go through the town and under the Autoroute, and turn left toward Nieuwpoort (N367). The Ramscapelle Road Military

Cemetery with 843 burials is on the corner. Continue to the Konig Albert I Monument.

On the night of 29 October, Hendrik Geeraert, Chief Lockkeeper, crept into no man's land with a small Belgian army patrol and opened the last of the sluice gates. The wartime gates have been replaced by their modern equivalent, but they are still there, under the watchful eye of a mounted statue of **King Albert I** surrounded by a memorial rotunda dedicated to him. A balcony around the top of the memorial offers views of the IJzer, the complex of sluice gates and canals, and the North Sea. The tower is open weekdays 1 March through 15 October from 08:45 to 12:00 and 13:15 to 18:00; 16 October through 28 February from 08:45 to 12:00 and 13:15 to 17:00. No admission charge; elevator.

The adjacent **British Memorial to the Missing** is guarded by three stone lions. The eight-meter stone records the 566 names of those who died in fighting at Antwerp in 1914 or in British actions along the seacoast in 1917 and have no known grave. Around the stone are inscribed words from Laurence Binyon's *For the Fallen*, 'They shall grow not old, as we that are left grow old: age shall not weary them, nor the years condemn. At the going down of the sun and in the morning, we will remember them.'

A stroll around the rim of the sluice gates reveals memorials to numerous military units, Belgian and French, and eventually leads to the La Belgique representing the **Belgian Memorial to the Battle of the Yser**.

Other Sites of Interest: In Ramskapelle the **wartime train station**, which became a concrete observation post, remains along the old rail line that was the front line after the flooding and which has been converted into a bicycling path. A nearby Albertina Stone marks the farthest German advance. The **Vladslo German Cemetery** is 3 km northeast of the village of Vladslo and contains the remains of 25,644 German soldiers. The cemetery is known for a pair of kneeling figures by famed sculptress Kaethe Kollwitz, whose son was killed in the 1914 fighting and is buried nearby. The figures have come to symbolize the grief of all parents who lost a child during the war.

#16

First Battle of Ypres (Ieper)
19 October to 22 November 1914

OBJECTIVE	To advance upon Ypres –the last barrier to the Channel ports – and upon Bruges and Kortrijk (Courtrai) – entries to the German border.
FORCES	
BRITISH:	Seven divisions of BEF (Field Marshall Sir John French)
FRENCH:	Two corps of Detachment of Belgium (général de division Victor d'Urbal)
GERMAN:	Sixteen divisions of Fourth Army (Duke Albrecht of Wurttemberg)

	and Sixth Army (Crown Prince Rupprecht of Bavaria)
RESULT	Greatly outnumbered the Allies were pressured into a salient around the city of Ypres.
CASUALTIES	
BRITISH:	7,960 dead, 29,562 wounded, and 17,873 missing
FRENCH:	50,000 killed and wounded
GERMAN:	103,050 killed and wounded
LOCATION	Ypres is 250 km north of Paris

In mid-September Erich von Falkenhayn, German Chief of the General Staff, considered his options for pursuing the war. Still believing that a successful conclusion was possible on the Western Front more rapidly than against Russia, he planned to threaten Britain by securing Belgian ports for use by German submarines and possibly capturing the British army embarkation cities of Calais and Dunkerque. He therefore moved the Crown Prince Rupprecht of Bavaria's Sixth Army from its initial positions in Alsace and new Fourth Army, under command of Duke Albrecht of Wurttemberg, into the open German right flank.

Général Joseph Joffre, Commander-in-Chief of the French Army, and Sir John French, commander of British Forces, agreed that the BEF should relocate from the Aisne to Flanders. Two French territorial divisions completed the line between Bikschote and the Belgian Army at Diksmuide.

By 20 October the Allies and Germans faced each other on an almost continuous line from the Swiss border to the North Sea. The 'Race to the Sea', which French général de division Joseph Galliéni described as being the British and French Armies 'always twenty-four hours and an army corps behind the Germans,'[3] ended the war of movement until the German Kaiserschlacht of March 1918. The opposing forces now engaged in the horrid trench warfare that was to characterize the next three years.

In a flat, horizontal battlefield like Ypres, any height brought the advantage of observation. A long, low ridge ran from Messines to Wijtschate; from there it began an extended arc through Passendale[4] and back west to Langemark. In its center was the city of Ypres.

The Ypres Salient is one of the more heavily commemorated battlefields of the world due to the enormous sacrifices endured by both sides during four years of the most exhausting trench warfare. From Armentières to Nieuwpoort, opposing forces suffered one million casualties. Over 145 military cemeteries dot the countryside, memorial stones to units and individuals appear everywhere, and even a few permanent fortifications in the form of concrete blockhouses remain. Since the fighting raged back and forth over the same ground, memorials to units and battlefield sites become intermixed.

Three locations have been selected as First Ypres battlefields, although the

---

[3] Joseph Galliéni, *Mémoires du Général Galliéni* (Paris: Payot, 1920), 197.
[4] Spelled Passchendaele during the war; the village's name is now recorded as Passendale but the older spelling is still frequently used in reference to the battle.

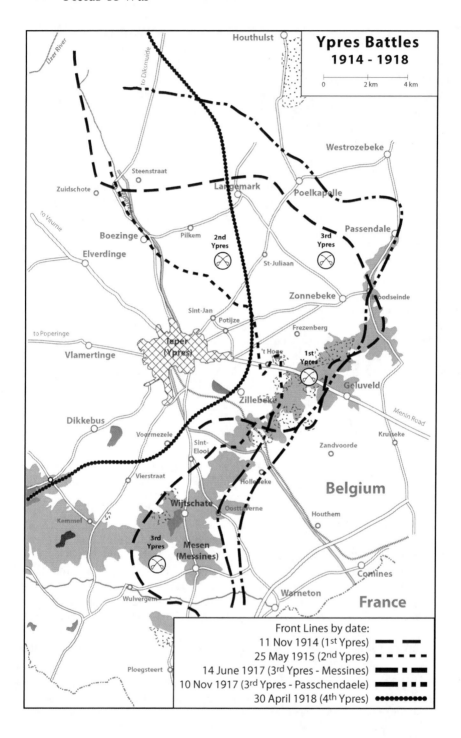

Ypres Battles
1914 - 1918

0   2 km   4 km

Houthulst

Westrozebeke

Steenstraat

Zuidschote

Langemark

Poelkapelle

Passendale

Boezinge

Pilkem

2nd Ypres

3rd Ypres

Elverdinge

St-Juliaan

to Veurne

Zonnebeke

Broodseinde

Sint-Jan

Potijze

Frezenberg

to Poperinge

Ieper (Ypres)

Vlamertinge

't Hooge

1st Ypres

Geluveld

Zillebeke

Menin Road

Dikkebus

Voormezele

Sint-Elooi

Zandvoorde

Kruiseke

Vierstraat

Hollebeke

Belgium

Wijtschate

Oosttaverne

Houthem

Kemmel

3rd Ypres

Mesen (Messines)

Comines

Wulvergem

Warneton

France

Ploegsteert

Front Lines by date:
11 Nov 1914 (1st Ypres) — —
25 May 1915 (2nd Ypres) - - -
14 June 1917 (3rd Ypres - Messines) —·—
10 Nov 1917 (3rd Ypres - Passchendaele) —··—
30 April 1918 (4th Ypres) ●●●●●●

to Diksmuide

IJzer River

fighting in October to November 1914 raged over far larger territory. The first site is Ypres, the locus of the three Ypres offensives and a city whose psychological import vastly outgrew its military significance. Although technically not a battlefield, its 'martyrdom', as the French would say, and the richness of its war sites earn placement in this book. The destruction of Germany's reserve battalions is commemorated at their cemetery at Langemark, and the stunning reversal of the German breakthrough at Geluveld is recorded in that village. Many other sites are worthy of visitation and some are covered later in this book under Second Battle of Ypres (1915) and Third Battle of Ypres (1917).

Ypres

The city of Ypres was a center of textile manufacturing during the 12th century, and the cloth trade brought great wealth. Its position across the trade route between Lille and Bruges supported commerce and added to the town's prosperity. Political unrest in the 14th century led the city's inhabitants into several wars, mainly against French domination. The plague appeared in 1316, and the loss of population combined with competition from Bruges led to the city's eventual decline. The textile trade moved elsewhere during the 15th and 16th centuries. By the 17th century Ypres was in French possession and important only as a frontier town. The great French military architect, Sébastien Le Prestre, Seigneur de Vauban, constructed the ramparts and associated fortifications. The creation of the state of Belgium in 1830 solidified the borders, and Ypres lost all strategic importance, once again entering into economic decline. The town's population had dwindled to approximately 17,000 by 1914.

On 7 October 1914, advance parties of German cavalry and cyclists (reconnaissance troops using bicycles) entered the city and levied a large fine on the townspeople. They occupied the city for three days before moving elsewhere. Although threatened during the German Lys Offensive in 1918, German troops would not enter the city ramparts again until 1940.

Major damage occurred in the spring of 1915, when the Germans moved up their super heavy artillery, including the 420-mm gun known as '*Dicke Bertha*' (Big Bertha) in preparation for the Second Battle of Ypres. By the end of the war most of the city's buildings had received substantial damage; many were completely destroyed. After much discussion, including Winston Churchill's proposal that the city be left as a ruin commemorating British sacrifices in its defense, Ypres was rebuilt, following much of the original design. Ypres today, therefore, gives the appearance of a medieval city with all the modern appurtenances and traffic congestion, thriving on tourists visiting the numerous battlefield sites surrounding the city.

The **Cloth Hall** (Lakenhalle) stands on the café-lined central square (Grote Markt) and still commands a central place in the life of the city's inhabitants. Although the original was started in 1201 by Baldwin IX, Count of Flanders, the massive Gothic structure was not completed until 1304. It was used as a warehouse and auction centre for the local textile industry, which converted English wool into fine cloth. At that time, the Ieperlee River extended directly to the hall where the loading and unloading of material took place. Used as a billet for British army troops and possibly as an observation point, it hence attracted German artillery fire. The first bombardment of the Cloth Hall took place in October 1914, with incendiary shells igniting the building on 22 November 1914. The shelling continued sporadically for the next four years. The hall was almost completely destroyed, with only sections of the exterior wall surviving. The townspeople insisted upon reconstructing the hall to its original design, but with the interruption of the Second World War, the building was not completed until 1958. It now houses some municipal offices, a very helpful tourist office, and the main Ypres battle museum called 'In Flanders Fields.' The 70-meter belfry houses a forty-nine bell carillon.

Besides presenting memorabilia of the Great War, **In Flanders Fields** brings the experiences of the combatants alive with audiovisual displays, short movies, and the unique assignment of a real wartime identity to each visitor. The museum reopened in 1998 after a complete renovation and it is the logical starting place for Ypres battlefield tours. All the materials are in four languages. The museum is open every day from 1 April to 15 November from 10:00 to 18:00; and from 16 November to 31 March every day except Monday from 10:00 to 17:00. The museum is closed during the first three weeks following the Christmas holidays. Fee.

Directly behind the Cloth Hall is **Sint-Maartenskathedraal**, which was started as a fortress chapel for the Count of Flanders' residence. Some of the existing piers around the ambulatory date from 1251. Although almost completely destroyed during the war, it was rebuilt to original specifications (although the original square tower was converted into a spire). The church is wonderfully colored with plaques that bear the coats of arms of various organizations adorning the walls, and its rose window is a British memorial to Belgian King Albert I. St-Martin is marvelously maintained and decorated with wood engravings and artwork.

Across the street and on Elverdingestraat is the smaller, more modern **St George's Church**. After the war the town was flooded with British visitors hoping to find remains of lost loved ones, ex-soldiers revisiting the fields of their memories, and workers constructing memorials and cemeteries. The British community constructed their own church, and over time the walls became lined with plaques dedicated to the memory of units or individuals who fought in the salient. Every chair has a cross-stitched kneeling pad with emblems of the fighting units, forming a colorful array across the church.

The **Menin Gate** was originally a gateway through the Vauban-designed fortifications, but by the nineteenth century its military importance had been reduced by modern artillery. The gate was replaced with a road opening marked by two stone lions through the ramparts, which were gradually converted into public gardens. Through this passage marched many of the soldiers who participated in the Ypres battles. After the war, a triumphal arch 25 meters high and 41 meters long was constructed with the intent to inscribe the names of the thousands of soldiers who were killed in the Ypres Salient but whose bodies were never found. The arch now presents the names of 54,896 of the missing on panels completely covering its interior walls and stairways. The designers ran out of space, and all those missing after 15 August 1917 are commemorated on the Memorial to the Missing at Tyne Cot Cemetery.

At 20:00 every evening since 1928 (except during the German occupation of the Second World War), the local fire brigade's buglers have presented a tribute to the missing by blowing '**The Last Post**.' The brief ceremony is usually heavily attended by visitors and schoolchildren, who frequently read short poems and present wreaths of poppies in one of the most moving commemorations on the Western Front. No admission charge.

Battle of Langemark
21 to 24 October 1914

OBJECTIVE	An encounter battle when both forces moved to attack.
FORCES	
BRITISH:	I Corps (Lieutenant-General Sir Douglas Haig) and IV Corps (Lieutenant-General Henry Rawlinson)
FRENCH:	IX Corps (général de division Pierre Dubois)
GERMAN:	Fourth Army (Duke Albrecht of Wurttemberg)
RESULT	The BEF held a thin line against repeated German assaults.
LOCATION	Ypres is 250 km north of Paris; Langemark is 10 km north of Ypres

Field Marshal French, still thinking that the BEF could outflank the Germans and move toward Bruges, sent General Haig's I Corps northeast of Ypres from Poperinge. They encountered the Germans along a line that stretched from the Ieperlee Canal west of Bikschote toward Langemark and even as far as Zonnebeke. French realized that his army was facing a much larger force than expected and ordered his corps commanders to establish defensive positions.

The battle of Langemark resulted from Falkenhayn's directive to the Fourth German Army to break through the Belgian/French forces along the Yser and proceed to capture the Channel ports of Calais, Boulogne, and Dunkerque. By 20 October, on a curved line from Armentières to the Yser, seven British infantry divisions augmented by five French and British cavalry divisions faced the onslaught of eleven German infantry divisions and eight German Cavalry divisions.

Battle

Duke Albrecht commanded five reserve divisions, which contained mostly volunteers including students who had been deferred from Germany's universal military training program as well as reservists too old for the regular army. Fifteen percent of the reserves were students, which led to the postwar legend of *der Kindermord bei Ypern*, or Massacre of the Innocents. The reserve divisions had received only one month of training; their arms were decidedly inferior, frequently being captured enemy weapons; and their artillery support was limited. They attacked British lines singing '*Das Deutschlandlied,*' which starts with the more familiar '*Deutschland über alles*' – a story greatly magnified by Nazi propaganda 25

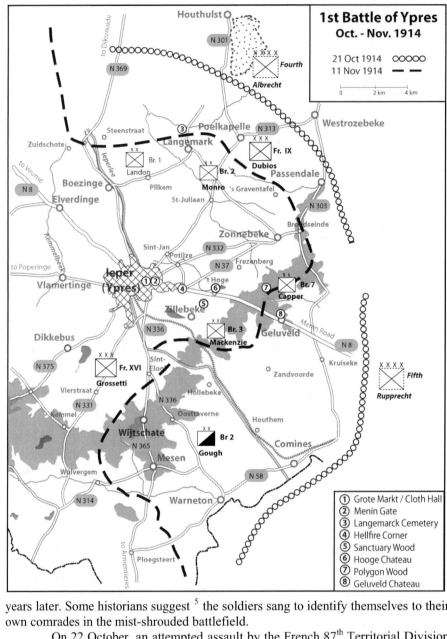

1st Battle of Ypres
Oct. - Nov. 1914

21 Oct 1914 ○○○○○
11 Nov 1914 ▬ ▬ ▬

0   2 km   4 km

① Grote Markt / Cloth Hall
② Menin Gate
③ Langemarck Cemetery
④ Hellfire Corner
⑤ Sanctuary Wood
⑥ Hooge Chateau
⑦ Polygon Wood
⑧ Geluveld Chateau

years later. Some historians suggest [5] the soldiers sang to identify themselves to their own comrades in the mist-shrouded battlefield.

On 22 October, an attempted assault by the French 87th Territorial Division

---

[5] Ian FW Beckett, *Ypres: The First Battle, 1914* (Harlow, England: Pearson Education, 2004), 76.

of général d'Urbal's Army Detachment of Belgium between Langemark and Steenstraat was easily dismissed in the early afternoon. The German XXIII Reserve Corps aimed its artillery at Langemark, targeting at first the church and its tall steeple, then any shelter in the village. The German batteries maintained a murderous rate of fire; trenches at this time were not the elaborate constructions that they became later in the war and thus offered little in the way of protection, especially from howitzer shells. British artillery was unable to respond adequately, shells of all calibers being in short supply. By the end of the day little remained except rubble, and the few remaining inhabitants were evacuated during the night. At dusk the German 51st Reserve Division charged southwest of Poelkapelle against the line of the 5th Brigade, British 2nd Division. They were cut down by intense rifle fire; the surge stopped only 50 meters in front of the British line. Near Kortekeer some territory was gained by the Germans, only to be reclaimed the next morning by reinforcements from the 2nd Infantry Brigade.

During the night of 23 October, the French 17th Division moved into position, relieving the British 2nd Division which went into reserve. Two battalions were called upon immediately to support the badly stretched the British 7th Division by counterattacking German elements in Polygon Wood, at the same time when events along the Yser were reaching their climax. By the end of the next day the French IX Corps took over the line from Langemark to Zonnebeke, freeing the BEF to consolidate its units in positions to the south, where an intense artillery barrage preceded the German infantry's advance. Through the organization of staff, clerks, and cooks, the 7th Division's commanding officer, Major-General Thompson Capper, was able to stem the tide and retain Polygon Wood. Three days of fighting reduced Capper's division to little more than one-half of its original size, and the assaults continued.

Battlefield Tour

The village of Langemark was not captured by German troops until the Second Battle of Ypres in April 1915. It became part of the German Wilhelm Line and was heavily fought over during the Third Battle of Ypres finally recaptured on 16 August 1917, when the surrounding territory was shredded by British artillery. The area offers little specific to the 1914 fighting, therefore, the tour is confined to the German cemetery and surrounding area.

Leave Langemark north toward Houthulst (Klerkenstraat).

Langemark German Military Cemetery was started in 1915 and was expanded during the years of German occupation. After the war, with the agreement of the Belgian government, the graves from 678 smaller cemeteries were consolidated. Langemark now contains 44,304 dead, including 3,000 of the student soldiers of 1914. The Alte Friedhof (Old Cemetery) is entered through a huge, red sandstone gateway known as a *Totenburgen*. Inside the entrance is a room with oak-lined walls which are inscribed with the names of the 6,313 known dead, who were buried when the cemetery was inaugurated in 1932. Immediately in front upon entering the cemetery is a shrub-covered ossuary containing the remains of 24,917 German soldiers and to which recently discovered remains are occasionally added. Sixty-eight adjacent bronze panels are covered with 17,342 names of the identified bodies in the mass grave. Surrounding it are insignia of the student regiments. Rows of horizontal grave markers fill the remainder of the tree-shrouded cemetery grounds. Due to Belgian restrictions on space, each grave contains up to twenty bodies, with the stone listing their names or '*Unbekannt Deutsche Soldaten*' for the unidentified. Groupings of three German stone crosses are randomly placed among the graves. Directly behind the mass grave along the rear border of the cemetery are four sculpted figures by Emil Krieger. These mourning soldiers continue their decades-long watch over the graves of their comrades.

On 9 October 1917, during the British advance upon Poelkapelle, the 4th Worcestershire Regiment came upon a defended pillbox that had survived the preliminary bombardment. While the troops were maneuvering, Private Fredrick Dancox VC became isolated among the craters and falling shells. He moved to the rear of the pillbox, primed his Mills bomb, and a few moments later emerged with forty prisoners and carrying the German Maxim machine gun. Dancox was killed in November 1917 during the battle of Cambrai.

To the right are three blockhouses that formed part of the front line. Next to these houses is a newer section of the cemetery created as part of a 1954 further consolidation of German cemeteries in Belgium. Before and during the Second World War, Nazi propagandists used the '*Kindermord*' story to encourage sacrifice of the individual for the state; Langemark eventually became a symbol of senseless sacrifice. Thus, it is now one of the most visited Ypres battlefield sites, frequented by tour groups and bus loads of schoolchildren.

---

200 meters farther on the Klerkenstraat is a rural road to the left.

A short distance along the rural road is a **1917 pillbox** that had been used as an Advanced Dressing Station. A white stone in front commemorates the men of the Royal Artillery and the Royal Engineer sections of the British 34th Division. Its walls bear the scars from the intense British bombardment.

Battle of Geluveld
29 to 31 October 1914

OBJECTIVE	To encircle Ypres and proceed west to capture the Channel ports.
FORCES	
BRITISH:	1st (Guards) Brigade (Brigadier Charles FitzClarence VC)
GERMAN:	Six divisions of Army Group Fabeck (Generalmajor Max von Fabeck)
RESULT	The British 7th Division repulsed the attack, saving the BEF from destruction.
LOCATION	Ypres is 250 km north of Paris; Geluveld is 8.5 km southeast of

Although the German Fourth and Sixth Armies had thus far failed to penetrate the allied line, the German Supreme Command believed that a fresh push would bring victory. Gathering together units released from other fronts, Falkenhayn created Army Group Fabeck, commanded by veteran of the Franco-Prussian War General Max von Fabeck and comprised of six infantry divisions, whose mission was to attack along the British line from Ploegsteert Wood to Geluveld. Continued pressure along the front from the two German armies would prohibit allied transfer of reserve troops. The attack came as a surprise to the British. Before a preliminary attack against Geluveld commenced on 29 October, Sir John French reported to Secretary of State for War Lord Kitchener that the Germans were incapable of launching any further attacks despite the interception of Group Fabeck's plans. British aerial reconnaissance on 28 October, however, reported a large movement of German troops astride the Menin Road.

Battle

A preliminary move on 29 October, the 54th Reserve Division, strengthened by a brigade of Bavarian reservists, struck west of Becelaere. The thin lines of the Coldstream Guards and the Black Watch were nearly overrun because the enemy suddenly appeared out of the dense fog. Both sides committed reserves as the fighting spread south of the Menin Road and against the British 20th Brigade. The intense struggle continued all day, with high losses on both sides until darkness and a heavy rain chilled the engagement.

The next day Fabeck unleashed his battalions with deadly consequences as German divisions south of the Menin Road attacked reinforced positions with deadly accurate fire that covered the landscape with grey-clad bodies. Fabeck's men were even more successful farther south, where they drove Allenby's 2nd and 3rd Cavalry Divisions back three kilometers.

Dawn on 31 October broke in a miserable rain. The German 30th Division pressed the attack on Geluveld from the south. They were ultimately stopped but retained a small orchard from which they could enfilade units to the north. At 10:00, sixteen battalions of German infantry moved forward toward thinly held British lines. Field batteries fired into the shallow trenches of the 1st Queens Regiment and set on fire the village behind them. While the Queens attempted to retire, they discovered that the reserve companies supposed to be 500 meters to their rear in Veldhoek were gone; the Germans surrounded and captured all but a dozen men of the battalion. Dense German artillery fire stopped the 1st Gloucestershire Regiment's counterattack. Farther south the 105th Saxon Regiment completely overwhelmed the diminished ranks of the 1st Loyal North Lancashire and the 2nd Royal Scots Fusiliers Regiments. The way to Ypres was open.

North of the road, British units already well below strength started to disappear. The initial bombardment from the 54th Reserve Division had so weakened the 2nd Welsh Regiment that it withdrew. On their left the second assault at 10:00

forced the 1st South Wales Borderers back through most of Geluveld and onto the château grounds, where they established a position near the church.

Brigadier FitzClarence, upon hearing of the loss of Geluveld, rode forward and ordered the last reserves – three companies of the 2nd Worcestershire Regiment, led by Major Edward Hankey, borrowed from the 2nd Division – to counterattack from what later became known as Black Watch Corner[6] in Polygon Wood. The 350 men moved out at 13:00, crossed a small creek, and halted momentarily in a belt of trees. Redeployed in two lines and fully exposed on open ground for the last 1,000 meters, they advanced 'at the double' through enemy artillery fire to a small protective wood, where they fixed bayonets. The surviving 250 men charged into a host of 1,200 Germans in and about the château, inducing panic in the young recruits, who were more interested in finding loot or water. After rescuing the Borderers, who were still firing from the château stables, they re-established the line along the sunken Geluveld-Kortekeer road. Enfiladed by the remaining Germans in the village, one company proceeded to occupy the church and churchyard, despite the flames and falling timbers of the burning houses. Some house-to-house fighting took place, but German artillery denied the occupation of the center of the village. Two weeks later FitzClarence was killed; his body was never found and he is commemorated on the Menin Gate.

South of the road a mixed unit including the 1st Gloucesters halted the Saxon advance, which was then routed by well-placed high explosive shells from the 54th Battery RFA. Extremely heavy fighting continued throughout the day, with the result always in doubt. That night British forces, needing to conserve their remaining resources, abandoned Geluveld to form defensive lines 500 meters farther west. Divisions of the French XVI and XX Corps arrived to man the line along Messines Ridge, freeing Allenby's cavalry for BEF reserves. Paris newspapers declared that 'the fate of Europe was decided' on 31 October 1914.

Four days of chaotic fighting left Messines in Fabeck's hands, though the great strategic position had been lost. (Messines and Wijtschate are reviewed in Third Battle of Ypres.) Despite the creation of another assault group (Army Group Linsingen) for a final push on 11 November, the Prussian Guards were routed in their assault upon Nonnebosschen (Nun's Wood). On 17 November Falkenhayn officially ended the offensive, although reciprocal attacks continued through December. Germany's best chance of breaking the BEF had failed.

Battlefield Tour

The approach from Ypres to Geluveld travels the famous **Menin Road**, down which many of the British units entered the fighting. On either side of the roadway some of the best-known engagements of the war took place. Names such as Sanctuary Wood, Hooge Château, and Hellfire Corner are burned into the lexicon of the First World War. While Geluveld is the ultimate destination for the First Battle of Ypres, a few short detours will bring one to these other sites.

---

[6] Later so named after the Black Watch's defense of the site against German Guards on 11 November 1914.

Leave Ypres through the Menin Gate toward Menen (N8), Due to single direction streets, this movement is possible only by accessing Bollingstraat, which runs along the inside of the ramparts south of the Menin Gate, and turning right onto Meensestraat. At the next major intersection, turn right and remain toward Menin (Meenseweg, N8).

The roundabout 2 km outside of Ypres is the notorious **Hellfire Corner**. Unfortunately, modern traffic has forced reconstruction of the intersection, and the Demarcation Stone of the Germans' farthest advance toward Ypres (except for their brief cavalry occupation in 1914) has been relocated to the northwest side of the roundabout.

Slightly more than 1 km ahead, turn right onto Canadalaan.

This quiet, rural road passes through Zouave Wood before arriving at **Sanctuary Wood Cemetery** and the **Sanctuary Wood Museum**. This private museum holds the usual collection of battlefield artifacts, presented in a rather haphazard manner, and a large collection of excellent stereoscopic photographs. Behind the museum is one of the few remaining original British trench lines, complete with cemented passageway, shell holes, and dead, bullet-ridden trees. A few cemetery monuments from early German graves are on the grounds. The trenches are frequently muddy so appropriate footwear is recommended. Open daily from 10:00 to 19:00. Small café and toilets for visitors' use. Fee.

Approximately 50 meters up the road is the **Hill 62** (referred to as Tor Top in older works) **Canadian Memorial**. Nondescript from the road, upon ascending the stairway, the large stone block comes into view. The inscription on one side states, 'Here at Mount Sorrel and on a line from Hooge to Sint-Elooi the Canadian forces fought in defense of Ypres April to August 1916.' The fight for this last piece of British-held high ground was particularly vicious. The German 13th Württemberg Corps captured it from 3rd Canadian Division on 2 June 1916, after a terrifyingly intense artillery bombardment which blew men and trees of Sanctuary Wood to pieces. The 1st Canadian Division retook Hill 62 and Mount Sorrel, a flat knoll approximately 600 meters southwest of Hill 62, on 13 June. The two Canadian divisions suffered 8,430 casualties; the Germans less than half that number. The view to the northwest includes the fields approaching Ypres and the towers of the Cloth Hall and St-Martin.

Return to the Menin Road and turn right.

Almost immediately on the left is the **Hooge ('t Hoge) Crater Museum 1914-1918**. Hooge Château was the scene of numerous engagements and changed hands several times, resulting in its complete destruction. The private museum was named after the nearby crater formed by the explosion of a British mine on 19 July

1915. The museum, located in what was once the chapel for the château, presents displays that cover the war year by year. An audio track relates not only events but also identifies the displayed equipment used by the combatants. Suspended from the ceiling is a replica of the Fokker aeroplane Baron Manfred von Richthofen ('The Red Baron'). A small café offers refreshments and souvenirs, unfortunately the location suffers from a scarcity of parking. Open 1 February through 1 December on Tuesday through Sunday from 12:00 to 16:00 (open at 11:00 on weekends). Fee.

Across the street is the overwhelming **Hooge Crater Cemetery**. The size is deceptive because it drops away from the road. Started in October 1917 and enlarged after the Armistice, the cemetery now contains 5,182 British, 105 Canadian, 513 Australian, 121 New Zealander, and 3 West Indian soldiers and airmen. Almost 3,600 bodies are unidentified. The back of the cemetery overlooks Zouave Wood and Sanctuary Wood.

Continue toward Menen.

The fork in the road is another of the famous intersections around Ypres that was continually under German observation and bombardment. Known as **Clapham Junction** to British soldiers after the London rail station, it holds memorials to the Gloucestershire Regiment, which fought here in 1914, and the 18th Division, which fought here in the opening stages of Third Battle of Ypres in 1917.

At the fork, bear left onto Oude Kortrijkstraat and cross the Autoroute to the wood. The wood ahead on the left is Polygon Wood, the southwest corner of which is known as Black Watch Corner. Turn left and follow the perimeter road and the Commonwealth War Graves Commission signs.

The first fight in Polygon Wood was in October 1914, when the Germans held the northern half and the British held the southern. Attacks by British Guards regiments were beaten back with heavy casualties. The wood was completely occupied by the Germans during their advances of 1915. It received its name from British soldiers due to the shape of the wooded area's boundary.

Before the war, a long, narrow butte on the northern end of the wood was the site of a Belgian army rifle range. From its summit, German riflemen and artillery observers held commanding views of the countryside in all directions. As part of the German defenses, the butte was interlaced with tunnels and dugouts. Advancing behind a creeping barrage, the 5th Australian Division captured Polygon Wood on 26 September 1917, during the segment of the Third Battle of Ypres known as the battle of Menin Road. The bombardment reduced the wood to shattered stumps.

Polygon Wood is now a large, forested park crisscrossed by walking lanes and containing several sites clustered in its northeastern corner. Directions to the cemeteries are well-indicated by Commonwealth War Graves Commission signs from Zonnebeke. Enter the area along a grass walk enclosed between stone walls. The path leads directly to the stairway up to the top of the butte where the **5th**

Australian Division Memorial is located. The 12-meter high obelisk bears the rising sun emblem of the Australian Imperial Force. Below and to the right are the gravestones of the large **Buttes New British Cemetery,** which contains 2,103 graves. The vast majority of the burials are a result of the 1917 fighting and remain unidentified. The **New Zealand Memorial to the Missing** is at the rear of the cemetery and records the names of 378 men who fell in the Polygon Wood sector and who have no known grave. Each end of the double colonnade has a square structure holding the panels upon which the names are inscribed. The remnants of one of the **German pillboxes** can still be visited approximately 500 meters along the main path behind the New Zealand Memorial, on the right identifiable by the fenced access path. The bunker itself is readily accessible and is much larger than one would anticipate; its walls are a solid 1 meter thick.

Originally the location of a German Military Cemetery, **Polygon Wood Cemetery** is across the road and contains a relatively small number of graves, the majority of which are New Zealand servicemen. Enter along a grass path to the Cross of Sacrifice and follow the steps down into a hexagon of irregularly spaced graves, a pattern typical of battlefield cemeteries.

> Reverse direction and return to Black Watch Corner; proceed west across the Autoroute on Oude Kortrijkstraat. Ahead on the right is Nonnebosschen, where the third and final engagement of First Battle of Ypres occurred on 11 November. Turn left almost immediately onto Polygonestraat and continue along the side of the Autoroute.

This route was taken by the 2nd Worcesters on 31 October, when they came to the rescue of the troops in Geluveld. The rural road dips in the slight valley of the Reutelbeek, where the Worcesters found their last piece of cover before proceeding. A line of poplars now marks the trees were Major Hankey deployed his men into a double line. From here the road diverges from the route of Hankey's advance; the Worcesters' charge took place across the open ground to the left.

> Continue until the intersection with the Menin Road and turn left toward Geluveld. In the village, turn toward the church and to its east is convenient parking in a small commercial area.

Geluveld stands upon a spur of the ridgeline that curves around from Messines to Passendale. The straight Menin Road (N8) bisects the spur and the village on its way to Menen. Behind the church are the gates to the long drive that approaches the restored and still private **Château de Geluveld**. On these grounds the successful German advance lost focus and became victim to the Worcesters' assault. A signboard gives a brief history of the château and the fighting on its grounds.

Opposite the shopping area to the east is a residential lane that ends at a ruined windmill, a replacement for the wartime mill. Two monuments commemorate the actions of individual regiments in the battle for Geluveld. A Celtic Cross was erected in memory of the officers and men of the **South Wales Borderers Regiment**. Near the bottom is the unit's insignia. To its right is a handsomely mounted stone dedicated to the men of the **2ⁿᵈ Battalion Worcestershire Regiment** who fell defending the village. Polygon Wood can be seen in the distance to the north-northwest by looking between the houses. Approximately half that distance away is the much smaller Polderhoek (wood). Even with the modern development the route seems very exposed when under enemy fire and hence speaks to the courage and, perhaps to some measure, of the desperation of the men who attempted it.

Geluveld was completely destroyed by the British bombardment that preceded the September 1917 offensive. It changed hands twice in 1918, when the Germans advanced during the battle of Lys and then were forced back during the Advance to Victory.

Recommended reading

Ascoli, David: *The Mons Star: The British Expeditionary Force, 5ᵗʰ August – 22ⁿᵈ Nov. 1914.* London: Harrap Limited, 1981.

Beckett, Ian FW: *Ypres: The First Battle, 1914.* Harlow, England: Pearson Education, 2004. A richly detailed account of the first months of the war, focusing upon events in Flanders.

Groom, Winston: *A Storm in Flanders: The Ypres Salient, 1914-1918.* New York: Grove Press, 2002. Very readable telling of the three Ypres battles, enlivened by eyewitness accounts.

Holmes, Richard: *Army Battlefield Guide: Belgium and Northern France.* London: Her Majesty's Stationary Office, 1995. An excellent book on four selected battlefields by a noted military historian – if you can find it.

Terraine, John: *Mons: Retreat to Victory.* London, Wordsworth Editions Limited, 2002. A reprint of the classic 1960 account of the British Army in the first month of the First World War.

Tuchman, Barbara: *The Guns of August.* New York: Macmillan Publishing, 1962. The definitive account of the prelude to and first months of the war.

Chapter Six

Trench Warfare
1915

The deadlock of 1914 led to the trench building of 1915 while both armies prepared themselves for a long conflict. The Germans were content to remain an occupying force on Belgian and French soil, while the Allies felt the need to evict them. The opposing armies developed different philosophies toward trenches and fortifications with the Germans constructing extensive and relatively secure emplacements and the French and British building temporary and rudimentary trench lines. The shallow water table and the chalky ground of Flanders prohibited the digging of deep structures except upon elevations, and those were predominantly held by the Germans. Allied trenches flooded easily and required constant maintenance. The soldiers' lives were characterized by dreary, mud-encased days of hiding from snipers followed by cold nights of repairing the fortifications.

The French, spurred on by Joffre's aggressive nature, launched costly attacks in Artois and Champagne against the flanks of the great German salient, in the Woëvre against the rear of the German forces, and along the Aisne River; each produced little besides more casualties. The British Imperial General Staff advocated attacking Germany's weaker partners and launched a terribly executed and therefore costly expedition against the Turks in the Dardanelles.

#17

Capture of Hill 60
17 April to 5 May 1915

OBJECTIVE	To deny the high ground to German artillery observers
FORCES	
BRITISH:	British 5th Division (Major-General T.L.N. Morland)
GERMAN:	Alsatian Infantry Regiment Nr 172
RESULT	After initial success, the British could not hold the position.
CASUALTIES	
BRITISH:	Approximately 3,100
GERMAN:	Undetermined
LOCATION	Ypres is 250 km north of Paris; Hill 60 is 4.5 km southeast of Ypres

The ridge line that runs from Passendale to Messines is bisected by the Ypres-Comines rail line near where the ridge changes direction south of Zillebeke. Nineteenth century engineers cut through the ridge, moving the spoil to a nearby site and thus creating an artificial mound that was only 60 meters in height, but still was a mountain relative to Ypres' flat terrain. The actions of October 1914 left Hill 60 defended by the French XVI Corps. On 10 December, the German 39th Division captured the hill, which provided them with a great advantage only 4.5 km from the center of Ypres. The British 28th Division took over the sector from the French in February, followed by the 5th Division in April. British Headquarters was anxious to reclaim the hill, and after traditional infantry attacks failed, they imported professional miners to dig tunnels from their lines to the German positions. After great hardship and with a constant fear of collapse, the tunnels were forked into five branches and packed with explosives.

Battle

At 19:05 on 17 April, the explosives were fired and the hill erupted in a shower of debris and German bodies. Rushing forward under the cover of an artillery barrage, the men of the Royal West Kent Regiment, 2nd Kings Own Scottish Borders, and 1/9th Battalion County of London Regiment (Queen Victoria's Rifles) quickly occupied the still-smoking craters after bayoneting most of the survivors of the German Infantry Regiment Nr 172; only twenty prisoners were taken. Then the real fight began. The Germans refused to forfeit the hill, and within hours they launched the first of many counterattacks. By morning they won a section along the railway cutting, only to be evicted that night. Artillery pulverized the already smashed dugouts and trenches, while machine guns fired into British positions from both flanks as the hill now presented a salient into the German line.

The British presented a heroic defense, repulsing attack after attack with bombs and bayonets while attempting to improve their positions. Reinforcing battalions were summoned to occupy trenches filled with the dead and dying. Particularly heavy fighting occurred on the night of 20/21 April, when artillery barrages alternated with grenade attacks. Testimony to the intensity of the battle is given by the award of four Victoria Crosses for actions on that day, three of them to two officers and a private of the East Surrey Regiment. On 5 May, with British dead totaling almost 2,000, the hill finally fell to the Germans after a huge bombardment followed by an infantry assault that may have also utilized gas. Further British efforts to regain the hill were repulsed by fire from the nearby Caterpillar position, which was across the railway cut from Hill 60.

Tunneling and counter-tunneling efforts continued through 1915, with deeper shafts being bored under the hill. The Germans held the hill until the British advance of June 1917, when enormous explosions rocked Hill 60 and the Caterpillar, killing 687 defenders of the German 204th Division. Yorkshire battalions quickly occupied the hill, suffering only seven casualties. As with much of the ground in the salient – except the city of Ypres – Hill 60 changed hands twice during the German advance and retreat of 1918.

Battlefield Tour

This tour is limited to sites on and near Hill 60.

Leave Ypres through the Lille Gate toward Wijtschate (N336); turn left on Komenseweg and left again on Blauwepoortstraat in Zillebeke. Leave Zillebeke toward Zandvoorde (Werviksestraat); turn right onto Zwarteleenstraat.

Hill 60 is on the left, with a parking area at the far end near the rail line. The hill has remained essentially unchanged since the great explosion and engagements of 1915. Whereas not officially a cemetery, most of the German and British soldiers killed remain buried beneath its grassy slopes. Today the small 110-meter by 230-meter hillock is rich in memorials and ruins of defensive positions scattered among the numerous craters of 1915 and 1917. Sheep graze peacefully among the shell and mine craters. The hill is not frequently visited, although modern housing encroaches upon the edges and young children play among the remnants of war.

Fronting the parking area is a huge stone block memorial to the **14ᵗʰ Light Division,** which was relocated due to subsiding ground. At the foot of the hill is a memorial which commemorates the **1ˢᵗ Australian Tunneling Company**. The Australians assumed responsibility from their British and Canadian predecessors for the digging operations in November 1916 taking over until the detonations of the battle of Messines in June 1917. The plaque still shows bullet holes from the Second World War. The craters formed during the 1915 explosions are discernible beyond the plaque. Up the hill and nearer to the rail line is the larger crater of 1917, which still contains chunks of concrete.

Continuing past the 1915 crater is the **Queen Victoria Rifles Memorial**. The regiment participated in the initial April 1915 assault; when 2ⁿᵈ Lieutenant Geoffrey H. Woolley VC, as the citation reads, 'During the night of 20/21 April 1915 … Woolley was the only officer on the hill at the time, but with very few men he successfully resisted all attacks on his trench, and continued throwing bombs and encouraging his men until relieved. His trench during all this time was being heavily shelled and bombed.' The battalion's veterans' organization owned the property for many years after the war, before it was transferred to the Commonwealth War Graves Commission, which now tends the ground. The memorial suffered damage from the Germans during the Second World War. Slightly below the memorial are the ruins of a concrete machine gun emplacement.

On the crest is a relatively complete **pillbox**. Originally constructed by the Germans, it shows British modifications – as would be expected on a site that changed hands so frequently. Scattered over the hillside are the ruins of several other fortifications, including a bunker with a barely discernible entrance. The trenches have mostly been filled, and even the craters are softening on their edges.

The Queen Victoria's Rifles Museum, which stood across the road for decades, has unfortunately been closed and demolished in favor of a restaurant. Between the parking area and the railway embankment stands a small memorial stone to **French Resistance fighters**, who were captured near Lille in 1944 and taken aboard a train bound for Belgium. Their bodies were later found trackside near this memorial.

Immediately across the rail bridge and to the left, a gated path crosses a pasture with a second gate on the far side. From the second gate the path enters the wood and proceeds to **Caterpillar Crater**, the remains of a second June 1917 explosion. Originally 30 meters deep and 110 meters across, Caterpillar Crater has become a water-filled pond set among lush trees. The surrounding forest hides other small pillboxes and observation posts.

#18

Second Battle of Ypres
22 April to 25 May 1915

OBJECTIVE	To test the use of poison gas
FORCES	
ALLIES:	Three British divisions of V Corps (Lieutenant-General Sir Herbert Plumer); two French divisions of Groupement d'Elverdinghe (général de division Fernand Quinquandon) and one Belgian division (Lieutenant-Général Baron De Ceuninck)
GERMAN:	Fourth Army (Generaloberst Duke Albrecht of Württemberg)
RESULT	The Germans advanced 3 km, eventually forcing the Allies to abandon much of the salient.
CASUALTIES	
BRITISH:	59,000
FRENCH:	Approximately 10,000
BELGIAN:	Approximately 1,500
GERMAN:	Approximately 35,000
LOCATION	Ypres is 250 km north of Paris; St-Juliaan is 6 km northeast of Ypres

Battle

At 17:00 on 22 April 1915, after nervously waiting all day, special *'Stinkpionere'* troops observed that the wind had finally turned toward the southwest. A German bombardment struck Ypres and numerous surrounding villages, an event that was unusual but not extraordinary. Six thousand gas cylinders had been secretly collected and placed in the south-facing German trenches from Langemark to Bikschote. A greenish-yellow cloud crept from the German forward trenches to engulf the positions of the French 87th Territorial and 45th Algerian Divisions along the northern shoulder of the Ypres Salient around Langemark. Despite its prohibition by the Hague Convention of 1907, the Western Front witnessed the first military use of poisonous gas.

French troops, gasping and coughing because the chlorine gas tore at their throats and filled their lungs with fluid, immediately began streaming to the rear. Major Andrew McNaughton described the French soldiers: 'They literally were coughing their lungs out; glue was coming out of their mouths. It was a very disturbing, very disturbing sight.'[1] The Belgian Grenadiers, who were no as severely affected, held their positions along the canal at the junction with the French and

---

[1] Winston Groom, *A Storm in Flanders: The Ypres Salient, 1914 – 1918: Tragedy and Triumph on the Western Front* (New York: Grove Press, 2002), 99.

limited the German advance to only a small bridgehead across the canal line. On the French right, the 3rd Canadian Infantry Brigade manned the front lines and held firm.

The panicked withdrawal of French troops left a 6.5 km gap in the front lines. With a single, fearsome action the Germans had opened an unopposed avenue to Ypres. Protected by only a crude respirator that many soldiers did not trust, the German infantry tentatively advanced 3 km and took up defensive positions. General Falkenhayn was so doubtful of the gas' effectiveness that he allowed for no reserves to carry on the fight. Using the gas late in the day also left little daylight during which to continue the advance. Fate had saved Ypres.

Wounded soldiers died quickly when they slumped to the trench floor, where the gas collected. For soldiers who reached the aid stations, the medics were puzzled by the symptoms since they had never experienced a gas attack and knew of no treatment. The worst cases died quickly, vomiting and suffocating. Others died days later after they slowly drowned in their own fluids and their extremities turned from blue to green to black. Those lightly exposed recovered only to suffer the effects for the remainder of their shortened lives.

The Germans' pause gave the Allies time to organize a defense. A French battalion attempted to counterattack from the area of Boezinge toward Pilckem but made little progress. In their country's first action on the Western Front, the 10th Battalion Canadian Light Infantry, supported by the 16th Battalion (Canadian Scottish), counterattacked the German 51st Reserve Division's positions just before

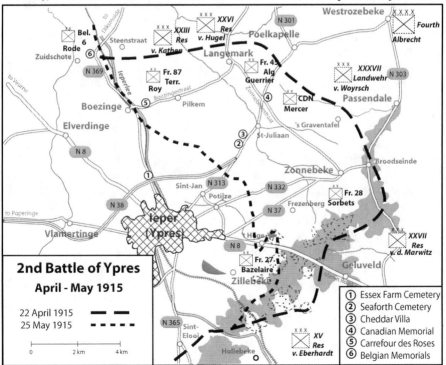

2nd Battle of Ypres

April - May 1915

22 April 1915
25 May 1915

0   2 km   4 km

① Essex Farm Cemetery
② Seaforth Cemetery
③ Cheddar Villa
④ Canadian Memorial
⑤ Carrefour des Roses
⑥ Belgian Memorials

midnight in Bois de Cuisiniers (Kitchener's Wood), 900 meters west of St-Juliaan. The wood, situated upon the forward slope of the ridge line, was critical territory for controlling the area south of the village. Facing massed machine-gun fire which scythed down the front line, the Canadians pushed on, entering the forest to engage the enemy in hand-to-hand fighting. They cleared the wood at a fearsome cost, losing 613 men out of a complement of 816. Holding the enfiladed position was impossible, however, so they moved back to a trench line on the south edge of the wood.

On 23 April, while the Germans moved slowly to extend their advance, allied battalions – many of them Canadian – struggled to establish a continuous front. At 04:00 on 24 April, the Germans released a second cloud against the now Canadian line. Without respirators, the troops desperately wet any available cloth, usually with their own urine, and placed it over their nose and mouth. Despite this crude protection and somewhat effective artillery support, St-Juliaan was overcome by the afternoon. The Canadians received the order to retire by nightfall; the Germans moved forward into a world of shriveled leaves, yellow grass and extinguished animal life, including the ever-present rats.

Counterattacks the next day were met with the usually effective German machine-gun and artillery fire. German batteries took up advanced positions with impunity because their British opponents were chronically short of shells. An assault by the 10th Brigade to retake St-Juliaan led to its almost complete annihilation.

Sir John French, highly encouraged by général Ferdinand Foch with promises of upcoming French offensives, was unfortunately taken with the idea of recovering the lost territory. In what was to become characteristic of First World War battles, the initially successful advance was followed by both sides throwing more troops into the engagement, resulting in escalating losses for little gain by either side. A hastily ordered counterattack against Mauser Ridge by the British Lahore Indian Division supported by British infantry was cut down by German artillery; however, they stopped the German advance.

Smith-Dorrien presented the costliness of the situation to General Sir William Robertson, Chief of the Imperial General Staff, who responded by relieving him of his command. Smith-Dorrien's subsequent offer to resign was accepted. General Plumer, Smith-Dorrien's replacement, executed on 4 May the withdrawal to the 'GHQ' line that Smith-Dorrien had so boldly suggested – with Generals Robertson and French approving. The Germans advanced against British positions along the Frezenberg and Bellewaerde spurs. The latter was the last ridgeline before Ypres; from there it was downhill all of the way to the city and beyond. At 06:30 on 8 May, the Suffolk Regiment, manning the forward slope of Frezenberg Ridge, came under heavy bombardment. The firing enveloped the entire salient, while the German assault quickly drove open a 3 km gap in British defenses between Bellewaerde and Mouse Trap Farm. Decimated battalions, random support companies, cooks, and orderlies were ordered into the fight. The line was slowly restored while the attackers settled for establishing their own defenses.

By 25 May static positions were once again established. The salient remained, though much reduced in size, and the Germans were only 5 km from

Ypres. The British were now compressed into a smaller space that provided German artillery with almost unlimited targets.

The use of poison gas became a fixture on the Western Front. Improved respirators were met with increasingly effective poisons such as phosgene and the notorious mustard gas. Fighting men struggled through engagements encumbered with gas masks that limited visibility and restricted breathing while giving them an extraterrestrial appearance. Could warfare become more horrific?

Battlefield Tour

The tour visits sites northeast of the city which figured in the famous German gas attack and other engagements.

Leave Ypres toward Diksmuide (N369); immediately after passing under the very busy N38 highway, the **Essex Farm Cemetery** is on the right. A new parking area is in front of the cemetery along the road.

A memorial in front of the cemetery commemorates **Lieutenant-Colonel John McCrae**, Royal Canadian Medical Corps, who wrote his famous poem 'In Flanders Fields' after the death of a close friend during the Second Battle of Ypres. McCrae later contracted pneumonia and died in January 1918, but his poem established the red poppy as a symbol of the sacrifices of the fighting men of the First World War. The dugouts which he used as a dressing station are down the lane, toward the canal, and they can be entered.

From here one can continue north to the French and Belgian memorials marking the armies' positions on the Second Ypres battlefield. Their descriptions are at the end of this section.

Return to the highway overpass and take the access ramp toward Brugge (N38). After 4 km this road merges with the N313; continue northeast to the next several sites.

The farms that are passed while driving along the modern highway northeast of Sint-Jan hide the battlefields of 1915. The names given to them by British soldiers – Mouse Trap, Cheddar Villa, Canadian Farm, English Farm, and Irish Farm – resonate through accounts of Ypres battles.

On the west side of the N313, approximately 1 km before entering St-Juliaan is Cheddar Villa Cemetery, now known as **Seaforth Cemetery**. The Canadian 10th Battalion formed-up here before their assault upon Kitchener's Wood. The location also experienced heavy fighting on 25 and 26 April 1915 when 2nd Battalion Seaforth Highlanders attempted to recapture St-Juliaan; their dead were buried here. As the site of later fighting, many of the original graves were obliterated. The stones in the open central area mark what are essentially mass graves. The surrounding flat and open terrain demonstrates the difficulty in advancing against an entrenched enemy, especially one who possesses artillery superiority as the Germans did in 1915.

Immediately adjacent to the cemetery is a farm known as '**Cheddar Villa**' to the British. On the far (northern) side of the farm is a large German blockhouse which was part of a string of pillboxes stretching across the field to the north. Captured at the opening of the Third Battle of Ypres, it became a British Advanced Dressing Station and suffered a terrible fate when a German shell entered the open doorway – since it was constructed by the Germans, the opening faced toward their lines – and exploded among sheltering soldiers, the wounded, and the medical staff.

West of St-Juliaan was Kitchener's Wood, marked only by a white stone memorial plaque along a rural road that proceeds north from the vicinity of Seaforth Cemetery.

Vancouver Corner, which was also the site of the Triangle defensive works, is 1 km past St-Juliaan, and on one corner of the intersection stands the famous **Canadian Memorial at St-Juliaan,** popularly known as 'The Brooding Soldier.' The 11-meter granite pillar is surmounted by the head and shoulders of a soldier with head bowed and hands resting upon arms reversed – the traditional funeral stance. The stone marked with directions to sites on the battlefield sits upon a stone court, which in turn is surrounded by a grass lawn and clipped hedges. The top is illuminated at night, adding to the already sorrowful yet determined mien of the battlefield's guardian. The attached plaque states: 'This column marks the battlefield where 18,000 Canadians on the British left withstood the first German gas attacks the 22nd – 24th April 1915. 2,000 fell and lie buried nearby.' In the two days that the Canadians defended the line against German artillery and gas, they suffered a total of 6,037 casualties but proved themselves as a formidable fighting force.

Proceed northwest from Vancouver Corner towards Langemark (Zonnebekestraat). In Langemark turn towards Boezingestraat. Continue to the parking area on the right.

French and Belgian commemorations of the Second Ypres gas attacks are located 1 km east of Boezinge toward Pilckem / Langemark (Langemarkseweg). The **Le Carrefour des Roses** contains the Breton Memorial, a commemoration of the two French divisions which experienced the initial gas attack of 22 April. The site also has a prehistoric dolmen and 16th century calvary, both relocated from Brittany, the home of the 87th Territorial troops.

Continue, cross the canal, and turn right towards Diksmuide (N369).

A memorial stone was erected 2.5 km north of Boezinge after the war, commemorating the French 418th Regiment. The stone's graphic depiction of gas victims holding their eyes in agony offended the Nazis, so German soldiers blew up the stone during their occupation in 1941. It has been replaced by a simpler, 15-meter aluminum cross erected upon a stone-banked earthen mound. The **Franco-Belgian Memorial** is inscribed with French and Belgian units which were subjected to the gas attacks. Within a short walking distance down Grenadiersstraat is a granite obelisk to the **Belgian 2nd Grenadier Regiment** who manned the extreme right of the Belgian line on 22 April and whose men fought off the effects of the gas to repel the German attempt to cross the canal. Returning to the highway and to the north just before the canal is a black sword mounted upon a white stone cross, dedicated to the men of the **Belgian 3rd Regiment** who fell defending the canal line.

#19

First, Second and Third Battles of Artois
27 September to 10 October 1914
9 May to 19 June 1915
25 to 28 September 1915

OBJECTIVE	To relieve Arras and seize the Douai Plain
FORCES	
FRENCH:	Eighteen divisions of the Tenth Army (général de division Victor d'Urbal)
GERMAN:	Sixteen divisions of the Sixth Army (Generalfeldmarschall Kronprinz Rupprecht of Bavaria)
RESULT	Although 64 square kilometers were gained and the German front was temporarily broken, the offensive was a strategic failure.
CASUALTIES	
FRENCH:	16,803 killed and 85,697 wounded and missing
GERMAN:	75,000 casualties including 7,450 taken prisoner
LOCATION	Arras is 180 km north of Paris; Notre-Dame de Lorette is 16 km north of Arras

Général Ernest Barbot's 77th Division composed of alpine troops and chasseurs arrived at Arras on 30 September 1914 and immediately went into action east of the city to stem the German advance. Although under heavy pressure from General der Infanterie Friedrich Sixt von Arnim's IV Corps, général Barbot ignored orders to withdraw and continued to defend Arras' eastern suburbs. The Germans brought up their 280-mm guns, and after setting the city ablaze, German infantry moved to capture the ruins. Amid the burning houses of the faubourgs St-Nicolas and St-Laurent, however, the attacks were defeated by the stubborn resistance of the Alpine Brigade. Unable to enter Arras, the I Bavarian Reserve Corps executed a flanking maneuver to the north, capturing the communities of Lens, Souchez, Neuville-St-Vaast as well as the strategic terrain of Vimy Ridge and Notre-Dame de Lorette Ridge. The front line around Arras stabilized, and the Germans turned their attention northward, continuing the 'Race to the Sea' toward Ypres.

Two months later, a long and bloody effort to drive the enemy from Lorette started at 13:10 on 17 December 1914. After a six-and-one-half hour artillery bombardment that was considered heavy at the time, French infantry began a three-pronged assault upon the German trenches in what became known as the First Battle

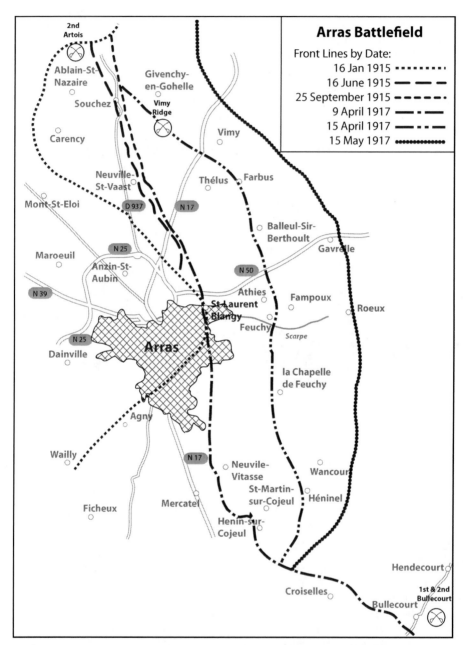

Arras Battlefield

Front Lines by Date:
16 Jan 1915
16 June 1915
25 September 1915
9 April 1917
15 April 1917
15 May 1917

of Artois. Général de division Paul Maistre's primary objective was the capture of the Notre-Dame de Lorette plateau for use as an artillery platform in support of général de division Philippe Pétain's assault on Vimy Ridge. The first German trench was quickly entered but the ever-present sticky mud and machine guns in the second trench line brought the advance to an abrupt halt. The assault officially ended after four days of useless bloodshed but localized fighting continued throughout the winter as French assaults attempted to recapture the ridge and the Germans improved their fortifications.

By the spring of 1915, the front line formed a double salient with the ridges of Notre-Dame de Lorette, Vimy, and Monchy-le-Preux in German hands. From these heights artillery observers and hidden batteries dominated French positions. Front line villages were transformed into fortresses, the cellars of the stone houses connected by underground passages. Armor plate and concrete reinforced critical positions. Général de division Ferdinand Foch, commander of Army Group of the North, organized the first grand French offensive with the objective of recovering the ridges. Success would open the way for a French advance across the open Douai plain into important mining centers around Lens as well as threaten the important German supply line using the Lille-Douai-Cambrai railway.

Battle

On 9 May 1915, a four-hour bombardment preceded the French attack along a 10-km front from Roclincourt to Notre-Dame de Lorette. The troops left their trenches at 10:00, entering a maelstrom of German artillery fire. They advanced rapidly in the center, where général Pétain's XXXIII Corps caught the defenders unprepared. The *Ouvrages Blanc* and *Sucrerie* strongpoints were taken, and Souchez was entered. The Moroccan Division reached crest of Vimy Ridge but their exhaustion and loss of officers made them vulnerable to counterattack. A temporary panic hit the German headquarters at Lille, where there were discussions of a mass withdrawal. Unprepared for the rapid advance, French reserves were slow to advance, meanwhile the superior German artillery pounded the regiments from atop the ridge and nine fresh divisions arrived to fill the gaps in the German front. Slowly the French troops were forced to withdraw and by 10 May they were back in the valley.

Progress was significantly slower on the flanks, where the ridge of Notre-Dame de Lorette in the north and the fortified villages of la Targette and Neuville-St-Vaast to the south proved to be difficult targets, even though each position had been deluged with artillery shells. The German wire remained intact in many places, especially in front of X Corps, XVII Corps, and the right of XX Corps. The left units of XX Corps slowly cleared La Targette, where grenade and bayonet were the weapons of choice in clearing each house. XXI Corps came under dense machine-gun fire from the Lorette, enfilade fire from Ablain, and artillery fire from Angres. The French took Ablain-St-Nazaire on 29 May and northern Neuville-St-Vaast on 9 June. Later assaults upon Souchez failed. After five weeks of continuous fighting, the one-square kilometer German stronghold known as 'the Labyrinth' was finally captured on 17 June. Minor trench engagements continued to consolidate positions, but the offensive was effectively over.

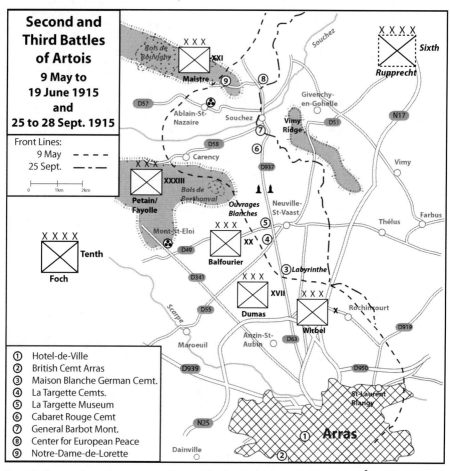

Second and Third Battles of Artois

9 May to 19 June 1915 and 25 to 28 Sept. 1915

Front Lines:
9 May ----
25 Sept. --- ---

0   1km   2km

① Hotel-de-Ville
② British Cemt Arras
③ Maison Blanche German Cemt.
④ La Targette Cemts.
⑤ La Targette Museum
⑥ Cabaret Rouge Cemt
⑦ General Barbot Mont.
⑧ Center for European Peace
⑨ Notre-Dame-de-Lorette

On 25 September, in conjunction with the British attack at Loos[2] and a French offensive launched in Champagne, the third Artois offensive began, with the objective remaining Vimy Ridge. At 12:30, after a five-day artillery barrage, XXI Corps attacked Souchez; XXXIII Corps, now commanded by général de division Emile Fayolle, attacked toward La Folie. Souchez was entered and cleared on the second day, after bitter fighting on the grounds of Château Carleul. The stiff resistance, a dreadful rain, and the destroyed terrain halted the advance. The heavy casualties caused the premature end of the Third Battle of Artois on 28 September. The area became relatively quiet until the successful British assault on Vimy Ridge in April 1917.[3]

---

[2] See battlefield #23: Third Battle of Artois (Loos)
[3] See battlefield #27: Battle of Vimy Ridge

Battlefield Tour

Arras

Arras was founded during Roman times, built upon a hill to protect trade routes in northern Gaul. Although briefly entered by German patrols on 6 September 1914, it remained unconquered throughout the war. Its proximity to the front and its position on critical transportation routes, however, made it a constant target of German artillery. Shells rained on the city while its inhabitants sheltered in a labyrinth of underground tunnels. The center of the city was in ruins by the end of the war. Postwar reconstruction followed the original plans, and today the city presents squares, both ancient and modern, for sightseeing, shopping, and dining. The **Hôtel-de-Ville**, its **Belfry**, the **Grande Place,** and the **Petite Place** are of special interest. On the boulevard Charles de Gaulle is the **Faubourg de Amiens (British) Cemetery Arras,** with 2,640 burials and its **Memorial to the Missing**, which lists the names of 34,726 soldiers who disappeared in fighting in this sector from 1916 to 1918. Behind the cemetery is the old Arras Citadel, containing the somber **Mémorial des Fusillés** to 218 patriots executed there by the Nazis during the Second World War. The citadel is restricted but the memorial is accessible via the avenue de Mémorial des Fusillés.

Leave Arras north toward Bethune (D937).

The tour passes along the battlefront of 1914 to 1917, the scene of so much hardship and death, and arrives at Notre-Dame de Lorette. The modern, tree-lined D937 highway passes through the Artois battlefield, with only the high-speed traffic breaking the pastoral prewar image. The enormous **Maison Blanche German Military Cemetery**, which with 44,833 bodies is the largest German cemetery in France, occupies the ground of the 'Labyrinth' defense system. Farther north are **La Targette British and French Cemeteries**. In the center of La Targette, a fortified village that was completely destroyed, is the **La Targette Museum**, which contains thousands of glass-encased artifacts. Open daily from 09:00 to 20:00. Fee. From the village center, signs provide directions to the Canadian Memorial at Vimy Ridge. Farther ahead are remembrances to Polish and Czech soldiers who fought for the allied cause. Before entering Souchez, the huge **British Cabaret Rouge Cemetery** with its 7,655 graves is on the left. The **Monument to général Barbot**, who was the savior of Arras and who died near this spot on 10 May 1915, is at the entrance to the town. The roadsides hold numerous sites from the several engagements fought across the neighboring fields.

Pass through Souchez and shortly after exiting, turn left toward Notre-Dame de Lorette (D58e3).

The **Center for European Peace** is opposite the D58e3 identifiable by the colorful First World War murals and numerous flags decorating its façade. The center contains a small exhibit of First World War trench art and a filmstrip of archival images as well as a commercial meeting center. Open every day, except Saturday and Sunday morning, from 10:00 to 12:00 and from 14:00 to 18:00. Fee.

Climb the hill, passing the statue of général Maistre, to the parking area.

Général Maistre's XXI Corps had been battering German defenses on Notre-Dame de Lorette in a succession of assaults since December 1914. The flat-topped ridge's southern slopes had five steep, finger-like spurs, and each had to be taken in its turn. The western-most spur was captured after fighting from December 1914 to January 1915; the second on 15 March 1915, after carrying three trench lines and beating back strong counterattacks; the third spur was taken the next month in preparation for the larger May offensive. Casualties were high when compared to the ground gained, and the Germans began to call the ridge '*Totenhilgel,*' or the Hill of Death.

On 9 May, three infantry regiments supported by chasseurs fought through five lines of trenches to close the last 1,000 meters to a small chapel that gave the ridge its name. The battle pitted grenades against machine guns, while the chasseurs leapt from shell crater to shell crater until the attack broke down under the intense fire. Huddling in an enormous mine crater, the attackers remained under German fire from 10 May to 12 May. During the night of 12 May, they crept forward, with enemy guns firing just above their heads, and stuffed sacks of earth into the loopholes to silence the machine guns temporarily while other troops climbed the parapet to capture the trenches. Once inside the chapel, the opponents engaged in hand-to-hand fighting in a darkness punctuated by grenade blasts. Each crater, tunnel, and underground shelter was cleared. By the time the fighting ended, the grounds were left littered with dead and dying soldiers, and the small rural chapel was but a low pile of broken stones. Ten more days of attacks were required to take the fourth spur.

Adjacent to the parking area, an overlook with a **table of orientation** provides views into the valley and of the steep hillsides that were conquered by the French. The ruins of the early 16th century church of Ablain-St-Nazaire can be seen below the hill. French forces attacked the fortified village on 12 May 1915 and completed its capture on 29 May. In the distance is the ruin of the Gothic-style Abbaye Mont St-Éloi, which was destroyed during the French Revolution, but whose high towers still served French soldiers later as an observation point. To the east, the Canadian Memorial at Vimy Ridge on the heights across *Vallée des Zouave* can be seen through the opening cut in the trees.

Notre-Dame de Lorette is one of the major French National Memorials and Cemeteries of the First World War. When entering the cemetery, the first grave encountered on the right is that of général Barbot. The simple prewar chapel has been replaced by an enormous **Byzantine-style basilica**. A colorful mosaic of the Risen Christ fills the rear interior wall, and the side walls are covered with memorial plaques to individuals as well as military units. The church sits amidst a sea of 19,987 white crosses neatly divided into large plots and occasionally punctuated by a Jewish or Muslim headstone. Facing the basilica is a 52-meter **Lanterne des Morts,**

whose light can be seen 70 km away at night. Its crypt holds the ceremonial coffins of a concentration camp deportee, unidentified Second World War soldiers from North Africa and Indo-China, and 3,028 additional unidentified bodies. To the rear of the Lantern Tower, two mass graves are surrounded by low, white stone walls and hold a total of 10,212 unidentified dead. The graves extend behind the basilica, where a Jewish section adjoins a Muslim section, both identifiable by their distinctive headstones. Finally, three mass graves on each side of the central path hold 6,758 more unidentified bodies.

Behind the cemetery is the **Musée Vivant 1914-1918**, which contains displays of French and German equipment and five full-sized dioramas of life in the trenches described in multilingual narrations. For a small extra fee, one can enter the small park behind the museum, which is the actual location of the fighting for the final section of the crest. The trenches have been reconstructed, and scattered about the grounds are examples of large equipment, including a rusted trench mortar and a nearly operational German 77-mm gun. Open every day 1 February through 15 December from 09:00 to 20:00. Fee.

#20

Battle of the Argonne
14 September 1914 to November 1915

OBJECTIVE	To encircle the Fortified Region of Verdun by cutting the Châlons-Verdun railway, which supplied the French fortress
FORCES	
FRENCH:	Third Army (général de division Maurice Sarrail until 22 July 1915, then général de division Georges Humbert)
GERMAN:	XVI Corps (General der Infanterie Bruno von Mudra)
RESULT	An extended stalemate
CASUALTIES	
FRENCH:	107,438, including over 15,000 evacuated with injuries or illness
GERMAN:	Estimated to be one half of the French casualties
LOCATION	Reims is 140 km east of Paris; Clermont-en-Argonne is 95 km east of Reims.

With Belgian neutrality violated, frontier defenses breached, and Paris threatened, French Commander-in-Chief Joseph Joffre ordered his forces into general retreat toward the Marne River. The German Fifth Army, commanded by Crown Prince Wilhelm of Prussia, followed the French, moving south along both sides of the Forêt d'Argonne in the valleys of the Aire and Aisne Rivers. The Germans advanced as far as Revigny and threatened to encircle Verdun. After the defeat at the Marne, they withdrew from this exposed advance position to establish scattered defensive positions near the forest of Argonne, facing the French Third Army, under général de division Maurice Sarrail. By late September 1914, the lines had stabilized, and the Germans were in possession of Montfaucon, Vauquois, Varennes, and

Servon. Opposing them was général de division Augustin Gérard's French II Corps, established in the western Argonne, and French V Corps, commanded by général de division Joseph Micheler, located to the east behind Vauquois. French forces also held the valley of the Biesme River, a route through the forest that they never relinquished.

General Falkenhayn set to neutralize the Région Fortifiée de Verdun. Falkenhayn knew he could not attack Verdun directly because its forts, strongpoints, and trench lines were among the strongest in France. His plan was to invest Verdun by cutting supply routes from the Forêt d'Argonne and from the valley of the Meuse. Two separate battles with one common objective thus developed in the forests of Argonne and Apremont.

Battle

The thickets and irregular terrain in the Forêt d'Argonne made fighting particularly difficult. Persistent rain, poorly drained clay soil, and natural springs inhibited the digging of deep trenches. The lack of roadways through the twisting ravines worsened the already difficult supply situation. Combat became an exchange of grenades and mortar shells. The night sky was lit by frequent rockets, and the ground was swept by machine-gun fire to prevent surprise. To gain advantage the Germans introduced both new weapons suited for trench warfare and the new 'Hutier' tactics of 'nibble and hold' – named after their proponent General Oscar von Hutier. For nearly one year, the opposing sides fought almost daily within the woods, each attempting to gain a localized advantage, threaten a salient, or secure a point of observation. General Mudra, who was an engineer by training, led the Germans, supported by enlarged ranks of pioneer troops and sappers (engineers). French soldiers persevered despite inadequate artillery and protection from poison gas.

On 29 September, German XVI Corps attacked the Biesme River valley at La Chalade, Le Four-de-Paris, and la Harazée. A French attack from the west on 2 October created a salient centered on two hunting lodges in the Bois de la Gruerie known as Bagatelle and St-Hubert, and cut the two roads which crossed the large wood. The Germans responded two days later using their new weapon, the *minenwerfer,* or trench mortar, advancing within 40 meters of Four-de-Paris. The next day the first use of a flamethrower in warfare occurred, with the Germans igniting enemy trench defenses and stored munitions. By 6 October, a front was established that would remain practically unchanged until 1918.

On 13 October, the Argonne sector was assigned to General Mudra, who dispensed with mass assaults in favor of small unit tactics. Each of these tactics started with an intense bombardment concentrated into a small area. Infantry, with a lavish use of grenades, then captured a section of forest and any defenders who remained alive. The process was then repeated, even though a counterattack usually followed each gain of ground. The skirmishes increased in frequency in both November and December. In the French assaults on 26 December and on 5 January, the Italian Garibaldi Regiment was nearly wiped out defending Courte-Chaussée for their French allies. Two grandsons of the famous unifier of Italy, Giuseppe

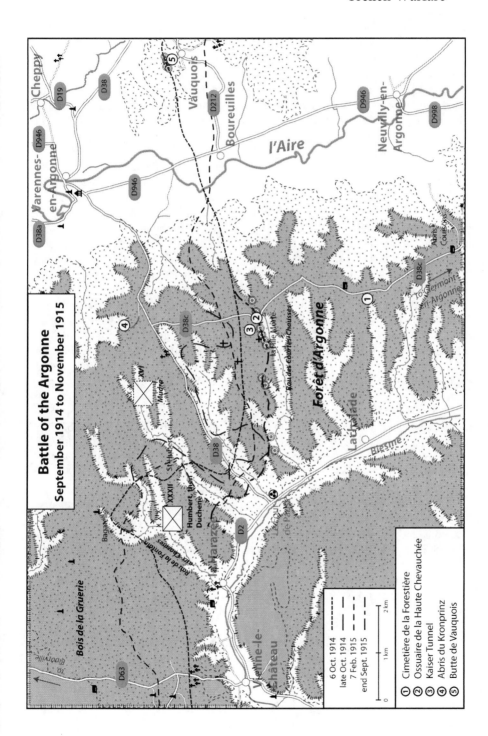

Battle of the Argonne
September 1914 to November 1915

6 Oct. 1914
late Oct. 1914
7 Feb. 1915
end Sept. 1915

① Cimetière de la Forestière
② Ossuaire de la Haute Chevauchée
③ Kaiser Tunnel
④ Abris du Kronprinz
⑤ Butte de Vauquois

Garibaldi, were killed. Eight additional German attacks were made that month, mainly upon Fontaine-aux-Charmes, Bagatelle, and Four-de-Paris.

French XXXII Corps replaced II Corps, and the fighting resumed on 29 January with a large attack targeting the Bois de la Gruerie. Through March and into May the battle for control of Bagatelle continued. Advances were measured in tens of meters, and each piece of ground was hotly contested. On 1 May, a German mine explosion coupled with the use of flamethrowers gained one entire trench line in what was a major victory by Argonne standards.

East of the Argonne, the French 10th Division of Infantry assaulted Butte de Vauquois, from which German artillery targeted the rail line that ran near Aubréville, in mid February. The deadly action continued until early April with little positive result.

The fighting culminated in the summer. After a bombardment heavy with the first use of gas shells on 20 June 1915, a mass German attack followed along both sides of the Binarville–Vienne-le-Château road. The advance was pushed back by a French counterattack on 24 June. A larger attack by the German Infantry Regiment Nr 124 (Württemberg) against Le Four-de-Paris commenced on 30 June. French 75-mm guns inflicted terrible casualties on the enemy, and once again the lost ground was regained. German Infantry Regiment Nr 67 finally captured Bagatelle on 2 July. On 13 July, Mudra ordered a seven-hour bombardment, heavy with the fire of large caliber mortars, followed by an assault by five regiments from Vienne-le-Château across the front to Haute Chevauchée. Initial progress was made, but the French counterattack soon recovered much of the ground at the cost of 26,419 casualties. French Third Army commander général Sarrail was relieved shortly thereafter.

French troops carried the first German line between Servon and Bois de la Gruerie in September as a subsidiary operation to the French Champagne Offensive; however, massed machine guns in the wood inflicted heavy casualties, and the French were forced to withdraw. The re-introduction of mine fighting began in November with underground explosions preceding both sides rushing forward to capture the resulting crater with fierce hand-to-hand fighting. Whereas the scale of these battles was small, the intensity and terror weighed heavily on the participants. With the massive struggle occurring at Verdun and the exhaustion of both armies which followed in 1916, only mine attacks and artillery duels occurred in the area until the Franco-American Offensive of 1918.

Battlefield Tour

The forest of Argonne is 60 km long and 12 km across and consists of tracts of beech, ash, and oak trees interspersed with plantations of fir trees. The underbrush is nearly impenetrable, providing shelter for the wild game that has attracted hunters for centuries. The terrain also includes narrow ravines, springs that feed the woodland streams, and boggy lowlands. Roadways are limited to the east-west route between Varennes and Vienne-le-Château, which intersects with the north-south chemin de la Haute Chevauchée. Much of the Bois de la Gruerie is now private land, barring access to locations such as Bagatelle, St-Hubert, and la Barricade. The road that once traversed the forest between Montblainville and Vienne-le-Château has disappeared. Four-de-Paris was destroyed and never rebuilt.

The area's natural beauty and interesting sites make it a good battlefield to visit; however, it is frequently ignored because of a shortage of tourist amenities and the lack English spoken in much of this part of France. Vauquois, Abris du Kronprinz, and the Kaiser Tunnel are worth the extra effort needed to see them.

Clermont-en-Argonne was a rear-area support base for French troops engaged in Argonne actions. Along with Ste-Menehould, it provides amenities for touring the Argonne. Both are on the National Road (N3) to Verdun.

Unfortunately, the Autoroute (A4) exits are not convenient for accessing the Argonne Forest; therefore exit at Ste-Menehould and proceed toward Verdun (N3, renamed D603). Leave the National Road (N3) between Clermont-en-Argonne and Ste-Menehould at Les Islettes (D2). North of the village, turn right towards Lochères (D2c, becomes Route de Lochères). Continue on this lonely, but scenic, forest road known as the **Haute Chevauchée** as it runs along the top of a north-south ridge, and forms the backbone of the Argonne plateau.

Ravines that cut into the plateau are visible to the left and right, and these were frequently the sites of desperate fighting. The Haute Chevauchée no longer traverses the full length of the Argonne because it terminates at the major east-west Varennes–Vienne-le-Château road (D38).

Almost immediately upon entering the **Haute Chevauchée,** one passes the roadside blockhouse dedicated to lieutenant Robert de Courson de la Villeneuve, a scion of a French aristocratic family, who was killed 20 km south of there on 19 September 1914. After 5 km, the **French Cimetière Nationale de la Forestière** is at the junction with a forest road to Lachalade. Planted between each of its 2,200 graves are hydrangea bushes, for which the cemetery is noted and which present a spectacular display when in bloom.

After another 2.5 km, the parking area for the **Ossuaire de la Haute Chevauchée** is on the right. For much of the war, the front line crossed the highway near this point. The German assault of 13 July captured the Bolante Plateau and parts of La Fille Morte to the west. The resulting positions were exposed to French fire, forcing the Germans to launch another assault on 27 September 1915. Wearying of the massive casualties that these attacks produced, the Germans and French then resorted to mine warfare. Although casualties decreased, the front lines hardly moved.

From the parking area, a gentle path that follows the old French communications trench approaches Cote 285, the highest point on the Haute Chevauchée and upon which stands the **Monument Ossuaire de la Haute-Chevauchée**, which is the major French memorial to the Argonne fighting. The 275 French regiments which participated in the battle are recorded on its sides; also included are lists of Italian, Czech, and American units. Entombed within the ossuary are the remains of 20,000 French soldiers who were killed in the Argonne from 1914 to 1918.

Immediately behind the ossuary is a 50-meter diameter crater, which is the result of a German mine explosion under a French dugout on 12 December 1916. This crater is the largest of a string of similar craters that runs 3.5 km along La Fille Morte to the edge of the Argonne plateau. They were formed during the mine warfare from October 1915 to June 1916 when this sector experienced 223 underground explosions.

The path curves around the north edge of the large crater, and the German first line is clearly indicated off to the left. One can see the narrow separation between opposing trenches. An Art Deco cross commemorates the 150,000 soldiers of all nations who died in the Argonne from 1914 to 1918. The path then continues through the replanted forest to a viewpoint from which the Lantern Tower on the Butte de Vauquois is visible. Multilingual signboards along the way explain warfare in this area. The path circles back below the rim of the craters, through the German trenches, and across the Haute Chevauchée to the Kaiser Tunnel.

After the last major attack of 27 September 1915, the French retained Cote 285 and the ability to fire into German-held ravines. Starting in November 1915, therefore, German infantry dug what became known as the **Kaiser Tunnel** to provide access to the front without exposure to French fire. The tunnel was twice expanded and became a major installation, with kilometers of galleries, storage facilities, a hospital, power station, and its own communications exchange. The tunnels were abandoned and their entrances destroyed by the Germans in September 1918. Due to the efforts of local volunteers, portions of the tunnel are now open for tours. The damp, slimy interior presents an image of what life was like for those forced to live underground for extended periods. The Kaiser Tunnel is open only on the first Sunday of each month and every Sunday in summer from 14:00 to 18:00. Fee. A walk in the nearby ravine presents numerous shell craters and trench lines in their unreconstructed state as examples of the difficult Argonne terrain.

Continue north on the Haute Chevauchée, then turn right toward Varennes-en-Argonne (D38).

Approximately 600 meters farther down a narrow track to the left are the **Abris[4] du Kronprinz**. Many protected and quite comfortable areas were constructed in the forest to provide shelter and recreation for German soldiers. Most of them are not easily accessible; however, the Abris du Kronprinz have been preserved. They were once used by German Crown Prince Wilhelm, although undoubtedly only temporarily due to their proximity to the front. Not visible from the parking area are four concrete shelters, one of which retains some of the decoration accorded to its royal inhabitant, specifically the frescoed fireplace. Single strands of wire make a feeble attempt to exclude visitors. Communications trenches still link the separated

---

[4] An abri is a small shelter frequently constructed of concrete to protect infantry from enemy small arms fire.

positions, and shell craters litter the area. The abris were captured by the US 77th Division on 28 September 1918 and renamed Champ Mahaut.

Return to the highway and continue toward Varennes (D38)[5]. After entering to the town, turn right toward Boureuilles (D946), then left toward Vauquois (D212). Before entering Vauquois, turn left onto the access road to the butte.

The **Butte de Vauquois** is located 4 km east of the Argonne Plateau and rises 70 meters to dominate the Aire valley. The Germans captured the site on 24 September 1914, and the hilltop village of 168 people was suddenly on the front lines. Preliminary French assaults in October and December failed to gain any strategic footing because German artillery in Bois de Cheppy applied flanking fire. Until February, French infantry assaults were essentially sacrifices of men due to the lack of artillery support.

French 10th Division assaulted Vauquois on 17 February, starting with the explosion of four small mines. Waves of attacks continued until 4 March when they were able to establish themselves on the crest of the hill. With each side controlling one half of the old village, the front lines were only 9 meters apart at certain places. Surface positions became so deadly that the underground 'war of the mines' commenced. Digging new tunnels and exploding mines under enemy positions continued until August 1917; by then the subterranean galleries were so deep that getting sufficiently large explosions became impractical, and the mine warfare essentially ceased.

From the parking area, walk to the crest through the French communications trench and past several of the French tunnel entrances. The butte has been frequently described as a giant termite nest, containing kilometers of galleries and hundreds of chambers – some reaching 100 meters below the surface. The contours of the hill have been reshaped by 519 explosions, and it is now several meters lower than in 1914. The prewar village was completely obliterated, and nothing remains except the mine craters. Only a few scattered stones in the craters mark the site of the village church.

The **Lanterne des Morts,** commemorating the soldiers killed fighting on the hill, is at the edge of the field of craters. The lantern is lit on special days, including 26 September to commemorate the beginning of the Meuse-Argonne Offensive on that day in 1918. A table of orientation describes the 'war of the mines' and its geographic relationship to the village. The largest crater is on the western side of the hill and measures 80 meters across. It was formed on 14 May 1916, when a German detonation of 50,000kg of explosives destroyed a French dugout, killing 108 inhabitants. Views to the north show Cheppy, Montfaucon, and other sites of the Meuse-Argonne Offensive. A walk down into the craters and up the other side brings one to the German side and a reconstructed entrance to their tunnel system.

The site is open to visitors at all times; however, tours of the tunnel system are offered by the volunteer *Les Amis de Vauquois* organization only on the first

---

[5] See battlefield #36: Meuse-Argonne Offensive for move information concerning this area

Sunday of each month from 09:30 to 12:00 and on 1 May and 8 May at 10:00 and 18:00. A small museum is adjacent to the parking area.

#21

Forêt d'Apremont
26 September 1914 to 14 April 1915

OBJECTIVE	To eliminate the St Mihiel Salient and reopen supply routes to Verdun
FORCES	
FRENCH:	15th and 16th Divisions of VIII Corps (général de division Jean de Mondésir)
GERMAN:	5th Bavarian Division of III Bavarian Corps (General der Kavallerie Ludwig von Gebsattel)
RESULT	Hardly any tactical advantage gained by either side.
CASUALTIES	
FRENCH:	60,000 in the entire salient during 1915
GERMAN:	Unknown
LOCATION	St-Mihiel is 300 km east of Paris; Bois d'Ailly is 5 km southeast of St-Mihiel

After the Franco-Prussian War of 1870, the French-German border was only 40 km from the Meuse River, the result of the German annexations of Alsace and parts of Lorraine. French military planner général Séré de Rivières established fixed defenses along the river, with a line of forts between Toul and Verdun. Falkenhayn attacked across portions of the Woëvre plain to outflank Verdun from the south. German strikes and French counterstrikes stabilized a front a along ridgeline known as Hauts de Meuse, which formed the western boundary of the plain. The Germans were in possession of a dominant height at Les Éparges. Farther south the Germans were more successful; bombardment by Austrian-made 305-mm howitzers destroyed fortifications protecting St-Mihiel at Camp des Romains and Fort des Paroches. Although the city was occupied and the river crossed, the enemy could advance no farther. At the end of September 1914 the Germans were in possession of a 22-km, arrow-shaped salient into French territory, which cut the French supply route to Verdun. Despite French attempts, the area was to remain in German hands until the American Offensive in 1918.

To protect Verdun, the French High Command ordered efforts to reduce the salient by attacking its shoulder at Éparges. Meanwhile, the Germans strove to protect their supply line to St Mihiel by evicting the French from the Forêt d'Apremont.

Because of the distance between these two locations on the Woëvre battlefield, they will be treated separately.

Battle

A new French bombardment opened on the morning of 5 April 1915. Five mine explosions destroyed German strongpoints, and the Brigade de Belfort rushed the enemy with mounted bayonets, advancing as far as the German third line. The Germans did not respond until mid afternoon with artillery and counterattacks, which continued into the next day, when the French repulsed eight attempts to dislodge them. Only a small amount of ground was exchanged.

On 5 May, a German counterstroke was successful in regaining most of the ground lost over the previous weeks. Within these trenches on 20 May 1915 at 02:00, a company of the French 172nd Regiment commanded by commandant André advanced very quickly through five German lines but was trapped by a heavy bombardment that isolated it from the supporting units to the rear. André and his eighty soldiers organized their resistance in the German fourth line trenches. Repeated attacks by Prussian Guard were repelled by the French, who were without

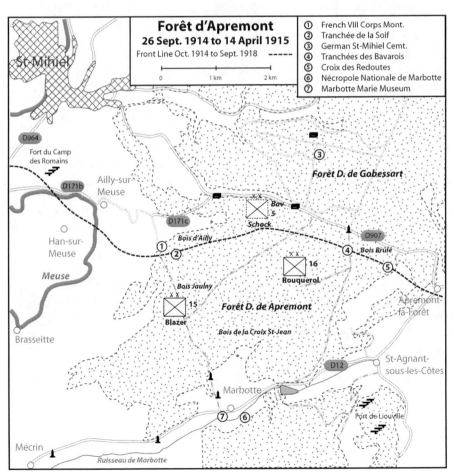

Forêt d'Apremont
26 Sept. 1914 to 14 April 1915
Front Line Oct. 1914 to Sept. 1918 -----

0   1 km   2 km

① French VIII Corps Mont.
② Tranchée de la Soif
③ German St-Mihiel Cemt.
④ Tranchées des Bavarois
⑤ Croix des Redoutes
⑥ Nécropole Nationale de Marbotte
⑦ Marbotte Marie Museum

food or water amid the May heat and suffocating dust of exploding shells. On 22 May at 18:00, with all their ammunition expended, the sixty-three exhausted survivors were captured, and the position became known as *Tranchée de la Soif* or 'trench of thirst.'

Battlefield Tour

Upstream from St-Mihiel to Commercy, the Meuse curves through a broad valley bordered by wooded hills. Above a 4-km stretch of the valley, on a plateau east of the river is the Forêt d'Apremont, which encompasses a number of smaller woods (*bois*). The front line bisected the forest, with French forces holding the southwest quadrant.

Leave St-Mihiel southeast toward Apremont-la-Forêt (D907). After 4 km turn right toward Ailly-sur-Meuse (D171c), then bear left at the junction toward Bois d'Ailly. A parking area near a monument offers great views down into the Meuse Valley.

Today the **Forêt d'Apremont** presents the best naturally preserved trenches and dugouts on the Western Front. The site has no re-creations, no artificial preservation, and very few restrictions on entering the actual positions where thousands fought and died amid the melting snow of the winter of 1914 and the spring rains of 1915.

The obelisk near the parking area is dedicated to the units of the **French VIII Corps,** which fought in the Forêt d'Apremont for two years. The four sides list the numerous regiments who were engaged in the deadliest sector of the St-Mihiel salient. In front of the obelisk is an ossuary containing bodies of French and German soldiers.

Nearby signboards give directions for a 20-km *Sentier Historique,* a network of paths that link four major sites within the Forêt d'Apremont and whose route is marked by orange and yellow signs with a barbed wire logo. The Bois d'Ailly is *Le Saillant de Saint-Mihiel Platforme* #1 on the *sentier.* The paths are sometimes difficult to follow; carrying a detailed map of the forest should be considered.

The path into the woods runs parallel to the German lines. The trenches are two meters deep in places, and a large number of underground concrete shelters still stand. Their entrances are barred for safety. Many are as much as 30 meters below ground, and their stairways descend at very steep angles. The path along the parapet is quite walkable and crosses from side to side as the terrain permits. A more difficult, alternative route is in the actual trenches, where years of fallen leaves now cushion the still muddy tracks. The sounds of mine and grenade explosions and the frenzied shouts of 'gaz!' have been replaced by the chirping of birds and the rustling of dried leaves. The path circles 400 meters through the wood and emerges at the **Monument of the Tranchée de la Soif**. The stone commemorates the steadfastness of commandant Andre, his men, and all the soldiers of the 172nd and 372nd Regiments.

An access road to the Bois d'Ailly continues past the wood and has a sign pointing to Marbotte, but do not take this route because it eventually becomes almost undrivable.

> Return to the road toward Apremont-la-Forêt (D907) and continue past the motocross course.

The road passes a well-constructed and rather extensive German first aid post on the right. Slightly farther ahead, a sign indicates the access road to the **German St-Mihiel Cemetery** on the left. The burial ground in the Forêt de Gobessart contains many original German headstones erected early in the war, when the Germans still had hopes of victory. The site is interesting, though the approach road goes through a foreboding abandoned industrial area.

> After 2.7 km on the road toward Apremont, turn right into the woods where a Second World War monument stands on the left shoulder.

This area is known as the **Tranchées des Bavarois et de Roffignac** (Trenches of the Bavarians and of comte de Roffignac), and it is *Le Saillant de Saint-Mihiel Platforme #4* on the sentier. The site presents one of the most fantastic First World War trench areas on the Western Front. Immediately on the right is a large shell crater. Approximately 300 meters farther on the left is a French sap entrance. The *'Abri Allemande'* (German outpost) is signed on the access road before the parking area. The concrete Bavarian outpost's entrance bears the inscription *'In Treue Fest'* (Firm in Loyalty), the slogan of Bavarian regiments. Continue to the parking area, where hundreds of meters of German trenches and concrete shelters built around a French salient are easily accessible. Trilingual signs identify and explain their uses and construction. The underbrush has been removed, and the pathways are mostly walkable. Among the strongpoints and shelter entrances are tangled sections of original barbed wire, some still supported upon their pigtail posts. Only 100 meters farther are the French first and second line trenches. The site offers numerous paths for exploration, a large parking area, and even picnic benches.

> Return to the main highway and continue toward Apremont (D907). Approximately 1 km farther, another turn to the right accesses a rough road up a hill to Bois Brûlé, which is *Le Saillant de Saint-Mihiel Platforme #3*.

A small French infantry strongpoint in the **Bois Brûlé** had the German supply route from Apremont to St-Mihiel under its guns. The Germans were determined to reopen the route. After three months of intense fighting – much of it hand-to-hand, an advance of 300 meters and over 15,000 casualties, the French bastions were captured, but the French retained positions in the forest.

Adjacent to the parking area is a ceramic **table of orientation**, overlooking the valley of the Meuse. Continuing up the farm road from the parking area, trench remnants are to the right and left. Follow the sign indicating the path to the forest. Just before the sign to enter the Bois Brûlé, two collapsed dugouts are on the left. Once under the shelter of the re-grown pine forest, one enters the first German trench line. The front line trenches ran hundreds of meters back into the wood and were only 50 meters apart at certain places. Signs, walkways, and railings have been placed for visitor safety, but these essentially unadulterated positions remain after 90 years. The original German installations are in excellent condition, with command posts and underground shelter entrances still intact. The German trenches are 1.5 meters deep and backed in concrete with fire-steps, ammunition caches, and parapets with loopholes. In contrast, the French trenches were backed with fascines (bundles of twigs) and sand bags. As a result, the French lines have almost disappeared, whereas the German positions are still quite strong. The reason for the difference is the French attitude toward the German occupation of their country. Permanent fortifications would indicate acceptance of the situation. The Germans believed the occupation to be permanent – at least until a suitable peace could be negotiated. They therefore designed and built their trenches using concrete, with deep underground shelters for comfort and safety.

Follow the trench line to the large wooden cross, the **Croix des Redoutes**, which was erected to commemorate the story of Adjutant Jacques Péricard. On 8 April 1915,[6] men of the 95th Regiment were defending a recently conquered trench against a massive German counterattack. Most of Péricard's force were wounded or dead, and the survivors were at risk of being overrun. With a spirited shout of '*Debout les Morts!*' (Arise, the Dead!), he inspired his remaining men to fight on and made the enemy believe that their strength was greater than it truly was. They successfully beat off the attack.

Return to the D907 and proceed into Apremont-la-Forêt. Along the steep slope down into the village was a quarry which the German defenders transformed into an extensive complex of shelters and tunnels. The remains are barely visible on the right from the roadway and are difficult to access. In Apremont turn right toward Marbotte/Mécrin (D12).

On the wooded heights south of St-Agnant-sous-les-Côtes is the **Fort de Louiville**. The fort was completed in 1878 as part of Séré Rivières's defenses along the Meuse. As with all late 19th century fortifications, however, developments in artillery shells soon made it obsolete. The fort was essentially destroyed by German heavy guns in September 1914, but it remained in French hands and was used as an important but dangerous observation post. The site was abandoned for decades and completely overgrown until recent efforts by volunteers to restore it. Now on private property, the fort is open for tours only on the third Sunday of each month during the summer. A sign indicates a turn toward the 'Massive Fortifiée du Liouville';

---

[6] The date inscribed on the plaque is incorrect.

however, the road quickly becomes undrivable. The alternative approach road south of St-Agnant is more easily navigated.

Before entering Marbotte, the **Nécropole Nationale de Marbotte à Apremont-la-Forêt** can be seen set back from the road on the left. The cemetery spreads up a gentle hillside and is sheltered by a wood to its rear. It holds 2,652 dead, mostly from the battles in Bois d'Ailly, Bois Brûlé, and Tête-à-Vache. A walk through the cemetery and up the incline arrives at an 11-meter memorial stele to the French VIII Corps, which incorporates an altar upon which a Mass is still held yearly. A table of orientation in front of the monument puts the entire battlefield into perspective, from the Camp des Romains down to Apremont. From the hillside, the forested plateau and village of Marbotte are clearly visible.

Marbotte (*Le Saillant de Saint-Mihiel Platforme #2*) was the village closest to the battlefield, but it was protected from German gunfire by the steep ridge to its north. It became a place of refuge for the wounded, and its **18th century church** was used as a mortuary for the dead. Scenes of blood flowing down the church aisle were common. The little church still stands upon the hillside and is noted for its glorious stained glass windows which depict the actions of Adjutant Péricard and commandant d'Andre. The walls are covered with the small memorial plaques frequently seen in French memorials.

A non-descript structure along the highway holds the three-room **Marbotte Mairie Museum**. Although the operating hours are not always convenient, a stop at this excellent little museum is suggested to view its collection of drawings and photographs of Fort de Liouville and the local fighting. The upper floor displays an evocative and fearful collection of soldiers' artwork. Open April through October daily except Tuesday from 14:00 to 18:00. Fee.

Above the town, a forest road enters a wood where numerous monuments to French units are located. This spot is the opposite end of the forest road that passed the Monument of the Tranchée de la Soif. The road should not be attempted without a four-wheel drive vehicle.

#22
Butte des Éparges
21 September 1914 to October 1915

OBJECTIVE	To eliminate the German fortified position atop the Crête des Éparges
FORCES	
FRENCH:	12th division (général de brigade Jean Paulinier)
GERMAN:	Elements of V Corps (General der Infanterie Eduard von Below)
RESULT	The French recaptured the butte.
CASUALTIES	Tens of thousands killed and wounded
LOCATION	Verdun is 265 km east of Paris; Les Éparges is 22 km southeast of Verdun

Battle

The Germans occupied Les Éparges on 9 September 1914, after it was abandoned by French soldiers withdrawn to defend Paris. Although forced from the village two weeks later, the Germans immediately fortified the crest of Butte des Éparges to the east with a vast network of trenches, tunnels, and concrete fortifications, eventually encompassing five defensive lines. With the stabilization of the front in this section, attention shifted to the west and the 'Race to the Sea.'

In February 1915, the French High Command ordered its First Army to capture these strong positions as part of the effort to reduce the St-Mihiel Salient. At 14:00 on 17 February, four 1,500 kg mines were detonated along the German first trench line, followed one hour later by an assault by the 106th Regiment. The soldiers leapt from their forward trenches, ran across the open field and entered the mine craters filled with debris and dead bodies. German artillery fire started almost immediately, and by the next morning guns as large as 305-mm were pounding the hastily improvised French defenses. The counterattack pushed the French back to their starting positions. The battle continued for four days until mutual exhaustion forced a halt. French assaults on the nights of 18 and 27 March were successful in capturing the western spur overlooking the village.

On 5 April 1915, as part of a larger offensive on German positions on both shoulders of the salient by Army Detachment Gérard, the French 12th Division again

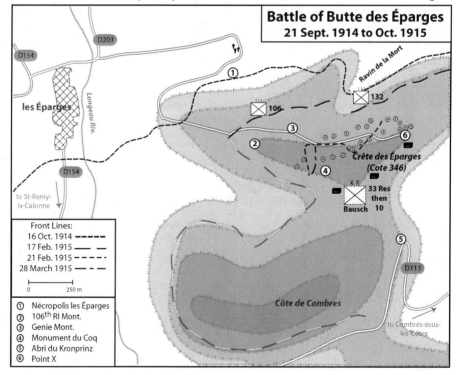

Battle of Butte des Éparges
21 Sept. 1914 to Oct. 1915

Ravin de la Mort

les Éparges

Longeau Riv.

to St-Remy-
la-Calonne

D203

D154

D154

① 106

132

③

② ⑥

Crête des Éparges
(Cote 346)

④

X X
33 Res
then
Bausch 10

⑤

D113

Côte de Combres

to Combres-sous-
les-Côtes

Front Lines:
16 Oct. 1914
17 Feb. 1915
21 Feb. 1915
28 March 1915

0   250 m

① Nécropolis les Éparges
② 106th RI Mont.
③ Genie Mont.
④ Monument du Coq
⑤ Abri du Kronprinz
⑥ Point X

attacked Éparges. Progress was meager with advances failing on uncut barbed wire and intact blockhouses despite the preliminary bombardment. The attacks continued for four more days, under appalling artillery bombardments and amid rain squalls. On 9 April, French efforts at Éparges were rewarded with the capture of the peak known as Point C, but the point of the spur, known as Point X, remained in German hands. The cost was enormous, with French casualties totaling 3,978. Général Gérard then decided against continuing mass attacks in favor of small-scale actions all along the salient. Whereas the intensity of fighting diminished, the shelling and mine warfare continued; however, the French were never dislodged.

Battlefield Tour

The Woëvre plain consists of undulating ground composed of poorly draining clay soil. Water collects in low spots, creating ponds and boggy fields. The western boundary of the Woëvre plain is formed by the Hauts de Meuse. Equidistant between Verdun and St-Mihiel, the Crête des Éparges was a 1,370-meter spur near the village of Les Éparges. It is 346 meters high and overlooks the Woëvre plain to the east and French defensive positions on the Hauts de Meuse to the west. Its sides were steep, slippery when it rained, and in the spring of 1915, it was described as a mountain of mud.

From the D903 east of Verdun at Haudiomont, turn right toward Les Éparges (D154). The road follows the valley of the Longeau River, which separates Éparges from the Hauts de Meuse. In the village of Les Éparges, turn right toward Trésauvaux (D203) and then continue straight toward the 'Site des Éparges' (D203a).

Follow this access road past the **Necropolis, Nationale Les Éparges** (also known as Cimetière Militaire du Le Trottoir), which was created in 1915 during combat in the Hauts des Meuse. The cemetery is near the *Ravin de la Mort*, which was used by the attacking French regiments in their assaults up the hill. A trail starts to the left of the cemetery and ascends the hill. The path is steep and slick when damp – exactly as it was for the attacking French. Driving up is preferred.

Proceed to a parking area at the foot of a steep 90-meter stairway.

Above the stairway is the **Monument to the 106th Régiment Infanterie,** which commemorates the regiment's losses in ascending this peak in February, March, and April 1915. The huge stone shows the closed eyes of a dead warrior, with a skeleton's hand creeping up the monument on the left and skulls on the right. Below the warrior is a bronze statue of France holding a fallen soldier. Trenches are on either side of the pathway.

Continue on the road toward Point X, past the **Monument to the Genie** (Corps of Engineers) which recognizes the seven specialist groups from bridge builders to camouflage experts, to the parking area on the right.

On the right is a signed path to Point C and the **Monument du Coq**. Climb through the pine forest see the remnants of the trenches and shell holes. The ground still holds the shattered remains of hundreds of soldiers who were never recovered. The Monument du Coq sits upon the lip of a large crater and commemorates the French 12th Division and its fellow soldiers killed at Les Éparges. Plaques on the base list all of the divisions engaged in the area, including the four American units from 1918. The obelisk is crowned with a golden rooster.

From the monument, a rugged trail descends the eastern side of the hill, utilizing the German communications trench, to the German medical blockhouse. This shelter is of typically German concrete construction, with one-meter thick roof and walls. Inside are several individual rooms as well as a second section that appears to have been added later. The shelter was built into the hillside, but passages to the tunnels have been blocked due to safety concerns.

The **Abri du Kronprinz** is 390 meters down the hill. This large bunker has three windows and an entrance all facing to the southeast. Its windows provide the same view of Combres was presented to the German Crown Prince in 1914. Access is permitted, although little remains except for empty rooms that housed command posts and storage. Deep tunnels extended into the hillside for protection from French artillery. The abri and the medical blockhouse were connected by an underground railway. Alternatively, the abri can be more easily approached by returning to Les Éparges and continuing south toward St-Remy-la-Calonne. Turn toward Combres-sous-les-Côtes (D113). The abri is at the hairpin curve on the road after St-Remy. Do not try to park at the bunker on the dangerous curve; a forest trail a short distance ahead provides a safer stopping point.

Return to the car still parked below Point C, and continue to the roadway's end, passing through a field of very large mine craters.

Although the French captured the peak in April 1915, the 'war of the mines' continued, with some of the largest explosions occurring in September and October 1915. The large craters on either side of the road are the results of those explosions. At the end of the road, arborvitae trees line the avenue de la comtessa de Cugnac to **Point X**. The comtessa donated the trees in memory of her fiancé, who was killed at Éparges. The ground on both sides of the path has trenches, craters, and remnants of concrete shelters. At the farthest point is a yellow sandstone monument commemorating the **302nd Régiment Infanterie**. Adjacent to the monument is a table of orientation which indicates the direction and distance to towns spread across the stunning Woëvre plain. A few steps beyond the monument on the very steep point of the spur is more concrete rubble, demonstrating the German determination to maintain a position on the spur.

#23

Third Battle of Artois (Battle of Loos)
25 September to 14 October 1915

OBJECTIVE	To break through the German line in coordination with French offensives in Champagne and near Arras to eliminate the German salient on the Western Front
FORCES	
BRITISH:	Six infantry divisions (73,500 men) of First Army (General Sir Douglas Haig)
GERMAN:	Four infantry regiments (10,400 men) of 14th and 117th Divisions; one Jäger division of Sixth Army (Generaloberst Kronprinz Rupprecht of Bavaria)
RESULT	The German second line was penetrated, but the breakthrough was not accomplished, and not all of the gains were held.
CASUALTIES	
BRITISH:	15,800 killed and 34,580 wounded
GERMAN:	1,837 killed, 21,000 wounded, and 3,000 taken prisoner
LOCATION	Lens is 200 km north of Paris

In the early summer of 1915, British attacks against Aubers Ridge, Festubert, and Neuve Chapelle – British actions in support the Second Battle of Artois – captured some ground but failed to reverse significantly German control of the strategic Aubers Ridge. A German salient in Picardy offered the tantalizing prospect of cutting off the German First, Second, and Seventh Armies. French général Joffre convinced Lord Kitchener that a coordinated attack by British troops north of Lens and by French troops against Vimy Ridge south of Lens would force the German abandonment of France's major mining center, threaten German transportation routes to the east, and possibly drive the enemy back behind the Meuse River. Joffre blithely ignored alternative suggestions and reports of the strong German defensive positions. Lord Kitchener insisted upon supporting the French attack, even against a prediction of substantial casualties.

British reinforcements, including the first of the New Army divisions recruited by Lord Kitchener, were arriving on the Western Front. The failure at Gallipoli, an expedition to Salonika, and troop commitments to East Africa and Egypt, however, drew off manpower. The BEF nevertheless expanded its responsibilities on the Western Front in August, taking over the Loos sector from the French.

Battle

Not long after the Allies' condemnation of the Germans' use of poison gas, the British Army investigated its potential as well. General Haig believed gas could augment his short supply of heavy artillery shells in the bombardment of German

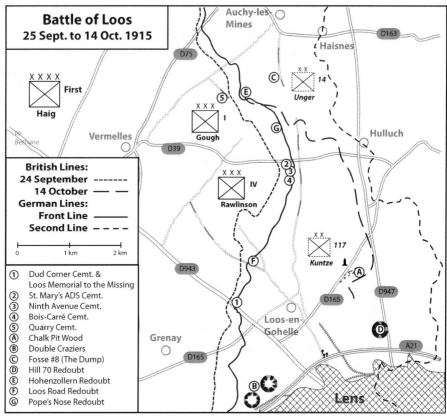

Battle of Loos
25 Sept. to 14 Oct. 1915

X X X X
First
Haig

British Lines:
24 September ----------
14 October —— —
German Lines:
Front Line ——————
Second Line – – – –

0   1 km   2 km

① Dud Corner Cemt. &
  Loos Memorial to the Missing
② St. Mary's ADS Cemt.
③ Ninth Avenue Cemt.
④ Bois-Carré Cemt.
⑤ Quarry Cemt.
Ⓐ Chalk Pit Wood
Ⓑ Double Craziers
Ⓒ Fosse #8 (The Dump)
Ⓓ Hill 70 Redoubt
Ⓔ Hohenzollern Redoubt
Ⓕ Loos Road Redoubt
Ⓖ Pope's Nose Redoubt

positions around of the mining center of Loos-en-Gohelle. In the subsequent assault, the six divisions of the British First Army had the objectives of breaking through two enemy lines and advancing 7 km to the Canal de la Deûle.

The German defenses had been improved during the summer of 1915 and included two main defensive lines, each studded with redoubts, wire entanglements, and well-positioned machine guns. In the north near Auchy lez la Bassée (now Auchy-lès-Mines), Hohenzollern Redoubt was a complex of concrete machine-gun emplacements and underground bunkers. Located only 200 meters east of the British front line, it was supported by strong, deep trenches connecting to the Fosse 8 and the Quarries strongpoints 300 meters farther east. Lens Road Redoubt sat upon the eastern side of Grenay ridge, across the main highway between Bethune and Lens. One km north of Lens Road Redoubt was Loos Road Redoubt, defending the farm track from Vermelles and the open Loos valley. Between Loos and Haisnes, the chalky plain was covered with long grass and stretched gradually but steadily uphill toward the German trenches. The open nature of the battlefield provided no cover from German observers.

A second, parallel trench line ran 500-1000 meters to the east and consisted of a series of German strongpoints (*stützpunkt*) that were connected by communications trenches and anchored in the south by the city of Lens. The Lens-La Bassée Road provided excellent lateral communications and transportation. The Germans overall had the advantages of good observation and clear fields of fire. Sir Henry Rawlinson, commander of the key IV Corps, foresaw the battle when he recorded in his diary, 'My new front is as flat as the palm of my hand. Hardly any cover anywhere. . . . It will cost us dearly, and we shall not get very far.'[7]

At 05:50 on 25 September, after a four-day artillery bombardment which was the most intense thus far in the war, the British released chlorine gas from 5,028 cylinders into less than optimum wind conditions. In the north, the gas drifted back over poorly protected British troops, producing confusion and panic. The British 2nd Division of Lieutenant-General Sir Herbert Gough's I Corps was prevented from advancing along the La Bassée Canal by German fortified brickworks and mine craters, which channeled troops into deadly, narrow gaps. Aided by a smokescreen that combined with the gas, 9th (Scottish) Division's 7th Seaforth Highlanders entered the southern section of the Hohenzollern Redoubt, attacking the German Reserve Infantry Regiment Nr 11. Bombing their way forward along the German communication trenches, they captured Fosse 8 within the hour. Meanwhile, the 5th Cameron Highlanders passed through the northern section of Hohenzollern Redoubt and also reached Fosse 8, where they suffered heavy casualties from enfilade fire. A gentle breeze in the south blew the gas so slowly that onrushing attackers entered their own cloud. The British 7th Division nevertheless progressed across the open terrain between Vermelles and Hulluch to capture the Quarries.

British IV Corps, commanded by General Sir Henry Rawlinson, made significant progress in the southern sector. 1st Division approached the Lens-La Bassée Road, threatening to crack the German second line. The 15th (Scottish) Division advanced over 3 km, capturing Loos Road and Lens Road Redoubts, and the town of Loos. The cellars in the houses of Loos had been made into underground fortresses, and each had to be cleared by grenade or bayonet. The fighting was hand-to-hand, and occasionally the surrendering enemy were executed.[8] The division's rapid advance was not matched by that of the adjacent units, exposing it to enfilade fire. It continued forward, however, to overcome the redoubt southeast of Loos on the commanding height of Hill 70; heavy casualties prohibited farther advance. 47th Division captured both the Double Crassier and the southern section of Loos and then formed a defensive flank facing southeast.

The initial British success penetrated the German first line, reached the Lens-La Bassée Road, and even entered the German second line trenches west of Haisnes. Considering the Germans' interlocking machine-gun fire and density of strongpoints, such progress was truly remarkable. Even the few veteran troops in the units were hard pressed to maintain the attack against such withering fire. Casualties were high; some units were all but annihilated. The Kings Own Scottish Borderers (KOSB) was one of six battalions that lost over six hundred men and most of the

---

[7] Captain B. H. Liddell Hart, *The Real War: 1914 – 1918* (Boston: Little, Brown and Company, 1964 ed.), 187.

[8] Trevor Wilson, *The Myriad Faces of War* (Cambridge: Polity Press, 1986), 260.

senior officers. The loss of entire companies left gaps between the British positions, which the German counterattack successfully exploited.

Personally commanded by Field Marshal Sir John French and stationed 9 km to the rear, British reserves were unable to provide the necessary support before German reserves reestablished the line. They spent the night of 25 September struggling through chaotic, narrow country roads that were crowded with supply trains moving forward, and ambulances and the walking wounded staggering rearward. Regiments of the German 8th Division were rapidly transported to positions around Loos. By evening two German Guard Reserve Regiments were entrained and were strengthening defenses near Haisnes, and together with the 15th Bavarian Division, they recaptured Hill 70 before the end of the day. British casualties on the first day were approximately fifteen thousand, whereas German losses are described as minimal.

The British situation at dawn on 26 September was tenuous. They had suffered heavy casualties and expended much of their ammunition; reinforcing units were starting to arrive but were exhausted after a long night march in constant rain; advanced units were mixed and in some cases physically isolated; and German reinforcements had considerably redressed the initial British manpower advantage. All of the tactical advantages from the first day had been lost, and no hope of achieving the original objectives remained; however, the fighting continued. The reserve 21st and 24th Divisions – each reduced in manpower by a brigade – finally arrived and were sent against positions between Hill 70 and Hulluch. German machine guns opened fire at 1,500 meters range, dropping their enemy by the hundreds. The advance continued until it encountered the still intact wire, at which point they turned and withdrew. The result was devastating for the two New Army divisions; eight thousand of the fifteen thousand infantrymen were casualties. German gunners, sickened with the slaughter or filled with admiration at the men's bravery, ceased fire, permitting an unopposed retreat.

On 27 September, German bombers applied steady pressure, forcing a withdrawal from Fosse 8 and the Dump. Positions north of Hill 70 along with the lower slopes were retaken by British Guards Division. All hope of a major advance was gone, however because in three days of fighting some units had suffered such great casualties as to be no longer viable fighting forces. Twelve battalions lost more than seventy-five percent of their nominal strength; twenty-three other battalions were reduced by approximately fifty percent or more.

After a week-long lull in the fighting, the Germans recaptured Hohenzollern Redoubt on the night of 2/3 October. A British plan to resume the attack was delayed by a strong German counter assault on 8 October. Despite a heavy preliminary bombardment on a narrower front, intact German wire and enfilade machine-gun fire from both flanks quickly ended the renewed assault on 13 October. Deteriorating weather brought the offensive officially to a close.

Hill 70 was taken the next year by a Canadian assault and held against repeated German counterattacks on 15-25 August 1917. Hohenzollern Redoubt would remain in German hands until 1918.

The nearly fifty-one thousand casualties proved nothing except the courage of the New Army soldiers. Strategic gains were nil, despite claims of gained experience in modern warfare. The battle of Loos became noted for its bad planning and poor staff work. Recriminations over the BEF's poor performance in the first year of the war cost Sir John French his job as commander-in-chief. Douglas Haig, later a subject of much controversy, was appointed as his replacement on 19 December 1915.

Battlefield Tour

Loos-en-Gohelle is located among depressed mining and manufacturing communities on a plain punctuated with clusters of factory chimneys, quarry pits, mine heads, and tailing piles. The northern boundary of the battlefield is the Bethune-La Bassée-Lille Canal, (actions north of the canal were merely diversionary in nature) and the southern is the congested districts of Lens. Bois Hugo, Chalet Wood, Puits 14 bis – all British objectives north of Hill 70 that were achieved and later lost – have been subsumed within the Lens Commercial Centre and Aérodrome de Lens. Hill 70, a chalk extension of one of the many spurs which reach northeastward from the Artois plateau, dominates Lens and the plain beyond Loos. Although significantly obstructed, a view of the Loos Valley is still possible along the D937 (Lens-La Bassée Road) east of Loos, especially from the eastern crest approximately 400 meters north of the A21 Autoroute. The plain has retained its openness and bone-chilling winds.

In the great mining district around Lens, a few definitions of French terms are helpful:

> Cité - company town of miners' housing
> Corons – miners' cottages
> Crassier - major mine waste piles; slag heaps
> Fosse - principle mine
> Puits - auxiliary mine shaft

The tour starts at the final resting place of some of the British casualties, then proceeds behind the British front line to approach the most contested terrain across an open plain.

Leave Lens toward Béthune (N43); after approximately 6 km, stop at the cemetery on the right.

Dud Corner Cemetery was the site of the German Lens Road Redoubt and was supposedly named after the large number of unexploded artillery rounds found nearby. The 15th (Scottish) Division captured Dud Corner and moved on toward Loos after Piper David Laidlaw VC, 7th Battalion KOSB, rallied the battalion to advance against German machine guns, despite the gaps being torn in their ranks and being twice wounded himself.

The cemetery now contains 1,812 graves, mostly from the 1915 fighting. The original five burials – and the only burials before the armistice – are halfway down the left side. Only 684 of the bodies are identified. The **Loos Memorial to the Missing** lines the cemetery's inner wall, with panels listing the 20,594 names of those who lost their lives in the 1915 battle as well as in the fighting at the Lys River in 1918. The roof of the left shelter presents unobstructed views of the plain to the north, creating an ideal location to view the terrain where the British attack moved from left to right. The stairs leading up to the Cross of Sacrifice provide an opportunity to look over the rear wall.

Continue toward Béthune (N43); turn right at the first rural road (chemin de Bully) and continue to the crossroad on the Vermelles-Hulluch Road (D39). Turn right toward Hulluch.

The open fields north of Dud Corner are marked with Crosses of Sacrifice at **St. Mary's Advanced Dressing Station Cemetery** (a post-armistice accumulation cemetery), **Ninth Avenue Cemetery** (an mass grave of 41 Cameron Highlanders), and **Bois Carré Military Cemetery** (a battlefield cemetery) – all originally in no man's land. These cemeteries can be accessed from the Vermelles-Hulluch Road (D39), which divides the battlefield at the boundary between the British I and IV Corps. To the south and visible from most of the battlefield are the ominous twin peaks of the Double Crassier.

Killed in the 27 September attack on Chalk Pit Wood east of Loos was 18-year-old Lieutenant John Kipling, 2nd Battalion Irish Guards, the only son of Rudyard Kipling. Despite exhaustive searches during and after the war by the frail young man's heartbroken father, his remains were not recovered. For 77 years, what may have been his body lay in a grave identified only as 'A Lieutenant of the Great War Irish Guards.' A 1992 investigation suggested that the unidentified body was indeed that of Lieutenant Kipling. A tombstone in St Mary's A.D.S. Cemetery now included Kipling's name, even though it also appears on the Memorial to the Missing; controversy as to the true identity of the grave's contents continues.

Reverse direction and continue to the entrance of Vermelles. Turn right toward Auchy-lès-Mines (rue Voltaire) and follow the CWGC signs.

Quarry Cemetery containing 139 graves is a sheltered depression used by field ambulances and other units of 9th (Scottish) Division during their attack upon the Hohenzollern Redoubt, now seen as a shrub-covered rise to the east. Little evidence remains of the famous redoubt and its craters are now used as a trash dump. Fosse 8 has been flattened since the battle, and the Dump also no longer exists. The open and windy area around the sunken cemetery demonstrates the exposure of the advancing British troops to German fire; the small cemetery now gives its inhabitants eternal shelter.

Recommended reading

Corrigan, Gordon: *Loos 1915: The Unwanted Battle*. Brimscombe Port Stroud, Gloucestershire, England: Spellmount Limited, 2006. A detailed account with British Army Order of Battle and detailed maps.

Macdonald, Lynn: *1915: The Death of Innocence*. New York: Henry Holt and Company, 1995. The story of several 1915 engagements in the words of the participants.

Warner, Philip: *The Battle of Loos*. Ware, Hertfordshire, England: Wordsworth Edition, 2000. A telling of the battle, organized by British army division.

Chapter Seven

Deadly Offensives
1916

After the stinging defeat of the Franco-Prussian War and the annexation of nearby Metz into the German Empire, the French began constructed concentric circles of stone fortifications around Verdun. Nine forts to the east of the Meuse River and ten to the west, augmented by scores of strongpoints, intermediary infantry shelters, artillery batteries, and ammunition depots, created the Région Fortifiée de Verdun.

During the initial German invasion of 1914, général Sarrail contradicted his orders and retained his forces at Verdun. The city became the focus of a large salient, around which the Western Front bent in its course from Belgium to the Swiss border. German efforts in 1914/5 to encircle and thus choke off the fortified region were defeated at Les Éparges and the Forêt d'Apremont. Germany did, however, interdict the main supply routes, and the region was constrained to a narrow-gauge rail line and a single roadway from Bar-le-Duc. Due to the devastating effect of German super heavy guns upon the Belgian forts at Liège and Antwerp, the French High Command had stripped the Verdun fortifications of men and transportable guns by 1915. The remaining garrison was much weaker than the Germans expected.

#24

Battle of Verdun
21 February to 19 December 1916

OBJECTIVE	To bleed the French Army to the point that France would sue for peace
FORCES	
FRENCH:	Initially two divisions of the Région Fortifiée de Verdun (général de division Frédéric Herr) growing to include sixty-six divisions of the Second Army (général de division Philippe Pétain, then général de division Robert Nivelle)
GERMAN:	Only six divisions launched the attack but grew to forty-two divisions of the Fifth Army (Generalleutnant Kronprinz Wilhelm von Preussen)
RESULT	An awful bloodbath without decisive victory
CASUALTIES	
FRENCH:	377,000–542,000 total casualties; 166,000 killed
GERMAN:	366,000–434,000 total casualties; 150,000 killed
LOCATION	Verdun-sur-Meuse is 270 km east of Paris; the battlefield is 7 km northeast of Verdun

In 1916, the Chief of the German General Staff, General Falkenhayn, believed that a massive German offensive was necessary to break the stalemate created by trench warfare. The opposing armies had already destroyed any opportunity for significant advance in both Flanders and Artois with heavy artillery bombardments, trench digging, and multiple lines of barbed wire. Falkenhayn's plan was to attack the French at a point that they would have to defend at all cost. He selected Verdun for that reason. His plan did not even require the capture of the city, just threatening it sufficiently to force a French counterattack, with the prediction that 'France will bleed to death.' He committed to the political leaders that he would call off the offensive if German casualties became greater than French.

Battle

An overnight snow squall had cleared by the morning of 21 February. At 07:15, 1,220 German cannon, including 13 of the super heavy 420-mm variety, began a furious nine-hour bombardment along an arc from Brabant-sur-Meuse to Ornes. German infantry then climbed out of their underground shelters and advanced rapidly through the wooden regions northeast of Verdun. Their *Sturmtroopen*, or assault troops, bypassed French strongpoints, which were to be cleared by the following infantry. The French 51st and 72nd Divisions were numbed by the ferocity of the bombardment, and the French commanders were similarly bewildered by the swiftness of the German advance.

By the evening of 24 February, the French second line had been breached, and 60 per cent of the men had been lost. Général de division Fernand de Langle de Cary, commander of Army Group Center, ordered the abandonment of the Woëvre Plain, believing his troops to be at risk of encirclement. The next day an event took place that even Falkenhayn could not have imagined. The key position in the entire Fortified Region of Verdun and the strongest fortification in Europe, Fort de Douaumont, was captured by a handful of Brandenburger infantry, who were driven into the fort to escape shelling from their own batteries.

Recriminations within the French command started immediately. Général Pétain was appointed commander of the French Second Army and given sweeping powers to restructure Verdun's defenses. Pétain took personal control of the artillery, established lines of resistance to be manned and defended at all costs, and created the massive supply operation which traveled along the sole highway available to Verdun, known after the war as *la Voie Sacrée*.

The German High Command failed to understand fully the French weakness and that the city was open for capture. French reinforcements started to arrive to strengthen the defenses, but the German front line had moved beyond the range of most of its artillery. As happened with most First World War offensives, the attacker's energy had been spent, and the advance ground to a halt 7 km short of the city.

French artillery batteries on the ridges along the west bank of the Meuse River were causing significant casualties within the German right flank. To relieve this danger, the Germans began the second stage of the Verdun offensive along a 10-km front from Brabant to Malancourt on 6 March. They advanced 4 km to the slopes of an aptly named hill, le Morte-Homme (the Dead Man), before being stopped by a spirited French counterattack. A deadly routine of bombardment, advance, counterattack, and retreat played out on the slopes of that hill and the adjacent Cote 304 for months until a German bombardment by 500 guns on 3 May obliterated any resistance and the Germans occupied the two hills.

Criticized by the French High Command for being too timid on the attack, général Pétain was promoted to command of Army Group Center, and général Nivelle assumed command of the forces at Verdun on 1 May. On 1 June, the Germans launched Operation 'May Cup' along a narrow 5-km front, intending to capture the final fortified positions between them and Verdun. After a week of

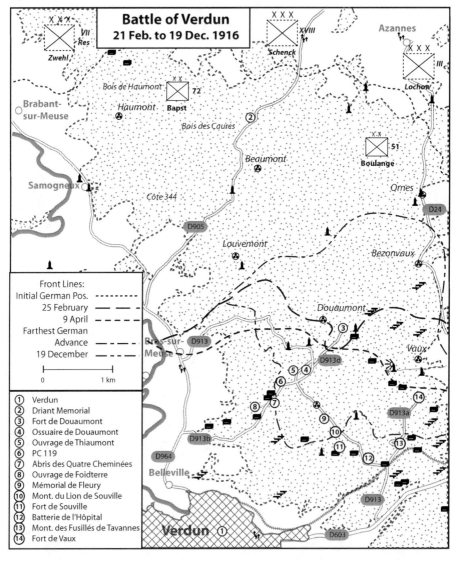

Battle of Verdun
21 Feb. to 19 Dec. 1916

Front Lines:
Initial German Pos. ----------
25 February —— ——
9 April —— ——
Farthest German
Advance —— · —— ·
19 December —— ·· ——

0   1 km

① Verdun
② Driant Memorial
③ Fort de Douaumont
④ Ossuaire de Douaumont
⑤ Ouvrage de Thiaumont
⑥ PC 119
⑦ Abris des Quatre Cheminées
⑧ Ouvrage de Foidterre
⑨ Mémorial de Fleury
⑩ Mont. du Lion de Souville
⑪ Fort de Souville
⑫ Batterie de l'Hôpital
⑬ Mont. des Fusillés de Tavannes
⑭ Fort de Vaux

fighting that cost the Germans 2,742 casualties, they captured Fort de Vaux. After a preliminary bombardment on 23 June that included their first use of phosgene gas,[1] the Germans sent seventeen regiments (50,000-70,000 men) against the remaining strongpoints at Thiaumont. Thiaumont fell, focused on Fort de Souville, the crucial battle that would decide the outcome at Verdun. Général Nivelle issued his stirring order of the day: '*Ils ne passeront pas!*' (They shall not pass!) – and the Germans did not. Although a few German troops later achieved the escarpment of Fort de Souville, the main defenses held. Weaker, and by now futile attempts to push forward, were defeated.

As early as April the Crown Prince had concluded that the continuation of the offensive was fruitless. Not until 28 August, however, did Falkenhayn, under pressure from his Kaiser, resign. Two heroes of the German forces on the Eastern Front now assumed command of the entire German Army. Generalfeldmarschall Paul von Hindenburg became Chief of the German General Staff and General der Infanterie Erich Ludendorff became the soon all-powerful First Quartermaster General. After a review of the battlefield several days later, Ludendorff ordered the German army at Verdun to adopt a flexible defensive posture.

Although suffering almost uncountable losses, the French Army had slowly established artillery and air superiority on the Verdun battlefield. On 24 October, they unleashed a 650-gun bombardment, preparing the way for a three-division assault which easily swept the annihilated German front line. Thiaumont, Fleury, and Douaumont were retaken in rapid succession. Fort de Vaux was abandoned as untenable against the French bombardments on 2 November.

Extensive infrastructure preparation preceded the next French move on 15 December. Eight divisions supported by 740 guns rapidly secured all objectives. On the eastern bank of the Meuse, the Germans had been pushed back, almost to near starting positions of February. The French had succeeded in retaining Verdun but the cost to both sides was unimaginable numbers of dead and wounded.

Battlefield Tour

The Verdun battlefield is along the Meuse River northeast of the provincial city. Four ridgelines provide a natural location for fortifications. Once a farming area with agricultural villages dotting the countryside, the battlefield today is heavily wooded. The combination of hilly terrain and military artifacts limits roadway access into and through the area. The statistical measures of the Verdun battle easily eclipse any other battlefield in any other war, except possibly the Somme. Over a 300-day period, 65 square kilometers of territory was shredded by 26 million artillery shells. Total casualty estimates range from 750,000 to over 1,000,000. Since the same ground was repeatedly fought over, a large number of the dead remained unburied, their remains still lying within the soil of Verdun. After the war, the entire site was declared a '*Zone Rouge*' by the French government because it was too dangerous to be inhabited or cleared. Nine villages were completely destroyed, and their ground was so peppered with unexploded munitions that they were never rebuilt. For all of

---

[1] The French had experimented with small amounts of the gas a few months earlier.

these reasons, the Verdun battlefield presents the most unique opportunity to witness the results of First World War warfare.

The battlefield sites are open at all times, the exceptions being guided tours of Forts Douaumont and Vaux, the Musée Mémorial de Verdun à Fleury and Ossuaire de Douaumont. Visitors are strongly advised not to touch or dislodge any munitions that might be found on the battlefield. Shells, grenades, or bullets could unexpectedly explode, causing injury or death. The removal of artifacts is strictly prohibited by French law, and severe penalties are applied for violations.

Verdun

The ancient city of Verdun dates back to Gallo-Roman times, when it was a wooden fortification situated upon a rock outcropping above the Meuse River. The Treaty of Verdun, which divided Charlemagne's Empire, was signed here in 843AD. Long part of an ecclesiastical domain, Verdun was on a hotly contested frontier and was not incorporated into France until 1552. Sébastien Vauban was responsible for building the town ramparts and citadel, but the town was nonetheless occupied by Prussians in 1792 and 1870.

Most sites of interest in Verdun are within an easy walk. An automobile is necessary to tour the battlefield; however, a number of one-day excursion tours are available. The Office of Tourisme is in the **place de la Nation** on the east bank of the Meuse River. Sharing the place de la Nation is the town's war memorial, a huge stone block in which are carved five figures representing the different branches of the French Army. Across the river is the **Porte Chaussée,** whose circular towers date from 1380 and through which many soldiers left the city for the battlefield. Verdun's commercial and historic center is visible directly across the river. Ample and convenient parking is available to the right, after crossing the bridge from the Office of Tourisme. The colossal **Monument de la Victoire** stands seventy-three steps above the city's commercial area in the place de la Liberation. The base of the obelisk is a chapel, in which three books record the names of the soldiers who participated in the defense of the city; its top is a mustached Gallic warrior, his hands resting upon the hilt of his sword. On the highest point in the city stands the **Cathédrale Notre-Dame,** which was started in 990 and modified numerous times in its long history. Columns supporting the crypt roof are carved with scenes of trench warfare. Farther to the west is the Vauban-designed **Verdun Citadel,** which offers a highly commercialized tour of its galleries. The **Carrefour des Maréchaux** stands in the fort's old moat and contains sixteen statues honoring marshals and generals from Napoleon's time to the First World War.

Verdun was never entered by German troops, although it underwent heavy shelling and suffered substantial damage. The recommended battlefield sites are northeast of the city and are located near each other with the exception of the command post of Colonel Emile Driant. They can be visited in any order, and many visitors may start with the fine Mémorial de Verdun à Fleury Museum. The tour below approximates the course of the German advance, starting with French field defenses at the time of the initial assault and coursing through the besieged strongpoints.

Leave Verdun to the north toward Belleville-sur-Meuse (D964) and continue along the east bank of the Meuse River through Bras-sur-Meuse. In Vacherauville bear right toward Ville-devant-Chaumont (D905) and continue 7 km to the Driant Memorial. Parking is ahead on the right.

Lieutenant-Colonel Emile Driant was a well-known and controversial figure who authored fictional war stories and served in the French parliament. He also made enemies by protesting the inadequacies of Verdun's defenses. On 21 February, 1,200 members of his 56th and 59th Battalions de Chasseurs à Pied occupied the Bois des Caures when the German bombardment began. The heavy shelling dropped 80,000 shells on a relatively small area, almost obliterating Driant's strongpoints. Reduced to 400 survivors, the colonel's men fought a delaying action against XVIII Corps, which continued into the next day. A second artillery barrage was followed by the assault of an entire German corps, which poured through gaps blown in the French line and captured position after position, despite suffering heavy casualties from Driant's well-placed machine guns.

After beating back several assaults by forces ten times their size, and holding to the last possible moment, a nearly encircled Driant and approximately eighty survivors left Driant's command bunker to seek shelter to the south in Beaumont. Driant stopped several hundred meters from the bunker to assist a wounded chasseur when a German machine gun tapped out its deadly staccato. The colonel was heard to exclaim '*Mon Dieu*' before he fell dead. His stubborn defense of the Verdun perimeter and sudden death made him an instant hero and symbol of the sacrifices of Verdun. Only 118 of his men survived, but they had upset the German timetable and inflicted serious casualties.

The rough stone **Driant Memorial** near the parking area commemorates the men of Driant's battalions and marks his final resting place. Across the road from the memorial, a path into the trees leads to a brick memorial marking the place where he fell. A path continues another 380 meters to the simple cross that marks the provisional grave where Driant was buried by the Germans immediately after his death. His personal effects and the facts of his death were forwarded to his widow by the wife of a German artillery officer through Swiss diplomats.

The sector is well-maintained for visitors, with several paths from the memorial to **Colonel Driant's command post**. Access into the command post is permitted from the west side, now marked by a huge chestnut tree. Inside are four bare rooms, and the concrete roof of the west end is partially collapsed from the blow of a German shell. The gun embrasures on the east side are all but obscured by vegetation, but they show the damage from the attack. The site is removed from the more popular central battlefield, but its solitude and state of preservation as well as the heroics of the chasseurs recommend a visit.

Reverse direction and return to Vacherauville. Turn south back toward Verdun (D964) and proceed to Bras-sur-Meuse.

French artillery batteries along the heights on the opposite side of the river had German forces within their range. Eliminating those guns caused the Germans to extend the battlefront to the west bank with the assault upon Morte-Homme in March 1916.

Before Bras-sur-Meuse center, turn left toward Fort de Douaumont (D913). Turn left toward Fort de Douaumont (D913d).

This sector is the most visited part of the battlefield. The Abri des Pélérins Café offers the only refreshments available on the battlefield. Picnicking is allowed only in designated sites.

Trenches, abri, and individual monuments abound in this area and numerous additional stops are possible. The *Association Nationale du Souvenir de la Bataille de Verdun* (ANSBV) has erected explanatory panels around the battlefield, most of which are trilingual. The roadway follows the route of the narrow-gauge railway once used to supply the fort.

Fort de Douaumont was constructed in 1885 upon a hill which overlooked ravines radiating from it in numerous directions. Its original limestone exterior was later strengthened by the application of 2.5 meters of reinforced concrete to survive the effects of newly developed explosives. The roof mounted 75-mm and 155-mm guns under retractable turrets, two machine-gun bells of 15-cm thick armor plate, and

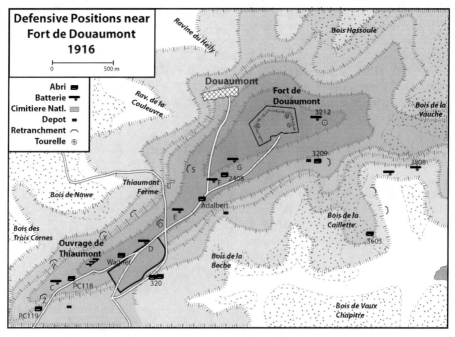

several observation bells. The entire fort was surrounded by a six-meter deep ditch, whose exterior corners held machine gun galleries. The superstructure housed a complex of storage rooms, barracks for 1,000 men, a bakery, and a hospital, with tunnels connecting them all. When the Germans attacked, it was grossly undermanned with only fifty territorial troops.

On 25 February, German infantry was approaching the fort and noticed its decidedly weak defensive fire. They sought shelter in the fort's ditch from a French machine gun, which was firing from the steeple of the church in the nearby village of Douaumont, and from German shelling of the fort. After climbing into the ditch through a hole in its iron fence, they scrambled up the glacis and entered the fort through an unguarded doorway. A second party of German troops entered through a machine-gun embrasure and captured the team operating the fort's 155-mm gun. The two German teams proceeded into the depths of the fort, and the French defenders, thinking that they were vastly outnumbered, quickly surrendered. The strongest fortification on the Verdun battlefield was suddenly in German hands with hardly a shot having been fired.

The Germans rapidly manned Douaumont and created embrasures to fire toward the French. An attempt to retake the fort the next day failed. Although frequently bombarded, the fort's roof was not penetrated until 24 October, when a shell from a newly arrived French 400-mm railroad gun caused an immense internal explosion. French colonial infantry attacked and quickly captured the stunned defenders.

Fort de Douaumont and its exterior concrete shell are now a grassy mound that is hardly recognizable as a military structure. Paths allow an ascent to the roof, however, which presents the panoramic views that made this location important defensively as well as the remains of the guns that made it a formidable installation. The 155-mm gun turret is frozen partially up and a machine-gun turret is fully up. Observation bells still exist, and the crater from the French shell that pierced the fort is still evident. Carefully avoid metal barbed wire supports, chunks of destroyed concrete, and other debris. The outline of the fort's ditch is discernible if the undergrowth has been recently cut. The long, narrow open area in the front is an active French army gunnery range.

The guided tour inside the fort does not access all of the galleries due to internal damage and structural weakness. The 155-mm gun's turret hardware, however, is still present as is the counterweight system which raised and lowered the gun. The depressingly crowded barrack galleries retain their metal bed frames. One gallery ends in a memorial to the 679 German soldiers, who were killed in a chain-reaction of internal explosions in May 1916. Unfortunately, only French and German are spoken, but a paper copy of the tour in English is available. The experience is unforgettable. Hours vary considerably by month: February and March from 10:00 to 13:00 and 14:00 to 17:00; April to August from 10:30 to 18:30; September and October from 10:00 to 13:00 and 14:00 to 17:30; November and December from 10:00 to 12:00 and 14:00 to 17:00. Closed in January. Fee.

Reverse direction and return to the ossuary.

The **Ossuaire de Douaumont** and adjoining French cemetery are located at what once was the Ferme Thiaumont. This intersection of two ridges includes the Ouvrage de Thiaumont and PC 118. The entire area was the scene of the most intense combat of the battle. Bavarian infantry captured the farm grounds and the ouvrage on 8 June, but possession was contested until 8 August, during which period it changed hands sixteen times. The site was permanently retaken during the French advance in October.

After the war the battlefield retained the remains of thousands of unidentifiable soldiers. The ossuary was constructed as a last resting place and monument to the futility of war. It is in the shape of a tunnel with a 50-meter artillery shell-shaped tower in the center. Inside are thirty-six vaults, one for each sector of the battlefield and in which were placed the bones of 130,000 French and German soldiers. Two additional vaults at either end of the ossuary contain additional remains. The interior has an appropriately solemn, funereal atmosphere. A small Catholic chapel has stained glass windows representing scenes from the fighting. The tower section has a small but useful bookshop, a film room showing footage of the battlefield, and access to the tower observation room, from which restricted views over the battlefield are possible. At the rear of the building is a row of windows permitting views of the soldiers' bones in the vaults. Public toilets are in a separate building behind the ossuary. The ossuary is open in December and February from 14:00 to 17:00; March from 09:00 to 12:00 and 14:00 to 17:30; April from 09:00 to 18:00; May to August from 09:00 to 18:30; September from 09:00 to 12:00 and 14:00 to 18:00; October from 09:00 to 12:00 and 14:00 to 17:30; November from 09:00 to 12:00 and 14:00 to 17:00. Closed in January. No admission charge for the ossuary; fee for movie and tower admission

Spread across the slope in front of the ossuary is the **Nécropole, Nationale de Douaumont,** which contains an additional 15,000 French graves. A large stone, which was supposed to be the location of the grave of général Philippe Pétain, sits in the front center of the cemetery. Due to his subsequent disgrace during the Second World War – when he led the Nazi-sympathetic Vichy government – controversy has prohibited his burial there. One corner contains the graves of Muslim soldiers, whose headstones are aligned to face Mecca.

Walk across the parking area to the west. The large **Wall of Remembrance** honors Jewish volunteers who fell while fighting for France. Across the shell-cratered field behind the wall is **Ouvrage de Thiaumont**. The small French strongpoint held only a handful of soldiers and mounted only a single machine-gun tower, but as an observation point at the critical junction of the Froideterre and Souville ridges, it was unsurpassed. The German preliminary bombardment of 6 May pierced the structure with a 420-mm shell. After the German attack of 23 June, it changed hands eight times until finally coming under German control.

The massive shelling of 1916 has left only a mound of broken concrete and twisted steel reinforcement bars. The destruction is almost complete and the remains are unrecognizable. A perilous climb onto its roof presents a table of orientation that shows the outline of the original structure along with distances and directions to nearby sites. The thick iron fragment behind the Casemate de Bourges is a segment of the machine-gun bell. The site can be hazardous, so be careful.

Immediately to the west is an example of one of the many abris or infantry shelters, to be found on the Verdun battlefield. This one was designed to house one-half of a company, or one hundred men, although that is difficult to discern in its present condition. Commonly called **PC 118** for *Poste de Commandement*[2], the position was taken by the Germans on 23 June. French counterattacks continued through July and into August in unbelievably bloody fighting. Now only vegetation-covered, broken concrete, the roof has two stone crosses to soldiers who disappeared in the fighting.

Leave the ossuary area and go to the roundabout to the south. Proceed toward Froideterre (D913b).

After 500 meters in the wood on the rise to the right is **PC 119**, a more complete example of a French abri. These shelters were not intended to be strongpoints but rather to provide protection for infantry from enemy shelling. They frequently were used as dressing stations for the wounded and resting points for messengers traveling across the exposed ground. This abri was attacked by Bavarian troops on 23 June, and the struggle for control continued throughout the summer. Signboards describe the abri, its function, and the ghastly fighting that occurred here. Although struck by large caliber shells, the abri's 2-meter thick roof and walls have survived, and it can be entered – although at some risk. Its three interior rooms held one hundred men and provided a kitchen area and commander's office; the latrine was external. On the signpost is a description of this area shortly after being retaken by the French but still under German fire:

> The bunker is a reinforced concrete redoubt which is reduced to a pile of rubble. The men crowd into it like salt herrings in a barrel and every inch of space in every corner of the chamber is occupied by the C-in-C's, the staff officers, the telephonists, pioneers, the runners, the liaison officers, the medical corps, etc. The troops pour into the outstretched arms of every opening and every crack. Their eyes expressionless – filled with the horrors that they have seen, their faces taunt with the superhuman suffering they have to bear. There is also the screams and heartrending cry of seriously wounded men, probably a mutilated soldier suffocating in the midst of the crowd of human beings.

A sentier continues along the ridge above the highway and eventually accesses Ouvrage de Froideterre in the course of passing several less dangerously

---

[2] PC118 is also called FT4 for the fourth abri between the strongpoints of Froideterre and Thiaumont; other structures are also so named.

damaged abris.

Continue on D913b.

Ahead on the left is the **Abris des Quatre Cheminées**, named for the four ventilation shafts which protrude above the 10-meter deep, underground bunker. This shelter was larger and more substantial than PC 119. It held a brigade headquarters with barracks for 350 men and a hospital. The Bavarians also attained this location in their advance of 23 June. Although in possession of the roof and entrances, they were not able to enter the abri. Four days of fighting ensued, with the German troops dropping hand grenades down the ventilation shafts. The attackers were finally driven off by shelling from the guns of Ouvrage de Froideterre 600 meters away.

The shelter entrances are not visible from the roadway because they are on the back slope of the ridgeline. The entrance gates are usually open, but signs warn of the potential hazard and prohibit entry to the 75-meter deep galleries. Guardhouses stand beside each of the two entrances and are in remarkably good condition, considering their age and history.

Continue to the access road to Ouvrage de Froideterre and proceed to the fortification.

Ouvrage de Froideterre was constructed between 1895 and 1905 on a spur of ground overlooking the Meuse Valley. Originally a simple shelter, it was expanded to include one turret housing two 75-mm guns and a machine-gun turret. Casemate des Bourges[3] were also added housing additional 75-mm guns to protect the French forts on the other side of the Meuse. The entire fortification was surrounded by a 10-meter wide and 5-meter deep ditch. In the June assault, German troops surrounded the structure and mounted the roof but were beaten off by machine-gun fire. Continued bombardment was unable to silence the fort's guns, and efforts to capture it were abandoned. Possession of Froideterre would have opened the Meuse valley to the Germans and almost certainly led to the fall of Verdun.

Froideterre did not suffer the extensive damage of Douaumont or Fort de Vaux and therefore presents the image of a Verdun fortification as it looked in 1916. The site is not as heavily visited as other sites. No guided tours are offered, but a walk around the fort and across its roof provides a stunning image of 1916 combat. The roof has a table of orientation, and its shell-pocked retractable turret is permanently up. A 75-mm gun remains in the Casemate des Bourges. Beware of the largely eroded ditch because numerous sharp stakes that were used to support the barbed wire entanglements protrude from the grass. Water-filled shell craters are in abundance. Replanted forests now block views of the Meuse, but it is only 2.5 km to the west.

---

[3] Casemate des Bourges were reinforced concrete bunker which contained guns in a staggered arrangement to provide flanking fire.

> Return to the roundabout south of the ossuary and turn toward Fleury-devant-Douaumont, which appears shortly on the right.

In 1916 **Fleury-devant-Douaumont** was a village slightly larger than most in the area. It was located on a section of high ground between Douaumont and Fort de Souville. Four regiments of German Alpine troops captured the village on 23 June, but a French counterattack retook the eastern part. With the village partially controlled by each side, a desperate struggle ensued, replete with intense artillery bombardments, bayonet charges, and massive assaults. The French finally captured the remainder after an assault by French Alpine Chasseurs and Moroccan Colonial Infantry on 17 August. The village changed hands sixteen times and was completely obliterated in the process.

Fleury is one of nine destroyed villages on the Verdun battlefield to be declared a *village détruit* and never rebuilt, except for a memorial chapel. Fleury is the most easily accessed and receives a good share of visitors. Fleury chapel has been renamed Notre-Dame de l'Europe and stands in memory of the 1,796 officers and men of the French 39th Regiment who died here. A few stones protruding from the ground are the only indication that a farming community once stood here. Small signs discretely mark the houseless village streets and the occupations of their inhabitants. Trees occupy the shell craters and provide peacefulness to the setting.

> Continue 500 meters to the Mémorial de Verdun à Fleury.

Originally the site of the Fleury train station, the **Mémorial de Verdun à Fleury** museum and monument was built by a private veterans foundation after the war. The entrance stairs are framed by several cannons and wartime vehicles. Inside is a high-quality collection of Verdun battlefield artifacts, propaganda materials, soldiers' artwork, and a life-sized re-creation of a section of Verdun trench using original materials. A theater presents English- and German-captioned filmstrips about the war. The lower level has larger items, including a French 75-mm gun and a German Maxim machine gun. All materials are identified in three languages. The museum is a good first stop if a battlefield overview or bookstore materials are desired. The museum is open in February and March from 09:00 to 12:00 and 13:00 to 18:00; April to August from 09:00 to 18:00; and September to mid-December from 09:00 to 12:00 and 14:00 to 18:00. Closed from mid-December to 31 January. Fee.

Continue to the next intersection, where the **Monument du Lion de Souville** is located. Parking nearby is difficult, and a walk from Fleury or from the parking area for Fort de Souville is recommended. The statue of a recumbent lion marks the farthest penetration of the German assault of 23 June, even though later research indicates that German troops did reach the roof of Fort de Souville. It was erected by the veterans of the French 130th Division who were garrisoned in Souville. The ground around the intersection is still marked by water-filled shell craters.

Continue ahead (D913) past Fort de Souville (not visible from the roadway) to the parking area, where trilingual signboards describe the fighting and display maps of the forest paths.

Fort de Souville was constructed of earthen-covered limestone in 1877. Modernization continued up to 1916. The main armament was a turret with two 155-mm cannons. Its position atop a ravine that leads down to Verdun made it the last major fortification between the Germans and the city in the summer of 1916. The fall of Souville meant the capture of Verdun. Bombardments by German 380-mm and 420-mm cannons disabled much of the fort's defenses. On 23 June, the German 103rd Division attacked but failed to capture the fort. In early July German Alpine Troops held the crossroads now identified by the Monument du Lion and launched an early morning attack on the fort. By 06:00, 150 Germans were on the fort roof when a French Chasseur counterattack drove them off amid the chaos of gas and high-explosive shells.

Since the location was critical to French defenses even after the battle, Fort de Souville underwent modifications before the end of the war. Three **Casemates de Pamard**[4] were added, including the one visible from the roadway. The earth-covered fort is barely discernible in the wood that now covers the site. By proceeding from the table of orientation, however, and following the Sentier de Souville, which follows the chemin de D S2 for a short distance, several interesting elements of the fort are accessible.

The **Tourelle Jumelée** was a disappearing turret designed by Lieutenant-Colonel Bussière. It held the fort's two 155-mm guns and first engaged the enemy on 24 February. An accidental internal explosion on 10 April rendered it inoperative until March 1917. The turret is in the full down position, but despite the German bombardments of the fort, it remains intact. To the right of the turret are an observation bell and the third Casemate de Pamard.

The dramatic **Entrée de Guerre** is deeply hidden by the re-grown forest on the sheltered, Verdun-facing side of the fort. The arched entrance is flanked by the latrine and washstand. Rifle embrasures to protect the entrance from enemy infiltration are evident as well as a large 'Keep Out' sign indicative of the dangers within the fort. The small gullies behind the fort hold numerous ammunition niches, some of which serviced open-air batteries located in the forest.

Continue on the D913.

On the left is a sentier that leads through the wood to the **Batterie de l'Hôpital**, a ruin of brick casemates from which French gunners defended Fort de

---

[4] A Casemate de Pamard, named after its inventor, is a small steel cupola mounted in concrete, which is designed to deflect incoming shells. Twenty-three such machine-gun positions were installed at Verdun.

Douaumont. The site was never captured but frequently came under artillery fire. The remains of earth-covered stone arches stretch about 250 meters along the forest path.

Continue along the path to the Batterie du Tunnel or return to the car and proceed to the next intersection.

On the left, amid one of the approved picnic areas on the battlefield, is the **Batterie du Tunnel**. This very solid structure housed French guns.

Follow the signs toward Fort de Vaux (D913a); after 1.3 km on a hairpin curve is a crushed-stone road to the right.

The road descends into the glade where the **Monument des Fusillés de Tavannes** stands. In August 1944, the German Gestapo executed one Belgian and fifteen French civilians at this spot and buried their mutilated bodies in the pit now encircled by the chain fence.

At the end of the road is Fort de Vaux.

Similar to but smaller than Fort de Douaumont, **Fort de Vaux** was more heavily contested. Early in the battle on 26 February, a German 420-mm shell destroyed the 75-mm gun turret. Two weeks later German infantry attacked as part of a brutal three-month effort to capture the fort, losing entire regiments to French rifle fire. German engineers reached the roof of the fort on 2 June, after most of the supporting batteries in the surrounding forests had been eliminated. French machine guns took a terrible toll before baskets of grenades lowered into a casemate blasted openings in the fort. One of the most gruesome actions of the war then began, with the opponents using every weapon from grenades to pick axes to flamethrowers in a deadly fight that ranged through the now-darkened galleries of the fort's interior. For six days French soldiers built sandbag blockades every few meters along the tunnels. The number of defenders slowly dwindled from the original 670 along with the drinkable water. The air turned fetid from human waste and decaying bodies. A final carrier pigeon message flew through poison gas with a message requesting immediate relief, but reinforcements were unable to fight their way through the surrounding Germans. Exhausted and without any means of continued resistance, the decimated garrison finally surrendered on 7 June. In a fitting tribute, the victorious Germans recognized and honored the survivors as they marched into captivity. A French assault on 25 October was stopped by massed German machine guns, but by then the heavily damaged and outflanked fort was untenable. The Germans abandoned it on 2 November. One French stretcher-bearer described the shell holes around Vaux, each of which contained at least one corpse:

Some, mown down in a bayonet charge, still clutch their rifle butts. Others have been felled at their machine-gun posts. Human remains everywhere, mangled limbs. Sticking out of the half-flattened trench we are following, here, there, an arm, a leg, a head.[5]

Vaux presents a picture of destruction much like Douaumont. Crushed by artillery, its façade and walls are barely recognizable. Near the entrance are commemorative plaques dedicated to the defenders as well as to the pigeon. On the right a Casemate des Bourges still contains its 75-mm gun. A destroyed section of the wall gives access to the roof. The 75-mm turret is in the raised position. Strewn about are enormous shards of iron blasted from the central observation post. Dangerously hidden pieces of reinforcement bar protrude from the surface. Fort de Douaumont is visible to the northwest, and the Woëvre Plain is to the east. Guided tours of the interior are offered, and they visit dormitories, the reconstructed commander's office, chapel, Casemate des Bourges, and interior passageways. Vaux is open February and March from 10:00 to 12:00 and 14:00 to 17:00; April to June from 10:00 to 18:30; July and August from 09:00 to 18:30; and September to December from 10:00 to 12:00 and 13:00 to 17:30. Closed in January.

Return to the intersection with the D913 and turn left toward Verdun. At the intersection with the National Road, turn right toward Verdun (N3) and return to the city.

Other Sites of Interest: The eight other *villages détruit* are poignant reminders of the effects of the battle on civilians. Monuments are found in the forest or along the roadside, including one to **André Maginot**, defender of French war veterans and after whom the defense line of the Second World War is named. The **Tranchée des Baïonnettes** commemorates two battalions of French infantry instantly interred by German shelling. On the opposite bank of the Meuse are the monument to *La Voie Sacrée* and the battlefields around **le Morte-Homme** and **Cote 304**. To the north and west are German military cemeteries, many containing personal or unit monuments from early in the war. A German experimental construction camp in the forest near Spincourt is nearly intact, and the site of the German super heavy **380-mm 'Gros Max' cannon** is in the Bois de Warphémont. French cemeteries surround Verdun, including the massive **Faubourg Pavé,** which has a circle of 75-mm cannon as well as memorials to French civilians executed by the Germans and to allied aviators. Other fortifications on both sides of the river remain in various states of decay or collapse.

---

[5] Ian Ousby, *The Road to Verdun* (New York: Doubleday, 2002), 323.

#25

Somme Offensive
1 July to 18 November 1916

OBJECTIVE	To break through three German positions and capture Bapaume thereby relieving pressure on the French at Verdun and possibly clearing occupation forces all the way to the French frontier.
FORCES	
BRITISH:	Twenty infantry divisions, 1,437 guns and 486 aeroplanes of Fourth Army (General Sir Henry Rawlinson) and Reserve / Fifth Army (General Sir Hubert Gough)
FRENCH:	Six infantry divisions of Sixth Army (général de division Emile Fayolle) and Tenth Army (général de division Joseph Micheler)
GERMAN:	Six infantry divisions of Second Army (General der Infanterie Friedrich von Below).
RESULT	The Allies captured 130 square kilometers, but nothing strategically important.
CASUALTIES	
BRITISH:	419,654
FRENCH:	194,451
GERMAN:	The initial allied estimate after the battle was 600,000 but the number has declined with further analysis.
LOCATION	Albert is 150 km north of Paris

The 1915 allied assaults upon German defensive positions achieved little besides casualties. Firmly ensconced on French territory, the Germans prepared for permanent occupation, while the French and British struggled to find the formula to evict them. During the winter coordination meetings between French and British commanders, their attention turned to a quiet sector in the Somme. General Haig preferred an attack against the Ypres Salient because it was closer to the Channel ports and his supply lines. Bowing to political pressure, however, Haig deferred to the French plan on the Somme. The February 1916 German Offensive at Verdun lessened the French commitment to the Somme Offensive, and the action became a predominantly British affair.

The British plan called for an attack along a 20-km front from north of Serre to the junction with the French Sixth Army at Maricourt. The hilly region north of the Somme River was bisected by the Albert-Bapaume highway. The sluggish Ancre River ran through a flooded, weed-filled valley. Above the Ancre, the heavily cultivated fields were dotted with unremarkable villages, farms, and sugar beet refineries. Being a former cavalry officer, Haig thought that once the trench line was broken, the terrain was ideal for cavalry to sweep through the enemy's rear. German defenses north of the highway, however, were among the strongest on the Western Front; their first position consisted of three trench lines protected by extensive wire entanglements, with a second position 2 to 5 kilometers to the rear, and a third

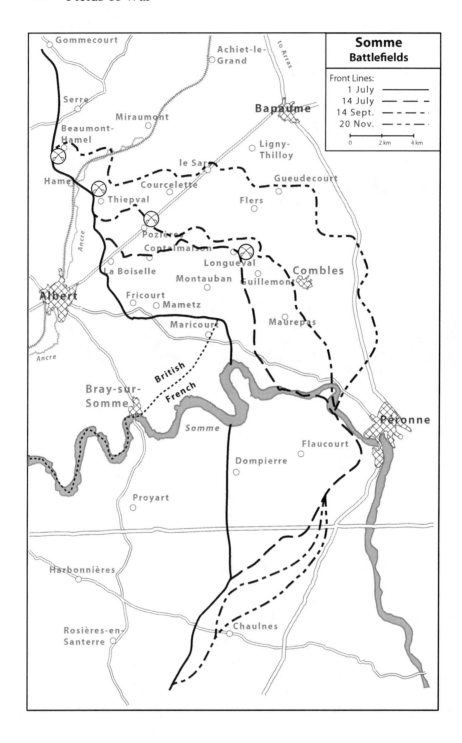

position under construction farther back. The French Sixth Army, now relegated to a subsidiary role, was to attack on either side of the Somme river valley to the south.

The initial attack force was to be the eleven divisions – six of which had never seen combat – of General Rawlinson's British Fourth Army. This assault was the first test of 'Kitchener's Army,' volunteers who answered the call of Kitchener. In a historic departure from Britain's traditional professional army, recruits joined battalions formed almost exclusively from their local community, trade, or factory.

Haig thought that the key to overcoming the stalemate of trench warfare was a preponderance of artillery. He amassed over fourteen hundred guns to prepare the battleground for seven days with artillery bombardment. Although the use of shrapnel shells proved ineffective against wire and dugouts, the bombardments did destroy German trenches and communications as well as constrained supplies and reinforcements. Its effect upon German troops was punishing, as revealed by a German infantryman, 'Five days and nights now this hell concert has lasted. One's head is like a madman's; the tongue sticks to the roof of the mouth. Almost nothing to eat and nothing to drink. No sleep.'[6] Unfortunately, Haig's artillery was inadequate to contend with the deep dugouts that Below's men had built.

At 07:30 on 1 July 1916, British infantry, confident of an easy victory, left their forward positions, intending to walk across no man's land and occupy the battered German positions. Upon the cessation of the artillery bombardment, German infantry raced from their dugouts, mounted their machine guns, and placed a withering stream of fire upon the attackers as wave after wave fell. In the northern sector, entire formations were destroyed before even engaging the enemy. Some units were all but wiped out in the first few minutes of the battle.

The British advance was more successful on the line from Fricourt to Maricourt, although casualties were still high. Brilliantly utilizing the creeping barrage and crossing a narrower no man's land, they captured the villages of Mametz and Montauban. Fricourt, now out-flanked, was abandoned during the night. On the first day of the Somme Offensive, however, British casualties exceeded 58,000 men, a slaughter unparalleled in British military history. German losses were estimated at only 8,000. Successfully using small unit tactics and accurate counter-battery fire, the French achieved their first-day objectives.

Despite the first day's staggering losses, Haig continued the offensive for four and one half months, converting the planned breakout into a battle of attrition, with the objective of destroying the enemy's ability to resist. Haig repeatedly launched assaults, including the first use of British tanks, against various German positions until the autumnal rains made the ground impassable. The German first and second lines were overcome, and the third line was penetrated, but the objective of Bapaume was never accomplished. The losses to the three nations were staggering – a total of over one million men. The British Army of volunteers was all but destroyed, and the government was later forced to resort to conscription to fill the ranks. The German army suffered a loss of unit commanders and trained NCOs that was unrecoverable. British strategy and tactics are still questioned, and disagreement

---

[6] Lyn Macdonald, *Somme* (London: Michael Joseph, 1983), 49.

about the impact of the offensive on the capacity of the Germans to continue the war still exists.

The Somme battlefield has retained a primary place in the memory of the British people, and it is one of the most revered and visited battlefields in Europe, second only to the Ypres Salient. The impact upon communities throughout the British Empire was felt for generations, and those losses are commemorated in numerous monuments, both impressive and simple, which were constructed to honor the acts of bravery and condemn those of butchery.

The landscape has mostly returned to its agricultural roots; tractors moving between barns and fields frequently slow the pace of traffic. The four Somme locations below have military significance as well as commemorate the sacrifices that took place. The Newfoundland Memorial Park commemorates the first day's horrendous losses, when the experienced 29th Division fell in front of the machine guns of one German regiment. The Thiepval Memorial, in the heart of the German defenses along the Ancre River, commemorates all those who fell 'with no known grave.' Pozières village and Mouquet farm were captured by Australian and Canadian forces at a great cost. Delville Wood typifies the violent struggle to capture a forest tract against a determined German oppo-sition; its memorial and museum commemorate South Africa's sacrifices in all wars.

Battle of Beaumont-Hamel
1 July to 13 November 1916

OBJECTIVE	To capture the German's first and second positions around Beaumont-Hamel
FORCES	
BRITISH:	29th Division (Major-General Henry de Beauvoir de Lisle)
GERMAN:	Reserve Infantry Regiment Nr 119 (Oberstleutnant Freiherr von Ziegesar)
RESULT	Complete failure with disastrous casualties
CASUALTIES	
BRITISH:	5,267
GERMAN:	423
LOCATION	Albert is 150 km north of Paris; Beaumont-Hamel is 9 km north of Albert

The regular army British 29th Division arrived on the Western Front to face the experienced German Reserve Infantry Regiment Nr 119 across Hawthorn Ridge. In the valley behind the ridge is the village of Beaumont-Hamel, its cellars and ravines a maze of underground tunnels constructed during the twenty months that the German Württemberg Regiment had been there. Hawthorn Redoubt, which dominated the Beaumont-Auchonvillers road 400 meters to the north, presented British commanders with an especially difficult objective. Welsh miners spent the winter tunneling under the redoubt and packing it with 40,000 pounds of ammonal explosive.

Given the week's-long artillery bombardment, the Germans could guess that an assault was coming. Sheltering in crowded dugouts 30 feet underground while deafening artillery explosions rattled both men and equipment was not pleasant, but the dugouts did offer the chance of survival; on the surface the landscape was churned by hot metal and shrouded in smoke.

Battle

At 07:20 on 1 July 1916, Hawthorn mine erupted in a violent explosion that blew earth, chalk, debris, and men into the air, creating a crater 50 meters in diameter and 15 meters deep. Hawthorn Redoubt was destroyed, killing two platoons of the 119th Regiment and trapping a third underground. Two platoons of Royal Fusiliers quickly rushed forward through a cloud of black smoke to occupy the near rim of the crater. German troops, rapidly exiting from their bunkers, also rushed forward to occupy the opposite rim. Calling for defensive artillery support, German flares illuminated the sky. A deadly fight for the still-smouldering earth commenced. By afternoon the British survivors were driven out by trench mortar fire, their reinforcements having been cut down by machine-gun fire.

The explosion had inexplicably resulted in the cessation of artillery fire along the entire front line manned by the British VIII Corps. At 07:30, 86th and 87th Brigades of the 29th Division used scaling ladders to surmount the parapets and started their trek across no man's land; each man carried sixty pounds of ammunition, food, trenching tools, and grenades. The 2nd South Wales Borderers targeted a bulge in the German trench line that was supported by deep dugouts in the sides of a depression known as Y-Ravine. Many of them did not survive the day. The German defenders won the race for the parapet, their Maxim machine guns cut down swathes of the heavily burdened and slowly walking men, who were easy targets because they were channeled into the open lanes in their own wire or they were struggling to cut the German wire. The German barrage caused heavy losses and delayed the second wave battalions – the 1st Borders, 16th Middlesex, and 1st KOSB – from leaving their trenches until 07:55. Few men survived to reach the German front line. A private watching from the command bunker described the field as 'a proper trap for our boys as the enemy just set the sights of the machine guns on the gaps in the barbed wire and fired.'[7]

Mistaking German signal flares for those of his men, General de Lisle believed that the lead battalions had been successful, and he ordered the reserve 88th Brigade to press the attack. The 801 members of the battalion-sized 1st Newfoundland Regiment had marched through the night from their rearward positions to occupy reserve trenches behind the first wave 2nd South Wales Borderers and second wave 1st Border battalions. At 09:15, the Newfoundland Regiment left St. John's Road trench; their objective was the German second position along the

---

[7] Anthony J. Stacey, *Memoirs of A. J. Stacey, a Newfoundlander at War* (Goulds, Newfoundland: the Staceys, 1986)

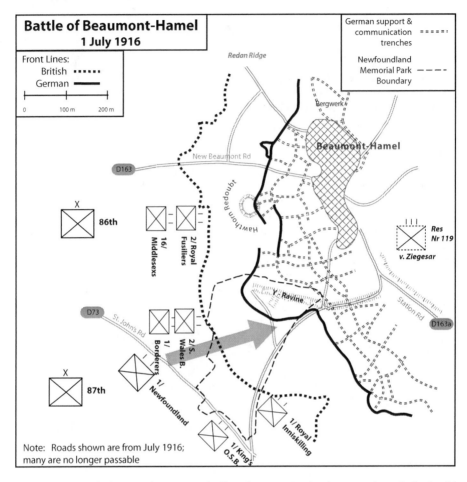

Battle of Beaumont-Hamel
1 July 1916

Front Lines:
British ·······
German ▬▬▬

0   100 m   200 m

German support &
communication ≡≡≡≡≡
trenches

Newfoundland
Memorial Park ▬ ▬ ▬
Boundary

Redan Ridge

Bergwerk

Beaumont-Hamel

New Beaumont Rd

D163

X
86th

16/ Middlesex

2/ Royal Fusiliers

Hawthorn Redoubt

Res Nr 119
v. Ziegesar

Y-Ravine

Station Rd

D163a

D73

St. John's Rd

1/ Borders

2/ S. Wales B.

X
87th

1/ Newfoundland

1/ King's O.S.B.

1/ Royal Inniskilling

Note: Roads shown are from July 1916;
many are no longer passable

Beaucourt Road almost 5 km east. Finding the communication trenches choked with dead and wounded, their commander, Lieutenant-Colonel Arthur Hadow, ordered his men to leave the relative safety of the trenches and continue the advance in the open. The Newfoundlanders were now the only troops moving over open ground, and they were exposed to the full fire of German machine guns of Redan Ridge, Y-Ravine, and Station Road embankment. Since they started from behind the front trench line, the additional ground they had to cover contributed to their losses. Few soldiers progressed more that 100 meters, most did not even attain no man's land. Those able to pass the forward trenches doggedly continued toward the 'danger tree,' a single stump in an otherwise open field that marked a forward observation post. The survivors were too few in number to press home the attack. General de Lisle described the scene as 'a magnificent display of trained and disciplined valour, and its assault only failed of success because dead men can advance no further.'[8] The

---

[8] Major-General Sir Beauvoir de Lisle, Commander of the British 29th Division reporting on the 1st

regiment lost 710 men in less than 30 minutes. There would be no further 29th Division assaults that day.

During the short night of mid-summer France, the moans of wounded men were punctuated by short bursts of fire or the sharp glare of Very lights[9]. An unstated truce allowed British stretcher-bearers to move about no man's land. Some wounded British soldiers were taken into German lines for treatment. The roads leading to the rear areas were choked with walking wounded and stretchers. Dressing stations treated cases as best they could, surgeons often making the butcher's decision of amputation or death. The next morning the two armies warily eyed each other across no man's land. A quiet settled over the ground along with the morning mist.

In this sector the assault was a total failure. The front lines had not moved, and the positions were to remain essentially unchanged until the last dreary days of the offensive, when the 51st (Highland) Division finally captured Beaumont-Hamel on 13 November.

Battlefield Tour

Leave Albert north toward Aveluy (D50); after approximately 7 km, turn left toward Auchonvillers, also signed as Mémorial terre-neuvien de Beaumont-Hamel (D73).

Newfoundland, a British territory at the time, selected 30 hectares (75 acres) of Hawthorn Ridge after the war as the site of the **Beaumont-Hamel Newfoundland Memorial**. The battlefield starts in what is now the parking area that is across the roadway from the main entrance. The jagged white line painted on the pavement represents the location of St. John's Road trench and the sheltered starting positions. At the entrance to the site is the red triangle of the 29th Division and an epitaph composed by John Oxenham which ends:

> For not one foot of this dank sod
> But drank its surfeit of the blood of gallant men
> Who for their Faith, their Hope, for Life and Liberty
> Here made the sacrifice.
> Here gave their lives, and right willingly for you and me.

The ground is truly hallowed because approximately 200-300 dead remain unrecovered beneath the surface.

A **bronze caribou** – the Newfoundlanders' regimental symbol – is sited atop a mound of native rock and shrubs near what once was the location of the battalion headquarters dugout. One of five on the Western Front, these bronze caribou mark the engagements of the Newfoundland Regiment. Near here the troops first became exposed to the German guns because they had reached the crest of the ridge and were silhouetted against the horizon. The caribou symbolically bellows defiance toward the enemy positions. Bronze tablets at the base of the mound record

---

Newfoundland Regiment at Beaumont-Hamel.
[9] Very Light was a flare shot from a specially designed pistol and named after the inventor

the names of 820 members of the Royal Newfoundland Regiment, the Newfoundland Royal Naval Reserve, and the Mercantile Marine who gave their lives in the First World War and have no known grave.

A short path circles around the mound and up to a platform, from which an excellent view of the battlefield is possible. Below are the remnants of British and German trenches. The Newfoundland attack progressed from the near left diagonally across the battlefield toward the right, where a clump of shrubs still mark the 'danger tree.' Below are the well-preserved communications trenches, which provided access to the second-line support trench of the British front line.

The path continues down the slope to **Y-Ravine Cemetery,** which holds 426 burials, including soldiers from many of the regiments who participated in the 1 July attack and those from the site's eventual capture in November. Many of the bodies lay unrecovered on the battlefield until the following spring and were unidentifiable; as a result cemetery has many 'unidentified' graves. The route proceeds down the hill, finally crossing the German front trench, which is clearly delineated and extends in both directions. The view back up the hill demonstrates the field of fire from German machine guns. On the right, a short finger of the ravine that gave the feature its name was used as a communications trench to the German front line.

Y-Ravine was a natural feature that ran west from the valley in which Beaumont-Hamel was located toward the British front line. Its depth and the steepness of its sides made it a difficult artillery target and an excellent defensive position. Its sides were honeycombed with dugouts and tunnels, some undoubtedly connecting to other positions on Hawthorn Ridge. Remnants of dugouts, tunnels, and unrecovered munitions still exist; therefore, it is too dangerous for visitors.

A stone plinth surmounted by a kilted Highlander commemorates the eventual capture of Hawthorn Ridge and Beaumont-Hamel by the **51st (Highland) Division**. The original German front line continued across the park in front of this statue. A path behind the statue leads around Y-Ravine, where a sunken road and folds in the terrain were used by the defenders to move from their deep dugouts in the village to the first trench line.

Ahead is **Hunter's Cemetery**, the smallest of the three, which is located in a large shell crater in which were buried forty-six dead of the 51st Division, who fell in the November assault upon the village.

On the far left boundary of the park is **Hawthorn Ridge Cemetery #2,** which consists of 214 burials. Directly north is Hawthorn Crater, barely visible but marked by the brush and trees growing around its perimeter. Although the crater can be reached at the end of a rutted farm road north of the park entrance – which also leads to **Hawthorn Ridge Cemetery #1** – the tangled undergrowth prevents access. The trek to the cemetery allows for views over the ridge of the Celtic Cross memorial to the captors of the village and of the numerous cemeteries dotting Redan Ridge.

The park is open every day, and bi-lingual Canadian students provide free tours from April to November. A brochure is available for self-guided exploration along the approved pathways. The park is immensely popular and receives approximately 125,000 visitors every year. 1 July, celebrated as Canada Day throughout most of that country, remains Memorial Day in Newfoundland in commemoration of the losses of the Great War and at Beaumont-Hamel in particular. Visitor's Center open May through October from 10:00 to 18:00; November through April from 09:00 to 17:00. No admission charge.

Battle of Thiepval
1 July to 9 October 1916

OBJECTIVE	To capture German strongpoints at Thiepval the German second line
FORCES	
BRITISH:	X Corps (Lieutenant-General Sir Thomas Lethbridge Morland)
GERMAN:	Reserve Infantry Regiment Nr 99 (Major Hans von Fabeck)
RESULT	Most of the day's gains were lost by evening.
CASUALTIES	
BRITISH:	9,053
GERMAN:	1,800
LOCATION	Albert is 150 km north of Paris; Thiepval is 10 km northeast of Albert

The Thiepval Plateau rises sharply from the valley of the Ancre River. To the north and northeast are gradual slopes across rolling, open fields that are occasionally broken by small farm communities. To the east is the village of Pozières, through which runs the Albert-Bapaume highway. The plateau provided dominating views across the river to the German stronghold at Beaumont-Hamel and as far as the city of Albert 10 km to the southwest. The British Army could hardly move without being under the eyes and guns at Thiepval.

Thiepval was historically dominated by the wealthy Count de Bréda, who lived in the two-story, brick and stone French manor house situated on the village's western edge. Fighting in 1914 had damaged the château, and its ruins were converted by German engineers into a mass of fortified gun positions and trench lines. The backside of the village was further enclosed in a series of strongpoints named Goat Redoubt (Feste Zollern), Stuff Redoubt (Feste Staufen), and Schwaben Redoubt. Projecting from the German front line was a blunt but well-fortified salient aimed at Bois d'Authuille[10] known as the Leipzig Redoubt.

The 36th (Ulster) Division was formed from the Ulster Volunteer Force, a Protestant group opposed to Irish rule from catholic Dublin. At the outbreak of the war, they volunteered to turn their German-supplied weapons against the enemies of the king. They were given the mission to attack out of Thiepval Wood through Schwaben Redoubt, which dominated the high ground between Thiepval and St Pierre Divion, and to continue toward Grandcourt. While the British 29th Division was suffering near annihilation to the north, 36th Division was hurtling its Irish battalions against the strongest German position attacked that day – and they made it.

---

[10] The wood is identified as Bois d'Authuille on British maps but as Bois de la Haie on modern French roadmaps; similarly 2 km north is Thiepval Wood to the British but Bois d'Authuille to the French

Battle

Supported by experienced French batteries, the troops had positions in no man's land before zero hour. At 07:30, the bugles blew, and with two battalions of Royal Irish Rifles on the left and two battalions of Royal Inniskilling Fusiliers on the right, they won the race for the parapet and overwhelmed the German front line manned by the Reserve Infantry Regiment Nr 99, a Prussian regiment in a Württemberg division. The Irish pushed forward 400 meters against increasingly stiff resistance, and by 09:00 Schwaben Redoubt was taken; by late morning advance parties reached as far as Grandcourt. The British established machine gun positions and prepared to defend the ground they had gained.

All over the battlefield, German counterattacks were hindered by the British preliminary bombardment's cutting of telephone cables as well as the overall condition of the shell-churned battlefield. Unit movement orders were carried by the slow process of runners – both unreliable and time consuming in such a fluid engagement. The Germans' response, therefore, could not be organized until 16:00. Meanwhile, German survivors engaged British troops in hand-to-hand fighting among the trenches, tunnels, and dugouts of the redoubt. Since the fighting continued through the afternoon, both sides lost effectiveness from shortages of ammunition. Heavy fire from undamaged German batteries blocked British attempts at reinforcing the forward units. They became trapped, taking machine-gun fire from three sides. German reserve troops were fed into the struggle, finally tipping it in the Germans' favor. At 22:00, a one-hour artillery barrage began, after which a final assault to recapture the Schwaben positions was launched. Resistance was finally overcome, and as a German officer reported, 'the British corpses of 700 courageous members of the Ulster division littered the redoubt, every foot of which was soaked in blood.'[11] As night fell British survivors crept back to the shelter of the German front line trenches. The 36th Division was relieved on 2 July by 49th Division, who were bombed back to the starting line five days later.

To the south was 32nd Division, whose various 'Pals' battalions were raised from communities in England. Comprised of the 96th Brigade fusiliers and 97th Brigade light infantry, their mission was to capture Thiepval, its dangerous château, and Leipzig Redoubt. The 96th Brigade faced the village and its heavily defended château. The lead battalions failed to make progress; machine-gun fire from the château ruins pinned down the 16th Northumberland Fusiliers in no man's land. Attempts by 15th Lancashire Fusiliers to leave Thiepval Wood were met with furious bursts of fire, and they failed to advance.

Just before 07:30, the 17th Highland Light Infantry left the trenches and crept within 30 meters of the German trench line in front of Leipzig Redoubt. Given the attack signal, they quickly occupied trenches near the redoubt, but additional progress was limited by machine guns in the next strongpoint at *Wundtwerk*. Further attempts to flank behind the redoubt were similarly driven back. Reserve Infantry

---

[11] Hauptmann von Wurmb, Bavarian RIR Nr 8 as quoted by Jack Sheldon, *The German Army on the Somme, 1914-1918* (Barnsley, England: Pen and Sword, 2005), 154-155.

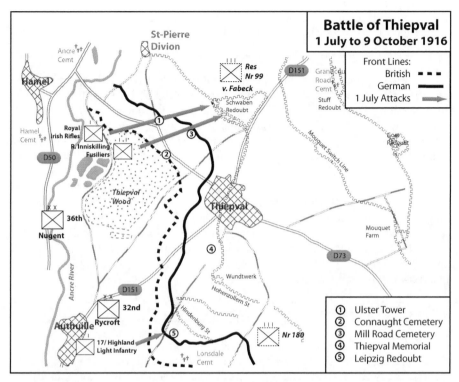

Regiment (RIR) Nr 99 and Infantry Regiment (IR) Nr 180 bombed the Highlanders out of Hindenburg Trench behind Leipzig Redoubt, but they could not recover the redoubt. The fighting was described in the Victoria Cross citation of Sergeant James Turnbull, stating 'he was subjected to severe counterattacks, which were continuous throughout the whole day. Although his party was wiped out and replaced several times during the day, Sergeant Turnbull never wavered in his determination to hold the post.'[12] Turnbull was killed later in the day. Progress south of Thiepval would remain so stopped for weeks because the attention of the British turned to more advantageous areas of the battlefield.

The 49th (West Riding) Division attempted to capture the Thiepval position that summer, but the assaults were repeatedly repulsed; however, advances via Pozières threatened Thiepval from the rear and made holding the position tenuous for the Germans. The 18th Division assumed the responsibility and with defined, limited objectives, strenuous training, and effective artillery, Thiepval finally fell on 26 September. After a series of costly attacks, Stuff Redoubt was captured on 9 October and held against further German counterattacks.

---

[12] Crown Copyright

Battlefield Tour

> Leave Albert north toward Aveluy (D50) and continue along the Ancre Valley for approximately 7.5 km. Turn right on Thiepval road (D73).

After a brief ascent, an apparently out-of-place Irish castle appears on the left. **Ulster Tower** was constructed as a memorial to the Irish Rifles, Irish Fusiliers, and Inniskilling Fusiliers that died in the 1 July assault, which started in the forest across the road on the right. Inside the boundary fence is a stone memorial to nine soldiers from the 36th Division who were awarded the Victoria Cross during the Somme fighting. The Gothic-style structure marks the location of the 1 July German front line trenches, and it was modeled after a tower near Belfast, where many of the troops trained. The walls of the memorial room on the first floor bear the emblems, flags, and awards of the units of the 36th Division. The tower observation room has unfortunately been closed for many years. Through a gateway behind the tower stands a memorial to the Orange Order of Northern Ireland. Open daily February through March and October through November from 10:30 to 16:30; April through September from 10:30 to 17:30; closed Mondays as well as in December and January. No admission charge.

> Continue on the D73 toward Thiepval.

Along the edge of Thiepval Wood is **Connaught Cemetery**, which is situated in front of the British front trenches. From here the 10th Royal Inniskilling Fusiliers, followed by the 8th and 14th Royal Irish Rifles, left the protection of the forest and moved against Schwaben Redoubt. Within an hour, they had advanced past the German stronghold. The cemetery holds 124 of their dead among its 1,262 graves.

Mill Road Cemetery is down the path on the left. Walking the grass path from the road to the cemetery duplicates the attack route of the Inniskilling battalions against Schwaben Redoubt. The redoubt itself was between the rear of the cemetery and la Grande Ferme, visible to the northeast. Many of the cemetery's 1,304 tombstones have been laid on their side due to the unstable nature of the underlying ground from German tunnels and dugouts. Among its graves are many of the young men who died that first day; almost 65 per cent are unidentified.

The short entrance road on the left leads to an exciting addition to the Somme battlefield, the newly constructed **Thiepval Memorial Visitors Center**. Located in a hollow to be unnoticeable from the great Thiepval Memorial, its large maps present the major events of the First World War and provide context for the assault upon Thiepval. Information, guides, books, and toilets are all available. The center is open daily from 10:00 to 18:00. No admission charge.

A short walk around a private farmhouse leads to the most impressive memorial structure on the Somme battlefield. The 45-meter high, brick and stone pillars of the **Thiepval Memorial** bear the names of 73,367 British and South African soldiers who fell between July 1915 and March 1918 and who have no grave. The missing from other Commonwealth countries are commemorated on other memorials. The structure is in the old château's gardens and represents the location of fierce fighting during the summer of 1916. Walk among the twenty piers, their surfaces covered with stone plaques listing the missing by regiment and rank. The upper portions of the piers are inscribed with the names of local battles – Albert, Courcelette, Longueval, among others.

Behind the memorial, the **Thiepval Anglo–French Cemetery** contains the graves of three hundred dead from each country – representative of the bond among soldiers fighting a common enemy. Most of the bodies were unidentified because they were gathered from the Somme and nearby battlefields after the war was over.

A walk down the tractor-rutted road that starts from the large lawn in front of the memorial leads to **Leipzig Redoubt**. Nothing remains of the defensive structures, the heart of which was in the brush-covered depression that once was a small quarry. Going the full distance is not necessary to appreciate the views over the Ancre Valley north of Albert and to witness Thiepval's command the countryside and the British positions to the west. Across the river and slightly to the right stands the still massive Bois d'Aveluy, a wood that sheltered allied artillery batteries and from where they battered the hilltop and surrounding German-held fields.

Near the exit from the memorial, a white obelisk commemorates the **18th (Eastern) Division**'s capture of the site in September 1916. The large farm buildings to the north mark the site of the old château, whose foundation stones are still visible.

Battle of Pozières and Mouquet Ferme
23 July to 26 September 1916

OBJECTIVE	To flank the German strongpoint at Thiepval.
FORCES	
BRITISH:	I Australian and New Zealand Army Corps (I ANZAC) (Lieutenant-General William)
GERMAN:	117th Division (Generalmajor Ritter Hermann von Burkhardt)
RESULT	The two objectives were achieved but with significant casualties
CASUALTIES	
BRITISH:	22,835
GERMAN:	Uncertain
LOCATION	Albert is 150 km north of Paris; Pozières is 7.5 km northeast of Albert

Battle

Pozières sits across the Roman road which connects Albert and Bapaume and is the major transportation route through the battlefield north of the Somme River. The village occupies a broad ridge that commands the terrain in every direction. Its defenses formed part of the German Second Line. Wire entanglements surrounded the village and concrete fortifications guarded each end along the highway. Heavy fighting continued through the first weeks of July, with British III

Corps' 48th Division making slow progress toward Pozières through the shallow valley from Ovillers and 34th Division through Contalmaison from the south.

After four previous unsuccessful attacks against Pozières, fresh troops were needed, and the 1st Australian Division of General Gough's Reserve Army entered the front lines. Starting before dawn on 23, July they launched an assault that entered Pozières along the main highway and captured the German strongpoint south of the village known as 'Gibraltar[13]'. By 05:30 the next day, small gains secured control over the entire village and along the road to Thiepval. A German corporal described the intense struggle for control of the village, 'The little group of fighters shrank steadily. Some of the men were gripped with trench frenzy and launched themselves at the enemy with spades, only to be beaten to death with rifle butts.'[14]

The advance created a dangerous Australian salient in German-held territory. They were exposed to shelling from three sides, especially from strong German lines anchored at a fortified windmill to the north. German counterattacks were unsuccessful but dramatically raised casualty figures on both sides. The efforts so exhausted the ranks of the 1st Australians that they were relieved by the 2nd

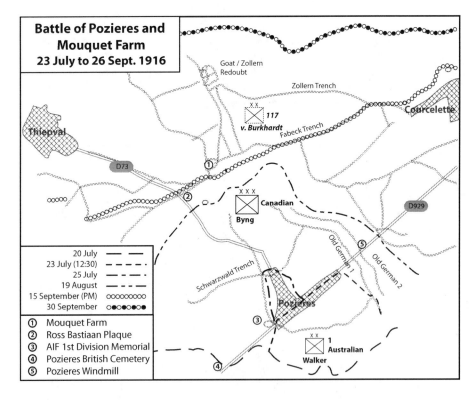

Battle of Pozieres and Mouquet Farm
23 July to 26 Sept. 1916

20 July	— —
23 July (12:30)	– – – – ·
25 July	— — — ·
19 August	— · – · –
15 September (PM)	oooooooooo
30 September	o●o●●o●o●

① Mouquet Farm
② Ross Bastiaan Plaque
③ AIF 1st Division Memorial
④ Pozieres British Cemetery
⑤ Pozieres Windmill

---

[13] In German called *panzerturm*, meaning armored turret.
[14] Sheldon, *The German Army on the Somme, 1914-1918,* 215.

Australian Division on 27 July. German losses, particularly from British 'drumfire[15]' were sapping the strength of their front line forces. Some regiments were reduced to less than 1,000 men; some battalions to less than 200; and some companies ceased to exist. German command became increasingly confused because Bavarian, Prussian, Guards, and Württemberg units were intermixed. Forty-two German divisions saw service in the Somme during July and August.

On 4 August, four attack waves of 2nd Australian Division finally penetrated the Old German (OG) Support Line, physically obliterating the windmill. After a continued assault, the mill was captured at 05:00 the next day. The 4th Australian Division then took over the front line. Pozières was secure, but the cost was high, with the three Australian divisions suffering 12,131 casualties. Four Victoria Crosses were awarded during the battle. The direction of the attack then turned northwest toward Mouquet Farm.

The daily reports throughout the month of August were dismal reading. Small gains were followed by German counterattacks. Slowly and against determined opposition, the Australians crept across the battlefield, bombing their way down trench lines and charging over open ground. Trench lines were obliterated during the constant exchange of artillery fire. With the battlefield barren of landmarks, troops frequently became lost or disoriented. Defenders occupied a ragged line of shell craters; the attackers leapt from shell craters in a dash to another a few meters ahead. Positions were taken and lost again, allied artillery bombardments fell on their own troops, and the Germans counterattacked every gain. Liddell-Hart described the fighting of July and August as 'the British made little progress at much cost, and the infantry of both sides served as compressed cannon-fodder for artillery consumption,'[16] The Australians, having already experienced poor British leadership during assaults against Gallipoli and Fromelles, felt like battering rams in their repeated frontal attacks.

Assaults upon Mouquet Farm by the Australian divisions continued through August and into September, when seven separate attacks raised the Australian casualty toll to 23,000. The Canadian Corps assumed responsibility on 3 September, and a relative quiet descended upon the front until 15 September, when another attempt to take the farm was coordinated with the first tank attack at Courcelette 2.5 km to the north. The tank attack was successful in capturing Courcelette, but Mouquet Farm held.

On 26 September, the last remaining farm position was the target of another major assault, this time by British 11th Division. At 05:30, smoke bombs drove the last fifty-six defenders out of the cellars of the farm. The battle was finally over. Despite the fact that they were not there at the end, it will be forever remembered as an Australian victory.

---

[15] Drum fire is a translation of a German term for artillery fire so intense that individual detonations cannot be distinguished.

[16] Liddell-Hart, *The Real War 1914-1918*, 243.

Battlefield Tour

From the exit of the Thiepval Memorial, continue toward Pozières (D73).

Between Thiepval and Pozières, **Ferme du Mouquet** is plainly visible in the field 500 meters east of the D73. Nothing of the great fortification remains to indicate the violent struggle that took place here during the seven weeks of late summer 1916. The ground is once again used for farming, and the land is private, so please remain on the roadway. It has a bucolic appearance that belies its history. Between the road and the farm, the terrain dips down before rising to the ridge crest where the farm buildings are located. The trees to the left of the current structures indicate the farm's original site. On the edge of the highway and under the shade of some trees, a **bronze plaque by Ross Bastiaan** quietly identifies the site and describes what happened there. The temptation is to pass it by, do not. Stop and read the inscription.

Continue into Pozières to the junction with the Albert-Bapaume highway (D929). The road is a heavily traveled, high-speed route frequented by large trucks, so be very cautious. Turn right, and within 400 meters on the right is a memorial obelisk. Turn onto the side road and into the parking area.

The white stone of the **AIF (Australian Imperial Force) 1st Australian Division Memorial** shines brilliantly in the sunshine, and it is surrounded by an iron and stone fence within a plot of manicured lawn. The Rising Sun emblem of the AIF sits above the memorial plaque, which commemorates the 5,285 men of the 1st Division who were casualties during Pozières' capture. The site is the location of 'K' trench, taken early in the attack on Pozières on 23 July and the first trench that the division captured on the Western Front. The division's battle honors are inscribed on the side and indicate the unit's participation in some of the bloodiest fighting of the entire war.

Ascending the wooden viewing platform across the side road enhances the view of Pozières Ridge, and the Thiepval memorial is clearly visible. The openness of the terrain shows how a few well-positioned machine guns would have a murderous effect upon advancing troops. Behind the platform are the underground remnants of the '**Gibraltar**' strongpoint, a concrete dugout with a tower that rose 2 meters above ground level, a machine gun position, and an artillery observation post. Its capture by fifteen men of the 2nd Battalion eliminated a dangerous German position on this side of Pozières. Recently excavated and gated for safety, the stairs and entrance into the bunkers are visible among the broken masonry.

Drive approximately 600 meters south along the highway (D929).

Behind the white stone entrance columns of the **Pozières British Cemetery** are 2,755 graves, with 50 per cent of the bodies unidentified; most were killed in the fighting around Pozières. Among the graves is that of Sergeant Claude Castleton, who was awarded the Victoria Cross for his repeated excursions into no man's land to rescue wounded comrades on 29 July; on the third such trip he was shot and killed. The cemetery's interior walls form the **Pozières Memorial to the Missing,** listing the names of over 14,300 men from the United Kingdom and South Africa who disappeared defending the Somme area against the great German advance from 21 March to 7 August 1918.

> Reverse direction and proceed through Pozières to the northern edge of the village.

The **German fortified windmill** was located at the memorial on the left side of the highway. Nothing remains of the windmill but a low, grassy knoll. The site now commemorates all Australians lost in the battle. The memorial is very simple and understated; white stone blocks are stepping stones to a small bench of reflection, which bears the inscription, 'The ruin of Pozières windmill which lies here was the center of a struggle in this part of the Somme battlefield in July and August 1916. It was captured on August 4th by Australian troops who fell more thickly on this ridge than on any other battlefield of the war.' The Old German (OG and OG2) Second Line and Support Lines ran across the highway in front of the windmill. Behind the bench is another of the fine plaques by Ross Bastiaan.

Across the road is an obelisk-topped stone plinth, the four corners of which radiate out to display bronze models various First World War tanks. The bronze plaque on the **Tank Corps Memorial** states: 'Near this spot the first tanks used in the war went into action on 15 September 1916.'

Battle of Delville Wood
15 July to 4 September 1916

OBJECTIVE	To occupy the wood and repulse any German attempts to regain the position.
FORCES	
BRITISH:	South African Brigade (Brigadier Henry Timsom Lukin)
GERMAN:	3rd Guards Division (Generalleutnant Arthur von Lindequist)
RESULT	The brigade held for six days, suffering almost complete annihilation.
CASUALTIES	
BRITISH:	766 dead and 1,632 wounded, equaling 76 per cent of the brigade's complement
GERMAN:	Unknown
LOCATION	Albert is 150 km north of Paris; Longueval is 12.5 km northeast of Albert

With the opening of the Somme offensive a disaster, General Haig decided to capitalize on the local success of XIII Corps, which captured Montauban and its surrounding area. In reaction to this British advance, the Germans established strong defensive positions in Bois des Fourcaux (High Wood), Bois des Troncs (Trones Wood), and Bois d'Elville (Delville Wood). To gain an advantage through surprise, the preparatory bombardment on 14 July, which was five times denser than on 1 July, was limited to five minutes, and infantry units were moved to the front line trenches during the night to be ready to attack at dawn. Moving troops in the dark was a risky procedure, but from Contalmaison to Trones Wood the attack was successful, and Bazentin Ridge was captured. The 9th (Scottish) Division led the attack on Longueval, with the attacking 26th and 27th Brigades in the village by 06:15 and occupying the southern half after a seesaw fight. German defenses then stiffened. The South African Brigade, nicknamed the 'Springboks' and comprised of four battalion-sized regiments, was held in reserve near Carnoy.

Battle

The South Africans advanced and on 15 July two regiments attacked German-held positions in the wood. The 1st Regiment was already engaged in northern Longueval, pushing into the wood from the west; 4th Regiment was in support. At 06:00, the 3rd Regiment entered the woods from the southwestern perimeter and proceeded north along Buchanan Street[17]. The 3rd Regiment continued to the eastern perimeter of the forest and established its positions; the 2nd Regiment turned toward the northern perimeter. Headquarters was established near Buchanan Street and Princes Street, the main east-west ride under the command Lieutenant-Colonel William Tanner. Confusion arose over who controlled the trenches to the east, but the question was answered approximately two hours later when a counterattack started from the east and against the southern perimeter, now manned by 4th Regiment. Scattered fighting continued throughout the day, and casualties increased while ammunition reserves dwindled. The thin soil and thick roots made digging proper trench positions nearly impossible. By mid-afternoon the 2nd Regiment was also under assault from the north and northeast perimeters. Although the lines held, the South Africans spent an uneasy night under enemy shelling and sniping.

By late afternoon on 16 July, the Germans were massing troops in trenches north and east of the east end of Princes Street. Repeated requests to Major-General William Furse, commander of 9th Division, for relief were met with orders to hold the woods at all costs. The assault commander, Lieutenant-Colonel Tanner, was wounded, and Lieutenant-Colonel Edward Thackeray assumed command. A German assault from the northwest corner advanced as far as Princes Street before being driven back. Responding to South African requests for help, British artillery dropped short rounds, hitting their own troops – a common problem in close-quarters battle. During the evening of 17 July, the Germans moved up additional artillery pieces transported from the Verdun battlefield.

The German troops withdrew next morning and at 08:00 two hundred guns blasted three square kilometers in Delville Wood from three sides. The South

---

[17] The open lanes or 'rides' cut through the forest, and were given English place names for ease of identification.

Africans held their ground as seven-and-one-half hours of German drumfire destroyed the forest around them. Trees fell on top of their meager defensive positions, and the ground was shredded with shrapnel. The depleted force's messages asking for relief and help in evacuating their wounded were repeatedly met with orders to hold as well as suggestions to retake the entire wood. After the artillery, the dwindling number of soldiers continued fighting, repelling German assaults with grenades and bayonets. The few survivors of 3rd Regiment's A and C Companies were overrun and forced to surrender.

Early on 19 July, Lieutenant-Colonel Thackeray made another request for relief, which was met with a promise of relief after the wood was cleared of the enemy. The German Reserve Infantry Regiment Nr 153 and elements of Reserve Infantry Regiment Nr 52 entered the woods from the north and penetrated to the southern perimeter where they turned east and captured B Company of 3rd Regiment from behind.

On 20 July, Thackeray sent a plea for help:

> Urgent. My men are on their last legs. I cannot keep some of them awake. They drop with their rifles in hand asleep in spite of heavy shelling. We are expecting an attack... Food and water has not reached us for two days – though we have managed on rations of those killed... but must have water...Please relieve these men today without fail as [because] I fear they have come to the end of their endurance.[18]

Relief finally did appear late that afternoon in the form of the 10th Royal Welsh Fusiliers. Thackeray led three wounded officers and one hundred forty men out of Delville Wood.

Although the South Africans were relieved, the ordeal in Delville Wood – now referred to as 'Devil's Wood' by the soldiers – continued. Not until 18 August did the British 14th (Light) Division push beyond the eastern boundary. Delville Wood was not completely cleared of Germans until 27 August, however, and even then the British struggled to regain control. On 31 August, the Germans launched a pincer movement from the eastern and northern corners, spearheaded by specially trained assault troops known as '*Sturm*' battalions. The assault collapsed under accurate British artillery fire, the mud of a battle-seared terrain, and British machine guns. Delville Wood was fully cleared on 4 September.

Battlefield Tour

East of Longueval toward Ginchy are a visitor's center and parking area.

A section of the wood was purchased by the South African government in 1922 as the site of the **National Memorial and the South African Museum.** After a short walk along the highway, the memorial and museum are approached across a

---

[18] IS Uys, *The South Africans at Delville Wood* (Military History Journal, Volume 7, Number 2)

magnificent oak-lined lawn. Whereas the forest has re-grown, plinths mark the road intersections and provide their wartime, English names. Trench lines and shell craters are faintly visible in the forest, but the dense undergrowth prevents wandering off the cleared lanes.

At the end of the lawn, the center of a fieldstone wall is crowned with a triumphal arch that bears a bronze statue representing Castor and Pollux with a single steed between them. The ancient warring brothers represent the antagonists of the Boer War, now joined in fighting a common enemy. The wall curves away to the left and right, ending in covered shelters.

After passing through the memorial's gate, one approaches the museum, which is a replica of the Castle of Good Hope in Cape Town. The museum commemorates the South African contribution to the First World War, the Second World War, the Berlin Air-Lift, and the Korean War. The structure surrounds a hexagonal open gallery. On its interior walls are four, large bronze panels. The first panel to the left of the entrance contains sixteen friezes depicting various aspects of the Great War; the next is devoted to the actions at Delville Wood. The final two present scenes from the Second World War and the Korean Conflict. The images are well done and display the fatigue and resolution of troops fighting in such inhospitable conditions. Etched into the glass of the inner wall are depictions of the Delville Wood battlefield. The courtyard contains a simple white stone cross. Photographs and a few relics complete the displays. The visitor center, which offers light refreshments and toilets, and museum are open every day except Monday and public holidays, from 10:00 to 15:45 (10:00 to 17:45 from 1 April to 14 October); closed in December and January. No admission charge.

To the west of the museum is Buchanan Street. A stone obelisk indicates the location of the brigade's **battlefield command post**. A trench line runs from it into the wood.

Across the road is **Delville Wood Cemetery**, which contains the remains of 5,493 men, approximately two-thirds of whom are unidentified. The cemetery is a post war accumulation site, and most casualties were the result of battles in the Somme during July, August, and September 1916. Surprisingly, it contains only 151 labeled South African graves, but many more South Africans probably lie under gravestones inscribed 'unknown.'

Other Sites of Interest: The highly recommended and very informative **Musée Somme 1916** is adjacent to the Basilica in Albert. Open daily February through mid-December from 09:00 to 12:00 and 14:00 to 18:00; extended hours June through September from 09:00 to 18:00. Fee.

The Albert-Bapaume road has many more fine monuments and memorials, and several are along or slightly off the highway. South of Pozières is the **Lochnagar Crater** in la Boisselle. North of Pozières at Courcelette is a **monument to the Canadian Corps** and the limit of the allied advance in 1916, near the German strongpoint on **Butte de Warlencourt**.

The **New Zealand Memorial** commemorates their actions between High Wood and Flers. Located on a farm track directly north of Longueval, its position marks the highest point on Crest Farm and sits directly on the German Switch Line. To the northwest is **High Wood**, a location as deadly to allied soldiers as Delville Wood. Although private and not accessible, it has a number of memorials on its periphery, including a stone cairn dedicated to the **1/9th Highland Light Infantry** (Glasgow Highlanders); a stone cross to the **47th London Division**, which eventually cleared the wood on 15 September; and a plinth to the **1st Cameron Highlanders**. **London Cemetery and Extension**, which is a bit unusual in its design, is across the road.

#26

Battle of Fromelles
(originally Battle of Fleurbaix)
19 to 20 July 1916

OBJECTIVE	To prevent enemy reserve units from entering the Somme battle.
FORCES	
BRITISH:	5th Australian Division and British 61st Division of British XI Corps (Lieutenant-General Richard Haking), totaling approximately 30,000 men and 395 guns
GERMAN:	6th Bavarian Reserve Division (Generalleutnant Gustav Scanzoni von Lichtenfels), approximately 12,000 men and 102 guns
RESULT	The Australians were slaughtered in one of the worst fiascos of the war.
CASUALTIES	
BRITISH:	5,533 Australian and 1,547 British casualties, including 481 taken prisoner
GERMAN:	1,500 killed or wounded
LOCATION	Lille is 220 km north of Paris; Fromelles is 17 km west of Lille and 19 km north of the 1915 Loos battlefield

The Fromelles attack was originally conceptualized as a feint to keep the enemy from shifting reserves to the Somme battlefield; however, the plan's objectives changed repeatedly before the battle, and what started as an artillery bombardment became a two-division assault. Some British commanders questioned its feasibility. The British Army's commitment to the Somme severely restricted the number of available guns and men. It was the Australian Imperial Force's (AIF) first major engagement on the Western Front.

Battle

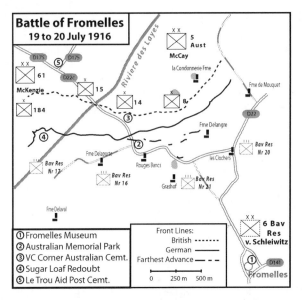

Battle of Fromelles
19 to 20 July 1916

In the summer of 1916, Fromelles was a quiet sector near the 1915 Aubers Ridge and Neuve Chapelle battlefields. The terrain was flat, boggy, and cut by innumerable drainage ditches and canals. Deep trenches were impossible, forcing men to crouch behind sandbagged parados which in some places were only 400 meters from the enemy's front lines. The attack force to the east was the untested 5th Australian Division, composed of hardy farmers and led by junior officers pulled from civilian life. On the west side was the weak British 61st Division, a territorial 'second line' unit frequently raided for replacements for other divisions. The British artillery bombardment included a series of breaks to entice the Germans to man their front line trenches. The Germans, having observed the assault's preparations over the preceding days from Auber's Ridge, manned only a few forward outposts, and the stratagem failed. The bombardments fell upon mostly empty positions.

The 6th Bavarian Reserve Division was on the high ground of Aubers Ridge. Its regiments were primarily filled with poorly trained men either under or over military age men along with some elderly reservists. Their first line was thinly held but strengthened by numerous machine guns and concrete bunkers.

After a seven-hour artillery bombardment, the troops started leaving the trenches and sap heads at 17:31 under a bright afternoon sun. The German guns responded, inflicting a rapidly growing number of casualties upon the massed troops. An NCO of the 14th Brigade afterwards said;

> The first thing that struck you, was that shells were bursting everywhere, mostly high-explosive; and you could see machine-guns knocking bits off the trees in front of the reserve line and sparking against the wire. . . . When men looked over the top they saw No-Man's Land [with explosions] leaping up everywhere in showers of dust and

sand . . . rather confirming our fears that the Germans knew something.[19]

The central objective was Sugar Loaf Salient, the strongest point in the German line. Converging attacks by the 15th Australian Brigade from the northeast and British 184th Brigade (61st Division) from the west were to pinch out the enemy. Four successive waves of the 15th Brigade fell upon Sugar Loaf and all were shattered by machine gunners who had survived the artillery fire in their underground shelters. German riflemen targeted officers depriving the Australians of leadership. Isolated groups reached the German parapet; however, they were too few in number and withdrew into shell craters.

The flanks of the attack made good progress. By 18:30, 8th and 14th Brigades were digging defendable trenches out of the water-filled and weed-choked drainage ditches which crossed the area where they had expected to find a second German line. German barrages and an occasional friendly fire shell hit the forward units as the work continued into the night.

The 61st Division's first assault was quickly driven back. They planned to renew the attack but quickly canceled without word reaching the Australians. 15th Brigade reserves assaulted Sugar Loaf at 21:10, meeting the same fate as their British mates. The brigade was so decimated that it ceased offensive action.

Bavarian Reserve Infantry Regiment Nr 21 launched a counterattack against the exposed western flank of 14th Australian Brigade, bombing their way along the original German forward trench. The advance was temporarily stopped by counterattack at approximately 23:00. A second, more powerful German counterattack struck both flanks at 02:00. German forces succeeded in recapturing their trenches behind the new Australian front line on the right. Similarly on the left, the Germans cut off Australian troops facing Ferme Delangré. The desperate fighting continued through the night, with both Australians and Germans bombing along opposing trenches. As dawn approached, the order to withdraw was received. Finding avenues for escape was difficult because German forces had established enfilade machine-gun fire. All localized resistance was eventually overcome, and the survivors were taken prisoner.

A German proposal of truce to collect the wounded was prohibited by British Headquarters' standing orders, although heroic efforts to rescue wounded mates trapped in no man's land continued for several days.

In less than 24 hours, the Australians had suffered over 5,000 casualties with no territorial gain. The smaller 61st Division incurred over 1,500 losses. British dispatches concealed the enormity of the disaster with the description, 'Yesterday evening, south of Armentieres, we carried out some important raids on a front of two miles [3.2 km] in which Australian troops took part. About fourteen German prisoners were captured.'[20]

---

[19] CEW Bean, *The Official History of Australia in the War of 1914-1918: Volume III The Australian Imperial Force in France, 1916* (Sydney: Angus and Robertson Ltd., 12th ed. 1941), 358.

[20] Ibid., 446.

Following the disastrous Gallipoli expedition in which Australian troops also suffered horrendous losses, Fromelles further damaged the Australian's faith in British leadership.

Battlefield Tour

The tour starts in the center of Fromelles at a local museum dedicated to the battle. It continues to the recently created memorial park, and then to battlefield cemeteries, which were areas of intense fighting.

Fromelles Museum is operated by the *Association pour le Souvenir de la Bataille de Fromelles en 1916* and spans the entire second floor attic of the combined municipal building / elementary school in the center of Fromelles. Do not be deterred by the location or the narrow stairway. The museum is the best municipal First World War museum in France and presents an overwhelming collection of armaments in its crowded rooms. The machine guns, with hoses and cooling-water cans still attached, appear to be still operational. A German corpsman's boots and uniform are mud covered, as if he had just climbed out of the trench. A few items from the Nazi occupation of Fromelles in the Second World War are also shown. Each display is labeled in three languages. Unfortunately, the museum's hours are limited to the 2nd Sunday of the month, April to December from 09:00 to 12:00 and 14:00 to 19:00; closed in August. Donations accepted.

Follow signs in town for directions to the *Mémorial Australien* 1.8 km to the northeast.

The area that is now the **Australian Memorial Park** was captured during the battle by the 14th Australian Brigade and held during the night of 19/20 July. The park stands on land donated by a local farmer and still contains the ruins of several German bunkers that were part of their first defensive line. The spacing between the German fortifications indicates how densely the area was fortified. The damage to the bunkers was not the result of the British bombardment but rather postwar efforts to clear the battlefield.

The focus of the park is the 'Cobbers' statue, which was unveiled in 1998 and depicts the rescue by Sergeant Simon Frazer of a comrade after the battle. Sergeant Fraser, 57th Battalion, 15th Brigade laconically described his exploits in a letter home:

> One foggy morning in particular, I remember, we could hear someone over toward the German entanglements calling for a stretcher-bearer; it was an appeal no man could stand against, so some of us rushed out and had a hunt. We found a fine haul of wounded and brought them in; but it was not where I heard this fellow calling, so I had another shot for it, and came across a splendid specimen of humanity trying to wriggle into a trench with a big wound in his thigh. He was about 11

stone weigh [154 lbs] and I could not lift him on my back; but I managed to get him into an old trench, and told him to lie quiet while I got a stretcher. Then another man about 30 yards [27.7 meters] out sang out 'Don't forget me, cobber.' I went in and got four volunteers with stretchers, and we got both men in safely. [21]

Frazer later became a commissioned officer and died in the battle of Bullecourt in May 1917. He is commemorated on the Villers-Bretonneux Memorial to the Missing. A **Ross Bastiaan bronze plaque** describes the fighting and provides a contour map of the British and German lines within the borders of the park.

VC Corner Cemetery is visible 250 meters to the northwest across the cornfield.

The location of **VC Corner Australian Cemetery and Memorial** was no man's land on 19 July and was crossed by the 14th Australian Brigade during their advance. The name apparently stems from four Victoria Crosses that were awarded for actions in the vicinity on 15 May 1915. VC Corner is a cemetery without gravestones because by the time the battlefield was cleared after the armistice, many of the Australian dead had simply disappeared or were not identifiable. The only all-Australian cemetery on the Western Front was thus created to honor the missing and bury the unidentified dead. The grave area consists of two mass graves covered with 410 rose bushes – one for each unidentified body. The Wall of Remembrance lists the names of 1,299 dead who have no known grave.

Continue 1.7 km on D22c to the crossing of the Rivière des Layes, a barely discernible brook that figured in the Fromelles action.

Sugar Loaf Redoubt was located west of the Layes, in the open fields southwest of where the brook crosses the D22. The site is not accessible; however, the clear fields of fire from German machine guns into the flanks of the retreating 14th Australian Brigade can be imagined from the highway.

Turn onto D175 and proceed to the cemetery on the left.

Le Trou Aid Post Cemetery was established in October 1914, only a few hundred meters to the rear of the British front lines. It was the location of Australian brigade headquarters during the battle of Fromelles. Burials continued through 1918, when bodies were collected from the battlefields of Aubers Ridge, Loos, and Fromelles after the armistice. The cemetery now contains 356 graves, a large number of which remain unidentified. Trou Aid is one of the most beautiful and tranquil cemeteries in France. Enter via a bridge crossing the moat that surrounds the cemetery, then proceed through a fieldstone portico. The path is lined with thyme,

---

[21] Ibid., 441.

and a border of weeping willow trees adds to the dramatic effect. The open area contains gravestones in two sections at right angles to each other. Alone under a willow in one corner, is the grave of a single, unidentified French soldier. A second French cross stands among the British tombstones.

Other Sites of Interest: Southwest of Fromelles toward Aubers (D141) is a **concrete blockhouse** said to have been used by Adolf Hitler. As a member of the Bavarian Reserve Infantry Regiment Nr 16, Corporal Adolf Hitler was stationed in the area from March 1915 through September 1916 and very likely took part in the defense of Sugar Loaf. In 1940, as the conqueror of France, he returned to this bunker, where he claimed to have spent time. Several additional First World War German constructions are visible in the fields around Aubers.

Recommended reading

Cave, Nigel (series editor): *Battleground Europe*. Barnsley, England: Pen and Sword Books, 1997. A series of guide books for Great War battle sites.

Holstein, Christina: *Fort Douaumont: Verdun*. Barnsley, England: Pen & Sword, 2002. A detailed account of the Fort de Douaumont and its capture as well as a description of the fort's construction. Tours of the fort and surrounding sites are presented.

Horne, Alistair: *The Price of Glory: Verdun 1916*. New York: St Martins Press, 1962. One of the best accounts by a great English-language writer of French history.

Keegan, John: *The Face of Battle*. New York: The Viking Press, 1976. A detailed understanding of the Somme as well as its military and political rationale.

Macdonald, Lyn: *Somme*. London: Michael Joseph, 1983. The entire offensive described and supported by individual British soldiers' recollections.

Sheffield, Gary: *The Somme*. London: Cassel, 2003. The battles of the Somme concisely described and generously illustrated.

Sheldon, Jack: *The German Army on the Somme 1914–1916*. Barnsley, England: Pen and Sword, 2005. A detailed account of the Somme battles told from the German perspective.

Uys, I.S.: *The South Africans at Delville Wood*. Military History Journal, Volume 7, Number 2. An account of the South African stage of the battle available at http://rapidttp.com/milhist/vol072iu.html. Also by the same author, *Devil's Wood*. Knysna, South Africa: Fortress Books, 2006.

Chapter Eight

Exhausted Armies
1917

The British did not achieve their desired breakout in the Somme, and the Germans had spent the winter of 1916/17 constructing a new line of defenses well behind the front lines of November 1916. The *Siegfried Stellung* – the Hindenburg Line to the British – use every advantage offered by the terrain, construction techniques, and weapons systems to produce the most formidable series of emplacements yet devised. Built in secrecy, the *Siegfried Stellung* was suddenly occupied when the German army executed a withdrawal from their front lines to occupy the new positions on 22 February 1917. In their wake they left the land devoid of every usable asset – orchards, houses, and farms were torched, villages looted, wells poisoned, and civilians herded eastward. These actions presented the Allies with a devastated landscape that was totally unsuitable for waging war.

At Verdun, the French had blunted the German advance just hundreds of meters short of the final French strongpoint defending the city. French counterattacks in October 1916 had driven the enemy back near its starting position. Only in the northern part of the battlefield did the Germans retain some captured ground.

The Allies' attention now turned to the Arras sector. In front of this ancient city the German advance of 1914 was stopped by French général Ernest Barbot's Chasseurs and Alpine troops. During 1915, the French executed a series of bloody assaults, recapturing the heights upon which Notre-Dame de Lorette was situated. Unsuccessful attempts to assault the nearby heights known as Vimy Ridge cost the French Army 150,000 casualties.

The allied planning conference held at French headquarters in Chantilly in November 1916 resulted in a general offensive north, east, and south of Arras as part of a larger plan to draw the German reserves away from the Aisne Valley west of Reims. The French planned to attack along the chemin des Dames, effect a breakthrough, and roll up the entire German line. The Allies were still contemplating a single stroke to win the war.

General Sir Edmund Allenby's British Third Army would attack east from Arras along the Scarpe Valley. Gough's Fifth Army would use its I ANZAC to attack Bullecourt on the southern flank. North of the Hindenburg Line was Vimy Ridge, and its capture was assigned to General Julian Byng's Canadian Corps.

#27

Battle of Vimy Ridge
9 to 13 April 1917

OBJECTIVE	To storm and occupy the strategic heights of Vimy Ridge
FORCES	
BRITISH:	97,000 men of Canadian Corps and 73,000 support troops

	(Lieutenant-General the Honorable Sir Julian Byng)
GERMAN:	52,000 men of *Gruppe Vimy* (General der Infanterie Karl Ritter von Fasbender)
RESULT	The Canadian Corps successfully drove the enemy from the ridge.
CASUALTIES	
BRITISH:	3,598 killed, 7,004 wounded and missing
GERMAN:	Estimated at 2,400 dead; 3,400 taken prisoner
LOCATION	Arras is 180 km north of Paris; Vimy Ridge is 13 km north of Arras

Viewed from the west and south, Vimy Ridge is not an imposing sight, rising gradually through fields and orchards. To the north, however, a steep drop which provided a view of the coal mines from Lens to Douai – the battleground of the abortive British assault upon Loos. To the east was the Douai Plain with its network of rail lines that was the backbone of the German defenses and transported German troops and materiel to 'hot spots' along the front. Nothing happened and nothing moved that was not under the careful watch of the occupants of Vimy Ridge.

The goal of a major breakout abandoned, Byng's instructions were to accomplish a limited set of objectives commensurate with the size of his forces. Intense training in new, small unit tactics gave the Canadians advantages which the British had lacked at Loos in 1915 and in the Somme in 1916. The use of artillery was as heavy as in the Somme, but alternating the level of intensity during the twenty days before the assault confused the Germans as to when the attack would commence as well as deprived them of replacements, rations, and repairs to damaged defenses. British aeroplanes outnumbered the German fleet three to one, assuring air supremacy with which to target their artillery.

To move troops forward without being attacked by German artillery fire, British coal miners dug twelve tunnel systems – called 'subways' – 5 to 20 meters beneath their forward trenches. Not only did these tunnels provide sheltered transportation, but they also accommodated unit headquarters, dressing stations, communications equipment, and storerooms. Eighteen additional tunnels were dug for mines under German front line positions, the explosives to be detonated immediately before the attack.

Battle

On Easter Monday, 9 April, the soldiers of four Canadian divisions took a tot of rum, and exited the subways directly into advanced trenches. A light sleet added to the cold and misery as the dawn's light crept over the ridge. At precisely 05:30, 1,462 guns spewed their shells in a single, massive explosion at the German positions. In a last-minute decision, only five of the eighteen mines were detonated; eliminating at least one German garrison. Three minutes later the artillery performed the war's first successful creeping barrage – the shells falling 100 meters farther forward every three minutes. As the Canadians surged forward, the German front trenches were quickly and easily occupied; strongpoints were bypassed, to be cleared of the enemy by the following units. The forward momentum was maintained in all but the northern most sector, where a decision to withhold the preliminary

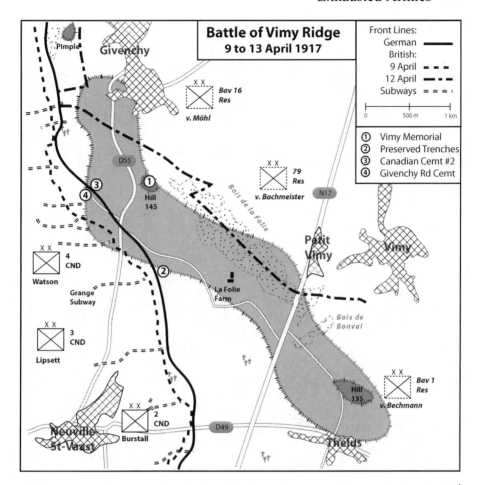

bombardment to preserve the trenches for Canadian occupation resulted in the 87th Battalion (Canadian Grenadier Guards) walking into the fire of prepared German riflemen. The battalion suffered fifty per cent casualties in sixty seconds. The German Maxim machine guns then swung around and tore into the advancing troops on either flank. 54th Battalion, the right most unit of 4th Division, was moving forward to replace the leading 102nd Battalion when machine guns applied enfilade fire and forced their withdrawal. The Maxims swung north, and the 78th Battalion was also caught in the enfilade while relieving the 38th Battalion. While the other three divisions were clearing their second objectives and moving toward the third, 4th Canadian Division had their battalions intermixed and their lines of communication broken. Two hours after the assault began, the 78th Battalion reached the Red Line (second objective); however, an hour later the weakened unit was driven back to the Black Line (first objective) by a company of the German Infantry Regiment Nr 261.

To the south 3rd Division sealed their northern flank and proceeded 1 km to the edge of Bois de la Folie. By 11:15, 2nd Division was through Thélus, the

Zwischenstellung (the German Intermediate Line), and at their Blue Line (3rd objective). Before noon the 1st Division achieved the Blue Line. At this point, the advance slowed. The 2nd Division faced an expanded belt of bared wire 20- to 50- meters thick. The creeping barrage, which had so effectively dealt with most of the German positions, was at its maximum range. Three brigades swept down on Bois de la Ville from the north and west, cutting their way by hand through sections of undestroyed wire. By sheer grit and determination, they broke through the entanglements to charge the German batteries firing from the wood. The gunners turned and ran but were gunned down in flight. The 1st and 2nd Division accomplished their objectives and began consolidating positions, improving trenches and reestablishing communications to the rear.

All was not well atop the ridge, however, where 4th Division had made little progress against Hill 145, the highest point on the ridge. Only a few of the front line trenches had been secured. The 11th Brigade commander, Brigadier Victor Odlum, ordered two companies of his reserve 85th (Nova Scotia) Battalion forward against the Black Line objective. With daylight fading and the temperature dropping, the advance faltered, only to be rescued by individual displays of heroism, including that of Private John Pattison VC, who single-handedly eliminated a machine-gun nest. The defenders, their lines thinned by twenty days of artillery bombardment and a full day of fighting, finally broke and ran. The crest of Hill 145 was taken.

The reserve battalions of 4th Division moved forward the next day, and at 15:15, under a repeat of the original barrage, they surged forward against weakened opposition. By 17:00, the Red Line objectives were captured, and the ridge was clear. The Germans withdrew to their *III Stellung* (Oppy-Mericourt Line) 6 km to the east, which was completed during the night of 12/13 April.

After the successful capture of Vimy Ridge, the offensive was temporarily suspended on 14 April, since the enemy was in prepared defensive positions, and allied artillery was stuck behind a shell-torn battlefield. The cavalry – no longer expecting a rapid advance but still hoping for a moderate breakthrough – was once again sent to the rear, unused. Nine days later a series of actions commenced that lacked the planning, training, and force of the initial assault. Intended to straighten the line rather than to achieve a breakthrough, advances were made but they were minor. The fighting dwindled and all actions stopped by 24 May.

The victory at Vimy Ridge was the first truly successful British army assault of the war. The Canadian divisions' participation as a unified corps in the Vimy attack is credited with developing a feeling of unity that many believe inspired the dominion's nationhood.

Battlefield Tour

Exit Arras toward Neuville-St-Vaast (D63, then D937); bear right toward Neuville-St-Vaast (D55) and follow the signs to the memorial.

A 91-hectare park now covers Vimy Ridge, the land granted to Canada in perpetuity by a grateful French people. The **Canadian National Vimy Memorial** (Mémorial Canadien de Vimy) is the country's main memorial to its troops who perished in the First World War. Visible from a great distance, the 27-meter twin pylons occupy the summit of Hill 145, where the 85th (Nova Scotia) Battalion pressed forward on 9 April. The Dalmatian stone monument bears the maple leaf of Canada on one pylon and the fleur-de-lis of France on the other, representing the unity of the two countries. They are accompanied by twenty larger-than-life-sized carved figures representing such concepts as Peace, Truth, and Sympathy. The lane from the parking area approaches steps flanked by statuary groups representing the defenders of peace and victory. At the base of the monument are recorded the Canadian accomplishment in very understated terms, 'The Canadian Corps on 9 April 1917 with four divisions in line on a front of four miles [6.4 km] attacked and captured this ridge.' The walls of the monument are inscribed with the names of 11,285 Canadians killed in France and who have no known grave. An evocative statue stands on the east side overlooking the Douai Plain and represents 'Mother Canada,' in the form of a sorrowful woman mourning her dead.

Vimy Ridge's modern appearance is muted from what it was like in 1917. Forests have covered most of the ridge, hiding the viewpoints onto the distant plain that were so important to the military planners. Grass has covered the churned ground, and erosion has softened the outlines of the mine and shell craters. The battlefields of Loos and Hill 70 are still visible to the north; the twin peaks of the Double Crassier rising above the level terrain. To the west, atop the crest of the Lorette spur, the towers of the commemorative Basilica of Notre-Dame stand amid the rows of crosses of the French dead from the 1915 capture of Lorette and the disastrous attack upon Vimy.

A second parking area approximately 1 km south is on the terrain of the 3rd Canadian Division's advance. Immediately in front of the information kiosk is the first group of sandbagged trenches. These are outpost trenches, the main line being 50 to 100 meters back. The exit from Grange subway led immediately into these front trenches. Movement around the battlefield is restricted to the marked lanes because the surfeit of unexploded munitions makes the land dangerous. The trenches can be entered, with the cement sandbags and duckboards providing a touch of reality. In between them and the German line, which is visible a very short distance ahead, are Grange and Winnipeg Craters. The German side includes a concrete observation post that was built into the trench wall and a *minenwerfer* position.

Tours of **Grange Subway** are offered, but group size is restricted. During the peak summer months, the tour can be filled quickly. The only modifications to the narrow tunnels have been for safety reasons, and the 250-meter walk gives the feeling of soldiers waiting for the start of the attack. Along the access road connecting the two sites are numerous mine craters which were the result of the mine war of 1916. Down a rural road – which essentially follows the German front – are **Canadian Cemetery No. 2**, containing the remains of 2,965 soldiers killed in the Vimy attack and others who died in later actions, and the **Givenchy Road Canadian Cemetery**, with 111 burials from the Vimy fighting. Both are worthwhile to visit.

The memorial is open every day May to October from 10:00 to 18:00 and from 09:00 to 17:00 the remainder of the year. Canadian volunteer students provide guided tours of the trench lines and Grange Subway during the summer. No admission fee or charge for the tours.

Other Sites of Interest: The area is dotted with memorials and sites marking the key locations of the war. In the woods east of the memorial are several memorials to Canadian divisions, and the **Canadian Artillery Memorial** in Thélus is along the N17 roadway.

#28

First and Second Battles of Bullecourt
11 April and 3 to 17 May 1917

OBJECTIVE	To capture the Hindenburg Line position around Bullecourt
FORCES	
BRITISH:	Four Australian divisions and three British divisions of the Fifth Army (Lieutenant-General William Birdwood)
GERMAN:	German 27th Wurttemberg Division, with other units of the XIV Reserve Corps as reinforcements (Generalleutnant Otto von Moser)
RESULT	The April assault was a complete disaster in planning and execution; the May assaults captured small amounts of territory, were costly and provided no strategic advantage.
CASUALTIES	
BRITISH:	3,289, including 1,170 captured during the April assault; an additional 7,000 Australian and 2,700 British casualties in May
GERMAN:	750 killed during April and 6,000 casualties in May
LOCATION	Arras is 180 km north of Paris; Bullecourt is 24 km southeast of Arras

Battle

General Hubert Gough, commander of the British Fifth Army, believed that tanks could be successful in penetrating German barbed wire. Forgoing the usual artillery preparation, he ordered the 4th Australian Division to assault the strongly held Hindenburg Line east of the village of Bullecourt. Unfortunately for the Australians, the tanks were early training models and not equipped for the rigors of battle. Most of the eleven tanks became disabled before reaching the front line; the others moved so slowly as to be passed by the attacking foot soldiers. The 4th and 12th Brigades of the 4th Australian Division attacked across open fields against prepared positions of the German Hindenburg Line at 05:15 on 11 April, after a night of huddling to keep warm during a snowstorm. The assault was flanked to the west by German positions in Bullecourt and to the east by machine guns in Quéant.

While the 12th Brigade waited for the arrival of the tanks, the 4th Brigade moved forward even though their left flank was highly exposed. Although they were able to enter the first German trench line, a feat thought by some to be impossible, German machine-gun fire and artillery stopped the leading 14th and 16th Battalions. The reinforcing 13th and 15th Battalions passed through and continued the advance toward Riencourt. A well-placed German machine gun at a road junction known as Six Cross Roads fired into the troops when they attempted to enter the German communications trench called Ostrich Alley.

The 12th Brigade was hardly more successful, its lead battalion also penetrating the German first line but farther progress was impossible. By 10:00, the inevitable German counterattack began, with the forward Australian units, especially the 48th Battalion, being cut off and the men either killed or captured. The abortive assault essentially wiped out the 4th Brigade, which suffered seventy-five per cent casualties; the 12th Brigade fared only slightly better, suffering forty-seven per cent casualties.

The German XIV Corps responded on 15 April with a substantial assault along a 12-km front from west of Quéant to Havrincourt, pushing the ANZAC troops back approximately 1 to 2 km across the entire attack line. A major incursion into Australian lines temporarily captured the village of Lagnicourt.

On 3 May, 2nd Australian Division repeated the April assault, this time with a preparatory artillery barrage as well as a creeping barrage as they advanced from the shelter of the sunken road east of Bullecourt. The British 62nd (West Riding)

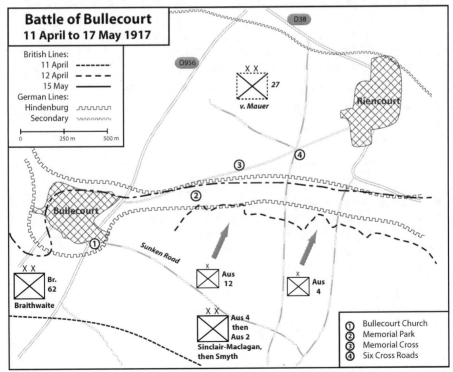

Division was again on the left flank advancing west of Bullecourt. The 5th Brigade, on the right side of 2nd Australian Division, was met with intense machine-gun fire and made little progress despite two attempts to achieve the German front trench. Although the battalions of the adjoining 6th Brigade penetrated the German second line, the lack of progress on both their flanks made the advance unsupportable, and they later withdrew.

The 62nd Division's attack upon the village faced the same intense machine-gun fire and was also forced to withdraw from any localized gains. By the end of the first day, the 7th Division took over for the 62nd, and the 1st Australian Division replaced the 2nd. The village, still in German hands, was now a salient in the British lines.

An assault on Bullecourt on 7 May ended with the British occupation of most of the village despite the machine-gun and artillery fire. The fighting for the now ruined buildings moved back and forth, with each British assault countered by the Germans. The British, supported now by the 5th Australian Division, finally controlled most of the village by 12 May, although the fighting continued until 15 May, when they repelled a German 3rd Guards Division attack. The Germans then abandoned Bullecourt as unworthy of further bloodshed. A final, isolated German strongpoint was captured on 17 May.

A British attack from within a salient in the German lines, even if successful, would have created only a deeper salient, with strong positions of the Hindenburg Line on each flank. The useless slaughter of so many fine Australian and British troops led to recriminations against British generalship and particularly against General Gough. Many Australians thought that the attack was ill-conceived and carried out either to satisfy French requests for support or to further Gough's hopes for promotion.

Battlefield Tour

Leave Arras on the national road toward Cambrai (N39, becomes D939); after passing through Vis-en-Artois, turn right toward Bullecourt (D956).

The Bullecourt battlefield shows no remnants of the intense fighting. The farmer's plow has returned the earth to productive uses, and the village has been rebuilt. It has become a pilgrimage site, however, for Australians, who are still warmly welcomed by the villagers. Several memorials have been constructed, and they are the scenes of annual remembrances.

In the center of **Bullecourt** is the village church, with its massive tower constructed of randomly sized stones. In front of it is a monument to the Australian and British troops who fought here in 1917. The stone wall has the rising sun emblem of the Australian force and the pelican emblem of the **British 62nd Division**. Other plaques commemorate the British 7th and 58th Divisions. The top of the low wall displays a bronzed 'slouch' hat, the distinctive headgear worn by Australian infantry. **Signboards** indicate the location of other memorials to the battle and a recommended walking tour. If the entire walk seems too long, a good alternative is to proceed to the left of the church on the rue de Quéant, which is the sunken road utilized in the second battle of Bullecourt. A short walk down this tractor-rutted lane provides a view over the terrain of the Australian assault. The two flags in the distance indicate the location of the memorial park as well as the German first line. The difficulty of advancing over such open ground against entrenched machine gun positions is evident.

Exit the village toward Riencourt-lès-Cagnicourt (rue de Douai).

Northeast of the village is the **Bullecourt Memorial Park**. To the left of the entrance walkway is a Ross Bastiaan Plaque which commemorates Australian participation in the battle. The German first line trenches ran near the plaque's location. A paved walk up a slight incline goes through a narrow, park-like setting bordered with recently planted trees. The French and Australian flags flank a memorial statue at the crest of the incline. The brass 'Digger Statue' is situated where the 12th Brigade suffered extensive losses. The statue receives its name from the nickname for Australian soldiers. It commemorates the more than 10,000 casualties that the four Australian divisions suffered during the two attempts to capture the area's trenches. Looking toward Bullecourt from this spot, the Australian attack was from left to right.

Farther ahead on the same road and located atop the rock embankment on the left is a **small memorial cross** mounted on a stone block plinth, commemorating 2,423 Australian soldiers who have no known grave. Attached to individual stones are private memorial plaques commemorating loved ones killed at Bullecourt. They make for poignant reading. Parking near the cross is perilous; walk from the Memorial Park. The terrain along this walk was the location of the German Second Line.

Farther northeast is the open road junction of **Six Cross Roads,** which now has only five roads. The open lanes that provided German machine gunners with deadly fields of fire remain.

#29
Second Battle of the Aisne (Chemin des Dames)
16 April to 9 May 1917

OBJECTIVE	To launch a breakthrough offensive against German positions
FORCES	
FRENCH:	Forty-four infantry and seven cavalry divisions, 128 tanks, and 220 aeroplanes of Fifth, Sixth, and Tenth Armies (général de division Joseph Micheler)
GERMAN:	Twelve front line and twelve reserve divisions of First Army (General der Infanterie Fritz von Below) and Seventh Army (Generaloberst Richard von Schubert)
RESULT	Small territorial gains at the expense of significant casualties

CASUALTIES	
FRENCH:	183,000 killed and wounded; 4,000 taken prisoner
GERMAN:	133,000 killed and wounded; 28,815 taken prisoner
LOCATION	Soissons is 130 km northeast of Paris; the Chemin des Dames (D18) starts 17.5 km northeast of Soissons

Political maneuvering in France forced général Joffre's resignation as commander-in-chief and his position was given to général de division Robert Nivelle. Nivelle's 'new' theories of warfare were based upon his successful recapture of Fort de Douaumont the previous year. Nivelle, a career artillery officer, believed that overpowering artillery was the answer to achieving the breakthrough necessary to resume mobile warfare and escape the trench-war stalemate. Nivelle chose the line between Soissons and Reims as the key target. Defensive lines had formed there after the German withdrawal from the Marne in 1914, when they had retraced their steps northward to favorable defensive positions along a high ridge. A brief and inconclusive encounter known as the First Battle of the Aisne followed. The front in this sector remained essentially stagnant until Nivelle's plan of 1917.

Nivelle planned to crush German defenses beneath a substantial bombardment, allowing infantry to rush up the hillsides and capture their positions. He amassed a truly impressive force of three armies supported by 5,350 guns, including 1,550 *Crapouillots* (trench mortars) and 128 newly arrived Schneider tanks. The Sixth Army was to attack between Chavonne and Hurtebise; the Fifth Army between Hurtebise and Reims. The assault troops were to crack the German line on the first day, allowing Tenth Army reserves and cavalry to pour through onto the Laon plain.

Not every commander shared Nivelle's enthusiasm. Some that did not, including général Pétain, voiced their concern to President Poincare, who brought the matter to a head. At first Nivelle threatened to resign, then he agreed to terminate the offensive if its goals were not reached within the first 48 hours.

French security was porous, and the German High Command knew of the planned general offensive as early as March. Parisian café gossips openly discussed the upcoming attack, and seized military documents spelled out the entire battle plan. The Germans accelerated efforts to strengthen the line, digging deep galleries into the face of the bluff. Trench lines were multiplied and supported with blockhouses. Front line divisions were strengthened, and reserve units were moved into place. In the days leading up to the attack, counter-battery fire took a toll on French guns because the ridge gave the Germans excellent observation sites.

Battle

Two postponements due to inclement weather hampered French artillery observation aeroplanes and balloons, and Nivelle extended the preliminary bombardment from ten days to two weeks. After another stormy night filled with heavy rain, nineteen assault divisions were finally launched on 16 April. The infantry immediately fell victim to the mud and was not able to keep pace with the creeping barrage. German positions in the underground posts were not as effected by the

French artillery as expected, and upon the cessation of artillery fire, they immediately began repositioning their machine guns for the slaughter.

The first news of the attack reached French *grand quartier général* (GQG) at 10:30 and was guardedly optimistic. That local commanders had ordered the creeping barrage to return to previous targets because the infantry had not maintained pace, however, soon became apparent. Despite orders to gain ground at any cost, the infantry was able to make only localized advances. By the end of the day the offensive was obviously a disastrous failure. The French suffered 40,000 casualties, but Nivelle ignored his own 48-hour time limit, and the fighting continued to 26 April before being halted. A secondary assault took place on 5 May with some minor successes.

The consequences of the battle were critical and far-reaching. Nivelle was removed from command and exiled to North Africa. He was replaced by the hero of Verdun, général Pétain. The inspiration given to the army by Nivelle's optimistic expectations of a breakthrough turned to depression and disillusionment. Mutinies that were officially described as 'collective disobedience' spread through the army because troops agreed in most cases to man defensive positions but refused to attack; some units refused to return to the front lines. Courts martial and executions followed, but Pétain instituted a series of reforms in food, leave, and medical care. Seven months passed before the French Army was again able to mount even a small-scale offensive action.

Battlefield Tour

A ridgeline runs east to west north of the Aisne River, upon which a roadway known as the Chemin des Dames had been constructed for the convenience of the daughters of the French king, Louis XV. To the north, the plateau gradually descends into the valley of the Ailette. To the south, however, the plateau was cut by numerous ravines and gullies, forming steep, finger-like projections into the valley of the Aisne. The Germans built substantial gun emplacements along the crest and into the many caves and galleries dug into the sides of the slopes.

The Chemin des Dames battlefield is one of the most informative French battlefield sites. A local association has preserved numerous monuments and erected several trilingual signboards to describe the fighting and aftermath of the offensive. The route is an easy day's drive from Soissons and ends near the famous cathedral and champagne city of Reims. The combination of historical, cultural, and gastronomic activities makes this battlefield tours a favorite.

Leave Soissons toward Laon (N2); after approximately 13 km, stop at the small café on the left.

An old windmill on the heights near Laffaux was attacked by the I Colonial Corps three hours after the general assault started on 16 April. Ignoring their flanks, they quickly captured the mill, but enfilade machine-gun fire made holding the position impossible. A new assault occurred after a second artillery barrage that

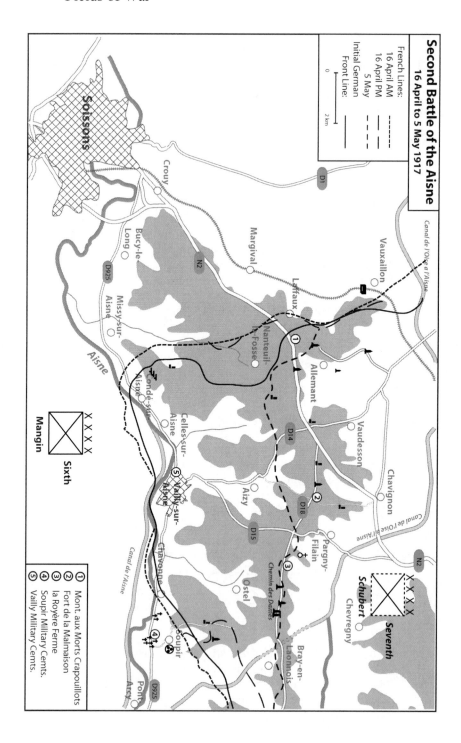

Second Battle of the Aisne
16 April to 5 May 1917

French Lines:
16 April AM
16 April PM
5 May
Initial German
Front Line:

0   2 km

Soissons

Crouy

Canal de l'Oise à l'Aisne

D1

Vauxaillon

Margival

N2

Laffaux

Bucy-le-Long

D925

Missy-sur-Aisne

Nanteuil-la-Fosse

①   Allemant

1

Vaudesson

Chavignon

Aisne

D14

Condé-sur-Aisne

Celles-sur-Aisne

Aizy

D18   ②

Pargny-Filain

Mangin

XXXX
Sixth

⑤ Vailly-sur-Aisne

N35

D15

Canal de l'Oise à l'Aisne

N2

Schubert

XXXX
Seventh

Chevregny

Chavonne

Canal de l'Aisne

Chemin des Dames

Ostel

③

Bray-en-Laonnois

Soupir
④

Pont-Arcy

D925

① Mont aux Morts Crapouillots
② Fort de la Malmaison
③ la Royère Ferme
④ Soupir Military Cemts.
⑤ Vailly Military Cemts.

evening, but no progress was made despite the effort, as attested by the 3,800 casualties suffered by the corps that day. The position was again attacked on 5 May and captured.

Behind the café is the towering, mortar bomb-shaped **Monument aux Morts Crapouillots,** which commemorates the 12,000 trench mortar troops (*de l'Artillerie des Tranchée les Crapouillots*) who died in the war. Images of trench warfare are inscribed around its top. Slightly to the north, on a side path that once was the original Soissons-Laon highway, are several individual memorials that were relocated in the course of highway reconstruction. In the café parking area is a concrete bunker which is now the **Moulin de Laffaux Memorial** to the 123,079 dead and missing from the Second World War.

Continue northwards toward Laon (N2) 4.5 km, then bear right onto the Chemin des Dames (D18).

Ahead on the left is the **Fort de la Malmaison Soldatenfriedhof**, an enormous Second World War German military cemetery containing 11,841 burials. Behind the cemetery is the ruin of **Fort de la Malmaison**, built by Séré de Rivières to protect the western end of the Chemin des Dames. Barely defended, the Germans easily occupied it in 1914 and held it until French Moroccan troops recaptured it in October 1917 during the first test of French offensive power after the mutinies. Although the fort is not open for tours, trilingual signboards in its parking area describe the construction and history of the fort.

Two km past Malmaison, a left turn leads to an overlook named after the nearby **la Royère Ferme**. Signboards lining a reconstructed slit trench, pay homage to the colonial troops which strengthened France's fighting capability during the war. The views to the north and of the Ailette Valley do not show the battlefield.

Many of the rural roads along the Chemin des Dames descend the ridge to the south and present an opportunity to visualize the difficult terrain experienced during the uphill assault. The road toward Braye-en-Laonnois (D883) passes through Braye and continues downhill to Soupir. The Aisne valley near Soupir contains a string of military cemeteries, including French, German, and Italian cemeteries at Soupir and French and British cemeteries at Vailly-sur-Aisne. From the chemin to Soupir and back is a 16 km excursion.

Continue to **Cerny-en-Laonnois**, which in 1914 was located south of its current position on the forward edge of the plateau situated above les Hurtemonts valley. The village was fortified by the Germans with machine guns and two artillery batteries in the adjoining wood. The sugar mill was a major bastion in this sector and was surrounded with multiple bands of barbed wire. Despite the dense defenses, the French 153rd Division quickly captured the sugar mill ruin on 16 April 1917, but was unable to advance farther.

The small, privately erected chapel located at the intersection of two highways in Cerny is the main memorial to the dead of the Chemin des Dames battle. In front of the chapel is a **Lanterne des Morts,** whose nighttime light can be visible

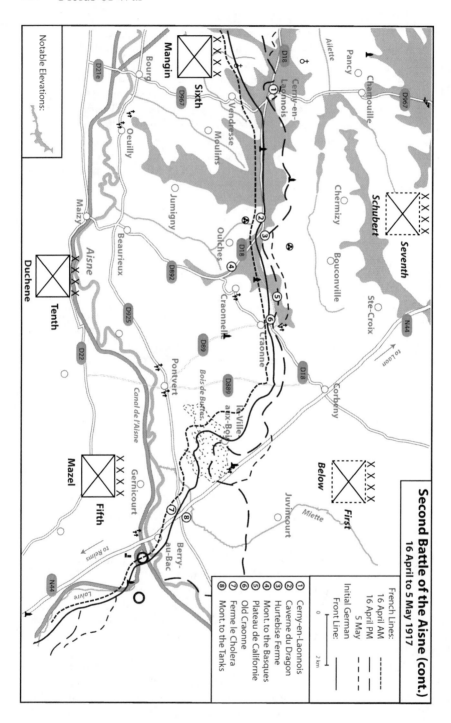

Notable Elevations:

Second Battle of the Aisne (cont.)
16 April to 5 May 1917

French Lines:
16 April AM
16 April PM
5 May
Initial German
Front Line:

0   2 km

① Cerny-en-Laonnois
② Caverne du Dragon
③ Hurtebise Ferme
④ Mont. to the Basques
⑤ Plateau de Californie
⑥ Old Craonne
⑦ Ferme le Cholera
⑧ Mont. to the Tanks

from the cathedrals at Laon, Soissons, and Reims. A plaque commemorates the **French 38th Division**, whose colonial regiments of Zouaves and Tirailleurs fought locally in 1914 and in April and October 1917. Across the road are French and German cemeteries. South on the D967 is a monumental column dedicated to the **1st Battalion Loyal North Lancashire Regiment,** whose attack upon the sugar mill during the First Battle of the Aisne in September 1914 was costly.

Continue on the Chemin des Dames for 5 km.

Caverne du Dragon Museum is on the right. Old quarry tunnels were extensively fortified by the Germans, starting with their occupation in 1914. The caverns below the museum were the scene of truly frightening underground warfare in the summer of 1917. At times fighters were only meters apart, attacking each other with grenades, rifle butts, and bayonets in the fearful darkness of an underground no man's land.

The modern museum's free reception area displays dramatic photographs of local fighting with captions in French only. Underground tours which demonstrate life and fighting in the tunnels and quarried rooms are offered in multiple languages at various times throughout the day. The rear terrace presents spectacular views into the Foulon Valley as far as the Aisne River as well as two tables of orientation. The museum offers the only refreshments and public toilets on the Chemin des Dames. Open daily February through June from 10:00 to 18:00; July and August from 10:00 to 19:00; September through mid-December from 10:00 to 18:00; closed Mondays February through April and September through December; and closed January. Fee.

Continue east less than 1 km.

The fortified walls of **Hurtebise farm** were the scene of a clash between Napoleon and an allied army commanded by Prussian General Blücher on 7 March 1814. The farm was critical to any combat in this area because it straddled the narrowest segment of the Chemin des Dames, a 75-meter wide isthmus joining two sections of the ridge. On 16 April 1917, the farm was attacked by the French II Colonial Corps. Its 10th Division climbed the muddy slopes from the Foulon Valley and stormed the farm. Heavy losses prohibited any farther advance.

At the nearby intersection stands the **Monument des Marie-Louise,** named after the young recruits in Napoleon's 1814 army. The original statue was destroyed in the war, and its replacement shows soldiers of two eras supporting the flag of France, thereby commemorating the soldiers of Napoleon and of Nivelle who died in attacks on the farm over 100 years apart. The brick walls of the farm hold plaques commemorating the actions of the 4th Zouaves Regiment in 1914 and 1917 as well as Colonel Charles de Gaulle's 4th Division's attack against the Germans in 1940.

East of Hurtebise, the Chemin des Dames road forks; proceed to the right toward Craonnelle (D18).

The 13-meter stone **Monument to the Basques** was erected by the men of the 36th Division to commemorate the fighters from that section of France along the Pyrenees. The beautifully landscaped area has more signboards and tables of orientation.

Return to the fork and proceed to the left.

The road passes through the Forêt de Vauclair and along the **Plateau de Californie**. The 16 April assault on the plateau by three divisions of I Corps was met with massed German machine-gun fire that wiped out entire regiments. Two divisions repeated the attempt on 5 May, and while they climbed the height, Germans streamed from underground positions in the Caverne du Dragon and attacked from the rear. After heavy losses the French were forced to retire. A parking area provides access to the plateau ridge, which now affords a gentle sentier along the edge that continues the entire distance to the destroyed village of Craonne.

Drive farther east and park immediately before the intersection with the D884.

This area is the **old village of Craonne**, destroyed by shellfire so completely that it became uninhabitable. The new village is down the slope to the south. From the parking area, a foot trail ascends the rather steep hill, and wooden steps continue the path to the top. Near the summit is a German machine-gun pillbox. From the interior of the bunker, views through its gun slit show the challenges facing the French in attacking such fortified positions.

Proceed toward Corbeny (D18) and turn right onto the Laon-Reims Road toward Berry-au-Bac / Reims (N44).

The road passes through the French Fifth Army's area of operations, where the terrain and effective tank support made a 3-km advance on 16 April possible.

After 7.5 km and before entering Berry-au-Bac, turn left onto the D925, and enter the monument grounds.

The French tanks were divided into two groups – one formation commanded by commandant Louis Bossut, supported XXXII Corps and attacked from **Ferme le Choléra**, which was located across the highway, the other, Groupement Chaubès in support of V Corps, attacked 4 km farther west. This engagement was the first French use of tanks in the war. Unfortunately, tank tactics were not well defined at this stage, and the terrain selected for their use was less than ideal. Bridge crossings and shell craters funneled the slow moving behemoths into channels targeted by German artillery. Although Bossut was killed, his unit was able to break passages in the German wire entanglements, permitting the advance of the infantry. The Chaubès group was almost totally destroyed with not one tank able to penetrate the German first line. Of those tanks not damaged by shellfire, many suffered mechanical breakdowns.

The **National Monument of the Tanks** consists of a huge granite stone which records the names of the tankers killed in the last two years of the war. The smaller memorial in front of the monument is to général Jean-Baptiste Estienne, credited with creating the Schneider assault tank. The parking area displays several armored vehicles; however, they are all of postwar vintage.

Return to Ypres

The great battles of 1916 at Somme and Verdun ground to a miserable, bloody, inconclusive halt. The losses in the Somme shocked the British public. British Prime Minister David Lloyd George's antipathy for General Haig was undisguised and he believed that the generals were murderous fools for their insistence on attacking strong German positions in a contest to see who could create more casualties. Lloyd George proposed attacking Germany's allies in an attempt to isolate and starve the enemy into capitulation. Prior experiences at Gallipoli and Salonika, however, discredited such proposals.

French général Nivelle's great offensive against the heights of the Aisne River proved to be an utter disaster that took all the fight out of the French Army. Although Pétain's leadership inspired enough aggressiveness in the selected units to push the Germans back to their start line at Verdun, the French became a purely defensive force.

After two and a half million deaths on the Western Front, the opposing forces were deadlocked, facing each other over shell-pocked, trench-drilled, and gas-drenched ground in which no living thing could survive for long. America had joined the war but with only an insignificantly sized army. Russia had all but exited the war, the soldiers laying down their arms and walking home. Responsibility for continuing the war hence fell to General Haig's British Army. Even in 'quiet' periods, trench warfare claimed an average of one thousand casualties per day in the Ypres salient. Haig had long held faith in a plan to wrest the Belgian port cities away from the Germans to halt their usage as bases for the German submarine war against British shipping. The breakthrough would be followed by mass cavalry pouring through the gaps.

The nomenclature of the Ypres battles can be somewhat confusing. The British Official History of the war breaks Third Battle of Ypres into the fol-lowing periods:

Battle of Messines:	7 to 14 June
Battle of Pilckem:	31 July to 2 August
Battle of Langemark:	16 August to 18 August
Battle of Menin Road:	20 to 25 September
Battle of Polygon Wood:	26 September to 3 October
Battle of Broodseinde:	4 October
Battle of Poelkapelle:	9 October

First Battle of Passchendaele: 12 October
Second Battle of Passchendaele: 26 October to 10 November

The entire conflict after 31 July is sometimes referred to as the Battle of Passchendaele.

#30

Third Battle of Ypres (Messines)
7 to 14 June 1917

OBJECTIVE	To eliminate the German presence upon the ridgeline that dominated the southern Ypres Salient
FORCES	
BRITISH:	Twelve divisions of the Second Army (Lieutenant-General Sir Herbert Plumer)
GERMAN:	Eight divisions of XIX Corps (*Gruppe Wijtschate*) (General der Kavallerie Maximilian von Laffert)
RESULT	Plumer's Army successfully captured the ridge as well as Messines and Wijtschate, its two dominant villages
CASUALTIES	
BRITISH:	Approximately 25,000
GERMAN:	Estimated at 25,000, including 5,000 prisoners taken the first day
LOCATION	Ypres is 250 km north of Paris; Messines is 10 km south of Ypres

The British positions west of Messines were the remnant of the 1914 battles, when the German advance halted with the possession of the ridge. The Germans formed a counter-salient, extending into the British held areas south of Ypres and north of Ploegsteert. From the heights the German *Gruppe Wijtschate* had almost complete observation over the British lines, precluding any attempt at attack in the open or even along trench lines. As early as 1915, therefore, the British employed tunnelers to dig a series of shafts beneath strongpoints in the German front line. By the spring of 1917, 20,000 men burrowing twenty-one tunnels under no man's land. In addition to the natural risks of air depletion, flooding, or collapse, German coal miners from the Ruhr were digging countershafts to intercept and destroy British tunnels. Small explosives known as *camouflets* were used to cave in enemy tunnels. Upon completion, the tunnel ends were packed with one million pounds of ammonal and sealed against blowback. When asked if the forthcoming battle would change the course of the war, Plumer's chief of staff, Major-General Tim Harrington, famously responded, 'Gentlemen, I do not know whether we shall change history tomorrow, but we shall certainly alter the geography.'[1]

General Plumer's force was a representation of the British Commonwealth: New Zealand 'Kiwis' and Australian 'Aussies' in ANZAC as well as Protestant 36th (Ulster) Division and Catholic 16th (Irish) Division in IX Corps. Plumer was known

---

[1] Leon Wolff, *In Flanders Fields: The 1917 Campaign* (New York: Viking Press, 1958), 97.

for meticulous planning, and the Messines attack was a masterpiece. All the requirements of a modern army, from artillery shells to drinking water, were accumulated in great supply. A scale model of the attack zone was built, and soldiers of all ranks were given their unit objectives. Air observation by 300 Royal Flying Corps planes pinpointed German batteries, supply points, troop concentrations, and other artillery targets. German batteries were identified in detail, and over two thousand British guns were concentrated for the initial barrage. For one week before the attack, the German lines were saturated with explosives and poison gas to deaden German responsiveness and strain their nerves.

The sector was defended by five divisions of *Gruppe Wijtschate*, with three additional divisions in reserve. Not noticing the British build-up of troops and equipment was impossible. The German batteries were therefore reinforced with 700 guns, adding to the original complement of 340. The German defensive arrangement exercised the principles of 'elastic defense.' Weakly held front positions utilized the terrain and shell holes to survive the enemy bombardment and inflict causalities upon the attacking force. The main defensive position, rich in concrete pillboxes and deep bunkers, was rearward, sited upon a reverse slope to avoid direct enemy observation. This placement offered the additional advantage of silhouetting the attackers when they passed over the crest of the hill. Farther rearward, reserves would launch counterattacks after the attackers' initial momentum was expended.

Battle

At 03:10 on 7 June, nineteen explosions of such magnitude as to be heard as far away as London erupted along the 16 km front from Hill 60 in the north to Trench 122 in the south. It was the most violent man-made event in history as tons of earth and debris along with 10,000 dead German soldiers were thrown into the air. While the remnants were still falling back to earth, the artillery barrage started, focusing on the enemy front lines and killing any survivors of the explosions. When British soldiers climbed out of their trenches, the barrage crept forward at an even pace as the infantry advanced close behind it. The German forward zone was quickly occupied. The German 204th Division, defending Hill 60 and Mount Sorrel, had little opportunity to contest the British 23rd Division's advance, and the heights were quickly occupied. The ruins of Wijtschate and Messines, mostly leveled by the British artillery fire, were quickly occupied, and isolated pockets of resistance were rapidly overcome.

The British Second Army commanded the crest of the ridge six hours later. German counterattacks quickly failed because now the British observers owned the high ground and they effectively directed gunfire onto approaching enemy columns. German reserve troops, however, directed machine-gun and artillery fire onto the ridge now crowded with British troops, causing many of the battle's casualties.

Plumer had established the final objective as the Oosttaverne Line, which was 2 km east of Messines, and the fighting resumed after the artillery had advanced. By day's end all the objectives were met, although the fighting continued for another week until the German High Command decided that their current positions were untenable and ordered a withdrawal to their *Flandern I* defensive line. The battle of

Messines was the best-planned and executed assault by the British thus far in the entire war.

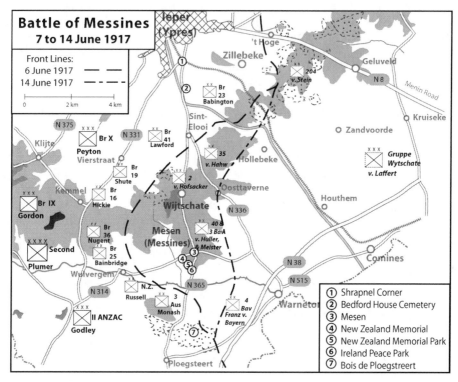

Battle of Messines
7 to 14 June 1917

Front Lines:
6 June 1917
14 June 1917

0   2 km   4 km

① Shrapnel Corner
② Bedford House Cemetery
③ Mesen
④ New Zealand Memorial
⑤ New Zealand Memorial Park
⑥ Ireland Peace Park
⑦ Bois de Ploegstreert

Battlefield Tour

The tour proceeds south from Ypres to Messines noting sites along the highway.

Leave Ypres through the Rijsel (Lille) Gate toward Armentières (N336).

Shortly outside of the city is the intersection with the Kemmelseweg (N331), known as **Shrapnel Corner** because it was under German fire for most of the war. Approximately 1 km farther on the left is the beautiful **Bedford House Cemetery**, most of which is not visible from the roadway but still worth a stop. Also on the left are the seven British dugouts of **Langhof Farm,** still surrounded by the moat of the destroyed château. Past Langhof 200 meters south on the opposite side of the road is the **Belgian Demarcation Stone,** marking the farthest German advance toward Ypres – only 3 km from the Grote Markt. The road passes through Sint-Elooi before reaching the gradual rise onto the plateau, then runs east of Wijtschate before traveling along the ridgeline to Messines. The Wijtschate sector was defended by the already depleted German 2nd (East Prussian) Division. On the front line since April, most of its members did not survive to be relieved as planned on 8 June; two regiments were destroyed, the third reduced to a few individuals.

The area in front of Messines was defended by the 40th Saxon Division, but it was in the process of being relieved on the night of 6 June by the 3rd Bavarian Division. The mine explosions and artillery barrage caught a number of troops in transit. As befitting its critical location, the village had been turned into a veritable fortress by the Germans. The cellars of residences were concreted into shell-proof dugouts, and five additional concrete bunkers were constructed in the village center. After the detonation of the mines, a stout defense was put up by the Bavarian Regiment Nr 18, with machine guns and riflemen sited among the rubble. Hand-to-hand fighting swept through the houses, each cellar a strongpoint needing to be cleared with grenades and each window or doorway potentially holding a sniper. The final Bavarian redoubt was the cellar beneath the church of the Institution Royale, which held the regimental headquarters. The New Zealanders took it, capturing the headquarters staff as well.

The **Messines central square** contains several monuments, including a Ross Bastiaan Plaque commemorating the 43,000 casualties which Australian units suffered in the Ypres Salient. Nearby is a simple white post which was presented to the village by the Japanese Peace Movement. The town hall holds a small museum of battlefield artifacts and is open weekdays from 09:00 to 12:00 and 13:00 to 17:00; between Easter and 11 November on Sunday afternoons from 14:30 to 17:30.

One block from the square is **De Sint Niklaaskerk** (Saint Nicholas Church), founded in 1060 by Countess Adela of France, a well-connected women who was the daughter of Robert the Pure, King of France; the wife of Baldwin V, Count of Flanders; and the mother of Mathilda, the wife of William the Conqueror. The foundation stones of the much larger original church are still visible in the parking area in front of the church. The rebuilt parish church sits over the 11th century crypt that was used by German medical units during the war. A wounded Adolf Hitler was rumored to have been treated here as a member of the Bavarian Reserve Infantry Regiment Nr 16. The crypt is the burial place of Countess Adela and still holds her tombstone. In a corner is the original wooden cross of 'Schneider, Anton, Musketier 17.09.18' – a type originally used in German cemeteries. The crypt is open to viewing; the access door is around the corner to the right of the altar.

Proceed on a well-marked turnoff in Messines toward Nieuwkerke (N314).

The road dramatically drops down Messines ridge to the **New Zealand Memorial to the Missing**. A beautiful stone entryway is formed by fieldstone walls centered upon a Cross of Sacrifice on a raised platform. Around the wall of the platform are 828 names of 'officers and men of New Zealand who fell in or near Messines in 1917 and 1918 whose graves are known only to God.'

Continuing on the stone walk is **Messines Ridge British Cemetery**, which stands on ground that once belonged to the Institution Royale. The post-Armistice cemetery contains graves dating from October 1914 to October 1918, but the majority died in the fighting of 1917. To the left is a colonnade with small shelters on either end, one of which displays a battlefield map. In the center is a bench which provides a resting place and a position to observe and contemplate not only the cemetery but also the ground outside the cemetery that drops into the valley, the direction from which the New Zealand troops advanced upon the village. To the west, the church steeple in Wulvergem is visible; slightly farther to the northwest are the Flanders Hills, the most notable being Mount Kemmel.

Return to Messines and proceed toward Armentières (N365); at the south edge of Messines is a well-signed turn down a narrow lane (Nieuw Zeelandersstraat).

Among the houses of Messines is the tree-shrouded entrance to the **New Zealand Memorial Park**. The white stone obelisk, which commemorates their participation in the battle of Messines, overlooks the Douve Valley to the south. In the lower corners of the park are two German pillboxes that were constructed as part of the German defenses at Messines. Note the two different construction techniques. The New Zealand attack progressed up the ridge and captured the two pillboxes before entering the village.

Return to the highway and proceed toward Armentières (N365).

At the southern exit of Messines is the **Isle of Ireland Peace Park,** containing a tower constructed in 1998 of Irish stone and dedicated to the memory of all those from the Isle of Ireland who fought and died in the First World War. The Peace Tower was erected as an act of reconciliation between nationalist and unionist factions who committed themselves to establishing a just peace for their people. Inside the tower are registries of Irish soldiers who were killed in the war. Beautiful bronze orientation maps showing the Ypres area from June to December 1917 and the attack routes of the various divisions on 7 June 1917 are mounted on gray stone pillars. The descriptions of the fighting by Irish authors, which are inscribed on stone tablets along the walkway, are especially moving. Chaplain Francis Gleason, Royal Munster Fusiliers, wrote, 'Spent all night trying to console, aide, and remove the wounded. It was ghastly to see them laying there in the cold, cheerless outhouses on bare stretchers with no blankets to cover their freezing limbs.' The war is never far away in Ypres; south of the tower, in the middle of the pasture, is an old pillbox.

Other Sites of Interest: South toward Armentières is **Bois de Ploegsteert,** a shelter area for British troops during much of the Ypres fighting and the final resting place for many in its five cemeteries. East of the highway on chemin du Mont de la Hutte, follow the CWGC sign toward the Ploegsteert cemeteries. A wooden cross marks the location of the famous **1914 Christmas Truce**, where soldiers of both sides, in disobedience to orders, mingled and shared small gifts in a few moments of sanity in an otherwise insane war. Back on the highway, a rotunda guarded by two lions is the **Ploegsteert Memorial to the Missing**, which holds the names of and commemorates

17. Bronze Caribou stands upon the Beaumont-Hamel Newfoundland Memorial.

Mill Road Cemetery sits upon the site of the July 1916 German front lines. The white stripe in the plowed field beyond the cemetery is said to be chalk spoil excavated during the digging of trenches. Thiepval Memorial is seen in the distance to the right; the village of Thiepval in the center.

18.   Thiepval Memorial dominates the area and is visible for kilometers. The white plaques on its lower walls list the names of the missing. Crosses of the Anglo-French Cemetery are partially visible at the bottom.

Canadian soldiers inspect the ruins of 'Gibraltar' strongpoint in Pozières. The tree stumps barely visible on the extreme left locate Mouquet Farm. LAC

All Australian divisional monuments on the Western front have the basic design of the 1st Division Monument at Pozières. Thiepval is barely visible in the woods to the left.

19.   The triumphal arch of the South African Memorial in Delville Wood near Longueval provides access to the museum beyond.

Shattered trees present the intensity of the shelling in Delville Wood in September 1916. *IWM Q1259*

An obelisk marking the brigade's command post stands along a shallow trench indicative of the poor shelter to be had in Delville Wood.

20. The 'Cobbers' Statue stands upon one of the German pillboxes in the Australian Memorial Park near Fromelles.

One of the two mass graves in VC Corner Cemetery near Fromelles and the Wall of Remembrance whose plaques hold the names of the missing.

21. Concrete 'sandbags' now preserve the trenches on Vimy Ridge. The foreground structure is a German pillbox; a mine crater is in the center, and the Canadian front lines were at the sign board on the left.
Inset: Unusual action photograph of Canadian 29th Infantry Battalion advancing through no man's land on a barren Vimy Ridge in April 1917. LAC

The inspiring Canadian National Vimy Memorial stands upon the highest point of Vimy Ridge. This photograph dates before a recent renovation removed the flagpoles.

22.   The Monument de Marie-Louise near Hurtebise farms along the Chemin des Dames marks the site of battles from three wars.

Detail from the Monument des Basques which commemorates the men from the Pyrenees.

Trench warfare is detailed on the Monument aux Morts Crapouillots (trench mortar troops).

23.   A German pillbox, located on the grounds of the New Zealand Memorial Park overlooks the approach up the Messines Ridge.

This example of the 'Iron Harvest' was photographed in 2003 near Passchendaele. The largest shell in front appears never to have detonated.

Village of Messines sits upon its ridge. On the horizon to the right is the tower of the village church. *Courtesy of Peter Folkers (http://pierreswesternfront.punt.nl)*

24. Left: Australian soldier on duckboards looks after a fallen comrade in Château Wood in October 1917. *LAC*

View from German position in Tyne Cot Cemetery against the direction of the Australian attack. Note the German pillbox among the four trees on the left.

The Memorial of the Missing curves around the rear of Tyne Cot Cemetery.

25. Tanks are mired in the heavily shelled approaches to Passchendaele. The village's name became synonymous with the worst First World War battlefield conditions. *LAC*

Canadian Passchendaele Memorial at Crest Farm; over 16,000 Canadians died capturing Passchendaele, marked by the village church ahead. It took almost two weeks of fighting to get from here to there.

26. 'Digger' Statue at Bullecourt Memorial Park representing Australians who fought to break the Hindenburg Line.

Right: The Germans rebuilt the bridge at Masnières near Cambrai using the English tank that collapsed it as support. *NARA*

Canadian Cavalry Brigade Memorial near the Masnières canal locks (in the distance) that were used by the Fort Garry Horse to cross the Canal de l'Escaut.

27.   The Belleau Wood Marine Memorial stands in the re-grown Bois de la Brigade de Marine.

Left: The German A7V tank Elfriede was captured during Somme 1918 fighting. *LAC*

Fouilloy Military Cemetery north of Villers-Bretonneux as viewed from the tower of the Australian National Memorial. Amiens is to the west and barely visible in the distance across the flat terrain.

28.   Crew from 23rd Infantry Regiment firing 37-mm gun during the advance of the US 2nd Division in the St Mihiel region. *NARA*

American Artillery firing upon German positions on Montsec. *NARA*

Circular colonnade of the American Memorial at Butte de Montsec.

29.   Ruins of the church of Montfaucon; a German observation bunker stands behind the doorway on the left. Courtesy of Peter Folkers (http://pierreswesternfront.punt.nl)

Entrance to German dugout below the Montfaucon summit; church ruins are on the horizon to the upper right. *NARA*

The Aire River passes through Varennes-en-Argonne below the Tour Louis XVI.

30. Roadside marker in the Forêt d'Argonne indicating the location of the Lost Battalion. American troops were trapped on the steep hillside below the roadway.

Meuse – Argonne American Cemetery now occupies a section of the Kriemhilde Stellung. The reflecting pool and slope up to the chapel were areas of intense fighting by the US 5th Division.

31.   Left: Brigadier General JV Campbell VC addresses troops of the 46th Division from the Riqueval Bridge on 2 October 1918. *IWM Q9534*

The bridge and St-Quentin Canal as they appear today – almost unchanged.

(Below) The American Memorial at Bellicourt sits upon the underground St-Quentin Canal and looks out upon the Hindenburg Line battlefield.

32. The agony of France is dramatically depicted in this segment of the Péronne War Memorial.

The anger of France is shown in the Alsace-Lorraine Monument at the Clairière de l'Armistice; the sword of France pierces the underbelly of the German Imperial eagle.

The railroad clearing at Rethondes held the railcars where the armistice was signed ending the First World War. Foch's car was on the foreground tracks and his statue is to the center rear.

'the memory of 11,447 Officers and Men of the Forces of the British Empire who fell fighting in the Years 1914 to 1918 between the Douve River and the towns of Estaires and Furnes whose names are here recorded but to whom the fortunes of war denied the known and honored burial given to their comrades in death.' Extending on either side of the rotunda is the **Berks Cemetery Extension** with 876 graves; **Hyde Park Corner (Royal Berks) Cemetery** with an additional 83 graves is across the road.

#31

Third Battle of Ypres (Passchendaele)
31 July to 10 November 1917

OBJECTIVE	To capture the Belgian Channel ports and force a German withdrawal from Belgium
FORCES	
ALLIES:	Twenty-eight divisions of the British Second (Lieutenant-General Sir Herbert Plumer) and Fifth Armies (General Sir Hubert Gough), and six divisions of the French First Army (général Francois Anthoine) totaling 500,000 men, 3,000 guns, 136 Mark IV tanks, and 500 aircraft
GERMAN:	Thirteen divisions of Fourth Army (General der Infanterie Friedrick Sixt von Armin), Fifth Army (General der Artillerie Max von Gallwitz), and Sixth Army (General der Infanterie Otto von Below)
RESULT	The British succeeded in wresting the strategic Passchendaele Ridge from the Germans.
CASUALTIES	
BRITISH:	450,000 for the entire Third Battle of Ypres
FRENCH:	Estimated at 20,000
GERMAN:	Estimated at 270,000
LOCATION	Ypres is 250 km north of Paris; Passchendaele is 12.4 km northeast of Ypres

For the breakout battle with which the British hoped to escape from the Ypres Salient, Haig replaced his most thorough and successful commander with General Sir Hubert Gough; Plumer's forces for the offensive were transferred to Gough's British Fifth Army. Personal differences between Plumer and Haig probably drove Haig's decision, but the change cost the British the momentum established during the Messines victory. The respite was a godsend to the reeling Germans.

Battle

Gough's first objective was to retake the ground captured by the Germans during the gas attack of 1915. On 03:50 on 31 July, the soldiers of Fifth Army left their trenches to march forward behind the creeping barrage. In the north initial progress was excellent, with advances across Pilckem Ridge. In the center, with

Menin Road as an axis of advance, the week-long preliminary bombardment had so fractured the ground that it was a sea of overlapping shell craters. Hundreds of German pillboxes nonetheless survived, and machine guns sprayed troops struggling through the clinging mud. Progress in the south was minimal – then it started to rain.

The offensive was on-again, off-again for the next several weeks. Dry weather was necessary to make the battlefield usable, but the August of 1917 was unusually wet. German guns on Geluveld Ridge, shielded from aerial observation by the continual bad weather, pounded British units with shells of all types, including the new and insidious mustard gas.

The great offensive to rid Belgium of the German invaders stalled. Haig responded by removing General Gough as commander – though he remained in charge of Fifth Army – and put General Plumer, who engineered the Messines success, in overall command. Although the weather cleared during September, Plumer halted the attacks to realign his forces. His first objective was Geluveld Plateau, from which any British move to the east was observed and subject to enfilade fire. Without the mines that he had had at Messines, Plumer amassed 1,200 guns to focus upon a narrow, 3-km strip of the front. The intensity of shellfire was unduplicated even by Somme standards, and after the troops moved forward the targets were adjusted to shield the captured ground from German counterattacks. The tactic was became known as 'bite and hold.'

On 26 September, Polygon Wood was taken; on 4 October, it was

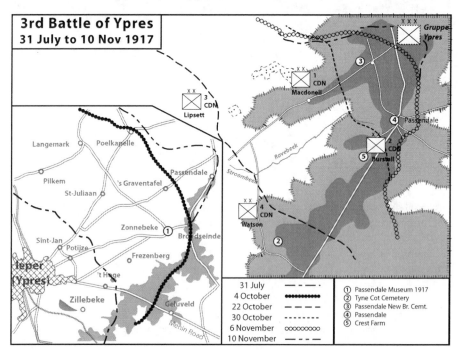

3rd Battle of Ypres
31 July to 10 Nov 1917

31 July	– ⋅ – ⋅ – ⋅
4 October	●●●●●●●●●●
22 October	– – – –
30 October	⋯⋯⋯⋯
6 November	∞∞∞∞∞∞∞∞
10 November	– ⋅⋅ – ⋅⋅ –

① Passendale Museum 1917
② Tyne Cot Cemetery
③ Passendale New Br. Cemt.
④ Passendale
⑤ Crest Farm

Broodseine's turn, and again Plumer's tactics were successful when his men advanced to within 2.2 km of a small village on the ridgeline. The good September weather, however, had run out, and by 7 October the land was thrashed by gale force winds and driving rain. Shell holes filled with water, and the streams and creeks overflowed the destroyed Flanders' drainage system. Plumer and Gough argued for an end to the offensive and to retire to winter quarters, but Haig would not consent.

On 9 October, Plumer's Second Army and Gough's Fifth Army attacked along a 13-km front targeting Poelkapelle due to its use by the Germans. Plumer's tactic of narrowly focused artillery barrages, however, was in jeopardy. Days of rain had turned the battlefield into soupy mud, making transporting guns and ammunition a dangerous and almost superhuman task. One wrong step on the slippery duckboards meant drowning in a flooded shell hole. Although the weather briefly cleared, the attack around Poelkapelle quickly floundered in the mud.

German resistance and unusually wet weather doomed Haig's breakout plan, but he could not enter winter quarters with his army under the German guns on the ridge. The final objective of the British offensive was the village whose name became synonymous with the worst of First World War fighting – Passchendaele. The rain, mud, stench, and death of Passchendaele seared the frustration, horror, and futility of trench warfare into the minds of both soldiers and civilians.

Haig's first attack upon Passchendaele commenced on 12 October, with ANZAC divisions starting from the area south of Crest Farm. Shells of the weak artillery bombardment targeting German pillboxes fell harmlessly into the muck. In the center, 3rd Australian Division moved from shell hole to shell hole, advancing past the pillbox at Crest Farm, a small detachment that reached the church in Passchendaele found the village abandoned. New Zealand troops to their north, however, were unable to make any progress against intact German pillboxes along Bellevue Spur. Enfilade German fire onto 3rd Division's positions caused severe casualties, including most of the officers. Having exposed flanks, lacking orders, and watching their battalions being annihilated, the men withdrew back to their starting positions. A similar fate befell 4th Australian Division on the right, and by the next morning all troops had returned to their starting points. Casualties for all three divisions totaled 13,000. German losses for the battles of 9 and 12 October were 3,325.

German Crown Prince Rupprecht noted in his diary, 'Sudden change of the weather. Most gratifyingly – rain; our most effective ally.'[2] Shell holes filled with water and the soil, pulverized by the frequent bombardments, took the consistency of porridge. Many of the wounded died where they fell, help unable to reach them. At night the Germans shelled British battery emplacements with mustard gas, further hampering the efforts to bring the artillery forward. The battlefield had become as close to hell as man could imagine.

Haig brought in fresh troops from four divisions of the General Arthur Currie's Canadian Corps. After completing an extensive rebuilding of roadways to

---

[2] C. E. W. Bean, *The Official History of Australia in the War of 1914-1918: Volume IV The Australian Imperial Force In France, 1917* (Sydney: Angus and Robertson Ltd, 1941), 928.

move artillery forward, Currie planned a series of 500-meter advances. With I ANZAC troops protecting their southern flank and Gough's Fifth Army to the north, 3rd and 4th Canadian Divisions advanced on 26 October against the 11th Bavarian Division, achieving the objective line. The success was repeated on 30 October with the capture of Crest Farm and other defensive positions against the German 39th and 238th Divisions, but high casualties and a violent rainstorm required the survivors to wait until replacements arrived. 1st and 2nd Canadian Divisions launched the final assault upon Passchendaele at 06:00 on 6 November against replacement German units. The honor of being first into Passchendaele went to the 27th Battalion (City of Winnipeg), its path cleared by Private JP Robertson VC, who wiped out an enemy post. Three hours later units were fighting over isolated piles of stone where houses once stood. On 10 November, the final effort took place for the possession of the crossroads and Hill 52 north of the village. Sixteen days of fighting cost the Canadians 15,654 casualties.

After the capture of Passchendaele, General Haig's chief of staff, Lieutenant-General Launcelot Kiggel, toured the battlefield for the first time. The shocked general reportedly broke into tears, stating 'Good God, did we really send men to fight in that?'[3]

General Haig had his ridge line, the advance to the Belgian seaports long since forgotten. Crown Prince Rupprecht still had the British Army trapped in an even larger salient with German guns on three sides. Accurate figures are difficult to ascertain, but the Third Battle of Ypres ranks with Somme and Verdun as one of the biggest bloodbaths of the war. The British War Office recorded total casualties on the Western Front from July through November as a staggering 450,000 men; the same report estimated German losses at 270,000. Postwar revisionists offered significantly different numbers, and the statistics remain controversial. Plumer was transferred to the Italian front; Haig's intelligence chief and chief of staff were removed. General Robertson, chief of the Imperial General Staff, was also sacked. Haig's strong connections to the royal family probably saved his position. Six months later, during the desperate resistance to the German offensives of 1918, the British evacuated the Ypres salient, which had been so desperately fought over and so costly to both armies – all for naught.

Battlefield Tour

As ground reclaimed from an ancient seabed, the terrain between Ypres and the ridges to the east is almost perfectly flat. To provide drainage for the water left by seemingly endless days of rainfall, local farmers had constructed a network of ditches which in turn fed a number of meandering streams. Along the roads are innumerable memorials to British military units and Commonwealth War Graves Commission cemeteries as befitting the length and intensity of the struggle that took place in these now pastoral fields.

---

[3] Groom, *A Storm in Flanders,* 231.

Leave Ypres toward Zonnebeke (N332) and proceed to the village church in Zonnebeke.

Zonnebeke was well within German lines from the Second Battle of Ypres in 1915 until the Polygon Wood phase of the Third Battle of Ypres in September 1917, when part of the village was taken. The liberation was not completed until the battle of Broodseinde on 4 October, when the numerous pillboxes manned by the German 6th Guards Division between Zonnebeke and Broodseinde were cleared by the II ANZAC.

Adjacent to the church is a stone archway leading to the grounds of the Château de Zonnebeke. The area is now a community park in which the 1924 building has been recently renovated and renamed '**Memorial Museum Passchendaele 1917**' (referred to in older works by its prior name – Streekmuseum). The museum is not nearly as large or elaborate as In Flanders Fields, but it has a good mix of photos, uniformed mannequins, monitors showing original film clips, and lighted map boards presenting a complete timeline for the 1917 battle of Passchendaele, including what happened each day and an indication of the weather – all labeled in four languages. The exhibit ends with a walk through a reconstruction of a trench and down a steep stairway to a British dugout which demonstrates aspects of underground life. As a German rear area early in the war, the grounds held German medical facilities; over 300 German soldiers were buried here, and the occasional memorial stone is still visible. The museum is open Monday through Friday from 10:00 to 18:00; Saturday and Sunday from 14:00 to 18:00; closed in December and January. Fee.

Continue thought Zonnebeke to the adjacent community of Broodseinde and turn left at the major intersection toward Passendale (N303). Approximately 1 km ahead, turn left at the sign for Tyne Cot Cemetery. Turn right onto the country lane (Tynecotstraat) to the entrance. Parking is a problem but will hopefully be solved with the construction of a new tourist center.

Tyne Cot Cemetery was named after a barn in the center of this strongpoint which resembled structures back home that the men of the Northumberland Fusiliers called Tyne Cottage or Tyne Cot. Below the crest of the ridge, on the ground now occupied by the cemetery, the Germans had constructed a line of strong, machine-gun pillboxes protected by bands of barbed wire. The cemetery ground was captured by 3rd Australian Division on 4 October 1917. One of the pillboxes was subsequently used as an advanced dressing station, and the first burials were made around it. By war's end the area behind the blockhouse held approximately 300 scattered graves. Most of the pillboxes along the ridge were blown up after the war, and the rubble was used as fill for local roads; however, those in Tyne Cot were left intact to avoid disturbing the nearby graves. The cemetery was enlarged by reburials from other battlefield cemeteries and is now the largest

Commonwealth War Cemetery in the world, containing 11,956 graves – including those of four Germans.

The Cross of Sacrifice is built over the dressing station pillbox, one of the five pillboxes that are still located within the cemetery. From the platform on its top, one can look back over the Steenbeek Valley to the towers of Ypres. Two pillboxes in the lower part of the cemetery are marked by poplar trees growing near their corners. The pillbox on the right was used by stretcher bearers as their headquarters during the assault on Passchendaele; the one on the left was used by the medical officers. Buried in the cemetery is Sergeant Lewis McGee (Plot XX, Grave D1), whose Victoria Cross was awarded posthumously for his efforts to seize the left pillbox.

Behind the cross and up a grass path between columns of yews is the **Memorial to the Missing,** bearing the names of 34,857 men who fell in the Ypres Salient after 15 August 1917 and whose graves are unidentified. The column breaks in the wall are entrances into circular alcoves that record additional names. A gated opening in the center allows access into a small garden that has the 1,166 names of the officers and men of New Zealand who fell in the salient and whose graves are unidentified. The final two pillboxes are beneath the pavilions at either end of the Memorial to the Missing and are used by gardeners as tool sheds.

Continue on the rural lane in front of the cemetery entrance until the junction with S'Graventafelstraat. Turn right and proceed to the cemetery on the left.

In front of the **Passchendaele New British Cemetery** is an **Albertina Marker** commemorating the end of the Passchendaele Offensive of September 1918, when the Belgian Army retook the area from the Germans for the final time. The cemetery truly represents the composition of the British Army, with graves of 1,026 British soldiers and sailors, 650 Canadians, 292 Australians, 126 New Zealanders, 5 South Africans and 1 Newfoundlander. Most were killed in the later stages of the 1917 Offensive.

Almost opposite the cemetery is Vierde Regiment Karabiniersstraat, which leads directly to the central square.

Passendale today is a pretty little village of houses, a few shops, and a church. Its appearance completely belies the events of both wars that forever scar its name. The Passendaleplaat in front of the church holds the *Stadhuis*, which is bedecked with plaques commemorating the village's liberation by the Canadian Corps in 1917, the Belgian Grenadiers in 1918, and the Polish Armored forces in 1944, as well as the members of the 43rd Regiment of the Line who died defending Passendale in May 1940. The square holds another of the fine **Ross Bastiaan bronze plaques**, which outlines the accomplishments of Australian troops.

Visible from the church steps at the far end of *Canadalaan* is the **Canadian Passchendaele Memorial at Crest Farm**. The Canadian 72nd Battalion (Seaforth

Highlanders) captured the fortified farm on 30 October and then turned the captured German machine guns upon the enemy on Bellevue Spur to the north. The single block of granite is inscribed: 'the Canadian Corps in October-November 1917 advanced across this valley – then a treacherous morass – captured and held the Passchendaele ridge.' The site marks the final starting line of the assault upon Passchendaele by the 1st and 2nd Canadian Divisions. Though difficult to imagine, 16,000 Canadians and an untold number of Germans died in the one-half kilometer from here to there.

#32

Battle of Cambrai
20 November to 7 December 1917

OBJECTIVE	To penetrate the German Hindenburg defenses and release cavalry into German rear areas.
FORCES	
BRITISH:	Eight divisions of the Third Army (General Sir Julian Byng)
GERMAN:	*Gruppe Caudry* of the Second Army (General der Kavallerie Georg von der Marwitz)
RESULT	Tanks destroyed the fixed defenses, but the lack of reserves hindered the exploitation of the success.
CASUALTIES	
BRITISH:	44,207, including 6,000 taken prisoner
GERMAN:	Estimated at 45,000, including 10,500 taken prisoner
LOCATION	Cambrai is 175 km north of Paris; Flesquières is 13 km southwest of Cambrai

The battles in Somme and Ypres had cost the British and German armies tremendous casualties. The Aisne Offensive had affected the French Army similarly, driving it nearly to mutiny. The battle of Arras had proved a limited success; the Germans had been driven from their positions, but once out of the range of protective artillery, the British Army's advance had slowed. The use of tanks in Somme in September 1916 had been a moderate success and presented allied military planners with a potential weapon. Their use during the Third Battle of Ypres had not been encouraging, however, because the shell-pocked, muddy fields of Flanders sucked the heavy vehicles into immobility. During the summer of 1917, Lieutenant-Colonel John Frederick Charles Fuller looked for terrain more suitable for the new weapon –a relatively flat battlefield not totally scarred by shell holes. He found it near Cambrai. General Haig and his staff were opposed to Fuller's proposal, their attention focused on Ypres. When that offensive stalled, however, the British Third Army commander, General Sir Julian Byng, combined the proposal with his own plans to attack that German transportation hub.

First World War tanks were not yet the weapon of speed and force that they became in the Second World War. Their slow rate of advance and precarious mechanical reliability made them more adept at tearing aside barbed wire entanglements than at rapid and prolonged advances deep into enemy territory. While the development of the Cambrai plans proceeded, their objectives became three-fold: to destroy enemy trench positions and other strongpoints; to pull aside barbed wire, permitting the advance of infantry; and to act as transport vehicles, supplying troops and guns. German soldiers responded as best they could to the new enemy weapon. Machine gun bullets could not penetrate the relatively thin armor plating, but they did cause flaking of metal bits which flew around the tank's interior. Infantry units did have a few steel-filled bullets that were capable of penetrating the light armor. Antitank ditches 5 meters deep and 6 meters across were dug in some areas, and artillery could target the slow-moving behemoths when they crept into range.

Divisions of III Corps and IV Corps of General Byng's British Third Army were allocated to assault Cambrai and were augmented by 374 tanks divided into thirteen tank battalions that were quietly accumulated in the forested areas around Gouzeaucourt and Havrincourt. An intermediate obstacle was the St Quentin Canal (de l'Escaut), which ran west and south of the city. The cavalry was once again assembled to exploit the breakthrough, with the plan of passing around Cambrai and advancing to the French frontier at Valenciennes.

Battle

At 06:20 on 20 November, one thousand guns opened fire in a brief but intense barrage. Then the tanks and accompanying infantry emerged from the morning mist and headed for the German wire 500 meters ahead. The initial German infantryman's response to the appearance of a tank was confusion mixed with fear. Most soldiers had never seen a tank, and the fearsome apparition was not even slowed by wire entanglements. They crushed the wire and then turned left or right, parallel with the trenches and firing Lewis guns or six pounder cannon at enemy troops emerging from their dugouts. Within two hours the main Hindenburg Line was taken.

Only at Flesquières did the advance not go well, and the location was an unfortunate one to have a failure. The village was situated upon a long, low ridge of the same name that commanded the ground to the southwest and shielded the approach to Cambrai to the northeast. Since the ridge was in the center of the battlefield and on the route of the 1st Cavalry Division, its capture was absolutely critical. Flesquières was in the assault sector of the tough 51st (Highland) Division, commanded by Major-General George Montague Harper. As an old-school general, Harper disdained the use of tanks, believing that they would attract enemy artillery fire that would kill his infantry. He ordered that a gap of 100 meters be maintained between the leading tanks and the following infantry. Without infantry for protection, the tanks were easy prey for the artillery. The separation allowed four batteries of German 77-mm guns to destroy sixteen tanks when they crested the ridge while the infantry was held under machine-gun fire. Every tank crewmember was killed. Without the tanks, progress in the 51st Division's sector was halted, and at the end of the day the Germans held the ridge. British advances on both flanks, however,

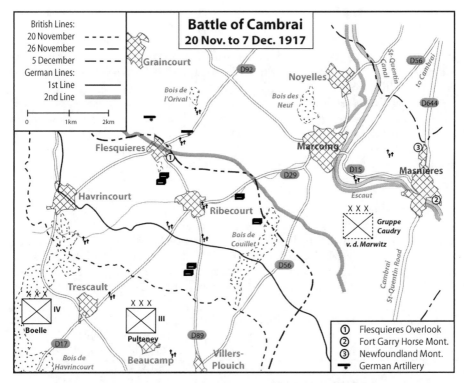

Battle of Cambrai
20 Nov. to 7 Dec. 1917

British Lines:
20 November - - - -
26 November - - -
5 December - - - -
German Lines:
1st Line ————
2nd Line

0   1km   2km

Graincourt

D92

Noyelles

Bois de
l'Orival

Bois des
Neuf

D56

to Cambrai

St-Quentin Canal

D644

Flesquieres

Marcoing

①

③

Havrincourt

D29

D15

Masnières

Escaut

②

Ribecourt

X X X
Gruppe
Caudry
v. d. Marwitz

Bois de
Couillet

D56

Cambrai St-Quentin Road

Trescault

X X X
IV
Boelle

X X X
III
Pulteney

D89

Villers-
Plouich

D17

Bois de
Havrincourt

Beaucamp

① Flesquieres Overlook
② Fort Garry Horse Mont.
③ Newfoundland Mont.
⟙ German Artillery

made Flesquières untenable, and the Germans abandoned it during the night. The Germans had been surprised and soundly beaten. The delay at Flesquières allowed the Germans a precious battlefield commodity – time – which they used to reassemble their shattered units and move reserves forward.

The cavalry, with the notable exception of a unit of the Fort Garry Horse, failed to cross the Canal de l'Escaut. The unfortunate destruction of a key bridge was a factor, but the real cause was a lack of specific orders from headquarters too far to the rear.

In the second day of the battle, some additional ground was captured. The now undefended Flesquières was occupied, and Masnières was cleared of the enemy, but the reduced number of available tanks and the strengthened resolve of German troops brought the advance to a standstill. British III Corps headquarters issued orders to consolidate positions, and the first phase of the battle ended.

To the north, IV Corps troops captured the strategic height of Bourlon Wood. With the British holding the wood and the Germans the village, a bitter struggle continued through 27 November, regardless of the nighttime snow and daytime rain.

On 30 November, a greatly restored *Gruppe Caudry* and the newly constituted *Gruppe Busigny* launched seven divisions against the southern flank of the British line. In addition, three divisions of *Gruppe Arras* moved west of Bourlon

Wood toward Flesquières. Using locally overwhelming force, *Gruppe Busigny* penetrated British 55th Division's line near Banteux, advancing as far as Gouzeaucourt and threatening the entire III Corps rear area. *Gruppe Caudry* fiercely attacked the 20th Division, and entire battalions were killed or captured. At Masnières, the stubborn defense of the 88th Brigade of 29th Division probably saved the entire British front.

Hastily assembled reserves comprised of British Guards Division, dismounted cavalry, and the thirty-six remaining operable tanks stopped the German advance west of Gouzeaucourt and recaptured the village. Local attacks continued for the next few days; on 4 December, General Byng ordered a withdrawal to the German's Hindenburg Support Line. The fighting dwindled until a blizzard on 7 December ended it for the winter.

Battlefield Tour

The undulating fields of Cambrésis contain attractive farming communities, and numerous divisional monuments and Commonwealth War Graves Commission cemeteries are scattered among the fields of wheat and oats. When the crops are short, dirty gray, reinforced concrete pillboxes of the Hindenburg Lines are visible deviations in the tractor's otherwise uniform plow furrows.

From Cambrai center, proceed south toward Péronne / St Quentin (N77); in the outskirts of Cambrai, bear right toward Marcoing (D56). In Marcoing, continue southwest toward Ribécourt (D29); then turn north into Flesquières (D89).

High spots offer excellent perspectives of the battlefield, and one such perspective is on the southern edge of Flesquières, where a **table of orientation** once stood east of the intersection of rue du Moulin (D89) and a farm lane. The spot is on the highest part of the Flesquières Ridge, which extends 10 km on an east-west axis. The main advance of III Corps took place in the fields in front of this location. The large forest to the southwest is the Bois d'Havrincourt, which was used as a staging area for tank battalions and from which the 51st Division emerged on 20 November. The long, low trough between the location and the forest is the Grand Ravine, a mostly dry gully that provided the approaching tanks shelter from observation until they started the climb up the ridge. Immediately behind is the chateau from which the machine-gun fire of the 27th Reserve Division hit the 51st Division's infantry. Four hastily repositioned German batteries located on the opposite side of the village crippled the assault when they destroyed the tanks cresting the nearby ridge. Hidden in the valley to the far left is the village of Ribécourt-la-Tour, and directly to the north, also hidden behind the village, is the massive forested area of Bourlon Wood.

Continue into the village.

The flags flying on the barn on the right mark the private display of **British female tank** D51 'Deborah.' The tank was hit by artillery fire on 20 November 1917, and it remained buried in a shell crater until excavated in 1998. The owner occasionally allows a viewing of this unusual relic.

In the center of Flesquières, turn right (D92, rue de Calvaire); after 2.6 km turn right toward Marcoing (D15) and follow through Marcoing. Turn toward Masnières (D15), crossing over the canal near the Marcoing locks. After the canal, turn immediately right and continue (D15) along the canal until entering Masnières. Turn right toward Péronne (N44); in a short distance, turn left onto rue des Dimeurs. Turn right on the first street (rue du 1st Mai), pass the school and park, and proceed to the canal.

In a small triangle of grass along the banks of the canal is the new **Canadian Cavalry Brigade Memorial,** which commemorates the feats of the Fort Garry Horse on 20 November. The old road bridge, located near the site of the modern bridge to the west, was designated a major crossing-point for the Canadian Cavalry in its plan to exploit the break in the Hindenburg Line. Damaged by a German engineer's attempts to blow up the bridge, it was completely destroyed when a tank tried to cross the canal. At 15:30, B squadron of the Fort Garry Horse crossed via a canal lock – visible to the east – and pursued the retreating Germans. When they disappeared over the next ridge, orders were received for the cavalry units to remain south of the canal, but the message failed to reach B squadron. Their commanding officer, Captain Duncan Campbell, was killed almost immediately. Now led with great bravado by Lieutenant Harcus Strachan VC, the horsemen charged and captured a German field-gun battery. They continued attacking isolated parties of German infantry on their way to Rumilly, 1.5 km to the north, where they were surrounded by enemy forces. When darkness fell, they scattered their horses to create a diversion, and the survivors straggled back to the British lines on foot, bringing their wounded comrades and nine prisoners. The unit had suffered sixty per cent casualties. The cavalry charge, almost unique in the First World War, became well-publicized, and the granite monument recalls the events with explanatory plaques. The canal, its banks, locks, and bridge location are only slightly altered and demonstrate the importance of capturing the bridge to the continued progress of the Third Army's advance.

Other Sites of Interest: The **Newfoundland Memorial** 0.5 km north of Masnières on the N44 commemorates the regiment's defense of the town during the German counterattack of 30 November. The **Canadian Bourlon Wood Memorial** northwest of Cambrai is the site of the Canadian attack in September 1918. The unusual British and German gravestones and memorials at the **Cambrai East Military Cemetery** northeast of the town are interesting. Cambrai itself is a charming market town with restaurants, shops and numerous memorials in the garden (Jardin).

Recommended reading

Buffetaut, Yves: *The 1917 Spring Offensives: Arras, Vimy, le Chemin des Dame*. Paris: Histoire & Collections, 1997. A brief history of the three spring battles, illustrated with numerous photographs.

Cave, Nigel: *Battleground Europe: Hindenburg Line*. Barnsley, United Kingdom: Pen and Sword. Two volumes (Cambrai and Villers-Plouich) that cover this sector are available in this popular series of First World War battlefield guides.

Cooper, Bryan: *The Ironclads of Cambrai: The First Great Tank Battle*. London: Cassel Paperbacks, 2002. An easy-to-read account that is also critical of British senior commanders for their handling of the battle.

Nicholls, Jon: *Cheerful Sacrifice: The Battle of Arras*. Barnsley, England: Pen and Sword Books, 1993. The battle of Arras as told through individual accounts.

Passingham, Ian: *Pillars of Fire: The Battle of Messines Ridge June 1917*. Stroud, England: Sutton Publishing, 1998. Detailed account of the opening moves of Third Ypres.

Prior, Robin and Trevor Wilson: *Passchendaele: The Untold Story*. New Haven: Yale University Press, 1996. A description of the action step by step.

Reed, Paul: *Walking the Salient*. Barnsley, England: Leo Cooper, 1999. One of the *Battleground Europe* series of battlefield walking guides.

Steel, Nigel and Peter Hart: *Passchendaele: The Sacrificial Ground*. London: Cassel, 2000. The Passchendaele story told in the words of the participants.

Walker, Jonathan: *The Blood Tub: General Gough and the Battle of Bullecourt 1917*. Staplehurst, Kent, United Kingdom: Spellmount, 2000. An account of the two battles at Bullecourt that is critical of British and Australian military leadership.

Warner, Philip: *Passchendaele*. Ware, England: Wordsworth Editions, 1999. A reprint of an account filled with participants' observations.

Wolff, Leon: *In Flanders Fields: The 1917 Campaign*. New York: Viking Press, 1958. A classic account of the battle.

Chapter Nine

America Joins the Fight
1918

As winter turned into spring in 1918, the Russian Revolution had ended the fighting on the Eastern Front, releasing forty-two divisions of German troops for

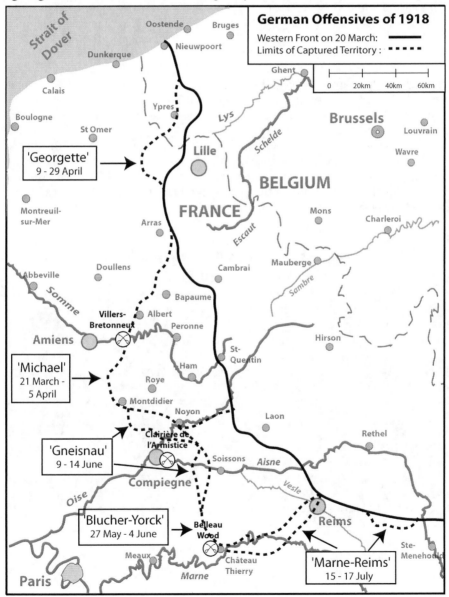

action on the Western Front. American troops were arriving in France by the thousands and would soon redress the temporary German manpower advantage. The German General Staff knew that they had a limited time frame within which to act. Their plan involved a series of massive assaults from Ypres to Reims with the hope that they would split the French and British armies, causing the French to sue for peace. On 21 March 1918, the first of these efforts, known as the *Kaiserschlacht* or 'Emperor's Battle,' struck General Gough's British Fifth Army and General Byng's British Third Army along a 90-km front from Arras to La Fère. Using ten thousand guns, Ludendorff's artillery fired nearly as many shells in five hours as Haig's had done in a week on the Somme. This was followed by an attack from forty infantry divisions. After the first two hours, forty-seven British battalions ceased to exist as operational units. The unprecedented ferocity of the attack ruptured the British line and began to drive apart the two British armies. For the next two weeks, wave upon wave of German infantry drove British units inexorably back across the Somme battlefield of 1916, until the line was finally stabilized on 4 April, just kilometers east of the critical transportation center of Amiens.

Losses to the Allies were catastrophic, numbering over 177,000 British and 77,000 French. Although the German army had recovered more territory in one 13-day period than the Allies had in three years of warfare, the 239,000 men lost were irreplaceable. In addition, they had captured no strategic site, and their exhausted men and equipment were well beyond the range of their supply infrastructure.

#33
Second Battle of Villers-Bretonneux
24 to 27 April 1918

OBJECTIVE	To push the German artillery out of range of the Amiens rail yards.
FORCES	
BRITISH:	7 divisions of III and Australian Corps of the Fourth Army (General Sir Henry Rawlinson)
GERMAN:	6 divisions of XI and XIV Corps of the German Second Army (General der Kavallerie Georg von der Marwitz)
RESULT	Villers-Bretonneux was recaptured after an aggressive nighttime assault.
CASUALTIES	
BRITISH:	For the period of 5 to 27 April, 9,529 British and 2,573 Australians killed or wounded; 2,400 taken prisoner.
FRENCH:	3,470 casualties from the Moroccan Division
GERMAN:	At least 5,783 killed and wounded; several hundred taken prisoner
LOCATION	Amiens is 130 km north of Paris; Villers-Bretonneux is 17 km east of Amiens

Battle

Ludendorff made a final effort to bring the bridges and rail yards of Amiens into the range of his cannon. At 03:45 in the foggy morning of 24 April, the German Second Army unleashed another intense bombardment on the roads and rear areas along an 11-km front east of Amiens. Two and one-quarter hours later, four divisions attacked astride the Amiens-St Quentin road, against the junction of the French First Army and the British Fourth Army. Unique for the Germans in the assault was the use of thirteen A7V tanks. The thirty-two ton behemoths carried one 57-mm gun, six machine guns, and a crew of up to twenty-two. They proceeded along either side of the railway line south of Villers-Bretonneux, attacking British 8th and 58th Division units defending the Bois d'Aquenne and the village of Cachy. Lacking any effective antitank weapon, the British soldiers immediately retired. Neighboring units became outflanked and were overwhelmed, with tanks to their rear.

In response, one male Mark IV tank with two 6 pounder guns and four machine guns as well as two female Mark IV tanks with only six machine guns each from 1st Tank Battalion moved from the Bois l'Abbé to southeast of Villers-Bretonneux, where they engaged an enemy tank. The lone German tank quickly knocked out the two female Mark IVs, accomplishing the first tank-to-tank kill in the history of armored warfare. Although also partially disabled by enemy artillery, the remaining male tank hit the German machine, forcing the crew to abandon it. The

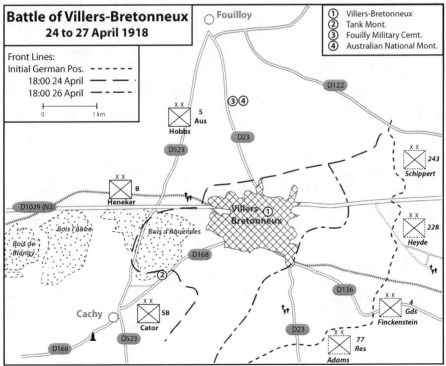

Battle of Villers-Bretonneux
24 to 27 April 1918

① Villers-Bretonneux
② Tank Mont.
③ Fouilly Military Cemt.
④ Australian National Mont.

Front Lines:
Initial German Pos. - - - - - -
18:00 24 April — — ·
18:00 26 April — · — ·

0   1 km

appearance of seven Whippet medium tanks armed only with machine guns halted the German infantry's progress. A salient that included Villers-Bretonneux, however, was pushed in the British line, and the Germans were only 13 km from the outskirts of Amiens.

As soon as Rawlinson heard of the loss of Villers-Bretonneux, he ordered reserve brigades of the Australian Corps forward to assist in its recapture. The 15th Brigade was to move north of the village, the 13th Brigade south of the village, and the 54th Brigade of British 18th Division was to attack farther south, forming the assault's right flank unit. At 22:00, the battalions of the 54th Brigade lost communications and encountered machine gun and artillery fire, thus accomplishing only a short advance. At 22:10, three battalions of the 13th Brigade moved forward without a preliminary bombardment, under the light of a cloud-covered full moon and the burning buildings of Villers-Bretonneux. Despite being enfiladed by machine-gun fire from the Bois d'Aquenne, the Australians eliminated or bypassed enemy positions to maintain their advance. By 01:00, the lead battalion halted in order to solidify a defense line east of the village.

At midnight, the 15th Australian Brigade attacked north of Villers-Bretonneux. The first mile was occupied before the Germans showed any resistance. The commander of the 59th Battalion ordered a charge, and the entire Australian line closed on the enemy, yelling and cheering. They broke through the German line and within 90 minutes accomplished their objectives. The village was nearly encircled but still occupied by elements of the German 4th Guards Division. Through the night some German troops escaped by moving east along the railway cut to the south. By dawn on 25 April, British artillery had become aware of the escape route and brought their guns to bear on it. Mixed units entered Villers-Bretonneux after daybreak and completed its capture, taking 472 prisoners. The two Australian brigades completed their juncture southeast of the village the next day. Colonel (later Brigadier) George Grogan VC described the successful counterattack across unknown and difficult ground, at night, and at short notice as 'perhaps the greatest individual feat of the war.'

In cooperation with the French Moroccan Division, the British 8th and 58th Divisions were to attack German positions in the Bois de Hangard, 2.5 km south of Villers-Bretonneux. Launched at 05:15 on 26 April, the Moroccans were severely mauled by a counterattack by the German 19th Division. The other units made little progress, and the attack soon ended. By noon on 27 April, the sector became relatively peaceful.

Battlefield Tour

Villers-Bretonneux sits upon a high plain bisected by an old Roman road that runs from Amiens to St Quentin. The wheat fields on the essentially flat terrain are occasionally cut by minor streams. East of Villers-Bretonneux, scattered forests mark the approach into the valleys of the Avre, La Noye, and Somme Rivers.

> Enter Villers-Bretonneux from the N29 (Amiens-St-Quentin Road) by turning south onto rue de Melbourne. Continue to the Mairie on the left.

The defense of the village on 4 April and the later liberation by Australian troops have formed a bond between the people of Villers-Bretonneux and Australia that has lasted to this day. The village is the site of an annual ANZAC Day celebration on 25 April (or the nearest Saturday) and is frequently visited by busloads of Australian battlefield tourists. A **Ross Bastiaan plaque** commemorating the Australians who fought in the area is on the grounds of the Mairie. Nearby is the town's **War Memorial,** with its commemoration to Australian troops.

> South of the Mairie, turn right on to rue Victoria and proceed to the village's school on the left.

Reconstructed after the war with assistance from the State of Victoria, Australia, Victoria School's upper floor contains the **Franco-Australian Museum**, one of the more attractive, small-town, municipal museums. Its displays contain the usual paraphernalia of weapons and uniforms, but they are professionally arranged. The walls are covered with enlarged photographs of Australian units fighting and recuperating. The museum is open Wednesday through Saturday from 10:00 to 12:30 and 14:00 to 18:00; Tuesday and the 1st and 3rd Sundays of the month from 14:00 to 18:00; closed holidays except 11 November and last week of December and first week of January. Fee.

> Continue to the southwest on rue Victoria, which becomes rue de Cachy (D168).

The road passes the southern border of Bois d'Aquenne, the closest point of the German advancement toward Amiens. The open fields to the south were the site of the **tank engagement**. No indication of the battle remains except for a small stone monument on the edge of the highway. The site has been bisected by the recently constructed Autoroute, but the bridge over the Autoroute provides a good perspective of the tank battle terrain.

> Reverse direction and return to Villers-Bretonneux; turn right toward Corbie (D23).

Three km north of Villers-Bretonneux is the **Villers-Bretonneux Military Cemetery**. The rows of 2,141 gravestones, which include 772 Australians, climb up the hill on either side of a wide grass lawn. In the middle stands the traditional Cross of Sacrifice with its bronze sword. In the rear, at the crest of the hill is the **Australian National Memorial**, which was erected in 1938 to commemorate all Australian servicemen who fought in France or Belgium in the First World War. Across the top of the U-shaped porch are inscribed the names of Australian Western Front engagements from Albert to Ypres. On its walls are the names of 10,749

Australian soldiers lost during the battles of Somme and Arras as well as of the 1918 battles who have no known grave. The structure retains bullet scars from Luftwaffe strafing in the Second World War. From the central tower, the city of Amiens is visible to the west, and when the fields are barren of crops, the irregular white streaks of trenches can be seen in the brown soil. The 15th Australian Brigade advanced from west to east across the ground between the memorial and the village during its assault on the night of 24/25 April.

Other Sites of Interest: **Adelaide Cemetery** west of Villers-Bretonneux toward Amiens is the last resting place of many Australian soldiers and where the country's Unknown Soldier was exhumed from in 1993 for reburial in Australia's War Memorial in Canberra. The empty grave remains and is marked with a special tombstone. From the Villers-Bretonneux Memorial, a tall brick chimney is visible on the horizon to the north. A roadside plaque near it marks an open field where **Baron Manfred von Richthofen** crashed his red Fokker tri-plane on 21 April 1918, after being shot by a gunner of the 24th Australian Machine Gun Company. Five km to the east is the newly constructed **Australian Corps Memorial Park,** commemorating the site of the 4 July 1918 assault on German positions overlooking the village of Hamel. General John Monash commanded a combined Australian-American force, which executed a carefully planned assault that was a forerunner of modern military coordination and resulted in the achievement of all objectives in ninety minutes.

#34

Battle of Belleau Wood
6 to 25 June 1918

OBJECTIVE	To reinforce the French and stop the German drive toward Paris
FORCES	
AMERICAN:	4th Marine Brigade (Brigadier General James Harbord)
GERMAN:	*Gruppe Conta*, also known as IV Reserve Corps (General der Infanterie Richard von Conta)
RESULT	Bois de Belleau was captured after suffering heavy casualties.
CASUALTIES	
AMERICAN:	Approximately 5,200 casualties
GERMAN:	Unknown killed and wounded; 1,600 taken prisoner
LOCATION	Château Thierry is 90 km northeast of Paris; Belleau Wood is 11 km west of Château Thierry

After the failed attempt to capture Amiens, Ludendorff's next move was to attack British positions in Flanders, threatening the vital Channel ports of Boulogne and Calais. Although Operation 'Georgette' failed to achieve its objective, it did cause General Sir Herbert Plumer, commander of British Second Army, to abandon the Passchendaele salient that had cost so many lives the previous year. The Germans also pushed the French off strategic Mt. Kemmel.

Ludendorff then turned his attention to the Chemin des Dames battlefield; on 27 May, he launched Operation 'Blücher-Yorck' with twenty-seven divisions of Seventh Army against French Sixth Army. Originally intended as a feint, the effort was so successful in overrunning five recuperating French and British divisions and occupying positions on the Marne only 90 km from Paris that Ludendorff decided to continue the offensive. The force of the attack panicked some French units, and with the road to Paris essentially open, général Pétain, now Commander-in-Chief of the French Army, petitioned General John 'Black Jack' Pershing for help. The only combat-ready troops Pershing could offer were the American 2nd and 3rd Divisions. Pershing immediately ordered both divisions to proceed toward Château Thierry. The 3rd Division took up defensive positions along the south bank of the Marne, east of Château Thierry, where its stubborn defense earned it the nickname 'Rock of the Marne.'

The 2nd Division was a hybrid unit composed of a brigade of regular army soldiers strengthened by volunteers and a brigade of American Marines. By 1 June, they were in position west of Château Thierry, where they became the only operational units between the Germans and Paris while dispirited French units passed through their line seeking safety. For three days, they, supported by the 6th Machine Gun Battalion, repelled repeated enemy attacks.

Battle

French and American commanders decided to recapture what they thought was a lightly defended Bois de Belleau to the marine's front. As part of a massive French counterattack against the exhausted Germans, the 2nd Division was assigned to attack Belleau Wood and the small villages of Bouresches and Vaux. To the west of the wood was Hill 142, which was attacked on the morning of 6 June by the Marine 5th Regiment. Standing practically shoulder-to-shoulder, the first waves entered the poppy-painted fields into the fire of Maxim machine guns. The charge was successful, although losses were substantial at 1,087. Attention now turned to Bois de Belleau and Bouresches to its east. Three battalions attacked from the south and west. The marines advanced in rows as if on a parade ground and were slaughtered, suffering over one thousand casualties. The wood was not as lightly defended as had been assumed – reconnaissance would have easily determined that fact. The first class, German 10th Division had established numerous machine-gun positions behind the huge boulders and downed trees. Interlocking fire made any progress through the open fields south of the wood a deadly experience. In an outstanding accomplishment, 96th Company of 6th Marine Regiment advanced along the road to Bouresches and captured the entire village except for a machine-gun position in the train station.

Due to the unfortunate international publicity, Belleau Wood became a cause for American commanders to capture and for German commanders to retain. The 81-hectare wooded hilltop assumed a psychological importance out of proportion to its military value.

On 10 June, the 6th Marine Regiment renewed the attack after an all-day artillery bombardment. Fighting in the dense forest, however, was extremely

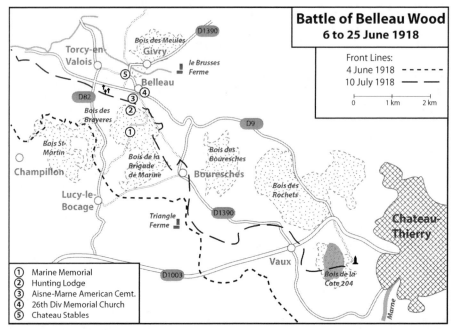

difficult. Units easily became disorientated; the enemy had well-established positions, and American commanders did not know how to dislodge them. By 14 June, the 4th Brigade had suffered fifty per cent casualties and could not even estimate how much of the wood it controlled. The exhausted men were given a seven-day reprieve, replaced by the 7th Infantry Regiment, which was unable to advance. The marines returned to Belleau Wood, and after another artillery bombardment, they captured the woods on 25 June. The next morning the report was received, '[Belleau] Woods now US Marine Corps entirely.'[1]

Though militarily unimportant, the American victory was significant to both sides. The French took heart that they had a new ally who was capable of fighting the hated Hun. A member of Pétain's staff, Jean de Pierrefeu, described the Americans as 'a wonderful transfusion of blood…to reanimate the dying body of France.'[2] The Germans had had five of their divisions, including the 5th Prussian Guards, mauled by the Americans. Ludendorff and his subordinates considered the arrival of American troops as a war-losing event.

---

[1] YANKS: The Epic Story of the American Army in World War I by John Eisenhower. Copyright © 2001 by John S.D. Eisenhower. Published by The Free Press, a Division of Simon & Schuster Adult Publishing Group, 148.

[2] Byron Farwell, *Over There: The United States in the Great War, 1917 – 1918* (New York: WW Norton & Company, 1999), 168.

Battlefield Tour

> The Bois de Belleau was once the hunting preserve of the Château de Belleau, which is in the village of the same name 1 km to the north. Approach it by leaving Château Thierry on the Paris road (N3), passing through the village of Vaux, and turning north toward Lucy-le-Bocage (D82). This quiet farming village served as the headquarters for Harbord's Marines. Exit the center of Lucy toward Torcy-en-Valois (D82) and after less than 1 km, turn onto the access road into the woods on the right.

The fields north of Lucy were the site of the 5th Marine Regiment's attack of 6 June. The huge boulders, large trees, and thick undergrowth of Belleau Wood are still present and provide vivid images as to the difficulty of this assault. The access road eventually leads to the open space of the **Marine Memorial**. Under a canopy of trees and in the center of the roadway, a black granite monolith displays a bronze bas-relief of a shirtless marine attacking with rifle and bayonet. The inscription declares that the woods be known forevermore as **Bois de la Brigade de Marine**. Around the periphery of the clearing are captured ordinance, aligned upon the marine as if aiming upon a target. Dirt paths wind through the surrounding woods, and remnants of shells or strongpoints are occasionally visible. The road continues to the border fence of the Aisne-Marne American Cemetery, which is below the ridge on the north side of the wood. Passage directly into the cemetery from here is not possible, but near the fence is the last defensive trench of the Germans that was captured on 25 June. To the left is the **stone hunting lodge** which was used as a German battalion headquarters until being overrun by the 43rd Company of Marines. The fighting over it was fierce because of the dominating views offered by its upper levels.

> Pass the Marine Memorial and follow the road down the hill. At the junction, to the right is Bouresches; turn left and continue into the village of Belleau.

Enter the **Aisne-Marne American Cemetery** through a massive gateway and proceed down a lane which passes the offices and visitor's center to the grave plots. Under its perfectly aligned rows of Latin Crosses and Stars of David are buried 2,288 men who died in regional fighting. At the southern end and 80 feet up the ridge, a **French Romanesque Chapel** sits upon the front line trenches dug by the 2nd Division after the battle. Inscriptions depict scenes of battle or insignia of the various units engaged in the area. The hole to the right of the entrance was made by a German tank shell in 1940 and has purposely been left unrepaired. The walls of the interior of the chapel are inscribed with the names of 1,060 soldiers who disappeared in the area and have no known grave.

A path leaves the left side of the Chapel and proceeds up the hill to the same boundary fence previously mentioned. The ground still bears the imprints of American artillery shells and German rifle pits. The land has been granted in perpetuity for use as a military cemetery by the government of France. All American cemeteries in Europe are open every day from 09:00 to 17:00, except 25 December and 1 January. Personnel are always on duty in the visitor's center to assist in locating gravesites or to provide information on the cemetery. Special commemorations of American Memorial Day are held every year on the fourth Monday in May and are worth attending.

Directly across from the cemetery entrance is the **26th Division Memorial Church**. The village church was destroyed in later fighting, and after the war this chapel was rebuilt by funds from the division's veterans organization. If it is not open, ask for the superintendent of the American cemetery, who has a key and will gladly provide admission. Inside the church are numerous plaques to American units and individuals. The stained glass windows are particularly striking. Across the intersection, is one of the remaining, albeit misplaced, Demarcation Stones indicating the limit of the German advance.

The road toward Givry (D1390) enters place du général Pershing, and across from the small Mairie are the château's stables – all that remain of the château that once dominated village life in prewar Belleau. Within its locked gates – the superintendent may provide access to the courtyard – is the famous **'Bulldog' fountain**. Sources of water were always scarce on a battlefield, and this fountain provided succor to thirsty marines after the battle. The Marine Corps symbol of a bulldog was added after the war, and the fountain carries the legend of providing increased longevity to any marine who drinks from its waters – and all who come here do.

Other Sites of Interest: The **German Military Cemetery** is west of Belleau toward Torcy (D9). Within the sound of the carillon in the American Cemetery are buried 8,630 German casualties in an almost treeless open field. Over 4,000 soldiers, most of them unidentified, rest in a mass grave. To the east and accessible from the Paris-Château Thierry Road (N3) is Hill 204, a promontory upon which stands the **American Aisne- Marne Memorial**. The huge double colonnade commemorates the sacrifices of French and American soldiers who fought in the sector. The larger-than-life-sized figures represent French-American friendship. A terrace on the side opposite the parking area offers dominating views of the Marne valley.

The Final Offensives

Ludendorff's fifth and last attempt to decide the war in Germany's favor started on 15 July. The plan was essentially a resumption of the Marne attack on both sides of Reims, but this time the Allies were prepared. Aware of the enemy's plans, allied artillery bombarded German preparatory lines, killing many of the tightly assembled troops. In contrast, German artillery shells fell upon essentially empty French and American lines as the Allies exercised the 'elastic defense' ordered by général Pétain. Whereas the Germans were still able to fight their way across the river, the losses sustained were substantial, and they were unable to progress. His infantry exhausted, Ludendorff called off the entire offensive days later. American troops were replacing British and French losses, but Ludendorff had no such reserves.

On 18 July, the French Sixth and Tenth Armies, strengthened by the addition of five oversized American divisions, attacked the throat of the salient that Ludendorff had created. The combined forces drove eastward, liberating the rail center of Soissons and threatening to cut off all German troops south of the Aisne. The Germans executed a masterful fighting withdrawal back to the Vesle River.

On 8 August, the British Army attacked across the front east of Amiens. Spearheaded by Australian and Canadian units and supported by 456 tanks, it advanced 13 km on the first day, once again crossing the Somme battlefields of summer 1916 and March 1918 and captured 16,000 prisoners. The German lines were still well within French borders, but the German High Command realized that the war could not be won. Ludendorff described it as the 'black day for the German army.' Successive attacks to the north and south drove the Germans back to their last strong defensive positions in France – the Hindenburg Line.

#35

St-Mihiel Offensive
12 to 18 September 1918

OBJECTIVE	To remove the German flank threat at St Mihiel before the Argonne Offensive
FORCES	
ALLIES:	Nine American divisions and five French divisions plus six divisions in reserve, totaling over 600,000 men (General John Pershing)
GERMAN:	Eight line divisions and five reserve divisions of Army Detachment 'C' (Generalleutnant Georg von Fuchs)
RESULT	All objectives were attained, and the salient was eliminated.
CASUALTIES	
ALLIES:	1,236 killed; 8,506 wounded and missing
GERMAN:	2,300 killed and wounded; 13,250 taken prisoner
LOCATION	Verdun-sur-Meuse is 270 km east of Paris; St Mihiel is 36 km south of Verdun

Allied planning for the fall of 1918 involved three great offensives to crush all German resistance. The French and Americans would advance through the Argonne Forest toward Mézières, cutting the main German supply route behind their front lines. The British would advance toward the French frontier at Maubeuge, and together with Belgian and French contingents, move toward Ghent in Flanders. Preceding these efforts would be an assault by the American First Army against the 1914 salient at St Mihiel, which had been a quiet sector used as a training ground for new American divisions before they were sent to other fronts.

The St Mihiel salient enclosed multiple German defense lines and was anchored across its base by the Michel Line, behind which was the *Kriemhilde*

Position. Running from Pont-à-Mousson to St Mihiel and then northward along the Hauts de Meuse was the 8-km wide Wilhelm Line. Seven divisions had had four years to string wire, dig deep dugouts, place machine guns, and range artillery. The relative peacefulness of the sector, however, had bred complacency, and many of the German defenders were weak *Landsturm* units. The area protected the strategic German lateral rail line that supported troop movements along the Western Front as well as the Briey coal fields, which were necessary for war production.

The Americans, who were transported to France, were mostly infantry soldiers, the speed of the build-up not permitting the formation of adequate support

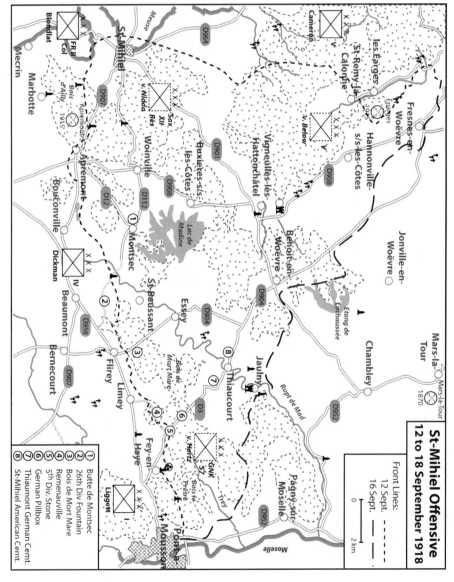

St-Mihiel Offensive
12 to 18 September 1918

Front Lines:
12 Sept.
16 Sept.

0   2 km

① Butte de Montsec
② 26th Div Fountain
③ Bois de Mort Mare
④ Remenauville
⑤ 5th Div. Stone
⑥ German Pillbox
⑦ Thiaumont German Cemt.
⑧ St-Mihiel American Cemt.

units. The Americans relied upon their British and French allies to supply much of the heavy equipment. Artillery pieces were thus of French manufacture, with one half manned by French crews. Thirteen hundred allied aircraft were piloted by British, French, and American crews. 267 light tanks were also of French origin, although the crews were mixed. The American attack plan assigned French II Colonial Corps to occupy the enemy in the nose of salient, while three American corps attacked the flanks. US I and IV Corps fell upon the southern face of the salient, intent upon driving north. Against the east face, US V Corps' 26th Division was to close the trap.

Before becoming aware of the American plans, the Germans had prepared to evacuate the salient to shorten the front and release troops for other sectors. They started an orderly withdrawal of their heavy guns, which was to be followed by infantry units on 13 September. In case of attack, commanders in the salient were ordered to resist until required to withdraw to the strengthened Michel Line in front of Metz. German reserves were held farther back than normal, restricting their use as counterattack troops.

Battle

General Pershing ordered the attack to commence at 05:00 on 12 September, after three thousand guns subjected the enemy to a crushing four-hour artillery bombardment. Shrouded in a heavy fog and misty rain, successive waves of Americans fell upon the enemy's wire entanglements, tossed grenades into dugouts, and rapidly advanced into the open country. The American force crushed the shoulders of the salient, and the German resistance faltered. Sensing that the enemy was attempting to escape, Pershing ordered the assault to continue through the night. Before dawn on the second day of the offensive, the US 1st and 26th Divisions effected a linkup near Hattonchâtel, closing the escape route. The cleanup continued for several days. The German High Command was greatly shocked by the American Army's fighting capabilities, long thought to be inferior to even mediocre German troops. Although the German units were not the best and lacked heavy guns and reserves, the victory was hailed as a great morale builder by the Americans. French and British military leaders remained skeptical, especially considering the excessive casualty rate. Almost immediately the Americans started relocating for more difficult challenges in the Argonne.

Battlefield Tour

The point of the salient was cut by the steep cliffs of the Hauts de Meuse, behind which were the open plains of the Woëvre. Lazy streams such as Rupt de Mad wound among the gentle hills that were dotted with woods and swampy areas. Dense forests hide trenches and dugouts; pillboxes stand as lonely sentinels over modern highways; the rubble of destroyed villages is softened by undergrowth. Small monuments erected shortly after the war by American veterans mark their achievements.

St Mihiel, after four years of enemy occupation, was entered by the French 25th Regiment on the morning of the offensive. They found the city relatively intact. Prewar French forts around St Mihiel remain ruins and are on private land. The town contains an interesting 17th century Benedictine Abbey with a great historical library as well as local churches with works by the famous sculptor Ligier Richier.

Leave St Mihiel toward Woinville (D119). The road winds down the face of the Hauts de Meuse. Follow the road through Woinville and on to the village of Montsec, where signs indicate the road to the *Mémorial Américain*.

The scale and scope of a battlefield can usually be best seen from high ground, and for St-Mihiel the best location is the **Butte de Montsec**, an isolated hill that rises 130 meters above the surrounding countryside and which becomes an increasingly dominant feature while approaching the small village. The southern side was studded with machine guns, and the approach slopes were strung with barbed wire entanglements. Tunnels into Montsec provided defenders with shelter and access to observation posts. A telephone exchange at its base transmitted sightings to batteries camouflaged in the woods. Montsec was too strongly defended for troops to attempt a frontal assault. Pershing reasoned that after being cut off from German reserves, the position would surrender. His plan therefore called for the dominant heights to be by-passed by 1st Division, which would then swing around behind it to establish contact with the charging 26th Division. The mount was shrouded by smoke shells to prevent the observers from reporting attackers' positions. On 13 September, surrounded by American forces and according to Pershing's plan, the Germans abandoned Montsec. Almost exactly 26 years later, Americans were again fighting Germans over Montsec. On 2 September 1944, American forces fired upon a German machine gun position on the hill.

Today the butte is crowned with the **Montsec American Monument** consisting of a circular colonnade surrounding a bronze relief map of the battlefield. The map shows the various sites, and from Montsec the full scope of I and IV Corps' 14-mile attack front can be seen from east of Thiaucourt on the left, as marked by its church steeple, to Seicheprey on the right. The huge Lac de Madine was lowland in 1918 and has since been flooded to support water sports and recreational activities. Always open. No admission charge.

Proceed east toward Richecourt (D119); turn left toward Lahayville (D33/D28), and after Lahayville make a sharp right toward Seicheprey (D28a).

The road passes through the village of Seicheprey, which was the scene of a German raid in the early morning of 20 April 1918, against the US 26th (Yankee) Division. Behind a rolling artillery barrage, 1,200 German assault troops overran the front line trenches, flanked the town, and captured the village. Hand-to-hand fighting raged in the narrow confines of Bois de Remières to the northeast before the Germans retired with 136 prisoners. Both sides claimed victory. Beside the church is a now unused **water fountain,** which was presented to the village by the people of Connecticut, from where many of the Yankee division soldiers came.

Continue to the highway and turn left toward Flirey (D958).

The front line of American 42nd and 89th Divisions was along the left side of the road. Across from the church in Flirey is a memorial to the American Army's first offensive. East of the town center and upon a hillock on the right are the ruins of the old church, left in its partially destroyed state to mark the position of the original village and to commemorate the local dead. In the woods north of Flirey and accessed from the road toward Essey (D904) is the **Bois de Mort Mare**. A monument along the road remembers French casualties in the mine warfare that occurred from February 1915 to April 1917, when the French and Germans sought dominance in the large forest. The wood retains craters from mines detonated in the vicious struggle as well as a few stretches of poorly defined trench.

Continue east toward Pont à Mousson (D958). On the eastern side of Limey-Remenauville turn left toward Remenauville (D75).

After the war some destroyed villages such as Remenauville were never rebuilt; however, their names were incorporated into neighboring villages to retain the village identity. At the bottom of the valley is one of the many **white boulder monuments** erected to the US 2nd Division. On the left ahead, is the destroyed and abandoned village of **Remenauville**. The village of 130 people had been occupied by the Germans since 1914, and its position on the front line all but assured its destruction. The US 2nd Division captured it on 12 September. The original church has been replaced by a small chapel, where signs describe the village before the war. From the memorial chapel a short walk leads along the narrow streets of a prewar French village, where now only scrub brush and vines occupy the sites of a butcher's or a farmer's home as identified by small placards.

Continue to the D3 intersection and turn toward Thiaucourt – now formally Thiaucourt-Regniéville to preserve the name of another destroyed village. Park at a convenient spot.

The intersection is studded with memorial stones; one, identified by the red diamond symbol, marks the starting point of the **US 5th Division's** assault upon Thiaucourt. A second plaque states that the same division passed through this area in September 1944 on its way to the Moselle River after fighting 1,100 km from the Normandy Beaches. Another **Demarcation Stone**, similar to the many seen along roadsides in Flanders, marks the limit of the 1918 German advance. Unfortunately, the rebuilt Regniéville chapel has become quite dilapidated, and most other reminders of the village have disappeared. Sharp eyes can still find a few village cellars along the roadway.

Proceed toward Thiaucourt-Regniéville (D3).

Three km ahead on the left is a **German machine-gun blockhouse** which defended the roadway. It remains in excellent condition despite the noticeable damage at its base caused by an artillery shell. The approach to Thiaucourt presents an example of the rolling hills and encroaching forests typical of the St Mihiel battlefield.

Near Thiaucourt, the road passes the enormous **Thiaucourt-Regniéville German Cemetery** on the left. Turn left before crossing the river and quickly left again to pass back under the rail bridge in order to enter. The cemetery contains 11,685 graves, a collection of private memorials in the northeast corner, and a special section with burials from the Franco-Prussian War.

Thiaucourt was an important German supply depot captured by the US 2nd Division at approximately 09:00 on 12 September, along with a vast quantity of German war materiel. In the town center, near the church is an imposing **War Memorial** depicting the unity of French and American soldiers. The church was reconstructed after the war as a remembrance by the parents of Captain Oliver Cunningham of Chicago, Illinois, who died on his 27th birthday near Jaulny. The exterior walls of the church and Hôtel-de-Ville still show damage from shell splinters.

> Leave Thiaucourt north toward Verdun (D67).

The **St-Mihiel American Cemetery** is the third largest of the First World War American Cemeteries in Europe and holds 4,153 dead, mostly from the St-Mihiel actions. An American eagle tops a sundial located at the intersection of the tree-lined walks that divide the cemetery into four plots. At the south end of the cemetery are a chapel, peristyle, and museum. The museum wall lists the names of 284 soldiers whose bodies were never found. The rear terrace overlooks the battlefield, through which the 89th and 42nd Divisions advanced; visible in the distance is the American Monument on Montsec. All American cemeteries in Europe are open every day from 09:00 to 17:00, except 25 December and 1 January. Personnel are available in the visitor's center to assist in locating gravesites or to provide information on the cemetery.

#36

Champagne Offensive
26 September to 28 October 1918

OBJECTIVE	To encircle the Forêt d'Argonne.
FORCES	
ALLIES:	Two American divisions; two French divisions of the French Fourth Army (général de division Henri Gouraud)
GERMAN:	Third Army's 12th Saxon Corps (General der Kavallerie Hans Krug von Nidda)

RESULT	Germany abandoned the Champagne Region.
CASUALTIES	
AMERICAN:	7,386 killed and wounded
FRENCH:	Unknown
GERMAN:	Unknown; 2,296 taken prisoner
LOCATION	Reims is 140 km northeast of Paris; Sommepy-Tahure is 50 km east of Reims

Champagne had been the scene of dreadful combat of four years with massive casualties on both sides. The elevated plains of Champagne's grain-growing region rank behind only Ypres, Verdun, and Somme in terms of casualties. Five great battles took place in the area: the winter battle of 1914 / 1915; a powerful French offensive of 25 September 1915; a French assault upon Moronvilliers in April / May 1917; defeat of the German *Friedensturm* Offensive on 15 July 1918; and the victorious Franco-American Offensive of 26 September 1918. These battles involved in total over one hundred French divisions, four American divisions, two Russian and one Czechoslovakian brigades and a Polish regiment.

By September 1918, the French Army was once again an offensive force after the dramatic consequences of the 1917 battles. Général Foch's plans for the fall of 1918 included attacks against the entire German front. Coordinated actions by the allied armies would prohibit their enemy from moving troops from quiet sectors against allied offensives – a feat that had served well in the past. In conjunction with the American Offensive in the Meuse-Argonne, the French Fourth Army was to attack between Reims and the Argonne Forest. Although they made progress, advancing 4 km in four days, they trailed behind the American advance in the Argonne, and the increasing separation concerned military planners. By 30 September, the French offensive was stalled by resistance south of Blanc Mont, a boomerang-shaped height that marked the last natural defensive position south of the Aisne River. With customary German thoroughness, it had been strengthened by a network of trenches, shelters, and barbed-wire entanglements. At général Pétain's request, two American divisions were sent to assist in taking the hill.

Battle

On 2 October, the US 2nd Division – they of Belleau Wood fame – arrived as part of the French XXI Corps and immediately cleared a section of the Essen Trench on the western end of their area of operation. 2nd Division's commander, Major General John Lejeune, had no intention of a frontal assault against the concrete pillboxes of Blanc Mont ridge. He split the division instead to effect a pincer attack with the unit's 3rd Infantry Brigade on the right and 4th Brigade (Marines) on the left. At 05:50 on 3 October, the soldiers and marines, accompanied by French tanks, left their trenches after a brief artillery preparation to follow behind a rolling barrage. The infantry brigade, however, first had to clear their front line trenches after a brief artillery preparation of Germans, who had launched a spoiling

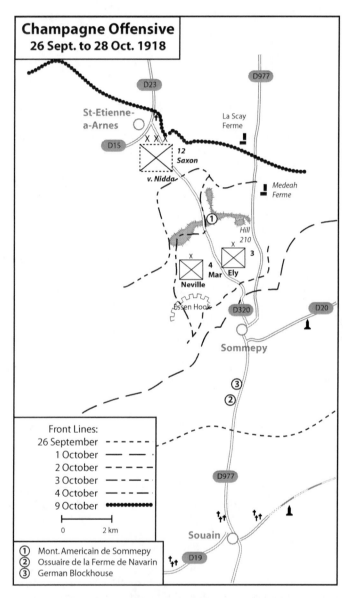

Champagne Offensive
26 Sept. to 28 Oct. 1918

raid earlier in the morning. Despite the initial setback, they were soon atop the ridge and moving along the arc of its summit. By 08:30, the eastern half of the ridge was in American hands, and a defensive front was established as far east as Médéah Farm.

The Marine Brigade also moved forward, taking position after position in hand-to-hand fighting, and reaching the summit at approximately 08:30. The French failed to retain Essen Trench, however, and were unable to advance on their left flank, leaving the western portion of the hill in enemy hands. The Americans were in a salient with enfilade artillery and machine-gun fire pouring on them while they sheltered in captured German trenches. While the infantry brigade continued its advance northward, the Marines dispatched forces to establish a left flank when counterattacks fell upon the line. German troops trapped in the triangle between the two American brigades eventually surrendered.

During the night the Germans moved machine guns and artillery forward to bring enormous firepower against the American flanks. Germany's air superiority supported effective targeting by the German batteries. At daybreak 15th Bavarian Division launched two counterattacks from Médéah Farm and St-Etienne-à-Armes, attempting a pincer of its own; both were beaten back with great losses. On 5 October, 3rd Battalion, 6th Marine Regiment stormed the last of the Blanc Mont strongpoints on the western end of the ridge, capturing 213 prisoners and 75 machine guns. The remainder of the day was spent consolidating their positions. With the French outflanking Notre-Dame des Champs and finally moving along the western slopes of the hill, the advance continued on 6 October. The Marines and French 22nd Division were stopped from entering St-Etienne-à-Armes by intense fire. The ridge before the village shielded enemy troop movements, and tunnels connected strongholds in the cemetery.

The 36th (Lone Star) Division took over for the 2nd Division; supported by two French tank battalions, they took the village the next day. The advance continued against weakening German resistance while units made their escape over the Aisne River. The 21-km pursuit was a vicious struggle against individual strongpoints manned by sacrificial rearguards. Allied attempts to pursue it across the river were defeated by strong German positions and by the lack of intact bridges. The American contribution to the offensive was terminated on 28 October, when the last German pocket south of the river was cleared of the enemy. The fearless capture of strategic Blanc Mont permitted the advance of the entire French Fourth Army in coordination with the American First Army in the Meuse-Argonne.

Battlefield Tour

The battlefield occupies 120 square kilometers of desolate waste caused by trench warfare, along a front running from Reims to the Forêt d'Argonne. In 1918, the front ran along an east-west line near the Ferme de Navarin, midway between Sommepy and Souain. Four km to the north was the 60-meter-high Navarin Ridge that stretched from near Orfeuil in the east, through Médéah Ferme, to Blanc Mont in the west. The extremes of the battlefield are now bordered by military cemeteries, including twenty-six French necropoles and ossuaries to the south and numerous German cemeteries to the north. The Camp Militaire de Suippes remains a restricted area of destroyed villages and shell-laden fields. The Champagne battles have largely disappeared from view, not even mentioned in some histories of the war. Despite the epic battles fought here during much of the First World War, remarkably few locations provide memorials. For Americans the exception is at Blanc Mont.

Leave Sommepy-Tahure to the north (D977); at the outskirts of the town, turn left toward St-Etienne-à-Armes (D320), and proceed to the monument.

The fields to the left are those crossed by the 4th Marine Brigade in its assault on the ridge. Even though the rolling hills that approach the monument from the south do not appear steep, their openness deprived attackers any opportunity for cover.

The summit of the crescent-shaped ridge has an American First World War battlefield **Monument Américain de Sommepy,** erected by the American Battle Monuments Commission after the war. The rectangular tower is emblazoned with the American eagle, and seventy-six stairs provide access to an observation platform, the parapet of which is decorated with bas-reliefs of military equipment. Still visible within the grounds of the monument are trench lines and entrances into underground dugouts. The Americans fought a desperate struggle to control these positions against repeated German counterattacks. Open every weekday throughout the year and on weekends 1 July through 15 September from 09:00 to 17:00; closed 25 December and 1 January. No admission charge.

To the north, visible at the edge of the road, is a white boulder monument erected to the 2nd Division – one of four such markers on the Blanc Mont battlefield. Located in a vale under a single tree, the site marks the forward advance achieved by the 2nd Division during the night of 4/5 October.

Return to Sommepy-Tahure and continue south toward Suippes (D977). Proceed to the large monument on the right.

The front lines ran across the Souain-Sommepy road at the **French Ossuaire, Ossuaire de la Ferme de Navarin,** the site of ferocious combat. The pyramidal structure holds the remains of 10,000 unidentified soldiers who died in the epic battles of Champagne as well as the body of général Gouraud, who was interred there in 1948. Three larger-than-life military figures top the monument; the soldier carrying a machine gun on the right is in American uniform and modeled after Lieutenant Quentin Roosevelt.[3] The ground behind the ossuary still retains faint impressions of trenches and craters. The ossuary is open on weekends and holidays mid-March through September, on Friday and Saturday from 14:00 to 18:00 and on Sunday and holidays from 10:00 to 12:00 and 14:00 to 18:00; 1 November and 11 November from 10:00 to 12:00 and 14:00 to 16:00. No admission charge.

---

[3] Lieutenant Roosevelt, youngest son of former United States President Theodore Roosevelt, was a pilot in the 95th Aero Squadron and was shot down near Château-Thierry on 14 July 1918. Originally buried where he fell with great honor by the Germans, his body now lies in the Normandy American Cemetery next to his brother and Medal of Honor winner, Brigadier General Theodore Roosevelt, Jr.

Other Sites of Interest: A **German blockhouse** remains at the intersection of the D977 and D220 highways, 200 meters to the north, and slightly hidden by recent road reconstruction. Southeast of Sommepy-Tahure is the **Camp Militaire de Suippes**. The large, brush-covered tract is an active military base and is closed to civilians; however, guided tours of the destroyed villages and other sites are occasionally offered.

#37

Battle of St-Quentin Canal
29 September to 2 October 1918

OBJECTIVE	To assault the St Quentin Tunnel as part of a larger action to penetrate the Hindenburg Line
FORCES	
ALLIES:	US II Corps (Major General GW Read); British IX Corps (Lieutenant-General Walter P Braithwaite); Australian Corps (Lieutenant-General Sir John Monash)
GERMAN:	Two corps of the German Second Army (General der Infanterie Adolph von Carlowitz)
RESULT	The Hindenburg Line was broken, and allied troops pushed the German Second Army back to the German Beaurevoir Line.
CASUALTIES	
ALLIES:	2,577 Australian casualties; 7,500 American casualties; significantly fewer British casualties
GERMAN:	Estimated 5,969 taken prisoner
LOCATION	Cambrai is 175 km north of Paris

During September 1918, the allied armies attacked the entire front from Ypres to Verdun. In Somme the Hindenburg Line incorporated the natural barrier of the St Quentin Canal, which connected the Somme and Scheldt Rivers. A vulnerable section of the canal was north of St Quentin, where the canal ran through a 5,670-meter long tunnel opened in 1810 by Napoleon I. This passage over the waterway was heavily defended. Barges moored in the tunnel provided shelter for a German division, including supplies and hospitals. The ground above it was honeycombed with galleries providing access to pillboxes, machine-gun nests, and escape openings. The steep banks of the canal were festooned with trenches and machine guns. The main defense line was west of the tunnel, where multiple lines of tangled barbed wire and strongpoints such as 'the Knoll,' le Tombois, Quennemont, and Guillemont Farms were situated.

As part of the five offensives ordered by Foch for the last week of September, General Rawlinson's Fourth Army attacked along a 19-km front between Cambrai and St Quentin. The underground sections of the canal provided a key crossing point. The British Third Army attacked on either side of Cambrai to the north and the French First Army did the same on either side of St Quentin to the south.

Battle

A bombardment from 1,634 guns started during the night of 26/27 September, with a heavy concentration of gas shells – including mustard gas – against enemy batteries. After a day of cold rain, assault units began the attack in the mists of the early morning of 29 September, with the US 27th and 30th Divisions (both National Guard units) and the British 46th (North Midland) Division in line

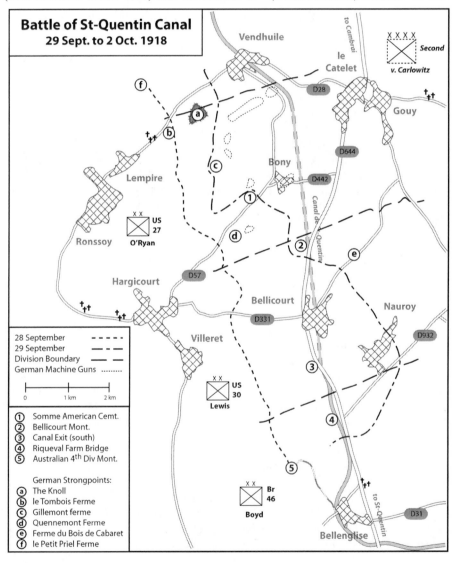

Battle of St-Quentin Canal
29 Sept. to 2 Oct. 1918

Vendhuile

to Cambrai

le Catelet

X X X X
Second
v. Carlowitz

D28

Gouy

f

a

b

c

D644

Bony

D442

Canal de St Quentin

Lempire

1

X X
US 27
O'Ryan

d

2

e

Ronssoy

Hargicourt

D57

Bellicourt

Nauroy

D331

D932

Villeret

3

X X
US 30
Lewis

4

5

28 September   - - - - -
29 September   - - - -
Division Boundary   — — —
German Machine Guns   ....

0   1 km   2 km

① Somme American Cemt.
② Bellicourt Mont.
③ Canal Exit (south)
④ Riqueval Farm Bridge
⑤ Australian 4th Div Mont.

German Strongpoints:
ⓐ The Knoll
ⓑ le Tombois Ferme
ⓒ Gillemont ferme
ⓓ Quennemont Ferme
ⓔ Ferme du Bois de Cabaret
ⓕ le Petit Priel Ferme

X X
Br 46
Boyd

Bellenglise

to St-Quentin

D31

from north to south. The men of British 137th Brigade scrambled down the sides of the 10-meter wide canal and swam the canal, using life jackets and whatever would float to cross the 2-3 meter deep water barrier. They fought their way up the eastern bank effectively piercing the Hindenburg defenses between Bellicourt and Bellenglise.

The US 30th Division overcame three lines of wire, as well as three trench systems and seized Bellicourt, the southern entrance of the tunnel, and entered Nauroy. Although they broke the line, they were attacked in the rear by German troops exiting the tunnel galleries. The 5th Australian Division responded and eliminated the enemy.

Farther north, however, the American 27th Division was in trouble. Replacing a British division only a few days before the attack, they arrived to find the planned jumping-off trenches still occupied by the Germans. Minor assaults on 27 and 28 September had failed to dislodge a stubborn German defense, and strongpoints such as the 'Knoll' remained in enemy hands. Their advance was delayed by these German positions, and they lost contact with the creeping barrage. The tanks allotted to them were quickly disabled with antitank fire. Pleas to the British artillery to call back the barrage were refused. German machine guns pressured the American left flank, behind which British troops to the north lagged. The units lost contact with each other in the dense fog and smoke and entered into confused fighting. The majority of the officers quickly became casualties, but the troops advanced up the slope of the tunnel in small, isolated parties, some of which crossed the canal line as far as Bony. Reserve battalions were attacked from the rear, while bypassed strongpoints remained centers of resistance and Germans emerged from the tunnel galleries. At noon the 3rd Australian Division was ordered to assault the many German positions bypassed by the American advance. Troops of the two countries mixed, many of the 27th Division refusing to leave the field. The Australians passed through the American troops and continued the attack. By midnight the main German line of resistance withdrew to behind the canal.

On 30 September, the 27th Division was ordered into support, but the front line troops continued to fight with the Australians. The remainder of the Hindenburg Line was cleared, and again Bony was entered but still not cleared until the following day. Ferme du Bois de Cabaret strongpoint was taken in a hand-grenade attack against desperate resistance. Constant pressure forced the defenders back through Joncourt and Estrées and pushed through the third of the Hindenburg defenses, known as the Beaurevoir Line, 4 km east of the canal.

At 01:30 on 1 October, the 27th Division was relieved and sent to the rear area. The men may have been lacking in coordination and leadership, but they were never short of courage. The 107th Regiment lost the equivalent of a battalion of men by sunset on the first day, the most casualties suffered by an American unit on one day in the war. The battle was short but intense, as demonstrated by the United States awarding nine Medals of Honor.

Battlefield Tour

Leave Cambrai south toward St-Quentin (N44, recently renumbered as D944).

The area consists of rolling farmland typical of Picardy. The Cambrai-St-Quentin road (N44) runs along a section of the underground canal, which is marked along the roadway by a line of brush and small trees. The village of Bony is accessed via a rural road (D442) approximately 1.5 km south of le Catelet. West of the village is the **Somme American Cemetery**, located on the site of strong German positions and thus a true battlefield cemetery. It contains 1,844 graves, including three Medal of Honor winners, arranged in a perfectly symmetrical pattern. The corner posts of the cemetery wall are topped with beautifully carved military scenes, and the small stone chapel displays an ornately carved bronze door. The chapel walls list the names of those 333 soldiers whose remains were never located or identified. All American cemeteries in Europe are open every day except 25 December and 1 January from 09:00 to 17:00.

Less than 1 km south of the Bony access road, on the west side of the national highway is **Bellicourt Monument**, which commemorates the sacrifices of 90,000 American troops who fought with the British Army during 1917 and 1918. From the east, a gated roadway approaches the broad stone stairway that ascends to the intricately carved face of the rectangular stone block. The western façade has a map of the actions of the 27th and 30th Divisions during their attack upon the Hindenburg Line as well as a table of orientation. Its position is directly on top of the underground canal and within the Hindenburg Line. The direction from which the Americans attacked can be viewed from the memorial's west terrace, which also overlooks the Vallée de Bony, which American troops used as shelter from enemy guns. The Quennemont Ferme defenses, which now appear as a brush-bordered plot, were on the high ground in the distance slightly north of due west. The British and American starting positions were approximately along A26 Autoroute, 2-3 km west of the canal. The German farm strongpoints are accessible only via farm roads and are of little interest.

The southern canal exit is 1 km south of Bellicourt which also has a small **barge museum and tourist information office**. A steep forest path leads down to the canal and its entrance. Access to the still-working canal is strictly prohibited. A **concrete pillbox**, apparently used as a command post, remains on the western shoulder, above the canal entrance; it can be entered, but bring a light. The northern exit of the canal near Macquincourt is more difficult to access and offers little of interest.

Approximately 2 km south of Bellicourt is the hamlet of Riqueval, where a rural road leads to the famous **Riqueval Farm Bridge** captured by the 6th Battalion, North Staffordshire Regiment before it could be destroyed. The structure remains almost exactly as it appeared in 1918 except for a few repairs. A plaque presented by the Western Front Association commemorates the event. Barely visible in the underbrush on the east end of the bridge is another ruined German pillbox.

Other Sites of Interest: Many small villages east of the Cambrai-St-Quentin road contain small memorials to their liberation by American divisions. The **Memorial Obelisk to the 4ᵗʰ Australian Division** is west of Bellenglise; unfortunately, it is accessible only over a rough farm road. Despite its isolated location, the site has beautifully manicured trees, shrubs, and lawn, and the high location offers views across the Hindenburg Line battlefield. A memorial obelisk to the **British 46ᵗʰ Division** is south of the **La Baraque British Cemetery,** approximately 100 meters east of the D644.

#38
Meuse-Argonne Offensive
26 September to 11 November 1918

OBJECTIVE	To cut German transportation routes around Sedan as part of a coordinated allied offensive.
FORCES	
ALLIES:	Nine American divisions and four French divisions plus six divisions in reserve; 384 aircraft and 215 tanks (General John Pershing)
GERMAN:	Army Group 'C', initially with five divisions and growing to twenty divisions (General der Artillerie Max Karl von Gallwitz)
RESULT	The Americans achieved the objective.
CASUALTIES	
AMERICAN:	26,277 killed and 95,786 wounded
GERMAN:	28,000 killed and 92,250 wounded; over 26,000 taken prisoner
LOCATION	Verdun-sur-Meuse is 270 km east of Paris; Meuse-Argonne battlefield is 30 km northwest of Verdun

Pershing's quarrels with Foch over dispersing American troops into French and British battalions resulted in a compromise by which the neophyte American First Army would undertake two offensives within two weeks on battlefields 100 km apart. The American logistics team, having resoundingly completed the first task at St Mihiel, prepared for the second.

The attack targeted the most critical point of the German railroad transportation network at Sedan. Loss of this choke point would separate the German armies in the north from those in the south and would make the supply or the withdrawal of German forces in Flanders nearly impossible. Recognizing the Argonne's strategic importance, the Germans strengthened the area with several defensive lines which formed an almost continuous, 16-km wide belt of machine guns, barbed wire, and dugouts nearly. The terrain provided numerous opportunities for gun emplacements with mutually supporting cross- and enfilade-fire possibilities. The hills along the Meuse valley and the wooded plateau of the Forêt d'Argonne provided excellent artillery positions, and the center of the battlefield was dominated by the Butte of Montfaucon.

The Preparations required the movement of over eight hundred thousand men and all of the related materiel. Even before the St-Mihiel operation had ceased, American infantrymen were moving north on three narrow roads and hiding during daylight to preserve secrecy. Forward positions were maintained by French troops until the last minute to hide the presence of American troops on the front. Some units arrived at the jump-off trenches just hours before the assault.

The American success at St-Mihiel could have been partially attributed to German plans for evacuation; however, the same could not be said about the Argonne. In the three years after the boiling battles against the French had quieted to a steady simmer, the Germans had developed the dense woods and steep buttes into a killing field. Enemy positions were so strong that général Pétain opined that the Americans should consider taking Montfaucon by Christmas as good progress. Defensive lines, named after characters in Wagnerian operas, culminated in the *Kriemhilde Stellung,* which ran from Brieulles through Romagne-sous-Montfaucon to Grandpré – 12 to 15 km north of the start line. Farther north, past the incomplete *Freya Stellung,* the fields were generally open.

The American First Army assault was to be three corps moving abreast along a line from the Meuse River to the western edges of the Forêt d'Argonne; III Corps on the right, V Corps in the center, I Corps on the left – each with three divisions up front and one division in reserve. To the east, across the Meuse French XVII Corps was to silence the German artillery on the heights along the east bank. West of the Argonne the French Fourth Army was to engage the enemy in a coordinated drive on Sedan.

Battle

At 02:30 on 26 September, 2,775 guns opened a three-hour bombardment along the 40-km front. The duration of the artillery preparation was short to minimize early enemy reinforcement. The infantry then followed behind the rolling barrage into the densely woven fabric of ravines, gun emplacements, machine-gun nests, trenches, and wire entanglements. A heavy fog hid some German strongpoints, which were by-passed. On the first day, US V Corps drove past the left of Montfaucon, and III Corps did the same on the strongpoint's right, leaving the height as a salient in American lines. I Corps moved swiftly along the Aire Valley but advanced only 1.6 km in the dense woods of the Argonne. Although Montfaucon was captured by noon on 27 September, the delay allowed the Germans to reinforce positions to its north and end America's hopes of a quick attack upon the main line of resistance. By the end of the third day, *Hagen* and *Giselher Stellung* had been penetrated after a 10-km advance, and American troops faced the *Kriemhilde Stellung.* Increased German resistance, supported by the transfer of seven fresh, first-class divisions and improved artillery support, forced a brief halt in the assault. The American advance, however, combined with British, French, and Belgian offensives elsewhere along the Western Front had sealed Germany's fate. On 3 October, Hindenburg

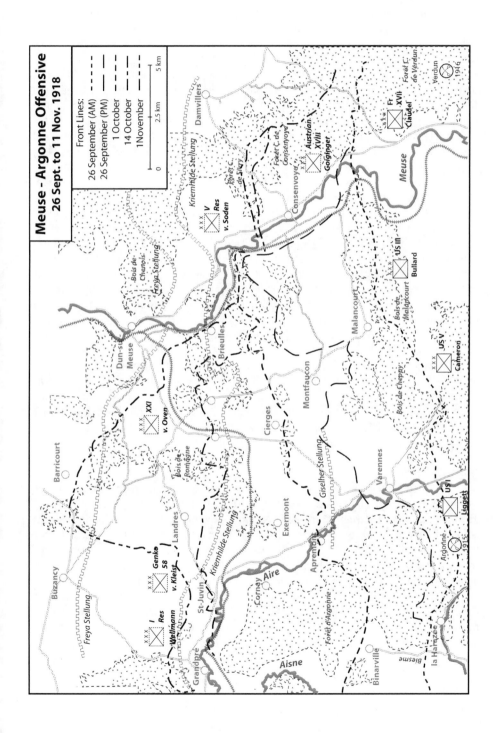

Meuse - Argonne Offensive
26 Sept. to 11 Nov. 1918

wrote, 'There is now no longer any possibility of forcing peace on the enemy.'[4]

Pershing replaced tired units with fresh divisions, and engineers constructed plank roads to cross the morass of no man's land. The assault was renewed on 4 October. The Germans were experts at using the terrain for defense, and each meter of progress was resisted by machine-gun fire and well-sighted artillery. The batteries on the heights of the Meuse were especially deadly to American troops on the right flank. On 5 October, Pershing ordered the French XVII Corps to attack those positions to relieve the pressure upon the III Corps. On 8 October, a stunning attack from the Aire valley west of Châtel-Chéhéry by the US 28th and 82nd Divisions and coordinated with the 77th Division coming up through the forest forced the Germans to abandon the Argonne for fear of being surrounded. The next day, the French / American divisions of the French XVII Corps drove the Germans from the hills east of the Meuse, ending much of the flank fire.

With the creation of the American Second Army, Major General Liggett was promoted to the American First Army, and Pershing became commander of American Army Group. On 14 October, after a two-day respite, the main Hindenburg Line came under assault. The German forces had increased to forty divisions, but they were unable to stop the relentless attacks. Strongpoints fell in succession after bitter and costly fighting, and the last defensive line was breached. The Germans continued to bring units from other battlefields along the Western Front to stem the advance but were unsuccessful.

A brief period of recuperation and replacement preceded a two-hour artillery bombardment and assault on 1 November. A rapid advance caused the German High Command to issue orders for a general withdrawal to the east of the Meuse River. The US 5th Division established bridgeheads across the river at Dun-sur-Meuse on 4 November. By 7 November, units of I Corps were on the heights above Sedan, and the ultimate objective of cutting the German rail lines around that city was achieved. The battle ended with the Armistice of 11 November – drawing to a close the greatest American military effort of that time.

Battlefield Tour

The Meuse-Argonne battlefield is bordered by the unfordable Meuse River to the east and the almost impenetrable Forêt d'Argonne to the west. The broad farming valley in between contained the slow-flowing Aire River. On the eastern banks of the Meuse were a series of bluffs and forests that sheltered German artillery batteries. The dense tangles of the trackless Argonne plateau provided similar cover for cannon and machine-gun emplacements. In the center of the battlefield was the elevation known as Montfaucon. The great German-French struggle of 1915 had hardened into a front line, cutting the Argonne in half along a line running east-west from Vauquois through the forest to the valley of the Biesme. As it moved northward, the Aire turned westward to join the Aisne through an opening that defined the northern limit of the Argonne and the southern limit of the Bois de

---

[4] Ibid., 255.

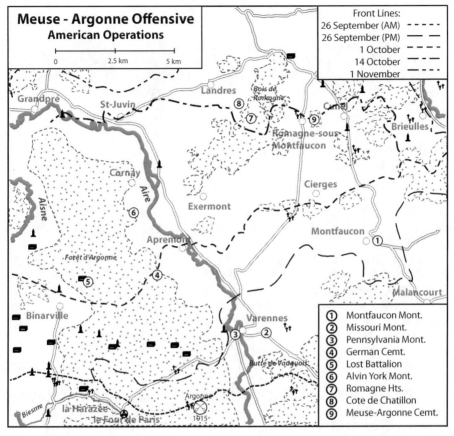

Meuse - Argonne Offensive
American Operations

0   2.5 km   5 km

Front Lines:
26 September (AM) ----
26 September (PM) ——
1 October ----
14 October ——
1 November ----

① Montfaucon Mont.
② Missouri Mont.
③ Pennsylvania Mont.
④ German Cemt.
⑤ Lost Battalion
⑥ Alvin York Mont.
⑦ Romagne Hts.
⑧ Cote de Chatillon
⑨ Meuse-Argonne Cemt.

Bourgogne. The series of ridgelines and high points in the terrain provided excellent defensive positions.

Since the Meuse-Argonne battlefield covers 1,500 square kilometers, the tour focuses on select locations critical to the initial success of the offensive. The countryside is dotted with divisional memorials erected after the war, and many of them are passed along the way, each having its own distinctive design.

Leave Verdun-sur-Meuse and follow the east bank of the river north to Samogneux (D964); then continue across to the west bank toward Regnéville-sur-Meuse (D123a). Remain on that road to Forges-sur-Meuse, turning toward Béthincourt (D160). Continue to Malancourt, turning north toward Montfaucon (D18 / D15).

From Forges to Malancourt the road travels along the valley of the Forges River, and the ridgeline to the left held the American front on the morning of 26 September. The final leg of the tour follows the attack route of the US 79th Division over a German defensive height known as Ouvrage du Démon and to Montfaucon d'Argonne. From the village of Montfaucon, follow the signs to the *Monument Américain.*

Montfaucon was originally the site of an ancient monastery reportedly to have been the scene of a great battle in 888AD against Norman invaders. It witnessed additional struggles in the Hundred Years War, the Religious Wars of the 16th century, and the passage of Prussian troops on their way to the battle of Valmy in 1792. The village of Montfaucon, which grew around the monastery, was obliterated during the four years of the First World War; however, the location was a key observation post for the German's second defensive line and was thus developed into a veritable fortress of above- and underground positions.

At 11:00 on 26 September, the US 37th Division emerged from the Bois Malancourt and entered the trench systems to the south. The first assault upon Montfaucon started at 18:00, and the lower slopes of the hill were reached, but the advance halted by nightfall. The assault renewed at dawn in a driving rainstorm, while two American divisions attacked from the front and right flank. By noon the hill was cleared.

The **American Monument on Montfaucon** is a 55-meter Doric column topped with the figure of Liberty, erected to commemorate the American First Army's victory in the Meuse-Argonne. It faces toward the American start lines of 26 September. Within the base of the column are 234 steps leading to observation rooms with splendid views over much of the battlefield as well as a table of orientation. Montfaucon is in the center of the American battlefield and can be seen from various points during the tour. Open every weekday throughout the year and on weekends 1 July through 15 September from 09:00 to 17:00; closed 25 December and 1 January. No admission charge.

Directly behind the American Monument are the ruins of the **church of Montfaucon,** destroyed during the fighting. Incorporated into the church walls is a German concrete blockhouse which was used as on observation post. The grounds around the church contain several additional wartime structures that were built during the four-year occupation of the village. Paths through the underbrush provide access, and a brief survey of the area demonstrates the strength of the position, even though vegetation now blocks the views of the surrounding countryside. A new village has been built below the hill.

Leave the village toward Cheppy / Varennes-en-Argonne (D19).

After passing Cheppy on the right but before merging with the D38 toward Varennes, the **Missouri Monument** is on the left. The elevated platform has a granite plinth topped with an Angel of Victory holding an olive wreath. It was erected by the State of Missouri to commemorate its sons who fought in the war, many of them members of the 35th (Missouri and Kansas National Guard) Division which advanced through this area. In the nearby woods Battery D, 129th Field Artillery, commanded by then-captain and future United States President Harry S

Truman, participated in the artillery exchanges with German batteries. During an attack upon a German observation post in Cheppy, Lieutenant Colonel George Patton received a serious wound while leading American 1st Tank Brigade.

Directly south of Cheppy is the **Butte de Vauquois**, which was bisected by the battle lines of 26 September and was the jumping-off point for the 35th Division. See battlefield #20 for a description of the 1915 fighting on the butte.

Follow the D38 into Varennes-en-Argonne.

Varennes is famous in French history as the place where the fleeing King Louis XVI was captured and returned to Paris during the French Revolution. Louis and his wife, Marie Antoinette, eventually were sent to the guillotine. Plaques near the stone bridge signify the event. Cross the bridge over the Aire River, and on the far side of the town is the impressive **Pennsylvania Monument**. It commemorates the men of Pennsylvania, particularly the 28th (Keystone) Division which captured the area west of the Aire. The double colonnade frames a large park and central urn.

Adjacent to the monument is the **Musée d'Argonne,** which is dedicated to the history of the area. The lower floor contains displays relating to the First World War and describing American and Italian participation. Dioramas of the mine warfare are included along with several original German trench maps. Although most of the signs are not in English, the displays are self-explanatory. Open weekdays 19 April through 30 June from 15:00 to 18:00; daily July through September from 10:30 to 12:00 and 14:30 to 18:00. Fee.

Return to the bridge over the Aire and proceed north toward Apremont (D38a).

The road travels along the eastern edge of the Argonne forest and follows the path of 28th and 35th Divisions in the beginning of the offensive. From Apremont the road toward Binarville (D442) is the only lateral route across the forest; it passes an interesting old **German cemetery** atop the heavily defended Le Chêne Tondu. On the west side of the forest, the road passes the location of the '**Lost Battalion,**'[5] now marked by a simple roadside stele.

Take the D42 north from Apremont, joining the D4 upon entering Châtel-Chéhéry.

West of Châtel-Chéhéry is the forest where acting **Corporal Alvin York** became famous as the conscientious objector who was awarded the Medal of Honor for capturing 132 enemy soldiers after shooting over 20. A stone was erected in his honor in the center of the village.

---

[5] The 1st Battalion, 308th Infantry Regiment, 77th Division was isolated under enemy fire for four days before being rescued. The inspirational unit became known as the 'Lost Battalion.'

> Proceed north toward Cornay (D4), after which cross the Aire River toward Fléville. Turn left toward St-Juvin (D946).

The 1st Division assumed responsibility for the eastern bank and drove north and east through some of the most heavily defended regions, including the powerful position known as the **Romagne Heights**.

> Before St-Juvin, turn right toward Sommerance (D54 / D123) and continue into Romagne-sous-Montfaucon.

The road traverses the area of the third German line, now with trees softening the contours of what were then sharp ridges. Three km after Sommerance and 1.5 km to the north of the highway was the strategic and strongly fortified **Côte de Châtillon**, captured on 17 October after extensive losses by 84th Brigade, 42nd (Rainbow) Division, commanded by flamboyant Brigadier General Douglas MacArthur. One of MacArthur's regimental commanders, Lieutenant Colonel William Donovan, was awarded a Medal of Honor for his actions in leading his men while under extreme enemy fire.

In the village of Romagne the road intersects with the D998; 50 meters to the north is a **German Military Cemetery**. The entrance is through a red sandstone gatehouse which contains a chapel. The cemetery holds 1,412 burials identified by slate crosses under mature pine trees.

> On the east side of Romagne, continue toward Cunel (D123).

Meuse-Argonne American Cemetery is the largest American military cemetery in Europe. Its location marks some of the most difficult fighting experienced by American troops in the war. The *Kriemhilde Stellung*, the strongest section of the Hindenburg Line, ran along the ridge behind the chapel. During the period of 9 to 13 October, five American divisions repeatedly attempted to dislodge the defenders, each time driven back by dense enemy fire. The village of Cunel and Romagne were taken and lost several times. On 14 October, despite a two-hour enemy artillery bombardment upon its front trenches, the US 5th Division fought through sweeping machine-gun fire from the Bois de Pultière north of Cunel and by 11:00, captured the slopes upon which the cemetery rests. Unable to advance farther, they sheltered in shell craters near the current reflecting pool and awaited the night. The US 32nd Division entered the village and held it despite an engulfing gas shell barrage during the night. The 5th Division continued its fight, requiring eight days to clear the enemy from the Bois des Rappes northeast of the cemetery. The seven divisions suffered a total of 27,000 casualties in the vicinity of the cemetery, cracking the Hindenburg Line.

The huge cemetery now contains 14,246 graves in 8 plots. The painstakingly groomed grounds surround the Carrere marble crosses or Jewish Stars which mark each grave. At the far end of the cemetery, opposite the Visitor's Center is the Memorial Chapel, a sanctuary for private reflection. Its stained glass windows display the insignia of divisions of the American Expeditionary Force. The arcaded walls of the chapel list the names of 954 dead whose bodies were never found. All American cemeteries in Europe are open every day from 09:00 to 17:00 except 25 December and 1 January.

#39

Rethondes Clairière de l'Armistice
8 to 11 November 1918

REPRESENTATIVES	
FRENCH:	Supreme Allied Commander maréchal Ferdinand Foch
BRITISH:	First Lord of the British Admiralty Admiral Rosslyn Wemyss
GERMAN:	Secretary of State Matthias Erzberger
RESULT	The Germans signed the armistice declaration, ending hostilities pending negotiation of the Treaty of Versailles.
LOCATION	Compiègne is 80 km north of Paris; the Forest of Rethondes is 7 km east of Compiègne

Although not a battlefield, the significance of Rethondes Clairière de l'Armistice to the two world wars and the colorful nature of the events that occurred here warrant a visit and this special tour section.

After the failures of the Champagne and Lys Offensives, Ludendorff knew that the war was lost. As early as 28 September, he had shared his opinion with Field Marshal Hindenburg, who had come to the same conclusion. Pressured by allied offensives along the Western Front and by the defeat of its Austrian, Turkish, and Bulgarian partners on other fronts, the German people were increasingly defeatist. Changes to the German government were intended to make negotiations with United States President Woodrow Wilson more palatable by reducing the control of the military and the Kaiser. The military prepared the new civilian government for the truce to preserve the 'honor' of the German Army. The new Chancellor, Prince Maximilian von Baden, initially refused to be the army's scapegoat, but then relented. Maximilian accepted conditions based upon President Wilson's Fourteen Points. The German military sought an armistice that would preserve what remained of the army in exchange for territorial concessions. Believing that the American conditions did not sufficiently punish the German people, French President Georges Clemenceau and British Prime Minister Lloyd George protested that Wilson was negotiating behind their backs. Wilson backed off, fearing a German attempt to split the Allies.

Faced with the dissolution of his armies, renewed allied offensives, and the lack of support from the now independent-minded civilian government, Ludendorff resigned on 26 October. Meanwhile, the allied Supreme War Council, headed by Foch, met in Versailles to establish the military's armistice conditions.

In the first week of November, German deserters marched in protest in Berlin, and Bolshevik elements in the German Navy seized several naval bases, refusing their admiral's orders to sail against the vastly superior British fleet. Workers' councils seized the main Rhine bridges and stopped the flow of men and supplies. At 05:00 on 10 November, the Kaiser left the Supreme Command Headquarters at Spa, Belgium to go into exile in neutral Holland. His abdication became official on 28 November 1918, ending the 250-year Hohenzollern Dynasty.

Events

On 7 November, the German delegation, led by Secretary of State Matthias Erzberger, a centrist politician, left the Kaiser's headquarters at Spa by motorcar. Generalmajor Detlev von Winterfeldt, the son of the man who had dictated the terms of France's surrender in 1870 and a former military attaché in Paris, was the army's representative. Field Marshall Hindenburg and members of the German General Staff had declined participation. Upon leaving Spa, Chancellor Prince Baden begged Erzberger to secure peace. The pressure on Erzberger was tremendous, and in addition, his son had died of influenza three weeks earlier. After a circuitous route through recent battlefields, the delegation arrived at the forest clearing at 05:30 the next morning.

Waiting for them was Supreme Allied Commander maréchal Ferdinand Foch, Chief of Staff général de division Maxime Weygand, and First Lord of the British Admiralty Admiral Rosslyn Wemyss, who had arrived earlier that morning. No Americans were present. Foch's demands were non-negotiable and were to be accepted as presented. The German delegation remained in the clearing for three days while their negotiations with authorities in Berlin took place. At 02:05 on 11 November, the new civilian government of Chancellor Friedrick Ebert in Berlin replied that they agreed. At 05:05, Erzberger signed the document on behalf of the German Government. The armistice took effect at 11:00 that morning. The guns finally fell silent.

Aftermath

With armistice declared, the German army demobilized itself; tired, sick, and disillusioned men walked home. Prince Max handed the Chancellorship to Fritz Ebert, an ex-cobbler and Social Democrat. In February 1919, he would declare himself President of the German Republic. President Wilson arrived in France on 14 December 1918 to participate in the Paris Peace Conference. Only the victors were present because political events in Germany made a military armistice an unconditional surrender. Wilson's Fourteen Points were ignored while Clemenceau, Lloyd George, and Italian Premier Orlando proposed punishing economic terms on Germany. Great Britain wanted to expand its Colonial Empire; France wanted a Germany on its knees and guarantees against future aggression; Italy – late to empire building – wanted overseas colonies. Wilson sacrificed his Fourteen Points in return for establishing collective security through the League of Nations. The leaders produced a document that was punitive and unworkable, filled with territorial contradictions. German Foreign Minister Count Brockdorff-Rantzau was appalled at the conditions when he arrived and initially refused to accept it. The allied blockade of German ports, however, was still in existence, and the population was on the verge of starvation. On 28 June 1919, the Treaty of Versailles was signed in the same Hall of Mirrors where the German Empire had been created only 48 years earlier. Wilson returned to the United States ill and disillusioned. Thirteen and one half years later, Adolf Hitler, the enemy the treaty had helped to create, was elected Chancellor of Germany.

Consequences of the War

In the decades after the First World War, recriminations abounded as to who was at fault for starting the great conflagration. Some historians believe that a system of alliances and predetermined army mobilization schedules forced the parties into fighting. The 'winners', blamed the 'losers' intransigence and militarism, but with over 20 million dead, blame is on both sides.

The war ended the dynastic houses of middle Europe that had ruled for centuries. The monarchial governments of Austria, Germany, and Russia were all replaced. The Ottoman Empire in Turkey disappeared. Like the Congress of Vienna at the end of the Napoleonic era, the Paris Conference redrew the political map of Europe, attempting to re-establish the balance of power. Germany lost industrialized Silesia, parts of Pomerania and West Prussia, and the Danzig Corridor to a reformed Poland. Alsace and Lorraine were returned to France. Minor adjustments were made to the borders with Belgium and Denmark. Germany's African colonies were occupied by Britain, and its Pacific Islands went under a Japanese Mandate from the League of Nations.

The human consequences of the war are measured by the casualty totals. On the Western Front, France suffered the most, with 1,385,300 dead or missing – 10 per cent of its male working population and 27 per cent of men between the ages of 18 and 27. It would take 35 years for the country to regain its prewar population level. British armies had 908,500 dead – 750,000 on the Western front – including 56,625 Canadians and 59,000 Australians. America's losses were significantly smaller in keeping with the late entry but were still a substantial 116,750. 85,000 fell on the Western Front, of which 52,947 were battle deaths. Belgium, with its much smaller population, lost 40,367. Italy's losses on its front against Austro-Hungary were a staggering 460,000. Totals for all allied armies on the Western Front were 2.3 million dead. Russian military deaths were estimate at 1,700,000, but an accurate number is not known.

German casualty figures were accurately tabulated until the army dissolved in the last months of the war. German losses for all fronts on all fronts for the entire war were 1,718,250. Today 768,000 German soldiers are buried in France. Germany's allies added 1,200,000 from Austria-Hungary, 335,750 from Turkey and 101,250 from Bulgaria to the death toll.

In total, the fighting resulted in 8.2 million dead, 7 million disabled, and 12 million carrying the physical or psychological scars of combat. Those classified as prisoners (many of whom returned) or missing (many of whom did not) totaled 7.5 million, of which a large percentage occurred on the Eastern Front. Western Europe added an additional 5 million civilian casualties, not including the effects of the influenza pandemic, which are estimated at 27 million deaths.

The monetary cost of the war has been estimated to be as high as $250 billion at today's valuation. Agricultural production and industrial output of the ravaged participants remained below prewar levels for a decade. France had 250,000 buildings destroyed and almost 10,000 square miles of land laid waste. Britain lost approximately 10 million tons of shipping to submarine warfare. At the end one side thought that it had won, but in reality both sides had lost.

Battlefield Tour

The forest of Compiègne is a lowland area bordered by the Oise and Aisne Rivers. The boggy woods are confined by a series of hills running from north to east to south. Once a favorite playground of French kings, approximately 1,500 kilometers of roads, horse trails, and footpaths still remain through the beech and oak groves. Just outside its borders are **Château Pierrefonds**, the famous residence of Napoleon III, and the early Gothic, 12th century church at Morienvald. The site is a popular tourist destination because of its historical significance and proximity to Paris. The city and forest offer numerous cultural, historic, and natural destinations.

Leave Compiègne center on rue de Solférino toward the Oise River (D332). Before crossing the bridge, turn right onto Cours Guynemer (N31). The road turns to the right and becomes rue de Soissons (still N31). After a curve to the left, its name becomes avenue de l'Armistice (still N31), and the route enters the Forêt de Rethondes. When the highway takes a wide turn to the left, continue straight on D546, which leads directly to the Armistice Clearing parking area.

A significant cause of France's going to war in 1914 was the return of the provinces of Alsace and Lorraine that Germany had annexed after the Franco-Prussian War in 1871. The **Alsace-Lorraine Monument** at the roundabout before the parking area commemorates the sacrifices of all French soldiers who fought for the return of those regions. A block arch of Alsatian sandstone stands over a sword, which is stabbing a prostrate German Imperial eagle. Inscribed in the top of the arch is the date 11 November 1918. Across the front of the stone platform are the words 'To the heroic soldiers of France – defenders of fatherland and right – glorious liberators of Alsace and Lorraine.' The monument so infuriated Adolf Hitler that in 1940 he had it destroyed and the pieces shipped to Germany. It was found and reconstructed after the Second World War.

During the war the Armistice Clearing was a boggy wood containing a network of rail lines used for heavy artillery installations bombarding the German lines 20 km away. The guns were cleared away to make room for maréchal Foch's private rail car on one side and that of the German representatives on the other. The two trains were no more that 300 feet apart. A short section of track remains, and memorial granite slabs resembling sarcophagi mark the spots where the cars stood. Between the two cars' locations a **stone terrace** commemorates the event with the words, 'Here on 11 November 1918 succumbed the criminal pride of the German Empire. Vanquished by the free peoples it sought to enslave.' Those powerful words fully represented the feelings of the allied peoples, especially those who had fought the war since 1914 and had suffered so terribly during four years of conflict, fear, and depravation. Since 1937, a statue of maréchal Foch looks over the clearing from among tall evergreen shrubs at the edge.

In 1940, Hitler had the slabs broken up and shipped to Berlin. The entire clearing was demolished, trees were cut down, and the earth was plowed over to remove any trace of Germany's humiliation. In respect for the French military leader, the **Statue of Maréchal Foch** was not damaged by the German occupiers during the Second World War. Compiègne was liberated on 1 September 1944, and the local population immediately forced German POWs to restore the clearing. The terrace blocks were recovered and reassembled.

Wagon Lits Company coach #2419D was originally a dining car. In 1918, it was at the service of maréchal Foch as a traveling office and accommodations. After the momentous events, it returned to regular service, but quickly became a popular attraction when installed in Les Invalids in Paris. In 1927, it was installed in a specially constructed museum at the edge of the clearing.

During the Second World War, Hitler ordered that Foch's rail car be removed from the museum and replaced in its 1918 location. On 22 June 1940, to the great glee of Hitler and his entourage, the French delegation, led by the aging maréchal Henri Pétain, was presented terms there by the German military, and France formally surrendered. The rail car was transported to Berlin as a trophy to be mounted in a new museum that was never built. After being briefly displayed at the Brandenburg Gate, it was housed in Anhalt Station until allied bombing raids on Berlin threatened its survival. Hidden in the forest at Orhdurf, Thuringia, 280 km southeast of Berlin, it was destroyed in the closing days of the war by SS troops.

A new **Mémorial du Wagon de l'Armistice** was constructed in 1950 and houses a replacement rail car of similar vintage as well as a room displaying artifacts from both the 1918 armistice and the 1940 surrender. Newspapers, documents, photographs, and the seating arrangements for the signing are included. Original documents from the First World War were hidden at the outbreak of the war and returned to the coach. An audio presentation describes the events. Open daily, except Tuesdays, October through March from 09:00 to 12:00 and 14:00 to 17:30; April through September until 18:30; afternoons only in December and January.

Recommended reading

Eisenhower, John: *Yanks: The Epic Story of the American Army in World War I*. New York: Simon & Schuster, 2001. Very readable account of American battles in the First World War.

Farwell, Byron: *Over There: The United States in the Great War 1917-1918*. New York: WW Norton & Company, 1999. The creation and development of the United States Army as well as its implementation in the war.

Macdonald, Lyn: *To the Last Man: Spring 1918*. New York: Carroll & Graf, 1998. An engrossing account of the *Kaiserschlacht* that preceded the Second Battle of Villers-Bretonneux.

Stallings, Laurence: *The Doughboys: The Story of the AEF, 1917-1918*. New York: Harper & Row, Publishers, 1963. The American Expeditionary Force story told by a participant at Belleau Wood.

Toland, John: *No Man's Land: 1918 – The Last Years of the Great War*. New York: Doubleday & Company, 1980. The events of 1918 in their political and cultural context.

Chapter Ten

Second World War
1939–1945

Germany's invasion of Poland in September 1939 again brought Europe into the conflict that the First World War was fought to end. The draconian terms of the Treaty of Versailles were intolerable to the German people. With his rise to power in January 1933, Chancellor Adolf Hitler began to re-arm the German military. In quick succession he re-occupied the Rhineland, merged Austria into a Greater German Reich, and occupied Czech Sudetenland, and then the remainder of Czechoslovakia. Poland's large but outdated army was destroyed by rapid, armored column movements that later became known as *Blitzkrieg*. Even before the fighting in Poland had ended, the emboldened dictator directed his military to prepare a plan for the invasion of France.

Fall Gelb (Case Yellow), the German General Staff's original plan for the invasion of France, copied the essentials of the 1914 Schlieffen Plan: a massive thrust through northern Belgium and Holland followed by a sweep down into France toward Paris. Generalleutnant Erich von Manstein proposed a reversal of emphasis that became Operation *'Sichelschnitt'* (cut of the sickle). He convinced Hitler that a strong armored force could sweep through southern Belgium and across northern France to the English Channel, cutting off the British Expeditionary Force (BEF) and major units of the French Army from their supply and communications. The plan included many additions, some of Hitler's own creation, to convince the Allies of Germany's intentions to make the main effort in the north. Specially trained airborne forces captured the Belgian fortress of Eben-Emael, which guarded the Albert Canal and the Maastricht appendix. Generalfeldmarschall Hermann Goering's Luftwaffe initially targeted Holland, wiping out the Dutch Airforce on the first day and dropping airborne troops to capture bridges across key waterways. Stuka dive bombers, sirens blaring while they dove upon targets, destroyed allied planes still on the ground and intercepted troop movements. Bombers laid waste to cities to terrorize civilians, and Messerschmidt 109 fighters provided air cover for the German columns of vehicles and marching men.

Belgian and Dutch military planning relied upon their forces executing a fighting retreat toward their population centers while the French and British advanced in support. The French trusted that the Maginot Line – a system of underground, concrete defensive installations lining the French-German border – was too strong for the Germans to consider attacking. After the fortuitous capture of German military plans on 10 January, commander of the French General Staff général Maurice Gamelin was convinced of the German intention to replicate the First World War's Schlieffen Plan. He instituted the Dyle-Breda defensive plan, which would bring the best units of the allied armies forward into Belgium upon the outbreak of the fighting to face the German invasion along the Dyle River-Gembloux Gap-Meuse River line. The French did not intend to fight a second war on French soil.

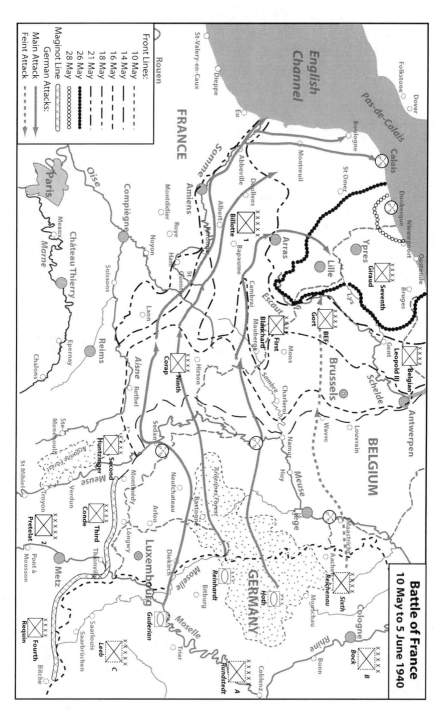

Battle of France
10 May to 5 June 1940

With the transmission of the code word '*Danzig,*' the invasion of Belgium, Luxembourg, Holland, and France started at 05:30 German time (04:30 French time) on 10 May. The German plan of attack was as daring in execution as it was thorough in its planning. To the north Generaloberst Fedor von Bock's Army Group 'B' was to appear to be the main assault group. Along the German-French border, Army Group 'C' was to pressure the Maginot Line and keep French defensive units from reinforcing other areas. Meanwhile, the real assault by Generaloberst Gerd von Rundstedt's Army Group 'A' was to pass through the Ardennes Forest with the intent of crossing the Meuse River before French Ninth Army commanded by général André-Georges Corap and French Second Army led by général Charles Huntziger could complete their defensive preparations. For this critical action, seven out of Germany's ten panzer (armored) divisions had been concentrated into three panzer corps. The principle force was on the southern flank, where General of Panzertruppen Heinz Guderian's XIX Panzer Corps targeted Sedan. On the northern flank General der Infanterie Hermann Hoth's two panzer divisions aimed at Dinant. XXXXI Panzer Corps, led by Generalleutnant Georg-Hans Reinhardt, was in the middle at Monthermé. The Luftwaffe provided massive air cover to shield the troops' movements from enemy eyes.

Allied attention was riveted on the actions against Holland and northern Belgium, just as the German High Command had hoped. Hitler later described his reaction while watching the allied divisions moving north, 'I could have cried for joy; they were walking into the trap. We calculated well to begin our attack on Liège. It made them believe we were carrying out the old Schlieffen Plan.'[1]

The German plan worked better than its military command expected. With the successful crossings of the Meuse on 13 May, the panzer divisions cut between the Maginot and Dyle Lines and headed for the English Channel. Allied responses were badly coordinated and usually late. On 15 May, the Dutch government surrendered, fearing additional bombings such as those that had destroyed Rotterdam. The German advance was so rapid that the execution of the Dyle-Breda Plan became impossible. On 20 May, the first panzer units reached the sea at Noyelles. In ten days they had accomplished what the Kaiser had not been able to do in four years. The cream of the French Army and the BEF were cut off; they were isolated and under attack from front, flank, and rear. On 28 May, the Belgian Army considered the situation hopeless and surrendered. The Belgian government continued functioning in London.

Attempts by the confused and exhausted troops to break out of the encirclement failed, and changes in senior command of the French Army added to the confusion. With the last British-held channel port within sight and remnants of the allied armies fighting doomed delaying actions, Hitler issued his famous 'Halt Order.' The British Navy, commandeering hundreds of private craft, launched the

---

[1] Adolf Hitler to Martin Bormann as quoted in William L. Shirer, *The Collapse of the Third Republic* (New York: Simon and Schuster, 1969), 638 footnote. Reprinted by permission of Don Congdon Associates, Inc. Copyright 1969 by William Shirer, renewed 1997 by Irina Lugovskaya, Linda Rae, and Inga Dean.

war's greatest sea rescue, evacuating 338,226 troops from the beaches of Dunkerque but abandoning their vehicles and equipment.

#40
Capture of Fort d'Eben-Emael
10 May 1940

OBJECTIVE	To neutralize the fortress, which barred German troops from utilizing the bridges across the Albert Canal
FORCES	
BELGIAN:	750 men (Major Jean Jottrand)
GERMAN:	85 men (Oberleutnant Rudolf Witzig)
RESULT	The fort was quickly neutralized
CASUALTIES	
BELGIAN:	23 dead and 59 wounded
GERMAN:	6 killed and 15 wounded
LOCATION	Liège is 370 km northeast of Paris; Eben-Emael is 25 km north of Liège

The fortifications at Eben-Emael were key to the Belgian delaying operations in front of the Dyle-Breda Line. The German plan to send its Sixth Army around Liège required that the river crossings west of Maastricht be captured intact. The bridges across the Albert Canal at Kanne, Vroenhoven, and Veldwezelt were under the fortress's guns, and they had to be neutralized for any invasion in this sector to succeed.

Built in 1935, Eben-Emael was thought to be the strongest fort in the world. Its armaments included two 120-mm guns and sixteen 75-mm guns – all of them in armored turrets or casemates. To the northeast, the canal cut's steep sides rose 40 meters above the canal waters and formed an ideal glacis for protection from attack across the canal. In other directions, antitank trenches, barbed wire, and bunkers provided protection. Machine guns swept the approaches. Defensive positions were linked by tunnels that also linked the underground barracks, storerooms, and hospital. Ventilation was provided through filters which offered protection from poison gas. Twelve hundred men commanded by Major Jean Jottrand were assigned to the fort, although many were billeted in the neighboring villages and hence not permanently within its perimeter.

A volunteer special force known as Storm Detachment Koch – named after its commander, Hauptmann Walther Koch – was established to capture the fort and the three critical bridges. Under tight security, training began in November 1939. A parachute sapper (engineering) detachment codenamed *Sturmgruppe Granit* was designated to capture the fort.

The attack relied upon surprise and the use of heretofore untried tactical weapons. Noiseless, unmarked glider aircraft, a weapon previously unused in military situations, seemed an ideal method to land men silently on top of the fort. Of special importance were the 25-cm thick, armored domes which sheltered the cannon. Able to survive a direct hit by large caliber artillery shells, the domes presented a special problem. The sappers carried 50-kg cone-shaped, hollow-charge explosives adapted from the mining industry to penetrate the domes. The special shape focused the explosive effect, resulting in an impact more powerful than otherwise achieved. In a ruse replayed by American Airborne troops on D-Day, the Germans airdropped dummy parachutists to the west to sow confusion within the Belgian command structure.

Battle

In the predawn darkness of 10 May, eleven gliders left airfields around Cologne. Their departure was timed for arrival at the fort at 05:30, H-hour for the invasions of Belgium, Holland, and Luxembourg. Towed behind fifty-two Junkers JU 87 transport aircraft, the gliders climbed to an altitude of 2,100 meters before being released 20 km from the Belgium frontier. Two of the attack gliders became lost during the flight, including that of the assault commander, Oberleutnant Witzig.

Major Jottrand had alerted his troops at approximately 03:00, when he received reports of German troop movements toward the border. The confusion

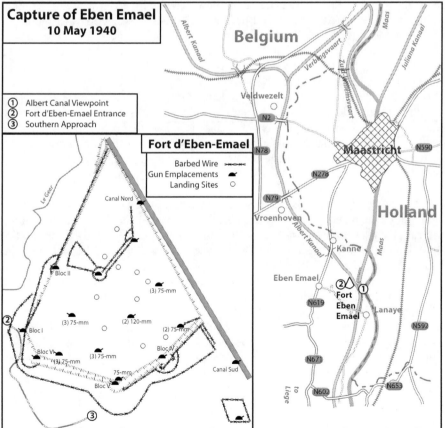

caused by the silent approach of the gliders and small arms fire from the direction of the canal bridges, however, had prevented the fortress from firing. Antiaircraft gunners hesitated to fire against aircraft that they could not definitely identify as hostile.

In Witzig's absence, Hauptfeldwebel Helmut Wenzel took command of the paratroopers, who disembarked immediately upon landing. First the antiaircraft guns were attacked and destroyed. Within ten minutes the fort's surface armaments were disabled, most through the use of the cone-shaped charges. Flamethrowers destroyed machine gun positions. The turret housing the twin 120-mm cannon was too well armored even for the special explosives. Before firing a single round, it was eliminated by placing charges into the cannon barrels. The northern gun emplacements, thought to be critical because of their proximity to the bridges, were found to be dummies.

Repeated attempts by Jottrand's fortress troops to exit the fort for reconnaissance or counterattack were met with fierce machine-gun fire and handgrenades. Since they were not skilled infantrymen, Major Jottrand called upon the Belgian 2nd Grenadier Regiment outside of the fort for assistance. Belgian infantry moved against the fort across its northwestern slopes; however, the defenses designed to protect against outside attack now benefited the Germans. In addition, the troops were strafed and bombed by Stuka dive-bombers. During the afternoon, the fort's exterior came under artillery fire from Belgian gunners, while the fortress troops continued to cower within the fort's interior. The paratroops assembled 55-kg charges and dropped them down cannon access shafts. The effect was devastating as explosions rocked the fort and convulsed the passages.

German reinforcements came under fire from canal-side emplacements that were still under Belgian control. During the night, elements of the German Infantry Regiment Nr 151 managed to cross the canal in inflatable boats and reinforce the small paratroop force on the fort. German artillery moved sufficiently close to keep the remaining casemates under fire. Around noon, with all hope of relief gone and at risk of suffocation from the contaminated air, the last shell-shocked defenders surrendered.

Although the bridge at Kanne was successfully blown, German paratroops had captured the other two bridges and defended them against counterattack until the arrival of the 4th Panzer Division. The Belgian 7th Division, which had responsibility for 18 km of the front, was completely overwhelmed, forcing King Leopold to issue an order for withdrawal. Allied bombers attempted to sever the German lifeline to its advanced troops by destroying the bridges. On 11 and 12 May, attacks by a total of thirty-nine aircraft resulted in twenty-eight losses and no damage to the bridges. Additional attempts were cancelled.

Propaganda Minister Joseph Goebbels celebrated the use of shaped charges, mysteriously describing them as a 'new method of attack.' Rumors of saboteurs and fifth columnists spread, but the truth was more poetic – and daring. The dramatic conquest of Europe's most formidable military installation brought the security of France's Maginot Line fortifications into doubt. Combined with attacks against other northern targets, the episode strengthened Germany's plan to misdirect allied efforts away from the primary attack through the Ardennes.

Battlefield Tour

Eben-Emael is situated on the west bank of the Albert Canal, north of Liège, and near the junction of the Albert Canal and Maas – the Dutch name for the Meuse River – only 8 km from the Dutch city of Maastricht. The triangular-shaped fort runs 900 meters from north to south and 700 meters from east to west at its wider, southern end. It remains a Belgian Army military establishment, and admission is restricted. Its position and surroundings are suitable for a tour even without an internal visit, but a fort tour significantly enhances the experience.

Leave Liège toward Maastricht on the E25 (A25) Autoroute. Just before entering Holland, take exit #1 toward Lixhe (N602). In that village turn north toward Lanaye (rue de la Croix); exit the highway to the left and proceed down the ramp before making the right turn toward Lanaye. The road changes names several times as it passes through Lixhe and Nivelle and proceeds into Lanaye. This mostly industrial area lies between the Albert Canal on the left and the Maas River on the right. Continue through Lanaye and proceed north (quai de Caster). Stop at a convenient location with views of the Albert Canal.

The canal divides at this point providing a connection to the Maas through the locks in the Canal de Lanaye to the right. The roadway crosses over the locks, and although the roadway looks private, it is accessible to the public. The left channel is the continuation of the **Albert Canal,** where it passes through the deep cut in the limestone hill known as the tranchée de Caster.

This route allows for observation of the defensive nature of the eastern side of the fort. The 40- to 60-meter limestone cliff face still has two casemates and multiple air intakes. Both casemates contained rapid-fire cannon, machine guns, and searchlights to illuminate nighttime targets. Visible on the summit of the cliff opposite is one of these casemates, showing its gun embrasures and armored cupola. During the afternoon of 10 May, fire from the casemate to the north frustrated elements of the German 51st Engineer Battalion in their attempts to cross the canal and reinforce the assault team. They were eventually successful the following morning.

Reverse direction, turn right and before re-entering Lanaye, toward the village of Emael (rue du Garage), and follow the zigzag road up into the village. Turn north on the main highway (N609) and proceed a few hundred meters to the signed access road to the fort. Turn right (rue du Fort).

Before reaching the **Fort Eben-Emael** entrance, memorials stand to the defenders of Eben-Emael and to the **Chasseurs Ardennais** artillery, which fired upon the German attackers on 10-11 May 1940. Heavy weapons line the approach to

Bloc I, which was the well-defended personnel entrance. If the fort is not open for tours, the entranceway may be blocked; however, much can still be viewed. The cannon and machine guns still visible on the pockmarked façade protected the fort from an attack from the direction of the village. To the right, the similarly shell-pocked Bloc VI guarded approaches to the main entrance, as did Bloc II, located farther to the left.

Inside the entrance, a long, ascending stairway provides access to the fort's 5 km of interior galleries. The fort tour visits various rooms, including the kitchen, hospital, and barracks. Seventy-five mannequins have been placed to demonstrate life in a 1940 underground Belgian fortification as well as the actions of the attacking Germans. Rooms have been outfitted with authentic artifacts, and sound effects have been added to heighten the experience. The damage wrought by German explosives remains mostly unchanged. The twisted blast door that the Germans destroyed to gain entry still hangs in place. Some corridors are blocked by wreckage from the charges dropped down the airshafts. Gun mechanisms for the operation of retractable turrets are visible. Open one weekend per month in March through November from 10:00 to 16:00; tours are conducted in French and Dutch only. Special tours of selected bunkers are available at certain times during the year. Fee. Call ahead for tour information. Tel: +32 (0)4 2862 861

The roof of the fort can be assessed via a path to the left of Bloc I. The fort's armaments remain mostly intact and the deadly effect of the German shaped charges is still visible on the armored cupola. The rotating turret containing the twin 120-mm guns remains in its down position, but the two shielded gun openings are visible. They were prime targets because their range covered all of Maastricht, to a distance of 15 km from the fort.

The northern approaches to the fort are not recommended because ditches and drainage canals block much of the way; however, the southern approach gives another impression of the fort's defenses. The western side and a portion of the roof are now heavily forested. Keep outside the fences and be mindful of the steep drops into the ditches that surround the landward sides of the fort. Avoid damage to any crops that might be in the fields. Before the path diverges from the fort, a good view of the defensive guns is possible. Bloc V is difficult to see because of the growth of new vegetation; however, Bloc IV protrudes into the ditch. Its two 60-mm antitank guns and machine guns provided defensive fire along the ditch and against the approaches to Bloc V.

The path leads away from the fort and approaches 'Eben 1,' a separate casemate which guarded the southeast approach from outside the fort. It was surrounded by tetrahedrons and barbed wire entanglements. Approach this site very carefully because the cliff edges are not protected and can be extremely dangerous. The casemate sits upon the cliff, above the point where the Albert and Lanaye channels split. Views are possible along the Albert Canal and across the flat countryside to the east, where the backwaters of the Maas create numerous lakes, islands, and channels. The shear limestone cliffs of the tranchée are visible.

Other Sites of Interest: The forts protecting Liège were captured or destroyed in the early days of the First World War. During the interwar years a second ring of forts was constructed at a greater distance from the city. Some of them can be visited. Of special interest is **Fort de Loncin**, northwest of Liège on the rue de Loncin near the N3 highway. This First World War fortification was hit by a shell from an Austrian super heavy mortar in August 1914, resulting in an internal explosion and its complete ruin. The fort shows the enormous destruction wrought on seemingly impregnable thicknesses of concrete and armored steel. Two hundred and fifty soldiers' bodies are still entombed in the ruins. Audio guides will soon be available to tell the story of the fort in four languages; guided tours are possible on Sunday afternoons. A small, adjacent museum, which is open every Sunday afternoon during April to October from 14:00 to 16:00, is very interesting and has displays on the construction of the fort and the operation of the fort's retractable guns.

#41

Battle of Dinant
12 to 14 May 1940

OBJECTIVE	To traverse the Forêt d'Ardennes, cross the Meuse River, and cut across the rear of the allied armies as they advanced into Belgium.
FORCES	
BELGIAN:	Group 'K' 1st Division Chasseurs Ardennais and 1st Cavalry Division (Lieutenant-General Maurice Keyaerts)
FRENCH:	18th Division (général de brigade Camilie-Léon Duffet)
GERMAN:	7th Panzer Division (Generalmajor Erwin Rommel)
RESULT	German armored columns crossed the river and sliced across northern France to the English Channel.
CASUALTIES	
ALLIES:	Unknown
GERMAN:	136 killed and wounded
LOCATION	Namur is 310 km northeast of Paris; Yvoir is 23 km south of Namur

The leading unit to emerge from the Ardennes Forest and reach the Meuse River was the 7th Panzer Division, commanded by then little-known General Erwin Rommel. Although he played only a secondary role to Guderian's assault upon Sedan, Rommel understood that the success of his country's invasion of France depended upon their ability to cross the river swiftly. The steep ridgelines along the river formed a formidable block to tank movements but were the last remaining major natural defensive feature between him and the excellent tank terrain that ran across northern France to the English Channel. The river valley, however, offered few exits. Well-placed antitank guns, supported by artillery and determined infantry, could provide an effective blocking force. Rommel had to win the race, or Germany's great gamble would be a failure.

Columns of Rommel's vehicles struggled through the narrow passages of the Ardennes Forest mostly unopposed, except for a stubborn stand by a company of the 3rd Regiment of Belgian Chasseurs Ardennais who delayed Rommel's progress for 15 hours. The Ardennes' reputation as impenetrable by modern military movements caused it to be defended by only Belgian Group K and two divisions of French cavalry.

Lack of coordination between Belgian and French units hindered the allied response. Belgian engineers destroyed bridges and cut roads passing through the narrow river valleys. While the slower-moving French infantry moved toward positions along the Meuse River, the French cavalry clashed with the leading German forces until ordered to retire. French military planning relied upon having five days to establish positions along the Meuse; the Germans arrived in two. The French 18th Division, assigned the sector from Anhée to Hastière, was at half strength and faced two German armored divisions.

Battle

The advance guard of 31st Panzer Regiment, part of the 5th Panzer Division but temporarily attached to Rommel's 7th Panzer Division, was the first German unit to reach the Meuse arriving at 16:30 on 12 May. The bridge at Yvoir was demolished as the first armored car attempted to cross. Ten minutes earlier, the bridge at Dinant had been dropped into the river; shortly thereafter the concrete road bridge at Bouvignes-sur-Meuse was similarly destroyed. The evening air was punctuated by the explosions from other bridges to the north and south. After rapidly passing through the difficult terrain of the Ardennes, the Germans were stopped only a few kilometers from the open plains beyond by the Meuse River.

During the night of 12/13 May, a motorcycle battalion discovered an undefended crossing point at Île de Houx and established a small bridgehead on the opposite bank. At 04:00 on 13 May, Rommel arrived at the Meuse River. The town of Dinant was under fire from French

Battle of Dinant
12 to 14 May 1940

① Chasseurs Ardennais Mont.
② Ile de Houx Crossing
③ Auberge de Bouvignes
④ Chateau de Crevecoeur
⑤ Leffe Crossing

0   1 km

artillery, and the streets were littered with dead and wounded men. Although some German troops had crossed the river while shielded by the early morning mist, efforts to reinforce the Dinant bridgehead were stopped by Belgian machine-gun fire from west bank and by French artillery batteries in the hills beyond. Rommel watched a fierce battle as the German 6th Rifle Regiment was blocked. Rommel later wrote, 'The situation was not very pleasant. Our boats were being destroyed one after the other by the French flanking fire and the crossing eventually came to a standstill.'[2] To provide a smoke screen, Rommel ordered the houses in the valley to be set on fire.

True to his credo of 'command from the front,' Rommel spent 13 May moving up and down the highway between Houx and Dinant, exposing himself to enemy fire – which wounded his adjutant – while scanning the opposite shore to get a perspective of the situation or identify targets. Only riflemen had been able to cross the river and remained without support from tanks or antitank weapons. Rommel crossed in one of the first boats and took command of 2nd Battalion, 7th Rifle Regiment. He personally led its defense against a tank attack, one of many such actions that he conducted. Although German forces west of the Meuse were weak and without their armored support, French attempts to repulse them were poorly coordinated and slow in execution.

During night of 13 May, the 58th Pioneer Battalion engineers ferried vehicles across the river, despite continued French fire that killed its commander. Eventually the resistance was overcome, and by 09:00 on 14 May, the 25th Panzer Regiment had thirty tanks moving toward the strategic village of Onhaye, west of Dinant.

Several sharp engagements ensued in the villages and woods west of the Meuse. Rommel criss-crossed the battlefield, at one point barely escaping capture when his command tank came under fire and was disabled. By 15 May, the French Ninth Army was routed and the Meuse defensive line was lost.

Battlefield Tour

In the region north of Dinant, the swiftly flowing Meuse is 75 to 100 meters wide between steep limestone shoulders. The approach from the east is slightly more gradual, as the roads leave the wooded terrain of the Ardennes and enter the river valley. On the opposite shore, railroad tracks run parallel to the river, along a narrow strip of ground below ragged cliffs.

Points of interest are best viewed from the east bank. The tour proceeds from the first attempted crossing at Yvoir and identifies crossing locations as it proceeds south toward Dinant.

Leave Namur toward Dinant along the west bank (N92), which is the faster route, or the east bank (N937). Cross to the east bank via the highway bridge at Yvoir, turn left (N937), and continue approximately 500 meters to a small turn-off on the left.

---

[2] Field Marshal Erwin Rommel, *The Rommel Papers*, ed. Sir Basil Liddell-Hart (New York: Harcourt, Brace, 1953), 8.

In the late afternoon of 12 May, Belgian engineers were assigned the task of blowing all of the Meuse bridges. 31st Panzer Regiment, after pushing through the rear guard of the French 4th DLC (light cavalry division), was making a mad dash to capture the nearest bridge between Sedan and Namur. While the bridge was being prepared for demolition, German vehicles started to cross. A 47-mm antitank gun disabled the first armored car with one shot, followed by the second car. Lieutenant René de Wispelaere, commander of the engineers, pushed the electric detonator to blow up the bridge, but it malfunctioned. In the face of enemy fire, he activated the manual igniter. At that moment he was shot and killed, but the bridge exploded, sending the two disabled vehicles into the river. The mad dash to capture the bridge had failed.

Only the cobblestone approach to the 1940 steel girder bridge remains, located at a small turn-off north of the modern highway bridge in Yvoir. A stone displaying the wild boar emblem of the **Chasseurs Ardennais** is on the riverfront wall. It commemorates the 1st Battalion, 5th Regiment assigned to protect the engineers assigned to destroy all the river crossings between Namur and Givet. Directly opposite on the western shore, a gas station now stands adjacent to the few remaining stones from the pillbox used by the chasseurs to defend the crossing. Next to the station, a stone block stele surrounded by a half circle of stone columns forms a memorial to the sacrifice and heroism of Lieutenant de Wispelaere and his men.

Reverse direction toward Dinant and proceed approximately 2 km to a parking turn-off south of the intersection of the Dinant-Namur road (N92) and the road to Purnode (Route de Blocqmont).

The railway bridge at the northern end of the Île de Houx had been destroyed earlier in the afternoon. While the Yvoir bridge was being blown, a German patrol discovered weir #5 near the south end of the island, its broken stonewalls giving perilous access to a mid-river island. From the island a lock gate spanned the channel to the west bank. The first attempt to cross was repulsed by a company from the French 66th Regiment. Later in the afternoon, however, that company was relieved by 2nd Battalion, French 39th Regiment. Contrary to orders, the replacements did not bring the defense down to the water's edge. They remained on the high ground, protected from German fire but unable to cover the Île de Houx adequately. During the night of 12/13 May, using the now undefended weir and flood control gate, several companies of 8th Motorcycle Battalion, 5th Panzer Division were able to cross to the opposite shore. By 01:00, the first German troops were west of the Meuse. At 03:00, the cyclists rushed the high ground, surprising and scattering then men of the 39th Regiment. By the next morning the advance guard of 31st Panzer Regiment reinforced the small unit and captured the village of Grange, extending the slim bridgehead to 2 km in depth but leaving their rear exposed to isolated pockets of enemy troops.

The current highway is postwar, but the turn-off pavement is the 1940 roadway. The narrow, brush-covered **Île de Houx** divides the waters of the Meuse into two channels. From the riverfront walkway, what appears to be the opposite shore of a narrow channel is the island. The old weir used by the Germans was later dynamited; several weirs now visible in the river are of postwar construction and are not at the original site.

At the highway intersection 200 meters north, Rommel stood on the grass verge, observing the efforts to reinforce the motorcycle battalion across the river. The Route de Blocqmont to the rear traverses open fields in which Rommel's vehicles were exposed to enemy antitank guns as they exited the forest. During preparations for the crossing, tanks, armored cars, and trucks lined this road and others, possibly for 75 km – almost to the Belgian / German border.

Continue south toward Dinant (N92) and stop in Leffe.

South of Île de Houx, the large, cream-colored stucco **Auberge de Bouvignes** standing below the exposed white rock cliffs marked the center of the 7th Panzer Division's area of operations. Although vehicles were ferried across at this locale, the main effort was not located here because the harsh rock face behind the auberge did not allow passage to the west. The auberge, rail line, and roadway appear as they did in 1940.

After Rommel's arrival at Dinant, he moved opposite Bouvignes, where he witnessed Oberst Georg von Bismarck's 7th Rifle Regiment stopped by concentrated fire from the French 66th Infantry Regiment. Rommel described the scene, 'enemy fire had then become so heavy that their crossing equipment had been shot to pieces and the crossing had to be halted. Large numbers of wounded were receiving treatment in a house close beside the demolished bridge. ... There was nothing to be seen of the enemy who were preventing the crossing.'[3] Rommel decided that he needed heavier weapons to dislodge the hidden defenders and left to confer with his superiors.

Towering above the river north of Bouvignes-sur-Meuse are the ruins of the **Château de Crèvecoeur**, believed to have been constructed in the 9th century to protect communications along the river. The ruins provided shelter for French artillery observers of the river crossing points. Under the watchful eyes in the château, Bismarck's regiment struggled to establish a crossing point where the three-arch, concrete footbridge had stood on the previous day. His infantry and engineers were shelled and fired upon from the numerous pillboxes that lined the opposite shore. Returning fire with their artillery regiment's 105-mm howitzers, the Germans set Bouvignes ablaze.

Bouvignes was rebuilt and appears much as it did in 1940. The church still dominates the small village, which has colorful buildings lining the riverbank. The

---

[3] Ibid., 9.

bridge was never rebuilt, but careful inspection will reveal its abutment on the western side of the river.

After a hurried conference at Army headquarters, Rommel returned to the Meuse near the Dinant suburb of Leffe – famed for the beer brewed by its monks, whose church building appears on the bottle label – finding more wounded and the crossing at a standstill. Rommel ordered forward several Mark III and Mark IV tanks. With their turrets traversed left, they drove at 50-meter intervals along the river road, throwing shell after shell into the structures on the opposite shore. Under continuous fire from their 37-mm and 75-mm guns, the defensive fire weakened, and the crossing resumed.

North of **Leffe** and slightly to the south of the church in Bouvignes-sur-Meuse on the opposite bank, a road tunnel goes under the rail embankment. A pontoon bridge was completed by 14 May in direct alignment with that tunnel, allowing movement of the infantry divisions that followed behind the armored columns. The river valley at Bouvignes provided the necessary exit along a highway toward Philippeville, Rommel's next objective. No trace of the pontoon bridge remains.

Continue into Dinant and park in its center near the road bridge.

The **Dinant** city bridge was destroyed by Belgian engineers at 14:30 on 12 May. Since access to the riverfront was difficult in the crowded city, the pontoon bridge at Leffe was constructed and became the division's main crossing point. Long since rebuilt, the bridge has a plaque commemorating the wounding of Lieutenant Charles de Gaulle on 15 August 1914, when he defended the city against invading Germans during the First World War.

The city of Dinant is dominated by its **Citadel,** which towers 100 meters above the onion-domed **Cathedral of Notre-Dame.** Views of the church and citadel are spectacular, especially from the opposite bank. The *Téléférique* is a cable car that goes up the side of the cliff from the south side of the cathedral, an ascent preferable to walking the 408 steps. Tours of the castle are guided, so arrivals must be timed accordingly. The open area in the courtyard does not provide the views of the Meuse valley that one might expect. Open daily 1 April to 30 October from 10:00 to 18:00 (17:00 in off season); closed Fridays from 1 November to 31 March; open weekends and schools holidays only in January. Fee.

#42

Battle of Sedan
12 to 14 May 1940

OBJECTIVE	To capture crossing points over the Meuse River at Sedan
FORCES	
FRENCH:	55th and 71st Divisions of French Second Army (général d'armée Charles Huntziger)

GERMAN:	XIX Panzer Corps (General der Panzertruppen Heinz Guderian)
RESULT	The French defenses were overcome, and the river was crossed.
CASUALTIES	
FRENCH:	At least 500 dead, thousands taken prisoner
GERMAN:	120 dead and 400 wounded
LOCATION	Sedan is 250 km northeast of Paris

A whistle blown at 05:35 on 10 May began the main German thrust, with over twelve hundred tanks and thirty-nine thousand vehicles of Panzer Group Kleist, which included Guderian's XIX and Reinhardt's XLI Panzer Corps, along four march routes. Movement plans quickly fell apart, and the resulting congestion created a traffic jam which was 250 km long and extended all the way back into Germany. The vehicles were perfect targets for allied aircraft, but despite reports from nighttime reconnaissance flights, the French High Command continued to believe that the Ardennes was not tank country. To protect the columns from air attack, the Luftwaffe provided an air umbrella which was never challenged.

The retiring Belgian Army destroyed bridges and cut down trees to delay the panzers' progress. A stiff resistance by a company of 1st Regiment, Belgian Chasseurs Ardennais at Bodange delayed the leading 1st Panzer Division for eight hours; however, most Belgian units retired toward Namur as planned. Working through the night of 10 May, German engineers hurriedly removed the barriers and filled demolition craters.

Upon notification of the German incursion, four cavalry divisions of the French Second and Ninth Armies crossed the French border into Belgium to act as a screen while French infantry divisions took up their positions. The lightly armed cavalry were no match for the German tanks, and after suffering heavy losses, they withdrew back across the Meuse.

Battle

After fifty-seven hours of uninterrupted advance, the 1st Rifle Regiment reached the Meuse west of Sedan between Floing and Glaire, at 18:15 on 12 May. The German army had achieved a total strategic surprise in one of the greatest logistics operations of the war. The French had no intention of defending the city, preferring instead to retire behind the 70-meter wide Meuse River and occupy blockhouses built on high ground. During the evening the French successfully demolished the highway and rail bridges as they left.

The French 55th and 71st Divisions, part of général Huntziger's French Second Army, were assigned responsibility for the Meuse line near Sedan. Since the French High Command believed that the Ardennes could not be penetrated by tanks, they thought that first class infantry units would be better used elsewhere. These two reserve divisions of poorly trained, older men, who suffered a shortage of antitank guns, mines, and antiaircraft weapons, thus defended the weakest sector in the entire French line.

Beginning at 11:00 on 13 May, over nine hundred bombers, fighters, and dive-bombers attacked French positions around Sedan in waves. Command posts and communications lines were destroyed, isolating units from their headquarters and cutting links to their artillery support. For five hours the howling sirens of Stukas added to the terror of exploding shells and the crack of machine-gun strafing. Despite the intense German aerial bombardment, the bunkers forming the riverside defense line remained intact; however, the psychological effect was crippling and contributed to the later rout. Deputy Chief of Staff of the French Second Army général de brigade Edmond Ruby described the effect:

> The gunners stopped shooting and hit the dirt; the infantrymen dove into the trenches and remained there motionless; they were deafened by the crushing of bombs and screeching of the dive bomber sirens. ... hours of this nightmare sufficed to shatter their nerves; they were no longer able to react to the approaching infantry.[4]

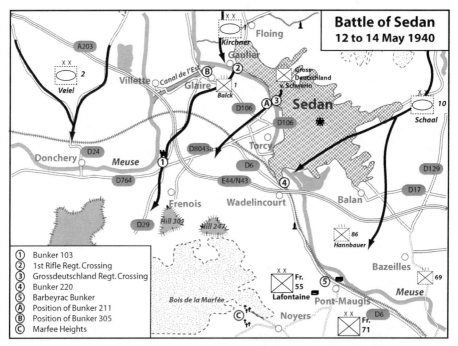

The 1st Panzer Division, augmented in its efforts by the elite *Grossdeutschland* Infantry Regiment and 43rd Assault Battalion, remained to establish the first bridgeheads across the Meuse. The first wave of twenty-four hundred men attacked under a covering smoke screen against the thinly held sector between Glaire and Torcy, west of the destroyed Pont Neuf Bridge. To the east, opposite Wadelincourt the *Grossdeutschland* Regiment faced Bunker 211, where a

---

[4] Karl-Heinz Frieser: *The Blitzkrieg Legend: The 1940 Campaign in the West* (Annapolis, Maryland: Naval Institute Press, 2005), 157-8.

25-mm antitank gun commanded the bridge and held firm until Guderian's gunners used antitank and antiaircraft guns to fire into the pillbox's gun embrasures. At 16:00, with the bunker silenced, the men crossed the river, paddling furiously in their inflatable assault boats.

Simultaneously at Gaulier, 1st Rifle Regiment assault troops, commanded by Oberstleutnant Hermann Balck, enjoyed a virtually uncontested crossing of the river and fought along the canal and river toward Château Bellevue, taking French pillboxes and machine-gun emplacements in succession. As night fell, they passed to the west of Frénois and proceeded to Hill 301, Graf Moltke's observation point during the 1870 battle of Sedan.

The French 55th Division crumbled under the pressure of the combined air and land assault, many of the inexperienced reservists fleeing. Their arrival in rear areas spread fear and confusion, which paralyzed French attempts to counterattack. The imminent tank attack frightened away French heavy artillery at Bulson, robbing the defenders of their most effective weapon against the amphibious river crossing.

Farther west, 2nd Panzer Division was halted in front of Donchéry because its approach was under the guns of casemates to the east and the batteries of the 55th and adjacent 102nd Divisions. Help arrived in the form of an engineering assault team from 1st Rifle Regiment, who eliminated a line of bunkers that were blasting German tanks and assault boats when they approached the river. With the bunkers along the Donchéry road disabled, the division infantry was able to cross at approximately 20:00.

The 10th Panzer Division suffered from a lack of artillery support because Guderian committed it to the main effort at Glaire. French artillery demolished most of the 69th Panzergrenadier Regiment's assault boats before they reached the water's edge. Their attack from Bazeilles toward Pont-Maugis thus failed. The 86th Panzergrenadier Regiment, which faced intact bunkers across the river and numerous artillery positions on the heights beyond, was only slightly more successful. Through the efforts of one platoon of engineers, they were able to seize seven bunkers, which allowed the division to establish a small bridgehead at approximately 19:30 at Wadelincourt.

By midnight of 13 May, engineers were constructing a pontoon bridge at Gaulier so that heavy vehicles could cross the river to strengthen and expand the bridgehead. The division's tanks were still in the Ardennes traffic, and the first armored vehicles did not cross until 07:20 the next day.

The critical choke point for the entire German effort was the single-span bridge at Gaulier. The Allies finally recognized the threat, and starting at dawn on 14 May, they sent one hundred seventy bombers with two hundred fifty fighter sorties as escorts against the bridge which Guderian now protected with seven flak battalions. One hundred sixty-five of the allied planes were shot down or severely damaged by the intense fire, and not one bomb hit the bridge; the losses were so severe that additional air attacks were cancelled. Sixty thousand men and eight hundred fifty tanks surged into the rapidly expanding bridgehead. The riskiest maneuver of the war was accomplished.

Aftermath

Général Huntziger ordered the remainder of his left flank formations to withdraw to the south. A 70-km gap consequently opened between the French Ninth and Second Armies at exactly the point of Guderian's axis of attack to the west. At 14:00 on 14 May, Guderian, in a daring move that defied direct orders, did not wait for the mechanized infantry support that was still crossing the Ardennes; instead, he ordered his 1st and 2nd Panzer Divisions to turn west toward the English Channel. On 15 May, elite units of the French 3rd Spahi Brigade fought the panzers to a standstill at La Horgne, 20 km southwest of Sedan, but they were exhausted and retired, leaving the way open for Guderian's tanks. By day's end Guderian's and Hoth's XV Panzer Corps columns were 60 km past the Meuse, with open territory before them. The assault destroyed the French Ninth Army, whose commander, général d'armée André Corap, was relieved of his command; his replacement, général Giraud, was also unable to contain the situation. Giraud was captured on 19 May.

After crossing the Meuse, the *Grossdeutschland* Regiment turned south to protect the main thrust's left flank. At Stonne, 22 km south of the river crossings, they faced a counterattack by the French XXI Corps. The French Char 'B' tanks were all but impenetrable to the standard German 37-mm antitank gun. The Germans nonetheless fought off the attack by targeting the huge tank's exposed radiator. German motorized infantry reinforcements arrived to relieve the *Grossdeutschland* Regiment, and the battle raged for eleven days, while the small village changed hands seventeen times. At the end, the Germans held the strategic heights.

Initial reports to the French High Command failed to recognize Guderian's daring implementation of Manstein's *Sichelschnitt* plan. Despite superior quantities of men and tanks, the slowness and confusion within the French command structure squandered opportunities to contain and destroy the German bridgehead. The Germans were too aggressive and too focused on their strategic objective. Guderian's evaluation of the French defeat concluded, 'the defense of France being systematically based on fortifications and carried out according to a rigid doctrine ... learned from the First World War, their experience of positional warfare, of the high value they attached to firepower, and of their underestimation of movement.'[5] The fate of France was sealed; French, British, and Belgian Armies totaling 1.7 million men had walked into a trap.

Battlefield Tour

The Franco-Prussian War battlefield tour focused mainly on sites to the north of Sedan; the 1940 tour's emphasis is south of the city and river. The two tours can be easily combined by starting the 1940 tour at the next to last stop of the 1870 tour near the Château Bellevue. A major east-west Autoroute traverses the 1940 battlefield; little remains to mark the German victory. No museums or monuments exist – only French and German cemetery headstones that line the crest and southern slopes of Marfée Heights as well as numerous concrete bunkers at Château Bellevue and along the D6 highway between Wadelincourt and Pont-Maugis. In 1940, the

---

[5] Heinz Guderian: *Panzer Leader* (Guderian: 1985), 96.

enemy attacked out of the wooded hills from the north and focused their forces upon a narrow '*schwerpunkt*' 'heavy point,' Guderian's term for the point of main effort) in the five kilometers between Donchéry and Wadelincourt.

Leave Sedan toward Donchéry / Charleville-Mézieres (D106, rue Thiers, avenue de la Marne); pass under the Autoroute and into the large roundabout. Turn toward Glaire (D29, route de Bellevue).

Bunker 103 is located in the château's park, south of the shuttered Château Bellevue and 200 meters north of the Donchéry-Sedan road roundabout (intersection of D764, D29, and D977). Invisible through the private park's vegetation, from the roadway it appears as a dark brooding hulk. Its fields of fire were to the east, covering the Donchéry-Torcy Road, and – more devastatingly – to the west, into the flank of the advancing 2nd Panzer Division. Along with the artillery located in the casemate southwest of the large roundabout, its fire prevented the 2nd Panzer Division's inflatable boats from crossing the river. Bunker 103 was attacked by advanced units of the 1st Rifle Regiment. The occupants surrendered only after intense hand-to-hand fighting. An attached assault engineering team then circled around to the west to attack the artillery bunker. Although temporarily stunned by a panzer hit upon one gun port, the French fortress troops continued to fire the remaining gun. Threatened with encirclement by the assault team, the French artillerymen evacuated the bunker.

Proceed north toward Glaire (rue de Bellevue, D29), crossing under the Autoroute and into Glaire. In the town center, continue onto the rural road past the Mairie until the pavement ends. Continue to the river's edge on foot.

The North Branch of the Canal de l'Est, which cuts across the loop in the Meuse, joins the river at this point. Across the river is the Sedan suburb of Gaulier. German reconnaissance identified a 1.5-km gap across a wide meadow between bunker 305, along the canal at Glaire, and bunker 211, which covered the Pont Neuf in Torcy. The two gun emplacements were defended by three hundred men of the 147th Fortress Infantry Regiment and one company of the 295th Infantry Regiment. This weakly defended sector was chosen by the Germans as the **first crossing site.** The 1st Rifle Regiment, 1st Panzer Division was assigned the lead in forging across the Meuse. Guderian crossed in the first boat of the second wave, regimental commander Oberstleutnant Balck greeting him with the words, 'Joy riding in canoes on the Meuse is forbidden'[6] – the same words Guderian had used during an earlier river crossing exercise. The rifle regiment continued through Glaire, took bunker 103 as afore mentioned, and advanced to the Donchéry-Sedan Road intersection, where the large roundabout now lies.

---

[6] Ibid., 102.

Very little remains to show the effects of the attack or defense. The river banks are straight and approximately three meters above the water level. The area's current appearance is one of quiet abandonment. The German pontoon bridge, over which three panzer divisions crossed, was built from the yard of the now abandoned cloth factory 150 meters east of the canal-river junction at Gaulier, at almost the exact same spot where the Germans had built one in August 1914.

Reverse direction and turn left on rue de maréchal Foch (D106). In approximately 500 meters, turn left onto an unpaved street (chemin de Prairie) and pass the grassy, flat flood plain. Continue as far as possible before parking and proceed to an unattractive track along the Meuse riverbank. Walk carefully.

Heavy fire from bunker 211 to the east and from a well-sited machine-gun bunker defeated all attempts by the *Grossdeutschland* Regiment to cross the river. Both positions were eliminated by fire from an 88-mm Flak gun. At 16:00 on 13 May, under cover of smoke shells, the 7th Company, 2nd Battalion, was the first unit to cross the river. The company continued southwest across the flood plain, over the D106 roadway, and the railway tracks, advancing against the reduced French 295th Infantry Regiment. The 1st and 2nd battalions quickly followed, engaging the French defenders in house-to-house fighting in Torcy and advancing toward Frénois. At approximately 20:00, the action culminated in a hand-to-hand battle for emplacements on the slopes of Hill 247. The German bridgehead was now almost 3 km deep.

Return to the highway (D106) and turn left. Continue into Torcy and follow either road (rue Vesseron-Lejay or the smaller rue Lambretèche) to the intersection with the main street (avenue des Martyrs de la Resistance). Turn right, then left in the large roundabout onto avenue Pasteur (D764). In the roundabout in front of the train station, continue southeast on rue de Wadelincourt. One km ahead on the left is bunker 220.

A second wave assault team of 86th Rifle Regiment, 10th Panzer Division crossed near the destroyed avenue Philippoteaux (D764) Bridge and silenced several emplaced machine guns in the area. They then attacked **bunker 220** from behind.

The square block of reinforced concrete appears in remarkably good condition on the side facing the roadway. The river-facing side, however, shows the blast hole and tangled iron bars created by the force of the German assault – a demonstration of the 88-mm gun's bunker-busting ability. A flower-covered granite plaque facing the road honors ten members of the 2nd Battalion, 147th Fortress Infantry Regiment and commemorates 'the defenders of Bloc 220, commanded by sous-lieutenant P. Leret, who were captured and shot by the Germans.' The flat fields between the rail line and the river provided excellent fields of fire for the bunker's 25-mm antitank gun and heavy machine guns.

> Cross the railroad tracks and turn left on Grande Rue (D6), continue through Wadelincourt. With the elimination of bunker 220, the 1st Battalion was able to storm Hill 246, located directly behind the First World War **US 1st Division Memorial** along the road. Continue to the entrance to Port-Maugis.

Port-Maugis marks the eastern limit of the German zone of attack. At the western limit of Pont-Maugis is a **Barbeyrac-type**[7] **bunker,** which is hardly damaged. Its position opposite a bend in the river allowed covering fire along the river to the north, northeast, and northwest. Bunker 12 is 0.2 km ahead on the left, between the road and the river, and several more bunkers are visible east of Port-Maugis. Against these positions the 69th Rifle Regiment failed in its efforts to cross the river. The marshy and open ground on the opposite shore slowed their advance and exposed them to the bunker's fire and accurate French artillery.

Other Sites of Interest: On **Marfée Heights**, French and German military cemeteries contain the bodies of soldiers from three wars. The scenic city of **Bouillon**, where the citadel built in 1050 and once owned by the First Crusade's Godfrey de Bouillon still stands in the river's loop, is 16 km to the northeast. The Hotel Panorama still presents dramatic views of the citadel from heights across the river. Finally, the tiny village of **Stonne**, which is 24 km to the south, contains monuments to the heroic attack of French armor against the *Grossdeutschland* Regiment.

#43

Maginot Line
18 May to 22 June 1940

OBJECTIVE	To defend northeastern France from German incursion
FORCES	
FRENCH:	Seventeen divisions of Second Army Group (général Charles Condé)
GERMAN:	Six divisions of First Army (Generaloberst Erwin von Witzleben)
RESULT	The defenses were rapidly outflanked and useless
CASUALTIES	
FRENCH:	107 killed at La Ferté
GERMAN:	80 killed at Fort du Fermont
LOCATION	Sedan is 250 km northeast of Paris; Villy is 25 km southeast of Sedan

The network of fortifications built along the French-German border was to provide France with early warning as well as a first line of defense against any

---

[7] Basic concrete machine gun and 25-mm antitank gun fortifications of which over one hundred were in position or under construction in the Sedan sector by May 1940. They were vulnerable to attack from blind spots not covered by their machine guns.

probable German invasion. The frontier defenses were designed in the tradition of the great French fort builders, maréchal Sébastien Le Prestre Vauban (1633–1707) and général Séré de Rivières (1815–1895), but adjusted by the fortifications which saved Verdun during the First World War. Their construction was championed by Andre Maginot, Minister of War and a veteran of the Verdun fighting, where he was wounded. After Maginot's death in 1932, when construction of the forts was starting, the system became known as the Maginot Line.

By 1940, a complex network of fortified artillery casemates, observation posts, machine-gun and antitank-gun pillboxes, and underground shelters – all costing over 3 billion francs – had been established, with over five thousand structures stretching 314 km from Montmédy to the Swiss border. Forward gun positions were linked to barracks and supply depots with over 100 km of underground tunnels, frequently using narrow gauge rail lines to transport men and munitions. Larger casemates held rotating, retractable turrets with 75-mm to 135-mm guns. The partially underground forts, or '*ouvrages,*' were manned with first-class fortress troops, supported in the gaps between forts by 'interval' infantry who were mostly second-rate reservists.

Unfortunately, the fortifications created a 'Maginot mentality' among the French High Command; who thought that their southern flank could securely shelter behind the forts while their best units forged into Belgium to meet the enemy as in 1914. The Germans, however, were able to exploit gaps in the fortifications opposite the Ardennes and along the Meuse.

Battle

German military plans did not involve penetrating the strong fortifications. Manstein's '*Sichelschnitt*' called for establishing a defensive shoulder at the western end of the line while armored columns moved westward to the English Channel. After the French collapse and evacuation of British troops from Dunkerque, the Germans launched a two-pronged attack south of the Somme. On 5 June, the western assault was launched, once again led by Rommel's 7th Panzer Division. Despite initially strong resistance, the French lines collapsed, and by 7 June German troops were closing in on Rouen. A second strike started on 9 June against French forces in Champagne. In eight days Guderian's tanks swept behind the Maginot fortresses to the Swiss border, trapping the defenders in a pocket. Although not one of the major forts was overcome by force of arms, on 22 June général Alphonse Georges, commander of the Northeastern Front, ordered four hundred thousand troops to surrender. Many of the Maginot garrisons refused to leave their positions and continued resisting for several days after the armistice.

The country was left in a catastrophic condition described as:

A result of the enforced evacuation there is an indescribable refugee misery and all of the cattle are dying. Everywhere places are plundered by refugees and French soldiers. Up until now we have come across only scanty civilian populations. The Middle Ages were humane compared with the present.[8]

This description is not from a Frenchman but from General Heinz Guderian.

After the surrender, some underground facilities were used by the Germans as bombproof factories for V-2 rocket assembles. After the war, a few were reoccupied by the French Army for training or communications purposes. Today the surviving structures have mostly been assigned to volunteer organizations, who keep their history alive.

Battlefield Tour

Twenty-two *grand ouvrages*, or artillery fortresses, supported by thirty-six *petit ouvrages*, or infantry fortresses, with 348 casemates and blockhouses ran along France's northeast frontier. Political and financial considerations delayed construction of the massive underground structures along the Franco-Belgian border, where eventually sixty-three casemates were constructed between Valenciennes and Avesnes. Many of these are still visible along the highways that run parallel to the border.

Of the many Maginot sites, two were chosen for inclusion in this book because of their proximity to the Sedan battlefields. La Ferté was one of the few sites captured by the Germans through force of arms; Fermont has a high level of preservation. Both sites are operated by local volunteers, and their tour hours are limited. The subterranean galleries are cold and often damp. Visitors are advised to bring appropriate clothing and footwear. Steep stairways or sloping ground are encountered.

Leave Montmédy or Sedan on the National Road toward Margut (N43). In Margut turn southwest toward La-Ferté-sur-Chiers (D44), pass through the village, and then turn right toward Villy (D52). An access road and small parking area are on the right.

Petit Ouvrage de La Ferté is located between the villages of Villy and La Ferté-sur-Chiers, on a hill known as 'La Croix de Villy.' It formed the northwestern-most fort of the Maginot Line. The structure consists of two combat blocks armed with machine-gun and antitank-gun turrets, connected by a 270-meter long underground gallery and surrounded by belts of barbed wire. La Ferté was defended by elements of the 155th Fortress Infantry Regiment, led by Lieutenant Bourguignon. Elements of the German First Army attacked La Ferté on 18 May. At 18:00, after a concentrated artillery preparation which included the use of two 210-mm mortars, German engineers of the 171st Pioneer Battalion reached the fort's exterior despite French fire from the neighboring Le Chesnois battery. Shaped charges destroyed the turret and observation bell, and the fort's guns fell quiet. Bourguignon received orders not to surrender. The next morning the Germans entered Block 1 and found

---

[8] Kenneth Macksey, *Guderian: Creator of the Blitzkrieg* (New York: Stein and Day, 1975), 150.

the bodies of the one-hundred-seven-man garrison in the gallery – all asphyxiated by the explosion's deadly fumes.

The path from the parking area to the entrance of Block 1 circumvents the remaining barbed wire and upright metal stakes of the tank defenses. It passes a small marble slab commemorating the fallen of the German 7th Division. A climb up the gentle slope to the block's roof reveals the three fixed 'cloche,' or armored cupolas, which show the impacts of high velocity shells from the German 88-mm Flak guns. The hills visible across the valley to the east mark the position of the attacking German artillery. Inside Block 1 the 47-mm antitank gun is still on display, mounted upon a swivel to fire through the block's embrasure. A stairway winds down 35 meters to the gallery which connects to Block 2 through the narrow, dimly lit passage in which the bodies of Lieutenant Bourguignon and his men were found. Exiting the block, the exterior blast door which was blown off by attacking Germans can be seen with the inner door protected by machine-gun embrasures. The dislodged turret on the roof of Block 2 remains unaltered. On the elevation alongside Block 2 is a table of orientation showing French infantry positions and routes of the German attack. Behind the block is the small **Nécropole Nationale de Villy-la-Ferté**, identified by the French flag which is always flown above it. Nearby is a French memorial to the defenders of Villy-La Ferté. Two casemates designed to protect the fort from attack from the west a short distance away along the road (D52), in opposite directions. La Ferté is open Sunday afternoons from Palm Sunday through October and every day except Mondays in July and August from 14:00 to 17:00. Fee.

Return to the National Road (N43) and continue to Longuyon. Once in the town, turn left onto rue R. Poincare (D17a) and follow it where the road continues into the countryside. Before the village of Fermont, bear right (D17a) toward the fort where indicated. After a short distance, turn right onto D174 and go through the forest, passing the fort's personnel entrance before reaching the parking area on the right.

Ouvrage de Fermont consists of seven combat blocks holding a total of five 75-mm guns, two retractable turrets with twinned machine guns, two 81-mm mortars, a 47-mm antitank gun, and numerous machine-gun embrasures. It was manned by 600 men of the 149th Regiment of Fortress Infantry under the command of capitaine Daniel Aubert.

On 17 June, Block 4 was attacked. Shells from 88-mm guns repeatedly struck the 1.75-meter thick, reinforced concrete wall, splattering shards of concrete into the casemate and driving the gunners to seek shelter. Not realizing how close they came to penetrating the structure, the Germans eventually gave up the effort, and repairs were quickly implemented. Four days later, Block 1, whose two 75-mm guns commanded the main highway through Longuyon, was attacked with heavy guns up to 305-mm. The effort was repulsed, leaving eighty Germans dead. Fermont's garrison surrendered when ordered after the armistice.

Fermont provides a more carefully preserved and detailed tour than La Ferté. A Nissen hut houses guns and vehicles from 1940 as well as retractable turrets which had been salvaged from another fort. A German 88-mm Flak gun guards the munitions entrance, inside which the ammunition magazine now houses the fort's museum depicting underground garrison life. An elevator descends 30 meters to the subterranean gallery where a narrow-gauge rail line takes visitors 1 km to Block 4. The block still holds three casemated 75-mm guns, the operation of which is explained. The tour exits the casemate through an emergency door to view the block's commanding position and the damage done by German 88-mm cannon. Block 1 is visible nearby, displaying its 265-ton retractable cupola that housed twin 75-mm guns. An underground return route visits other rooms, including the infirmary, power station, barracks, kitchen, and numerous other facilities which provide an impression of life within the fort. Guided tours are available in April on Saturdays and Sundays at 14:00 and 15:30; May and June on Mondays through Fridays at 15:00 and Saturdays and Sundays at 14:00 and 15:30; July and August everyday from 14:00 to 16:30; first three weeks of September every day at 14:00 and 15:30; rest of September and October at 14:30 and 16:00; closed November through March. Tours are conducted in French with English handouts. Fee.

Other Sites of Interest: Around Thionville, the **Maginot fortifications** were particularly strong. Near the village of Veckring, 18 km east of Thionville, one of the best and most toured fortresses is **Fort du Hackenberg,** with its 17 combat blocks connected by a network of underground galleries. Unlike many other forts, much of Hackenberg's equipment remains intact and operational. The tour includes a demonstration of the operation of the fort's 135-mm howitzer's retractable turret and diesel-powered generators. Trilingual guided tours are offered from April through October on Saturdays, Sundays and public holidays from 14:00 to 15:30.

#44
Defense of Calais
23 to 26 May 1940

OBJECTIVE	To delay the German advance sufficiently for the embarkation of British troops from Dunkerque
FORCES	
BRITISH:	3,300 men (Brigadier Claude Nicholson)
FRENCH:	1,000 men (commandant Raymond le Tellier)
GERMAN:	10th Panzer Division (Generalmajor Ferdinand Schaal)
RESULT	The Anglo-French contingent held off an armored division for three days.
CASUALTIES	
BRITISH:	292 killed, 500 wounded, 2,400 taken prisoner
FRENCH:	Casualties are unknown, but few of the 1,000 soldiers and marines escaped.
GERMAN:	Unknown
LOCATION	Calais is 290 km north of Paris

During the so-called 'Phony War,' German and French forces faced each other across their frontier, and Great Britain transported its British Expeditionary Force (BEF) commanded by General Lord Gort, across the Channel. By May 1940, reservists and territorial troops had expanded its four regular army divisions to nine, and the BEF was assigned to be part of French First Army Group. With the German invasion of Holland and Belgium, the BEF moved north to pre-assigned positions on the Dyle River Line, arriving on 11 May. With the movement of German armored units across the Meuse to the south, the entire BEF was at risk of being cut-off; on 16 May, it began executing three successive nighttime withdrawals to the Escaut Line along the canal, south of Oudenaarde. Général Maxime Weygand replaced général Gamelin as Commander-in-Chief of the French Army and after three days of decision-making, produced a plan for joint Anglo-French thrusts aimed at breaking the 'Panzer Corridor.' The plan was unsupported by the battlefield situation. The units involved could not disengage from their active fronts and attack in an altogether different direction. Gort felt the decision to be foolhardy and refused. The plan came to naught.

The French government feared a strike toward Paris and planned for a relocation of the government to Tours. Defeatism was in the air, as exemplified in a dramatic scene witnessed and described by Winston Churchill, when clouds of smoke drifted over the Quai d'Orsay (French Foreign Office) while officials stoked bonfires with sensitive documents.

By 20 May, only ten days after the Germans had crossed the Belgian frontier and, according to French Military planning, were supposed to be amassing forces in front of the Meuse river barrier, the men of the Spitta Battalion, 2nd Panzer Division wet their feet in the English Channel, west of Abbeville near Noyelles-sur-Mer.

Days later the BEF was in full flight toward the channel ports, and its Imperial General Staff was already drafting plans to evacuate as many men and resources as possible from the port of Dunkerque. To implement those plans the British Army needed time, and they received it – partially due to Hitler and his High Command's fear of counterattack and partially from the dogged defense of Calais by a few thousand men, who fought through the streets of the city until overwhelmed.

Battle

Scattered French infantry and naval units were stationed in the citadel, Fort Risban, Fort Lapin, and several of the ancient bastions which surrounded Calais. On 21 May, reinforcements arrived from England, consisting of 30th Infantry Brigade – known as the Green Jackets – and 3rd Battalion Royal Tank Regiment with 48 light and medium tanks. The units had been grabbed piecemeal and shipped across the channel with no advance preparation to face an enemy force of underdetermined size. From the moment of their landing on the docks at Calais, they were starved for essential supplies and equipment. Communications units had no radios, tank units had no tanks, and motorcycles troops had few weapons. They were to do their best.

French forces were even more disparate, consisting of one machine-gun company, a partial battalion of infantry, two platoons of antiaircraft guns, a battery of self-propelled guns, and miscellaneous artillery troops without weapons. French naval units manned guns at Fort Lapin and several seaside bastions, but many of their guns fired only toward the channel. Brigadier Claude Nicholson was put in charge of the Anglo-French contingent and established defenses along an outer perimeter formed by the city's 19th century moat and an inner perimeter formed by

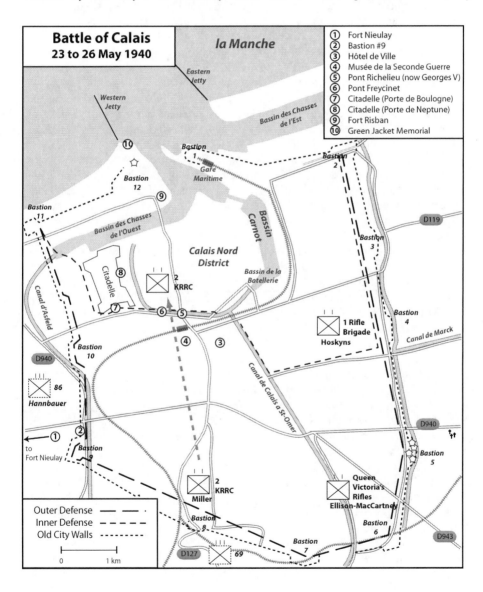

Battle of Calais
23 to 26 May 1940

la Manche

① Fort Nieulay
② Bastion #9
③ Hôtel de Ville
④ Musée de la Seconde Guerre
⑤ Pont Richelieu (now Georges V)
⑥ Pont Freycinet
⑦ Citadelle (Porte de Boulogne)
⑧ Citadelle (Porte de Neptune)
⑨ Fort Risban
⑩ Green Jacket Memorial

Eastern Jetty

Western Jetty

Bassin des Chasses de l'Est

Bastion 1

Gare Maritime

Bastion 2

Bastion 12

Bastion 11

Bassin des Chasses de l'Ouest

Bassin Carnot

Calais Nord District

Bassin de la Batellerie

Bastion 3

D119

Canal d'Asfeld

Citadelle

2 KRRC

Bastion 4

1 Rifle Brigade
Hoskyns

Canal de Marck

Bastion 10

④ ③

D940

86
Hannbauer

Canal de Calais à St-Omer

D940

to Fort Nieulay

Bastion 9

Bastion 5

2 KRRC
Miller

Queen Victoria's Rifles
Ellison-MacCartney

Bastion 8

Bastion 6

Bastion 7

D127   69

D943

Outer Defense ——— ·
Inner Defense — — —
Old City Walls ··········

0   1 km

the canals around the old Calais-Nord district.

The engagement started on 23 May west of Guines with an encounter between an armored column of 1st Panzer Division's Assault Group Kruger, which was bypassing Calais for their assault on Dunkerque, and a detachment from the tank regiment attempting to make contact with British GHQ in St-Omer. Severely outgunned, the British force beat a hasty retreat after losing seven tanks. Kruger's group continued northeast, to an encounter with the men of the British Searchlight Regiment holding a key bridge across the Canal de Calais at Les Attaques. The German tanks took three hours to push aside the vehicular roadblock and continue toward their lodgment area east of Calais. Late that night a British tank regiment had another unfortunate encounter while, trying to accompany a rations shipment to Dunkerque. They were in the midst of the 1st Panzer Division lodgment; more tanks were lost, and the rations never left Calais.

At dawn on 24 May, 69th Rifle Regiment, 10th Panzer Division began the assault upon the outer perimeter by attacking along roads from the southwest. Over the course of the day they fought their way through Calais to the canal barrier around Calais-Nord. At the same hour, 86th Rifle Regiment, supported by the 90th Reconnaissance Battalion, moved east from Coquelles, planning to enter the city from the west. In order to advance, they would have to take Fort Nieulay, an obsolete 17th century fortification occupied by a small garrison of French soldiers and, augmented the previous night by British troops. Nieulay blocked approaches to Calais from the west, and the Germans took twelve hours to overcome stiff resistance by the combined Anglo-French force. The defenders held their ground until surrendering to an overpowering mortar, artillery, and infantry force in the late afternoon.

German riflemen, supported by tanks, then moved against the western outer perimeter. Around the ancient Bastion #9 they were met by 2nd Battalion, 2nd King Royal Rifle Corps (KRRC), who, despite taking direct tank fire, held off the advance into the night.

With his troops thinly spread and without reserves, Brigadier Nicholson decided that the outer perimeter could not be defended for another day and ordered a withdrawal to within the ship basin and canals around the old district. Key to this new defense line were the three bridges across the Bassin de Batellerie.

By 08:00 on 25 May, the 69th Rifle Regiment had pushed through Bastion 8 south of the city, crossed most of the city center, and captured the Hôtel-de-Ville and its clock tower. They now had an excellent observation and sniper platform with visibility over the key bridges.

British infantry barricaded the bridges with trucks, busses, and whatever else was available. Houses fronting the waterway bristled with rifles and machine guns. Nicholson's headquarters was in the citadel, where the mayor of Calais brought an ultimatum from General Schaal to surrender or see Calais destroyed. Nicholson's refusal triggered artillery and Stuka attacks upon the citadel and Fort Risban.

In the early afternoon, a German officer crossed Pont Richelieu (now Pont Georges V) under a white flag to demand surrender once again. Schaal was following Guderian's instructions to take Calais and avoid unnecessary losses. Nicholson again refused with the words, 'The answer is no as it is the British Army's duty to fight as well as the German's.'[9]

On the opposite side of the city the battle progressed similarly, with house-to-house fighting gradually pushing the 1st Battalion, Rifle Brigade and 1st Battalion, Queens Victoria Regiment back from the outer perimeter and up the narrow isthmus toward the Gare Maritime. Artillery bombardments alternated with small arms fire for most of the day. By 19:30, a deadly silence fell over Calais-Nord, to be broken by the steady rumble of tank engines and the clank of their treads. The panzers were going to force their way across the bridges.

Assaults upon the left hand Pont Richelieu and Pont du général Faidherbe were repulsed with heavy fire from the houses fronting the canal, driving back supporting infantry. One tank, however, forced Pont Freycinet, and 1st Battalion, 86th Regiment infantry streamed across in its wake. A counterattack stopped the tank, but the infantry took up positions in the houses along esplanade Jacques Vendroux and brought the citadel under small arms fire. In the late evening, the Stukas returned to bomb the port facilities and the citadel, cutting the water supply and setting the food stores, hospital, and ammunition dump on fire. The fighting ceased when night approached, the darkness punctuated by the glare of burning buildings. The British repositioned their meager forces while the two German regiments moved heavy weapons in for the kill.

On 26 May, the Germans again unleashed their artillery and Stukas. After two hours, much of Calais-Nord was in flames. Tanks finally pushed aside the bridge barricades, now manned only by the dead and dying. By the afternoon ammunition was almost completely expended, and water was scarce. The eastern defenses consolidated, slowly withdrawing toward final positions around the harbor. At 15:30, 1st Battalion, 69th Rifle Regiment surrounded the remnants of the Rifle Brigade at Bastion 1, and they surrendered. Across town at 16:30, the citadel fell when the Boulogne Gate was battered down; shortly thereafter the French at Fort Risban were taken.

Calais remained under German control for five years, becoming a center for German naval activity and defensive works to thwart the allied invasion that was expected in the Pas de Calais. The city was liberated by Canadian forces on 1 October 1944, after a week of bitter fighting.

Battlefield Tour

Calais has been a port of entry for English warriors and tourists since its conquest by King Edward III in 1347. Since the construction of the train tunnel under the English Channel and its terminal at nearby Sangatte, new construction on the outskirts of Calais has accelerated. Nevertheless, the areas included on our tour are easily navigated and still present the city that was so stubbornly defended by rag-tag elements of the British Expeditionary Force and French Army.

---

[9] JE Kaufmann and HW Kaufmann: *Hitler's Blitzkrieg Campaigns* (Conshohocken, Pennsylvania: Combined Books, 1993), 251.

Start by approaching Calais from Coquelles, as did the men of Generalmajor Schaal's 10th Panzer Division. The *Centre de l'Europe* should be avoided due to the confusing and complicated road network servicing this commercial hub and terminal for the EuroTunnel train.

If coming from Boulogne, exit the A16 Autoroute at exit #12 and proceed toward Calais. If approaching from Boulogne by departmental roads, follow D243e3 into Coquelles. If coming from Calais, exit the city on the rue Leon Gambetta and pass Fort Nieulay into Coquelles. In all situations enter the large roundabout south of Coquelles on the avenue Charles de Gaulle and exit toward Calais to the east. Unfortunately this area has become highly commercialized. Before the sweeping curve where the road turns to the east, a white château and woods is on the right. In those woods the German artillery established itself on the night of 23 May before beginning its bombardment of Fort Nieulay. Continue along the road (its name changes to avenue Roger Salengro) around the large curve to approach Fort Nieulay. From this perspective its defensive position along the roadway is obvious. The defenders were unfortunate to be totally lacking in heavy weapons besides one antitank gun and two heavy machine guns. Proceed into the parking area.

Fort Nieulay was constructed in 1525 with a rather peculiar application. Originally designed as a tollgate to levy fees for entering the city, it became a defensive area because the fort stands upon locks in the Hames River, which could be opened to flood the surrounding countryside. In 1940, the French commander, capitaine Herremann, led the small garrison of forty-eight French soldiers and seven marines, supplemented by the fifty-nine-man British contingent. They positioned their 25-mm antitank gun in Porte Dauphine. At 05:00, German heavy artillery opened a mild bombardment while infantry moved across the fields to the west of the fort. Intermittent machine-gun exchanges continued. The weak assault was easily repulsed, and a game of probe and fire continued for the rest of the morning. At approximately 14:00, German artillery fire resumed, eliminating the French antitank gun with a direct hit upon Porte Dauphine. The artillery fire continued for over an hour, answered by allied warships off the coast until Luftwaffe bombs sunk *HMS Wessex* and severely damaged the Polish destroyer *Burza* forcing a withdrawal of the ships. The German fire gradually reduced the fort's bastions and ramparts. At 16:30, German troops approached the fort under a leading mortar barrage. Capitaine Herremann surrendered the fort.

The damage of 1940 and of RAF bombing in 1944 to the stout walls has been repaired, and the iron gates at each of the major entrances have been replaced. Grass fields inside the fort are crossed by arched bridges, under which floodwaters were channeled. Only one lonely segment of the chapel's façade still stands. The *Poudrière* has been repaired and now contains a small museum of the fort's history. Tours are available 1 July to 31 August, from 13:00 to 18:00, except weekends and holidays. From 1 September to 30 June, reservations are required. Tel: (0)321466641.

Continue east on avenue Roger Salengro, which becomes boulevard Leon Gambetta after a large roundabout. The boulevard immediately crosses the Canal de la Rivière Neuve, where the Pont Jourdan was located. Along the quai Catinat on the right members of the KRRC established the outer perimeter near **Bastion #9** during the night of 23 May. Continue on boulevard Leon Gambetta and then turn left onto boulevard Jacquard. (One-way streets will require a slight loop around to the right, ending with a left turn onto boulevard Louis Pasteur, which becomes boulevard Jacquard after passing through place Albert 1st). Park in front of the Hôtel de Ville, around the Parc de St-Pierre, at the SNCF regional train station, or on the esplanade Jacques Vendroux near the citadel.

Boulevard Jacquard runs between the Parc St-Pierre and the ornately decorated Flemish Renaissance **Hôtel de Ville** and its equally ornate, 75-meter bell tower. Both were captured and occupied by German troops during the street fighting early on 25 May and provided observation positions during the attack on the old district.

In the park in front of the town hall stands the late 19th century masterpiece *'Les Bourgeois de Calais'* (Burghers of Calais) by Auguste Rodin, which commemorates the offer in 1347 by six town fathers to sacrifice themselves to save the city's inhabitants from the army of Edward III; they were spared through the entreaties of Edward's wife, Philippa of Hainault. The sculpture shows the six when they emerged from the city walls, thin and haggard from the effects of the eleven-month siege, sullen and worn as they prepared themselves for death, with nooses already around their necks.

Under the trees in the Parc St-Pierre across the street, the Germans built a bunker to house their military telephone exchange. The building's twenty-two rooms have been converted into the **Musée de la Seconde Guerre Mondiale**. The long central corridor accesses themed rooms containing numerous objects, some weapons, and a multitude of newspapers, drawings, postcards, maps, and letters illustrating the hardships of the people of Calais during the occupation. In the main corridor an impressive collection of First World War propaganda posters as well as soldiers' drawings from the Second World War. They really should not be missed. One room contains an excellent model of the Batterie Lindemann, the colossus of German cross-channel gun emplacements, the three casemates – named Antoine, Bruno, and Caesar – each housed 406-mm guns which were capable of firing shells weighing more than a ton across the channel. The structures were cleared for the construction of the Channel Tunnel terminal at Sangatte. Most displays are labeled in French only. Open every day from 1 May to 30 September from 10:00 to 18:00; open every day except Tuesdays, February through April and October through November from 11:00 to 17:00. Fee.

Immediately north of the park is **Pont Georges V**. German tanks made their first attempt to enter the old district here. The houses and shops lining the basin provided cover for British riflemen, whose intense fire stopped the Germans' first attack. After the two hour bombardment on the morning of 26 May, their smoking rubble afforded less cover to the survivors, and the panzers were able to force their way across the bridge and down rue Royale to the boulevard des Allies, where they divided to attack the remaining defenders at Fort Risban and at the harbor.

To the west is the smaller **Pont Freycinet**, over which the Germans made their advance on 25 May. Proceed west on avenue Pierre de Coubertin, which is the first street south of Pont Freycinet. 500 meters ahead on the right is the non-descript Porte de Boulogne entrance into the citadel.

Construction of **Calais' Citadel** began in 1560, almost immediately after the expulsion of the English from Calais. The city's importance encouraged succeeding monarchs to improve its defenses, culminating in the current design by Louis XIV's master fort builder, Sébastien Le Prestre, Seigneur de Vauban. Within the inner gate is a dark gray **stone memorial** to the '19 officers, and 185 warrant officers, NCOs and men of the King's Royal Rifle Corps, the Rifle Brigade, and Queen Victoria's Rifles who fell in the defense of Calais 23-26 May 1940.' The memorial's date of May 1945 makes it one of the earliest Second World War commemorations erected on the continent. The fort's interior was completely destroyed during the war and never rebuilt. It has been converted to a stadium and sports fields with a perfunctory dedication to war heroes. The tunnels in the northeast bastion held Brigadier Nicholson's headquarters. Always open; no admission charge.

Pass through the sports field to the eastern (Neptune's) gate. Inside the gate is a memorial to the soldiers of France who fought in the defense of Calais. **Neptune's Gate** is a more picturesque entrance to the citadel, the approach being through a beautifully landscaped demi-lune. The gate is known for its relief of the god Neptune, seen above the entrance. Return to the three bridges via the esplanade Jacques Vendroux (esplanade de la Citadelle in 1940). In houses along this street German infantry established itself on the evening of 25 May.

Return to the car and proceed north on rue Royale, crossing directly over the double spans of the Ponts Henri Hénon. On the right immediately after crossing the second bridge is a small parking area.

Fort Risban's existence dates from King Edward III, who ordered the construction of a defensive tower on this location in 1346 to block re-supply of the town during the siege. The fort was reconstructed many times over the centuries, its latest incarnation during the Second World War. Facing the roundabout in front of the fort is black granite stone with a plaque erected by the friends of the veterans of the **Maritime Dunkerque** 'In the memory of commandant Carlos de Lamdertye and his marines, soldiers, and allies killed in the defense of Calais May 1940.' De Lamdertye led 800 French volunteers to man guns at the fort and at bastions 11 and 12. He died during the battle of a heart attack.

The fort is now under reconstruction, and entry to the interior is prohibited. A walk around the southern quarter is possible to view the harbor as well as a German bunker constructed to defend the harbor. From here clear views of the significant orientation markers of Calais are possible; from left to right, they are the lighthouse, the spire of église Notre-Dame, and the belfry.

From the large roundabout in front of Fort Risban, proceed on avenue Raymond Poincaré and turn right in the next roundabout, into the large parking area servicing the Calais beach. Proceed to the right-most point closest to the harbor entrance.

A Cross of Sacrifice marks the **Green Jackets Memorial** on the harbor jetty, right at the corner where the ships enter the harbor. Appropriately, every cross-channel ferry that enters Calais passes it. On the wall behind the Cross of Sacrifice is a plaque which commemorates the sacrifice of the Green Jackets of 30th Brigade. A rather desolate caravan park occupies the site of Bastion 12, which is to the landward side of the monument. The site is enlivened by the gaily decorated walls of another German defensive bunker.

Across the harbor entrance from the Green Jackets Memorial is the ferry terminal which was the location of the Gare Maritime. Here the survivors of the 1st Rifle Brigade and 1st Queen's Victoria Rifles made their last stand until, with ammunition expended and engulfed in wounded comrades, they surrendered.

#45
Battle of Dunkerque (Operation 'Dynamo')
26 May to 4 June 1940

OBJECTIVE	To evacuate the British Expeditionary Force from France
FORCES	
BRITISH:	Nine divisions (General Lord Gort)
FRENCH:	Two divisions (amiral Jean Abrial)
GERMAN:	Ten divisions (General der Artillerie Georg von Küchler)
RESULT	200,000 British and 125,000 French were rescued
CASUALTIES	
BRITISH:	8,061 casualties, including 2,000 lost at sea
FRENCH:	1,230 casualties and 40,000 taken prisoner
GERMAN:	Unknown
LOCATION	Dunkerque is 290 km north of Paris

On 23 May, the 1st Panzer Division, commanded by General der Panzertruppen Friedrich Kirchner, swung around Calais, cutting through British detachments to move against Dunkerque. That night the division reached the Aa Canal and established four bridgeheads on its opposite bank. On 24 May, Hitler issued the much-debated 'Halt Order,' stopping his panzer divisions. The explanations offered for this action differ, but the three-day delay gave allied units an opportunity to consolidate the pocket's perimeter. At this time the port was part of the northern coastal defenses commanded by amiral Abrial; Dunkerque was defended by général Robert Fagalde's French XVI Corps and other units of the Secteur Fortifié

de Flanders. The German thrust to the channel modified the dynamics of the air war because German ground units were farther away from their air support and closer to RAF bases across the channel in Kent.

German armor resumed its movement toward Dunkerque on 27 May, but its progress was slowed by the strengthened defense. Two days later leading panzer divisions were withdrawn to be conserved for the final push south of the Somme River; the remainder became the anvil upon which the second-rate infantry divisions of the less-mechanized Army Group B would be the hammer.

The Belgian Army held the line along the Lys River; however, German pressure caused nearly to collapse. On 28 May, the Belgian Army surrendered; British II Corps quickly moved into the gap. Four days later the French at Lille surrendered after a valiant resistance that won praise from their German attackers.

Battle

Since the French High Command seemed unable to establish or implement a plan of action against the encircling German divisions, as early as 19 May, Gort suggested that plans be made for evacuation of the BEF. Vice-Admiral Bertram Ramsey, British naval officer in charge of channel operations, gave the order to commence Operation 'Dynamo' at 15:00 on 26 May, four hours before receiving Admiralty approval. At risk were 200,000 men of the BEF and an unknown number of French, Belgians, and other allies. Général Fagalde assumed responsibility for the western perimeter from the English Channel to Bergues, and the British assumed responsibility for the eastern perimeter from Bergues along the Canal de la Basse-Colme to Nieuwpoort. Purposeful flooding reduced the distance of British defense to a small section of the canal bank east of Bergues. The evacuation effort started slowly, and expectations that much of the BEF could be successfully rescued were low.

Intense Luftwaffe bombing of the port facilities had rendered much of them useless; the main lock gate was disabled, a blazing tanker already blocked access to the inner harbor, and other wrecks made navigating the narrow seaward approaches hazardous. On 27 May, the Luftwaffe attacked the city of Dunkerque, using incendiary devices to set the town on fire. Naval officers directed evacuees to beaches east of the harbor, between Dunkerque and La Panne, to avoid the blazing buildings, crumbling walls, and blocked streets. Small boats began a shuttle between the beaches and larger vessels in deeper water, but the process was slowed by difficulties in hauling near-drowned men into small boats driven by large tidal swings and offshore currents. That night, the French 68th Division shortened the western perimeter defense by withdrawing to the stronger Canal de Mardyck Line.

At the western end of the evacuation beaches, the 1.6-km long East Mole – the British soldier's name for the lengthy jetty – jutted straight out to sea from the harbor entrance. Much of its length consisted of piles driven into the sand bed, upon which was a wide wooden walkway. Evacuation from the East Mole began during the night of 27 May and continued off and on for seven days until 200,000 men escaped along its occasionally teetering planks.

Rain began on 28 May, and low clouds mixed with greasy smoke of burning oil tanks provided air cover from the Luftwaffe. Passenger ships, warships, fishing boats, and coastal ferries continued the dangerous task of navigating minefields and sand bars to reach the mole, all the while avoiding bombers and shore artillery. After unloading the men at Dover, they returned to do it all over again.

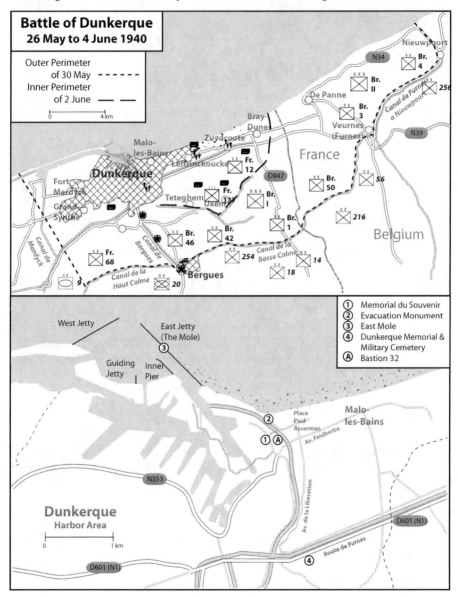

Not until 29 May did Lord Gort meet with his counterpart, amiral Abrial, at his headquarters in Bastion 32 and disclose to him that the BEF was leaving France. After a flurry of communications between Dunkerque, London, and Paris, the Allies agreed that further evacuations would have French and British soldiers removed in equal numbers. The French felt betrayed by British plans to abandon what they saw as the Dunkerque redoubt. That afternoon the wind shifted and skies cleared, permitting the Luftwaffe to sweep in on targets lining the East Mole. Three destroyers and numerous other craft were lost.

British infantry units continued their fighting retreat, while their comrades made for the escape beaches. By 30 May, all retiring British units were within the perimeter. Since the terrain around Dunkerque was not suitable for armored operations, responsibility for Dunkerque operations was transferred to the infantry divisions of Eighteenth Army.

31 May marked the high point for the evacuation, when 68,014 men boarded boats – the East Mole contributing almost two-thirds of the total because it was deemed usable once again. The evacuation rate slowed after 1 June, when the Luftwaffe returned, forcing the cancellation of daylight sailings. The final British troops left during the night of 2 June; the next night the last 52,921 French troops left the port at 03:45 on 4 June. At 08:20, général Beaufrère, now commanding the remaining French forces, surrendered the town.

The evacuation totaled 338,226, of which approximately 125,000 were French. The achievement by the soldiers, sailors, airmen, and the naval reservists who manned many of the smaller boats were spectacular. Ship losses totaled 228 craft, including nine destroyers and 60 French naval vessels. The RAF lost 177 aircraft in their engagements with the Luftwaffe, who lost an approximately equal number.[10] The evacuated army left all of their materiel behind, including tanks, transport, artillery and antiaircraft guns, ammunition, rations, and even most of their rifles; however, much of it was rendered useless, since the guns were spiked, the engine blocks holed, and munitions detonated. Winston Churchill put the success in proper perspective, however, in his address to Parliament on 4 June, 'We must be very careful not to assign to the deliverance the attributes of a victory. Wars are not won by evacuations.'[11]

In September 1944, the Canadian Army, sweeping up the coast, bypassed Dunkerque, considering its canal defense too strong to risk attack. The German garrison finally surrendered on 10 May 1945 – two days after the war was officially over.

Aftermath

With the action north of the Somme ending, the *Wehrmacht* turned its attention to the rest of France. The main attack started on 9 June with Rundstedt's Army Group A and consisted of another tank-led *Blitzkrieg*. The French established

---

[10] Aircraft losses remain a contentious point with air combat and ground antiaircraft fire double or triple counting enemy losses and propagandists of both sides giving the totals a favorable slant.

[11] Winston Churchill: *Their Finest Hour* (Boston: Houghton Mifflin Company, 1949), 115.

strong defensive points called 'hedgehogs,' but their lack of mechanized units prohibited effective counterattacks. The Germans crossed the Somme, the Aisne, and then the Marne; river barriers that had held them 25 years previous now provided only temporary delays in the age of mobile warfare. The government, having previously moved to Tours and then to Bordeaux, declared Paris an open city and on 14 June, the Germans repeated their march down the Champs d'Élysée as in 1871. The French government was re-formed with the hero of Verdun, maréchal Henri Pétain, as the new premier; however, French units were rapidly collapsing. A delegation led by General Huntziger finally met with the Chief of the German *Wehrmacht*, Generaloberst Wilhelm Keitel, in the forest at Compiègne, in the same railway car in which the Armistice of 1918 had been signed. The site selection demonstrated Hitler's desire for revenge upon France. No negotiations were allowed, and at 20:50 on 22 June 1940, the armistice was signed. The conquered countries thus entered their four-year purgatory of occupation.

Battlefield Tour

Dunkerque presents the visitor with the usual difficulties of navigating any unfamiliar urban locale. Dunkerque compounds these issues with an almost bewildering array of canals and waterways. The sites most related to the events of 1940 are fortunately clustered on the eastern edge of the city, near its junction with the resort community of Malo-les-Bains. Along the evacuation beaches east of Malo-les-Bains are the communities of Bray Dunes and La Panne, with their long brick esplanades and water-facing apartment blocks. Separating the towns are undulating sand dunes sparsely covered with grass and the occasional French fort or German Atlantic Wall bunker.

The Anglo-French defensive lines, often based on waterways and their bridges, offer little to visit. Obsolete fortifications at Forts Castelnau, Vallières, and Dunes played small parts in the battle and have been converted to other private or public uses. Clusters of blockhouses dot the outskirts of the city but are generally of later construction and not easily accessible.

Dunkerque can be entered from east or west, utilizing exit #30 from the A16 Autoroute. Proceed toward Malo-les-Bains (D916). Shortly after crossing the Canal de Dunkerque à Furnes, a confusing network of roadways and roundabouts exists. Proceed toward Malo-les-Bains on either rue des Fusiliers Marins, which passes the inner shipping basins, or boulevard Alexandre III. The two streets join farther ahead in the place du Minck. Continue on the rue du Leughenaer to the place de la Victoire; turn north on avenue des Bains, then left on rue des Chantiers de France.

Ahead on the left is the brick façade of the **Operation Dynamo Museum (Mémorial du Souvenir)**, which is housed in the concrete and steel casemates of Bastion 32. The 19th century fortification became the French Command Post of amiral Abrial and général Fagalde, and from there they left the city for England during the night of 3 June. Most of the defense works are gone, having been demolished during the construction of the Zone Neptune industrial / maritime center.

The arched roof, bunker-like building holds twelve rooms of artifacts, weapons, a diorama of the evacuation, and enlargements of photographs from the period. The museum is open every day May to September from 10:00 to 12:00 and 14:00 to 17:30. Fee.

Continue on rue des Chantiers de France to the next intersection and then turn right. Just before crossing the bridge, on the wall to the right, is a plaque identifying this landscaped hill as part of Bastion 32. Fortifications spread along the northeastern side of the harbor, providing a number of casemates, bastions and other constructions. Cross the bridge over the drainage channel, turn left onto rue Marcel Sailly, and continue to the Plage des Allies.

On the edge of the beach at the harbor entrance is a **stone block memorial** to the soldiers, sailors, and airmen – both British and French – who made the rescue possible. To the east stretch the beaches and dunes where long lines of soldiers wound while they waited to embark from the mole or sought shelter from Stuka bombs or Messerschmidt machine guns. The broad expanse of sand expanded and contracted with the tides, bringing grief to the sailors handling the shallow draft boats used to transport the men to larger vessels. To help with the loading, artificial jetties were constructed by driving long rows of lorries onto the beach at low tide.

To the northwest is the long **East Mole,** along which orderly groups of men sprinted to board rescue vessels. Bombs pierced the wooden walkways in places, but soldiers used whatever was available, including stretchers or ship's doors, to bridge the gaps. By the end of the evacuation the waters around the mole were a ship's graveyard, with dozens of funnels from sunken vessels sticking out of the water.

One of the myths of Dunkerque is that civilian sailors crossed the channel to effect the beachfront rescue operation. Most evacuees left via military or large passenger craft using the mole. The small boats necessary for the beach evacuation were manned by naval reservists, although the occasional fisherman did participate.

Walking along a shortened section of the causeway leading to the East Mole is possible. From the end, the West Mole on the opposite side of the port entrance is barely visible. In 1940, the West Mole bordered upon the port's oil storage facilities and was therefore deemed too dangerous for the ships to use.

Reverse course back over the Canal de Dunkerque à Furnes. Turn left toward Furnes (N1) and continue across the two canal bridges to the Cimetière de Dunkerque.

The **Dunkerque Memorial** is accessed across a gated lawn flanked by ten stone and brick tablets that list the names of the 4,534 British men who were lost during 1939-1940 operations and who have no known grave. At the end of the walk is an enclosure with etched glass panes depicting the evacuation. Adjacent to the memorial are 793 burials from the Second World War, the majority from the battles around Dunkerque. Since the city was a port during the First World War, separate plots in the Dunkerque Civilian Cemetery and in the Commonwealth War Graves Section contain 460 burials from that war. A short distance away from the British Memorial and separated by the communal cemetery is a French cemetery from 1914 to 1918.

Recommended reading

Churchill, Winston. *Their Finest Hour*. Boston: Houghton, Mifflin Company, 1949. The second volume of the prime minister's account of the Second World War.

Ellis, Major LF. *The War in France and Flanders, 1939 – 1940*. London: Her Majesty's Stationary Office, 1954. Detailed history of the BEF's operations.

Goutard, Colonel Alphonse. *The Battle of France 1940*. New York: Ives Washburn, 1958. A hard-to-find account by a French military historian who analyzes the French Army.

Guderian, Major-General Heinz, trans. Christopher Duffy. *Achtung! Panzer!* London: Arms and Armour Press, 1992. First published in German in 1937, it presents theories on the use of panzers by Germany's foremost armored forces theoretician and general.

Horne, Alistair. *To Lose a Battle: France 1940*. Boston: Little, Brown and Company, 1969. A descriptive and thorough account of the 1940 campaign.

Kemp, Antony. *The Maginot Line – Myth and Reality*. New York: Military Heritage Press, 1988. An account of the fortifications, with details on sections that can be visited.

Rommel, Field Marshal Erwin. *The Rommel Papers*, ed. by Sir Basil Liddell-Hart. New York: Harcourt, Brace, 1953. Rommel's career in his own words, edited and annotated by a foremost authority on the Second World War.

Shirer, William L. *The Collapse of the Third Republic: An Inquiry into the Fall of France in 1940*. New York: Simon and Schuster, 1969. A comprehensive telling by the American correspondent who witnessed the events.

Chapter Eleven

Raids and Invasion
1942–1944

Less than one month after the French surrender, Hitler ordered planning for the cross-channel invasion of Britain, codenamed Operation 'Sealion'. Any such action, however, required control of the skies, therefore the air war known as the Battle of Britain commenced. The RAF's success in bringing down German planes and, more importantly, German pilots led to the cancellation of 'Sealion'. Hitler turned his attention instead to Russia and North Africa. The Japanese attack upon Pearl Harbor and Germany's subsequent declaration of war on the United States created a now truly global conflict.

Churchill recognized the need for a large-scale operation in Europe during the summer of 1942. After a string of military setbacks, public opinion and the Russian and American Allies pressured the British for some positive action. After a review of potential target locations, the port of Dieppe was chosen. Dieppe represented the typical coastal port city, replete with military targets such as port facilities, rail yards, oil depots, and factory districts.

#46

Amphibious Assault on Dieppe (Operation 'Jubilee')
19 August 1942

OBJECTIVE	To conduct a reconnaissance-in-force, practice amphibious landing procedures, and destroy military targets.
FORCES	
BRITISH:	6,100 men of 2nd Canadian Division (Major-General John Roberts) and two British Commando troops
GERMAN:	302nd Division (Generalleutnant Konrad Haase)
RESULT	A disaster with heavy casualties for no benefit.
CASUALTIES	
BRITISH:	962 killed, 774 wounded or missing, and 1,946 taken prisoner; 550 Royal Navy seamen killed or wounded
GERMAN:	345 killed and 268 wounded
LOCATION	Dieppe is 190 km north of Paris

British intelligence estimated the German garrison in Dieppe at not more than fourteen hundred men. German intelligence predicted, however, that sea and weather conditions would be favorable for an amphibious landing during the month of August. They reinforced the Dieppe sector with the second-rate 302nd Division. Dieppe's defenses, however, were first-rate and included heavy coastal batteries at Berneval and Varengeville-sur-Mer, 75-mm guns covering approaches to the town from land and sea, 37-mm antitank guns facing the beachfront, two Luftwaffe heavy antiaircraft batteries, barbed wire entanglements lining the beach, and concrete antitank barriers blocking exits from the esplanade into the town. Dieppe was thus protected by a formidable array of weapons.

British Commandos were assigned responsibility for silencing the two coastal batteries. The assault was assigned to six battalions of the 2nd Canadian Division and supplemented by the 14th Tank Battalion, with all units operating under the auspices of a British service branch known as Combined Operations, commanded by Lord Louis Mountbatten, whose responsibilities included such raids against the continent. Transport was provided by landing craft flotillas of the Royal Navy, with an eight destroyer escort and air protection afforded by sixty-seven RAF squadrons of fighters and bombers, including four squadrons of American-flown B-17 bombers.

The objectives were to seize Dieppe, destroy military targets, obtain intelligence on the port defenses, and then return to waiting landing craft for evacuation. The main force was to land on the beaches in front of the city, the landing areas codenamed White Beach and Red Beach. In addition to the assault against the city, landings at the nearby seaside villages of Pourville and Puys were to silence the heavy guns, howitzers, and antiaircraft batteries that protected the city from the east and west.

Battle

Under moonlight on 18 August 1942, the convoy of ships silently moved across the English Channel and along the previously swept path through an enemy minefield. In the only successful part of the entire operation, No 4 Commando, personally led by Lieutenant-Colonel Lord Lovat, landed two contingents near Varengeville and proceeded inland to attack 'Hess' battery of six 150-mm coastal guns. Mortar rounds fell amid the battery's munitions stores, igniting a huge explosion. With Lovat's men in front and to the rear of the German position, a stirring charge crossed the last 100 meters of open ground; the defenders were killed, the guns spiked, and the two groups returned to the beach for re-embarkation. Casualties were minimal.

Events elsewhere did not go as planned; landings at Pourville, Puys, and Berneval all failed to reach their targets, the latter two never leaving the beachfront because heavy German crossfire trapped the men on the beach. In all three locations, evacuation attempts were also unsuccessful against the German fire, and the troops were forced to surrender or face annihilation.

The main attack started shortly after 05:00 with a naval bombardment by four destroyers and one gunboat. The bombardment targeted the wire entanglements on the beach and crept forward toward the buildings lining the sea. Hurricane aircraft applied cannon-fire onto the headlands while Spitfires raked gun positions. The entire pre-invasion bombardment lasted only twenty minutes. A covering smoke screen was laid down, through which landing craft approached the beach hidden for all but the last few hundred meters. Landing craft discharged the Essex Scottish on the eastern Red Beach; the Royal Hamilton Light Infantry was brought to the western White Beach.

Upon landing on the beachfront, both battalions came under frontal and

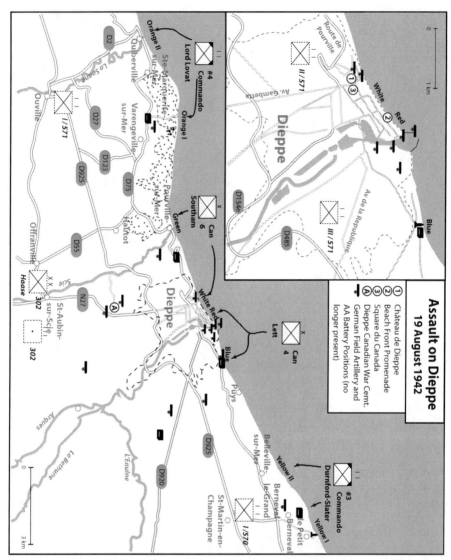

enfilade fire from German machine guns, mortars, and rifle fire. The honeycomb of caves on the east headland held guns sheltered from the aerial and naval bombardment. The Essex Scottish could not advance past the seawall. The Puys attack was to have engaged the headland defenses from the rear, but their failure allowed these strong positions to bring the full weight of their fire upon White Beach and Red Beach landing zones.

The first of twenty-eight Churchill tanks arrived ten minutes behind the trapped infantrymen, directly into fire from well-sited guns. Many of the vehicles were hit, but a few reached the esplanade. The concrete barricades erected at the end of the narrow streets were still intact, and the tanks were unable to enter the town. Several cruised back and forth, firing at targets of opportunity in frustration until all gas and ammunition were expended.

At the opposite end of the beach a three-story casino occupied the space between the seawall and the city buildings. The casino was flanked by two pillboxes containing antitank guns, which were knocked out by the Hamiltons. They cleared the building of enemy troops in hand-to-hand fighting that took approximately one hour. They then established fire positions within its walls. This action was the singular success of the Dieppe city landings. A few hours later the position was abandoned while the survivors made desperate bids to return to the beach for re-embarkation.

At 07:00, reinforcements were sent to Red Beach in the form of the Fusiliers Mont Royal. Their landing craft were met with heavy fire immediately upon leaving the protective cover of the naval smoke screen. In the confusion one-half of their craft landed at a small beach below the western headlands. They were trapped and separated from the battle, ultimately surrendering. The remainder suffered heavy casualties upon reaching the beach.

The Royal Marine Commandos attempted to reach White Beach but encountered such intense fire upon leaving the smoke screen that their commander signaled for the boats to abort the landing. At 11:00, Major-General Roberts decided to initiate a withdrawal. Rescue landing craft again encountered intense shelling, and few survived to make way out to sea. By 12:20, the evacuation was terminated. Only approximately 400 men were rescued.

The landing was labeled an informative reconnaissance-in-force, but much of what was learned involved how not to conduct an amphibious landing against a defended port. The effort did convince Hitler to increase Germany's expenditure of men and materiel on defenses along Europe's Atlantic coast.

Two years later on 1 September 1944, the same 2nd Canadian Division liberated Dieppe.

Battlefield Tour

The French coast from Dieppe to Cap Gris Nez is formed by high cliffs broken at intervals only by the occasional river mouth. Dieppe is located at one such exit, where the Arques River cuts a 1.6-km gap in the cliffs to provide the harbor, beaches, and seafront esplanade. Dieppe remains a busy port and tourist site, despite the narrow, one-way streets of the old town that make driving difficult. The suggested route skirts the pedestrianized Grande Rue shopping district, which, however, can make for a pleasant additional stop. Parking is always an issue.

The city can be approached from east or west on D925 or from the south on N27. These roads intersect south of the city in the large intersection named 'Rond-Point des Canadiens.' Proceed north (avenue des Canadiens, becomes rue Gambetta) through much of the city to the place des Martyrs; turn left (D75) and follow up the hill, around the hairpin turn; then turn right onto avenue de l'Esplanade, which leads directly to the west headlands.

The **Château de Dieppe** was reconstructed in 1433 on 12th century ruins, and was headquarters for the German 2nd Battalion, 571st Regiment. The ground near the chateau held three 75-mm beach defense guns and two antitank guns. The cupola now located here is of post-1942 construction. The overlook provides the views of the German gunners, indicating how the beachfront and entire esplanade came under their direct fire. White Beach is in the foreground, and Red Beach is in the distance. The dominating German position was duplicated on the opposing east headlands, demonstrating the futility of the Canadian assault. Below the cliff an aquatic center marks the former site of the casino, which was demolished by the Germans after the assault to improve their fields of fire. The chateau now houses a maritime museum and religious artifacts.

The 1.6-km long beachfront and the inland park are popular locations for walks and various forms of recreation. To the right of the park, a wall of commercial and residential structures separates the sea from the city proper. The two round medieval towers of Les Tourelles were built in the 15th century and form the only remaining example of the seven ancient town gates.

The east headlands are identifiable in the distance by the steeple of **Notre-Dame de Bonsecours**, a chapel dedicated to those lost at sea. Not visible from this position, the harbor is below the east headlands and inland from the city. The jetty, which extends into the sea from near the mouth of the harbor, held a French tank turret embedded in concrete, positioned to fire its 37-mm gun into the rear of the landing troops.

Reverse direction down the hill and loop around the place des Martyrs to continue northeast (rue de la Barre). The narrow, single direction streets make the remainder of the route difficult; therefore, it may be preferable to find parking, which is generally available around the esplanade, and walk the remainder of the tour. After 80 meters turn north (rue des Bains) and after a similar distance, turn east (rue St-Remy). Turn left at the 'T' junction (rue de la Morinière), finally reaching the open space of the esplanade; turn right (boulevard de Verdun).

Pass along the seafront park, noting the narrow streets where the Germans had constructed 2-meter high concrete walls to seal off the beach from the city. Small groups of infantry were able to dodge through the buildings to escape the seafront, but they were usually overcome in vicious street fighting with German patrols or well-hidden snipers.

At the eastern end of the boulevard, a partial view of the harbor entrance, which was one of the objectives of the Essex Scottish landing on Red Beach, is possible. The intensity of the fire kept all but a few isolated troops from approaching it.

> Turn left (boulevard du maréchal Foch) and proceed along the beach side of the esplanade, stopping to view the beachfront monuments.

The sleek, black monolith seen along the beach promenade is a memorial to the **Essex Scottish Regiment**. It displays a Canadian Maple Leaf in silhouette and states only '19th August 1942' above the unit's insignia. The memorial marks the location of Red Beach. Of the battalion's 553 officers and men who participated in the raid, only 52 returned to England that day. The monument is oriented so that on each 19 August at 13:00, the sun shines through the maple leaf shaped-opening and illuminates a second maple leaf inlaid in the promenade.

Several hundred meters farther down the beach is a stone monument to French Canadians who fought here under the banner of the **Fusiliers Mont Royal Regiment**. The monument lists all the locations where this regiment fought, starting with Ypres in 1915, Dieppe in 1942, and through to locations in Germany.

At any of the beachfront openings, a walk onto the smooth oval stones known as shingle shows how the material was capable of jamming tracked vehicles and disabling many of the Canadian tanks. Continue to the water's edge for a soldier's view of the city, noting from this perspective the previously identified gun positions. Without control of the headlands, any frontal assault was doomed to inevitable destruction.

A gray granite stele on the west end of the boulevard du maréchal Foch, where the boulevard curves back toward boulevard de Verdun, commemorates the landing of the **Royal Hamilton Light Infantry**. They had only slightly more success than the men at Red Beach, being able to obtain some cover in the casino.

> Turn right (boulevard de Verdun), then left (rue de Sygogne) to the **square du Canada**, directly below the château.

A memorial pillar records the long historical relationship between Canada and France beginning in the early 16th century, and includes the Dieppe Raid and the liberation of Dieppe by Canadians on September 1, 1944. The base of the monument is inscribed with the words *'nous souvenons'* ('we remember'). Above the monument, the Canadian Maple Leaf flag is flown side-by-side with that of France. A plaque commemorates the men lost in the raid of 19 August, and the **Monument des Flammes**, a stone topped with metal tongues of flame, memorializes those who became prisoners of war.

Other Sites of Interest: The **Dieppe Canadian War Cemetery** in the village of Hautot-sur-Mer, 4 km south of the city center toward Rouen (N27), contains 783 men killed in the attack. Over forty flying officers are buried along the south wall, a result of the ongoing air war.

#47

Atlantic Wall and 'V' Weapons

OBJECTIVE	To protect occupied France from cross-channel invasion and to house weapons capable of striking London
RESULT	The combined effect on the outcome of the war was marginal.
LOCATION	Calais is 290 km north of Paris; Cap Gris Nez is 28 km southwest of Calais. St-Omer is 260 km north of Paris and 40 km southeast of Calais

The massive concrete structures erected to house Hitler's defensive Atlantic Wall are some of the most impressive remnants of the Second World War. Constructed of reinforced concrete, most were impenetrable to even specialized bombs or the largest naval shells. They presented postwar landowners with a significant demolition problem. In some cases, farmers made the best of the situation using them as barns or animal shelters; a few were converted into museums; many remain abandoned, graffiti-marred hulks. The largest, Batterie Lindemann near Sangatte, was destroyed in the course of the public works project for the construction of the EuroTunnel terminal; others were exploded by British engineers after the war and have been left as piles of rubble. A few survived and stand as representatives of the massive building program initiated by the Germans to protect their '*Fortress Europa.*'

Two of the most feared weapons used by Germany in the later stages of the war were the V-1 'Flying Bomb' and the V-2 rocket. They brought London within range of incessant bombardment not seen since the 'Blitz.' Most V-1 launch sites were destroyed by extensive bombing raids or the advancing allied armies in the autumn of 1944. A few heavily damaged examples survive. Due to their need for extensive infrastructure, the Germans decided to harden V-2 rocket launch sites against allied bombing by housing them inside enormous reinforced concrete bunkers. Relatively impervious to aerial assault, V-2 sites survived the war, and two of the largest are open for tours.

These facilities are interesting, each in their own way, and can easily be included with any battlefield tour of the Calais / Dunkerque area.

Atlantic Wall

To keep the British fleet out of the English Channel during the planned invasion of England, the Germans moved their heaviest guns from opposite the Maginot Line to positions between Boulogne and Calais. With the abandonment of invasion plans, Hitler and the German High Command assumed that the allied invasion of occupied Europe would occur at the channel's narrowest point, along the coast of Pas-de-Calais. These naval batteries were thus tasked with keeping the channel closed to allied shipping and occasional firings upon the southern English coast. The long-range cannon ranged from 170-mm to Batterie Lindemann's three mammoth 406-mm guns, the barrels of which had originally been manufactured for a

33.   The Meuse River and Île de Houx from Château de Poilvache; note the level approach to the river from the east (left) and the steep embankments to the west.

Entrance (Block #1) to Fort d'Eben-Emael (below) and its appearance in 1940 (right). NARA

34. Flemish Renaissance belfry of the Hôtel de Ville in Calais

German communications bunker in Parc St-Pierre which is now the Musée de la Seconde Guerre Mondiale

The broad slopes of Malo-les-Bains beach.

Inset: Abandoned British and French vehicles cover the evacuation beach at Malo-les-Bains. *NARA*

35. Ouvrage de Fermont Block #4 (left) and Block #1 (right) house turrets and embrasures as part of the Maginot Line.

French Armistice delegation in front of the Nazi flag shrouded Alsace-Lorraine Memorial in the Clairière de l'Armistice. *NARA*

The historical railway car in which the 1918 armistice was signed is again in use for France's 1940 surrender. *NARA*

36.   Bodies of Canadian soldiers lying among damaged landing craft and 'Churchill' tanks of the Calgary Regiment; the headlands south of the city are barely visible through the smoke. *LAC*

Dieppe's beachfront today retains the open park along the waterfront and 'wall' of buildings inland; the cupola was a post-invasion addition.

Batterie Todt's Casemate #1 now houses the Musée du Mur de l'Atlantique

37. The replacement Pegasus Bridge at Bénouville retains the design of the original, now in the museum nearby; German anti-tank gun position is right foreground.

The 'Flame' monument and memorial to the French Commandos under the command of Commandant Kieffer stands on the beach in Ouistreham.

38.   German 50-mm AT gun on Gold Beach in St-Aubin-sur-Mer is inspected by soldiers after its capture and (inset) as it appears today. *IWN B5252*

Nan White sector of Juno Beach now known as place du Canada after capture by the Queen's Own Rifles of Canada. The dark structure on the left was a German bunker, part of Widerstandnest #28.

39.   One of four Longues Battery casemates and its 155-mm Czech naval gun.

Right: Aerial view of the Mulberry
Harbor at Arromanches; floating piers
facilitated unloading of supply ships.
IWM C4845

The town of Arromanches and
remnants of the artificial harbor as
viewed from St-Côme.

40.   Easy Red sector of Omaha Beach looking up the bluff to Normandy American Cemetery; the 5th Special Engineer Brigade stele sits on the upper of the two bunkers; note the shingle in the foreground.

1st Division troops hunker down as their LCVP approaches Omaha Beach on D-Day; the bluff is barely visible through the smoke from naval fire. *NARA*

Aerial view of Normandy American Cemetery and Memorial with Omaha Beach to the left. *Courtesy of American Battle Monuments Commission*

TO THE HEROIC RANGER COMMANDOES
D 2RN E 2RN F 2RN
OF THE 116TH INF
WHO UNDER THE COMMAND OF
COLONEL JAMES E. RUDDER
THE FIRST AMERICAN DIVISION
ED AND TOOK POSSESSION OF
HE POINTE DU HOC

41. Above: Bombers of the US Ninth Airforce attack Point du Hoc before D-Day. *NARA*

The shaft and plaque of the Ranger Monument at Point du Hoc; this photo was taken before seaside erosion prohibited access to the command bunker upon which they stand.

German Military Cemetery at La Cambe displays clusters of five stone crosses, characteristic of German war cemeteries; the mound holds a mass grave.

42. The church in Ste-Mère-Église; hanging from the tower is a dummy representing Private John Steele.

Voie de la Liberté bollard 'KM 00' stands at an exit from Utah Beach.

The 1st Engineer Special Brigade Memorial sits upon a German bunker at Utah Beach.

43. A Churchill tank of the Royal Tank Regiment on Hill 112.

Canadian troops carefully work their way through the rubble strewn rue St-Pierre in Caen in July 1944. *LAC*

Operation Goodwood battlefield north of Cagny: the monument commemorates all members of the Guards Division who perished attacking across these open fields.

44.   Forest road used by German armor in the Ardennes Offensive.

Peiper's troops on the road towards Malmédy.

Malmédy Massacre Memorial

45.   Roadside marker indicates the farthest advance of Peiper's column. Three German tanks were disabled on the curve in the road. Stoumont Station is in the distance.

German Panzer Mark VI (King Tiger tank) stands outside Museum Décembre 1944 in La Gleize.

46.   Morning mist shrouds the rather dilapidated Patton memorial in Bastogne. The famous general's profile is on the white stone to the rear.

The town square now known as the place du Général McAuliffe immediately after the Luftwaffe's Christmas Eve bombardment. *NARA*

The place is now a parking area in the commercial center of Bastogne. A Sherman tank and other memorials are on the left.

47.   One of the tank turrets that now mark the limits of the German advance into the city. This one is at Marvie.

Mémorial Mardasson stands upon a hill over-looking the city and commemorates the American defenders of Bastogne.

48. Belgian Army pillbox along the road to Assenois where Bastogne defenders and Third Army relief column broke the encirclement of the city.

Right: Regimental command post in camouflaged pillbox in the forest; most troops had no such shelter. *NARA*

Foxholes dug by the men of the 101st Airborne Division in the Bois Jacques survive sixty-four years after the defense of Bastogne.

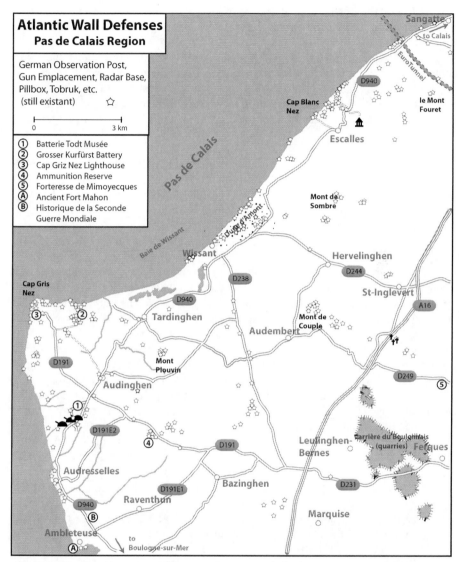

Atlantic Wall Defenses
Pas de Calais Region

German Observation Post,
Gun Emplacement, Radar Base,
Pillbox, Tobruk, etc.
(still existant) ☆

0 ——————— 3 km

① Batterie Todt Musée
② Grosser Kurfürst Battery
③ Cap Griz Nez Lighthouse
④ Ammunition Reserve
⑤ Forteresse de Mimoyecques
Ⓐ Ancient Fort Mahon
Ⓑ Historique de la Seconde
  Guerre Mondiale

super-heavy class of battleship that was never constructed.

At first the guns were mounted in open emplacements, but air attacks led to their being housed in massive concrete casemates. Most of this construction was carried out by the civilian *Organization Todt,* named after its founder and the builder of Germany's Autobahns, Fritz Todt. Upon his death in February 1942, he was replaced by Albert Speer, Hitler's favorite architect and the man who eventually organized German industry for total war as Reichsminister for Armaments.

In late 1943, responsibility for the Atlantic Wall, now spanning 2,000 km of coastline from Norway to the Spanish Pyrenees, was given to Generalfeldmarschall

Erwin Rommel. Construction at the batteries continued, transforming them into fortresses surrounded by minefields, barbed wire, antitank ditches, and barracks for supporting infantry.

By September 1944, First Canadian Army, moving north along the coast, contained the batteries within a coastal pocket. Most of the big guns were designed to fire only upon channel targets and could not rotate sufficiently to fire landward. One by one they were overcome by assault troops using flamethrowers and special 290-mm tank-mounted mine launchers. By the end of the month they were all captured.

Vengeance Weapons

The V-1 jet propulsion 'Flying Bomb' and the V-2 rocket were both products of the German research establishments at Peenemünde, a resort area on the Baltic coast in northeastern Germany. The island's facilities were divided between two fiercely competitive factions – the German army working on the V-2 and the Luftwaffe working on the V-1.

The V-1's pulse jet engines propelled an 800-kg bomb at 700 kph, nearly the speed of the fastest fighter aircraft. One week after D-Day, the first flying bombs landed in East London. Soon they were falling all over the city, with their approach forewarned by the buzz of their pulse jet engine – followed by deadly silence when the engine cut off and the explosive-laden missile fell to the earth. Whereas the targeting of the bombs was crude, the approximately seventy-five hundred successful launches hit all areas of London, killing over six thousand people and wounding almost eighteen thousand. RAF countermeasures were limited to fighter aircraft getting close enough to disturb the aerodynamic flow and send the V-1 crashing to the ground. Aerial balloons and antiaircraft batteries were relocated to intercept their course south of the capital with some success. Massive bombing raids began against launch sites and storage facilities in France. The threat to England ended when advancing allied armies overran the coastal launch sites.

Meanwhile Wernher von Braun was developing the first true rocket, named A-4 by the Germans and V-2 by the British. The first experimental firing of a V-2 rocket at Peenemünde on 13 June 1942 went out of control, nearly killing Speer and Braun. The second test on 14 October 1942 was successful, and by the end of the year mass production was approved by Hitler. The V-2 was considerably more expensive to manufacturer than the V-1, and extensive facilities were required to handle assembly and the liquid oxygen rocket fuel. Its range was 320 km, however, sufficient for launch sites to be in more secure territory; its speed was 6,400 kph – or almost four times the speed of sound –allowing no counter-measures and no warning of its arrival.

A total of thirteen hundred V-2s were launched, of which five hundred reached London, killing over twenty-seven hundred people and wounding over six thousand. Later attacks against the allied-held cities of Antwerp, Liège, and Brussels were even more devastating, with larger numbers of V-1s and V-2s killing thousands of civilians and military personnel.

Neither a jet-propelled bomb nor a rocket, the *Hochdruckpumpe,* or V-3, was designed to be a long-range cannon capable of firing a 150-mm shell 165 km across the channel – three times the range of Germany's largest cannon. Propulsion was accomplished through sequential explosive charges in side tubes of the 127-meter long barrels. The advantage was low cost and rapidity of fire. In actual practice the shells were aerodynamically unstable and began to tumble after firing, falling well short of their specified range. It never became operational in its original form.

Atlantic Wall

To bring English shores within range, the big guns were placed on Cap Gris Nez, the spit of land that points like an arrow across the channel toward Dover. These guns enforced a no travel zone in channel waters and presented an intimidating threat to any cross-channel invasion fleet. The three recommended sites are all within 30 km of Calais. The entire Pas-de-Calais coastline is rife with smaller anti-invasion bunkers and pillboxes that can be seen at almost any seaside resort.

Along the scenic Calais-Boulogne-sur-Mer coastal road (D940), 750 meters south of Audinghen, a rural road to the right leads to a large casemate.

Batterie Todt was originally named Siegfried Battery but was renamed for Fritz Todt after his death. The battery had four 380-mm naval guns mounted in separate armored turrets encased in concrete casemates. The 19.6-meter long barrels were intended to be replacement barrels for the battleships *Bismarck* and *Tirpitz*. The guns were capable of firing an 800-kg shell a maximum distance of 52 km, bringing the southern English coast within range – Dover and Ramsgate being frequent targets. The battery's participation in defending Normandy against invasion was rather limited.

The North Nova Scotia Highlanders attacked the battery on 29 September 1944, supported by armor from the 79th Armored Division. The defense was brief, and white flags appeared after a few hours. The Germans had already prepared the battery's installations for demolition when the Allies approached, but only the command bunker was detonated. The explosives remained in place, and after the war two Frenchmen died after accidentally setting off explosives in casemate #3, thereby destroying that installation.

The privately owned **Musée du Mur de l'Atlantique** is located in the northern-most casemate #1, and its rather disorganized but interesting displays contain an array of small arms, including handguns, rifles, bazooka, *panzerfaust*, handgrenades, and an array of shells – including a two-meter tall 380-mm shell. The two-story casemate held the gun and munitions stores above and crew accommodations and equipment rooms below. A self-guided tour leads through the blast doors to access most of the casemate's rooms, although the guns have long since been removed. The square openings in the rear wall are ventilators to release firing gases. The gun rotated on its mount, and the rear rested on running rails which encircled the gun platform. The stepped overhang provided protection to the gunners from bombs. Outside the museum is one of only two remaining 280-mm K-5 German railway guns, which were hidden in railway tunnels during preparation and rolled out to fire at targets in the channel. Numerous vehicles as well as flak and antitank guns line the rear of the casemate. The pieces are inadequately labeled, and many of the outdoor pieces are in dilapidated condition. Open every day June through September from 09:00 to 19:00; October to May from 09:00 to 12:00 and 14:00 to 18:00; closed December and January. Fee.

The three other Batterie Todt casemates are visible across the reclaimed farmland, but they are not open for visits. The partially collapsed casemate #3 is in particularly dangerous condition.

Return to the Boulogne-Calais road (D940) and at the first roundabout turn left (D191).

Upon entering Framezelle, the first right turn toward Floringzelle leads to the site of **Grosser Kurfürst** battery, the gun platforms, defenses, and support buildings of which extended for 1 km to the opposite side of Floringzelle. The ruins of twelve bunkers are within 100 meters of the roadway, with another nine between the road's end and the sea, 500 meters farther.

The Grosser Kurfürst battery, named after the Great Elector, Friedrich Wilhelm Duke of Prussia, was built during the spring of 1943 on Cap Gris Nez, near the cliffs above the English Channel. The battery held four 280-mm guns mounted atop concrete bunkers which could rotate a full 360 degrees. The bunkers held munitions stores, ventilation equipment, a power generator for the hoists, and quarters for the crew of six. Numerous pillboxes and tobruks[1] for machine and antitank guns, flak towers, as well as command and fire control posts dotted the surrounding landscape. On the cliff at the tip of the cape was a Würzburg radar and rangefinder.

During 1943 and 1944, the battery fired more than 400 shells at targets in southern England and occasionally exchanged fire with British long-range guns stationed near Dover. Aerial attacks in September 1944 scored hits on the bunkers, but the 2.5-meter thick walls and roofs were unaffected. A direct hit on the 100-mm thick armored turret failed to disable the gun. Canadian infantry and armor attacked the position on 29 September 1944, and the battery surrendered after a violent bombardment. British engineers destroyed the bunkers after the war, leaving only broken blocks of concrete.

Return to the highway (D191) and continue to the lighthouse parking area.

The cliffs at **Cap Gris Nez** are France's closest point to England, only a mere 34 km. From the cape the white cliffs of Dover can be seen across the English Channel as Rommel saw them when he visited the Atlantic Wall fortifications in December 1943.

Around the lighthouse, along the shoreline, and farther inland the terrain is

---

[1] Tobruk: an concrete-lined, open pit defensive position

dotted with a variety of bunkers in various states of decay. At least fourteen ruins are within the circle formed by the access road and coastline. Cap Gris Nez held 'M4' battery, with three 170-mm guns mounted in open-air firing pits located north of the lighthouse. The large, intact fire control post on the cliff south of the lighthouse has a slit-opening facing the sea. The terrain still displays the slowly fading craters created by allied bombing and naval shelling. The massive bunker with the slit opening in one corner was also a fire control bunker. Looking back to the south, the casemates of Batterie Todt are visible, with their dark gun ports open toward the sea. The nearest and left-most is casemate #1; casemate #2 is hidden by woods; casemate #3 can be seen with its partially destroyed roof; to the farthest right is casemate #4, identified by its rooftop soil mounds.

The GR *(Grande Randonnée)* du Littoral public walking trail continues along the cliff's edge to the south. Approximately 2.5 km from the lighthouse are the ruins of the **Würzburg Radar** installation used to target the guns of Batterie Todt. The terrain is strewn with additional tobruks, bunkers, and observation posts.

Return toward Batterie Todt (D191), crossing the Boulogne-Calais road in the roundabout north of the battery. Continue toward Onglevert / Marquise (D191).

Approximately 1 km after Onglevert, the road passes a field on the right which contains a large number of bunkers and sheltered **Battery Todt's ammunition reserve**.

Follow this numbered highway 8 km, passing over the A16 Autoroute, shortly after which bear left toward Ferques (D231). In less than 1 km turn left toward Leulinghen-Bernes and continue on this rural road for 3.6 km. Turn right toward Landrethun-le-Nord (D249), and in approximately 2 km is the entrance to Musée de la Forteresse de Mimoyecques.

The V-3 plan at **Forteresse de Mimoyecques** called for three batteries of five tubes each to fire five hundred 150-mm shells per hour on London. Digging the tunnels into the side of the ridge began in April 1943, with a railway tunnel running parallel to a main gallery connected by eleven branch tunnels. At the ends of three of the branch tunnels were the breeches for the long barrels. Angled at 45 degrees, the barrels exited the surface embedded within a 5-meter thick concrete slab. The entire matrix of tunnels was 30-meters below the surface to offer protection from allied bombers. After aerial photographs identified that the openings pointed directly toward London, bombing raids started in November 1943 and continued for eleven months. The dropping of seven of the Allies' heaviest bomb, the 5,500-kg 'Tallboy,' on 6 July 1944 caused rock falls within the tunnels. All work was stopped three weeks later. British engineers detonated explosives in the empty tunnels in 1945.

Mimoyecques is not a museum in the traditional sense, rather a tour that is little more than a walk through damp galleries cut into the ridge, 30 meters below the surface. The main tunnel was 600 meters in length to accept complete trains loaded with construction materials. Three of the cannon shafts are visible, the final one still showing a segment of the barrel. The site is also a burial ground because when the Tallboy struck, water flooded the lower levels housing the laborers and guards' bomb shelter. Their bodies are still entombed below. The museum is open every day April through June from 11:00 to 18:00; July and August from 10:00 to 19:00 and September through 11 November from 11:00 to 18:00. Fee.

Other Sites of Interest: The **Historique de la Seconde Guerre Mondiale** is located along the D940 in Ambleteuse, 8 km south of Cap Gris Nez. This very professionally structured museum contains the private collection of war memorabilia of a local resident, much of it displayed in life-sized dioramas. The weapon comparisons are illuminating, and a reconstructed street scene shows life in occupied France. A small theatre presents archived film of the D-Day landings. The museum tells the history of the global war from beginning to end in English and French and is one of the better such sites in France. Highly recommended and well worth the visit. Open every day 1 April to 15 October from 09:30 to 18:00 (until 19:00 in July and August); March and November on weekends only from 10:00 to 18:00; closed December through February. Fee and handicap accessible.

Vengeance Weapons

From Cherbourg to Pas-de-Calais, over 450 V-1 launch or storage sites were started. Many never became operational. Since construction was usually of concrete block rather than the reinforced concrete of weapons casemates, they have mostly been destroyed by landowners, the materials used to reconstruct destroyed dwellings, fill bomb craters, or grade roadways. A few that remain are in heavily forested areas or on private land. One of the exceptions is **Bois des Huit Rues** in the state-owned Forêt Domaniale de Nieppe, 20 km east of St-Omer near Hazebrouck.

Leave St-Omer toward Hazebrouck (D211, then N42); 7.5 km east of Renescure, turn toward Wallon-Chappel. A short distance farther, bear left (D138) and enter the forest; proceed to the parking area on the left.

The central path through the site starts at the parking area and continues past workshops and staff buildings to the launch bunker. The launch ramp has the characteristic 'ski jump' shape used to gain take-off velocity. Only the overgrown blast walls that flanked the ramp remain. To the right, back 100 meters is the important compass alignment shed, where the bomb's navigation gyroscopes were calibrated. These sites always instill a feeling of quiet discomfort; once they teemed with focused activity, now the silence is broken only by the songs of forest birds. The launch ramps are still aimed at the heart of London.

The Wizernes V-2 launch site was constructed in a chalk quarry 5 km southwest of St-Omer. Return to St-Omer, leaving the National Road (N42) toward Arques (D211). West of central Arques follow the road where it turns left toward

Blendecques/Wizernes (avenue de la Libération, D211). Follow for 4.5 km, then turn left upon entering Wizernes (rue du Pont d'Ardennes, D198). Follow across the D210, where it makes a slight bend to the left. Turn right toward the entrance. Numerous signs provide directions once south of St-Omer.

In a quarry, a 72-meter diameter concrete dome houses **La Coupole**, a modern, publicly funded rocketry and space exploration museum. The immense concrete dome was to shelter V-2 rockets when they were taken from a horizontal position to a vertical position, their explosive charge added, guidance system calibrated, and the propulsion – a combination of liquid oxygen and alcohol – added. They were then taken out on a moving platform through blast doors into the quarry, where they were to be launched much like current day rockets. The ignition lasted only sixty-five seconds, until the rocket achieved full velocity. Construction started in July 1943 and continued undisturbed until 11 March 1944, when the structure's purpose was identified. After 3,200 tons of bombs were dropped around it, the quarry walls were so damaged that the dome became unstable and construction ceased.

La Coupole contains four museums, covering secret weapons, local life under the Nazi occupation, man's need for peace, and space exploration. Two theaters present a film on the development of V-1 and V-2 rockets and a slide show on life in the region under the Nazis. Displays include an external V-2 housing and an actual V-2 engine. Multi-language headphones describe stops along the self-guided tour in the site's partially completed tunnels. A very modern reception building houses a bookshop and cafeteria. Open every day from 09:00 to 18:00; July and August from 10:00 to 19:00; closed Christmas through early January. Fee.

The Watten V-2 launch site is located in the Forêt d'Éperlecques, only 10 km north of St-Omer. Leave St-Omer north toward Watten (D928). In the roundabout near St-Momelin, exit toward Watten (D213). Upon entering Watten, turn left toward the SNCF train station and Bleue-Maison (D207, rue de la Gare); in Bleue-Maison, before reaching the D300 highway, turn right (chemin de la Vlotte). At the 'T' junction, turn left (rue de St-Gilles, becomes rue du Fort Wesques) and follow it to the entrance.

The private **Le Blockhaus d'Éperlecques** is one of the most impressive V-2 sites to visit because of its size and the damage wrought to it by USAF and RAF bombers. Construction started in March 1943 by conscripted foreign laborers. The objective was a complete facility where pre-assembled V-2 rockets could be received, fueled, and calibrated in bombproof bunkers and then launched from underground silos. The facility also included a liquid oxygen plant to supply V-2 fuel. Its 5.5-meter thick concrete roof was designed to withstand the Allies' Tallboy bomb. Watten was repeatedly bombed while still under construction, culminating in thirty-two Tallboys between mid-June and late July 1944. One bomb struck the roof, causing a section to be blown off; another caused extensive damage to one corner of the bunker. The numerous near hits destroyed construction materials and created craters which made the site unusable; it was abandoned, never having become operational.

The approach to Le Blockhaus d'Éperlecques is through the woods, in which armaments, old torpedoes, and a two-man submarine are displayed. A V-1 bomb is on its launch ramp. The numerous craters demonstrate how the area was devastated by allied bombing. Le Blockhaus claims to be the largest bunker in northern France, measuring an enormous 70 meters by 40 meters. The entrance is through the 2.3-meter thick west blast door. The self-guided tour directs visitors into the damp and stark interior of poured concrete walls, but much of the tour is around the exterior due to the blockage of internal shafts and galleries. The lower levels remain flooded and inaccessible. The damage done to the north roof and west wall by Tallboy bombs is very evident. At various locations buttons initiate multi-lingual messages explaining the bunker's history and function, but the site is relatively underdeveloped as a museum. Open daily March 14:15 to 17:00; April and October from 10:00 to 18:00; May through September from 10:00 to 19:00; November from 10:00 to 17:00; closed December through February. Fee and handicap accessible.

Blockhouse d'Éperlecques and La Coupole tell complementary stories of V-1s and V-2s with many redundancies. At d'Éperlecques the tour focuses on the blockhouse and its construction; at La Coupole the emphasis is on the history and development of rocketry.

#48
Normandy Invasion (Operation 'Overlord')
'D-Day' 6 June 1944

OBJECTIVE	To mount an amphibious assault and begin the liberation of Europe.
FORCES	
ALLIES:	Nine divisions of Twenty-First Army Group (General Bernard L Montgomery)
GERMAN:	Six divisions of Seventh Army (Generaloberst Friedrich Dollmann)
RESULT	The landing did not accomplish all its objectives, but it firmly established the allied armies in continental Europe.
CASUALTIES	
AMERICAN:	6,603 total casualties
BRITISH:	2,839 total casualties
CANADIAN:	961 total casualties
GERMAN:	9,000 total casualties
LOCATION	Caen is 240 km northwest of Paris; Bénouville is 10 km north of Caen

The British Isles became a veritable island fortress, brimming with military hardware, naval vessels, aircraft and their landing fields, as well as personnel in training for the upcoming invasion of Hitler's *Festung Europa*. The decision of the Quebec Conference in August 1943 was to be fulfilled with a cross-channel amphibious invasion of Western Europe, codenamed 'Overlord.' A guessing game as to the actual site of the invasion continued through the spring of 1944, while allied and German intelligence tried to ferret out the opposition's intentions amid false information and conflicting military opinions. Geographical limitations were assessed, and meteorological conditions were monitored.

The Allies selected the shores of Normandy's Seine Bay, from the Orne River to the east coast of the Cotentin Peninsula, as the invasion site. The area possessed excellent landing beaches and seemed a better alternative than the more obvious and more strongly defended Pas-de-Calais. The important issue of harbor facilities for post-invasion supply and reinforcements had been resolved by floating portable harbors, called Mulberries, across the channel to establish disembarking facilities until the port facilities at Cherbourg and Le Havre could be brought on line. Over 176,000 men, 3,000 guns, and 1,500 tanks, supported by 284 major naval combat ships and 4,300 landing craft, were posed to cross the rough waters of the English Channel under an air umbrella of 7,770 aircraft. They had been training for as long as two years for this event. All units were held in closed encampments along Britain's southern shores to assure security.

The invasion force, commanded by British General Montgomery, targeted five invasion beaches, codenamed, *Sword, Juno, Gold, Omaha*, and *Utah,* from east to west. They were further divided into sectors with codenames such as *'Dog White'* and *'Queen Red.'* Sword and Gold would have landings by the British 3rd and 50th Divisions, and Juno would be taken by the 3rd Canadian Division – each supported by large contingents of commandos, demolition engineers, tank battalions, and special function forces. Omaha and Utah, on either side of the confluence of the Aure and Vire Rivers, were landing sites assigned to the Americans. The US 1st and 29th Divisions would land on Omaha, and the US 4th Division would take Utah. To capture and hold critical areas before the water-borne troop landings, the British 6th Airborne Division and American 82nd and 101st Airborne Divisions would land by parachute and glider in the early morning darkness.

Hitler and the German High Command expected the invasion to occur in Pas-de-Calais, where the journey across the channel was shorter and Boulogne and Calais could provide port facilities. German generals disagreed on the utilization of Germany's panzer divisions against the invading forces. Field Marshal Erwin Rommel, as commander of Army Group B responsible for coastal defenses, thought that Germany's only chance of victory was to smash the invaders at the water's edge. Others, led by Generalleutnant Leo Freiherr Geyr von Schweppenburg, commander of Panzer Group West, argued for waiting until the allied intentions became clearer. The controversy, plus Hitler's personal control of the panzer troops, would contribute to Germany's muddled reaction. Rommel nonetheless led the construction of the Atlantic Wall defenses, which included casemated armaments, antitank walls, seaside pillboxes, resistance nests called *Widerstandnesten*, millions of mines, and beach obstacles designed to sink landing craft when they approached France's shores.

The German Seventh Army was responsible for the coastal defenses in Normandy and Brittany. Although reserve troops in the form of II Parachute Corps

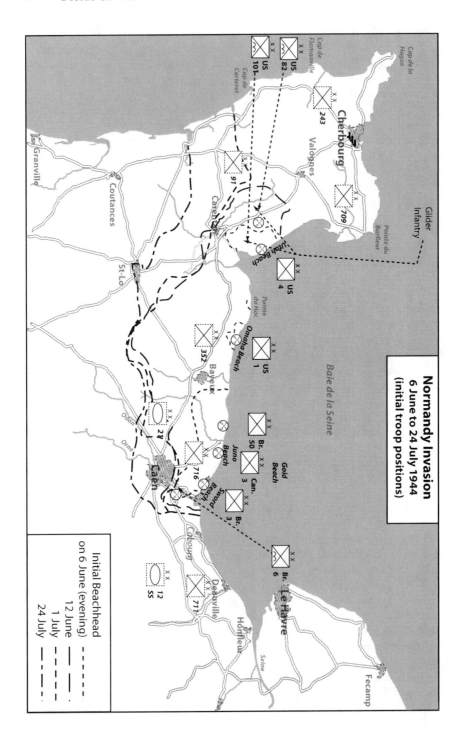

Normandy Invasion
6 June to 24 July 1944
(initial troop positions)

Initial Beachhead
on 6 June (evening)

12 June
1 July
24 July

and the 21st Panzer Division were first-rate units, most of the other units were decidedly second-rate, composed in many cases of Russians and ethnic Germans from conquered lands who volunteered to fight for the Reich. They consisted mainly of older Germans with little combat experience or training units which may have had experienced cadres but were not fully operational.

In the early morning of 5 June, amid unsettled weather conditions that had already delayed the invasion for one day, the Supreme Allied Commander, General Dwight Eisenhower, made the decision to proceed with the invasion the next day. He also wrote a note accepting full responsibility if the invasion failed and spent the evening visiting the airborne troops that would lead the invasion, fearful of the appalling casualty rates as projected by his staff. He returned to his headquarters to await the outcome of the largest amphibious invasion in history, on a day that has since been called 'the longest day.'

Battle
Airborne Landings
The first allied unit to set foot upon French soil in large numbers since the abortive Dieppe landings of 1942 was the British 6th Airborne Division. Its primary targets were the bridges across the Orne River and the adjacent Caen Canal as well as the Merville Battery, 9 km to the north. Control of the bridges and the highlands to their east was crucial to protect the massive invasion's eastern flank from potential attack by the armor of the German Fifteenth Army.

One company of glider troops secured the bridges over the Orne River and captured the powerful Merville Battery, which enfiladed Sword Beach. Pathfinders were assigned to identify landing and drop zones for other elements of the division which parachuted into France only minutes later. The 5th Parachute Brigade captured the high ground to the east of the bridges, near Ranville, to establish a firm perimeter east of the Orne. Late in the day, gliders arrived with the reinforcing Airlanding Brigade.

Thirteen thousand men of the America's two airborne divisions left southern England's airfields in nine hundred forty-five C-47s. They executed a dangerous night drop, parachuting behind enemy lines at approximately 01:30. The individual planeloads, or 'sticks,' were widely scattered by a variety of navigation errors, heavy German antiaircraft fire, and the failure of beacons identifying the drop areas. Time was lost while the sticks accumulated into viable fighting units. The targeted drop zone of Major General Maxwell Taylor's US 101st Airborne Division's was 3 km behind Utah beach, and their mission was to secure the causeways leading inland from the beaches over flooded ground. Major General Matthew Ridgway's US 82nd Airborne Division was not far behind, landing two regiments at 02:30 between the Douve and Merderet Rivers. Their objective was to capture or destroy bridges over the Merderet River, prohibiting German reinforcement of the invasion areas and establishing Utah Beach's western perimeter. South of the drop zones and based in the strategic transportation hub of Carentan was the highly regarded German 6th Parachute Regiment, commanded by Colonel Freiherr Friedrich-August von der Heydte. The newly formed German 91st Airlanding Division was to their west, on the

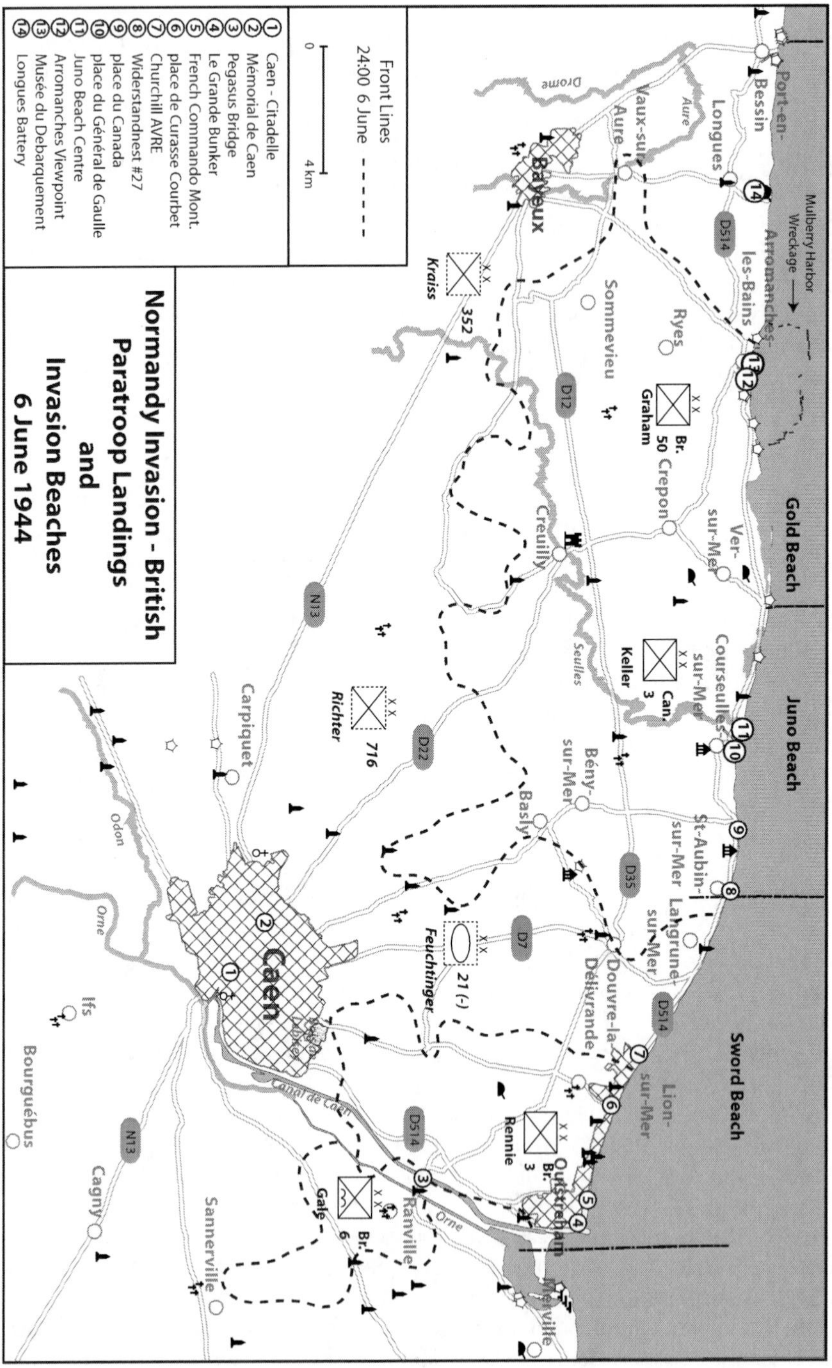
Normandy Invasion - British
Paratroop Landings
and
Invasion Beaches
6 June 1944
Front Lines
24:00 6 June
0
4 km
1 Caen - Citadelle
2 Mémorial de Caen
3 Pegasus Bridge
4 Le Grande Bunker
5 French Commando Mont.
6 place de Curasse Courbet
7 Churchill AVRE
8 Widerstandnest #27
9 place du Canada
10 place du Général de Gaulle
11 Juno Beach Centre
12 Arromanches Viewpoint
13 Musée du Debarquement
14 Longues Battery
Gold Beach
Juno Beach
Sword Beach
Mulberry Harbor Wreckage
Port-en-Bessin
Longues
Arromanches-les-Bains
Bayeux
Vaux-sur-Aure
Ryes
Sommervieu
Crepon
Ver-sur-Mer
Creully
Courseulles-sur-Mer
Bény-sur-Mer
Basly
St-Aubin-sur-Mer
Langrune-sur-Mer
Douvre-la-Délivrande
Lion-sur-Mer
Ouistreham
Ranville
Merville
Caen
Carpiquet
Ifs
Bourguébus
Cagny
Sannerville
Canal de Caen
Orne
Odon
Seulles
Aure
Drome
D514
D12
N13
D22
D35
D7
Kraiss
352
Graham
Br. 50
Keller
Can. 3
Richter
716
Feuchtinger
21 (-)
Rennie
Br. 3
Gale
Br. 6

far side of the Merderet River. Both units presented considerable threats. The dropping of American parachutists helter-skelter across the Norman countryside, however also brought confusion to the German response. When morning approached, the airborne positions came under pressure from the German 709th Division from the north, the 91st Division from the west, and the 6th Parachute Regiment from the south. The units were reinforced later in the day by five hundred Waco glider aircraft carrying glider infantry, support weapons, and communications gear.

Sea Based Landings

Minesweepers led the allied naval flotilla across the channel. Nine battleships, twenty-three cruisers, and ninety-five destroyers and gunboats were arrayed to fire upon the beaches and coastal defenses while over four thousand landing craft held near their transports, loading men and then circling offshore. Firing against the British beach defenses began at 05:30; twenty minutes later, it started along the American beaches. At 07:30, one hour after the start of the American landings at Omaha and Utah, the British and Canadians began their assaults under the protection of complete air supremacy.

Sword Beach

Offshore rocks limited the Sword Beach landings to only one of the four identified beaches. The British 3rd Division's tanks led the first landings at 07:30, with infantry following. Although encountering heavy fire from units of the German 716th Division, flail tanks cleared the beach of mines, and the lead battalions moved inland. The 2nd East Yorkshire Battalion and No 4 Commando moved toward Ouistreham. Lord Lovat's 1st Special Service Brigade rapidly reinforced Major John Howard's men at the Orne bridges, who had been holding out since before dawn. The division's 185th Brigade moved off toward Caen at approximately noon, but when almost within sight of the city, they were met with a counterattack by panzergrenadiers of 21st Panzer Division and stopped near Lebisey Wood. The failure to capture Caen on the first day would have far-reaching consequences.

Juno Beach

Centered upon the village of Courseulles-sur-Mer, Juno Beach was narrowed by offshore rocks that constricted the seaward approach. The landing area was defended by Richter's 716th Division, which was well equipped with eleven batteries of 155-mm guns and nine batteries of 75-mm guns. *Widerstandnesten,* or resistance nests, guarded St-Aubin, Bernières, and Courseulles. Preliminary bombings failed to destroy most of the German emplacements; however, two of the defending battalions were *Ost* troops from Russia and Poland. Although stiffened by their German officers and NCOs, they were third-rate troops. The 3rd Canadian Division's first wave landed at 07:49 and took dreadful casualties while they advanced to the protection of the sea wall. The beachfront pillboxes sprayed withering machine-gun and cannon fire. The arrival of the 'DD'[2] tanks provided the infantry the cover and firepower necessary to overcome small arms and machine-gun resistance. Strongpoints were eliminated by tank and grenade. The Canadians dealt with the beachfront defenses and pushed inland over open ground on either side of Courseulles.

The Canadian's objective was to move inland, capturing Carpiquet Airfield west of Caen. The landing of additional units led to congestion on the beaches and a delayed start toward Carpiquet. Although the division made the greatest progress inland of any of the invasion forces, the airfield was not taken, and the failure would contribute to later difficulties in capturing Caen.

Gold Beach

British 50th (Northumbrian) Division landed on the low-lying coast between Asnelles and Ver-sur-Mer, where enemy resistance was concentrated on the two extremities. The division was augmented by additional armored and infantry brigades as well as the No 47 Royal Commando, whose mission was to capture Port-en-Bessin and link with the Americans coming from Omaha Beach.

The first wave landed at 07:25, and although the 1st Hampshire met with stiff resistance on the western-most 'Jig' sector, the beaches were quickly cleared. The main delay was from German strongpoints at Le Hamel. Elsewhere the division advanced swiftly inland, flanking and finally taking Le Hamel by mid-afternoon. The main German reserves in the area were *Kampfgruppe* Meyer stationed near Bayeux. Their divisional commander, Generalleutnant Dietrich Kraiss, sent the unit chasing the false paratroop landing reports before recalling it toward the beach invasion; it spent the day marching instead of fighting. By the evening of 6 June, the British had landed 25,000 men and had moved inland an average of 10 km. Bayeux was captured without resistance the next day.

Omaha Beach

The landing force at Omaha Beach started transferring from transports to landing craft at 02:20. Whipped by a strong northwest wind the sea, was rough, but by 05:30 the first LCTs[3] carrying sixty-four DD tanks were crossing the 5.5 km of open sea. Behind them came fifty LCVPs[4] carrying fifteen hundred infantry of the 1st Division and attached units of the 29th Division. The tidal beach and dominant bluff were as heavily defended with concrete positions – including blockhouses, trench lines, tobruks, mines, and barbed wire – manned by the static 716th Division but strengthened by elements of the more experienced 352nd Division to a total of

---

[2] The Duplex Drive or DD swimming Sherman tank consisted of a collapsible canvas shield to provide buoyancy and a secondary gearbox and propeller system for propulsion. Other special purposes tanks were designed for detonating mines (flails), laying collapsible bridges, flame throwing (crocodiles), and for throwing huge explosive packages against blockhouses (petards).

[3] Landing Craft, Tank

[4] Landing Craft, Vehicle or Personnel

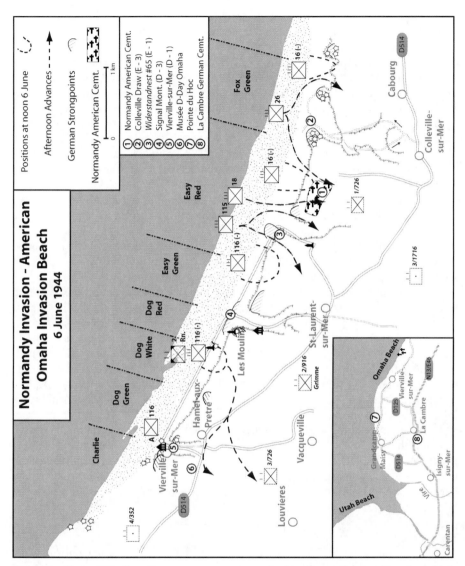

Normandy Invasion - American
Omaha Invasion Beach
6 June 1944

Positions at noon 6 June
Afternoon Advances - - - -
German Strongpoints
Normandy American Cemt.

1 Normandy American Cemt.
2 Colleville Draw (E - 3)
3 Widerstandnest #65 (E - 1)
4 Signal Mont. (D - 3)
5 Vierville-sur-Mer (D - 1)
6 Musée D-Day Omaha
7 Pointe du Hoc
8 La Cambre German Cemt.

eight battalions. The first German response was the battery at Port-en-Bessin, which opened fire at 05:30, quickly followed by other batteries.

The allied naval task force started to fire at every German battery and blockhouse at 05:50. The Americans hoped to retain some element of surprise and therefore limited the preliminary naval bombardment to forty minutes. The cloud and dust raised by the naval bombardment obscured the formidable defenses at Omaha Beach, making targeting difficult. Shortly after 07:00, while the landing craft approached the beach thirty minutes behind schedule, German units received orders to hold fire until the invaders touched the shore. When the first boat ramp fell into the water, machine guns burst into action, swinging back and forth in arcs of interlocking fire. The first wave of 1,450 men was annihilated.

The DD tanks were launched from their LCTs but almost immediately started to flounder in the heavy seas. Only five of the thirty-two vehicles supporting 116th Regiment reached the beach, and the regimental armor transported in the DUKWs[5] were lost, depriving the infantry of much-needed firepower. Many of the landing craft were swamped, discharged their men in water too deep, or were struck by accurate German mortar and machine-gun fire. Some units suffered the loss of their entire command structure. Those who reached dry sand cowered behind beach obstacles, the fortunate ones behind the sea wall. With radios destroyed, demolition equipment lost, and officers killed, Omaha was becoming a disaster. The tide was coming in, shortening the beach.

At 08:30, Lieutenant General Omar Bradley, commanding American forces, contemplated shifting the landings to Utah because of the strong enemy resistance and congestion. Determination to survive slowly drove individual soldiers to band together to infiltrate between strongpoints, conquer them, and gain the high ground between the well-defended beach exits. The official military plan was a disaster; the men, led by junior officers and NCOs, made their own invasion.

At approximately the same time, while the first reports were reaching offshore command vessels, men of the elite 2nd Rangers Battalion reached the top of the bluff. The narrow lodgments expanded, eventually wedging between the German strongpoints. The Germans were being outflanked. By 11:00, Vierville was captured, and by afternoon men were starting to encounter the *bocage,* the network of small, brush-edged fields particular to Normandy, that was to bedevil the advance in the weeks to come. By evening the beachhead was 3,650 meters wide but only 900 meters deep, and the American positions were isolated pockets without artillery or long-range communications.

Command decisions contributed significantly to the near collapse at Omaha. The assault upon the most heavily defended of the landing beaches was a direct frontal attack; the DD tanks were dropped off too far from land and into water too deep; the infantry had been held on the bobbing craft for too long, making the overburdened men seasick; and the naval and aerial bombardments proved to be ineffective.

Utah Beach

Despite landing 2 km east of their targeted landing site but only minutes after the scheduled time of 06:30, 2nd Battalion, 8th Regiment of the US 4th Division became the first American seaborne troops in France. In contrast to what would later occur at Omaha, they found Utah Beach lightly defended. Naval and air bombardments had cut German communications lines and battered the few positions so that the landing was immediately successful, with only one hundred ninety-seven casualties. Simultaneous landings of army and navy demolition teams made possible the detonating of charges against obstacles, consisting mainly of steel and concrete

---

[5] DUKW: a six-wheel-drive amphibious truck capable of traveling over land or water

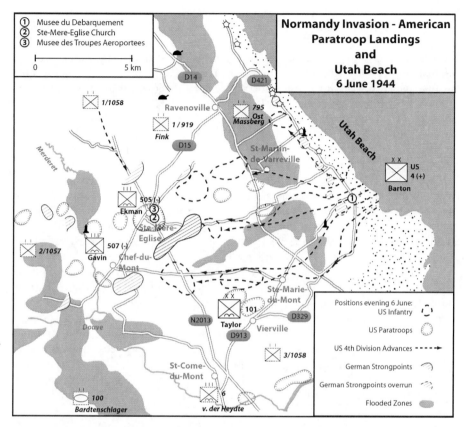

Musee du Debarquement
Ste-Mere-Eglise Church
Musee des Troupes Aeroportees

0   5 km

**Normandy Invasion - American
Paratroop Landings
and
Utah Beach
6 June 1944**

Positions evening 6 June:
US Infantry
US Paratroops
US 4th Division Advances
German Strongpoints
German Strongpoints overrun
Flooded Zones

pikes, steel tetrahedra, and hedgehogs. A link with the 101st Airborne holding the causeways was quickly established, and the 4th Division moved inland.

The Germans

The most notable German response to the D-Day landing was their lack of response. Believing the weather to be unsuitable for an invasion, Rommel had left for Germany to celebrate his wife's birthday, and General Dollman had scheduled war games in Rennes, to which many unit commanders had already departed. Although intercepted messages had caused the German Fifteenth Army, responsible for Pas-de-Calais, to be on alert, the Seventh Army in Normandy was not, although the paratroop landing caused General of Artillerie Erich Marcks to alert his LXXXIV Corps at approximately 01:00.

Generalfeldmarschall Rundstedt made repeated requests early on to OKW[6] headquarters for the release of panzers reserves; however, Generaloberst Alfred Jodl,

---

[6] OKW: *Oberkommando der Wehrmacht* – directed operations for all branches of the German Armed Forces (OKH: *Oberkommando des Heeres* – German Army High Command, whose authority diminished in favor of the OKW as the war progressed.)

the OKW Chief of Staff, refused to wake a sleeping Hitler to obtain the Führer's personal approval as required. Rundstedt nevertheless sent the 12th SS Panzer Division to assemble east of Caen. Normandy Reserves, in the form of the strong 21st Panzer Division, was gripped by some degree of indecision in the absence of its commander, who was said to be with his mistress in Paris. Not until five hours after the first paratroop landings were orders given for deployment against the British landings at Sword and Juno beaches. Later in the day the Panzer Grenadier Regiment Nr 192 successfully penetrated the gap between Sword and Juno beaches, reaching the coast and giving British commanders some uneasy moments; however, the failure of the 22nd Panzer Regiment's tanks to run the gauntlet of British and Canadian antitank guns and Hawker Typhoon aircraft forced the infantry's withdrawal.

In the early afternoon, OKW responded to Rundstedt by releasing the 12th Panzer, the elite Panzer Lehr, and the 17th SS Panzer Grenadier Division as 1st SS Panzer Corps, commanded by one of Hitler's favorites, SS Obergruppenführer Josef 'Sepp' Dietrich. The latter two units, however, were scattered across western France, and their movement toward the invasion front was greatly disrupted by allied air attacks and French Résistance demolition of bridges and communications.

By day's end, the landings at four of the five beaches were secure. Only at Omaha Beach did American troops continue to hang on precariously. Approximately one hundred fifty thousand men had landed at a moderate cost of nine thousand casualties. The beaches were not linked, and the British had failed to take a main D-Day objective of Caen. The Germans had fortunately been unable to mount a serious counterattack, and Rommel's direction 'to beat off the enemy on the coast and to fight the battle in the more or less strongly fortified coastal strip'[7] was not fulfilled. The Allies continued to feed German doubts that Normandy was even the main invasion, still presenting information that the main landing would be in Pas-de-Calais.

Battlefield Tour

The British invasion beaches are along a 30-km stretch of oceanfront, from the mouth of the Orne River to the heights east of Arromanches. Some sections were essentially barred to landings because of steep cliff faces such as at Lion-sur-Mer. Most, however, were sandy beaches with vacation cottages or fishing villages marking outlets of the many streams draining Normandy. The ground rose island gradually, ideal for the variety of multipurpose vehicles known as 'Hobart's Funnies' from 79th Armored Division; however, the buildings and seawalls also offered the Germans opportunities for the construction of strongpoints. Queen Sector of Sword Beach consisted of a wide, sandy beachfront, with the eastern shoulder guarded by high ground running along the Orne River. Juno Beach landings, where the beaches rose gradually from the water, were more impacted by offshore reefs than onshore terrain. Gold Beach was edged by low dunes backed by boggy wetlands. Once through the narrow seafront developments, the land consisted of open plowed fields.

---

[7] Rommel, *The Rommel Papers*, 455.

West of Arromanches, the cliffs rose again and continued for 12 km to the eastern limits of Omaha beach. The landing zone was almost 10 km long and terminated at each end with cliffs. The sand beach was narrow and covered with a thick layer of slippery pebbles known as 'shingle.' Inland was a steep, 50-meter high ridgeline. Utah Beach was approximately 2 km long and consisted of gently sloping sand before the 1- to 3-meter high sea wall. Behind the dunes were the flat lowlands subjected to German flooding.

Yellow sign in the British zone identifies the *'Overlord-L'Assaut'*; purple signs at Omaha beach follow the *D-Day Le Choc* route to Carentan. Almost every village and seafront protuberance seems to have a memorial, bunker, or other identified site – possibly as many as three hundred such in Normandy. More detailed listings can be obtained from locally available tourist guides.

Start the tour in the city of Caen.

Caen

An ancient city of major proportions, Caen sat upon the transportation and communications nexus for much of Normandy and other routes toward Paris. The Orne River, which passes through the city, was the major obstacle between the Normandy invasion beaches and the strong German Fifteenth Army guarding the Pas-de-Calais. For those reasons it was a primary D-Day objective for Montgomery's army.

Allied aircraft first struck German installations in the city of 60,000 inhabitants on the morning of 6 June, bombing barracks and river bridges. The resulting fires burned for eleven days, destroying whole districts of the city. Confusion and paranoia led to eighty French civilians being executed by the Germans as saboteurs. Caen's real martyrdom, however, was to come days later, when British forces, unable to penetrate German defenses, ordered a massive bombing of the city's northern section. The destruction was complete yet fruitless because the bombs fell behind the German lines, creating a desolate city whose ruins later provided the Germans with excellent shelter. Caen was not captured until 19 July, when British forces struggled against strong panzer divisions. The Germans shelled the allied-held city until pushed beyond artillery range one month later.

Caen, one of the most historic cities in France, is known as the home of William the Conqueror. Signs in the city center indicate the 'Château Garage' underground parking, which is conveniently at the Porte St-Pierre entrance to the Château de Caen. William constructed the **citadel** in the center of the city, which was repeatedly enlarged over the centuries. The château was massively damaged during the 1944 bombings and now presents ramparts, the Porte des Champs, a moat, and the outlines of the foundations of the donjon. An elevator provides access to a raised terrace for views over the château ruins and sections of the city.

William was buried in the **Église St-Étienne**, the parish church for the *Abbaye-aux-Hommes,* which he founded in 1077. Since it was not completed until the 13th century, the architecture is a mixture of Romanesque and Gothic styles. The interior stonework reflects the 12th century Norman style, supplemented by Gothic elements especially in the ambulatory and radiating chapels. The structure was used as a shelter for the citizens who did not evacuate during the battle for the city. Fortunately, it survived relatively unscathed.

The Abbaye-aux-Hommes monastery buildings can be toured by entering through the Hôtel de Ville. The warming room, chapter house, sacristy, and other rooms can be visited; the cloisters and the view of the church from them are not to be missed. Views of the exterior are best from the east side of the place Louis-Guillouard, where the ruins of the old St-Etienne are also located. Open daily from 09:30 to 11:00 and 14:30 to 16:00. Fee.

Memorials to the British and Canadian liberators as well as the military and civilians who suffered German occupation dot the city. Walking the streets between the Abbaye-aux-Homme and the ruins of the ancient castle, commemoration steles are frequent. Maps of their specific locations can be obtained at the tourist office, which is located down the rue St-Jean from the Porte St-Pierre.

For an understanding of the battle of Normandy, including the D-Day landing, visit the **Musée le Mémorial de Caen**. The modern building stands upon the site of General Richter's personal bunker. The museum displays photos and objects from the occupation and liberation of Normandy. The 35-minute film on D-Day uses a very effective split screen to contrast the allied and German preparations before the actual invasion. More of a peace memorial than a war museum, le Mémorial de Caen also addresses the late 20th century issues of the Cold War and the terror of nuclear warfare. Large dedicated gardens offer contemplative space. The large bookstore provides additional tourist materials and histories of the battle. The memorial is north of the city, on esplanade General Dwight Eisenhower, and is well-signed as '*Le Mémorial*'; take exit #6 from the ring road (Périphérique / E48 / N814). Open every day 11 February through 11 November from 09:00 to 19:00; open daily except Mondays 12 November through December from 09:30 to 18:00; closed 25 December and January through 10 February. Fee and handicap accessible.

Leave the Caen ring road (E46) at exit #3 toward Ouistreham (D515). After 7.6 km, exit toward Bénouville (D514). Proceed through the village, cross the Caen Canal (Pegasus Bridge), and turn left in place du Commandant Kieffer onto avenue Major John Howard toward the museum parking area ahead on the right.

Pegasus Bridge

At 22:56 on 5 June, six Halifax bombers towing Horsa gliders left Tarrant Rushton Airfield in Dorset, England, on a dangerous, even foolhardy assignment. The one hundred eighty men of the 2nd Oxfordshire and Buckinghamshire Light Infantry were to land on a moonlit night in German-occupied France to capture two bridges that were critical to the success of the invasion. The Bénouville Bridge over the Caen Canal and the Ranville Bridge over the Orne River were strategically important because they were the only crossings along the coast road north of Caen. They were guarded by fifty men, mainly eastern European enlisted men commanded by German officers and NCOs, of the Grenadier Regiment Nr 736.

The lead glider cast off its towline at 00:07, when it crossed the Norman coastline. The mission was simple: capture the bridges and hold them until relieved. Navigating only by stopwatch, compass, and airspeed, the glider pilots performed a remarkable feat of flying, bringing the first three craft down at 00:16 in a boggy field just meters away from the east end of the bridge and the antitank pillbox. In quick succession grenades were tossed through the apertures on the machine-gun pillbox across the road, and a burst of fire killed one bridge sentry – but not before he had fired a warning Very flare. German troops in slit trenches on both sides of the canal jumped into action, but quick bursts from Sten guns and a few grenades ended their resistance. Meanwhile, the Ranville Bridge, 400 meters to the east, was taken against only nominal opposition.

A panzer engineering company moved to retake the bridges. Arriving in Bénouville at approximately 01:30, the lead Mark IV tank was ignited by a British PIAT,[8] and the massive explosion of fuel and ammunition convinced the Germans that they were facing a much stronger force, thus delaying their attack. The formidable 125th Panzer Regiment, commanded by Oberst Hans von Luck, was stymied, first awaiting orders from headquarters, which was then undergoing heavy naval bombardment.

At approximately 13:00, announced by the blowing of bagpipes, Lord Lovat and his 1st Special Brigade reinforcements arrived, accompanied by Churchill tanks. The bridges were now secure, and the Bénouville Bridge would afterward be known as 'Pegasus Bridge' after the airborne division's flying horse emblem. Despite the early success, the British would not advance more than 5 km past the bridge toward Caen, while fighting swirled around the intervening French villages.

A path leads from the parking area to the bridge. The original **Pegasus Bridge** was replaced in 1994 by an upgraded, wider and longer version that retained the original shape. The German antitank position is still on the east side of the bridge along the water's edge, near where the gliders landed. Amidst the swampy ground southeast of the bridge, a path connects the three **stone lectern-like monuments** on the actual glider landing sites. Each monument bears a plaque naming the officers and men that landed there. The glider that landed nearest the bridge contained Major Howard, and a bust of him commemorates the occasion. On the banks of the canal, just above the first of the glider tablets is a stone table of orientation showing the location of the antitank cannon, café, and three glider landing spots with respect to the canal and bridge. Nearer to the canal bridge is the first of ten Signal Monuments, erected at strategic sites by Comité du Débarquement, the French agency created in 1946 to foster commemoration of the events in Normandy. On each monument is inscribed, 'Here, on June 6th 1944, the heroism of the Allied Forces liberated Europe.' This **Signal Monument** specifically states, '6 June 1944 – the banks of the Orne the first parts of France are liberated by the allied forces.'

The small café on the left across the bridge is still owned by descendants of the Gondrée family, who were the proprietors on 6 June. It claims to be the first

---

[8] PIAT: Projector Infantry Anti Tank weapon fired a high explosive charge, but was also heavy, difficult to aim, hard to arm, and with a limited effective range of 50 meters.

liberated building in France and became known as 'Pegasus Café.' Madame Gondrée, a trained nurse, assisted British medics while the café became a first aide post. Monsieur Gondrée was helpful in his own way by digging up the ninety-nine bottles of champagne that he had buried in his garden in 1940, when the Germans approached. The tank across the road is a Centaur/Cromwell which landed at la Bréche d'Hermanville.

Return to the parking area of the **Mémorial Pegasus,** which contains artifacts from the taking of Pegasus Bridge and other engagements of the British 6th Airborne Division in the area. Many items were collected over the years by the Gondrée family, augmented by contributions of the participants, including Major Howard. The original steel girder bridge is now located on the grounds of the Pegasus Museum. The dent in the side of the original bridge was made by a German bomb dropped to destroy the captured bridge. The bomb was a dud and fell harmlessly into the canal. The grounds also hold an original Bailey bridge and other vehicles. The Horsa glider is a full size replica. Open daily February and March, October and November from 10:00 to 13:00 and 14:00 to 17:00; April through September from 09:30 to 18:30; closed December and January. Fee.

Return through Bénouville and enter the ramp to the main highway toward Ouistreham (D514). Continue for 2.4 km to the roundabout (Rond-Point de la Paix); D514 goes to the left; however, continue straight into Ouistreham (D84), through the place du général Charles de Gaulle, and bear left (rue des Dunes) just before the ferry port entrance. Continue where the road curves to the left (boulevard Maritime) and park opposite avenue de la Plage.

Sword Beach

The port of Ouistreham and the entrance to the Caen Canal were protected by a German strongpoint known as the Casino, so called because of the *Casino de Ouistreham* demolished by the Germans to make way for the defensive emplacements. Farther east and positioned at the shoulder of the canal entrance was a German battery of 155-mm guns. German defensive positions in the form of machine guns and antitank guns guarded the beachfront to the west. No 4 Commando, strengthened by two French troops commanded by capitaine de corvette Philippe Kieffer, was in the second landing wave behind the 2nd East Yorkshires. Kieffer, although wounded during the landing, led his men among the seaside villas of Riva Bella against the Casino strongpoint until they came up against effective fire from a German 88-mm gun. Kieffer scampered back to the road, where he solicited the assistance of a British tank. The German gun was quickly silenced, and the position taken.

The British Commandos moved farther east along the Lion-sur-Mer Road (now D514) to attack the battery from the rear. One of the British troop leaders was Major R Porteous, who had been awarded the Victoria Cross for his actions attacking the Hess Battery during the Dieppe Raid. Gunfire kept the Germans' heads down while the commandos rushed over planks conveniently left across the antitank ditch and overcame the gun pits in succession. When the gun emplacements were reached, the commandos found to their amazement that the guns had been removed and replaced with telephone poles. The German inland observation tower called down artillery fire on the small group, causing serious casualties.

No 4 Commando then completed their assignment by moving through the fields and forests to reinforce the paratroopers holding Pegasus Bridge, which was still under fire from German snipers and machine guns on both sides of the canal. The expected strong German response never came, and the men settled down for an uneasy night.

Many of the houses in this area were destroyed by the Germans to provide lines of fire for the gun emplacements. They, as well as the modern ferry facilities to the east, have been rebuilt. Just over the dunes to the north, however, and parallel to boulevard Maritime, a **pleasant promenade** now runs along the beachfront that was lined with German machine-gun positions. Between the road and the water, bunkers still remain, although they are now largely covered by shifting sand and dune grass. From the roofs of the artificial hills, the water is nearly 0.5 km across flat open sand, explaining why these positions had to be eliminated from the rear.

Down the now tree-lined avenue de la Plage, the prominent element at this site is the five-story concrete observation and control tower, known today as '*Le Grand Bunker.*' In 1944, the area was dominated by this 16-meter high flak and observation tower. The buildings between it and the sea had been cleared, except for, ironically, the residence immediately in front of the bunker. From its roofs, the Germans lobbed grenades on Major Porteous' men, while the lightly armed commandos were helpless against the 3-meter thick concrete walls. The shells of their heaviest weapon, the antitank PIAT, failed as well. Although temporarily silenced on D-Day by the commandos, the tower was not captured and remained a threat until 9 June, when four Canadian engineers blew open the armored entrance door, and the fifty-two man garrison surrendered.

The museum entrance is guarded by a German 88-mm gun of the type Kieffer's men faced. The machine-gun emplacements protecting the entrance demonstrate the difficulty in capturing such a position. The six floors of rooms present the facility as it appeared on 6 June, including a telephone exchange, dormitory, infirmary, armory, and the observation post – each a filled with artifacts demonstrating the room's function. The top floor allows a 180-degree view over Sword Beach through a wartime stereo-telescope, which helps orient the visitor to D-Day sites. The museum is dedicated to the Atlantic Wall and contains numerous photographs and documents pertaining to its construction and the life of German occupation troops. Open daily from February through December from 10:00 to 18:00; extended hours from April through September from 09:00 to 19:00. Fee.

Return to boulevard Maritime and continue west for approximately 750 meters; the road changes its name to boulevard du Commandant Kieffer, then to boulevard Aristide Briand.

'The Flame' monument commemorates the landing of French Commandos led by Commandant Kiefer. The tall, steel sculpture resembles tongues of fire and rests upon a rotating machine-gun cupola. The stones at its base bear the names of the commandos killed in the operation. Approximately 1.4 km farther on the left is avenue du 4éme Commando, at the far end of which is a **statue of Field Marshall Bernard Montgomery**. On the beachfront just ahead is a bas-relief commemorating the **landing site of No 4 Commando** at the western edge of 'Queen Red' beach. Directly opposite the stone is an ivy-covered **German blockhouse,** the gun embrasures of which were aligned to fire down the beach.

Continue west; the road joins the main highway (D514) which passes through the seaside villages of Sword, Juno, Gold, and Omaha beaches.

Although the driving may be more tedious than the high speed Caen-Bayeux-Carentan Highway (E46 / N13), the route provides greater opportunities to view the battle zone terrain, numerous monuments and memorials, and the stunning Norman villages. Many of the communities are simple farming villages without tourist amenities, especially those farther west; a variety of cafés, restaurants, and museums exist to satisfy a visitor's needs.

In la Bréche d'Hermanville, turn toward the sea on the rue du 6 Juin (D60B).

The **place du Curasse Courbet**, in front of the tourist office, contains several monuments, including the large red-and-black triangle of the British 3rd Division, who landed on Sword beach. Unlike the landings at Colleville-sur-Orne – renamed Colleville-Montgomery, the field marshal being honored by having his name added to the village's after the war – where the 2nd East Yorkshire Regiment met stiff resistance and suffered numerous casualties, the South Lancashire Regiment landing here had few difficulties, and Hermanville farther inland was cleared by 10:00.

Highway (D514) curves away from the water to circle around Lion-sur-Mer and then returns closer to the water near the western edge of the town.

British No 41 Commando landed at 08:45 near Hermanville with the mission to move around Lion-sur-Mer and join with No 46 and No 48 Commando coming from Juno Beach. The German resistance was stiff, their final positions not taken until the evening of 7 June. Just after the roundabout (D221), a group of memorials commemorate the events. Most prominent is a steel, pointed **sundial memorial to No 41 Commando**. At its base is a plaque recalling events of 6 June and an extract from President Franklin Roosevelt's 'Four Freedoms' speech. Adjacent is a **Churchill AVRE** (Armored Vehicle Royal Engineers) tank of the type used by armored support units.

Continue west (D514) through Luc-sur-Mer and Langrune-sur-Mer to the center of Aubin-sur-Mer.

Juno Beach

St-Aubin-sur-Mer was on the eastern edge of the Juno Beach section codenamed 'Nan Red' and is notable for the beachfront pillbox in the place des Canadiens which retains its 50-mm antitank gun and was part of the network of minefields, wire entanglements, trenches, and roadblocks that formed *Widerstandnest* #27. German riflemen poured fire down upon the North Shore Regiment of Canada as its men scrambled across 100 meters of open beach to the shelter of the sea wall. The stronghold fell to the fire of a Churchill tank, the 290-mm demolition gun of which hurled forty-pound shaped charges against the concrete walls while antitank guns battered it from the rear. Two Fort Garry Horse tanks added to the pounding before white flags appeared. Adjacent memorials commemorate the landings of the **North Shore Regiment**, The Fort Garry Horse (armored), and No 48 Commando. The latter stele occupies the position of a well-fortified group of houses which was overcome, taking thirty-one prisoners.

Continue west (D514). Upon entering **Bernières-sur-Mer**, turn right on any one of several streets to access the seafront Promenade des Français. Turn left to continue proceeding west, noting the tobruks built into the seawall.

This beach was designated as 'Nan White' and was the landing site of the Queen's Own Rifles of Canada Regiment and the tanks of the 10th Armored Regiment (Fort Garry Horse). The houses and strongpoints of Bernières were silent while the landing craft approached, only to erupt with machine-gun, mortar, and antitank fire when the ramps dropped, shredding B Company when it attempted to cross the sand. Casualties to the unit soon totaled fifty percent. Almost miraculously, a misdirected landing craft struck a quiet stretch of beach. The platoon immediately went inland and attacked the strongpoint from the rear. The defenders soon surrendered.

In the **place du Canada**, a pillbox that greeted the Queen's Own Rifles of Canada, one of five of *Widerstandnest* #28, still remains. The site, called 'La Cassine' by the Canadians, was one of strong resistance. The bunker holds memorial plaques to several other units, including the Fort Garry Horse and Regiment de la Chaudière of Canada, a unit formed by French-speaking Canadians.

The next location is 250 meters west and can be reached by car or on foot. By car, turn left on rue du Queens Own Rifles of Canada, then right to regain the highway (D514), and then shortly right again into **place du 6 June**.

A **Signal Monument** adjacent to the 'Maison du Queen's Own Rifles of Canada' has a metal plaque which states:

This house was liberated at first light on D-Day 6 June 1944 by the men of the Queen's Own Rifles of Canada, who were the first Canadians to land on this beach. It may very well have been the first house on French soil liberated by sea-borne allied forces. Within sight of this house over one hundred men of the Queen's Own Rifles were killed or wounded in the first few minutes of the landing.

Both St-Aubin-sur-Mer and Bernières-sur-Mer provide opportunities to see dramatic **Norman village churches**. To find the church in Aubin, turn south at the pillbox (rue Canet), right on rue du maréchal Foch, and then a quick left on rue de l'Abbé Bossard. In Bernières, west of place du 6 June, turn left from the D514 onto rue du Royal Berkshire Regiment, then turn left toward Bény-sur-Mer (D79a). The 13th century bell tower is easily seen from much of the town.

Return to the highway (D514) and continue west into Courseulles-sur-Mer. Follow the highway (rue de la Mer) and continue straight to the waterfront (place du général de Gaulle).

On the eastern side of the Seulles River estuary is the wooden, sword-in-a-stone **monument to the Royal Winnipeg Rifles,** who landed in this section of 'Mike Red' Beach. An example of a **Sherman DD tank** is also there; this one was sunk during the run toward the beach, only to be recovered twenty-seven years later and restored. The side of the tank has a row of regimental plaques from units involved in the landings. Directly across from the tank is a 50-mm antitank gun that occupies the site of what was a tobruk. The flag-surrounded mount holds a stele commemorating **général Charles de Gaulle's return to French soil** on 14 June 1944. On a brass plaque affixed to the rear of the monument is de Gaulle's famous 18 June 1940 speech that he gave via radio from London after the collapse of French resistance to the German invasion.

Proceed inland along the river (quai des Allies) to the bridge across the river (Pont de Goldbach / D514). Follow the signs to the Juno Beach Centre.

The **Juno Beach Centre** stands west of the outlet of the Seulles River. The beach in front of the Juno Centre was identified as 'Mike Red' and was assigned to B and D Companies of the Royal Winnipeg Rifles. B Company was on the left to secure the bank of the Seulles River, where a pillbox scythed landing parties on the beach to the west. The dunes held five concrete blockhouses and numerous concrete emplacements. Four DD tanks of the 1st Hussars landed in the area and immediately came under artillery fire. While Captain John Powell directed his Sherman through the beach obstacles, a 50-mm shell ripped through the gun. Armed with only a machine gun, Powell steered directly toward the pillbox, killing the crew and earning a Military Cross. Fearlessly exposing himself to the enemy, Captain Phil Gower coordinated his infantry in attacks against one strongpoint after another, eventually silencing the all, and also earning Gower a Military Cross. D Company met little opposition and was able to reach the dunes relatively unscathed. Using bangalore torpedoes, they cut a gap in the tangles of barbed wire to exit the beachfront.

Juno Beach Centre is noted for the architecture of its building, six sections of which represent Juno, Gold, Omaha, Utah, Sword and Canada connected in a star fashion around the center that houses the reception area. In front of the Centre entrance is a unique sculpture of soldiers with blank faces wearing the traditional British-style helmet, their bodies rising out of a single mass. The museum's rooms cover the invasion of Normandy and the entire Canadian participation in the war, both on the home front and in Europe. In a hallway, the names of the 45,000 Canadian soldiers that were killed in the Second World War are slowly projected across the curved ceiling. The plaque nearby says that it takes 13 ½ hours for all of the names to appear. Open April through September from 09:30 to 19:00; March and October from 10:00 to 18:00; February, November and December from 10:00 to 13:00 and 14:00 to 17:00; closed in January and on 25 December. Fee.

Between the museum and the sea are the **German bunkers** attacked during the landing. In 1944, the dune was narrower, and the defensive structures were closer to the sea and could be reached by the waves at high spring tide. The bunkers were located every 500 meters along the beach, providing overlapping fire, and housed antitank guns varying from 50-mm to the formidable 88-mm cannon positioned at the entrance to the port. One-meter stone blocks set in the ground indicate the path of a tunnel that linked the seaside observation bunker to bunkers farther inland at the site of the Juno Centre. The blocks lead to a bunker sitting near the water that has been pitched sideways at a 35-degree angle by the undermining action of the waves.

Return to the highway (D514) and continue west.

Gold Beach

The seawalls in **Ver-sur-Mer** and **Asnelles** hold large German gun emplacements, but they are less interesting than those already viewed. This does not detract from the numerous memorials in both villages. If desired, the avenue du Colonel Harper, named after the commander of 2nd Battalion Hertfordshire Regiment, in Ver-sur-Mer and rue du Débarquement in Asnelles provide access to the waterfront. Turn left in both instances to proceed to the blockhouses.

The highway (D514) passes inland of the small village of St-Côme-de-Fresné, which was the western limit of the British invasion beaches. The road ascends the ridge which separates St-Come from Arromanches. At the summit is a parking area that requires a small fee.

The cliffs had a commanding **view of Gold Beach** to the east and therefore contained German bunkers which were destroyed before the invasion by British naval fire. The field also contains the pyramid-shaped concrete foundations of a **German Würzburg radar station**. An allied air raid weeks before the invasion destroyed the installation, rendering the Germans blind to the approaching sea armada. Atop the intact German blockhouse is a much-abused **table of orientation**.

The esplanade du général d'armée aérienne Michel Fourquet, named after the commander of the Free French Air Force, leads to the **Cinéma Circulaire Arromanches 360 Cinema**. The cinema uses multiple projectors to present an eighteen-minute film on the events of 6 June, especially those at Arromanches, on a 360-degree screen. Open daily June through August from 09:40 to 18:40; April, May, September and October from 10:10 to 17:40; February, March, November and December from 10:10 to 17:10; closed January. All presentations are at 10 and 40 minutes past the hour. Fee.

The sea cliffs between Gold and Omaha Beaches were unsuitable for amphibious landings, but the fishing port of Arromanches provided interior access for vehicles. The harbor was unfortunately not sufficient to accept the volume of men and materiel planned. British planners devised the tactic of transporting pre-manufactured concrete caissons across the channel and constructing temporary port facilities codenamed 'Mulberry' at Arromanches. Floating roadways were attached to floating docks, and vehicles off-loaded equipment from the ships. The first caissons arrived and were sunk into place on 9 June. By 15 June, the facilities were operational and continued until 19 November 1944. A similar harbor was constructed for American use off Omaha Beach, but a violent three-day storm completely destroyed the facility on 19 June. The Americans reverted to small craft to off-load the larger transports and successfully supplied their armies accordingly.

The height in front of the cinema offers a stunning **view of the Arromanches**, the cliffs to its west, and the waves breaking over the remnants of the Mulberry artificial harbor. From this height the village was attacked and captured by the Royal Hampshire Regiment, which had landed at Gold Beach and proceeded overland. Whereas following the path down to the village is possible, driving is preferable. The stele visible part way down the path commemorates a Napoleonic naval battle in the waters near Arromanches in 1811.

Continue west (D514) into Arromanches and follow the signs to the Musée du Débarquement.

On the seafront at low tide a walk among the ruins of the hollow concrete caissons sunk to form a harbor wall is possible. Across the parking area is the popular **Musée du Débarquement**, the entrance of which is guarded by twin 25-pounder guns and which focuses on the construction and operation of the Mulberry Harbors with a diorama, film, and working model. Explanations are trilingual. Open daily February, November and December from 10:00 to 12:30 and 13:30 to 17:00; March, April and October from 09:00 to 12:30 and 13:30 to 18:00; May, June, July and August from 09:00 to 19:00; September 10:00 to 19:00; open later on Sundays; closed Christmas holidays and January. Fee.

Return to the highway (D514) and follow into the village of Longues-sur-Mer. Turn right (D104) and continue to the access road to the Longues Battery.

Longues Battery held four 155-mm Czech naval guns set in reinforced concrete casemates and directed by a multistory concrete observation post on the edge of the cliff. The battery was relatively unscathed by the tons of bombs dropped before the invasion. During the initial naval bombardment, Longues Battery engaged in a duel with the British cruiser *HMS Ajax,* which was 11 km offshore. British naval fire struck close enough to the casemates that the blasts drove the gunners from two of the four positions. In a third casemate, a naval shell appears to have struck the gun's breech, destroying it. The resulting explosion ripped through the casemate's lower floors, igniting the stored ammunition, killing all of its crew, and blasting the casemate apart. The fourth gun recommenced firing in the afternoon but was quickly silenced by a French cruiser.

One of the better sites along the coast, the battery's four reinforced-concrete, earth-embanked casemates still contain their Czech guns. Their weapons rooms and rear storage rooms can be explored, except for those of the heavily damaged third casemate. Remnants of ammunition storage bunkers, barracks, and other facilities are barely discernible in the surrounding fields. Longues Battery produces some of the most dramatic photographs of German defensive emplacements in Normandy. The site is popular, always open, and requires no admission fee.

A path across the field leads to the coast where the battery's multilevel **observation bunker** is located. The lower floor held a direction finder, chart room, and telephone exchange. The upper floor, the one-meter thick, reinforced concrete roof of which is supported by four metal posts, held the range finder. The views from the lower floor are now partially obstructed by new vegetation; however, a rather perilous climb to the upper floor permits views of Gold and Omaha Beaches.

Follow the exit road from the battery parking area and return to the D104, then on to the D514. Turn right toward Port-en-Bessin. Continue for 13 km, passing through Colleville-sur-Mer, and turn right toward Cimetière Américain.

Omaha Beach

The **Normandy American Cemetery and Memorial** is the premier site for all visits to D-Day landing beaches and receives over one million visitors each year. On 6 June 2007, a new visitor's and interpretive center was ceremoniously opened in a discretely hidden wooden site east of the cemetery. The center provides an explanation of Operation 'Overlord' through personal stories, photos, films, and artifacts. All American military cemeteries are open daily from 09:00 to 17:00, except on 25 December and 1 January.

Among its finely manicured lawns and shrubs are buried 9,387 men and women, including 307 which remain unidentified; all but 8 are Americans. The precisely aligned graves are marked with white marble headstones in the shape of the Star of David for those of the Jewish faith or the Latin Cross for all others. Among the graves are those of three Medal of Honor recipients, identified by the gold lettering on their headstones, including that of Brigadier General Theodore Roosevelt

Jr. The rotunda in the center of the graves area is a memorial chapel, and at the far end of the central mall are two Italian granite figures representing the United States and France. General Roosevelt is buried on the outside end of Row 28 in Plot D, next to his brother Lieutenant Quentin Roosevelt, a pilot who died in the First World War and who is the only serviceman from that war buried in a Second World War cemetery. A short distance behind the Roosevelts in Plot F, Row 15 are 2nd Lieutenant Robert Niland and Sergeant Preston Niland, two of the three Niland brothers killed in the same week and who inspired the motion picture *Saving Private Ryan*. Tragically, thirty-eight pairs of brothers are buried in the cemetery. Father and son Colonel Ollie Reed and Lieutenant Ollie Reed J are buried in Plot E, Row 20.

At the eastern end of the cemetery, behind the reflecting pool, is a semicircular memorial with a loggia that houses battle maps of the Western European campaign with inscriptions describing its events. In the center of the open arc is a 7-meter bronze statue representing 'The Spirit of American Youth Rising from the Waves.'

Behind the memorial is the **Garden of the Missing**, upon whose curved walls are 1,557 names of those who gave their lives for their country and whose graves were never located. Included are the Morelands, twin brothers who were both killed on 6 June while serving with the 149th Engineer Combat Battalion. The spaces between the memorial and the wall are landscaped with American Peace rose bushes.

The walk along the sea-facing side of the cemetery was the location of a German slit trench which held numerous machine-gun positions. The waves of the English Channel below crash against the sands of Omaha Beach, the most difficult and deadliest of the landing sites. Strong winds invariably blow inland, providing an appropriate hushed whisper among the pine trees lining the road. Toward the eastern end, a small overlook protrudes from the walkway and provides a view down a steep path to Omaha Beach.

The beach below the cemetery was code-named **'Easy Red'** and was the targeted landing area of the 16th Infantry Regiment, US 1st Division, known as 'The Big Red One.' Whereas most of the landings drifted eastward due to the prevailing current, a mixture of partial companies from the 16th and 116th Regiments landed on 'Easy Red.' The German fire was intense and accurate, ripping the groups of men before they exited their landing craft.

A handful of men from E Company, led by Lieutenant John Spaulding, and elements of G Company, led by Captain Joseph Dawson, both of 16th Regiment were fortunate in landing midway between the heavily defended draws. They were able to get their men across the beach and seawall, through the minefield and swamp, to reach the base of the bluff with few casualties. Finding a faint trail, the men cautiously ascended. The brush that covered the hillside was on fire from the naval bombardment. The smoke and folds of land offered cover for the troops as they climbed. Eliminating a machine-gun nest with two grenades, the men arrived at the bluff top amid enemy soldiers retreating from their trenches. They were the first troops to reach the flat land above the German positions.

While Dawson and Spaulding were ascending the bluff, the 16th Regiment's commander, Colonel George Taylor landed with his staff, crawling through the chaos to the seawall. Taylor said to his staff, 'There are only two kinds of people on this beach; the dead and those about to die. So let's get the hell out of here!'[9] Men like Spaulding and Dawson leading small groups up the bluffs made the invasion successful, not the deadly draws as the generals had directed.

The paved path that goes down the bluff to the beach approximately follows Spaulding's and Dawson's route. Walk down the path to access the beach, and do not be intimidated by the low, bolted gate because it is to keep animals out of the cemetery, not the visitors in. The trek can be arduous, making one wonder how the seasick, terrified young men made it up carrying their 60-pound packs. Driving down to the beach, as described below, may be more desirable.

Return to the cemetery parking area and drive back to the D514. Turn left to enter Colleville-sur-Mer and then left at the sign indicating '*la Plage.*'

The 6.5-km cliff between Colleville and Vierville was broken by five draws created by water running to the sea. Each held a single roadway protected by all the military ingenuity of the German army, and they were the only means of escape from the beachhead for vehicles of any type. To the east of the cemetery is **Colleville Draw,** identified as 'E-3' by military planners. The long, broad draw made a natural killing field for the German resistance nests which flanked its entrance. The narrow road goes down the draw in the opposite direction of the planned American advance. Just above the beach, the one-lane road forks; bear left into an unpaved parking area. A walk down to the water's edge leads to 'Easy Red' beach. Face the bluff and imagine enemy small arms fire, rapid-fire MG 42 machine guns, and antitank weapons firing from the heights.

Approximately two-thirds of the way up the bluff are the fortifications of *Widerstandnest* #62, manned by twenty-eight soldiers of the 3rd Company, Grenadier Regiment Nr 726 plus thirteen soldiers who were artillery spotters from the 352nd Division's battery located 4.5 km inland, near Houtteville. The position consisted of two artillery casemates, each holding Czech 76.5-mm field guns (Model 1917), facing along the beach to the west; five tobruks with either machine guns, 50-mm shell throwers or riflemen; one machine gun bunker; seven open-air positions holding a 50-mm antitank gun, three machine guns, one antiaircraft machine gun, and two flamethrowers. A bunker held a Polish machine gun and flamethrower. The entire position was surrounded by a barbed wire fence; in addition, two barbed wire fences and a water-filled antitank ditch protected approaches from the water.

The walk up to *Widerstandnest* #62 from the beach can be strenuous; the underbrush has been removed, but the path is not paved. Though not steep, it can be rocky and slippery when wet. The best view of the eastern end of Omaha Beach is from the upper bunker, on the roof of which a stele commemorates the **5th Special Engineer Brigade.** Numerous plaques on the stele memorialize engineer units that landed before the infantry, with the special mission to demolish the beach obstacles.

---

[9] Stephen E. Ambrose, *D-Day June 6, 1944: The Climactic Battle of World War II* (New York: Simon & Schuster, 1994), 356.

Behind the upper bunker is a tobruk which still contains the cement mounting-platform that once held its 50-mm mortar. The zigzags in the ground give faint evidence of slit trenches which ran up the hill from the tobruk, past a second tobruk, to the underground barracks bunker, and through to the southwest entrance.

On top of the hill is the pointed **column to the Big Red One**, surrounded by a small brick court. On the three sides of the column are listed the six hundred and twenty-seven members of the US 1st Division who died, their names listed by unit and rank. Five soldiers who received the Medal of Honor for their actions on 6 June and 10 June have their names printed with gold lettering. In the distance is the church in Colleville-sur-Mer. Behind the column is an asphalt pavement that leads 150 meters to the new interpretive center.

On the opposite side of the draw, 320 meters away, was *Widerstandnest* **#61**, where a blockhouse, now on private land, a short distance east of the draw held one of the feared 88-mm guns. It was destroyed by an American tank at 07:10, only a few minutes after the landing began. This section of beach, codenamed 'Fox Green,' is the only one that retains the shingle barrier of oval stones. These stones caused problems for tracked vehicles because they became wedged in the tracks; however, they were the only beach shelter from enemy fire for the landing soldiers.

Return past the US 1st Division obelisk and the cemetery parking area to the D514 highway. Turn right (D514) and after passing the village entrance sign for St-Laurent-sur-Mer, turn right and follow the signs for the '*la Plage*' (rue de Quincangrogne); proceed along what was draw 'E-1.'

Just before the sharp left curve, a casemate is up the hill on the left, and parking is on the right. This nearly intact emplacement still retains its gun, which effectively covered this beach exit. The draw has been obscured significantly by vegetation, but by 10:00 on 6 June, hundreds of men were stuck on this beach among the destroyed landing craft. In front of them, the small Ruquet Valley was protected by *Widerstandnest* **#65**. The blockhouse was hit by fire from an approaching vessel 1 km away and was permanently destroyed by fire from a half-track. Engineers immediately opened this road, and by 15:00, heavy equipment took the first cleared exit from Omaha Beach.

On top of the casemate is a plaque to the **467th Anti-Aircraft Artillery Automatic Weapons Battalion**, who landed on this beach on the morning of 6 June 1944 and suffered heavy casualties while neutralizing this enemy position. In front of the casemate is a simple yet elegant monolith to the **US 2nd Division**, which landed here on 7 June, with Indianhead unit insignia and the words, 'For those who fought and died for freedom, 1944- 1945.'

Continue along the road through Les Moulins, continuing toward Vierville-sur-Mer (D517).

The beaches are obscured by housing and dunes, but the plateau behind the beach is visible on the left. A **Signal Monument** marks 'D-3' Draw in Les Moulins. The side is engraved with symbols of beach barricades as well as men dying among the waves, lying on the beach, and fighting inland. The inscription states, 'Erected in memory of those of the 116th Regiment, 29th Division, who landed here June 6, 1944.'

Continue to Vierville-sur-Mer, to where the road turns inland and where there are two more casemates with parking behind them.

The draw at **Vierville-sur-Mer ('D-1')** was as well-fortified as any position at Omaha protected by *Widerstandnesten* #70 to #73. The machine guns and artillery were in concrete bunkers, capable of subjecting every foot of the beach to flanking crossfire. The strongpoints were connected by deep, narrow trenches. Barracks and ammunitions stores were well placed in bunkers eight meters underground.

'A' Company, 116th Regiment, 29th Division, a unit comprised of men from the Virginia National Guard, was the only unit which landed at their planned location on 'Dog Green' beach. The other units of the regiment's first wave landed farther east, missing their designated beach and leaving A Company to bear the full brunt of German resistance. When the landing craft reached the beach and dropped their ramps, the German positions erupted in a wall of fire. In a few minutes, of the two hundred men of A Company, twenty-two of whom came from the small town of Bedford, Virginia, only eight survived.

The division's assistant commander, Brigadier General Norman Cota, landed a few hundred meters to the east at 07:30. His aide, Lieutenant J Shea described the scene:

> Although the leading elements of the assault had been on the beach for approximately one hour, none had progress [sic] farther than the sea wall at the inland border of the beach. [They] were clustered under the wall, pinned down by machine-gun fire, and the enemy was beginning to bring effective mortar fire to bear on those hidden behind the wall.[10]

Cota realized immediately that the planned movement through the draw was impossible. He personally organized fire on the defenders while bangalores were placed under a belt of barbed wire. The blast opened a narrow passage that allowed Cota and a mixed troop to reach the base of the bluff. The men immediately started to climb to the high ground near Hamel-au-Prêtre, from which they could bring effective fire down upon the German positions.

Cota's small group and a mixed group from 116th Regiment and 5th Rangers Battalion reached the east side of the Vierville Draw. With the help of destroyers

---

[10] Ibid., 339.

firing directly on the pillboxes, position after position was cleared of the enemy. The Germans had erected a massive concrete wall that was four meters thick across the mouth of the Vierville draw. Although repeatedly hit by 14-inch shells from the battleship USS *Texas*, the wall still blocked the exit. The defending infantry was eliminated, and a bulldozer delivered one thousand pounds of TNT that finally destroyed the wall. At 17:00, Vierville draw was open.

The upper casemate near the parking area held a German 88-mm gun that dueled thirty American tanks, knocking many of them out before it was destroyed. A Memorial to the **American National Guard** has been built on top and explains the National Guard system in English and French. It closes with a quotation from President Franklin D. Roosevelt which ends, 'We, and all other who believe [in freedom] as deeply as we do, would rather die on our feet than live on our knees.' The beach below was the landing area for A Company and the men who paid for that freedom.

To the west of the second bunker are three examples of concrete tetrahedron beach obstacles and a short cement pier that goes out over the water, providing a beautiful, waterside view of the landing beaches. The first few steps of the pier are on a remnant of the Mulberry built here to service American forces.

The steeps cliffs west of Vierville block farther waterfront travel and extend all the way to Pointe du Hoc. More gun emplacements (*Widerstandnest #72*) can be seen on the hillside above; one housed a 75-mm cannon and can be reached up a steep, concrete walkway. Above the bunker, very treacherous, steep stone steps set into the side of the hill approach a grass area that provides a wonderful view of Omaha Beach and a partial view of another bunker that is even a little higher. The very dangerous, grassy cliff edge retains impressions of a slit trench.

Follow the road (D517 / avenue de Bedford Virginie, USA) where it turns inland and enters into Vierville Draw.

Between the road and a parallel street, a gray granite block commemorating the **29th Division** marks the location where the regiment's command post was established before the draw was opened. Its inscription starts with, 'From north and south in our land we came that freedom might prevail.' Across the road is a metal plaque on the road embankment wall which says:

> **Ranger 5th Battalion**. On D-Day 6 June 1944 the US 5th Army Ranger Battalion landed on Omaha Beach near Vierville-sur-Mer under intense enemy fire. Responding to General Cota's historic order 'Lead the Way, Rangers' the 5th Ranger Battalion and A, B, and C Companies of 2nd Ranger Battalion advanced against strongly held and defended enemy fortifications.

Turn around and face the 29th Division stone, look up the bluff to find two more machine-gun positions. One is aimed directly across the draw, and the other is aimed inland up the draw.

> Continue up the Vierville draw. The fabrication on the right side of the road is the remains of Mulberry 'A' from Omaha beach. Turn right (D514).

On the right is the **Musée D-Day Omaha**, its presence first identified by the cannon barrel that almost overhangs the highway. This private museum has one of the best weapons collections in Normandy. The Quonset (Nissan) hut building is itself historic because it was once on the beach at the end of the Mulberry and served as an army hospital. It was later moved inland and acquired by the museum owner. German equipment is in abundance including Pak 40s, Quad 50-mm machine guns, automatic flamethrower, Enigma Machine, Goliath miniature, remote-control tank, several range-finding apparatus, and an English motorbike that folds down and fits into a large suitcase. It appears to be all in a jumble, but photographs help to identify the major pieces. Open daily March through May from 10:00 to 12:30 and 14:00 to 18:00; June through September from 09:30 to 19:30; October through 11 November from 10:00 to 12:30 and 14:00 to 18:00. Fee.

> Continue 7 km before turning right toward Pointe du Hoc (D514a). Enter the new parking area.

Pointe du Hoc

German batteries on the spit of land known as Point du Hoc completely enfiladed the Omaha and Utah landing beaches. The battery was constructed in 1942, when six 155-mm guns were placed in open-air pits. The reinforced concrete fire control bunker was later built near the very tip of the point. The site eventually included underground barracks and ammunition stores, antiaircraft-gun positions, and barbed wire and minefields. The garrison numbered two hundred men. Two casemates had been built for the guns, and a third was under construction when a violent bombardment on 15 April 1944 destroyed one of the guns.

From these positions the five remaining guns believed to be on the point could bring annihilating fire on the American landing craft and their support ships at sea. Their capture and elimination were a critical requirement for the success of the invasion. Although the installation was severely bombed and bombarded, especially by the big guns of the battleship USS *Texas*, three companies from 2nd Ranger Battalion were assigned to scale the cliffs and destroy the guns. In the case of their failure, a second Ranger battalion augmented by three additional companies was to land near Vierville and attack the point from the landward side.

One hundred fifty men, led by Lieutenant Colonel James Rudder, used ladders and ropes fired from landing craft-mounted rocket launchers to climb the 36-meter vertical cliffs. Despite the rocket-propelled ropes becoming too heavy from the soaking they took during the run in and the grenades tossed over the cliff edge, most of the rangers climbed in fifteen minutes. They used the numerous shell and bomb craters for cover while they moved against the lightly defended height. While the small Ranger force fought its way across the point, they discovered that the feared guns were only dummies, the actual cannon having been moved to safer positions inland. A patrol eventually found the guns and rendered them useless with thermite grenades. They established a perimeter on the landward side of the site and roadblocks on the Grandcamp-Vierville Road. The strongest resistance came from the critical observation bunker nearest the point. A slit trench housing a machine gun was taken out with three hand grenades; a bazooka round fired through the bunker's firing slit only temporarily silenced the bunker. Unable to destroy the position, the Rangers kept it under fire while the Germans continued with harassing small arms fire. The bunker was not cleared until the next day, when satchel charges were thrown through the entrance.

Whereas they had succeeded in their mission and had already lost one third of their number as casualties, their struggle was not over yet. A few stragglers from other units arrived, but the unit was isolated and under siege, fired upon by snipers hidden within the point's underground tunnel system. The Germans recovered sufficiently to launch a counterattack, and intermittent, vicious firefights continued through to the next day. The Rangers were finally relieved on 8 June, after men of 5th Ranger Battalion and 116th Regiment fought their way from Vierville through stiff German opposition in St-Pierre-du-Mont. The Rangers' casualties by then totaled over sixty per cent.

From the **Point du Hoc Visitor's Center** the gravel path winds back toward the actual battlefield. First one large bomb crater is passed, then several more. The path then enters the only D-Day battlefield that remains unchanged since 1944. The lunar landscape of overlapping shell and bomb craters that greeted the Rangers has been softened by the intervening years, but the violence of the place is still evident.

The gravel path continues among the open-air and casemated gun positions and provides easy walking; however, broken rubble and craters make movement off the path much more difficult. Two positions have observation platforms built on top for better views. The command bunker, which once held the **memorial plaque to Colonel Rudder**, has been closed due to erosion; however, a more intact casemate and a garrison bunker are open for exploration. The **Ranger Monument**, a granite pylon with tablets at its base, stands atop the command bunker. Nothing on the Pointe du Hoc battlefield is signed or identified. The site can be visited even when the information center is closed.

Return to the highway (D514) and reverse course, turning left toward Vierville. In less than 1.5 km, turn right (D204) and follow this road over 6 km before turning right toward La Cambe (N13). Avoid entering the new Autoroute. In La Cambe turn left (D113), pass under the Autoroute, and enter into a large roundabout. Follow the signs to the Cimetière Militaire / Deutsche Soldatenfriedhof.

The access road to the **German Cemetery at La Cambe** follows a long, tree-lined lane that runs parallel to the high speed N13. Adjacent to the cemetery entrance is a building called the 'Peace Garden,' where exhibits show the work of the German War Graves Commission. The toilets are five-star. The cemetery proper is entered through a gatehouse constructed of enormous gray granite blocks. Everything in the cemetery is made of gray granite, including the grave markers, the symbolic clusters of five crosses scattered among the oak trees, and the mourning parents sculptured atop the mount that is the mass grave. Steps to the top of the mount provide a better view of the cemetery, which is very different from that of other nationalities. The cemetery contains 21,160 dead, including the 296 in the mass grave, but has only a fraction of that number of graves because the German custom was to bury several bodies in the same grave. This is a somber and solemn place but the most visited German military cemetery in France.

Return to La Cambe and continue west (N13) to enter the high-speed highway (E46 / N13). Continue for approximately 22 km, exiting toward Ste-Marie-du-Mont / Vierville (not to be confused with Vierville-sur-Mer) (D913). The high-speed road now bypasses Carentan and crosses the Douve River to its north. Pass through Vierville.

This area was the drop zone of the 101st Airborne Division's 506th Parachute Infantry Regiment (PIR), commanded by Colonel Robert Sink, whose objectives were the critical southern exits #1 and #2 (now roads D913 and D329) from Utah beach. They advanced along both highways to within 2.5 km of the beaches before being repelled by heavy machine-gun fire. The Germans eventually surrendered to the 4th Division advancing from Utah Beach.

Pass through Ste-Marie-du-Mont and continue toward Utah Beach.

The roads in this area have been dedicated to individual soldiers of the 1st Special Engineer Brigade who were killed on D-Day or the ensuing Normandy battles. Blue and white roadside signs identify them. The final approach to Utah Beach crests a hill approximately 1.5 km from the beach to enter flat lowlands. These pastures were flooded by the Germans, emphasizing the importance of capturing the causeways that crossed the flooded ground.

Utah Beach

The initial landing unit was the reinforced 8th Regiment of the US 4th Division. German mines sunk approaching landing craft and guiding patrol boats. At 06:30, the strong current brought the first landing craft almost 2 km east of their target, but the miss was inconsequential those defenses were weaker than at the original target. Assistant Divisional Commander, Brigadier General Theodore Roosevelt Jr., son of former President Theodore Roosevelt and veteran of the First World War, immediately took charge and stated, 'We'll start the war from right here.'[11]

---

[11] Roosevelt was awarded the Congressional Medal of Honor for his leadership, but unfortunately died five weeks later of a heart attack.

The division's other two Regimental Combat Teams[12] landed during the next four hours, supported by a RCT from the 90th Division. Defenses for Utah Beach were relatively incomplete, with few beach obstacles and only one completed *Widerstandnest*. An attack by three hundred sixty medium bombers and the subsequent naval bombardment had destroyed the position's 50-mm antitank guns and 75-mm cannon. Twenty-eight of the thirty-two DD tanks reached the shore, providing the armor support necessary to eliminate the remaining 88-mm cannon and Renault tank turret dug into the sand.

The men rapidly moved over the sand dunes, but the flooded pastures slowed their progress despite the four crossings held by the 101st Airborne at the western ends. Twenty-three thousand men landed at Utah that day, with only one hundred ninety-seven casualties.

'La Madeleine,' as Utah Beach was called before D-day, holds numerous monuments, including those to the 4th and 90th Divisions, 1st Special Engineer Brigade, and an 8-meter high granite column erected by the American government to pay homage to all of its sons who landed here. The memorials are constructed upon the partially completed German defensive works.

The prominent building is the **Musée du Débarquement**. In front of the museum parking area are several machine-gun and mortar positions which formed *Widerstandnest #5*. In front of the museum are a couple old landing craft that are damaged from the war and exposure to the elements.

The museum shows maps, artifacts, and photos of the ceremonies that have commemorated the events through the years. Many of the maps were used to plan the offensive. A large table shows the assault beaches at 06:30 on 6 June, and the German fortifications are well-identified. A film on the landing is shown every hour in three languages. In the center of the museum's main hall, under a large dome, is the tobruk bunker designed for the Renault tank turret. It can be entered, although the entrance is only three feet high. Amphibious vehicles fill the hall. The front of the main hall has large windows which allow 180-degree viewing onto the beachfront. Open February, March and November from 10:00 to 12:30 and 14:00 to 17:30; April, May, and October from 10:00 to 18:00; June through September from 09:30 to 19:00; closed in December and January. Fee.

To the west of the museum is the draw through the dunes now identified by a Sherman tank and *Borne 00*, marking the beginning of the *Voie de la Liberté* that follows the victorious advance of Patton's Third Army's march across France to Bastogne, Belgium. Every kilometer of the route is marked with a *Borne*. The store across the beachfront road is now a café called the 'Roosevelt'; it was a house on 6 June and was converted into a defensive position, with a bunker added onto its rear. Slightly farther west of the café is another large blockhouse.

Leave Utah Beach, driving parallel with the water, toward Ravenoville-Plage (D421). After approximately 2 km, turn left toward Ste-Mère-Église (D67). Follow

---

[12] Regimental Combat Team (RCT) – an infantry regiment combined with tank battalions and engineering brigades to attack beach fortifications and obstacles.

this numbered highway for approximately 10 km, directly into the center of Ste-Mère-Église; park near the church.

American Airborne Landings

At 01:15, two sticks from 506th Parachute Infantry Regiment (PIR) came down in **Ste-Mère Église** to find the town and its German garrison awakened by a burning barn. Thirty minutes later F Company, 505th PIR landed among the alerted Germans. Many were shot as they floated to earth or hung by their parachutes from trees or poles around the village.

Later that morning, the 82nd Airborne's, 505th PIR drop concentrated around Ste-Mère-Église. The 3rd Battalion, commanded by Lieutenant Colonel Edward Krause, gathered up one hundred eighty men and advanced toward the town. With the fires out and the dead paratroopers thought to have been a minor raid, the German garrison had returned to bed. The paratroopers quickly captured the village with hardly a fight. Krause unfolded an American flag in front of the Hôtel de Ville on 04:30 June 6 1944, thus making Ste-Mère-Église the first town in France to be liberated. *Borne 0* marks the village's opinion of the start of the *Voie de la Liberté*.

The village's strategic importance astride the Caen-Cherbourg highway made it a critical objective for the only large-scale counterattack that the Germans launched that day. At approximately 10:30, two companies supported by self-propelled guns and tanks, attacked from the direction of Neuville-au-Plain in the north. A detachment from 2nd Battalion withstood the attack for eight hours until accurate enemy mortar fire reduced its ranks. It withdrew into the town, but the Germans failed to press the advance. Meanwhile, the German 795th *Ost* Battalion moved from west of Utah Beach to attack the airborne troops in Ste-Mère-Église from the south. The Georgian (Russia) Battalion was supported by its fierce 88-mm cannon. Krause sent a reduced company to flank the enemy force from the west. The attempt led the Germans to overestimate the size of the American force, and they withdrew. In the surrounding countryside, small groups engaged larger German formations, the Americans always on the run because they were outmanned and outgunned. German artillery pounded the town for most of the afternoon and evening while the paratroopers dug deeper holes. Any movement attracted German shelling. During the evening, glider regiments came in carrying the heavy weapons necessary to beat back the German tanks. Although still isolated, the 82nd was growing stronger in its Ste-Mère-Église positions. They joined the next day with the advancing 4th Division from Utah Beach in time to repulse a German panzer battalion attack.

Ste-Mère-Église is the quintessential Norman market town, with a lively town center of shops around its old Norman church. It revels in its invasion history, with every building seemingly serving tourists or carrying plaques which commemorate invasion events. Information boards labeled in French and English contain battlefield photographs compared to the same site today. A **Signal Monument** stands in front of the church.

The **church's famous stained glass window** dedicated to the parachutists is in the rear of the nave, above the entry door. During the summer, a dummy precariously hangs from a parachute snagged on the church roof. It represents the eventful landing of Private John Steele, who hung from a flying buttress for hours while the church bell tolled the invasion. Private Steele was captured by a German observer in the steeple but later escaped. His experience was made famous in Cornelius Ryan's book *The Longest Day*.

Musée des Troupes Aéroportées (Airborne Museum) is across the street from the back of the church, on the site of the burning barn that roused the townspeople before the paratroop landing. It consists of two buildings that are shaped like parachutes. Immediately inside the gateway is a Sherman M4 tank. The Waco building, named after the glider used by American airborne troops, maintains a collection of excellent photographs of gliders, paratroopers, and everyday life in Ste-Mère-Église after the liberation. Displays around the exterior windows contain the paraphernalia carried by the troops that morning. An appropriate collection of German weaponry also exists. The second, slightly larger building holds a Douglas C-47, America's major transport plane during the war and the craft used to tow the gliders. A great map of Ste-Mère-Église shows what the town looked like in August 1944. The airborne museum is an excellent site in terms of the story it tells and how would tells it. Open February, March, October, and November from 09:30 to 12:00 and 14:00 to 18:00; April through September from 09:00 to 18:45; closed December and January. Fee.

Other Sites of Interest: The Normandy invasion area presents the visitor with opportunities to visit many more museums and exhibits. The aforementioned locations are particularly interesting and are located at the battlefield sites. The following list expands upon the mentioned sites lists from east to west. Sites indicated with an * are described in more detail in the preceding text. Hours of operation are repeated for convenience. The purchase of a 'Normandie Pass' provides a discount at most of the museums; passes are available at any of the sites which honor them and are worth the investment.

* Mémorial de Caen (Caen): Invasion and Peace Museum with photos and film on D-Day; open every day 11 February through 11 November from 09:00 to 19:00; open daily except Mondays 12 November through December from 09:30 to 18:00; closed 25 December and January through 10 February. Fee and handicap accessible.

Musée de la Batterie de Merville (Merville-Franceville): Celebrates the capture of bunkers by 9th Battalion of British paratroops; open daily 15 March through 15 November from 09:30 to 18:30. Fee.

* Musée Mémorial Pegasus (Bénouville): Celebrates the actions of British 6th Airborne Division; open daily February and March, October and November from 10:00 to 13:00 and 14:00 to 17:00; April to September from 09:30 to 18:30; closed December and January. Fee.

* Le Grand Bunker (Ouistreham): German observation bunker overlooking Sword Beach; open daily from February through December from 10:00 to 18:00; extended hours from April through September from 09:00 to 19:00. Fee.

Musée du Débarquement & Musée No 4 Commando (Ouistreham): Artifacts from Sword Beach, focusing on No 4 Commando; open March through November from 10:30 to 18:00. Fee.

Musée Radar (Douvres-la-Délivrande): Explores the use of Würzburg radar in a fortified base; open every day except Monday 15 June to 15 September from 10:00 to 17:30. Fee.

* Juno Beach Centre (Courseulles-sur-Mer): Celebrates Canada's contribution to the war effort, overlooking Juno Beach; open April through September from 09:30 to 19:00; March and October from 10:00 to 18:00; February, November and December from 10:00 to 13:00 and 14:00 to 17:00; closed in January and on 25 December.

Musée America Gold Beach (Ver-sur-Mer): Celebrates the British landings on Gold Beach and the beginning of France-America airmail in 1927; open daily April through September from 10:30 to 17:30; closed Tuesdays. Fee.

* Cinéma Circulaire Arromanches 360 Cinema (Arromanches): 360-degree film of the invasion; open daily June through August from 09:40 to 18:40; April, May, September and October from 10:10 to 17:40; February, March, November and December from 10:10 to 17:10; closed January. Fee.

* Musée du Débarquement (Arromanches): Focuses on Mulberry artificial harbors; open daily February, November and December from 10:00 to 12:30 and 13:30 to 17:00; March, April and October from 09:00 to 12:30 and 13:30 to 18:00; May, June, July and August from 09:00 to 19:00; September from 10:00 to 19:00; open later on Sundays; closed Christmas holidays and January.

* Longues Battery (Longues-sur-Mer): German casemates and observation post; always open and no admission charge.

Musée des Épaves sous-Marines (Port-en-Bessin): Displays of wreckage salvaged from the channel; open daily June through September from 10:00 to 12:00 and 14:00 to 18:00.

Musée Mémorial d'Omaha Beach (St-Laurent-sur-Mer): Recalls the allied landing at Omaha Beach and Pointe du Hoc; open daily 15 February to 15 March from 10:00 to 12:30 and 14:30 to 18:00; 16 March to 15 September from 09:30 to 18:30 (19:00 mid-May through mid-September); 16 September to 15 November from 09:30 to 18:30.

* Musée D-Day Omaha (Vierville-sur-Mer): Weapons and equipment collection; open daily 15 February through 15 March from 10:00 to 12:30 and 14:30 to 18:00; 16 March to 15 May from 09:30 to 18:30; 16 May through June from 09:30 to 19:00; July through August from 09:30 to 19:30; 1 through 15 September from 09:30 to 19:00; 16 September through 15 November from 09:30 to 18:30. Fee.

Musée des Rangers (Grandcamp-Maisy): Dedicated to American Rangers; open daily except Mondays 15 February to 15 May from 13:00 to 18:00; open daily except Monday mornings 16 May through October from 09:30 to 13:00 and 14:30 to 18:30; closed November through 14 February. Fee.

* Musée du Débarquement (Utah Beach): Celebrates the Utah landings in a building overlooking the beach; open February, March and November from 10:00 to 12:30 and 14:00 to 17:30; April, May, and October from 10:00 to 18:00; June through September from 09:30 to 19:00; closed in December and January. Fee.

* Musée des Troupes Aéroportées (Ste-Mère Église): Dedicated to American Airborne troops; open February, March, October, and November from 09:30 to 12:00 and 14:00 to 18:00; April through September from 09:00 to 18:45; closed December and January.

La batterie d'Azeville (near Azeville): Tour inside German casemates; open daily 7 February through April and October through 11 November from 14:00 to 18:00; May, June and September from 11:00 to 18:00; July and August from 10:00 to 19:00; closed December and January. Fee.

Musée de la batterie de Crisbecq (near St-Marcouf): Self-guided tour of the massive installation for 210-mm casemated guns; open April, October and November from 14:00 to 18:00; May, June, and September from 11:00 to 18:00; July and August from 10:00 to 19:00; closed December through March.

Musée de la Liberté (Quinéville): Reviews the German occupation and invasion from Utah Beach to Cherbourg; open daily April to 11 November from 10:00 to 19:00.

#49

Battle of Caen
7 June to 22 July 1944

OBJECTIVE	To capture the crucial transportation hub of Caen and establish a defensive wall against German forces east of the Orne River.
FORCES	
BRITISH:	326,000 men of Second Army (Lieutenant-General Sir Miles Dempsey)
GERMAN:	180,000 men of Panzer Group West (General der Panzertruppen Freiherr Geyr von Schweppenburg, then General der Panzertruppen Heinrich Eberbach)
RESULT	The city was liberated after a long and costly battle.
CASUALTIES	
BRITISH:	45,795 total casualties
GERMAN:	100,000 total casualties through 16 July
LOCATION	Caen is 240 km northwest of Paris; Bayeux is 30 km northwest of Caen

An important element of the plan to drive the German army out of France was the capture of the city of Caen because it controlled the roadways and bridges used by the Germans to resupply their troops on the Cotentin peninsula. On invasion beaches in the British sectors, the Germans were reeling without an organized response. The congestion on the beaches and the excessive caution displayed by British commanders unfortunately delayed the advance inland until afternoon. The lack of action allowed the German 21st Panzer Division to move into position in front of Caen, and an extended and costly struggle for control of the city began.

Battle

Despite the early German sluggishness and constant harassment by allied aircraft, armored divisions of 1st SS Panzer Corps, led by SS-Obergruppenführer Josef 'Sepp' Dietrich, were arriving from their bases in the French interior.

Allied efforts to advance on Caen persisted after the D-day landings. British 185th Infantry Brigade continued its frontal assault on 7 and 8 June, directly upon the 21st Panzer Division in the area of Bois de Lébisey, north of the city. The Canadian 9th Infantry Brigade advanced toward Carpiquet and its airport, west of Caen, from the direction of Authie. The tanks and panzergrenadiers of 12th SS Panzer *Hitlerjugend* Division's *Kampfgruppe Meyer* counterattacked, driving the Canadians back to near their starting points. Additional attacks over the next four days were repulsed, and the Germans assumed defensive positions in front of Caen that they were to retain for weeks.

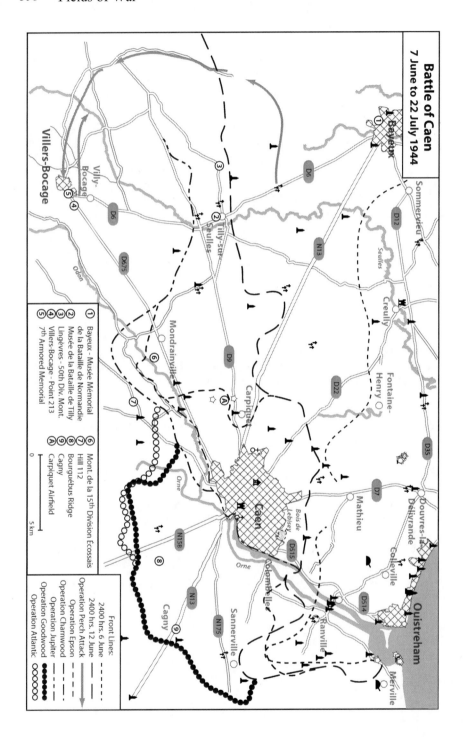

Battle of Caen
7 June to 22 July 1944

Villers-Bocage

Bayeux

Sommervieu

D6

Villy-
Bocage

Tilly-sur-
Seulles

D12

Seulles

Creully

N13

D675

Odon

Mondrainville

D9

Carpiquet

D22

Fontaine-
Henry

D35

Orne

Caen

Bois de
Lebisey

Mathieu

D7

Douvres-la-
Délivrande

Coleville

D515

Orne

Colombelles

Ranville

D514

Ouistreham

N158

Cagny

N13

Sannerville

N175

Merville

Legend:

① Bayeux - Musée Memorial
② Musée de la Bataille de Normandie
③ Musée de la Bataille de Tilly
④ Lingèvres - 50th Div. Mont.
⑤ Villers-Bocage - Point 213
Ⓐ 7th Armored Memorial

⑥ Mont de la 15th Division Écossais
⑦ Hill 112
⑧ Bourguébus Ridge
⑨ Cagny
Ⓐ Carpiquet Airfield

0   5 km

Front Lines:
2400 hrs. 6 June
2400 hrs. 12 June
Operation Perch Attack
Operation Epson
Operation Charnwood
Operation Jupiter
Operation Goodwood
Operation Atlantic

Battle of Tilley-sur-Seulles (8 to 19 June)

The British XXX Corps, led by Lieutenant-General Gerard Bucknall, tangled with Panzer Lehr, commanded by Generalleutnant Fritz Bayerlein, near the village of Tilley-sur-Seulles in a battle against the best of the German armored divisions. The village changed hands over twenty times, with the 50th (Northumbrian) Division and additional infantry and armored brigades eventually forcing a German retreat. The loss of men and armored vehicles permanently reduced the effectiveness of Panzer Lehr, a heretofore elite and over-strength unit.

Battle of Bréville (10 to 12 June)

On 10 June, the German 346th Division, the first of the Fifteenth Army's divisions to be drawn into the battle, launched an attack on Bréville. The village's position along a critical ridgeline that overlooked British positions east of the Orne was thinly held by 6th Airborne Division troops. The 51st (Highland) Division reinforced the airborne troops, and on 12 June, accumulated troops from several units launched a bloody assault which successfully recaptured the village. The battered men of both sides then took up defensive positions.

Operation 'Perch' (13 June)

General Montgomery ordered the first of a succession of operations, each designed to crack the German wall in and around Caen, starting with a daring flanking maneuver from the southwest. On 13 June, 7th Armored Division, known as 'the Desert Rats' and commanded by Major-General Erskine, found the seam between the German units and drove untouched through Villers-Bocage. Their leading tank unit passed through the village and advanced to a dominating hilltop position to the east. An attack by five German Tiger tanks led by Germany's premier tank ace, SS-Obersturmführer Michael Wittmann, destroyed fifty vehicles and stopped the British advance. The 2nd Panzer Division attacked, and the battle in the streets of Villers-Bocage continued for most of the day, with infantry scampering about the buildings as well as tanks and antitank guns engaging at near point-blank range. Toward evening the British withdrew to safer ground to the west. That same day, the first V-1 flying bomb landed on London.

Bad weather and the Channel storm of mid-June grounded aircraft and delayed further operations while Montgomery assembled a larger force to batter his way through the German front.

Operation 'Epsom' (26 to 30 June)

The next attempt to capture Caen was led by the entire VIII Corps. In the rain and gloom of early morning on 26 June, sixty thousand men and six hundred tanks crossed the Odon River southwest of Caen and fell upon elements of three panzer divisions – 12th SS Panzer, Panzer Lehr, and 21st Panzer. An initial, intense bombardment by seven hundred guns left the defenders stunned, but they recovered while the VIII Corps developed a 5-km deep salient within the enemy line. In the worst tradition of the battles at Ypres and Somme a generation earlier, three famed British divisions – the 15th (Scottish), 43rd (Wessex), and 11th Armored – advanced in formation while concealed machine guns supported by Tiger and Panther (Mark IV) tanks added to the firepower. After three days, 11th Armored crossed the Odon to take possession of Hill 112. The same day, 9th SS Panzer (*Hohenstaufen*) and 10th SS Panzer (*Frundsberg*) Divisions launched a major counterattack against the salient's western flank. The threat of pinching off the forward troops convinced General Dempsey to pull the troops back and shut down the operation.

The failure of the German generals to stem the invasion and Geyr von Schweppenburg's insistence that the Caen bridgehead be abandoned led to his dismissal on 1 July in favor of Heinrich Eberbach. The next day, after hints from Berlin, Rundstedt resigned, to be succeeded by Generalfeldmarschall Günther von Kluge.

Operation 'Windsor' (4 to 5 July)

At 05:15 on 4 July, the 8th Canadian Infantry Brigade attacked Carpiquet after a bombardment by field artillery and the nine 16-inch guns of the battleship *HMS Rodney*. The village was taken, but the bunkers around the airport control tower and hanger area, stubbornly held by a one hundred fifty-man detachment of SS Panzer Grenadier Regiment Nr 26, presented a harder target. Advancing tanks of the 10th Armored Regiment (Fort Garry Horse) fell to the 88-mm guns of a Flak battery. For two days the assault raged, every Canadian pause met with a German counterattack, ending with the Canadians in control of the village and the Germans still on the airfield.

Operation 'Charnwood' (7 to 9 July)

On the night of 7 July, British Bomber Command delivered a saturation bombing on Caen in preparation for Operation *Charnwood*, the next day's ground assault by one hundred fifteen thousand men of British I Corps. Four hundred fifty heavy bombers dropped their loads 6 km in front of allied lines to avoid hitting their own troops. The bombs fell between the German front line and reserve troops, causing only minor military losses but killing one thousand French civilians and filling the cratered streets of Caen with impassible rubble. For two days the Germans resisted, while the British 3rd and 59th Divisions fought through the ruins of the destroyed city to attain the banks of the Orne River. Carpiquet airport finally fell to the 3rd Canadian Division attacking from the west.

Operation 'Jupiter' (10 to 12 July)

General Dempsey ordered a renewed attack upon Hill 112, which was long thought to be the key to the entire Normandy battlefield. The 43rd Division, with massive air and artillery support, broke through between Verson and Baron-sur-Odon to move toward the hill. By 08:00 on 10 June, the leading Somerset Light Infantry crested the north slope, but further progress was impossible against concentrated German fire. The 5th Duke of Cornwall's Light Infantry passed through the Somersets and took the hilltop, only to suffer a counterattack by surrounding SS troops that night. By late the next day, when the intense fighting eased, each side held half of a hill that was littered with bodies and smoldering tanks.

Operation 'Goodwood' (18 to 20 July)

Operation 'Goodwood' was developed as an opportunity to use the numerical superiority of British armor in a massed attack east of the Orne. The intermediate objective was the dominating Bourguébus Ridge, 11 km south of the front line. The open fields approaching the ridge were perfect tank country, and similar terrain past the ridge promised rapid movement toward Falaise, 30 km south. German intelligence, however, had picked up the plan, and Panzer Group West responded by establishing five defensive lines across the British axis of attack which were well supplied with assault guns, 88-mm guns, and heavy tanks.

For three hours in the morning of 18 July, nineteen hundred medium and heavy bombers and eight hundred fighter-bombers delivered concentrated explosives on predetermined kill zones, shattering German tank battalions and panzergrenadier regiments. Three armored divisions fielding thirteen hundred tanks then attacked in succession. 11th Armored Division led the way following a tightly scripted rolling barrage. Initial progress against the dazed survivors of the bombing was swift. Since a traffic jam slowed the advance of the Guards Armored and 7th Armored Divisions, lead units fell victim to seventy-eight 88-mm guns stationed on Bourguébus Ridge and in the village of Cagny. The first Tiger tanks made an appearance that greatly exaggerated their real importance. British tankers so feared the nearly impregnable armored behemoths that they assumed any dot on the horizon was a Tiger. Their presence on the eastern flank of the advance further squeezed British units into a narrow front west of Cagny. By early afternoon, Eberbach strengthened the defenses by ordering the 1st SS Panzer *Leibstandarte* Division from reserve onto the ridge. One hundred eighty-six tanks were destroyed that day by German artillery and antitank guns. British armor continued for two more days, incurring fifty-five hundred casualties and a total of four hundred destroyed tanks. 7th Armored captured part of the Bourguébus Ridge, and the operation was halted. Goodwood secured Caen but was criticized as a failure by Supreme Allied Command.

Operation 'Atlantic' (18 to 22 July)

The newly created Canadian II Corps supported Goodwood by capturing the critical Colombelles steelworks northeast of Caen. By 22 July, the Canadians had cleared Caen's suburbs east of the Orne and continued the pressure against strengthening German resistance down the east bank as far as St-André-sur-Orne.

Aftermath

Whereas Caen was cleared of Germans, not until Operation 'Totalize' on 7 August was the German Seventh Army driven to annihilation at Falaise. Montgomery's descriptions of his intentions during the battle for Caen remain controversial. He insisted that every attempt to take the city and the expenditure of men's lives were all part of the plan to engage Germany's best armored divisions while the Americans achieved a breakout in the west. Members of Supreme Allied Command accused him of slowness to respond. Whether planned or not, the British did keep the Germans occupied.

On 17 July, Rommel's staff car was strafed by an allied warplane. His wounds were serious and required hospitalization. Three days later, anti-Nazi members of the German military attempted to assassinate Hitler. Rommel's prior knowledge of the plot became known, but because of his hero reputation, he was offered the option of suicide rather than a trial which would threaten his entire family. Rommel swallowed poison on 14 October.

American forces struggled to escape the bocage country, but when they finally did attain open ground, their progress was swift. German efforts to mount a counterattack near Mortain were defeated by stubborn American units which refused to surrender. The newly formed Third Army, commanded by Lieutenant General George Patton, swept around from the south and east; the British fought their way south, and the noose around the German Seventh Army was closed near Falaise, resulting in its annihilation. German survivors were on the run, and the Allies entered Paris on 24 August, led by général de brigade Philippe Leclerc's French 2nd Armored Division. The rapid pursuit continued, and logistical issues rather than German resistance halted the allied armies at the Rhine River.

Battlefield Tour

With the exception of the museum and numerous unit memorials, few formal recognitions of the battle for Caen exist. The Caen battlefield has been significantly impacted by the expansion of the city. Many of the woods and hedge lines have disappeared; Bois de Lébisey has shrunk considerably, and the Caen-Troarn rail line has been removed. Sites outside the city to the south and east have been less affected. The open fields around Caen did not bring the miseries of the bocage, but the small villages with their stone houses did provide the Germans with effective defensive opportunities. The city of Bayeux played little part in the battle for Caen, but it holds an excellent museum describing the entire struggle.

If approaching Bayeux from east or west, do not enter the A13 Autoroute. Approach the southern outskirts of the city on the ring road (D613 or D5a, depending upon direction of approach). Follow the ring road until it becomes boulevard Fabian Ware and turn into the museum parking area.

The grounds of the **Musée Mémorial de la Bataille de Normandie** hold a number of heavy vehicles of types used in Normandy, including a German Jagdpanther (tank destroyer), an American M4A1 Sherman tank, an American M10 tank destroyer, and a British Churchill Crocodile flamethrower. Also located outside the museum are a series of memorials dedicated to the units who liberated Bayeux on 7 June 1944. In the museum, the entrance hall recognizes the actions of allied and German commanders. Distinctive maps present the chronology of the battle of Normandy in 2-3 day increments. A 35-minute film depicts the events in French and English. The maps and a diorama of the Falaise Pocket show the allied progress as well as German attempts to escape the Allies. Themed displays present artifacts and personal mementos. Open daily January through April and October through

December from 10:00 to 12:30 and 14:00 to 18:00; May through September from 09:30 to 18:30; closed the last two weeks of January. Fee.

Leave the museum grounds and walk the short distance west on boulevard Fabian Ware. The **Bayeux War Cemetery** is the largest Commonwealth cemetery of the Second World War in France, with over four thousand graves and including relocated battlefield burials brought in from the surrounding districts and nearby hospitals. The Cross of Sacrifice is located at the far rear of the cemetery. Four hundred sixty-five German graves on the left boundary of the cemetery are distinguished by their slightly different headstones. Across from the British cemetery, on the east side of the boulevard, is the columned arch of the **British Memorial to the Missing,** the inside surfaces of which bear the names of more than eighteen hundred men who went missing from the time of the assault on Normandy's beaches until the approach to the Seine River and who have no known grave.

Other Sites of Interest: Bayeux is famous for the **Bayeux Tapestry,** which depicts William the Conqueror's victory at the battle of Hastings in 1066 and which is displayed in the 18th century former seminary now known as **Centre Guillaume le Conquérant**. The 70-meter long, embroidered linen cloth gives an account of the events that led to the Norman victory, and is viewable on a self-guided audio tour. The visit is enhanced by a series of short films describing events in the Middle Ages. To visit the center, continue from the war cemetery on boulevard Fabien Ware (becomes boulevard du maréchal Leclerc), turn left in the large roundabout onto rue Sadi Carnot, and proceed to a right turn onto rue Nesmond. Open daily February through December from 10:00 to 18:00 (until 19:00 in July and August); closed on 25 December and in January. Fee. The reception area is handicap accessible.

From the Centre Guillaume le Conquérant, walk a short distance west along the rue Nesmond (becomes rue Leonard-Lambert le Forestier) to the front of the Norman Gothic **Cathédrale Notre-Dame** the towers and crypt of which date from 1077. Other portions of the building are 12th and 13th century. The interior is decorated with Norman sculptures, an intricately carved stringcourse, and 15th century frescoes. Many of the old, half-timbered buildings along the narrow streets in the center of the city have been restored.

The **Mémorial du Général de Gaulle** celebrates général de Gaulle's return to France with a presentation of photographs and documents. Open daily April through October from 10:00 to 12:30 and 14:00 to 18:00; closed December through February. Fee.

From the war museum, continue southeast on boulevard Fabian Ware (D5a, becomes boulevard maréchal Leclerc D572) into the large roundabout, exiting to the right on boulevard Sadi Carnot. Turn right (D6) and continue approximately 12 km into Tilley-sur-Seulles. The small but beautifully landscaped **Jerusalem War Cemetery** is on the left, shortly after passing through Chouain. The first burials originated early in the fight for Normandy, from a clash between a German armor column moving toward Bayeux and the Durham Light Infantry on 10 June.

The **Musée de la Bataille de Tilly** is located in the small, stone Romanesque Chapelle Notre-Dame du Val in the heart of Tilley-sur-Seulles, just off the main road and easily identified by the line of flags. The area around the chapel holds several unit memorials, and the interior presents artifacts, maps, and documents chronicling the struggle for control of the destroyed village. Open only weekends and holidays May through September from 14:00 to 18:00. Fee.

Leave Tilly west toward Lingèvres (D13) to the cemetery on the left.

The **Tilley-sur-Seulles War Cemetery** is located on the heart of the Tilley battlefield, although most of the burials occurred because of later fighting. From the small parking area across the road, the entrance is framed by two stone block pillars. The cemetery presents the typical format of Commonwealth War Graves Cemeteries, with the Cross of Sacrifice in the center and the Germans in the right rear. It contains nine hundred ninety Commonwealth burials, almost all from Great Britain, and two hundred thirty-two German graves.

Continue into Lingèvres and stop at the church.

On 14 June, **Lingèvres** became a major objective of 50th Division's 9th Durham Light Infantry Battalion. The terrain was heavy bocage and offered Panzer Lehr the particularly effective use of their *panzerfaust*[13] antitank weapon in the scattered woods around Verrières to the northeast. Suffering heavy casualties, the infantry occupied the village, only to face a counterattack led by German Panther tanks. Sherman Fireflys[14] of 4th / 7th Dragoon Guards engaged the enemy in the streets of the village. One Sherman, commanded by Sergeant Wilf Harris, knocked out five of the nine Panthers destroyed during the long afternoon. The burning hulks were abandoned along the D13 highway east and west of the village. Fighting would continue in this area for weeks, with each small advance met with a counterattack until the German withdrawal on the night of 18 / 19 July.

In front of the church, guarded by British and French flags, stands a stone slab with a metal plaque commemorating the 50th (Northumberland) Division's liberation and defense of the village.

Return to Tilly and continue south toward Juvigny (D6). West of Juvigny, less than 1 km toward Hottot-les-Bagues (D9), is **Hottot-les-Bagues War Cemetery**. It contains over one thousand Commonwealth and one hundred German burials, most collected from the battlefield burials in the vicinity. Continue toward Villers-Bocage

---

[13] *Panzerfaust* was a hand-held, one-shot, antitank weapon similar to the British PIAT or American bazooka. It fired a hollow-charge rocket capable of penetrating 200 mm of armor.

[14] Sherman Firefly was a Sherman tank mounting an upgraded 17-pounder gun; it was the only allied tank capable of penetrating Tiger armor if close enough.

(D6). In the eastern fringe of the town, turn left toward Caen (N175, renumbered as D675). Pass under Autoroute A84 and continue to the summit of the hill. A small sign on the right indicates Point 213 (Point 217 on modern maps). Stop along the roadway.

East of Villers-Bocage, a high ridge dominates the area, and its slopes run steeply down to the Odon River to the south. At approximately 08:00, A Squadron of the 4th County of London Yeomanry, commanded by Lieutenant-Colonel Lord Cranley, leading element of 22nd Armored Brigade, advanced up the road to stop at the high ground at **Point 213**. The unit deployed in the field now occupied by reservoirs and radio transmission towers. Unseen 220 meters to the right was the overnight leaguer of five Tiger tanks of 101st SS Heavy Panzer Battalion, led by SS-Oberstumführer Michael Wittmann. In a stunningly daring maneuver, Wittmann's tank charged out from the rural road to the southwest, near the *Poste electrique,* into the British column. After eliminating a Cromwell and a Sherman tank at the rear of A Squadron's column, he turned left onto the highway toward **Villers-Bocage**. Driving toward the village, he fired shell after shell at point blank range, destroying three more Cromwells, three Stuarts, two command tanks, and thirteen soft-sided half-tracks and personnel carriers. Wittmann then exchanged fire with a Sherman Firefly, from which his vehicle received some damage, before withdrawing back toward the hill. The action was the most brilliant feat of tankmanship in the war. Meanwhile, the remainder of Wittmann's company moved along a mud rut road south of the *Poste electrique*, engaged and eliminated the spearhead of the British force at Point 213, and eventually captured Lord Cranley. Wittmann later received the Swords addition to his Knight's Cross of the Iron Cross with Oak Leaves, one of Germany's highest military awards.

Reverse direction and return to the junction with the highway coming from Tilley-sur-Seulles (D6).

The approach into Villers-Bocage descends a hill typical of this region of Normandy. The **7th Armored Division Memorial** is in the intersection and consists of a roughly cut, gray granite block with a bronze plaque recalling, 'with pride in gratitude those of the Seventh Armored Division who fought and died here for freedom on 13 June 1944.' In this intersection a British 6-pounder antitank gun crew damaged the drive sprocket of Wittmann's tank, forcing Wittmann to abandon his vehicle and make his escape on foot.

Continue into Villers-Bocage, following rue Clemenceau (becomes rue Pasteur) into place du général Leclerc.

The town has been mostly rebuilt and bears little resemblance to its 1944 appearance. In the place du général Leclerc a new Hôtel de Ville and a reconstructed church face each other across an open square. On its eastern side, after Wittmann's withdrawal from the village, Lieutenant William Cotton established an ambush. With his four tanks and a nearby 6-pounder antitank gun, 7th Armored got some measure of revenge knocking out two Mark IV tanks and five Tiger tanks before infiltration by German infantry forced their withdrawal.

From **place Jeanne d'Arc** farther ahead, a Sherman Firefly tank engaged Wittmann's Tiger when it was at the opposite end of the commercial district. Fighting brewed through the streets of Villers-Bocage for most of the day before the tanks and panzergrenadiers of Panzer Lehr and 2nd Panzer Division forced the British to extract themselves and establish a leaguer north of Tracy-Bocage, 3 km to the west. They suffered 378 casualties and lost twenty-seven tanks, twenty-eight other vehicles, and the chance to outflank Caen due to the daring of one experienced tanker and his comrades.

The village's punishment was not complete; to cover its retreat the following night, the British Airforce pounded Villers-Bocage. In the evening of 30 June, during Operation 'Epsom,' 250 heavy bombers completed the destruction of the village. The ruins were finally liberated on 4 August.

Reserve direction again, proceed back toward Point 213, and continue toward Caen (D675). The arrow-shaped monument at the entrance to Noyers-Bocage is dedicated to the **151 Typhoon pilots** who died during the battle of Normandy. The stele behind the monument lists their names. The Canadian-built fighter-bomber gained a reputation as an antitank weapon during the battle of Normandy. After 10.5 km, turn right toward Baron-sur-Odon, signed as Monument de la 15th Division Écossais (route de Baron, D89). Stop at the memorial on the right; parking is difficult.

The **Monument de la 15th Division Écossais** commemorates the units and actions of the 15th (Scottish) Division, which engaged the troops and tanks of the 2nd SS Panzer Division over control of the bridges over the Odon River during Operation 'Epsom'. On the afternoon of 27 June, the stone bridge a short distance ahead was captured, allowing 11th Armor Division's tanks to cross the river.

The monument, a gray granite obelisk topped by a crying lion, carries plaques on all sides from divisional units familiar from First World War engagements, including the Gordon, Seaforth, Argyll and Sutherland Highlanders, Royal Scots, King's Own Scottish Borderers and many more. The plaques are surmounted by the simple words 'Scotland, the Brave.'

Continue toward Esquay-Notre-Dame (D89), crossing the stone bridge over the Odon that was captured by the **2nd Argyll and Sutherland Highlanders**. Turn left toward Caen (D8). Stop at the memorial near the top of the hill.

Operation 'Jupiter' started at 05:00 on 10 July, with the 43rd (Wessex) Division assuming the bridgehead near Baron-sur-Odon from the 15th Division and driving east toward Maltot. Initial attacks upon **Hill 112**, however, could not secure the crest against machine guns and hulled down Tiger tanks. At 22:30, the 5th Duke of Cornwall Light Infantry launched a night attack and took the crest against the 9th SS Panzer *Hohenstaufen* Division. They fought off ten counterattacks that night before finally being pushed off the top, having lost 40 per cent of their men and most of their officers. A nineteen-year-old Somerset corporal reported:

> When we attacked it later [Hill 112] was like a second Verdun. We attacked at 0400hours and reached our objective at 2000hours covering about 1,500 yards [1.4 km] that day and by that time I was the senior rank in the company which had just twenty-three men left. We were then counterattacked and reduced to just 18 men but we held the hill.[15]

As a measure of the intensity of the fighting, over fifty Churchill tanks were destroyed that day. In coordination with Operation 'Goodwood', 43rd Division renewed the assault, and by 29 July had pushed into Maltot, 3 km to the east.

The stone block stele topped with a dragon plaque commemorates the memory of all ranks 43rd (Wessex) Division and marks the center of the boomerang-shaped Hill 112, a broad, flat highland that commanded the wheat and rapeseed fields between the Odon and Orne Rivers. The location is completely surrounded by plowed fields, the devastated landscape of 1944 having returned to peaceful uses. The copse behind the memorial is known as Cornwall Wood, in memory of the men who fought so desperately to hold it.

Across the rural road (chemin Hausée) is a larger memorial park marked with flagpoles along the highway. A Churchill tank is prominently displayed, and a gray granite **table of orientation** marks the movements of the 5th Battalion Cornwall Light Infantry and the Royal Tank Regiment in their struggle for the hill.

Continue toward Caen (D8). At the next intersection, a stele commemorates the **5th Battalion Dorsetshire Regiment**, which fought near here on 10 July. At the intersection with the Caen *Périphérique* (N814), proceed east, exiting (#13) toward Ifs (Route de Falaise, N158). After 750 meters, turn left toward Ifs Bras (D120). Pass through Ifs Bras and Hubert-Folie, stopping at a convenient high point.

Operation 'Goodwood' was fought across open fields between Escoville and Bourguébus, east of Caen. The terrain was not the bocage country of narrow lanes and high-walled fields. Whereas the open plain offered mobility to armored units, it also provided villages and woodland suitable for hiding antitank guns and the superior German Tiger tanks. The northern sector is now cut by the A13 Autoroute near the railway embankment that played an important part in the encounter.

On 18 July, after four hours of the most intense combined naval and aerial bombardment of the war, British tanks from three armored divisions, flanked by two infantry divisions, swept from the north, across the fields in front of this position,

---

[15] Robin Neillands, *The Battle of Normandy 1944* (London: Cassell, 2003), 176.

toward the **Bourguébus Ridge**. By moving ahead of their supporting infantry, however, the British tanks became victims to a German defense in depth and especially their antitank guns.

Despite reports that Hubert-Folie was undefended, the leading British 29th Armored Brigade's 3rd Royal Tank Regiment, which had advanced 10 km almost unscathed in four hours, fell under heavy fire north of the village just before noon. Eleven tanks were immediately lost, and more fell in an afternoon-long engagement with German assault guns. German counterattacks down the slope from Hubert-Folie were met by Typhoon fighter-bombers, and a stalemate developed. By evening the advance was stopped because the regiment had lost forty tanks.

The Germans rushed 1st SS Panzer Division forward from Falaise, and by afternoon it counterattacked, reoccupying some of the captured ground. The next day, the battle continued – with the heaviest action in the highly exposed ground north of Ifs Bras, Hubert-Folie, and Bourguébus –while 11th Armored Division faced-off against arriving German panzer units. By early evening Ifs Bras and Hubert-Folie were cleared, with the Germans withdrawing to Verrières Ridge.

Turn left toward Bourguébus (D89) and follow through Bourguébus, exiting to the east toward Bellengreville (rue Vallée Ès Dunes, D89). Stop at a convenient high point.

To the north, 2nd Fife and Forfar Yeomanry advanced on the eastern flank of 3rd Royal Tank Regiment. Hidden among trees and shrubs and occupying the high ground, the Germans were unseen by the exposed British tankers in the fields. After crossing the Caen-Vimont rail line and advancing as far as the current position, the tankers were caught in a cross fire from soldiers on their right (your forward left) and the hamlet of Four. Continuing to advance toward Bourguébus, they fell victim to frontal fire and were forced to withdraw under counterattack by 1st SS Panzer Division units. By the end of 19 July, Soliers, Four, and le Poirier were held, but farther advance was impossible.

Follow the highway into the hamlet of la Hogue and turn left toward Frénouville (D225a). Pass through that town and turn left onto a frontage road that leads to a large roundabout. Proceed toward Cagny (N13, now renumbered D613). Turn right toward Démouville (D228) and stop at the first convenient location.

2nd Fife and Forfar Yeomanry passed through these fields on the first morning of Operation 'Goodwood'. Central to the battlefield was the village of **Cagny,** where Oberst Hans von Luck, commander of 125th Panzergrenadier Regiment, found a Luftwaffe antiaircraft unit near the church. He ordered the battery to use their 88-mm guns against the approaching tanks. When the airmen refused the orders of an army officer, Luck drew his pistol and made the Luftwaffe officer an offer, 'Either you are a dead man or you can earn yourself a medal.'[16] The gunners acquiesced, and after being personally directed to an apple orchard north of Cagny, the four guns applied devastating fire into the flanking Yeomanry and, later in the afternoon, the Grenadier Guards tanks, setting aflame forty tanks whose burning hulks were scattered across the fields to the north and west. The exposed nature of the terrain and the well-camouflaged German guns explain much of the difficulty the tankers faced in maintaining momentum.

By late afternoon, pressured by approaching British infantry, the guns were destroyed, and the village was abandoned. Stopped to the west, the 5th Guards Brigade flanked Cagny to the east from Émieville, 2.5 km northeast, eventually entering and liberating the village. On 19 July, a battle group from 12th SS Panzer Division recaptured Émieville, which remained under contention for almost one month. Goodwood was essentially over.

Continue, passing le Prieuré Farm on the right and le Mesnil Frémentel Farm on the left, both sites of batteries of 75-mm antitank guns that blocked the route of 29th Armored Brigade. Cross over the Autoroute to the next roundabout (N175, renumbered D675) without entering Démouville. A left turn returns toward Caen; a right turn toward Sannerville leads to the **Banneville-la-Campaign War Cemetery,** located on the right before entering Sannerville. The cemetery entrance path is heavily landscaped with flowering shrubs; the grounds contain 2,170 burials, many from the Goodwood operation, in plots centered upon a vine-covered pergola. The graves with touching stones in front on the right front hold members of an RAF flight crew who died together. A counterattack in the afternoon of 18 July by six Mark VI (King Tiger) tanks from the fields south of the cemetery was repulsed by accurate antitank gunfire.

Other Sites of Interest: Carpiquet airfield was converted by the 26th SS Panzergrenadier Regiment into a virtual killing field. The approaches were mined and wired. The area was dotted with pillboxes and covered by crossing machine-gun fire and antitank guns. Mortars and artillery had pre-targeted every significant site. During Operation 'Windsor,' three Canadian battalions attacked from the west, north of the current D9, toward the village and terminal area, while a single battalion of the Royal Winnipeg Rifles attempted to cross the open fields toward the hangers on the southern edge of the airfield. An intact Luftwaffe barrack and command bunker remain adjacent to the regional airport's terminal, although the ground around it has been raised, and it cannot be entered. Approximately 50 meters on the opposite side of the terminal is a memorial stele to commemorate the battle and the Canadian units which participated.

---

[16] Hans von Luck, *Panzer Commander* (New York: Praeger, 1989), 173. It is unknown as to whether the Luftwaffe officer ever received his medal.

Recommended Reading

A list of books concerning D-day is almost endless; these are a few recommendations.

Ambrose, Stephen: *D-Day June 6, 1944: The Climactic Battle of World War II*. New York: Simon & Schuster, 1994. An account filled with personal stories of the men that made it happen.

D'Este, Carlo: *Decision in Normandy: The Unwritten Story of Montgomery and the Allied Campaign*. London: Penguin Classics, 2001. Critical evaluation of the politics and performance of Montgomery during the Normandy campaign.

Hasting, Max: *Overlord: D-Day & the Battle for Normandy*. New York: Simon & Schuster, 1984. Gripping historical account of the invasion and the battles that followed.

Neillands, Robin: *The Battle of Normandy 1944*. London: Cassell, 2003. Detailed description of the British battle for Caen and a defense of Montgomery's actions.

——. *The Dieppe Raid: The Story of the Disastrous 1942 Expedition*. London: Aurun Press, 2005. A critical review of the planning and execution of the Dieppe raid.

Ryan, Cornelius: *The Longest Day June 6, 1944*. New York: Simon & Schuster, 1959. Classic and popular account of D-Day.

Trew, Simon (editor): *Battle Zone Normandy*. Gloucestershire: Sutton Publishing. A series of fourteen books by various authors each of which describes a particular Normandy battlefield in great detail.

Zuehlke, Mark: *Juno Beach: Canada's D-Day Victory: June 6, 1944*. Vancouver: Douglas & McIntyre, 2004. The action of the Canadian landings on Juno Beach.

Chapter Twelve

The Final Offensive
1944–1945

By the winter of 1944, the Allies remained unable to penetrate Hitler's West Wall, the last great German defensive barrier. In the north, General Montgomery's 21st Army Group suffered a disastrous failure in Operation 'Market Garden', its attempt to jump across the Rhine River in September by capturing the bridges at Arnhem, Holland. From September 1944 to February 1945, the US First Army, commanded by Lieutenant General Courtney Hodges, fought a costly action in the Hurtgen Forest to capture the Roer River dams, a necessary prequel to any attempt to cross the Roer River east of Aachen. In the far south, General Patton's Third Army was preparing to launch an attack in Lorraine to enter the Saar basin. Between Hodges and Patton lay the heavily wooded, trackless hills of the Ardennes Forest. Throughout history the Ardennes region was considered an impenetrable barrier to invasion, but it actually had been a German avenue into France in both 1914 and 1940.

By December 1944, most of Germany's senior military commanders realized that Germany had lost the war. Adolf Hitler's eastern armies were crumbling under brutal attacks by the Red Army, and the Russians were on the frontiers of East Prussia, 300 km from Berlin. The Americans and British threatened the capture of Germany's main industrial centers in the Ruhr valley and Saar basin. Despite acute shortages of fuel and experienced junior officers and with an army that was increasingly manned by under- and over-age soldiers, Germany's only chance at survival was a desperate counteroffensive sufficiently successful to lead to an armistice in the west.

#50

Ardennes Offensive (The Battle of the Bulge)
16 December 1944 to 28 January 1945

OBJECTIVE	To break through the allied line, capture the port of Antwerp, and trap the British 21st Army Group.
FORCES	
AMERICAN:	Twenty-six divisions, 830,000 men, and 1,580 tanks (Lieutenant General Omar Bradley)
GERMAN:	Twenty-four divisions, 500,000 men, and 960 tanks (Generalfeldmarschall Walter Model)
RESULT	The German army was stopped and driven back to its start line.
CASUALTIES	
AMERICAN:	10,733 killed, 42,316 wounded, and 22,636 taken prisoner or missing; 733 tanks, 1,300 vehicles and 592 planes lost
GERMAN:	12,652 killed, 38,600 wounded, and 30,582 taken prisoner or

	missing; 324 tanks, 5,000 vehicles and 320 planes lost
BRITISH:	200 killed, 239 wounded, and 969 taken prisoner or missing
BELGIAN:	2,500 civilians dead
LOCATION	Liège is 370 km northeast of Paris; Malmédy is 60 km southeast of Liège; Bastogne is 330 km northeast of Paris

Under the utmost secrecy, the last of Germany's manpower and armor were gathered into three armies along a 60-km front from Monschau, Germany to Echternach, Luxemburg. Their intent was to puncture through the thinly held Ardennes, cross the Meuse River, capture supply depots around Liège, and drive to the North Sea, capturing the major allied supply port at Antwerp. The cut-off British 21st Army Group and US 12th Army Group could then be attacked from two fronts. Only Hitler, in his deluded, drug-induced state, could believe in the plan's potential for complete success – what some generals referred to as the 'grand slam'; however, many of the senior army commanders did believe a 'small slam' – encircling Liège and trapping the American force occupying the German city of Aachen – was possible.

To the Allies, the Ardennes sector was considered 'the ghost front,' manned by only four divisions; in the north were the 99th and 106th Divisions, neither of which had ever seen combat. To the south were the experienced 4th and 28th Divisions, both of which had fought in Normandy but had been badly mauled in the Hurtgen fighting and were undergoing replacements and refitting. In both sectors, the troops were thinly spread, often occupying forward observation positions during daylight hours only.

The German Sixth Panzer Army, commanded by SS-Oberstgruppen-führer Josef Dietrich, had the shortest route to the Meuse before targeting Liège and Antwerp and, mustered two-thirds of the offensive's armored vehicles, with six hundred forty tanks in four panzer, one parachute, and four infantry divisions. Fifth Panzer Army, led by General der Panzertruppen Hasso von Manteuffel, with three panzer and four infantry divisions, was to secure Meuse crossings between Namur and Givet as well as protect the main attack's left flank as it progressed to Antwerp. Seventh Army, under General der Panzertruppen Erich Brandenberger, was to form a blocking shoulder to protect the offensive's flank from Patton's Third Army in Luxembourg.

Battle

Although Dietrich's Panzer Army had the key role of penetrating allied lines, the limited road network channeled his armored columns between forested hillsides. After the opening minutes of artillery bombardment in the pre-dawn darkness of 16 December, the Ardennes was illuminated by an eerie glow from German searchlights reflecting off low clouds. While the bombardment continued, it crept backwards against secondary targets and key crossroads. At 07:00, German armor moved forward along five designated *Rollbahns,* or avenues of attack, identified as A through E. The battle began inauspiciously for the Germans. On *Rollbahns* A and B, two battalions of the US 393rd Regiment, 99th Division refused to be dislodged from the approaches to the twin villages of Rocherath / Krinkelt and inflicted heavy casualties upon the German infantry. Armored vehicles followed the infantry, sheltered from allied aircraft in the darkness of the winter-shortened day. The next day, reinforced by elements of the neighboring US 2nd Division, the defenders faced a determined attack by 12th SS-Panzer *Hitlerjugend* Division that raged house-to-house amid snow squalls and rolling fog before the Americans withdrew under the cover of night on 18/19 December. The German troops on the shortest route to the Meuse were already three days behind schedule, and the delay enabled the strengthening of the allied flank at Elsenborn Ridge.

Rollbahns C and D, which passed through the Losheim Gap, an 8-km sector of the frontier devoid of the sharp ridgelines of the terrain to the north and south, was opened by the 12th *Volksgrenadier* Division only after two days of resistance by the US 394th Regiment. On *Rollbahn* E, the advance of the main Sixth Army unit, the 1st SS-Panzer Division, was delayed for nearly one day because an ill-led German paratrooper regiment was held off by a reconnaissance platoon entrenched behind the village of Lanzerath.

In contrast, Manteuffel attacked along a wide front, led by his two panzer corps. Assault detachments used First World War 'Hutier' infiltration tactics to

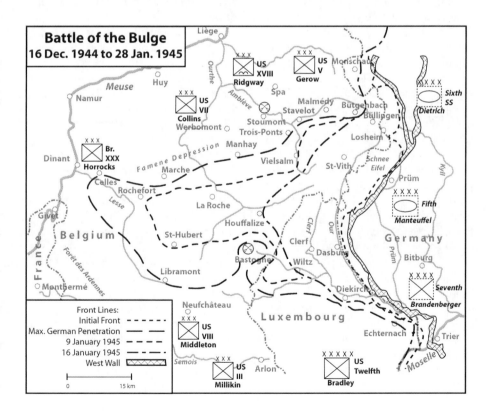

penetrate American lines before the initial bombardment, which in this sector did not begin until 08:30 and lasted only a brief 20 minutes. The American units lost communications and became disorganized. By 17 December, the 18th *Volksgrenadier* Division exploited gaps in the front lines, turned the American flanks on the wooded Schnee Eifel, and trapped the inexperienced US 106th Division's 422nd and 423rd Regiments, resulting in the surrender of seven thousand men on 19 December. The US 28th Division, led by Major General Norman Cota, hero of the D-day landings, fared little better. Thinly dispersed along the ridges west of the Our River, individual units were heavily outnumbered and completely overwhelmed. Only in the south of their sector did Cota's 110th Infantry Regiment engage in a stubborn, two-day resistance at Marnach and Clervaux (Clerf) to delay 2nd Panzer Division.

Although 12th Army Group's intelligence staff had completely failed to detect the offensive's preparations, Eisenhower and Bradley quickly recognized the implications of the assault and sent orders releasing the 7th and 10th Armored Divisions and their two experienced airborne divisions from Supreme Allied Command Reserve. The armor headed towards St-Vith, whereas the 101st Airborne Division, under Brigadier General Anthony McAuliffe as acting commander, was directed toward the road center at Bastogne and the 82nd Airborne Division moved toward Werbomont. Other American units were rushed into the conflict, in what rapidly grew into the largest American battle of the war.

To spread disinformation and confusion, small groups of SS-Obersturmbannführer Otto Skorzeny's English-speaking commandos, riding in captured American jeeps, raced ahead of the advancing army, cutting telephone lines and misaligning road signs. Their impact became over-exaggerated because nervous sentries became suspicious of anyone moving along the roadways. The ruse was eventually discovered, and a process of answering questions on Americana, especially sports trivia, was used to establish identities. Eighteen of Skorzeny's men were captured and executed by firing squad as spies.

Dietrich's *schwerpunkt*, 'heavy point,' was the elite 1st SS Panzer '*Leibstandarte* Adolf Hitler' Division, which strengthened its four thousand-man *Kampfgruppe* Peiper led by SS-Obersturmbannführer Joachim Peiper, with thirty 68-ton King Tiger tanks. His task force was to seize Meuse River crossings at Huy by driving west without regard to his exposed flanks. Repeatedly blowing bridges when Peiper's men approached, a small force of American engineers trapped the *kampfgruppe* in the Amblève River valley.

The attempt to secure the critical Elsenborn Ridge was stopped by the men and artillery of 26th Regiment, US 1st Infantry 'Big Red One' Division's defense of a small, ancient farmstead known as Domaine Bütgenbach, where it repulsed repeated armored attacks, destroying forty-seven enemy tanks and tank destroyers.

While Dietrich's advance was becoming bogged down, Manteuffel pressured the key road centers of St-Vith and Bastogne. US 7th Armored Division rushed into St-Vith on 17 December to defend the road junction against repeated German attacks. Whereas the town was eventually taken four days later, the delay denied the enemy a quick advance. The time lost proved to be decisive.

On 19 December, the 101st Airborne took up positions east of Bastogne, joining combat commands[1] of the 9th and 10th Armored Divisions in defense of this key crossroads city, where seven roads passing through the town controlled access to the flatlands to the west. After a brief effort to capture the city, Manteuffel's lead units by-passed Bastogne, leaving it to the encirclement by 26th *Volksgrenadier*[2] Division.

The German penetration disrupted communications between Bradley and his subordinate commanders. On 20 December, Eisenhower transferred allied forces on the northern flank to Montgomery, who moved the reserve British XXX Corps to guard the Meuse bridges.

The German efforts were aided by 'Hitler weather,' low cloud cover which prohibited American air superiority from attacking German columns or air dropping supplies to frontline units. On 23 December, 'Hitler weather' finally broke briefly, with bright, clear skies filled with swarms of American aircraft. Two thousand bombers protected by nine hundred fighters fell upon German frontline battlefield positions and rear supply areas, while nine hundred transports dropped tons of supplies into the Bastogne perimeter.

By 24 December, the German advance was fully blunted; American reinforcements strengthened their lines of defense, and allied aircraft retained control of the skies. Panzer movements were restricted to nighttime actions and limited by lack of fuel. 2nd Panzer Division's *Kampfgruppe* Böhm achieved the farthest penetration, reaching the woods near Foy-Notre-Dame, only 8 km from the Meuse.[3] On Christmas Day, the US 2nd Armored 'Hell on Wheels' Division attacked 2nd Panzer Division's flank near Celles. The unit was trapped and utterly destroyed over the next two days. On 26 December, Patton's 4th Armored Division broke through the German encirclement of Bastogne and established a narrow supply corridor. Hitler remained determined, however, to capture the city, and three weeks of brutal, cold weather fighting followed.

Allied troops on the northern flank passed over to the offensive on 3 January, and the long struggle to reclaim the lost territory began. Allied forces from north and south rejoined at Houffalize on 16 January, not until 28 January was the 'bulge' fully eliminated.

Aftermath

The American victory was made possible by the heroic efforts of small groups of soldiers who held their ground in the first days of the battle. Tank destroyers saved the crossroads town of Bütgenbach; engineers stopped Peiper's

---

[1] American armored divisions formed regimental combat teams composed of tanks, armored infantry, and artillery, emphasizing mobility and independence of action similar to German kampfgruppen.

[2] Whereas *Volksgrenadier* units were usually inferior in nature and typically manned by older personnel or transferees who were ill-trained and barely supplied with support equipment, the 26th was an exceptionally competent unit.

[3] Three German soldiers driving a captured American jeep were able to approach the river 1 km south of Dinant. They were killed when their vehicle struck a road mine while attempting to force a British roadblock.

tanks by destroying bridges at Trois-Ponts and Habiémont; and airborne troops refused to surrender Bastogne. Artillery support played a strong role in the victory, stopping infantry and armor attacks with a rain of shells. The grim hours of 16 December turned into the finest days of the American forces in Europe.

Patton wanted to trap large segments of the German forces within the bulge; however, the allied response was tempered by Montgomery's control of the northern flank and his penchant for 'tidying-up' the battle lines. Once again his after-action press interviews spread discord by suggesting that the British had come to the Americans' rescue. Relations between the field marshal and American commanders became as frosty as ever and never really thawed.

The German army suffered an enormous loss of matériel. The devastating effect upon the *Wehrmacht* permanently weakened its defensive capabilities and contributed to its eventual collapse. The air battle over the Ardennes effectively destroyed the Luftwaffe. The debilitated *Wehrmacht* was still capable of inflicting casualties upon the Allies, but all pretense of victory, or even survival of the Nazi regime, was gone.

On the Western Front, the great armies of Bradley and Montgomery had more bitter winter battles to fight, but the engagements were marked by hundreds of thousands of surrendering German soldiers. The Rhine was crossed at Remagen on 7 March 1945; pincers closed upon the Ruhr Pocket on 4 April, trapping 430,000 German troops. By 11 April, allied armies halted at the Elbe River. Nineteen days later, with Berlin under a massive Red Army infantry and artillery attack, Hitler committed suicide in his underground bunker. The war in Europe was over eight days later.

Consequences of the War

After the destruction and misery of the First World War, a worse conflagration would follow a mere twenty years later seemed inconceivable. The 'shell shock' of the First World War became 'battle fatigue' in the Second World War and then 'post traumatic stress disorder' afterwards. Whatever the name, the stress, loneliness, physical discomfort, and mental anguish of fighting men were universal. Casualty figures are fraught with imprecision. Allied military deaths on the Western Front totaled approximately one million. Germany, fighting on two fronts, incurred 3.5 million military deaths, 2 million permanently disabled, and over 3 million civilian casualties. Great Britain suffered 326,000 military and 62,000 civilian deaths, predominantly in Europe; the United States suffered 417,318 military deaths worldwide. The greatest atrocities, both military and civilian, occurred on the barbarous Eastern Front, where Germans and Russians sought to annihilate each other's culture. Soviet casualty figures are impossible to determine and were greatly increased by the brutal conditions inflicted upon Soviet prisoners of war by the Germans as well as Russian officers' barbaric treatment of their own troops. Estimates run as high as 13 million killed and an equal number wounded. Unlike warfare since the 17th century's Thirty Years War, however, the civilian populations suffered the most, especially in Russian and China. The global conflict produced 40 million civilian deaths, 25 million refugees, and 60 million homeless. Poland suffered the greatest percentage of losses with over 17 per cent of its total population – approximately 5 million civilians, including 3 million in the Jewish Holocaust.

As at Vienna in 1815 and Paris in 1919, political leaders redrew the map of Europe; just as in those previous conferences, the seeds of future conflict were sown. Estonia, Latvia, Lithuania, parts of Bessarabia, East Prussia, and Finland immediately came under Soviet control. In the postwar years, the Soviet Union gained dominance over Bulgaria, Czechoslovakia, East Germany, Hungary, Poland, Romania, and Yugoslavia. As described by Winston Churchill, an 'Iron Curtain' fell across the heart of Europe. The next European war, a battleless but not bloodless Cold War, would rage until the Soviet Union's economic collapse led to its political and military demise. Like Wellington at Waterloo, it too was 'a close run thing.'

Battlefield Tour

The initial German success of the Ardennes Offensive created a salient, or 'bulge,' in the allied defensive line, which gave the battle its better-known American name. For many Americans, the 'Battle of the Bulge' represents the definitive engagement of the Second World War. The snowy and cold weather, tank versus tank encounters, and early defeats followed by eventual triumph, generated numerous heroes – some named, but many unidentified. The size of the bulge and the number of battle sites prevent a comprehensive tour, although a listing of museums specializing in the battle is provided at the end. Two routes are suggested; the first tour covers the route and actions of the controversial SS commander Joachim Peiper and his *kampfgruppe*; the second tour reviews the famous defense of Bastogne. Because of the back and forth nature of Peiper's engagements, the tour does not follow strict chronological order but instead is structured to minimize driving time. The forested hills, stream-cut valleys, and ancient villages of the mostly French-speaking Walloon Region of Belgium provide visitors with an abundance of scenic views and outdoor activities.

Start the tour at Baugné (Baugnez) crossroads, 4 km from the town of Malmédy. If proceeding from the Normandy region, Malmédy is 640 km (400 miles) from Caen via Le Havre, past Rouen, through Amiens, across the First World War battlefields of Somme, and finally through Namur to Liège. This route avoids the congestion of Paris and can be accomplished in one day of easy driving by using France and Belgium's extensive network of Autoroutes. From Paris, the quickest route passes Cambrai and Mons before reaching Liège. Malmédy is best approached bypassing Liège on the E40/A3 Autoroute (direction Aachen) to reach the E42/A27 Autoroute toward Verviers (exit #1). After approximately 30 km, exit toward Malmédy (exit #11, leave the large roundabout on avenue du Pont de Warche, N62). If coming from southern battlefields near Sedan or Metz, reverse the order of the tours and visit Bastogne before proceeding north to Malmédy / Baugné.

The Advance of Kampfgruppe Peiper
17 to 24 December 1944

Obersturmbannführer Peiper's lead units passed through Buchholz Station at 03:30 on 17 December. Scattered American units were quickly overcome while *Kampfgruppe* Peiper passed through Lanzerath, Honsfeld, Büllingen, and Moderscheid in its approach toward Stavelot. Seasonally heavy rains had made farm fields sticky quagmires, and crossing open fields with tracked or wheeled vehicles was impossible. Peiper ordered his armored spearhead to proceed via the Baugné crossroads.

Leave Malmédy toward Waimes (N62). After 4 km, turn toward Ligneuville (route de Luxembourg, still N62); on the left is a sign indicating Mémorial Américain. [Highway N23, mentioned in older accounts of the battle, has been renumbered N62].

As Peiper advanced, trucks from Battery B, US 285th Field Artillery Observation Battalion were at the tail of a long column of 7th Armored Division vehicles moving toward St-Vith. When two German Mark IV tanks on a rural road from Thirimont crested a rise as they approached the N32 (now N632), they spotted the convoy 800 meters to the west. They shelled the lead trucks, setting some on fire and causing others to crash, thereby effectively blocking the road. The lightly armed Americans sought shelter in roadside ditches or escaped into the woods. Machine-gun fire from the approaching tanks forced their surrender. The black uniformed SS troops herded one hundred thirty soldiers into a farm field 100 meters south of the crossroads. Peiper left to oversee the progress of the column toward Ligneuville. What followed was one of the battle's most shameful episodes, as German machine gunners opened fire on the unarmed prisoners. After the firing ceased, SS troops then methodically walked among the wounded, executing them with a bullet to the head. In the confusion, twelve prisoners made their way into a small café at the highway intersection. The Germans spotted them and set the café on fire, shooting the men when they attempted to escape; the café proprietress also perished in the flames. Forty-three men nevertheless survived their wounds by playing dead and told the tale of what became known as the Malmédy Massacre.

Weeks later, when the site was recaptured by American troops, the bodies of eighty-six dead were uncovered from the snow. It was the worst such event in the American experience in the European war and was broadly publicized among allied troops. Such brutality was a pattern that Peiper's Waffen-SS men brought from their experiences in Russia, where prisoners were routinely executed. Although Peiper's force did send hundreds of prisoners safely to German POW camps, by 20 December the *kampfgruppe* had 'murdered approximately 350 American prisoners of war and at

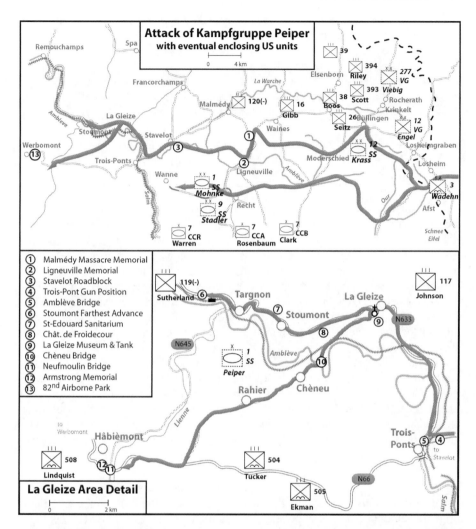

Attack of Kampfgruppe Peiper
with eventual enclosing US units

0   4 km

① Malmédy Massacre Memorial
② Ligneuville Memorial
③ Stavelot Roadblock
④ Trois-Pont Gun Position
⑤ Amblève Bridge
⑥ Stoumont Farthest Advance
⑦ St-Edouard Sanitarium
⑧ Chât. de Froidecour
⑨ La Gleize Museum & Tank
⑩ Chêneu Bridge
⑪ Neufmoulin Bridge
⑫ Armstrong Memorial
⑬ 82nd Airborne Park

La Gleize Area Detail

0   2 km

least 100 unarmed Belgian civilians … at twelve different locations along Peiper's line of march.'[4]

The **Malmédy Massacre Memorial** consists of a curved fieldstone wall centered upon a rose garden and American flag. Individual black stones mounted in the wall carry the names of the men killed in the massacre. The open stone chapel on the left has a small altar and crucifix, where remembrances from individuals and military groups can frequently be found. The memorial is across the road from the actual slaughter site, which was approximately 100 meters south of the intersection on the west side of the road toward Ligneuville. The tree-shaded site, which was

---

[4] Hugh M. Cole, *The Ardennes: Battle of the Bulge* (Washington: U.S. Government Printing Office, 1965), 262.

once open country, is unfortunately being encroached upon by commercial buildings and can be easily missed on the busy highway.

Adjacent to the massacre site is the **Baugnez 44 Historical Center**, a new museum dedicated to presenting the Ardennes Offensive through two floors of displays and artifacts, a 25-minute multi-language film focusing upon Peiper's penetration, and a diorama of the massacre. Open daily from 10:00 to 18:00; closed Christmas and New Year's Day; handicap accessible.

Proceed south toward Ligneuville / St-Vith (N62). The highway descends sharply into the Amblève River valley and retains many turnoffs of the original narrow and twisting roadway.

An American armor service company was repairing vehicles in Ligneuville when German tanks appeared around the blind curve at the north entrance to the village. The lead Panther was set on fire by a 76-mm shell from a disabled tank dozer, but the following tanks and panzergrenadiers quickly overpowered the poorly armed Americans and sent a column of prisoners marching up the hill. Eight POWs were ordered to dig graves behind the Hôtel du Moulin for three German soldiers killed in the brief encounter. When they finished, a German SS-sergeant marched the soldiers to the roadside near the church cemetery and executed each man with a bullet to the head. Peter Rupp, the Belgian hotel proprietor, saved fourteen other American prisoners held in the hotel by supplying the Germans with lavish quantities of wine and cognac. Unknown to all, Rupp was a member of the Belgian underground that smuggled downed allied fliers to safety using his hotel as a way station. The surviving POWs were later moved rearward to captivity in Germany.

The **Hôtel du Moulin** is near the entrance to the village, where the road takes a sharp curve. The old country inn survived the battle despite being used as 1st Panzer Division headquarters. To its right is a weatherworn memorial, the central pillar of which lists the names of the eight executed soldiers.

Continue through Ligneuville and on the opposite side of the village, bear right toward Pont (N660). After Pont the road passes under the Autoroute; turn right toward Beaumont / Stavelot and follow for 7 km. This very scenic route rises high above the Amblève and offers fine views of the valley and the opposite hillside.

This unnumbered rural road follows the exact route taken by Peiper when he approached **Stavelot**. Unlike most roadways on the tour, it remains mostly unchanged and provides a good example of the narrow passages and numerous sharp curves of the tree-lined, 1944 roadway. *Kampfgruppe* Peiper exercised a technique called 'reconnaissance by fire' in which the passing vehicles sprayed roadside buildings with machine-gun fire to discourage potential snipers or observant civilians. Some structures along this road still bear traces of those bullets.

Lieutenant Colonel David Pergrin commanded one of the isolated forces in the region – the 291st Engineer Battalion. His companies were scattered around the region in the villages of Trois-Ponts, La Gleize, Werbomont, and Malmédy, all locations of importance to Peiper. Receiving reports describing the size of the German attack and the presence of German armored columns, Pergrin quickly ordered that roadblocks be established in Trois-Ponts and Stavelot. An accident of fate placed one hundred eighty of his men directly in Peiper's path.

The road to Stavelot reaches a point where a guardrail runs along the downhill side of the road but is unsafe to stop.

A squad from Pergrin's engineers established a roadblock, forcing vehicles to slow down in order to maneuver a sharp bend in the road. The roadway was mined, and a bazooka team supported by a .30 caliber machine gun established itself above on the hill. When the leading Panther tank approached in the darkness of 17 December, a bazooka rocket struck and inflicted some damage. The exhausted men took a few hours rest before continuing, bivouacking to the rear near Vaulx-Richard. The small squad thus delayed the panzer attack into Stavelot for one full night and unknowingly gave a company of the 526th Armored Infantry Battalion, commanded by Major Paul Solis, an opportunity to establish itself in the town.

Proceed down the hill into Stavelot.

The ground opens where the road approaches Stavelot, allowing tremendous views over the city and its 16th century Benedictine Abbey. Skirmishes started early on 18 December, with a full attack at dawn led by Panthers down this road, toward the river. Despite Major Solis' tank destroyers knocking out four panzers when they descended the roadway into town, panzergrenadiers stormed across the bridge. Initial American attempts to blow the bridge may have been thwarted by soldiers who were part of Skorzeny's German infiltrators and dressed in American uniforms. American forces were driven from the town, which was in German hands by 10:00.

Most of Stavelot is north of the **stone bridge,** which still crosses the Amblève River and is guarded by a US 30th Division M3A1 half-track vehicle in the place du 18 Décembre 1944 on its southeastern side. The battle for Stavelot reignited and continued for the next seven days, when arriving task forces of the US 30th Division engaged trailing units of 1st SS Panzer Division. As one of the few remaining crossings of the river, the bridge was heavily contested as American and German forces swept back and forth over its spans. The bridge was eventually blown on 19 December to block the possible reinforcement of Peiper's spearhead. The current bridge was rebuilt to resemble the original, which dated from the mid-16th century.

Cross the bridge to enter the city center. Follow the rue du Châtelet, then the rue Chaumont to the intersection with the highway bypass and turn left toward Trois-Ponts (N68).

The highway bypass around the old center of Stavelot did not exist in 1944. The main road went through the old cobblestoned streets that still exist in the center of town. Faced with one of Solis' 76-mm antitank guns in the marketplace, the panzers turned left and, after crossing the bridge, emerged on rue Neuve, one of the wider streets to the southwest and which is now one-way. They then joined the portion of the N68 which did exist at the time and continued toward Trois-Ponts. The **Hôtel de Ville** has a plaque dedicated to the 133 civilian victims of the Nazi occupation of the town.

Some of the survivors of the short battle for Stavelot retreated northeast to Malmédy; others proceeded north, where one million gallons of fuel were stacked in 5-gallon cans spread along 8 km of the road to Francorchamps (N622). To keep the precious fuel from falling into German hands, a roadblock of Jerricans was built, ignited, and kept aflame until the German threat had passed.

At midnight on 17 December, one hundred forty men of Company C, 51st Engineer Combat Command joined Pergrin's engineers to prepare the Amblève and two Salm River bridges – from which **Trois-Ponts** received its name – for demolition. During the nighttime movement, a single 57-mm antitank gun and crew became detached from the 526th Armored Infantry Battalion. Commandeered by the engineers, the antitank gun and its crew were positioned near a stone tavern east of a tunnel carrying the Stavelot-Trois-Ponts road under the rail lines. Ignorant of the presence of the burning fuel dump, approximately twenty tanks comprising the advance guard of Peiper's main column rolled along the 6 km from Stavelot to Trois-Ponts shortly before noon. The 57-mm antitank gun was no match for a Panther's frontal armor, but a lucky shot damaged a track on the lead tank, halting the entire column. The tank fired once, destroying the gun and killing its crew, but the gunfire signaled the Germans' approach. In rapid succession the engineers blew up the three bridges, denying the *kampfgruppe* the main highway route to Huy through Werbomont. Amid growing feelings of despair, the attack force turned north on the minor road toward La Gleize.

Upon entering Trois-Ponts, approach the double rail tunnels on the road from Stavelot; the lone building on the left is near the location of the antitank gun.[5] Pass through the double railway tunnels and turn to the left after exiting the second tunnel; proceed to the nondescript highway bridge that crosses the Amblève River.

The 1944 bridge was wooden, replacing the original stone bridge that was destroyed by the Belgian Army during Rommel's advance in 1940. On the left side of the highway is a memorial to twenty civilian victims of the battle, many of whom were executed by the Germans during the fighting that raged after Peiper passed. The list of names includes one thirteen-year-old victim. The high railway bridge behind the memorial existed in 1944 but was unusable by armored vehicles. The road bridge now has a small plaque dedicated to **Company C, 51st Engineer Combat Battalion**

---

[5] The exact location of the gun is controversial. Some reports put it on the roadside between the double rail tunnels and the Amblève River highway bridge.

and states, 'The engineers at Trois-Ponts stopped elements of the German Sixth Panzer Army from breaking out to the Meuse River until reinforced by the 82nd Airborne Division.' The destruction of this small highway bridge completely altered the outcome of the battle. Later efforts to resupply Peiper via Trois-Ponts were repulsed by the arrival of elements of 30th Division and 505th Parachute Infantry Regiment, 82nd Airborne Division.

Reverse direction and proceed north toward La Gleize / Aywaille (N633). Continue through La Gleize (to which we will return), Stoumont, and Targon. A few hundred meters west of the remains of the Stoumont rail station, a small stone marker is on the left. Park on the forest road on the right.

Kampfgruppe Peiper became enmeshed in the narrow valleys of the Amblève River. The twists and turns of the road following along the rapidly flowing river frequently brought the tanks almost back upon themselves. Villages slowed the tanks' movements as they maneuvered between stone houses that crowded upon the roadway. Their next objective was a small rural road that led to a bridge over the Amblève, near the village of Cheneux. The bridge unguarded and easily crossed by 14:00; 6.6 km farther they rejoined the original route from Trois-Ponts to Werbomont. Another critical bridge over the Lienne stream, however, was blown by American engineers while the leading unit approached. *Kampfgruppe* Peiper, now cut off from reinforcements and running low on fuel for its gas-guzzling tanks, bivouacked that night between La Gleize and Stoumont, on the grounds of Château Froidecour.

On the morning of 19 December, the *kampfgruppe* moved westwards toward Stoumont, attacking the recently arrived 3rd Battalion, 119th Infantry Regiment, 30th Division. The morning mist rising from the river hid much of their approach until Panthers entered the town. The American unit was badly mauled, suffering 350 casualties in the ensuing two-hour battle despite bazookas and 90-mm antiaircraft-gun fire that knocked out six Panther and two Tiger tanks. German armor continued to work its way along the road against the slowly retreating infantry and a few remaining American tanks. Peiper's objective was a road only 1 km ahead that led to the last remaining bridge over the Amblève which was within his grasp. West of Targnon, the highway moved away from the river, providing a flat, marshy area on which a small rail yard and station were located.

At a curve west of **Stoumont Station**, where the road pinches between the river and the rising hillside, 1st Battalion, 119th Regiment decided to make a stand. Shortly after noon, amid the fog rolling up from the river, a roadblock of infantry supported by a 90-mm antiaircraft gun and the hastily assembled Shermans and tank destroyers of the 740th Tank Battalion, under Lieutenant Colonel George Rubel, ended Peiper's advance by knocking out the three leading Panther tanks. Peiper ordered a return to Stoumont, his final hopes dashed.

West of Stoumont Station the valley is only 300-meters wide, with the road, river, and rail line running through it. The small, rough-cut **boundary stone** is one of twenty-six such stones erected by the Belgian Touring Club, marking the limits of the German Ardennes breakthrough. Each stone carries an inscription of a tank and the words (in French) 'The invader was stopped here – winter 1944 – 45.' This stone marks the location where the three panzers were disabled, thereby identifying the farthest advance of *Kampfgruppe* Peiper in its attempt to reach the Meuse at Huy; it fell 38 km short.

Reverse direction toward Stoumont; before entering the center of the village and approximately 0.5 km west of the church, a long row of shrubs on the left hides Maison St-Edouard, a home for the handicapped.

During the attack of 19 December, the Germans overcame a small American outpost established in a Catholic sanatorium for sick children and the elderly. The sanatorium's staff and patients were herded into the large building's cellar, while the Germans fortified the site overlooking the roadway into Stoumont. In the early hours of 20 December, an American counterattack on Stoumont began; however, progress was slowed by antitank mines on the road, and German infantry dug into the hillside. In the evening, hidden by swirling fog from the river, American infantry climbed over the wall at the base of the hill and successfully stormed the building. While celebrating their liberation, the relieved inhabitants were shocked by a German tank and infantry counterattack from the hill above the sanatorium. A horrific duel erupted inside the building, with men fighting from room to room and throwing hand grenades down hallways. German tanks fired into the building through broken window frames. The German force retook most of the building, with the Americans holding isolated positions on the grounds.

Before dawn the next day, the Germans attacked down the road, setting three American tanks on fire with *panzerfausts*; the burning and exploding hulks effectively blocked the road. After noon on 22 December, 1st and 2nd Battalions of the 119th Infantry tried to overpower the sanatorium position, but tanks again firing through the windows drove them back. Rubel's tankers finally built a ramp of shell casings to get their tanks over the embankment. Attacked at point-blank range, the Germans fled, and the terrified but unharmed civilians were rescued from the cellars of the destroyed building.

A row of shrubs blocks the view of the sanatorium from the highway, and the building can be easily passed without notice. At the entrance driveway a sign identifies the institution as the St-Rafael local school, although the St-Edouard home for the disabled remains on the grounds. A plaque on the wall of the old central building states the building once was the **St-Edouard Sanatorium**. Views from the grounds certify its dominant position overlooking the western and northern approaches to the village and the Amblève valley.

Continue back toward La Gleize. Before re-entering the village, **Château de Froidecour**, a 20th century replica of a medieval castle, is best seen in the vale on the right. The château grounds became the leaguer for Peiper's tanks after his defeat at

Neufmoulin Bridge. In the center of La Gleize, turn right toward the church and musée (rue de l'Église).

On 19 December, 1st Battalion, 117th Regiment, US 30th Division advanced down the highway from Spa, recaptured Stavelot, and cut Peiper's supply line. The next day, Combat Command B (CCB) from 3rd Armored Division arrived from the north, while units of the 82nd Airborne reached Werbomont and proceeded toward the Amblève valley at Trois-Ponts. *Kampfgruppe* Peiper was trapped. The much-reduced force spent the night in La Gleize's stone buildings. American attempts to force passage into the village were defeated by mined approaches covered by direct fire from dug-in tanks and antitank guns. By 22 December, American artillery had advanced to ring La Gleize and with unobstructed views pounded the poor village's buildings and the Germans sheltered in their deep cellars.

Surrounded and subjected to increasing artillery fire, Peiper's remaining force of approximately fifteen hundred men was desperately low on food, ammunition and especially fuel, unable to reach the two million-gallon depot in the forest north of La Gleize. His armor, especially the King Tiger tanks, defeated American attempts to penetrate the village from west and north. From his headquarters in the stone building at #43 route d'Amblève, Peiper's repeated requests to Sixth Panzer Army for permission to attempt a breakout were denied. Continued American pressure upon the German perimeter made their positions untenable. On 23 December, approval to withdraw was finally received. Abandoning all heavy equipment, wounded, and prisoners, eight hundred men from Peiper's total force of six thousand left the village at 02:00 on 24 December to make their way on foot through the woods to the south. The small force regained the German lines the next day.

By the time of Peiper's departure, many of La Gleize's buildings had been reduced to roofless shells. Twenty-five abandoned German tanks and fifty-three half-tracks littered the small village's narrow streets and courtyards, left destroyed by the withdrawing Germans amid the structures where they hid. The fields southeast of La Gleize, where many of the panzergrenadier half-tracks stood among the fruit trees, retain depressions from American shelling.

La Gleize has been rebuilt to much of its 1944 appearance and size. Sturdy stone buildings still encroach upon its narrow roadways. After the battle, the short rue de l'Église was lined with four Panthers and an equal number of halftracks. In the small square behind the church is a well-preserved **Panzer King Tiger**, one of six abandoned by the *kampfgruppe*. During the battlefield clean up, this tank was to be towed away for scrap. A few bottles of cognac supplied by a local resident convinced the military to leave it, and although refurbished, it remains the only one to survive the salvager's torch. Its enormous bulk and nearly impenetrable 185-mm thick armored turret still inspire amazement. This fearsome machine is the symbol of the museum, the village of La Gleize, and the Battle of the Bulge.

Museum Décembre 1944 is dedicated to the local battle. Photo boards with explanations in four languages and display cases filled with a variety of battlefield artifacts describe the events. The small explanation book, available for an additional fee, is recommended. The quality of the materials qualifies this as the best museum on the battlefield. Open daily 1 March through 21 November from 10:00 to 18:00 and weekends and holidays during the remainder of the year. Fee.

Follow the rue de l'Église leaving La Gleize toward Cheneux. Stop at the bridge over the Amblève River.

On 18 December, after passing through La Gleize, Peiper sent out patrols to find intact bridges capable of supporting his heavy armor and allowing his force to reach the opposite bank of the Amblève. They found a bridge where the shallow river flowed through a broad valley and the approaches to the bridge were not steep. While the first vehicles crossed, the skies cleared sufficiently to allow American P-47 Thunderbolts to locate and attack the German column, destroying ten tanks and half-tracks further delaying the *kampfgruppe's* progress for two hours. On the far side, a Belgian army bunker defended the crossing, but it was unmanned during the battle. Peiper is said to have sheltered in the bunker during the American air attack.

Continue into Cheneux.

Peiper's force returned to Stoumont to attempt the aforementioned breakout to the west. After the destruction of the Neufmoulin Bridge, a heavily reinforced battalion of armored SS troops was left in Cheneux to guard their flank and the bridge. On 20 December, two companies of the 504th Parachute Infantry Regiment, 82nd Airborne Division executed a costly nighttime attack across the open fields from the south which – unbeknownst to them – were crossed with barbwire fences. Exposed to German machine-gun fire, waves of paratroops assaulted the town, suffering heavy losses. After hand-to-hand combat in the village streets, they gained a foothold in a few houses. A second effort on 21 December involved a company circle around the village to bring the German 20-mm Flak wagons under fire. The Germans then withdrew.

In the center of the farming community, the old stone houses of which have hardly changed since the battle and present an image of 1944, stands a fieldstone with a plaque displaying the insignia of the **American Army Airborne** (AA). It recognizes the bravery of the men of Companies B and C, 504th Parachute Infantry Regiment, 82nd Airborne Division, who suffered 223 casualties in capturing the village.

Continue on the rural road past Rahier to the intersection with the Trois-Ponts-Werbomont Road (N66). Turn right toward Werbomont and proceed 2.6 km to the small highway bridge before Habiémont.

Near nightfall on 18 December, the first of Peiper's tanks approached the curve east of the bridge. Pergrin's 291st Combat Engineers were once again present having been dispatched from their base in Werbomont to wire the bridge for demolition. At this time of year, the vegetation along the river was without leaves, so the American engineers could see the approaching vehicles 200 meters up the inclined road. While a Panther tank fired on the men with its 88-mm main gun, Corporal Fred Chapin twisted the key, detonating twenty-five hundred pounds of TNT. After a bright flash, the timber trestle bridge settled into the river, and the *kampfgruppe* advance was stopped. Peiper came to the river personally but observed that fording the stream near the bridge was not possible because the approach was too marshy. He was overheard saying, 'The damned engineers!'[6]

On the left of the current **Neufmoulin Bridge,** a monument marks the location of the old bridge; the asphalt approach is a remnant of the old highway. The inscription commemorates the 291st Combat Engineer Battalion, 1111th Combat Engineer Group, who stopped the advance of the tanks of the 1st SS-Panzer Division on 18 December 1944.

Proceed toward Werbomont (N66). Cross the intersection with the N645 to the white building on the right.

The rural road crossing the highway (now N645) that runs west of La Lienne stream would have provided German armor with a path around the destroyed bridge. Peiper, after returning to Rahier, sent a party to reconnoiter this road. They followed this route on the west side of the creek and successfully bypassed the Neufmoulin Bridge. They did not return until night, however, and they traveled without lights, so when the group reached the crossroads with the N66, they continued straight across, missing the road to Werbomont. By the time the German scout party realized their mistake and returned, a reinforced battalion had reached Lienne creek and quickly established defenses on the downhill slope from Werbomont. From there, they ambushed and destroyed the German scouting party.

In front of the white building, a cement guard post was positioned to protect the Neufmoulin Bridge from German invasion. On the white house, a bronze plaque mounted toward the west end of the building states:

> On December 18, 1944 from this house **Pfc. Mason Armstrong**, bazooka man of F Company, 119th Regiment, 30th U.S. Division knocked out two German half tracks of SS-*Kampfgruppe* Peiper and so stopped the forward spearhead of Hitler's great attack upon Antwerp. For this heroic action he was awarded the DSC [Distinguished Service Cross].

A few meters farther up the road, past the white house, is a Belgian Touring Club stone similar to the one at Stoumont Station which identifies the farthest German advance.

---

[6] Colonel David Pergrin, *First Across the Rhine: the 291st Engineer Combat Battalion in France, Belgium, and Germany* (St.Paul, Minnesota: Zenith Press, 2006), 134.

> Continue toward Werbomont / Huy (N66) and where the highway exits to reach the plateau, stop at the small park on the right.

The park commemorates the arrival of the **US 82nd Airborne** on 18 December and its subsequent actions in clearing Cheneux and the southern banks of the Amblève of the enemy. An inscribed stone set upon a star-shaped platform notes the event and asks that 'their sacrifice not be in vain.' Behind the stone is a 105-mm howitzer of the type carried by airborne troops.

> Pass through Werbomont to the E25 / A26 Autoroute and enter toward Bastogne. After 46 km, leave the Autoroute at exit #54 (N4) and proceed into Bastogne by following the rue de Marche (N84) directly to place du général McAuliffe.

Siege of Bastogne
19 December 1944 to 6 January 1945

The US 28th Division had engaged the leading German units in a series of holding actions. Many of the delays were imposed upon the advancing Germans by a squad or platoon of infantry firing from a wood or village, by a tank destroyer hitting a lead tank, or by engineers holding a bridge. Hasso von Manteuffel's spearhead division, Panzer Lehr, commanded by Generalleutnant Fritz Bayerlein, approached Bastogne on 18 December entering the village of Mageret, 6 km east of Bastogne, slightly after midnight. Misinformed by a Belgian civilian that a strong American force had earlier passed through the village in the opposite direction toward Longvilly, Bayerlein delayed resuming progress towards Bastogne until the following morning. The delay was fateful because that night the US 101st Airborne Division arrived in the city. The paratroops were immediately deployed despite their hurried departure from their camp near Reims and the resultant shortage of weapons, ammunition, and winter clothing. The next morning, in an uncharacteristic mistake, Bayerlein mistook the sound of the paratroop's 105-mm light howitzer for the fire of American tanks. Believing that he was facing an armored division, Bayerlein went on the defensive. The veteran of Rommel's Afrika Corps lost his second opportunity to capture the key road network to the Meuse and thereby lost the battle of Bastogne.

On 19 December, Panzer Lehr was joined by 26th *Volksgrenadier* Division, which now assumed responsibility for capturing Bastogne. By midday 21 December, Panzer Lehr, bypassed Bastogne to the south and cut the last open road from the city. Bastogne was surrounded. The next day, two officers approached the American lines offering terms of surrender to the embattled defenders. McAuliffe gave the most famous one word retort of the war, 'Nuts.' The reply confused the English-speaking German officer, who requested clarification as to whether the response was negative or affirmative. Colonel James Harper, commander of the 327th Glider Infantry Regiment, which was responsible for the sector around Remoifosse, answered, 'The reply is decidedly not affirmative … in plain English it means the same as "Go to

Hell"… we will kill every goddamn German that tries to break into this city.'[7] Harper meant what he said, and all subsequent attempts to penetrate the perimeter were defeated by stubborn infantry and accurate artillery fire.

The morning of 23 December was greeted with cold crisp air and clear blue

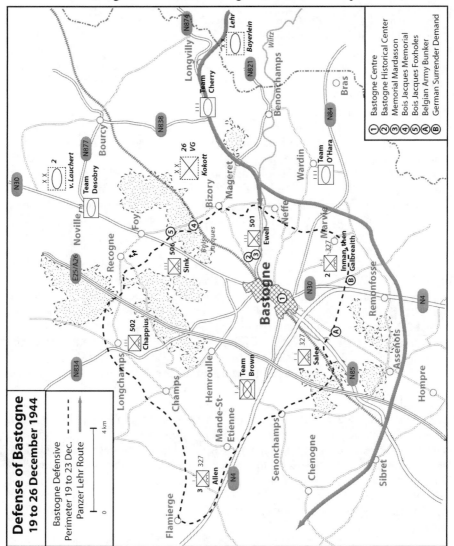

skies. C-47s and their fighter escorts arrived over Bastogne, bringing badly needed medical equipment and artillery shells. Surrounded by a German force incapable of mounting a sufficiently strong attack to break into the city, the Luftwaffe subjected

---

[7] Charles MacDonald, *A Time For Trumpets* (New York: Bantam Edition, 1985), 513.

Bastogne to two heavy bombing raids on Christmas Eve. The strongest ground attack was on Christmas day against the 502nd Parachute Infantry Regiment near Champs, northwest of the city. The paratroops enfiladed the panzer grenadiers' advance, and their machine-gun and antitank fire littered the snow-covered fields with bodies and smoldering armor.

On 26 December, Combat Command R, 4th Armored Division advanced along a narrow, rural road, fighting their way through Assenois, south of Bastogne, against German paratroopers being used as ground infantry. By late afternoon the lead tank approached a prewar Belgian Army pillbox along the road held by the 326th Airborne Engineers. The meeting of tankers and paratroops opened a narrow corridor to the still mostly encircled Bastogne.

Manteuffel, still hoping to effect the 'small slam,' deployed a major force to break the supply corridor and capture the city. The Führer Begleit Brigade, 3rd Panzer Grenadier Division, Führer Grenadier Brigade, and remnants of the badly beaten 1st SS-Panzer Division moved into the area. Pounded from the air by American fighter-bombers and on the ground by American artillery using their new proximity fuses for more effective airbursts, the massive German attack of 30 December made hardly any progress. Assaults along the Bastogne-Houffalize highway continued until 6 January, but the defensive perimeter held.

Battlefield Tour

Inhabited since the time of Julius Caesar, **Bastogne**, in the Belgian Province of Luxembourg, lies on a broad plateau that commands the surrounding countryside. It became an important trade town on roads linking England, Flanders, Champagne, and Italy. Bastogne received its city charter in 1332 from Jean de Luxembourg, of battle of Crécy fame. It has been an important defensive position since its walls were constructed in the 14th century. French troops of Louis XIV captured the city and razed the town's wall in 1688, although the current *Porte de Trèves* still exists.

In the heart of Bastogne is the **place du général McAuliffe** (formerly place du Carré), now a parking area for the town's vibrant shopping district and the location of the city's tourist office. In one corner of the square is a M4A3 Sherman tank which still displays the hole punched in its left side by a German 75-mm shell as well as the jagged damage from a *panzerfaust* in its rear, which disabled the tank during the German attack at Renuamont on 30 December. The stone wall behind the tank is festooned with plaques of units which participated in the defense as well as relief of the city and a bust of the town's hero, General McAuliffe. A Borne, or kilometer marker, of the *Voie de la Liberté* is also there marking the memorial highway that began in Ste-Mère Église and follows General Patton's Third Army route to Bastogne.

The city of Bastogne takes immense pride in its historic defense. Tank-gun turrets mounted upon concrete bases mark the closest German approaches to the city, at one point within 2 km of the place McAuliffe. Many of the city's streets are named after heroes of the defense; look for their distinctive identification signs. A tourist route (Circuit Historique) has been established with distinctive information boards at fifteen selected locations around the city, ranging from Noville to the north,

Champs to the west and Villers-la-Bonne-Eau to the south. These well-executed signs provide multi-lingual descriptions of local events, historical photographs, and directions to the next site.

> Leave the center of Bastogne to the northeast via rue du Sablon (N30 / N85). In the roundabout turn right toward Bizory / Longvilly (also signed to Mémorial Mardasson (N874)), bear left toward Bizory (rue de Clervaux), and continue to the museum parking area.

The first of the seven tank turrets identifying the 1944 roads leaving the city is on the approach to the museum. This Sherman turret is from the up-gunned T23 model with a 76-mm gun. Near the memorial entrance is the final **Borne #1147,** marking the end of the *Voie de la Liberté* and Patton's race across France and Belgium.

The **Bastogne Historical Center** is constructed in the shape of a star and is dedicated to the Battle of the Bulge. The displays include uniforms, weapons, and vehicles. Two dioramas present battle scenes from the American and German perspective. A film shows battle footage shot during the actual engagement. Outside the museum stands a M10 tank destroyer. Open daily March through April and October through December from 10:00 to 17:30; May through September from 09:30 to 18:00; closed year-end holidays, January and February. Fee and handicap accessible.

Over a slight rise from the historical center is the **Mémorial Mardasson,** constructed by the people of Belgium in gratitude to the Americans killed or missing in the battle to liberate their country. Legend has it that a German patrol crossed the hill on 19 December in their nearest approach to the city. The memorial's columns form a five-pointed star around a central open gallery. Across the top of the memorial are the names of the American states. The walls list the names and insignia of the units that participated in the fighting and a description of the battle that ends with the memorial's seminal sentence, 'Seldom has more American blood been spilt in the course of a single battle.' A staircase ascends 12 meters to provide access to the rooftop-viewing platform, where each point of the star holds a table of orientation to battlefield sites. The memorial is on a hill above the city of Bastogne, and the panoramic view from it provides an understanding of the military advantages of the site. Always open and no admission charge.

Other Sites of Interest near Bastogne: A small park along the road to Arlon (rue Joseph-Renquin, N30) contains a stone block wall inscribed with the image of **General Patton** to commemorate his force's liberation of the city. **Renee Lemaire**, a Belgian nurse who tended to the 10th Armored Division wounded and died in the Christmas night bombing, is commemorated by a plaque on a store front, marking the location of the hospital on the route de Neufchâteau (N85), 100 meters from place du général McAuliffe. The nondescript **Belgium Army bunker,** where the encirclement of the city was broken by the arrival of Lieutenant Colonel Creighton

Abrams' tank battalion, stands 3 km from the city toward Assenois / Remichampagne, along the rue d'Assenois.

From the museum exit, turn toward Bizory (N859a) and continue to the center of the village. Turn north (left) toward Foy, cross the bicycle path that was previously the railway line, and stop at the memorial on the left.

The rail line crossed before the memorial was the boundary between 501st and 506th Parachute Infantry Regiments during much of their defense of Bastogne. The memorial commemorates the actions of **Company E, 2nd Battalion, 506th PIR, 101st Airborne Division** and records the names of those killed from this unit during the defense of Bastogne. The company's actions were depicted in the *Band of Brothers* television miniseries. The center pier proudly displays the Screaming Eagle emblem of the 101st, but the engraved scene below is more emblematic of the fight for Bastogne: cold, weary soldiers with glazed eyes, passing the upturned rifle of a dead comrade. In the distance behind the memorial is the Bois Jacques, where the 101st fought off I SS-Panzer Corps' attempts to penetrate the Bastogne perimeter.

Continue toward Foy and where the road approaches the far side of the forest, turn left onto a muddy logging road and park. Walk approximately 100 meters into the woods and turn right, down a secondary logging road; continue another 15-20 meters until depressions can be seen on the right.

Hidden in the dark and foreboding **Bois Jacques**, where the sun rarely penetrates and undergrowth is absent, are the remains of shell craters and the foxholes of the men of the 101st Airborne. The rectangular and gradually disappearing depressions were two-man foxholes in which the paratroops attempted to shelter from the numbing cold, fearsomely quiet nights, and the air bursts of German artillery shells. Just inside the tree line overlooking the road to Foy is a particularly strong line of eight to ten foxholes dug facing the Germans, who at times were as near as the opposite side of the road. Toward the wood's front, the farming village of Foy can be seen in the distance.

The village of **Foy** was first occupied by 1st Battalion, 506th PIR in the early afternoon of 19 December, when they passed north to Noville to reinforce Team Desobry of Combat Command B, 10th Armored Division. Coming under heavy tank and infantry fire from the 2nd Panzer Division, which was passing north of Bastogne to continue toward the Meuse, the mixed detachment was driven from Noville and Foy with heavy casualties. Strategic to the control of the highway, Foy changed hands numerous times in the battle for Bastogne. On 13 January, E Company, after defending the Bastogne perimeter since 18 December, attacked and captured Foy, opening the road between Bastogne and Houffalize. The buildings in Foy have been rebuilt to be as they were at the time of the battle; close observation will reveal bullet scars on their walls.

Turn left onto N30 and return to Bastogne to conclude the tour.

Other Sites of Interest: Over two hundred fifty memorials, plaques, steles, obelisks, statues, stained glass windows, and bells are dedicated to the soldiers and civilians who defended and finally liberated Belgium and Luxembourg from the Nazis. Battlefield monuments incorporate thirty-two tanks, tank destroyers, howitzers, and other large caliber guns.

The town of Ettelbruck, Duchy of Luxembourg, 40 km southeast of Bastogne, has a memorial park dedicated to **General George S. Patton Jr**. It holds a Sherman M4A1 tank and a larger-than-life statue of the general peering over the battlefield. Patton's grave can be seen at the head of his men 37 km south of Ettelbruck, in the Luxembourg American Cemetery and Memorial in Hamm, outside the capital city of Luxembourg.

The nine **museums** listed below have collected and currently display artifacts from the battle. Those museums indicated with an * are described in more detail in the text.

* Bastogne Historical Center (Bastogne): Displays authentic weapons and uniforms and shows a 30-minute, multi-language film on the defense of Bastogne. Open daily March through April and October through December from 10:00 to 17:30; May through September from 09:30 to 18:00; closed year-end holidays, January and February. Fee and handicap accessible.

General Patton Memorial Museum (Ettelbruck, Luxembourg): This small museum presents the German occupation of the Grand Duchy of Luxembourg. A separate room shows some Patton artifacts. Open daily 1 July through 15 September from 10:00 to 17:00; open Sundays only 16 September through 30 June from 14:00 to 17:00. Fee.

Musée de la Bataille des Ardennes (La Roche-en-Ardenne): The displays present mannequined uniforms, artifacts from participants in the battle, armaments, and 20 vehicles. Wall maps show the progress of the battle. Open daily except Monday and Tuesday from 10:00 to 18:00; closed Christmas and New Year's Day as well as weekends January through March. Fee and handicap accessible.

Musée de la Bataille des Ardennes (Clervaux, Luxembourg): Located in the 12th century château, the small museum's entrance is marked by an American Sherman tank and a German 88-mm antitank gun. The crowded displays show weapons, uniforms, and artifacts of the battle. Open Sundays and holidays March through June from 13:00 to 17:00; daily 1 July through 15 September from 11:00 to 18:00 and 16 September through 31 December from 13:00 to 17:00. Fee.

Musée de la Bataille des Ardennes 1944/45 (Wiltz, Luxembourg): Located in the château, the museum has documents, weapons, and uniforms of the American and German units engaged in Luxembourg. Open daily 1 July through 14 July from

13:30 to 17:00; 15 July through 15 August from 10:00 to 12:00 and 13:30 to 17:00; 16 August through 31 August from 13:30 to 17:00.

Musée National d'Histoire Militaire Diekirch (Diekirch, Luxembourg): Recently expanded, the museum offers a large selection of detailed, full-scale dioramas featuring uniforms and equipment from the battle in realistic battlefield scenes. Displays of other artifacts, maps, and photographs tell the story with emphasis on General Patton's Army. Open daily 2 January through 20 March from 14:00 to 18:00; 21 March through 1 November from 10:00 to 18:00; 2 November through 31 December from 14:00 to 18:00. Fee.

* Museum Décembre 1944 (La Gleize): Contains thousands of artifacts and photographs, including dioramas; features a King Tiger tank in the village square. Open daily 1 March through 21 November from 10:00 to 18:00; and weekend and holidays during the remainder of the year. Fee.

Museum Poteau 44 (Poteau): Situated on the Poteau crossroads battlefield, where one of the largest armored engagements of the battle took place, the museum displays its collection of armor and vehicles – some operational – both outdoors and inside the barn-like structure. The artifacts and dioramas are described in four languages. A tour of the battlefield in an original half-track is available. Open weekends only 1 April through 14 June and 16 September through 31 October from 13:00 to 17:00; daily 15 June through 15 September from 13:00 to 17:00. Fee.

Truschbaum Museum (Elsenborn): Located in Camp Elsenborn, the museum traces the 100-year history of military operations at the camp through its displays and dioramas. Open all year Monday through Thursday from 09:00 to 16:00; Fridays from 09:00 to 12:00 only; closed weekends and holidays.

Recommended reading:

The Ardennes Offensive is one of the most written about engagements of the Second World War. Numerous individual accounts have appeared over the years, each telling of the bitter winter weather, shortages of almost every necessity, and the grim determination of the men who were outnumbered and outgunned. Historians debate the failure of American intelligence to recognize the signs of the impending assault, German errors in planning and execution, and American commanders' options to counter the assault. The following represent only a few suggested titles, many more are worthy of study.

Astor, Gerald: *A Blood-Dimmed Tide: The Battle of the Bulge by the Men Who Fought It.* New York: Donald I. Fine, 1992. The battle told in the words of the participants, from generals to foot soldiers.

Dupuy, Trevor N., David L. Bongard, and Richard C. Anderson Jr.: *Hitler's Last Gamble: The Battle of the Bulge, December 1944–January 1945.* New York: Harpercollins, 1994. Noted military historians analyze events from the operational perspective.

Eisenhower, John S.: *The Bitter Woods: The Battle of the Bulge*. New York: G.P. Putnam's Sons, 1969. Analysis of command told by a fine military historian and the son of the Allied Supreme Commander.

MacDonald, Charles B.: *A Time for Trumpets: The Untold Story of the Battle of the Bulge*. New York: William Morrow and Company, 1984. Richly detailed telling of the battle by an infantry officer who participated in it.

Reynolds, Michael: *Men of Steel I SS Panzer Corps: The Ardennes and Eastern Front 1944-45*. Staplehurst, UK: Spellmount, 1999. The details of *Kampfgruppe* Peiper from German sources.

Toland, John: *Battle: The Story of the Bulge*. New York: Random House, 1959. Classic telling of the stories of individuals participating in the battle.

Acknowledgments

The author wishes to thank the people who assisted in researching or writing this guide. There are a few without whose help, advice, or encouragement this work would never have been started or completed. Of primary importance among those is my wife and constant travel companion, Nancy, who provided the original idea and continued to know that I could complete the project when even I did not. My three children all supported the effort in differing ways and magnitudes. Nora for her improvement and, sometimes, complete overhaul of the text; Peter for insight and direct implementation of many of the business and communications issues; and Charles for redirecting my efforts on the target audience. Close friends offered their time to evaluate formats and bore my constant discussion of the subject with good grace.

Military enthusiasts must be a special breed. It has been a continual and pleasant surprise how generous many have been in contributing to this work. A few, such as Jean-Marie Castermans, Xavier Leriche, Sir Philip Preston, and Craig Rahanian spent hours escorting me to battlefield sites, pointing out significant terrain, or editing the text for historical accuracy. Vince Martinez contributed his skills by generating the cover artwork. Others assisted for fewer hours, but not in less valuable ways. The superintendants of the American military cemeteries in Europe and the employees of the American Battle Monuments Commission have been singularly helpful in relating local history or suggesting important sights to be reviewed. The workers at the United States National Archives in College Park, Maryland and at the Library and Archives Canada in Ottawa acquiesced to our numerous requests to view photographs with forbearance. The Imperial War Museum in London provided access to their extensive collection of photographs without which no book on the First World War can be illustrated.

Finally and of course, I thank the people of France and Belgium who accepted strangers into their communities and sometimes into their homes based upon our common interest in local battlefields. In particular, Martial Delebarre greatly enhanced my understanding of Australian contributions on the Fromelles battlefield. 'Shrapnel' Charlie was engaging in his discussion of the First War's devastation around Ypres and I thank Charlotte Cardoen-Descamps at Varlet Farm for her battlefield advice and for introducing me to him. Philippe Gorcznski provided local history and allowed me to view his recovered First World War tank.

I thank the farmers across whose fields I traipsed across looking for memorials, gravesites, and long disused pillboxes and other structures; the citizens of the small villages who tolerated my blocking traffic to read road signs uncertain of my intended direction and the shopkeepers who understood my requests for bread and wine and cheese despite my fractured french and who were not upset when I did not weigh our fruit before entering the checkout line.